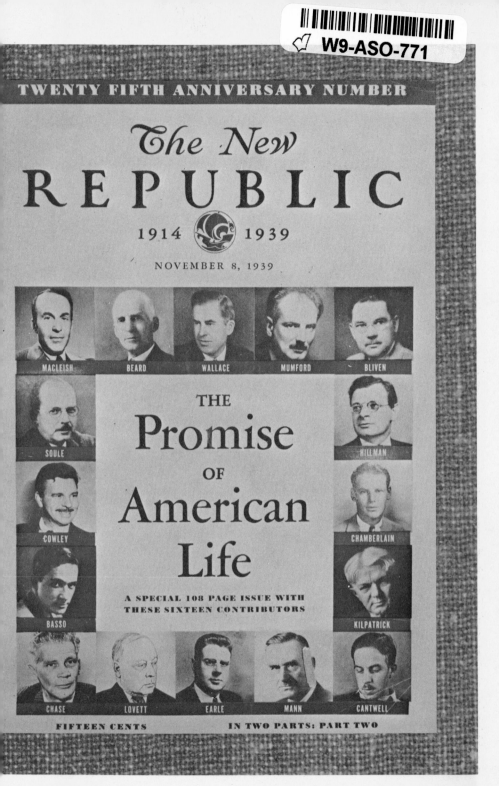

*The 25th anniversary issue, November 8, 1939*

# THE FACES OF FIVE DECADES

SELECTIONS FROM FIFTY YEARS OF

*The New Republic*

1914-1964

EDITED BY *Robert B. Luce*

COMMENTARY BY

*Arthur M. Schlesinger, Jr.*

SIMON AND SCHUSTER · NEW YORK

THE NEW REPUBLIC wishes to thank the following copyright holders for their
permission to use the following articles:

*Equality,* by Walter Weyl. Reprinted by permission of the Viking Press, Inc.
*Billy Sunday,* by Francis Hackett. Reprinted by permission of Signe Toksvig.
*Books and Things* by Philip Littell. Reprinted by permission of Mrs. Philip Littell.
*Meditation in E Minor,* by H. L. Mencken. Reprinted by permission of Alfred A.
  Knopf, Inc.
*Calvin the Silent,* by Edward G. Lowry. Reprinted by permission of Edward G.
  Lowry, Jr.
*Émile Coué; Henry Ford,* by Robert Littell. Reprinted by permission of Mrs.
  Anita Damrosch Littell.
*Duse Now; What Maisie Knows,* by Stark Young. Reprinted by permission of
  William McKnight Bowman.
*The Birth Control Raid,* by Margaret Sanger. Reprinted by permission of Dr.
  Stuart Sanger.
*Loom Dance,* by Sherwood Anderson. Reprinted by permission of Mrs. Sherwood
  Anderson.
*The Freight-Car Case,* © by Edmund Wilson, from *The American Earthquake,*
  published by Doubleday and Co., Inc., 1958.
*Ring,* by F. Scott Fitzgerald. Reprinted by permission of Mrs. Samuel J. Lanahan.
*Eugene O'Neill,* by Lionel Trilling, © 1936, 1964 by Lionel Trilling. Reprinted
  by permission of the Viking Press, Inc.
*I Have a Thing to Tell You,* by Thomas Wolfe, © September 1937. Reprinted by
  permission of Harper & Row, Inc.
*The Right People,* by Heywood Broun. Reprinted by permission of Constance M.
  Broun and Heywood Hale Broun.
*The Great Durante,* by Otis Fergusson. Reprinted by permission of Miss Dorothy
  Chamberlain.
*Amy Lowell,* from *New England: Indian Summer,* by Van Wyck Brooks, © 1940,
  1950 by Van Wyck Brooks. Reprinted by permission of E. P. Dutton Co., Inc.
*Leonardo da Disney,* by David Low. Reprinted by permission of the Estate of
  Sir David Low.
*Down Under in Harlem,* by Langston Hughes. Reprinted by permission of Harold
  Ober Associates.
*The "Stevenson Spirit,"* by John Steinbeck, © 1953 by *The New Republic.* Re-
  printed by permission of McIntosh and Otis, Inc.
*Lawrence Vindicated,* by Robert Graves, © 1955 by International Authors N.V.
  Reprinted by permission of Willis Kingsley Wing, Inc.

# Contents

# DECADE THREE : 1934–1943

# DECADE FOUR : 1944–1953

# DECADE FIVE : 1954–1964

8    *Contents*

# Preface

When information can be bounced off a satellite from one continent to
another, when news magazines sell in the millions and TV commentators reach millions more, what public need is there for such journals of
opinion as The New Republic? *The only answer I know is here—in
writings selected for this volume from over 2,500 issues of The New
Republic over the past fifty years. Taken together they are, I believe,
journalism at its best. Many are deadline pieces, written for this and
not next week. That they retain their immediacy is all the more remarkable. It is remarkable, too, how many of the controversies that engaged
the moral concern of The New Republic twenty-five or fifty years ago
still do. Indignation and disillusionment move in and out of these pages,
but these seem to me reflections of an indestructible confidence that
free men, humane and generous, can make something finer of life. In
this sense,* The New Republic, *though critical in temper, has been a
continuous affirmation.*

*No selection from fifty years of publishing can do justice to many
writers who have appeared in the magazine. This volume is primarily
a gallery of portraits; in no sense is it a chronology of events. Yet, because men shape events and are shaped by them, a picture of what we
Americans have been doing and thinking since 1914 becomes visible.
Most of the articles appear as originally written. Where a portrait was
part of a larger essay, editorial cuts in some instances have been made,
and deletions are indicated by the use of ellipsis. However, no text has
been added to or revised, and each is identified by the date it was first
published. "T.R.B.," whose reports from Washington appear throughout this book, is a pseudonym for no one person. The first T.R.B. was
the late Frank R. Kent of the Baltimore Sun; the current T.R.B. recently
celebrated his twentieth anniversary with* The New Republic—*anony-
mously.*

*Herbert Croly,* The New Republic's *founding editor, believed that
the vitality of this kind of journalism depended upon "the maintenance
of an extremely delicate balance between being specific and being general, being aggressive and conciliatory, and between being practical
and being visionary." The effort to embody this ideal in consecutive
weekly issues cannot, as Croly knew, "be more than occasionally successful."*

*I wish to thank the authors, or their heirs, who readily granted per-
mission to include copyrighted work in this book. We are indebted also*

*to Anne Fredericks, whose discriminating taste was invaluable in making the initial selections, and to Miss Caryn Levy and Miss Holly Shumway for their help in preparing the manuscript for the printer.*

–GILBERT A. HARRISON
Editor-in-Chief, *The New Republic*

*Washington, D.C., 1964*

# THE FACES OF
# FIVE DECADES

A Dinner *of* Introduction
*and* Anticipation *given at*
The Players *on the night of*
April *the* Ninth, Nineteen
hundred and fourteen *by the*
Republic *to its* Counsellors
Contributors *and* Friends

*The menu and guest list for a dinner at which* The New Republic *was formally organized. The dinner was held at* The Players, *April 19, 1914.*

## The Dinner

Smith Island Oysters

Chicken Gumbo Soup

Shad

Spring Lamb

Asparagus

Cheese

Coffee

## The Diners

| | |
|---|---|
| Felix Frankfurter | Charles Platt |
| George Rublee | Frederick Swift |
| Willard Straight | Albert Boyden |
| Philip Littell | Robert Hallowell |
| Walter Lippmann | Royal Cortissez |
| Arthur Willert | Dean Langmuir |
| Frank Colby | George Marvin |
| Herbert Croly | Robert Valentine |
| Learned Hand | Garet Garrett |
| Ogden Mills | George Brett |
| Lloyd C. Griscom | Francis Hackett |

Martin Egan

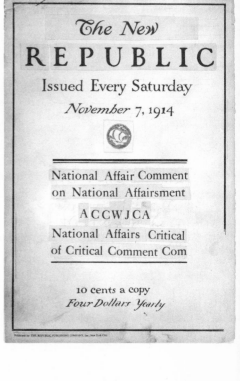

*Preliminary sketches for the first cover of*
The New Republic *(attributed to Ingalls Kimball).*

Dorothy Whitney Straight (now Mrs. Leonard Elmhirst) founder, with her husband, Willard, of The New Republic. Sketched by Mr. Straight, about the time of their marriage in 1911.

Willard Straight, about 1914

*Five members of the original Board of Editors of* The New Republic. *(The sixth member, not shown, was Charlotte Rudyard.)*

*Francis Hackett*

*Herbert Croly*

*Philip Littell*

Walter Lippmann

Walter Weyl

*The original offices of* The New Republic, *421 West 21st Street, New York*

*The Editors' Dining Room*

*The Living Room*

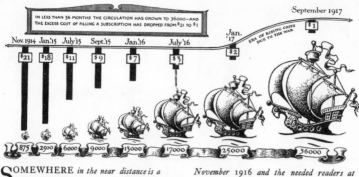

September 1917

Nov. 1914 $21   Jan.'15 $18   July'15 $11   Sept.'15 $9   Jan.'16 $7   July '16 $3   Jan. '17 $2   ERA OF RISING COSTS DUE TO THE WAR   $1

875   2500   6000   9000   13000   17000   25000   36000

SOMEWHERE *in the near distance is a point where there are no more red bars. It is a point The New Republic will have to reach in order to continue the voyage with that economic justification that comes with paying your way. It is a point in time as well as a number of readers. Last year we put the time as*

[8]

*November 1916 and the needed readers at 30000. But the cost of publishing the paper turned abnormal, and the date and number ceased to hold. Any prediction made to-day to be sound must leave both open. One thing is plain: it is readers alone and still more readers who have the destiny of the New Republic ship in hand.*

[9]

*A spread from an early appeal for subscribers, charting the circulation growth of* The New Republic *in its first three years.*

THE NEW REPUBLIC IDEA
By HERBERT CROLY

O TO SAIL TO SEA IN A SHIP !
PASSAGE TO MORE THAN INDIA ,
PASSAGE TO YOU ,
TO MASTERSHIP OF YOU ,
YE STRANGLING PROBLEMS .

— WALT WHITMAN

THE NEW REPUBLIC, DECEMBER 6th, 1922     VOL. XXXIII . No. 418 . PART 1"

*Bruce Bliven, member of the Board of Editors of* The New Republic *from 1923 to 1946. (RIGHT) Edmund Wilson, literary critic and member of the journal's Board of Editors from 1926 to 1940.*

*Michael Straight, youngest son of Dorothy and Willard Straight, who served as editor and publisher of* The New Republic *from 1941 to 1953. (RIGHT) Gilbert A. Harrison, present owner and editor-in-chief of* The New Republic

# DECADE ONE
# 1914-1923

**The New**
# REPUBLIC
*Published Weekly*
**Saturday September 9th 1916**

## The Two Mr. Wilsons

French Opinion on the War
The New Profession of City Manager
The Stockholm Conference
Lazy Verse

TEN CENTS A COPY
FOUR DOLLARS A YEAR
VOL. VIII. NO. 97

**The New**
# REPUBLIC
*Published Weekly*
**Wednesday March 22nd 1922**

Robert Littell on Our Senators
*"The Cave of Winds"*

Bruce Bliven on the Follies
*"Slaves of the Roof"*

CARL SANDBURG ON CHICAGO
*"THE WINDY CITY"*

Bertrand Russell on America
*"Hopes and Fears, II."*

Stark Young on Eugene O'Neill's
*"The Hairy Ape"*

FIFTEEN CENTS A COPY
FIVE DOLLARS A YEAR
VOL. XXX NO. 381

**The New**
# REPUBLIC
*Published Weekly*
**Wednesday January 11, 1928**

*A Prosperous New Year?*
*Smith's Valedictory as Governor*
*What Are the New Cruisers For?*

Justice Holmes and the Liberal Mind
by JOHN DEWEY

The Real Issue at Havana
by MAURITZ A. HALLGREN

Trees and Art
by STARK YOUNG

FIFTEEN CENTS A COPY
FIVE DOLLARS A YEAR
VOL. LIII. NO. 684

**The New**
# REPUBLIC
*Published Weekly*
**Wednesday June 27, 1928**

## How Is Hoover?
by HERBERT CROLY

## A Pasteboard Platform
EDITORIAL

## The Utilities Make Opinion
EDITORIAL

## Gigantic Dreams
by CONRAD AIKEN

FIFTEEN CENTS A COPY
FIVE DOLLARS A YEAR
VOL. LV. NO. 708

*1914-1923*

*The year 1914 can be said to have marked the high noon of American progressivism. More than a decade of political and intellectual ferment seemed at last to be reaching happy fulfillment.* The New Republic, *founded late in that year, appeared above all as the child of the enlightenment.*

*Yet it was a child with many fathers. Progressivism, as historians have subsequently discovered, was more complicated than it looked. It was, in essence, a spirit of critical inquiry into established ideas and institutions—this, and a conviction that events could be shaped by reason. But though the progressive spirit cast a bright light, it did so with a confusion of beams. It was at once innocent and sophisticated, idealistic and skeptical, moralistic and relativist, self-righteous and self-accusatory. Some progressives were Hamiltonians, some Jeffersonians. Some favored the acceptance and control of industrial concentration; others wanted an economy of freely competing small units. Some were internationalists, others isolationists. Some were* avant-garde, *others conventional or even reactionary in artistic matters. Progressivism, in short, was a bundle of contradictions held together by a common middle-class ethos and by a common moral energy.*

*In years to come, as the West entered its time of cumulative crisis, the contradictions would clash and thereby dissipate some of the energy—a process which* The New Republic *would faithfully reflect and record. But in 1914 this was still in the future. The present was a season of political hope and of artistic release. Woodrow Wilson was well launched in a reform program which promised to complete the work of Theodore Roosevelt in humanizing industrial society. James and Dewey had begun the reconstruction of American philosophy. Beard and Robinson were bringing new excitement to the study of history. The arts were in a state of exuberant creativity, discarding the exhausted forms of the past in the quest for a new immediacy of experience.* The New Republic *was conceived in this atmosphere of confidence. Only the offstage noises of the guns of August threatened the prevailing optimism.*

*The new magazine was particularly the voice of Eastern, metropolitan progressivism. It was intellectual, stylish, urbane—remote in mood, if not in politics, from the evangelical progressivism of La Follette in Wisconsin or Hiram Johnson in California. Its editor, Herbert Croly, had written five years before, in* The Promise of American Life, *the most substantial essay in progressive political thought; he had attended*

*Harvard and had been an editor of the* Architectural Record. *The magazine's backer, Willard Straight, after graduating from Cornell, had worked for such pillars of the Eastern establishment as J. P. Morgan's and the Department of State; his wife, Dorothy Whitney, came from a fashionable New York family. Two of the other editors, Walter Lippmann and Philip Littell, were Harvard men; Walter Weyl had gone to the Wharton School at the University of Pennsylvania; Francis Hackett was an Irishman; Charlotte Rudyard a Vassar girl. Together they proposed to patrol the fields of politics and culture, seeking, through reasoned analysis and muted wit, to raise small insurrections, as Croly liked to put it, in men's minds.*

*The First World War broke out on the day* The New Republic *opened its offices—a portent for the future. By the time the first issue appeared on November 7, 1914, a shadow had begun to fall across the progressive enlightenment. But for a time, the magazine retained a sober confidence that reason could influence events. Its editors were close to men of power, first to Theodore Roosevelt, later, if not to Wilson, at least to Colonel House. As the European war became more insistent,* The New Republic *followed Wilson in supporting neutrality and then in demanding participation. But war brought disenchantment, and the progressive hope began to falter. Walter Weyl and John Maynard Keynes saw Wilson's trip to Paris as a pilgrimage of betrayal, while Charles Merz, later to be editor of* The New York Times, *discerned the future on a front porch in Marion, Ohio. By the end of the decade, with the Treaty of Versailles and the election of Harding to the Presidency, disillusion was well advanced.*

*Defeated in the hope of direct influence on public policy, the magazine in the twenties turned an increasingly caustic look on the foibles and excesses of American life in the age of Calvin Coolidge, Henry Ford and Émile Coué. H. L. Mencken sounded the anarchic keynote in his "Meditation in E Minor" (and in his meditation on Mencken, Philip Littell added a characteristic* New Republic *caution about the dangers of anarchy). S. N. Behrman, dissecting the advertising man as "the genius of America," anticipated the attack on the gray flannel suit by a generation. At the same time,* The New Republic *enlarged its concern for culture. Two distinguished critics, Stark Young and Paul Rosenfeld, wrote brilliantly about the theater and music; and Bernard Shaw and Clive Bell brought transatlantic viewpoints to the discussion of the arts. Beginning hopefully in 1914 as the organ of a progressive majority in a progressive era, the magazine saw itself a decade later as the voice of a civilized minority in an era of Babbitts. Progressive idealism was now less a cause than a refuge.* —ARTHUR M. SCHLESINGER, JR.

*December 5, 1914 [Vachel Lindsay]*

# SINCERITY IN THE MAKING
by Randolph Bourne


You must hear Mr. Lindsay recite his own "Congo," his body tense and swaying, his hands keeping time like an orchestral leader to his own rhythms, his tone changing color in response to the noise and savage imagery of the lines, the riotous picture of the Negro mind set against the weird background of the primitive Congo, the "futurist" phrases crashing through the scene like a glorious college yell—you must hear this yourself, and learn what an arresting, exciting person this new indigenous Illinois poet is. He has a theory of his work, which Miss Monroe has supported in *Poetry* [Magazine], that he is carrying back the half-spoken, half-chanted singing of the American vaudeville stage to its old Greek precedent of the rhapsodist's lyric, where the poet was composer and reciter in one. After hearing the now so well-known "General Booth Enters into Heaven," and the "Santa-Fé Trail," and "The Firemen's Ball," one's imagination begins to run away with the idea of this Greek rhapsodist-vaudeville stage, where one could get the color and the smash of American life interpreted on a higher and some-what more versatile plane than is now presented. One finds oneself beginning irresistibly, "Fat black bucks in a wine-barrel room," or "Booth led boldly with his big bass drum," and whirling along to rhapsodic improvisation of one's own. The explicitly poetical stage directions which accompany these poems "to be read aloud or chanted" initiate the reader at once into the art, and rather spoil him for the tame business of reading. One hopes that these verses must have come in sweeps of improvisation as the poet swung along on one of his vaga-bond walks through the interminable prairies of the West. They sound as if they had been shouted to the winds and the clouds, their gaudy rhythms marking time for the slow roll of the sun over the blistering sky. . . .

Mr. Lindsay has tried every variety of verse from children's poems to political and up-to-date war poems. . . . He has reminiscences of every kind of poetic diction and philosophy and creed and moral atti-tude. One poem stamps him Christian, the next agnostic, the next socialist, the next aesthete or rapt vulgarian at the "movies." It is all tumbled in with an astonishing insensitiveness to what is banal and what is strong. . . .

Mr. Lindsay is concentratedly American, and his work and career are an illumination of the American soul. If that American soul had ever had any genuine hunger for the beauty of town and countryside which Europe clothes itself in, it would long ago have created that beauty, and not left itself to starve in shabbiness. The poet on his walk seems not to have found natural American beauty down through that long stretch of Missouri and Kansas, nor does he seem to have been saddened at its absence. One thinks of the visual richness of English vagabonds like Borrow and Jeffries, and is amazed at the thinness and poverty of these impressions. A few flowers along the railroad track, plenty of queer people, wheat interminable, but little hint of the quality of the life lived and the highhearted scenery. Perhaps it is because Mr. Lindsay is too much of a poet not to require verse, for several of his Kansas poems do send long vistas down the mind that has never seen the West, and one still feels through these lines the torturing violence of a nature almost too big for man. The powerful orginality of all this later work means the hope that he will leave this other apprenticing with ideas alone forever, and enter at last into his sincerity.

*January 23, 1915 [The Unemployed]*

# EQUALITY
by Walter E. Weyl

Last evening I happened by accident upon a strange coming together of the ends of New York. Seated on couches and chairs in the spacious, unpretentious drawing room were unemployed men, recruited from the bread line and the lodginghouses. These unemployed—there were some thirty of them—were the guests of men and women prominent in the city government and in social reform. They had been called in to give their advice to experts, to explain how relief work should be organized, to discuss the infinitely complex problem of unemployment. It seems absurd and sentimental, does it not? And yet it was evident that the expert learned much from these harassed men, who knew how unemployment hurts, and I took pride in city officials willing to study in such a book.

As I listened to these unemployed, as I heard these famished wanderers tell of the monotonous horrors of their life, of trudging night after night through cold, empty streets, of sleeping amid vermin on foul lodginghouse floors or on chairs in the stench of low saloons, of deprivation, of degradation, of despair, I felt infinitely abased. I looked about me at the well-clad solicitous men and women who had come to meet them, and in their faces read the same shame that I found in my own heart, the same leaden guilt of living in such a world. But for the happy bulwark of circumstance they too might have sunk into the abyss and joined this despised regiment, useless because unused. What could the fed say to the unfed? What hope could they extend? What did their slow plans for social regeneration mean to wretches whose life would be crushed out long before such plans could mature?

Only the unemployed were without constraint, for they had the tragic dignity of hopelessness. They stood up boldly, spoke not unwisely, and showed no humility before men who might have housed and fed them for months without noticing the cost. It struck me suddenly that these unemployed men, being Americans, possessed more self-assurance than Englishmen or Germans in like case would have possessed. These wanderers, despised even by pickpockets, held the stubborn conviction that after all they were human beings and citizens, equal to the others in all respects except the accident of money.

Of course they were not equal, if that word means anything. They had not the health, the vigor, the firm intellectual grasp. They could not reason a thing out; they were too obsessed by the sordid trifles that had become their life. Some were weak because they had grown up in an evil environment; some, no doubt, were handicapped before birth by a fatal heredity. What does equality mean when men are as unequal as these? What equality could exist between us, who sat apart, secure and fed, and these friendless unemployed, soon to be let out again upon the street, soon to be redelivered to the life that skirts the land of beggary and crime.

We tried desperately to be equal; it was the least we could do. Were we not all men and brothers? We used the title "brother" as men do when in the absence of all social bonds they appeal to the last shred, our common humanity. But though our will was excellent, though we were all engaged upon a single problem, it was not possible even for the short space of three hours to keep down the barrier. The two groups instinctively separated. The unemployed were addressed as "you fellows," "friends," "boys," but the title "gentlemen," which is in vogue in almost every section, was not used. Could it have been used without derision? Is a man a gentleman with whom society deals so ungently? To use that term of equality to one whom you can save from slow starvation or permit to starve, whom you can raise by a nod or condemn to misery is to mock him, as though you offered a flask of perfume to a wretch dying of hunger.

There can be no equality, nor any approach to equality, except among men economically independent and economically comparable. You may talk of equality and fraternity, of equal civil rights, of equal political rights, of the brotherhood of man and all the rest, but unless your man has a secure economic position, a chance to earn his living in dignity and honor, he has no rights whatsoever. Political equality is a farce and a peril unless there is at least some measure of economic equality. What does it avail the poor devil trudging the streets without a chance of bed or breakfast, that he is an equal American citizen with a vote? For what or whom shall he vote? What interest has he in all our fine political schemes, in economy and efficiency, in democracy and progress, when he himself after election as before is without a job and hungry? If such a man sell his political influence for whatever he can get, who is there to blame him?

We shall not advance far in working out our American ideals without striking hard at this inequality which has grown with the growth of society and which produces insane fortunes at the top and destitution at the bottom. When we talk of inequality, we mean inequality of possessions, inequality of income, inequality of industrial opportunity. It is not an easy task to eradicate this inequality, nor is it one which can be solved in a year or a decade, for the evil is rooted in complex conditions and in strong human instincts, and some of it is an inevitable result of quite healthy economic processes. Inequality, even in its worst manifestations, will last long, for the very reason that it means political inequality, for the very reason that the man of great fortune is the controller of other men's lives and other men's opinions and votes, and that those who have absolutely nothing join with those who have too much. The road to equality is difficult and long. We shall not even approach our goal without a national understanding of this problem, nor without radical economic readjustments, which will prevent excessive private accumulation at its source, and give to men at the bottom of society the economic as well as the educational bases of independence.

*January 30, 1915*

# MR. ROCKEFELLER ON THE STAND

by Walter Lippmann

Mr. Rockefeller seemed terribly alone on Monday when he faced the Industrial Relations Commission. There was an atmosphere of no quarter. A large crowd watching intensely every expression of his face, about twenty cameras and a small regiment of newspapermen, a shorthand reporter at his elbow, and confronting him the Commissioners led by the no means reassuring Mr. Walsh—except for an indefatigably kindly police sergeant who gave him one glass of water after another, not much was done to pamper the witness. He met what he knew to be his accusers with the weary and dogged good humor of a child trying to do a sum it does not understand for a teacher who will not relent.

From the first Mr. Rockefeller was on the defensive. He began by reading the long statement which was printed that evening in the newspapers. The statement was very carefully prepared; much thought and labor had evidently gone into it, but as a matter of style it did not sound in the least like anything that Mr. Rockefeller had to say on his direct oral examination. Perhaps we did him an injustice, but it never occurred to us to suppose that Mr. Rockefeller had written the document himself. Nevertheless, Mr. Rockefeller read the paper well.

But it was much too smooth to be convincing. When he read with warm emphasis that "combinations of capital are sometimes conducted in an unworthy manner, contrary to law and in disregard of the interest both of labor and the public," we wondered whom he had in mind. Nor were we any more enlightened as to what he really stood for when he said that "such combinations cannot be too strongly condemned nor too vigorously dealt with." He read those sentences with sincere indignation and without betraying the slightest self-consciousness. To the charge that he has enforced an industrial absolutism in Colorado, he replied with much feeling that "an attitude toward industry and toward labor such as is here implied is so abhorrent to me personally and so contrary to the spirit of my whole purpose and training that I cannot allow these allegations to pass unnoticed. . . . While it has been said that I have exercised an absolute authority in dictating to the management of the Colorado Fuel and Iron Company, it has also been said that I have been too indifferent, and that as a director I should have exercised more authority. Clearly, both cannot be true."

Yet it seemed to me as I listened to him that both could be true, and that in fact it was just such a dilemma which was the truth. For while the reality of the Rockefeller power could hardly be questioned, the use of that power appeared to have been secondhand and inadequate. For ten years Mr. Rockefeller had not seen his property; his relation to it was by letter and by conference with the officials. What he knew of it must have come to him from them, and, as he has confessed, he trusted their word. Now when we speak of the despotism of the Czar of Russia, we do not mean that he in person acts despotically in every province of his empire. We mean that a despotic hierarchy exists owing allegiance to him as its titled head. We know that if the Czar wished to liberalize his government he would find himself hampered by his subordinate officials. But he has to bear the responsibility for the things that are done in his name, and because he has potential power he is blamed not only for what he does but for what he doesn't do.

This seemed to be the predicament of Mr. Rockefeller. I should not believe that he personally hired thugs or wanted them hired; I should not believe that the inhumanity of Colorado is something he had conceived. It seems far more true to say that his impersonal and half-understood power has delegated itself into unsocial forms, that it has assumed a life of its own which he is almost powerless to control. If first impressions count for anything, I should describe Mr. Rockefeller as a weak despot governed by a private bureaucracy which he is unable to lead. He has been thrust by the accident of birth into a position where he reigns but does not rule; he has assumed a title to sovereignty over a dominion which he rarely visits, about which his only source of information is the reports of men far more sophisticated and far less sensitive than he himself.

His intellectual helplessness was the amazing part of his testimony. Here was a man who represented an agglomeration of wealth probably without parallel in history, the successor to a father who has with justice been called the high priest of capitalism. Freedom of enterprise, untrammeled private property, the incentives of the profiteer, culminate in the achievements of his family. He is the supreme negation of all equality, and unquestionably a symbol of the most menacing fact in the life of the republic. Yet he talked about himself on the commonplace moral assumptions of a small businessman. There never was anybody less imperial in tone than John D., Jr. The vastness of his position seemed to have no counterpart in a wide and far-reaching imagination. Those who listened to him would have forgiven him much if they had felt that they were watching a great figure, a real master of men, a person of some magnificence. But in John D. Rockefeller, Jr., there seemed to be nothing but a young man having a lot of trouble, very much harassed and very well-meaning. No sign of the statesman, no quality of leadership in large affairs, just a careful, plodding, essentially uninteresting person who justifies himself with simple moralities and small-scale virtues.

His tragedy is that of all hereditary power, for there is no magic in inheritance, and sooner or later the scion of a house is an incompetent. Yet the complicated system over which he presides keeps him in an uncomfortably exalted position, where all men can see its absurdity. It is the weak monarch who finally betrays the monarchy. It is the unimaginative, blundering, good-natured king who pays for the acts of his predecessors. Those who rule and have no love of power suffer much. John D. Rockefeller, Jr., is one of these, I think, and he is indeed a victim. The failure of the American people to break up his unwieldy dominion has put a man who should have been a private citizen into a monstrously public position where even the freedom to abdicate is denied him.

*March 20, 1915*

# BILLY SUNDAY
by Francis Hackett

Before I heard Billy Sunday in Philadelphia I had formed a conception of him from the newspapers. First of all, he was a baseball player become revivalist. I imagined him as a ranting, screaming vulgarian, a mob orator who lashed himself and his audience into an ecstasy of cheap religious fervor, a sensationalist whose sermons were fables in slang. I thought of him as vividly, torrentially abusive, and I thought of his revival as an orgy in which hundreds of sinners ended by streaming in full view to the public mourners' bench. With the penitents I associated the broken humanity of Magdalen, disheveled, tearful, prostrate, on her knees to the Lord. I thought of Billy Sunday presiding over a meeting that was tossed like trees in a storm.

However this preconception was formed, it at least had the merit of consistency. It was, that is to say, consistently inaccurate in every particular. . . .

The two men whom Sunday most recalled to me at first were Elbert Hubbard and George M. Cohan. In his mental caliber and his pungent philistinism of expression he reminded me of Hubbard, but in his physical attitude there was nothing of that greasy orator. He was trim and clean-cut and swift. He was like a quintessentially slick salesman of his particular line of wares.

Accompanying one of the presents [brought by members of the audience] there had been a letter referring to Billy Sunday's great work, "the moral uplift so essential to the business and commercial supremacy of this city and this country." As he developed his homely moral sermon for his attentive middle-class congregation, this gave the clue to his appeal. It did not seem to me that he had one touch of divine poetry. He humored and argued and smote for Christ as a commodity that would satisfy an enormous acknowledged gap in his auditors' lives. He was "putting over" Christ. In awakening all the early memories of maternal admonition and counsel, the consciousness of unfulfilled desires, of neglected ideals, the ache for sympathy and understanding, he seemed like an insurance agent making a text of "over the hill to the poorhouse." He had at his fingertips all the selling points of Christ. He gave to sin and salvation a practical connotation. But while his words and actions apparently fascinated his audience, while they laughed eagerly when he scored, and clapped him warmly very often, to me he appealed no more than an ingenious electric advertisement, a bottle picked out against the darkness pouring out a foaming glass of beer.

And yet his heart seemed to be in it, as a salesman's heart has to be in it. Speaking the language of business enterprise, the language with which the great majority were familiar, using his physical antics merely as a device for clinching the story home, he gave to religion a great human pertinence, and he made the affirmation of faith seem creditable and easy. And he defined his own object so that a child could understand. He was a recruiting officer, not a drill sergeant. He spoke for faith in Christ, he left the rest to the clergy. And to the clergy he said: "If you are too lazy to take care of the baby after it is born, don't blame the doctor."

It was in his platform manners that Sunday recalled George M. Cohan. When you hear that he goes through all the gyrations and gesticulations of baseball, you think of a yahoo, but in practice he is not wild. Needing to arrest the attention of an incredibly large number of people, he adopts various evolutions that have a genuine emphatic value. It is a physical language with which the vast majority have friendly heroic association, and for them, spoken so featly and gracefully, it works. Grasping the edge of the platform table as if about to spring like a tiger into the auditorium, Sunday gives to his words a drive that makes you tense in your seat. Whipping like a flash from one side of the table to the other, he makes your mind keep unison with his body. He keys you to the pitch that the star baseball player keys you, and although you stiffen when he flings out the name of Christ as if he were sending a spitball right into your teeth, you realize it is only an odd, apt, popular conventionalization of the ordinary rhetorical gesture. Call it his bag of tricks, deem it incongruous and stagey, but if Our Lady's Juggler is romantic in grand opera, he is not a whit more romantic than this athlete who has adapted beautiful movements to an emphasis of convictions to which the audience nods assent.

The dissuading devil was conjured by Sunday in his peroration, and then [Sunday] ended by thanking God for sending him his great opportunity, his vast audience, his bouquets and his towels. When he finished, several hundred persons trailed forward to shake hands and confess their faith—bringing the total of "penitents" up to 35,135.

Bending with a smile to these men and women who intend to live in the faith of Christ, Billy Sunday gives a last impression of kindliness, sincerity, tired zeal. And various factory superintendents and employers mingle benignly around, glad of a religion that puts on an aching social system such a hot mustard plaster.

*December 4, 1915 [Henry Ford]*

# A LITTLE CHILD SHALL LEAD THEM
Editorial

Mr. Henry Ford's peace trip has aroused violent resentment in America since the day it was announced. Men laugh at it with helpless anger. They regard it as humiliating. They want to break something at the thought of it. Yet there is hardly one of Mr. Ford's opponents who doesn't long for peace, and hope secretly that America may help to bring it about. Something in the protests seems a little too loud. May it not be that we are shouting at Mr. Ford because he has done us the inconvenience of revealing some of the American character a little too baldly? Is our indignation like that of the man making faces at himself in a mirror?

The first fact about Mr. Ford is that he is a very rich man. Whatever he says is therefore sure of a hearing in America. We have always acted instinctively on the theory that golden thoughts flow in a continuous stream from the minds of millionaires. Their ideas about religion, education, morality, and international politics carry weight out of all proportion to their intrinsic importance; and though we have not admitted that riches make wisdom, we have always assumed that they deserve publicity.

This automatic obeisance to wealth is complicated by our notions of success. We Americans have little faith in special knowledge, and only with the greatest difficulty is the idea being forced upon us that not every man is capable of doing every job. But Mr. Ford belongs to the tradition of self-made men, to that primitive Americanism which has held the theory that a successful manufacturer could turn his hand with equal success to every other occupation. It is this tendency in America which installs untrained rich men in difficult diplomatic posts, which puts businessmen at the head of technical bureaus of the government, and permits businessmen to dominate the educational policy of so many universities. Mr. Ford is neither a crank nor a freak; he is merely the logical exponent of American prejudices about wealth and success.

But Mr. Ford reveals more of us than this. He reflects our touching belief that the world is like ourselves. His attitude to the "boys in the trenches" is of a piece with his attitude to the boys in the Ford plant, kindly, fatherly, and certain that Mr. Ford knows what is best. His restless energy and success appear as a jolly meddlesomeness. He gives his boys good wages and holds them to good morals. He is prepared to do likewise for the boys in Flanders and around Monastir. Why shouldn't success in Detroit assure success in front of Bagdad? If Mr. Ford is unable to remember that all men are not made in his own image, it is not strange. Have Americans ever remembered it? Has our attitude toward the old world ever assumed that Europe was anything but a laborious effort to imitate us?

Mr. Ford serves as a reminder of another amiable trait in our character, our belief in the absolute validity of moral judgments. We have never taken much stock in the theory of Socrates that the good man to be really good must really be wise.

> Ez fer war, I call it murder,—
> There you hev it plain an' flat;
> I don't want to go no furder
> Than my Testyment fer that;
> God hez said so plump an' fairly,
> It's ez long ez it is broad,
> An' you've gut to git up airly
> Ef you want to take in God.
> —The Biglow Papers

These verses were written by an American about the Mexican War of 1845, but they express Mr. Ford and Mr. Bryan today. They go no further than their Testament, and what they will not see is that you have to go further than your Testament if you are ever to realize the principles which it embodies.

In common with most Americans Mr. Ford believes that evil can be eradicated by the spontaneous recognition of it. "The two notes that will be sounded," says Mr. Ford's secretary, "are faith and moral suasion." Oh, America! home of Christian Science, of blue laws, of the Sherman act, of letter-writing diplomacy, of moral indignation, of "prosperity" and "sunshine," of Prohibition and Billy Sunday and the new freedom and the promises of the Republican party. We are too good for this wicked world.

*March 4, 1916*

# THE NEW MANNER IN
# MODERN POETRY

by Amy Lowell

We hear so much about "the new poetry" today, and see it so injudiciously lauded in publishers' catalogues, and so nonunderstandingly reviled and jeered at in the daily press, that it is no wonder if most people think it a mere advertising term, with no basis in fact.

This is most unfair and uncritical, for there is a "new manner" in the poetry of today which sets it quite apart from the poetry immediately preceding it. I am not referring to the extreme fads so prevalent in Europe before the war, such as futurism, headed by Marinetti, with its pronunciamento that verbs should only be used in the infinitive, and its algebraic signs of "plus" and "minus," etc., to eke out a language it had intentionally impoverished; or "Fantaisisme," with Guillaume Appolinaire as chief priest, who wrote so-called "ideographic poetry," or poems printed so as to represent a picture of a railroad train with puffing smoke, or some other thing of the sort. That these "notions" (to .borrow a phrase from the country shopkeeper) will survive the war is inconceivable, but that the real, sane "new manner" will persist cannot admit of a doubt. For the "new manner" is not a dress assumed at will, it is the result of changed surroundings, of a changed attitude toward life.

The "new manner" is made up of so many elements that to give all these elements one specific name is a little difficult, but elsewhere I have called it "externality," and that name will quite suffice to show its antagonism to the "internality" which is the most marked quality in the poetry of the Nineties.

There is not space in a brief paper to show the steps by which poetry arrived at the introspective state against which the "new manner" is a protest. That the poets of the late Victorian epoch were extraordinarily subjective, no one will deny. And this subjectivity led to a refining and ever refining upon their emotions, until the emotions themselves became somewhat tenuous. With this, growing all the time, went a most beautiful technique. There seems to have been something a little faded about these men; perhaps jaded would be a better term. Were they really so melancholy, or was it just a fashion? Some of them were pensively sad, some were despairingly enraged, they looked at gray and old-rose landscapes and sighed a languid appreciation, or they whipped up their jaded mental appetites with minute descriptions of artificial, insinuated suggestions of quite ordinary vulgarities. But whatever they did they made beautiful, literary backgrounds for a gigantic ego. Each man's ego was swollen to a quite abnormal size, and he was worshiped by his other self, the author, with every conceivable literary device and subtlety.

Egoism may be a crime in the world of morals, but in the world of the arts it is perfectly permissible. It makes very good and very interesting poetry. In mentioning it I am not condemning it, I am only labeling it. It was the manner of the Nineties, it is not the manner of today.

Now, by "externality" I mean the attitude of being interested in things for themselves and not because of the effect they have upon oneself. The poet of the "new manner" paints landscapes because landscapes are beautiful, not because they chime with his mood. He tells stories because stories are interesting, and not to prove a thesis. He writes narrative poems because his range embraces the world and is not confined to himself. He is ironic, grotesque, ugly at times, because he has the feeling of the universality of life.

Some critics are forever measuring the modernity of poetry by what they call its "social consciousness." When a poet really writes in the "modern manner," social consciousness becomes one facet of his feeling of universality. The greater included the less, and "externality" includes the universe and everything in it. But Milton and Dante were universal, it may be said, were they therefore modern? Certainly not. They were universal, but they were not "external." Man stuck out in high relief all over their work. Man and his destiny—man completely out of focus, in short—was their theme. The "new manner" attempts to put man in his proper place in the picture; that is why it is so at variance with the method of the so-called "cosmic" poet.

Now "externality" shows itself in two ways: in choice of subject matter, and in treatment; and this last again may be subdivided into general arrangement and ordering of particulars, and style.

First, as to subject matter. "Externality" is the main trend of the "new manner," but of course that does not mean that no poet ever writes subjective verses. He could hardly be universal if he excluded himself. It is a fact, however, that modern poetry of the new kind does not concern itself primarily with introspection.

Another characteristic of the "new manner" is humor. Pensive melancholy is no longer inevitably to be worn, like a badge of office. It has gone, with many other obvious fripperies, such as leonine hair and visioning eyes. Is it because poets are more sincere today that they have less "side"? I do not know, but certainly in the Nineties, in England at least, they were a very carefully put together lot. It is this sincerity, I believe, which has brought back humor. To many poets of the preceding generation, melancholy must have been a fashion. I really think that if there is a fashion today it is sincerity.

Another striking tendency of the "new manner" is its insistence upon the poetry in unpoetic things. The new poet is never tired of finding colors in a dust heap and shouting about them. Sometimes the colors so occupy him that he takes them separately, unrelated to the dust heap, as it were. This taking colors, and light and shade, in planes and cubes, with practically no insistence on the substances which produce them, be they men or houses or trees or water, is often called futurism by the ignorant. Probably because the real futurists, Marinetti and his followers, never employ it.

The poets of the "new manner" have another distinguishing mark. They endeavor to write poetry in the syntax of prose. Inversions are abhorrent to them, except when used purposely for accent. They try to write in the ordinary phrase construction of everyday speech and make it poetry just the same. How difficult this is, only those who have tried it know. When at a loss for a rhyme they do not permit themselves to drop suddenly into a simile for three lines—a cunning simile, neatly devised to give the necessary rhyme. They use colloquial language; "poetic diction" has sunk into ill repute, only newspaper poets and their ilk employ it. Poets no longer "fain" to do anything, nor "ope" their eyes to the "ethiope splendor of the spangled night," when "they themselves had lain upon a couch to woo reluctant slumber."

Still a third characteristic is the presentation of facts and images without comment. If there is one thing which the "new manner" is more against than another, it is preaching in a poem. And this care not to point a moral is one of the most pronounced features of the "new manner." It is this very thing which leads so many poetry lovers of the older generation to find it cold. An old-fashioned editor once said to me that what he missed in modern poetry was its lack of noble thoughts. The poetry which is a pepsin to weak intellects to whom crude life is indigestible has nothing in common with the "new manner." "Noble thoughts," neat little uplift labels wrapped in the tinfoil of pretty verse, have their place in the scheme of existence, no doubt, but to the modern poet they are anathema. He seeks to give life, the world, as it is, as he sees it, at any rate; and the lesson of his poem, if there be one, must be inherent in the poem itself. He takes the intelligence of his readers for granted and trusts to their getting the meaning of the poem as it unfolds, refusing to bellow it at them through a megaphone in impertinent asides.

Why do people refuse to take art as organic and insist upon considering it as merely explanatory? When these same people walk in the garden on a fine morning, do they feel chilled and depressed because the little flower buds are not tagged with texts? But there! We shall never agree, and for people who like to be drugged with fine, conventional sentiments there is no cure in heaven or earth, that I am aware of.

Now as to form. It is the belief of most people that interest in metrical experiments is a distinguishing feature of the "new manner." But do you suppose that there has ever been a time when real poets were not interested in metrical experiments? Poets have been widening and deepening and freeing their prosody ever since there was a prosody to tinker with. In experimenting, the modern poet is merely following tradition.

As the word "new" has been "wished on" to contemporary poetry, so are its metrical experiments dubbed and condemned as "new." *Vers libre* in particular is constantly called "new" and hooted at; or poets who employ it are told that they think it is new, and it is not. Of course it is not; only the paragraph writers in the newspapers ever supposed it was. So far as I know, the only metrical experiment which is in the least new is "polyphonic prose," and that had its beginnings in France, in the work of Gustave Kahn, and Saint-Pol-Roux, and Paul Fort. I believe I am the first poet who has ever employed it in English, and it had to be so adapted in bringing it over from one language to another that it only retains a partial resemblance to the French form.

Now the "new manner" does not consist solely in any one of these characteristics; it consists in all. Some poets have one of them, some another; it may be subject, it may be form. The "new manner" is as characteristic as the manner of differing peoples. All Americans are not alike, but all Americans have something which sets them together, and apart from other nationalities. So the change in poetry is easily distinguished. And it is an inevitable change, reflecting the evolution of life.

*March 4, 1916 [The Elegant Woman]*

# SCARLET BERRIES*

by Rebecca West

I have tried to tell how the elegant woman is but the shadow of a man that vanishes into nothingness when the candle of his interest in her is blown out. I have told how women infected with elegance hand down the bad tradition in our schools and teach girls to live not for life's sake but to be desired. I have told how elegance makes women dangerous as producers, because they stand tittering together when they should be joined in labor's fierce fight to wrest industry from the hands of men maddened by ownership, and not less dangerous as consumers because they demand luxuries that confuse the economic arrangements of the earth and keep them from the concentration upon life which is the necessary prelude to genius. I have told how elegance softens women's will so that they cannot brace themselves to the hard decisions which are the gates to a glorious life or death. To every woman who desires her sex to be more than a perishable article hawked to uneager buyers at a penny plain and twopence pretty, who would have her sex engage in humanity's conspiracy to thrust order on the dark disordered universe, elegance is the enemy.

The half of the world that despises women thinks of this preoccupation with elegance as a pastime which keeps them quiet and does not overstrain the mechanism of their intelligence. And the other half, that believes women to be capable of all honor, has been divided by the circumstances of the feminist movement into two parties which on different grounds deny the existence of the problem. There is the grimmer type of feminist acidulated by controversy like milk soured by jolting, who scowls at the suggestion that anything upheld by a large

* The fifth article in a series entitled "The World's Worst Failure."

number of women can possibly be wrong, and remarks tartly that men have been known to take thought over the crease in their trousers. On the same line of argument one might defend foot-binding; and if the assumption that everything about women is perfect were correct we would have no need for their further emancipation. There is the other type of feminist whom controversy has made not grim but evasive, and who, instead of admitting the justice of the antisuffragist's claim that free women will cease to be pretty toys for men and pointing out how bad it is to be or have a pretty toy, tries to confute it by a decorative existence. Thus it was that Miss Christabel Pankhurst belied her physical courage and her administrative ability by smiling fluffily at audiences over Annunciation lilies; and thus it was that Mrs. Philip Snowden, a woman as shrewd as a horse dealer, would appear before a working-class audience in the Potteries to plead the cause of free and responsible womanhood in a shining satin robe and a prodigious hat of ostrich feathers that were higher than anything else in the Five Towns except the factory chimneys and her own heels. It was this acceptance of emphatic garnishings of the self as part of the campaign that brought the suffrage movement to the egotism and dashing autocracy of which it died; and that so many intelligent women fell before it is an indication of how lightly the world takes elegance. What more is elegance, it asks, than the modern manifestation of the eternal instinct of the female to attract the male? Didn't the cave woman twine scarlet berries in her hair as she sat by the fire and waited for her mate?

The instinct of the female to attract the male is life's first essential, now, as it was in the beginning; but that does not sanctify all the botched work the instinct does when it works through imperfect instruments. Half our legislation is directed toward checking and confining to legitimate channels the developments of instincts the free play of which was absolutely necessary to humanity at its birth. The desire of the strong man to set weaker men to work and to fight according to his wiser will was a sword in the hand of life so long as man was wresting a habitation from wild nature. But when that desire leads men of our time to send children into the mines of Silesia or the mills of South Carolina or the sweated home industries of England, then it becomes a sword in the side of life. Similarly the rightness of the cave woman when she twined scarlet berries in her hair does not imply the rightness of the London lady who spends five guineas on a petticoat or a hundred guineas on an evening cloak. Indeed the cave woman must start in her long sleep when the lady passes over her dust, as at some delicate white beast of prey that tracks the children descended from her body, that leaps upward at the torch of life she lit. For in her time she too had the capacity for dreaming of the future that shines in the brain of humanity like a jewel in the head of a toad. At night she lay awake while her mate slept, watched the firelight playing on the walls, listened to the howling of the wolves. "When all the wolves are dead," she used to think, "how good life will become! My man and I will walk where we will in the forest, and we will be great friends, and very tender and wise with each other. And what children we shall rear, when I know all the magic herbs that cure their sickness and they need never die of famine!" With such dreams she smiled and slept.

Well, all the wolves are dead. But women do not yet walk freely with men in the forest. Most men bid them not gad about looking for wisdom and tenderness but stay by the campfire twining scarlet berries in their hair; and most women obey. And children still die from famine and sickness, for the world seeks more busily for more scarlet berries than for food and healing herbs. But, bitterest of all to the dead cave woman, though the world has concentrated so extravagantly upon the adornments she invented, it has forotten the meaning that set her whole body glowing as her fingers twined them in her hair. Those berries were the badge of courage of the heart and of the body; they were an invitation to love and motherhood. These things have had no deadlier foe than elegance.

For love is a journey into a new country; and like any other journey its length depends entirely on what the country has to show. There should be woods with silent undergrowth, where comfort lives; bright rivers of vitality; clean cities built on foundations of fine tradition and splendid with the towers of learning and religion; green fields where simple thought and senses play like young cattle, and mountains so high that as one climbs one breathes quickening air not known to ordinary men—so high that by day the earth lies clear beneath like an open map, and by night the stars are just beyond arms' length above. In such a country a man can live forever.

With an elegant woman love is little more than a visit to Trouville: there is a bright little place and a bright little restaurant and a bright little casino—a tiny pocket of public brightness in the blackness of an unexplored, uncomprehended world. Of such a visit a man wearies and goes on, suffering a depreciation of his value not only as a lover but as a human being, because the transference of love blunts the nerves, and the beloved admits another man to her inadequate love and starts upon a cycle of humiliation. At best they commit the sin against the Holy Ghost, which is the sin of being contented with little things, and cling to this frail perch above the perilous universe, when it is the plain duty of every human being to build himself a surer stronghold. Even so they are not safe, for the limits of the earth's productivity may at any moment turn their relationship into a wrangle. "Beware," said Mohammed to his followers, "of marrying a toadstool woman, a woman that sits and sits, and spends all thy substance on jewels and perfumes and rich stuffs . . ."

Nor do the arms of the elegant woman carry her lover's child more safely than his soul, for she is altogether at odds with life and will not bear burdens at its will. It is the physical aim of [her] life to be fragile, to be so little that a man could pick one up in his arms; and like the lap dog, the lap woman can only be produced by interfering with the way of nature. In that age of elegance, the reign of Marie Antoinette, the waists of women were like the stalks of flowers; as women are not flowers but human beings of a solidity suited to the adventures of humanity, this appearance was contrived by means of cruel gripping stays. That this period of crippled bodies was also the period of weakly babies carelessly handed over to peasant foster mothers is the sign of a universal truth. Wherever women concentrate upon sex they fail at it. If we look to the East, where decorated women sit apart and seal up their souls to all but love, we think how fertile a land it should be that is watered by such a reservoir of grace. And true it is that children are there brought proudly into the world; for it is something to do in the scented dullness of the harem, and a baby is a sweet toy to play with. But their pride will not lift these women to the sterner task of keeping them in the world. So the babies slip, wailing, back; pushed out of life by bad feeding, by fever ill-tended, by infection cheerfully conveyed in ignorance, by sanitation never protested against.

We look from that so carelessly accepted motherhood to the too carelessly rejected motherhood of the luxurious West, and we see that feminists can submit to the test of their theory against which in the earlier days of the movement they used to rebel. Those of us who believe that women should play their part in the intellectual and industrial process of the world can admit that the condition of the child is a test of the rightness of the position of woman; indeed we are anxious that it should be taken so. We know that the woman the windows of whose soul are blocked by mirrors cannot look out at the world and love it so that she desires to maintain it by her body; and the Western birth rate and the Eastern infant-mortality rate prove our case. We can show that she fulfills no function save, by her costliness, her public exquisiteness, her incapacity for revolt, to satisfy the sense of propriety; and that—grievously cries out the poor social system, so rotted by poverty and prostitution—should not glut itself with human beings. This is the chief cause of joyousness in the feminist movement. The freedom that feminists desire will not be a wrenching away to personal freedom from the immemorial duties of women; it will be an added strength of function, another sinew that shall make the arm of humanity, as it brings down the hammer of its will on the world, mold it more beautifully than it had ever dared to think.

*June 7, 1919 [Woodrow Wilson]*

# PROPHET AND POLITICIAN
by Walter E. Weyl

The simple faith of Mr. Wilson in his Fourteen Points, unexplained and unelaborated, was due, I believe, to the invincible abstractness of his mind. He seems to see the world in abstractions. To him railroad cars are not railroad cars but a gray, generalized thing called Transportation; people are not men and women, corporeal, gross, very human beings, but Humanity—Humanity very much in the abstract. In his political thinking and propaganda Mr. Wilson cuts away all the complex qualities which things possess in real life in order to fasten upon one single characteristic, and thus he creates a clear but oversimple and unreal formula. As a consequence he is tempted to fall into inelastic categories; to see things black and white; to believe that similar things are identical and dissimilar things opposite. Mexicans seem to him to be Anglo-Saxons living in Mexico, and Frenchmen, Italians and Russians Anglo-Saxons on the continent of Europe. His thinking rarely concerns itself with concrete differences; it is never a quantitative thinking; it is never inductive. And this abstractness of Mr. Wilson is part of a curiously a priori metaphysical idealism. His world stands firmly on its head. Ideas do not rest upon facts but facts on ideas. Morals and laws are not created out of the rub and wear of men and societies but are things innate, uncreated, immutable, absolute and simple; and human relations arise out of them. "In the Beginning was the Word: and the Word was with God: and the Word was God." The Keeper of the Word, the Utterer of the Word is the man who creates. If Mr. Wilson could proclaim the Eternal Verities—the Ten Commandments of International Life—lesser minds might be entrusted with the humbler work of exegesis. His Fourteen Points would, by the mere fact of their expression, work themselves into the body of international life and re-create it in their image.

I do not presume to belittle this philosophy nor to deny to it all validity. Undoubtedly the impressive, half-true generalizations of our Declaration of Independence did contribute to a change in political thought and conditions. Between the Declaration and the Fourteen Points, however, lay a deep gulf. The first was an appeal, and what it lacked in precision it gained in eloquence. The Fourteen Points, on the contrary, were conceived as the basis of an organic constitution of the world, and as such should have been exactly determined and made to conform with each other and with the specific needs of the nations. I fear, however, that Mr. Wilson never understood his "points" in detail—either their extent or their mutual limitations. Was his idea of "the freedom of the seas" consonant with his League of Nations? Should self-determination have the right of way when an alien hinterland clamored for access to the sea? You cannot lay down fourteen general formulas without raising innumerable questions in political casuistry, important questions which must be answered. Mr. Wilson apparently did not see that his Fourteen Points were not an explicit program but were something less and infinitely more—a splendid but vague summary of decades of thought—not of Mr. Wilson's thought but of the thought of the world, derived from the long-perceived needs of millions of ordinary men and women. Having restated his philosophy, Mr. Wilson refrained from taking the next step of working out a plan of action. He went into the jungle with a map of the world but without a compass.

Because of this abstractness, because of his emphasis upon generalization and his neglect of the concrete facts and particular instances upon which the generalization should have been based, Mr. Wilson sat down at the peace table knowing nothing of the things he should have known. He knew nothing of Shantung, Fiume, Dalmatia, Silesia, Macedonia, and cared little about them so long as his principle of self-determination prevailed. He knew nothing of the complex economic interrelations, friendly and hostile, between various European nations, for he trusted to his not very clearly defined principle concerning "economic barriers." He did not even want to know these "details."

Had the President rightly conceived what minute special knowledge and what practical realistic judgment it required to write the Fourteen Points into the treaty, he would have selected his peace colleagues from the best informed and most responsible and independent thinkers in the United States. He would also have provided himself with a group of experts with whom he himself would have been in daily communication and at whose feet he would have sat. Instead he employed a body of special students, most of them capable and all conscientious, but a body apart, without instructions, without authority, without real contact with the President, disconnected. The expert who studied Kiaochow was not supposed to know what the President thought, though what the President thought on the morning of the day of decision was the decisive thing. Mr. Wilson's theory was that all determinations must be his and all must be based if not upon direct inspiration then upon evidence sifted by him. But he completely failed to perceive the magnitude of such a task. No mind, however capacious, could possibly have grasped all these intricacies, and where the greatest man would have failed Mr. Wilson failed. He was ignorant by reason of his chosen method of work, his love of political abstraction, his distaste for concrete, complex, coordinated research, by reason finally of his voluntary intellectual isolation. Working alone he worked too slowly and never finished anything. No wonder he was swamped by the impossible and uncongenial task. . . .

At last in these painfully delayed negotiations a day came when he would retreat no further. On Sunday, April the sixth, he publicly announced that he had cabled for the *George Washington*. A thrill of intense excitement ran through Paris; friends and enemies of the President asked, "What will he do?" To his friends the President revealed his intentions. He had compromised too much; hereafter he would take his stand on the Fourteen Points. These friends described to me the President as marvelously calm, with set jaws and "no bend in him anywhere." I went to bed that night hoping that at last the President would stand firm—there in the center of the world. He did not stand firm. He wavered, accepted small compromises, gave in more than before. The European correspondents smiled ironically. Doubtless they thought of Bismarck's cruel characterization of Salisbury: "A lath painted to look like iron."

It was not cowardice; had the President known at that late day, after innumerable concessions and self-betrayals, how to bring the vital matter of internationalism to a clear issue he would, I feel confident, have risked all and stood up against the world. He had, however, already surrendered too much; he was bound by as many slight threads as Gulliver in Lilliput. He would not now strain at a gnat or even a camel after having swallowed a whole menagerie. He might save his face by making a final stand on the question of Fiume, but the Italians would prove that he himself had already countenanced much harsher violations of his own principles. All he could gain was a spectacular tactical success; the main battle was already lost.

There was a still more compelling reason, as I take it, why Mr. Wilson failed to make this heroic decision. There are three sorts of minds in the world. The first can see only one side of every question; it is the mind of the very simple man and of the fanatic. The second sees both sides but sees them alternately, never together. The third, which one may call the synthetic mind, sees both (or all) sides and sees them contemporaneously, weighs them, balances them against each other and comes, perhaps slowly, to a final, firm judgment. Mr. Wilson's mind seems to be of the second order. Granitelike though it sometimes appears, it is wax to receive and wax to retain, eminently impressionable and unstable. It is perhaps because he himself knows this that he seeks to escape from the rude conflict with other minds and thinks alone—which means to think with the people who agree with what he thought yesterday. Again it is this mind of his with its alternating current that explains the amazing contradictions of his career, his disconcerting changes of front, his infinite self-reversals. To such a mind his seemingly friendly antagonists at the Peace Conference could present an argument of great cogency. To throw over the peace negotiations now would be to desert Europe and to push her down into anarchy. Better a small sacrifice of internationalism, better even the worst peace with order than utter disruption, decades of bloody revolution and in the end a Bolshevik world.

This argument, we may readily believe, was no part of the President's intellectual equipment when he left Washington in December. It represented a recession from his earlier thought, a violent fluctuation. For reasons, not at all occult, Mr. Wilson was more than usually liable at Paris to such fluctuations of conviction and will. He stood alone. He had no "unmannerly" Kent at his elbow to talk bluntly to him and no group of intellectual equals with him, upon whose independent judgment boldly given he could try out new ideas. Not only had Mr. Wilson, with what he has called his single-track mind, to shunt problems constantly arriving on many tracks but he was forced to oppose his individual, impressionable mind to more effective, more stable and much less impressionable group minds. The English mind at the Conference was a compact, articulate group mind, a mind of a hundred minds, taking up each other's slacks, a mind elastic, comprehensive, persistent and working harmoniously. It did not waver like the mind of an individual. The French mind, also a group mind, though febrile was constant and unfluctuating. The Japanese mind was concrete, concentrated and amazingly firm. Back of each of these group minds, moreover, was a national will; back of President Wilson, with his dummy colleagues and his unconsulted experts, was nothing with which he was in touch, nothing from which he knew how to draw support. He had no ballast. An individual arguing against nations, he was subject to the enormous pressure of national wills. Even the American people no longer knew what Mr. Wilson thought, and not knowing ceased to care. He might therefore swiftly change his mind or even pocket his whole philosophy without America or himself quite knowing.

There was a final reason, I suppose, besides his self-induced impotence and his too ready adoption of principles opposed to his own, that made Mr. Wilson accept his aborted treaty with little show of reluctance. He had his League. It was, he probably permitted himself to believe, the one permanent result of the negotiations, the one curative agent. Let the treaty pass; in time it might die of prenatal defects. The League would not only live but would cure the treaty or create a new one.

It was natural for Mr. Wilson to adopt this compensatory theory which seemed to convert his defeat into a victory. His pride was involved. Though he has in fact contributed little to the detailed elaboration of the League plan (and that little has not always been good), still the impulse was largely his, and he is therefore properly associated in the public mind with the League, which is almost spoken of as Mr. Wilson's League. We are optimistic where our own children are concerned and Mr. Wilson may well have persuaded himself that the League, though weak, faulty, and in some respects reactionary, was still sound enough to redeem the treaty. The truth, I fear, is the exact opposite. Even a poor League would have been better than none had the treaty been tolerable. But a vicious treaty, making for war and anarchy, must of necessity destroy the League to which it is in principle opposed. How can this League, based on the doctrine of unanimity, be much better than the Peace Conference itself? How can it, for example, undo the iniquitous gift of Shantung to Japan, when such recession requires Japan's own consent? I do not wish to prejudge the new Covenant but it is surely a sign of Mr. Wilson's faraway abstractness and of his failure to grasp near realities that he was willing to bargain the treaty for the League, instead of offering the League (and with it America's moral and material support to Europe) for the only sort of peace that we should be willing to maintain. It is even in doubt whether the President looked very closely at his League or assured himself that it was real and not counterfeit.

Thus comes to an inglorious end the quest of Woodrow Wilson in search of a new world. There also comes to an end—for a time at least —the hopes of millions of men.

*August 20, 1919*

# THE ADVERTISING MAN
by S. N. Behrman

The advertising man, the genius of America, is usually young, good-looking, sartorially perfect, with sleek hair and parti-colored shoes. Consciousness of the eminence of his position in American business has made him as complacent as Douglas Fairbanks. He does not conceal his awareness of the fact that he is the cornerstone of the most respectable American institutions; the newspapers and magazines depend on him; Literature and Journalism are his handmaidens. He is the Fifth Estate. . . . James Cabell speaks with accuracy of the great

American weekly which prints fiction among its advertisements. Yet, for all his dignity, the advertising man is a good fellow none the less. At lunch time he is lavish and fluent, fecund in anecdote. He is on the right side of things, the optimistic side. He has no use for morbidity, irregularity. He is as patriotic as George M. Cohan. Usually he is married and does not conceal from you the fact that his salary is twice that of the president of the university from which he didn't graduate since he deserted academic maunderings for the actualities. But he is likely to respect college presidents. Since they are themselves, along his own line, not meanly equipped. . . .

Not only would our newspapers not be without the advertising man; they would not be so funny. If there is some question as to whether he relieves the monotony of subway kiosks there is no doubt whatever that he relieves the monotony of newspapers. When you get tired of the ironic invectives against Claude Kitchin on the editorial page of the newspaper which is by no means your favorite but which you nevertheless read because your favorite isn't published yet (since it probably couldn't get the ads!) you can turn to an ingenious article on Gladstone, headed by a great picture of the G.O.M., which tells you that his success as a statesman was due to the fact that he used a razor, in all essentials exactly like the Durham-Duplex. Precisely like, that is, except for the "safety" of the later instrument. Or to the theatrical columns and be invited to see Theda Bara in *Cleopatra*. "Why," you are asked, "did Caesar leave Rome?" You speculate. You wonder. You are led to believe that Theda Bara had something to do with it. She must be an interesting person to attract so celebrated a weekender. Or, you are slyly told of Cleopatra, by way of historical diversion, that "her tailor was a florist." This, too, suggests that Theda is an interest ing person, orchidaceous and amiable.

"Publicity" is the reigning philosophy, the magic conjuring word. The extent to which you employ it is the mark of your success. The advertising man is as necessary to the undertaker as he is to the actor and the politician. Recently the family of a well-known dramatic critic, a modest man with simple notions about interment, was horrified to read in the newspapers, a few days after his death, the statement that the deceased had left a "sealed envelope" with esoteric instructions as to his funeral. When he investigated the story, the son of the dead man found that it had been circulated by the publicity man of the fashionable undertaking establishment which had charge of his father's body and had to write a privately published pamphlet in which he disposed of the story. The advertising man is the *enfant terrible* of the time, unabashed before the eternities. Even war needs him, to say nothing of Swift and Company. No doubt we should have seen, were it not for the emergence of the League of Nations, an increasing specialization in "war publicity." America would probably have developed the snappiest war publicists in the world. The first act of a South American revolutionist would be to wire a New York agency for a publicity man, a live wire, who could put a revolution over, with neatness and dispatch. This is one of the greatest undeveloped professions, which a lasting peace will render stillborn as it will stifle the activities of the munition makers.

*December 24, 1919 [Woodrow Wilson]*

# WHEN THE BIG FOUR MET
by Maynard Keynes

When President Wilson left Washington, he enjoyed a prestige and a moral influence throughout the world unequaled in history. His bold and measured words carried to the peoples of Europe above and beyond the voices of their own politicians. The enemy peoples trusted him to carry out the compact he had made with them; and the Allied peoples acknowledged him not as a victor only but almost as a prophet. In addition to this moral influence, the realities of power were in his hands. The American armies were at the height of their numbers, discipline and equipment. Europe was in complete dependence on the food supplies of the United States; and financially she was even more absolutely at their mercy. Europe not only already owed the United States more than she could pay; but only a large measure of further assistance could save her from starvation and bankruptcy. Never had a philosopher held such weapons wherewith to bind the princes of this world. How the crowds of the European capitals pressed about the carriage of the President! With what curiosity, anxiety and hope we sought a glimpse of the features and bearing of the man of destiny who, coming from the West, was to bring healing to the wounds of the ancient parent of his civilization and lay for us the foundations of the future.

The disillusion was so complete that some of those who had trusted it most hardly dared speak of it. Could it be true? they asked of those who returned from Paris. Was the Treaty really as bad as it seemed? What had happened to the President? What weakness or what misfortune had led to so extraordinary, so unlooked-for a betrayal?

Yet the causes were very ordinary and human. The President was not a hero or a prophet; he was not even a philosopher; but a generously intentioned man with many of the weaknesses of other human beings and lacking that dominating intellectual equipment which would have been necessary to cope with the subtle and dangerous spellbinders whom a tremendous clash of forces and personalities had brought to the top as triumphant masters in the swift game of give and take, face to face in Council—a game of which he had no experience at all.

We had indeed quite a wrong idea of the President. We knew him to be solitary and aloof and believed him very strong-willed and obstinate. We did not figure him as a man of detail, but the clearness with which he had taken hold of certain main ideas would, we thought, in combination with his tenacity, enable him to sweep through cobwebs. Besides these qualities, he would have the objectivity, the cultivation and the wide knowledge of the student. The great distinction of language which had marked his famous Notes seemed to indicate a man of lofty and powerful imagination. His portraits indicated a fine presence and a commanding delivery. With all this he had attained and held with increasing authority the first position in a country where the arts of the politician are not neglected. All of which, without expecting the impossible, seemed a fine combination of qualities for the matter in hand.

The first impression of Mr. Wilson at close quarters was to impair some but not all of these illusions. His head and features were finely cut and exactly like his photographs, and the muscles of his neck and the carriage of his head were distinguished. The first glance at the President disclosed, in fact, that, whatever else he might be, his temperament was not primarily that of the student or the scholar; that he had not much even of that culture of the world which marks M. Clemenceau and Mr. Balfour as exquisitely cultivated gentlemen of their class and generation. But more serious than this, he was not only insensitive to his surroundings in the external sense—he was not sensitive to his environment at all. What chance could such a man have against Mr. Lloyd George's unerring, almost mediumlike sensibility to everyone immediately round him? To see the British Prime Minister watching the company, with six or seven senses not available to ordinary men, judging character, motive and subconscious impulse, perceiving what each was thinking and even what each was going to say next, and compounding with telepathic instinct the argument or appeal best suited to the vanity, weakness or self-interest of his immediate auditor, was to realize that the poor President would be playing blindman's bluff in that party. Never could a man have stepped into the parlor a more perfect and predestined victim to the finished accomplishment of the Prime Minister. The Old World was tough in wickedness anyhow; the Old World's heart of stone might blunt the sharpest blade of the bravest knight errant. But this blind and deaf Don Quixote was entering a cavern where the swift and glittering blade was in the hands of the adversary.

But if the President was not the philosopher-king, what was he? After all, he was a man who had spent much of his life at a university. He was by no means a businessman or an ordinary party politician, but a man of force, personality and importance. What then was his temperament?

The clue once found was illuminating. The President was a non-conformist minister, perhaps a Presbyterian. His thought and his temperament were essentially theological, not intellectual, with all the strength and the weakness of that manner of thought, feeling and expression. It is a type of which there are not now in England and Scotland such magnificent specimens as formerly; but this description, nevertheless, will give the ordinary Englishman the distinctest impression of the President.

With this picture of him in mind, we can return to the actual course of events. The President's program for the world, as set forth in his speeches and his notes, had displayed a spirit and a purpose so admirable that the last desire of his sympathizers was to criticize details —the details, they felt, were quite rightly not filled in at present, but would be in due course. It was commonly believed at the commencement of the Paris Conference that the President had thought out, with the aid of a large body of advisers, a comprehensive scheme not only for the League of Nations, but for the embodiment of the Fourteen Points in an actual Treaty of Peace. But in fact the President had thought out nothing; when it came to practice, his ideas were nebulous and incomplete. He had no plan, no scheme, no constructive ideas whatever for clothing with the flesh of life the commandments which he had thundered from the White House. He could have preached a sermon on any of them or have addressed a stately prayer to the Almighty for their fulfillment; but he could not frame their concrete application to the actual state of Europe.

He not only had no proposals in detail, but he was in many respects, perhaps inevitably, ill informed as to European conditions. And not only was he ill informed—that was true of Mr. Lloyd George also— but his mind was slow and inadaptable. The President's slowness amongst the Europeans was noteworthy. He could not, all in a minute, take in what the rest were saying, size up the situation with a glance, frame a reply and meet the case by a slight change of ground; and he was liable, therefore, to defeat by the mere swiftness, apprehension and agility of a Lloyd George. There can seldom have been a statesman of the first rank more incompetent than the President in the agilities of the council chamber. A moment often arrives when substantial victory is yours if by some slight appearance of a concession you can save the face of the opposition or conciliate them by a restatement of your proposal helpful to them and not injurious to anything essential to yourself. The President was not equipped with this simple and usual artfulness. His mind was too slow and unresourceful to be ready with *any* alternatives. The President was capable of digging his toes in and refusing to budge, as he did over Fiume. But he had no other mode of defense, and it needed as a rule but little maneuvering by his opponents to prevent matters coming to such a head until it was too late. By pleasantness and an appearance of conciliation, the President would be maneuvered off his ground, would miss the moment for digging his toes in, and, before he knew where he had been got to, it was too late. Besides it is impossible month after month in intimate and ostensibly friendly converse between close associates to be digging the toes in all the time. Victory would only have been possible to one who had always a sufficiently lively apprehension of the position as a whole, to reserve his fire and know for certain the rare exact moments for decisive action. And for that the President was far too slow-minded and bewildered. . . .

*January 21, 1920 [H. L. Mencken]*

## BOOKS AND THINGS

by Philip Littell

Put cotton in your ears and listen to the noise of Mr. Mencken's vocabulary: slobber, hocus-pocus, softies, popinjays, flapdoodle, flubdub, poppycock, balderdash, pish-posh, clapper-clawing, rumble-bumble, sissified. I cannot think of his vocabulary without wondering whether he is a shrew. "A Birmingham anthropologist, Dr. Jordan," says William James in *The Varieties of Religious Experience*, "has divided the human race into two types, whom he calls 'shrews' and 'non-shrews' respectively. The shrew type is defined as possessing an 'active unimpassioned temperament.' In other words, shrews are the 'motors' rather than the 'sensories,' and their expressions are as a rule more energetic than the feelings which appear to prompt them." Yet Mr. Mencken is not one of Dr. Jordan's shrews. He only looks like one. In spite of his vocabulary, so appropriate to nobody but a man trying to hide his lack of energy behind it, his feelings really are energetic. No one can doubt his energy who reads his *Prejudices* through, though many single sentences sound as if he were faking it.

Equally irrelevant to Mr. Mencken's real gifts is his desire to *épater le bourgeois*. I use the shopworn phrase because the desire is just as shopworn. Long ago there was a split in the bourgeois party. Every writer of Mr. Mencken's rank, except Mr. Mencken, knows that some of them, at that remote date, enrolled themselves in *Les bourgeois inépatables*, and that the left-behind others are not worth shocking, being such easy marks. But Mr. Mencken cannot let the poor bourgeois alone. He has a point, and a good point, to make against Mr. Veblen's belief that we hire men to cut our lawns, instead of putting cows there to crop them, because "to the average popular apprehension," Mr. Veblen says, "a herd of cattle so pointedly suggests thrift and usefulness that their presence . . . would be intolerably cheap." And here is part of Mr. Mencken's comment: "Has the genial professor, pondering his great problems, ever taken a walk in the country? And has he, in the course of that walk, ever crossed a pasture inhabited by a cow (*Bos taurus*)? And has he, making that crossing, ever passed astern of the cow herself? And has he, thus passing astern, ever stepped carelessly, and— But this is not a medical work, so I had better haul up." Such a putting of his finger to his nose, such a winking and grimacing, read suspiciously like flourishes to something Mr. Mencken regards as brightly daring. Now I deny that it is daring to object to cow dung on lawns. Was Mr. Mencken afraid nobody would be offended if he made his objection simply?

When I began this article my plan was to write each paragraph so that the end would contradict the beginning, but I can think of no passage in *Prejudices* which effaces the impression left by what I have just quoted. Let me add, however, that the quotation is in a class by itself, that to be "daring" is not one of Mr. Mencken's besetting faults, that for every once he tries to shock *les bourgeois* he scolds them and flouts them twenty times. His dislike of the crowd has the same origin as his dislike of the men he calls the professors, namely, in a generous anger. He is angry or contemptuous or exasperated whenever he sees good books ignored and feeble books exalted. In other words, he is often angry. When "the professors" unite in praising an author he esteems, for example Poe, Mr. Mencken is uneasy, and his uneasiness takes him back to the time when "the professors" gave Poe the cold shoulder. "If it ever occurred," he says, "to any American critic of position, during Poe's lifetime, that he was a greater man than either Cooper or Irving, then I have been unable to find any trace of the fact in the critical literature of the time."

Let us be glad, on Mr. Mencken's account, that his search was unsuccessful, for success would have made him rather unhappy. And here, I think, we have one of the contradictions he interests us by revealing. In the spring which feeds Mr. Mencken's critical activities, most of the boiling and bubbling is done by a love for the books he thinks good, a hatred of the books he thinks bad. His business as a critic is to communicate this hatred and this love, and if he were successful on a large scale, if he found either the professors or the highbrows or the crowd in agreement with him often, then he wouldn't much like his company. The strongest critic, he appears to believe, is the critic who stands most alone.

For practical purposes the best critic is he who does most to increase a reader's enjoyment, either by giving him new books to enjoy or by intensifying and differentiating his enjoyment of old ones. This a critic cannot do for you unless he has the art of inclining you to agree with him. For me, Mr. Mencken is not that kind of critic. He seldom persuades me to feel I shall like a book by saying that he likes it. Of "The Purpose," a Sudermann story in the volume called in English *The Indian Lily,* Mr. Mencken says: "Here, in less than fifteen thousand words, Sudermann rehearses the tragedy of a whole life, and so great is the art of the thing that one gets a sense of perfect completeness, almost of exhaustiveness." To my taste, "The Purpose" is a workmanlike story, without any of Sudermann's worst faults. Another story in the same book, "Autumn," is "almost a fit complement to Joseph Conrad's great paean to youth triumphant." Never, I say upon reading that incredible comparison, never will I take Mr. Mencken's word for anything remotely related to life or letters. Then I turn the page, and I'm not so sure, for I come upon Mr. Mencken's admirable characterization of George Ade, which is both generous and wise, and at once I want to read George Ade over again.

But the book I most wanted to read, just after finishing *Prejudices, First Series,* was *Prejudices, Second Series,* by the same author. The second series will be as readable and sincere as the first. It will have the same defects. Mr. Mencken will put into it extraordinarily able things, like his articles on Mr. Wells, Mr. Bennett and Mr. Nathan, and he will put in howlers. He doesn't know the difference. He will never know.

*April 14, 1920*

# STRAVINSKY
by Paul Rosenfeld

The new steel organs of man have begotten their music in *Le Sacre du Printemps*. For with Stravinsky, the rhythms of machinery enter musical art. With this, his magistral work, a new chapter of music commences, the spiritualization of the new body of man is manifest. Through Debussy, music had liquefied, become opalescent and impalpable and fluent. It had become, because of his sense, his generation's sense, of the infirmity of things, a sort of symbol of the eternal flux, the eternal momentariness. It had come to body forth all that merges and changes and disappears, to mirror the incessant departures and evanescences of life, to shape itself upon the infinitely subtle play of light, the restless, heaving, foaming surface of the sea, the impalpable racks of perfume, upon gusts of wind and fading sounds, upon all the ephemeral wonders of the world. But through Stravinsky there has come to be a music stylistically well-nigh the reverse of that of the impressionists. Through him, music has become again cubical, lapidary, massive, mechanistic. Scintillation is gone out of it. The delicate sinuous melodic line, the glamorous sheeny harmonies, are gone out of it. The elegance of Debussy, the golden sensuality, the quiet classic touch, are flown. Instead, there are come to be great weighty metallic masses, molten piles and sheets of steel and iron, shining adamantine bulks. Contours are become grim, severe, angular. Melodies are sharp, rigid, asymmetrical. Chords are uncouth, square clusters of notes, stout and solid as the pillars that support roofs, heavy as the thuds of trip hammers. Above all, there is rhythm, rhythm rectangular and sheer and emphatic, rhythm that lunges and beats and reiterates and dances with all the steely-perfect tirelessness of the machine, shoots out and draws back, shoots upward and shoots down, with the inhuman motion of titanic arms of steel. Indeed, the change is as radical, as complete, as though in the midst of moonlit noble gardens a giant machine had arisen swiftly from the ground, and inundated the night with electrical glare, and set its metal thews and joints relentlessly whirring, relentlessly functioning. . . .

Stravinsky is one of those composers, found scattered all along the pathway of his art, who augment the expressiveness of music through direct imitation of nature. His imagination seems to be free, bound in no wise by what other men have adjudged music to be, and by what their practice has made it. He comes to his art without prejudice or preconception of any kind, it seems. He plays with its elements as capriciously as the child plays with paper and crayons. He amuses himself with each instrument of the band, careless of its customary uses. There are times when Stravinsky comes into the solemn conclave of musicians like a gamin with trumpet and drum. He disports himself with the infinitely dignified string quartet, makes it do light and acrobatic things. There is one interlude of *Petrouchka* that is written for snare drums alone. His work is incrustated with cheap waltzes and barrel-organ tunes. He makes the orchestra imitate the quavering of an old hurdy-gurdy. Of late he has written a ballet for eight clowns. And he is reported to have said, "I should like to bring it about that music be performed in streetcars while people get out and get in." For he finds his greatest enemy in the concert room, that rut that limits the play of the imagination of audiences, that fortress in which all of the intentions of the men of the past have established themselves, and from which they dominate the musical present. The concert room has succeeded in making music a drug, a sedative, has created a "musical attitude" in folk that is false, and robbed musical art of its power. For Stravinsky, music is either an infection, the communication of a lyrical impulse, or nothing at all. And so he would have it performed in ordinary places of congregation, at fairs, in taverns, music halls, streetcars, if you will, in order to enable it to function freely once again. His art is pointed to quicken, to infect, to begin an action that the listener must complete within himself. It is a sort of musical shorthand. On paper, it has a fragmentary look. It is as though Stravinsky had sought to reduce the elements of music to their sharpest and simplest terms, had hoped that the "development" would be made by the audience. He seems to feel that if he cannot achieve his end, the communication of his lyrical impulse, with a single strong motif, a single strong movement of tones, a single rhythmic start, he cannot achieve it at all. So we find him writing songs, the three Japanese lyrics, for instance, that are epigrammatic in their brevity; a piece for string quartet that is played in fifty seconds; a three-act opera performed in thirty minutes.

But it is no experiment in form that he is making. He seems to bring into music some of the power of the Chinese artists who, in the painting of a twig, or a pair of blossoms, represent the entire springtide. He has written some of the freshest, most rippling, delicate music. Scarcely a living man has written more freshly or incandescently. April, the flowering branches, the snowing petals, the clouds high in the blue, are really in the shrilling little orchestra of the Japanese lyrics, in the green gurgling flutes and watery violins. None of the innumerable Spring Symphonies, Spring Overtures, Spring Songs, are really more vernal, more soaked in the gentle sunshine of spring, are more really the seedtime, than the six naïve piping measures of melody

that introduce the figure of the *Sacre* entitled "Rondes Printanières."
Is any slumbersong really fuller of sleep than the few pages of *L'Oiseau
de Feu* that precede the death of Kastchei the Immortal? No doubt,
in venturing to write music so bold and original in aesthetic, Stravinsky was encouraged by the example of another musician, another
Russian composer. Moussorgsky, before him, had trusted in his own
innocence instead of in the wisdom of the fathers of the musical
church, had dared obey the promptings of his own blood and set down
chords, melodies, rhythms, just as they sang in his skull, though all
the world rise up to damn him. But the penning of music as jagged,
cubical, barbarous as the prelude to the third act of Stravinsky's little
opera *The Nightingale*, or as naked, uncouth, rectangular, rocklike,
polyharmonic, headlong, as some of that of *Le Sacre du Printemps*
required no less perfect a conviction, no less great a self-reliance. The
music of Stravinsky is the expression of an innocence comparable,
indeed, to that of his great predecessor. *Le Sacre du Printemps* is what
its composer termed it. It is "an act of faith." . . .

Whatever Stravinsky's future accomplishment, there can be no doubt
that with this one work, if not also with *Petrouchka*, he has secured a
place among the great musicians. It is doubtful whether any living
composer has opened new musical land more widely than he. For he
has not only minted music anew. He has reached a point ahead of us
that the world would have reached without him. That alone shows
him the genius. He has brought into music something for which we
had long been waiting, and which we knew must one day arrive. To
us, at this moment, *Le Sacre du Printemps* appears one of those
compositions that mark off the musical miles.

*September 8, 1920 [Politicians]*

# MEDITATION IN E MINOR*

by H. L. Mencken

I

I seem to be the only sort of man who is never heard of in politics
in the Republic, either as candidate or as voter. *Also*, I must write
my own platform, make my own speeches, point with my own pride,

* Passed reluctantly by the censor. —The Editors

view with my own alarm, pump up my own hopes and ideals, invent my own lies, posture and grimace upon my own front porch. . . .

II

Politically I am absolutely honest, which is to say, as honest as possible; which is to say, honest more or less; which is to say, far more honest than the general. My politics are based frankly and wholly upon what, in the dim light now shining in the world, I take to be my self-interest. I do not pretend to any pressing interest in the welfare of any other man, whether material or spiritual; in particular, I do not pretend to any interest in the welfare of any man who belongs to a class that differs clearly from my own. In other words, I am intensely class-conscious—almost the ideal citizen of the radical vision. Virtually all of the men that I know and like and respect belong to my own class, or to some class very closely allied to it. I can't imagine having any active good will toward a man of a widely differing class—say the class of professional politicians and bureaucrats, or that of wealthy manufacturers, or that of schoolmasters, or that of policemen, ordained and lay. Such men simply do not interest me, save as convenient targets for the malevolence that is in all of us. I like to vex them; beyond that, as old Friedrich used to say, I hand them over to statistics and the devil. If all the members of such a class were deported by Dr. Palmer and his blacklegs tomorrow, my indignation would be transient and theoretical; if I yelled, it would be as I yell occasionally about the massacres in Ireland, Haiti, Armenia and India, hoping all the while that the show doesn't stop.

Here, of course, I wallow in platitudes; I too am an American, God save us all! The blather of politics is made up almost wholly of violent and disingenuous attempts to sophisticate and obfuscate those platitudes. Often, of course, the bosh-monger succumbs to his own bosh. The late Major General Roosevelt, I have no doubt, convinced himself eventually that he was actually the valiant and aseptic Bayard of Service that he pretended to be—that he was a Lafayette sweating unselfishly and agonizingly to protect, instruct, inspire, guide and lift up the great masses of the plain people, his inferiors. He was, perhaps, honest, but he was wrong. What moved him was simply a craving for facile and meaningless banzais, for the gaudy eminence and power of the leader of a band of lynchers, for the mean admiration of mean men. His autobiography gives him away; what he left out of it he babbled to the deacon of his mass, Leary, and to the subdeacon, Abbott. Had Roosevelt been the aristocrat that legend made him, his career would have presented a truly astonishing spectacle: Brahms seeking the applause of organ-grinders, piano tuners and union cornetists. But he was no such aristocrat, either by birth or by training. He was simply a professional politician of the democratic kidney, by Harvard out of the Rotary Club bourgeoisie, and his good was always the good of his well-fed, bombastic and extremely shallow class. Immediately his usual victims became class-conscious on their own hook, he was their enemy, and showed all the horror of them that one would look for in John D. Rockefeller, Jr., Judge Gary or Frank A. Munsey.

III

The class that I belong to is an interior subclass of the order of capitalists. I am not rich, but my ease and welfare depend very largely upon the security of wealth. If stocks and bonds became valueless tomorrow, I'd be forced to supplement my present agreeable work with a good deal of intensely disagreeable work. Hence I am in favor of laws protecting property and am an admirer of the Constitution of the United States in its original form. If such laws can be enforced peacefully, i.e., by deluding and hornswoggling the classes whose interests they stand against, then I am in favor of so enforcing them; if not, then I am in favor of employing professional bullies, e.g., policemen, soldiers and Department of Justice thugs, to enforce them with the sword. Here I borrow the morality of the radicals, who are my enemies: their arguments in favor of an alert class consciousness convince me, but I stick to my own class. I borrow even more from the liberals, who are also my enemies. In particular, I borrow the doctrine that peace in such matters is better than war—that it is foolish to hire gunmen when it is so much simpler and easier to bamboozle the boobs with phrases. Here, of course, a trade interest helps out my class consciousness; I am a professional maker of phrases and delight in displays of virtuosity. The liberals feed me with that delight. This explains why I like them and encourage them, though their politics usually depress me.

But though I am thus in favor of property and would be quite content to see one mob of poor men (in uniform) set to gouging and hamstringing another mob of poor men (in overalls) in order to protect it, it by no means follows that I am in favor of the wealthy bounders who now run the United States, or of the politics that they preach in their kept press. On the contrary, I am even more violently against them than I am against the radicals with their sticks of dynamite and the liberals with their jugs of Peruna. And for a plain reason. On the one hand, these swine oppress me excessively and unnecessarily— by putting up prices, by loading me with inordinate taxes, by setting hordes of bureaucrats to looting me, by demanding that I give my assent to all their imbecile and dishonest ideas, and by threatening me with the cost of endless wars, to them extremely profitable. On the other hand, and even more importantly, their intolerable hoggishness threatens to raise the boobery in revolt and bring about a reign of terror from which only the strongest will emerge. That revolt would ruin me. I am not large enough, as a capitalist, to make a profit out of wars and turmoils. I believe that the rising of the proletariat, if it ever comes in this country, will end in a colossal victory for capitalism— that capitalism, as at present and in the past, will play off one mob against another, and pick the pockets of both. But it will also pick my pockets. It will also force me, who had nothing to do with the row and protested against it bitterly, to pay a tremendous price for getting out alive. I'll have my naked hide, but everything else will be lost, including honor.

Ah, that my vision were a mere nightmare, the child of encroaching senility and bad beer! Unluckily, the late lamentable war showed its terrible reality. That war was fought against my advice and consent, and I took no part in it whatever, save as spectator. In particular, I made no profit out of it—not a cent, directly or indirectly. Well, what is my situation today? In brief, I find that my property is worth, roughly speaking, no more than half of what it was worth at the end of 1916, and that, considering its ratio to the total national wealth, and the differences between the national debt then and now, I owe, as a citizen of the United States, something between $8,000 and $10,000. To whom? Who got it, and how, and for what? . . . Let us not go into the question too particularly. I find my class consciousness wobbling!

IV

Meanwhile, however, I still manage to eat without too much labor, and so I incline to the Right, and am a Tory in politics, and trust in God. It would give me great pleasure to vote for a Tory candidate for the Presidency—not a hollow ass like General Wood, but an honest and unashamed Tory, one voicing the sincere views of the more civilized section of the propertied class, not a mere puppet for usurers. Unfortunately, no such candidate ever offers himself. The men put up by these usurers are always such transparent frauds that it is impossible, without anesthetics, to vote for them. I admire liars, but surely not liars so clumsy that they cannot fool even themselves. I am an old hand at political shows, and witnessed both the nomination of Harding at Chicago and that of Cox at San Francisco. It would be difficult to imagine more obscene spectacles. Who, being privy to their disgusting trimming, their mean courting of mean men, their absolute lack of any sense of dignity, honor or self-respect, could vote for either? It will take me all the time between now and November, abandoning all other concerns, to work up the necessary cynicism—and no doubt I'll fail even then. But could I vote for Christiansen? He is a Knight of Pythias; allow me my prejudices! Debs? Please don't suggest it in plain words. It would be anguish unspeakable; I am probably the only man in Christendom who has never been a Socialist even for an instant. An idiot, this Debs, but honest, and he says plainly that he is against me. I'd be a worse idiot if I voted for him.

My dilemma, alas, is not unique. Thousands of other men must face it—men of my class, men of related classes, perhaps even men of classes far removed. It visualizes one of the penalties that democracy, the damnedest of frauds, inflicts upon every man who violates all its principles by trying to be honest.

*October 6, 1920 [Warren G. Harding]*

# THE FRONT PORCH IN MARION
by Charles Merz

Another week or two, and no more pilgrims. In Marion the dusk is falling. Delegations come and go; when Marion's day is done it will be said that Senator Harding has managed to align himself with the best of them. Out of the variety of his early experience and the capacity of his memory he has attained that personal touch which makes each stranger feel at home. For the band, he recalls days when he himself once blew upon a horn. He tells the railway workers of boyhood longings to become an engineer and of a day he helped "wood up" on the old Atlantic and Great Western. The schoolteachers he reminds that once upon a time he taught a country school. For baseball players from Chicago, he recalls his own experiences at first base. For veterans of the Spanish War he can recall "emotions in my breast the day the boys from Marion marched away . . . I remember also when the *Maine* was sunk." For delegates from certain native Indian tribes, he has this message: "I wish I could take you about here and introduce you to the musical names in this section that all come from the Indian days. . . . I was raised along the banks of the old Olentangy." And for visitors from Richland County, he can recall a Richland County grandmother on her way to market pursued by wolves—"I feel myself almost a part of Richland County."

The Senator is the ideal host.

You feel that, when you arrive in front of the green house in Mount Vernon Avenue with the wide porch that runs around the corner. There is a policeman on duty near the hedge. He does not warn you off the gravel lawn. He does not bid you keep your distance. To those visitors gathering on the walk before the house he points out marks of interest. "Yes, that flagpole came from Canton. Yes, it used to stand on President McKinley's lawn. That's all right, lady. You can go right up and take the little fellow's picture on the steps. Senator Harding doesn't mind a bit. What's that? No, that's not the Senator. I reckon it's one of the newspaper writers. On the porch? That lady? Let's see. Yes, the lady's Mrs. Harding." Mrs. Harding, eh? Two visitors especially are interested. They reveal themselves to the policeman. Between them, he is informed, they constitute the Court of Pettis County, Missouri—Republican now, thank God, and likely to stay Republican forever. They happen to be out looking at courthouses. Their own, not long ago, burned down. If that is really Mrs. Harding . . . ? Sure, says the policeman; go right up and introduce yourselves.

He is only the symbol, this Chesterfield in uniform, of Republican principle in 1920. For a party that may fly apart, whenever it attempts to reach agreement upon a definite issue, self-preservation advises postponement of the possible catastrophe. . . . There is more of a crowd now, and it surges respectfully across the lawn as the Senator appears with the newspapermen who have followed him from his office. He is still answering questions. The crowd holds back. The Senator disengages himself from the newspapermen and comes to greet his callers. He takes the nearest hand. "And what portion of the state do you come from?" he asks. "Ashland," replies his happy guest, and adds: "Motored in this morning." "Roads good?" asks the Senator. "Fine." The Senator turns to an elderly woman. She has been teaching school for forty years, she says, and she wants the Senator's interest in a teachers' pension bill. The Senator assures her that while he recognizes in America no special classes, and while he conceives the Presidency as at best co-equal with the legislative and judicial powers, nevertheless he is ready to promise that the teachers' pension bill will have his close attention. More handshaking follows. But the Senator sights his campaign manager, Mr. Daugherty, and wants a game of quoits. Bolder portions of the crowd adjourn with the contestants to the Harding alley. The Senator removes his coat. The crowd whispers its recognition of a democrat when it sees one, and the moving-picture men start grinding. The Senator pitches six horseshoes. Mr. Daugherty pitches six. It cannot truthfully be said that any of the twelve arrive. But the Senator is declared a winner. The crowd accompanies him around to the front of the house again. And the moving-picture men remain. They push their cameras nearer to the little stake and start taking close-ups. The finished picture must show at least one bull's-eye. So they grind away while an understudy stands just outside of camera range and drops horseshoes accurately upon the hitherto neglected stake. A knockout, the moving-picture men agree.

The Senator now has disappeared. There are delegations coming, delegations from six Ohio counties, and an official porch reception is to follow. Crowds are gathering along Mount Vernon Avenue, awaiting the parade. There are people sitting on the curbstones, sandwich boxes open on their knees. Come upon a crowd waiting like this anywhere else in America and you would guess that Barnum and Bailey themselves were the attraction. But all Barnum's horses and all Bailey's men could not tempt these people from their present posts.

Down the street at the head of a procession comes the first band on its way to the front porch in Mount Vernon Avenue. The Harding-and-Coolidge Club of East Liberty, Ohio, wheels in sight. The Logan County Women's Club for Harding follows. "Save the Constitution," its banners read. "League of Nations? No, We Know Our Business." Other delegations follow, from Ottawa County and from Tuscarawas. They march four or five abreast. They have come to greet the next President of the country. The Champaign County delegates appear with white-and-green-striped parasols. The crowd sends up a cheer. A moment later there is is a second burst of cheering. Knox County has arrived with a bandmaster who can throw his great baton above his head and catch it, spinning, with an arm behind his back.

The long line of pilgrims has been marshaled into position for a battery of cameramen, told to take its standards down, told to close its ranks up, told to take its hats off. Various minor celebrities have appeared upon the porch. The crowd has guessed at their identity. There is a moment of suspense. The Senator appears upon the porch. The crowd cheers. There is an ovation which lasts four seconds by the watch. Without difficulty the crowd is silenced by the unidentified celebrity who acts as master of ceremonies. "Ladies and Gentlemen," he announces, "we will first hear from the Tuscarawas County Quartet." The quartet follows with a lively song. There is another cheer. Various chairmen of county delegations are introduced. They tell the Senator he will win overwhelmingly in November. He is, they wish to assure him, the greatest statesman of his party. He will restore the country from the decay of Democratic rule, bring down prices, harmonize capital and labor, safeguard American honor and fan the sacred fire of the Fathers. He is the greatest statesman since Lincoln. To each generous tribute the Senator bows, not in false modesty, but as a man conscious of his worth and humbled by it. Between compliments he stands erect, eyes raised above the heads of those who watch him. On his face is stamped an almost tragic resignation. The times have summoned him: very well, he will obey the call. An octet of Negro singers leaps up the steps and bursts into ragtime. Here is a real sensation. The octet sings an encore. The crowd shouts its joy again. And then, suddenly, and with no more preparation, the Senator himself. . . .

"Fellow citizens of the Republic—America uncovers today in observance of the 133rd anniversary of the birthday of the nation. I do not say the birthday of American freedom which we celebrate variously though always patriotically on July Fourth in reverence for the Declaration of Independence, but this is the anniversary of the literal birthday of our American nation. . . . In that first convention were men of every type of mind. . . . It was difficult timber out of which to erect the enduring temple of the Republic which I think it worth our while to recall to lead us to greater appreciation. . . ."

Heads bared to the summer sun, they hear him out. They do not cheer especially, except when he has finished. It is his turn now, and he shall have it. He has been the perfect host. It has been a splendid day. They have come chiefly for the purpose of saying that they have been, and with this philosophy nothing can take the edge off their satisfaction. They pack banners, balloons and tired children into trains and motorcars and start back home again. Only a few more pilgrims will stand upon that gravel lawn. In Marion the dusk is falling. Not alone the merchants and innkeepers of Marion, but all those—everywhere—who cherish the performance of a perfect act will mourn the passing of the day.

*July 27, 1921*

# GANDHI: AN INDIAN SAINT

by W. W. Pearson

A PERSONAL STUDY
> We will grow strong by calmness and moderation; we will grow strong by the violence and injustice of our adversaries.—ABRAHAM LINCOLN

When a man is described by Rabindranath Tagore as "the greatest of living men," and by the governor of a province of the British Empire as "a dangerous and misguided saint," it is worth while studying his personality even if his policy does not interest us. And this is how the Indian leader M. K. Gandhi has been spoken of. Gandhi is undoubtedly a remarkable man, remarkable in the fact that he differs so greatly in policy and public life from all those who guide the nations. Statesmen and politicians are seldom guided by the motives which compel Gandhi to action. He has said of himself:

"Most religious men I have met are politicians in disguise; I, however, who wear the guise of a politician, am at heart a religious man."

This is the secret of Gandhi's overwhelming influence in India. It is not because he stands for a definite policy in regard to the British Raj, but because he is a saint, a man of austere and ascetic life who follows Truth at whatever cost to himself. Not even his worst enemy has ever doubted Gandhi's sincerity. His friends know him to be so stern in his loyalty to a principle once accepted that even friendship cannot divert him from a course which he regards as right.

I first met him in South Africa early in 1914, just after he had been released from prison for leading the Indian community in his Movement of Passive Resistance against the government. I remember my first glimpse of him as, surrounded by other Indians, he stood on the wharf upon the arrival of the steamer in which I had come from India. He was dressed in simple homespun, had no hat on his head and was barefoot. He is not striking in appearance though on closer acquaintance with him it is impossible not to be struck with the singular sweetness of his expression. As I saw him working for the coolies on the sugar planations and greeting them often by name, I was forcibly reminded of Saint Francis of Assisi. Whenever he traveled he went by the third class which is usually patronized by the Kaffirs, and he always preferred to walk, except when time made it advisable for him to drive.

As an example of his unswerving allegiance to a principle of action, I recollect his attitude before the commission which had been appointed by the government of South Africa to inquire into the grievances of the Indian community in that colony. It was to give Gandhi and other leaders an opportunity of giving evidence before this commission that they had been released from jail. But the Indian community had not been consulted in the matter of the personnel of this commission and Gandhi consequently refused to give evidence and persuaded all Indians who followed him to refuse likewise. He persisted in his refusal, although the Honorable Mr. Gokhale, a man for whom he had the very greatest reverence, was almost daily cabling to him from India urging him to reconsider his decision, as his refusal was being construed as a virtual confession of the weakness of the Indian point of view. But he regarded the appointment of such a commission, without consultation with the Indian community whose interests were at stake, as a direct blow at the self-respect of India. So he turned a deaf ear to the urgent plea of one whom he reverenced and esteemed. He was right, though he may not have been diplomatic. Gandhi never is diplomatic. He always lays all his cards on the table and his opponent is often unable to believe that he has nothing ulterior in his motives. Open diplomacy has always been Gandhi's strength.

Another characteristic is his chivalry to an opponent. Just when he was to start the Passive Resistance campaign again early in 1914 as a protest against the appointment of a commission without adequate Indian representation, a strike broke out among the white workers on the Rand. Gandhi immediately announced that his Passive Resistance would be indefinitely postponed until the government was no longer embarrassed by this strike. This chivalry proved to be a stroke of diplomacy, for it won the admiration of General Smuts and of many who would not otherwise have sympathized with his political ideals. But it was not intended as a diplomatic move.

Mr. Gandhi originally had a lucrative legal practice in Johannesburg bringing him in over $15,000 a year. This he gave up when the call of his country came to him with impelling force. He gave all the money that he had to the founding of a settlement at Phoenix, near Durban, modeled on Tolstoyan lines of simplicity and service. He himself felt that a life of poverty would give him the freedom necessary for his work for his countrymen.

I visited him at this settlement where every member of the community does some service for the whole. Gandhi himself was exceptional only in that he did far more when he was there than any other individual member. It was at Phoenix that his characteristic unselfishness of conduct was most evident. Often did I protest against the way in which Mr. Gandhi in the midst of great public responsibilities spent his valuable hours in menial tasks which could so easily have been carried out by less prominent members of his community.

When the Honorable Mr. Gokhale was a guest at Phoenix he had the same experience and he often told humorously of the heartless tyranny of his host, who insisted upon doing the most menial tasks, including that of a sweeper, for his guests. To such protests he would reply that as regards a piece of work which had to be done and got through with, there was no highness or lowness about it—if a piece of work was thought to be too dirty for him (Gandhi), it should be regarded as too dirty and low even for a poor sweeper, who was just as much a human being as he himself.

It is this readiness to make the same sacrifices which he asks of those who follow him which gives him his extraordinary moral authority. As a recent interesting writer on India has said of him:

Mr. Gandhi has always been prepared to accept and has always actually accepted for himself the direct logical outcome of his principles, whatever hardship and breach of social convention it may involve. This, combined with his utter sincerity, the austere simplicity of his life and his readiness to serve the people at all costs and sacrifice, explains his unparalleled hold over his countrymen. No trick or posing can give such influence to any leader.

Mr. Gandhi is a strict vegetarian, and when I first met him he was taking only one meal a day which consisted of fruit, nuts, olive oil and whole-meal bread, often baked with his own hands at the settlement. Even when he went to Pretoria to interview the heads of government he wore the plain homespun garments which he always wears, believing, as he does, in a revival of hand weaving in protest against the present industrial system. As he sat at his meal in a large store in Durban, he would ask the coolies who had come to see him and to consult with him about their troubles to sit beside him so that he could give them more time for talk. And in all his dealings with the simple uncultured people he showed the same courtesy and patience. He was always accessible to the poor and unfortunate, and even when affairs of the utmost importance weighed upon him he would give them some of his time.

Mention has been made of his settlement being started on Tolstoyan principles and it should be stated that Gandhi has always had the greatest admiration for the teachings of that great Western prophet. From him he adopted the term Passive Resistance, and the spirit of much of his public work shows the influence of Tolstoy. But there is no doubt that the doctrine of nonresistance which he preaches also has its foundation in the teachings of his own religion, a religion which teaches ahinsa, or aversion to slaughter and violence. He was born a Jain and the Jains will not destroy any life, even that of the most insignificant animal. Like strict Buddhists they will not eat animal food.

He has, where possible, cooperated with the British government, as is shown by the fact that he has been decorated several times with war medals for his services in the Zulu War, the Boer War and the war against Germany, in connection with ambulance work. But lately he has lost faith in the promises of British statesmen, and even in the justice of the British people. In an open letter addressed "To Every Englishman in India" occur the following words, which explain his present position:

> In my humble opinion, no Indian has cooperated with the British government more than I have for an unbroken period of twenty-nine years of public life in the face of circumstances that might well have turned any other man into a rebel. I ask you to believe me when I tell you that my cooperation was not based on the fear of punishments provided by your laws or any other selfish motives. It was free and voluntary cooperation

based on the belief that the sum total of the activity of the British government was for the benefit of India. I put my life in peril four times for the sake of the Empire. I did all this in the full belief that acts such as mine must gain for my country an equal status in the Empire. So late as last December (1919) I pleaded for a trustful cooperation. I fully believed that Mr. Lloyd George would redeem the promise to the Mussulmans and that the revelations of the official atrocities in the Punjab would secure full reparations for the Punjabis. But the treachery of Mr. Lloyd George and its appreciation by you, and the condonation of the Punjab atrocities have completely shattered my faith in the good intentions of the government and the nation which is supporting it.

He goes on to explain the meaning of his noncooperation policy:

I am engaged in evoking bravery of soul. Noncooperation means nothing less than training in self-sacrifice. Why should we cooperate with you when we know that by your administration of this great country we are being daily enslaved in an increasing degree? This response of the people to my appeal is not due to my personality. You are in search of a remedy to suppress the rising ebullition of national feeling. I venture to suggest to you that the only way is to remove the causes. You have yet the power. You can repent of the wrongs done to Indians. You can compel Mr. Lloyd George to redeem his promises. The other solution, namely repression, is open to you. I prophesy that it will fail.

In a recent number of his paper, *Young India,* dated March 30th, 1921, he writes as follows:

The problem before us, therefore, is one of opposing our will to that of the government, in other words to withdraw our cooperation from it. If we are united in purpose, the government must obey our will or retire. It is the disturbing factors of which the government avails itself for the consolidation of its power. When we are violent, it resorts to terrorism; when we are disunited, it resorts to bribery; when we are united, it resorts to cajolery and conciliation; when we are clamant, it puts temptations in the way of those who cry out the most. All, therefore, we need do is to remain nonviolent, united, and unresponsive to bribery and cajolery.

Let us not waste our resources in thinking of too many national problems and their solutions. A patient who tries many nostrums at a time dies. A physician who experiments on his patient with a combination of remedies loses his reputation and passes for a quack. Chastity in work is as essential as chastity in life. All dissipation is bad. We have hitherto all pulled our own way, and thus wasted away national strength in a most extravagant manner. To boycott foreign cloth within a year is a practical feasibility. To bring into being a working organization for the Congress is an easy thing for honest workers. Drink and untouchability must vanish. The education movement is steadily going forward. The national institutions that have sprung up will, if they are efficiently managed, make headway and attract students who are still hesitating. Boycott of the lawcourts by the public is making fair progress. These things do not now require concentration of universal effort.

My strong advice to every worker is to segregate this evil government by strict noncooperation, not even to talk or speak about it, but having recognized the evil, to cease to pay homage to it by cooperation.

Gandhi has been able to unite the people of India as they have never been united before, not only because of his unfaltering loyalty to a moral ideal and his austere and ascetic personal life, but because the British government has itself by repeated acts fed fuel to the fires of national aspiration.

Confronting the most powerful empire in existence stands this one man who cares nothing for his own personal safety, who is uncompromising and fearless in the application of principles which he has once accepted, and who scorns any longer to receive or beg for favors from a government which he regards as having "forfeited all title to confidence, respect or support." He believes in conquering hate by love, in the triumph of right over might, and all the effort of his public life is directed toward persuading the masses in India of the truth of this ideal.

*September 28, 1921 [Calvin Coolidge]*

# CALVIN THE SILENT
by Edward G. Lowry

The elections of 1920 imported into the City of Conversation, as one of its necessary consequences, perhaps the oddest and most singular apparition this vocal and articulate settlement has ever known. A politician who does not, who will not, who seemingly cannot talk. A well of silence. A center of stillness.

Moreover, it appears from the meager record that he thinks of himself as Peter Pan, the boy who never grew up to be a man.

We had, of course, all heard of Calvin Coolidge; that he had been City Councilman, City Solicitor, Court Clerk, State Representative, Mayor, State Senator, Lieutenant Governor and Governor, one after another virtually continuously since 1899; that being in place and in politics was with him both a vocation and an avocation. But the man himself as a social human being was not known at all. There was a bright curiosity to be satisfied.

Presiding over the Senate is the least of the duties of the Vice-President of the United States in the Washington scheme of things. What time he spends at the Capitol saying: "Does the Senator from South Dakota yield to the Senator from Mississippi?" or "The Senator from New Hampshire suggests the absence of a quorum, the clerk will call the roll," or when the calendar is being called, "The bill will be passed over"—is his period of reflection and digestion. His day's work really begins when he gets to his hotel in the evening and finds his dress clothes laid out on the bed and Mrs. Coolidge tells him, "We are dining with Senator Whosis tonight and you must be dressed and ready to leave here at a quarter to eight." His dress clothes are his working clothes; the overalls of a Vice-President.

By tradition and precedent the Vice-President has become the official diner-out of the Administration. Every night from November until May he must sally forth in his glad raiment and eat for his party and his chief. He and the potted palms that the close observer of official life notes being hauled from one house to another every afternoon during the season are social fixtures. No big dinner is complete without both of them.

The palms stand in the corners and on the stairways. Anciently it was a game, mildly diverting, to scratch one's name on the under side of the fronds and then keep tab to see how many times one encountered the same palms during the winter season. The palms are background, but the Vice-President is essentially foreground. He sits on the right of the hostess. He is the chief figure of the feast. The palms are, or are supposed to be, decorative. The Vice-President seldom or never is. The theory is that he is witty and amusing, or learned and informative, or a well of deep inside stuff about current political affairs.

Now as it turns out Mr. Coolidge is none of these things. To the whole of Washington, social and political, at this juncture, he presents an impenetrable blank. He dines out with the best of them. Never a night elapses that the big closed car placed at his service by the fond taxpayers does not convey him to a dinner party. No soup, however thick or thin, deters him, no fish, however disguised by the pallid, viscous goo the chefs seem to like, daunts him, and thence south through the entree to the ice, leaving only a waste behind him. And all in perfect silence.

No hammer fell, no ponderous axes rung;
Like some tall palm the noiseless fabric sprung.
    Majestic silence!

But I must say it is hard on the ladies. They often talk about it. They are supposed to make him have a good time. And having a good time at dinner is popularly supposed to be indicated by a light rattle of small talk. One hears that Mr. Coolidge feels sometimes that he is not doing all that is expected of him, for there are vague current reports that he asks wonderingly, "What do they talk about? I hear them and see them all about me, all at it, but what do they find to say?" One agreeable woman was the nine days' wonder and envy of all Washington because she made him laugh one night at dinner. She never would give the recipe or tell what she said. "I am going to use it again next winter," she declared thriftily.

In common with everyone else at Washington I have been eager to pluck out the heart of Mr. Coolidge's mystery, to discover what sort of man he is, to establish a basis for appraisal. All in vain, for he has revealed nothing, disclosed nothing. He has been described and observed as intently as possible under the circumstances, in the crush preceding the largest and noisiest of dinner parties, standing quite still and saying not a blessed word though all about him was babble and laughter and conversation. He didn't seem ill at ease or embarrassed or tongue-tied. He was just still. Silent upon a peak in Darien is no name for it. He gave no appearance of being about to say something presently. It was an absolute calm. *Old Ironsides* at anchor lay in the harbor of Mahon. The waves to sleep had gone. Not a leaf stirring. It was impressive—and he so small. A big man can be monosyllabic as he pleases, but more is expected of slight men.

One sought in vain an account of the experiences of those veterans of forlorn hopes who in the devoted pursuance of social duties had dashed themselves against the ice barriers. They had nothing to tell. Over the Alps lay Italy, they thought, but none of them had won the summit, and so they couldn't be sure that the view was worth the climb.

*January 25, 1922 [George Bernard Shaw]*

# THE CREED OF AN AESTHETE

by Clive Bell

Mr. Bernard Shaw is an admirable writer and a wit; he is one of the dozen living Englishmen whose prose is perfectly respectable; to compare him with Swift though unkind is not absurd; but he is not an artist, much less an aesthete. The difference between an artist and an aesthete is, I suppose, the difference between one who can create and one who can appreciate beauty: most artists are aesthetes as well—but not all. However, the difference does not concern me here, because I am going to deal exclusively with appreciation, and, confining myself to the term "aesthete"—under which may be ranged most artists—modestly draw attention to the fact that there are in the world quite a number of people to whom it may be applied, though apparently Mr. Shaw is unaware of their existence.

Mr. Shaw is a didactic; and one of the differences between didactics and aesthetes is that, whereas the latter rejoice in the knowledge that it takes all sorts to make a world, didactics are unable to believe that there are people who, without malice or stupidity, are fundamentally different from themselves. Thus Mr. Shaw, one of the cleverest men alive, comes out, on the fortieth page of his new book *Back to Methuselah*, with a statement so astonishingly false that I read it through four times before I would accept its obvious import. After stating quite fairly, so far as I can judge, the Darwinian theory of natural selection and survival—a theory as to the validity of which I have no opinion, not being deep in science—Mr. Shaw rejects it on the ground that it makes nonsense of "Beauty, Intelligence, Honor," etc. "When its whole significance dawns on you," says he, "your heart sinks into a heap of sand within you": and he is quite sure that "this hideous fatalism," as he calls it, will never be accepted by people who care for Beauty, Truth, Love, Honor, etc., etc., because, by depriving these things of their divine origin and purpose, it deprives them of their value. If Life be a mere purposeless accident, the finest things in it must appear to everyone worthless. That is what Mr. Shaw thinks, and the sooner he knows that it is not so the better. Whatever he may feel, the people who really care for beauty do not care for it because it comes from God or leads to anything. They care for it in itself; what is more, that is how they care for all the fine things in life.

The advantage of being an aesthete is that one is able to appreciate the significance of all that comes to one through the senses:

one feels things as ends instead of worrying about them as means. And this intrinsic significance of external reality is so intensely moving and so various that it completely satisfies those who can apprehend it. Mr. Shaw may be right and the neo-Darwinians wrong; life may be Heaven-sent and Heaven-directed toward some inconceivably glorious future; but, whether this be so or not, always life will be worth living by those who find in it things which make them feel to the limit of their capacity. Whatever its origin, beauty exists and so does the sensibility which reacts to it. A rose is a development of a briar which is a development of God-knows-what—and, incidentally, it grows out of manure; its beauties of form and color and smell appeal to a sense in me which may have grown out of primal lusts and appetites; but when I contemplate a rose I am not enjoying a chapter of natural history and I am using my sense of beauty and not my palate. Odd as it must seem to Mr. Shaw, I at this moment am enjoying a yellow rose, my contemporary; and though men of science assure me that both the rose and the I of this moment are the products of all preceding moments, our disgraceful past no more destroys my present pleasure than does my conviction that before long both the rose and I must perish.

Whatever is precious and beautiful in life is precious and beautiful irrespective of beginning and end. I have no patience with the snobbery that is forever deploring or denying our disreputable ancestry in a fortuitous concourse of atoms, or with the sentimentality that cannot do without a happy ending. Not long ago, one of that nasty brood of pseudo-scientists who nestle like wood lice in the decaying doctrine of Freud produced a theory with an unprintable name from which it seemed to follow that our romantic and passionate feelings were merely developments of a disgusting habit which, if really common amongst German children, is probably the symptom of some mental disorder induced by underfeeding. Would you believe it, the sentimentalists who happened to come across this theory were up in arms against it, not on account of its manifest improbability, but because, if true, it would make nonsense of their emotions? As if every amorous experience, from the grandest passion to the flutteringest flirtation, were not a real and complete thing as distinct from its origins as a glass of champagne is distinct from the chalk hills of the Tardenois. Long before the neo-Freudians came pestering us with their ill-founded generalizations, men of science had demonstrated the probability that all that is most rare and complex in our spiritual make-up can be traced back to the most elementary animal desires. What difference does that make? The pleasure I take in listening to the music of Mozart may, possibly, be derived from the anticipatory orgasms of a cave dweller listening to the bird he hopes to catch and eat. Mozart is not a pigeon on that account, neither are my feelings esurient. The antecedents of Mozart's music and of my feelings have nothing to do

with the present value of either. And though it should be proved
up to the hilt that the world in which we live was created by a fluke
and by a fluke will be destroyed, that would detract nothing from its
aesthetic significance.

The great good fortune of aesthetes is their capacity for seeing things
as ends whereby alone is one able to taste this significance. To Mr.
Shaw their capacity for enjoying life seems childish, and aesthetes, I
fancy, will accept the epithet as complimentary and not inexact.
Certainly children have a direct sense of things; and that is why gutter-
snipes playing on a dust heap appear to people like Mr. Shaw unrea-
sonably and irritatingly happy. Certainly, about the happiness of those
who appreciate the beauty, romance and fun of life there is a tipsy
lightheartedness which reminds me of the irresponsible gaiety of
schoolboys. These are merry because they have something to be merry
about—the fullness of life and the glory thereof: whereas those unfortunate people who can never feel things in themselves but only can
take an interest in their causes and effects are naturally worried, seeing
that of ultimate causes and effects we can really know nothing at all.
We can comprehend—embrace, that means—only the present; the rest
is shadowy and unsure: wherefore, I am sorry to say, those who cannot
live in the moment but must worry about the past and future are
obliged to "make up." My grandmother did it: she made up a nice old
gentleman with a long white beard who caused all, directed all, and
would in the end make us all happy. Mr. Shaw does not like him, and
has made up instead a, to my taste, less attractive figure, called "The
Life-Force," of whom he knows precisely as much as old Mrs. Bell
did of Jehovah. When Mr. Shaw's "grownups" are asked what they
want, they reply, "Immortality"; and when Mr. Shaw, who has ruled
out as "childish" Love and Art, is asked how they will spend their
immortality, he replies "in thought"; and when we pull a wry face at
the prospect of endless and unmitigated cogitation, he sternly gives
us to understand that we shall like it when we get there: my grandmother did the same when we, skeptical brats, protested that we
should weary of playing on harps and casting our golden crowns upon
the glassy sea.

It is only natural, I suppose, that those who cannot find happiness
in the present because they want the power of appreciation should
clamor for immortality—need I say that it is not for personal immortality but for the immortality of the race, the endless continuity of life,
that Mr. Shaw clamors? Yet it seems to me that even this betrays a
lack of courage. If we can enjoy our individual lives, knowing them
finite, surely it should not be impossible to face the fact of universal
death. Men of science, whom of course Mr. Shaw cannot allow himself
to trust, assure us that life, as we understand it, can exist only in conditions which have not always existed and will not exist always; that

Man is doomed as inevitably as Everyman. It may be so. Meanwhile
I am finishing this article and I have finished *Back to Methuselah*. The
sun is blazing into the square, but into my cool room it comes pleasantly filtered through blinds. It is lunch time; and after lunch I shall
light a pipe and sit reading, not Mr. Shaw's admirable treatise, but the
penultimate volume of Proust—an artist if ever there was one. I shall
dine with a charming companion and go to the ballet where they give
*Petrouchka, Sacre du Printemps,* and *Carnaval:* Lopokova will dance.
Later to a gay supper, with a dozen delightful people in a house full
of beautiful objects: if Artur Rubinstein is in good humor surely he
will play the piano. And so home under stars, smoking a cheroot in
the warm stillness of the sleeping streets and squares, sauntering up
all the long loneliness of Piccadilly, and only at the beginning of ugly
Shaftesbury Avenue picking up a "taxicab." The fruit and flowers go
rumbling into Covent Garden. It is dawn almost. "And tomorrow we
die?" So be it.

*February 22, 1922*

# SHAW'S COMMENT ON CLIVE BELL'S ARTICLE

by George Bernard Shaw

As will be seen in the [preceding] article, my friend Clive Bell is a
fathead and a voluptuary. This a very comfortable sort of person to be,
and very friendly and easy and pleasant to talk to. Bell is a brainy
man out of training. So much the better for his friends; for men in
training are irritable, dangerous, and apt to hit harder than they know.
No fear of that from Clive. The layer of fat on his brain makes him
incapable of following up his own meaning; but it makes him good
company.

A man out of condition muscularly not only dislikes rowing or boxing, but cannot conceive anyone liking them. A man out of condition
mentally not only dislikes hard thinking, but cannot conceive anyone
enjoying it. To Falstaff, Carpentier is an object of pity. To Clive, Einstein is the most miserable of mortals. So am I.

He is mistaken as to both of us. Intellect is a passion; and its activity and satisfaction, which can be maintained from seven years old to 107 if you can manage to live so long, are keenly pleasurable if the brain is strong enough for the exercise. Descartes must have got far more pleasure out of life than Casanova. Hamlet had more fun than Des Grieux, who tried to live on his love for Manon Lescaut, relieved by cheating at cards. Clive tells us how he poisons the clear night air of London with his cheroots after an evening of wine, woman and song; and he is contemptuously certain that he has enjoyed himself far more than a handful of old gentlemen in a society of chemists, mathematicians, biologists or what not, discussing the latest thing in quantums of energy, or electrons, or hormones. It is the interest of the tobacconist, the restaurateur, the theatrical manager, the wine merchant and distiller, to suggest that delusion to him. And what a silly delusion it is! No pleasure of the first order is compatible with tobacco and alcohol, which are useful only for killing time and drowning care. For real pleasure men keep their senses and wits clear: they do not deliberately dull and muddle themselves. I have not the smallest doubt that when the human mind is as fully developed as the human reproductive processes now are, men will, like the ancients in *Back to Methuselah*, experience a sustained ecstasy of thought that will make our sexual ecstasies seem child's play.

Clive is troubled—you know it when he cries Who cares?—because a rose grows out of manure. This comes of taking hold of things by the wrong end. Why not rejoice because manure grows into a rose? The most valuable lesson in *Back to Methuselah* is that things are conditioned not by their origins but by their ends. What makes the Ancient wise is not the life he has lived and done with but the life that is before him. Clive says why not live in the present? Because we don't and won't, and can't. Because there is no such thing as the present: there is only the gate that we are always reaching and never passing through: the gate that leads from the past into the future. Clive, meaning to insist on static sensation, slips inevitably into talking of *"the significance* of all that comes to one through the senses." What then becomes of his figment of sense without significance? "Whatever is precious and beautiful in life," he says, "is precious and beautiful irrespective of beginning and end." Bosh! The only sensations intense enough to be called precious or beautiful are the sensations of irresistible movement to an all-important end: the only perceptions that deserve such epithets are perceptions of some artistic expression of such sensation or prefigured ideal of its possibilities. The pain with which a child cuts its teeth, though felt, is not suffered because the child feels it as Clive pretends to feel his pleasures: that is, it cannot anticipate the next moment of it nor remember the last; and so, fretful as it may seem, it does not suffer at all. If Clive ever gets his pleasures down to the point at which he also does not anticipate the future or remember the past, he will not enjoy it in the least. In short, his imaginary present and its all-sufficing delight is unconsidered tosh.

The reason Clive enjoys his suppers is that he first works hard enough to need relaxation—at least I presume and hope he does. If he did not he would be miserable, and would probably have to take to drugs to enable him to bear his pleasant evenings at the Russian Ballet. Even now he cannot get through them without the aid of cheroots. I never eat supper; I never smoke; I drink water; and I can sit out *Petrouchka* and enjoy the starlight in Piccadilly all the same. But clearly, if I could be persuaded that *Petrouchka*, instead of being a relaxation, is as creative as the Piccadilly starlight is recreative, I should enjoy it a thousand times more. So would anybody.

No, my Clive: in vain do you sing

Sun, stand thou still upon Gibeon,
And thou, Moon, in the valley of Ajalon.

They will not stop for you. Lopokova will dance, as you say; but when you stretch your arms to her and cry

*Verweile doch, du bist so schön*

you cannot stop, either of you, any more than Paolo and Francesca could stop in the whirlwind. You delight in the music of Mozart; but does it ever stop? It ends; but your delight ends with it. You are a destinate creature, and must hurry along helter-skelter; so what is the use of waving your cheroots at us and assuring us that you are motionless and meaningless? There is nothing in the world more ridiculous than a man running at full speed, and shouting to everyone that he is in no hurry and does not care two straws where he is going to.

*January 24, 1923*

# ÉMILE COUÉ
by Robert Littell

It is much easier to see the President than to see Émile Coué.

M. Coué is going to be allowed to talk to the newspapermen in a big New York hotel. Downstairs you show your credentials; you show them again to the phone girl on the seventh floor; you show them again at the door of a room with a piano and many empty rows of flimsy hotel chairs. At the White House, if you are a newspaperman, you walk right in.

But then M. Coué is a greater man than the President. At any rate, thoughts of him possess many more minds than thoughts of Harding. Or rather, thousands of people are frantically thinking and feeling about themselves to the tune, as it were, of Coué. If he isn't a great man, at any rate he is a great word. There is some kind of magic, of mystery here, or else the word would not be epidemic. There must be some kind of healing aura about the man, some saintly or medicinal current in this magnet which has drawn thousands to itself.

Here he comes. Moving in and out among so many tall, young, modern Americans, this round little figure with the face of a de-hydrated fox seems extraordinarily small, old, and of the soil. He shakes hands patiently, with perfect courtesy, but without joy. One of the tall hearty Americans comes up to him. M. Coué, it appears, dined with him once in Nancy. M. Coué's manner warms through friendliness toward recognition, but does not quite get there. He is hunting for a name, but gives it up, with a sudden wizened gesture of one hand sketching the attempt to pull something forgotten from a wrinkled forehead. *"Les noms ne me reviennent pas,"* he states more than apologizes.

Now we are all sitting down, and M. Coué is about to explain his method. Some hopes are raised by the presence of the piano, but this turns out, unfortunately, to have been cast for no role. Before M. Coué begins we are given a brief and slightly solemn introduction, with lantern slides of M. Coué at home in Nancy. He lives in the nearer half of that large, ugly, comfortable stone house. There is a small crowd outside. Here is part of the same crowd, inside. A long room, furnished between 1860 and 1880, in those happy days when iron dog and iron deer first began to lie down together on American lawns. A hideous chandelier. Under it, M. Coué, very wise and solid and un-self-conscious, flanked by what might be all his sisters and his cousins and his aunts—some of them rather wild-eyed—come to be cured. Another picture: M. Coué alone in his study, behind a heavy desk. Heavy curtains, pictures in heavy frames, all of them decorated with an unblushing profusion of scrolls and curves. An atmosphere homely, restful, unchangeable.

But here is the man himself. He is just as he was in those pictures, he has only been lifted out of them for a bit. He does not say anything about America. Except that his words are English, a clear English with a French accent, he might be talking to patients at Nancy, and he might, to judge from his steady, matter-of-fact tone, be talking about invoices instead of sudden and remarkable cures.

His fingers press the table. They are thick, strong, clumsy hands, hands that might belong to a mason, to a farmer. They are entirely normal. The little body in a black suit, the little black tie, the high collar—all are quite normal. There is no magic here, nor, in the absence of magic, any faintest attempt to counterfeit a magician's presence. M. Coué has absolutely no make-up, physical or mental. His beard is less of a beard and more a part of his appearance than any beard I have seen. You cannot imagine the face without it. You cannot imagine any chin behind the beard which would have an equal truth.

M. Coué doesn't tell us anything new. We have read all about his method of autosuggestion. The few simple maxims and explanations sound even simpler, more obvious, when they come from his stolid, friendly, normal figure. "Imagination is vastly more powerful than will." What could be simpler than that to understand, or, once understood, easier to act on? M. Coué develops the inevitable deductions from this premise, with no air of discovery, with no assumption of prophecy or magic. One looks in vain for that magnetism which other saints and healers of other times have possessed. M. Coué is not magnetic. He does not fix you with his eye. He makes no attempt to draw all the threads of attention in the room into his hands. He tells you several times that he is not a healer, that he helps people heal themselves only, and has no singular powers of his own. This is not hard to believe. If you didn't know who he was, had never heard of him, and happened to drop into that hotel room, you would find yourself listening to a very plain, genuine little Frenchman, with a face curiously impenetrable, pudgy, wrinkled in repose; a face all sharpened and pointed down to a ridiculously individual beard, a face that often lights up in an engaging way, seemingly suddenly to open and show, not depths and mysteries, but a simple human twinkle of friendliness and common sense. You would think of a number of solid, peaceful, shrewd French shopkeepers, *députés,* retired majors you had seen, but never of a healer.

If everything else about him were to deny it, M. Coué's trousers would prove that he was not a healer. They are wide, and substantial, and durable, and creased with the innumerable wrinkles of common use. Every wrinkle shouts that there is no bunk about the owner of those trousers.

The more one listens to M. Coué, the more one likes him, and the more his theories and methods exchange mystery for simplicity. He believes people can help make themselves feel better by exorcising the defeatism in their own hearts. He makes no pretentions to cure organic troubles. But he has a naïve faith in the cures which people tell him he has made. Any man with the faintest touch of charlatanism, any man who had the slightest reason to fear suspicion, would not dare read the letters of testimonial which M. Coué takes from his pocket. He reads them with the warmth of feeling of a man who is justly proud of a good deed done partly with his help. Here is a letter from someone who was cured without ever having seen him, and of this letter M. Coué is perhaps prouder than he is of any of the others. Your opinion of his sincerity goes up tremendously at this, for he seems to have no idea how much he is laying himself open to the attacks of the doctors by accepting such letters as proof.

How lightly the weight of his prodigious fame rests upon him. You look in vain for the taint of solemnity. The solemnity is elsewhere. There is a hush over the room as we hear the awful words issuing from their source: "Day by day, in every way, I am getting better and better." Some of us feel as if we had just heard the voice of Moses issuing a commandment. We shall be telling our grandchildren that we heard "Day by day . . ." from Coué himself. Yet as he says it himself, how unimpressive, how merely sensible it sounds. And still it fails to impress—it is not meant to—when M. Coué begins to intone it in a religious monotone as one must say it on his pillow before sleep. He is far too normal and sensible a person to seem mysterious to anyone who does not come to him with a cloak of mystery already prepared to throw over him. What a contrast is this geniality of his to the expression on the face of the lady to whom he is repeating that she "cannot, cannot, cannot" unclench her hands—a stare of pained, beatific intensity, as of some decidedly nonequestrian saint placed suddenly on horseback, an expression which collapses into almost tearful relief as soon as M. Coué allows her hands to separate.

O wizened and solid and twinkling and inscrutable and shrewd and winning face, you might belong to the most honest stationmaster in all of France.

*June 20, 1923*

# DUSE NOW

by Stark Young

Duse, closer to seventy now than sixty, preserves still her old art of featuring nothing, but only of conveying the necessary truth. If you see one of the occasional performances that she is giving now in Italian theaters, you get the impression neither of a woman remarkably young-looking for her age nor of a woman on whom age has set an absorbingly interesting record. What you get is the impression of a slender woman with an extraordinary, interesting mask, with beautiful hands, gray hair and a low, poignant voice.

All through the performance that I saw, Duse did not suggest age so much as she suggested a diminished endurance. There was no question of quality but only one of quantity. That is to say, you could see clearly that the actress might not be able to go on for so long or so many performances or for prolonged, violent scenes; but it was also equally clear that for what she does do her body lacks nothing and is entirely adequate in the most exact meaning of the word: Duse's body keeps its old coordination, the flow of lines is still perfect and continuous; there is no sense of stiffness or angularity, or, as happens with age, of that lessening in the capacity of the muscles to carry out the immediate intention of the thought and will. The voice is something less clear and vibrant than once but no less dramatic and poignant. Looking at Duse's figure there on the stage you get pretty much what you always got, the sense of a body that has no existence apart from its idea and that is inseparable from what she means to express. Now as always Duse's art is connected with the external, the visible and audible aspect of her, as music is connected with sound. And the ideas and qualities that Duse expresses show still no sign of fatigue, of grayness, of doting egotism, of drouth, but only that old, quivering, subtle, profound passion of absorption with life and response to it that occurs in human living in its most complete moments whether in art or in other manifestations. . . .

Duse does not exemplify the art of acting so much as she illustrates the fundamentals of all art. All art, obviously, is concerned with the expression of life. To this purpose the artist is the first means, and after the artist the medium—color, words, sound, whatever it may be—that he works in. Duse's art illustrates first of all the principle in art of the necessity of the artist's own greatness, his sensitivity and power in feeling, in idea, in soul, in the education and fine culture of all these.

Her art illustrates the necessity for a fierce and subtle and exact connection between the artist's meaning and his expression of it. It illustrates the universal problem of rhythm in art, of line, emphasis, mood, all rhythm. It illustrates supremely the nature of the poetic as it applies not only to poetry but to every art. And it illustrates the nature of realism in general, especially of that best Italian realism which, as it occurs most of all in sculpture, is so capable of rendering by means of only actual or possible external details the inmost idea.

And so it is that you cannot easily get from Duse's acting a pure acting delight. She is not the actor's actor, as Velázquez is the painter's painter, or Spenser the poet's poet. That is to say, you cannot delight in her performance as supreme craft, something that delights whether it is deep or flitting, delights because of the perfection of its brush, its tone, its manner, because of its competency, because of its happy application of the art and the possibilities of pleasure in it by reason of its sheer technical purity and perfection, independent, so far as that is possible, of everything in life outside itself. And it is difficult to take any academic delight in Duse's acting. Something in you withholds you from saying what a beautiful gesture that was, what a tone, what a contrivance in that scene, what reading in this, what technical facility. All these things are good in themselves, of course; they too may be almost in themselves a kind of art. They are means of speaking, dialects for ideas; and, after all, art is art, not life. Style, however, in the sense of an added elaboration and distinction of method, of something in itself creative and separable, style in that separable aspect of technical felicity or skill or tact, Duse rarely has. Style in the sense of a medium which, like a glass over a laboratory experiment, disappears before the matter which it isolates and exhibits, Duse is never without. It is only slowly and almost unwillingly that Duse's art will allow you a stylistic or academic enjoyment. It will not allow that separation of the craft from the meaning; it will not yield itself to the mere choice judgments of a sophistication in taste. Duse will not grant you that kind of appreciation. It is as if she would accept no love but the love for all herself and the cost that follows.

It is only slowly that you see what labor and skill has gone to make up that creation of Duse's soul in the outer forms of an art. You see her bending over the child, you see her carry the pilgrim's staff, the lines of her long garment, the pity of her hands, the wandering of her hands among the lights on the altar. You see suddenly that dumbness, and then that flutter of life through the body. You see that the entire moment has revealed itself to you. You see what this woman knows; and you wonder whether such a knowledge of the human life and soul resolves itself in her finally into tears or into light. But it is only slowly that you perceive this artist's years of study of the lines of statuary— and especially of sculptors like Mino da Fiesole and Desiderio da

Settignana and those more delicate realists of the earlier Renaissance—to discover the inevitable lines of grace and meaning, to learn how to study the rhythms of the form in order to free them of all but that last beauty of its own characteristics. And you gradually observe that Duse suggests perpetually a state of music which must have come from a long love and study of that art. And most of all you will see that such a gradation of emphasis throughout the play and so fine and so elusive but unforgettable a comprehension of the entire meaning of the character and theme could come only from a remarkable ability and association with culture and ideas, combined with a poetic and reflective nature, with a courage of mind, and, finally, with something throughout the personality, quiet and taken for granted, a kind of untouched and unstressed and constant spiritual audacity.

*August 8, 1923 [Child Labor]*

# WLAD OF THE BEETS

by Frances B. Williams

Wlad is pretty much a man of the world, so his experience ought to count for something. Of course, he is only eleven now; but what difference does that make in a land where children are not prevented from getting an active start in business because of the mere handicap of youth? Wlad has had five good years in American agriculture, for he was not quite six when he came over with his parents from Poland. Wlad is only an incident in the Czylowitz family; there are eight or nine others—it is sometimes hard to keep track of them.

It was late winter when the Czylowitzes arrived in America. They used the money that was left from their steerage passage to take them straight to Detroit; for Wlad's mother had a cousin there. They had been in Detroit only a few days when Wlad's father received a very flattering offer from a gentleman who spoke Polish and was extremely kind to all the newcomers. This gentleman offered to take the whole Czylowitz family out on a nice farm in Michigan for the summer. He'd pay their carfare there and back; he'd supply them with a home and water and firewood and a place to grow vegetables—and in return Mr. and Mrs. Czylowitz would work on this nice farm, where they were to grow beets for the sugar company; and the children would help out, too; it would be so good for them to have the healthful exercise out in the pure air—just like play. How many children were there? Nine? All the better! The country was a great place for large families.

Wlad's father was immensely pleased with this. Hadn't he said all along that America was the land of promise—even when his wife had shown signs of wavering at making the plunge into the new country? Of course he signed the contract that the gentleman showed him—the contract that promised him home and carfare and other fine things besides good pay—eighteen dollars for every acre of beets that the Czylowitz family took care of. He was sorry that the children were going to miss the chance to get started in the American schools this spring; but then the life in the country would be so good for them, and it would be time enough for schooling when they came back to the city in the fall with lots of money saved up.

The Czylowitzes were taken to the sugar-beet-growing district of Michigan the first week in April. They were rather disappointed when they found that their home was to be a two-room wooden shack that had been used as a cow stable until a few seasons before. Still, by dividing the rooms up carefully they managed to make space for all eleven to sleep, and leave a little room for cooking. When they went to get water for their first supper, they discovered that their water supply was half a mile away; but, as the field boss explained, "with so many children to take turns carrying it, it wouldn't be very much work for any one of them." Half a dozen boughs of blown-down trees were lying outside the door. These constituted the "free fuel."

Wlad was six years old that summer (this was in 1917), and a man of six is quite old enough to be a big help in the beet fields. Of course Wlad's mother was much too valuable a worker to be allowed to stay at home except to cook the meals, so his younger sister, who was four, was the housekeeper for the family. That means that she took care of the year-old baby and the two-year-old brother, and did whatever cleaning-up there was done. There was to be another baby in October, but that oughtn't to keep Mrs. Czylowitz out of the beets for more than a couple of weeks. After that she could keep the baby near her out in the fields.

The first stage in Wlad's American education was known as "thinning." Each beet contains a number of smaller seeds which germinate and come up very close together so that they form almost a solid row. The superfluous plants must be removed by hand. The first part of this removing process, the "blocking," consists in cutting off the roots of the plants below the surface of the ground with a seven-inch hoe, leaving the plants standing in tufts or bunches from eight to ten inches apart.

Wlad was too young that summer to help with this work, so he and his next-older sister crawled along the rows after the blockers. They had old bags tied around their knees to prevent them from being scratched and irritated by the rough plowed ground. Wlad's job was to pull up the weaker plants and the weeds with one hand while with the other he grasped the best plant in the bunch and held down the earth around it so that it would not be uprooted. Of course, this kept him constantly bending or crawling, but, as the field boss said, "It's not hard for the little kid to do that; he's so close to the ground already."

During the first week or so of thinning, Wlad brought down frequent scoldings upon his head because he had a tendency to pull out the biggest plants in the bunch and leave the poorer ones to grow. These costly errors may possibly be explained on the ground that this was his first job, despite the fact that he was already six years old.

In June and July when the beets had to be weeded and hoed, the Czylowitzes had good long stretches of daylight to spend in the open air. They would have breakfast at four o'clock and go right to the fields, and often the mother would make lunch for the little sister to bring to them right at their work. By eight or nine o'clock they were usually ready to stop for dinner. They got so that they welcomed the rainy days, which at least obliterated the constant burning sunshine.

The Czylowitzes were already in debt at the country store where they had to buy all their food, for the space which had been promised for the kitchen garden turned out to be nothing but a few feet of rocky hill, impossible of cultivation.

It was when the "pulling and topping" began, late in October, that Wlad found working with the beets truly exciting. It was exciting to see how many tons of beets you could pull before you dropped over from sheer exhaustion. Wlad wasn't tall enough to straddle the row when he was pulling as his father did—but then of course he "didn't have so far to lean over." The beets weighed from two to nine pounds apiece, so Wlad had a lot of good exercise that summer.

But the most exciting part of it all was the topping, when you picked up each beet by spearing it with the hook on the end of the great big knife you carried and then, resting the beet across your knee, topped it by chopping off its crown just at the base of the last leaf. The knife you used was a formidable weapon such as any small boy would be proud to have as a plaything. It was fifteen inches long—almost big enough to look like a sword alongside a boy of six.

Wlad still has good reason to remember his first season of topping the beets—two shortened fingers on his left hand will always bear testimony to the valiant efforts of a six-year-old. A cold day, numb hands, a beet that was eight inches thick and a chopping stroke that was deflected an inch or so to the left tell the story of an instant's happening that made Wlad useless as a topper for the rest of the season.

A working man of six in his first industrial accident! But there is no workmen's compensation on the beet farms.

Perhaps it was just as lucky that Wlad was brought in from the fields just at this time though, because Mrs. Czylowitz had just given birth to the youngest Czylowitz and there was much that Wlad, even with his bandaged hand, could do to help about the shanty. His mother had been working in the beets the day before the baby was born.

School had started now in the little schoolhouse a mile away, but Wlad's parents figured there was no use in letting any of the children attend, because they'd have to be moving back to the city anyway as soon as school got fairly started and their work was worth good money at home.

When, sometime after Thanksgiving, the Czylowitzes left the beets and went back to Detroit it was too late in the year for Wlad's father to get any good employment. City employers did not like to hire men who worked in the beets. Luckily, perhaps, this turned out to be a "white winter" and he was kept busy almost constantly for three and a half months shoveling snow for the city.

The same state laws which had given the little Czylowitzes the privilege of doing such healthy work in the open air of the beet fields now prohibited them from working in the factories of the city. And Wlad's father thought he saw the chance to give them the education he coveted for them. They can go to school now till it's time to go back to the beets in the spring, he thought. (Despite the hardships of the last year's experience it never occurred to him not to return to the beets the next summer. One season's work had already stamped him as a "beet hunky"; this was now the only profession America offered him.)

School for the Czylowitz children was a constant effort at "catching up" and a constant failure to do so. The other children had already been having classes for three months when the Czylowitzes came in fresh from the beet fields and still visibly bearing the "old country" stamp—for possibly beet farming is not the best means of Americanization. Education proved from the start a losing struggle and in March, when Wlad's oldest sister reached her sixteenth birthday, she gave up the fight and went into a factory. She received better pay there than her share of the family's earnings in the beet fields, so when April came she remained in Detroit to board while the rest of the family went back to the country and its beets.

But all of that happened five or six years ago. Wlad is now a veteran beet laborer of eleven—almost twelve. In fact he would be beginning to feel almost superannuated if he could realize that already he is beyond the average age of the thousands of child beet workers in Michigan. But Wlad cannot realize this, for his horizon is bounded by the few acres of beets that occupy all his hours. Strange as it may seem, Wlad possesses not a vestige of a social conscience. He and his family are interested not at all in the problems of the sugar-beet industry in Michigan; they are interested only in making enough money from the beets in summer to see them through the following winter.

Ever since Wlad arrived in America he has spent seven months of each year down in the Michigan sugar-beet fields. In between times he has gone to school in Detroit. He is now in the second grade, and the teacher, who finds it annoying to have to bother with a boy who is so far behind his grade, looks forward to the spring, when she will be rid of him again. The hours Wlad spends in school are agony for him, for he is immensely sensitive about his size and his backwardness, and though he is anxious to learn he doesn't like to have to learn "along with a lot of little brats half his size." So Wlad joins the teacher in looking forward to spring with its labor in the beet fields. He doesn't mind it much now anyway, for he's used to the one big ache in his back and the burning in his knees, and he's long since ceased to mind the twitchings in those left-hand fingers that have no tips.

Last summer when someone asked Wlad what he was going to do when he grew up he looked perfectly blank. The future was something that had never seemed worth while to plan. It couldn't mean anything but more work, which would take care of itself when the time came. The only plan he has is that he'll go to work in a factory as soon as he's sixteen. That ought to be lots more fun than the beets. Wlad has never read a newspaper, so he doesn't know of any world outside of beet fields and Detroit.

So we leave Wlad now: a veteran worker of eleven; a normally bright boy who will enter only the third grade in school next year; a stoop-shouldered miniature man who does not know how to play; a boy who would be lonely now if he had ever tasted the wealth of companionship, of books, of recreation, of ambition.

Yet Wlad is not a lonely figure. There are thousands of others like him in Michigan.

*November 14, 1923*

# HENRY FORD
by Robert Littell

"What is the secret of Henry Ford?" people often ask, and expect an answer as complete and simple as if one lifted the mainspring out of a watch to show them how it worked. Of the many answers that have been given ("He's a mechanic"; "He's a farmer"; "He's a sort of economic John the Baptist") no one can be true, and even taken all together they are far from the truth, for Henry Ford is the sum of a great number of contradictory things which by their nature cannot be added up. A portrait of that side of himself which Ford the successful manufacturer presents would be puzzling enough, for it would have to contrive to show him as at once brilliant, hardheaded, flexible, obstinate, fearless, ruthless, domineering. Such a view would be only a profile. Another side of him, the part of him which has said and done a great deal that is quite apart from his business, reveals unplumbable depths of idealism, suspicion, good will, simple-mindedness, foresight and credulity, imagination and utter lack of it. And these two views would represent only two profiles of what is, after all, a very three-dimensional personality. A psychological sculptor who tried to do Henry Ford in the round would soon find that however faithfully he caught his likeness from any number of particular angles, the whole head would somehow not resemble Henry Ford. Any art of portraiture that tried to fix his traits so immutably would have to resign before some process that would catch contradictions and swift change as accurately as a moving picture. Ford cannot be judged by what he has done, for what he has done in general he has often done the reverse of in particular, nor can he be judged by what he has said, for what he says may not correspond with what he thinks, and in the common acceptance of the word he does not think at all. From the distance of the factory or of the outbursts quoted in the newspapers, Ford may seem comprehensible—even if the factory is complicated, and the outbursts bewildering. But when one has passed those public and visible outposts to find that the owner of the factory is a good deal like a small boy with a toy, and the author of the quotations very much like an old farmer sitting on a fence ready to pass pithy judgment on anything in the world—then Ford becomes a real puzzle. Then one learns that there is no "secret" of his character, but only clues to it.

One of the most helpful clues to any man's personality is his experience. Ford's narrow, but profound experience hangs over almost all that he does, like a shadow. He moves forward, normally, in this shadow, and when he ventures out of it he is blinded. At times it seems impossible that so capable a man should have strayed so little beyond the boundaries of his own experience, that a man who has done so much to a big world should still manage to live in such a small one. The terms he has learned in his world are those in which he thinks of the world outside. As an example, his answer to someone who was asking him about religion, that he "believed in it, but didn't work at it much," is highly characteristic. If his advocacy of $75,000 salaries for judges was startling, it was so only to people who didn't realize how much Ford had in mind the equal or greater salaries he has been accustomed to pay to his own assistants. It was quite like him to say that "when a man dies, it means that a part has worn out." And there is nothing strange in his saying proudly, while giving a copy of the "Jew Menace" pamphlets to a friend: "This came out of our factory." Nor in the boast, by the man who told customers they could have their cars painted any color so long as it was black, that there was "no choice of anything" in his hospital—where the nurses punch time clocks just as the reporters used to on the *Dearborn Independent*. Nor at his dealings with the wrens and sparrows. He was fond of birds even before he became fond of metal. But he used metal to solve trouble among the birds. Wrens liked the boxes which Ford nailed for them on his cherry trees, but the sparrows kept driving them out. Sparrows prefer immovable nests; wrens, nests that sway in the wind. "So we mounted a number of wren boxes on strips of spring steel," says Ford. "The wrens liked the idea. The sparrows did not."

But most characteristic of all, as an illustration of how Ford may not grasp an idea until put into his own terms, is the story of the early days of the *Dearborn Independent*. Not long after he had bought it, Ford found out that, as is the way with newspapers, Brown was writing news articles, Jones was contributing editorials, and Smith humorous sketches. Ford went to the editor, and, with his own conveyors in the back of his mind, told him that each article should be treated as a unit, and as it moved across the editorial desk—like an ungarnished cylinder block—Brown should attach the news to it, Jones screw on the opinion, and Smith insert the humor. The editor—also with the conveyors in the back of his mind—replied: "No, Mr. Ford, don't you see, the magazine is the unit, and not each article. As the magazine comes along, Brown's news article goes into it, then Jones's editorial, then Smith's piece of humor." Ford understood this and went away satisfied.

But one must not imagine Ford as an inhuman machine, intent only on things mechanical. In his dealings with other people he is very human indeed, in the several senses of the word. He has put on no airs because he is powerful or fabulously wealthy. The country around Detroit is full of old acquaintances whom he has far outdistanced, but whom he loves to drop in on from time to time. There are still men in the plant who call him Henry, as does his chauffeur. Every once in a while he gives somebody an automobile, or rescues a stray pup, or at some county meeting mingles unassumingly with the farmers, who often do not recognize him. He is naturally democratic. After he bought the railroad, his first act was to scrap the official car. (And he used to have on his desk a large photograph of the Prince of Wales!) He doesn't care a rap for the automobile millionaire society of Detroit. Indeed, money has not gone to his head, for he lives simply, spends little on himself, has built an ugly but not terribly large house, and a check for several hundred thousand dollars once lay for weeks forgotten in his vest pocket. People hold it much against him that he has never given anything to charity, nor done any public service to Detroit except build a huge hospital which he runs to suit himself. "Whoever offers charity," Ford says, "offers insult," and believes that if every employer ran his business as it ought to be run, charity would be unnecessary. It is quite characteristic of him to vary between what his enemies label as downright stinginess and a sudden, impulsive, handout generosity. If charity does not appeal to him, individuals do, sometimes very successfully. This generosity is returned, for when the company seemed to be in diffiulties in 1921, dozens of letters were received from owners of Ford cars all over the country offering to help him out, in amounts anywhere up to a hundred dollars.

Generosity and the reverse of it, openness and secretiveness, tolerance and prejudice characterize his relations with other people. It is quite like him to remark that so-and-so "is a good man, but he eats too much," and from Ford, who only eats when he is hungry, this is serious criticism. Neither does he smoke. So smoking is absolutely barred in the factory, and even in the office. Several of his best lieutenants could not give up the habit. "They'll smoke themselves," said Ford, and those men have left him long ago. They weren't fired, neither did they freely resign. Ford has his own way of smoking people out when their usefulness has expired. One of the heads of departments made a phenomenally rapid rise, announced that he would give courses in the methods of his department, and assumed a rather too distinct role within the company. Then he began to discover that gradually his functions and authority were being invisibly whittled away. When he could stand it no longer he said to Ford, "Am I the head of this department or am I not?" and was told, "No, you are not, and you haven't been for the last two years." He resigned. Another man who was driven to the same point stayed away from the office three days in disgust, then made an appointment with Ford to talk things over. He turned up, but Ford never came. When told later how the other fellow had been kept waiting, Ford only laughed. "Ha ha! That's funny." When he is dissatisfied with one of his executives, the latter often doesn't know it, but sits secure in his office, while Ford prowls about among the men and the machines, entering over low window ledges, or as unobtrusively straddling them with his long legs on his way out.

He has a way of surprising strangers with outbursts of the most unexpected, frank friendliness. A young reporter who had talked with him a few times ventured to try for a scoop by asking Ford what his platform would be in the Michigan senatorial election. Ford hesitated a minute, then: "My platform? Why, I guess you know what it would be as well as I do. Go ahead and write my platform for me, young man, and I'll sign it. Say anything you want." The platform was written, with some care and more excitement, and duly sent to Henry Ford. But he didn't sign it, nor perhaps even saw it.

No regular businessman would have said that. Nobody but Ford would have. And just as the regular businessman has his routine, his office hours, his mail, his appointments, his golf, so Ford's day is something quite different and quite his own. He will get up very early and perhaps chop a tree, often not eating anything till the middle of the morning. Then climb into the little wire-wheel Ford coupé, and drive like the mischief down to the River Rouge plant, or somewhere in his factories where something new is going on. He may go down to the river to see Edsel's new power boat and perhaps avoid the office altogether all day long, though people may be waiting there to see him. If it is summer, we may find him giving orders not to cut the crop on the farm until some fledglings he has seen in nests on the ground have grown strong enough to fly; if winter, he may be skating, with great skill and energy, or taking a walk, and jumping all the fences. If indoors, he will kick as high as the chandelier to show friends he still can do it, or cook for them a meal of synthetic foods in his laboratory, or turn on one of his vast collection of mechanical musical instruments, or even sit down to the automatic organ, which he likes to play with all the stops pulled out. He doesn't like to read and still "wouldn't give five cents for art." Work is amusement for him. Perhaps he has never known what work is, in the ordinary sense. He can never grow weary of watching things happen, wheels go around, and he is as engrossed in all his vast network of machinery as if it were a toy, and he himself young enough to worry about nothing else. And while he enjoys it, he takes awfully good care that the toy stays well oiled, and makes more and more money every year.

But Henry Ford—in the advertising phrase—"must be seen to be appreciated." Face to face, new traits appear, and traits already familiar are underlined, even if the "secret" remains unsolved.

I became one of the two hundred people who arrive daily in Detroit to see Henry Ford, usually on a something-for-nothing errand, or in furtherance of some cause which seems to them good and which they think Ford would like too. Since my errand was publicity, I had no trouble in getting an interview, to which, be it said to his credit, he was only forty minutes late.

He came into the office almost surreptitiously, and before I knew it we had shaken hands, and Ford was tilting back in a chair in the corner, with his feet on the radiator. He seemed absent-minded, and as I launched a series of questions he kept looking out of the window. Perhaps he had heard people say that in his factory there was no skill left, but that the men underwent a deadening repetitive grind of work? "There's nothing to it. If the men don't like their particular job, they can ask to be transferred. We shift men from job to job all the time." I tried to make him argue the point, whether the deadly monotony of labor necessary to efficient production wouldn't, in the long run, be an extremely bad thing for a society which he, notably, was anxious to improve. It was a point he would not or could not meet. He didn't want to argue, his first answer was clear, and he returned to it. The question stuck fast on the reef of his mind, where it was followed by all the others. Doubts as to the durability of the V-shape eight-cylinder motor he dismissed in a few words. "There's nothing to it." He was still looking out of the window, and every now and then rubbed his face with both hands, a nervous gesture of weariness and indifference.

We drifted onto the war, which brought from him a wonderfully complete, rapid and rather violent explanation of the whole business in two sentences, laying it all on the "international bankers" and the "diplomatists." "Europe had too many diplomatists. That's all there was to it." So much for the war. The Jews? An equally final and sweeping judgment. "The Jews are the scavengers of the world. They are necessary where there's something to be cleaned up. Wherever there's anything wrong with a country, you'll find the Jews on the job there." This statement quite satisfied him, and he could not be induced to add to it. Try the Negroes. How shall we settle the Negro problem? "We have several thousand in our plant, and no trouble. Whenever there's trouble, it's to somebody's advantage. There's always somebody making money out of it." Wherever I turned, I met this sudden, baffling tendency to pass complete and instantaneous judgment in a brief phrase. If Henry Ford's mind is an oyster, I failed utterly to open it, and I incline to believe that it is not so much an oyster as a stone. When an old farmer on a fence talks so dogmatically, one is not surprised, and one knows no harm will come of it. In Henry Ford, so attractively like the farmer in his unassuming simplicity, his directness, his plain American speech, this hardness of mind is peculiarly sinister, and when one remembers his vast power to put his beliefs into effect, it inspires something like fear.

It is almost the only thing about him that, when one sees him, inspires fear. His low, matter-of-fact voice, accurate and positive, his unaffected bearing, his almost graceful figure, his freedom from all the deadly marks of greatness, make one feel he could never do harm to anybody, and maybe a great deal of good. The face is more difficult to read. It is several faces all at once—ascetic, gentle, shrewd, humorous, sensitive, obstinate, delicate, invulnerable and unprotected, melancholy and serene, old and young, the face of a hardheaded Yankee horse-swapper, of a boy, of a minor saint. In it can be read by turns eagerness and age-old indifference, childlike content and profound restlessness.

The restlessness, the nervous rubbing of his face, the gazing out of the window continued as long as we were on general topics. So did the pat elusive answers to all questions. Sometimes they verged on epigram, sometimes they were condensations of prejudice. We were speaking of D——, a man who had once been associated with him, and quit in a huff, and later had criticized him publicly. "The trouble with D——," Ford burst out, "was that he wanted to get rich too quick and couldn't stop smoking." The war was mentioned again. "The Germans," said Ford, "would have been better off if they had had eyes like the woodcock. The woodcock has eyes so near the back of his head that he can see behind. Did you ever see a young woodcock?" Ford is no longer bored, and he turns away from the window. He starts to describe the young woodcock and asks if there are any pictures of the bird in the office. In a few minutes a book is brought in. Not the right book.

Somehow Ford has disappeared. Later his alert head is seen through the glass door of the next office, examining some sort of gun. When the biggest and best bird book arrives, he is gone. By gradual degrees he has slipped away, for good.

Ford slips away. "You can't pin him down," people who know him often say. You go to see him, maybe he does not meet the appointment —maybe he does, and in the end gets away from you. The very definiteness of his brief statements is an evasion. He hates to be tied down. Nobody has any strings on him. He has bought railroads, forests, factories, coal and iron mines because he hates not to be free. He gets rid of men when they threaten to invade his own power or his own mind. He resists compromise with things or men, and he is right, for his power lies in keeping his mind to himself. A president is powerful only by making other men share their minds with his, which means giving large pieces of his mind to theirs, and abandoning much purpose for sake of little result. This is absolutely contrary to Henry Ford's nature. He has always had his way, and he knows no other way but his to get things done. He is aware of this, and at one time he realized what troubles would meet him in the White House, where he would not be boss, but a political chief who could accomplish things only by endless talk and compromise with other men. It was then that he said he "wouldn't walk across the street" for the Presidency. Nearer to his present feelings is the later statement to a friend as they were walking by the White House: "That's where I'll be some day." When asked about it publicly, his eyes twinkle, but that's all. Undoubtedly he wants to be President, against his own better judgment, and that of those nearest him, who say, "If you're a friend of Henry Ford don't work for him," but quite according to the desires of his assistants. At one time they formed a group of hardheaded, capable, fearless men whose independence finally caused them to leave him. The men now around him are of distinctly inferior caliber, but perhaps just as useful and efficient wheels in the Ford system. They know how to keep well within his favor, and how to influence him at the same time; they understand what he wants done, and carry it through mercilessly, without question; they do not let him forget that he is one of the greatest men in the world. The former pioneer atmosphere of the Ford personnel is gone, and the give and take among self-made men who were opening up a new country together has been replaced by something much more like the court of an Oriental monarch in its combination of sycophancy and ruthlessness. Perhaps these men know what possibilities of terrible disaster to Ford as President he has within himself, but since the reflected glory they would reap is immeasurable, they help to suppress his doubts, they fan his desire to be a candidate, and it is from their midst that are pulled the skillful and invisible wires which are helping to spread the Ford boom.

If ever a man needed good advice, it was the Henry Ford of the Peace Ship, of the Jew Menace, of Presidential ambitions. If ever a man existed for whom the advice of others was destructive of his own brilliant intuitions, it was the Henry Ford who made the car that most of America rides in. There seldom has been a man at once so capable and incompetent, so shrewd and so credulous, so admirably self-sufficient and so appallingly isolated. One would like to be able to split him and use the capable and far-seeing half. Unfortunately, the bad in him is the inseparable complement of the good, and useful to it, and we must take him as he is, one and indivisible, a hard-boiled idealist.

# DECADE TWO
# 1924-1933

**The New**
# REPUBLIC
*Published Weekly*
Wednesday December 24, 1924

SAMUEL GOMPERS
*AN EDITORIAL*

Main Street in the Theatre
*by* ROBERT LITTELL

Travelling in America
*by* REBECCA WEST

The Banker's Lament
*by* DAVID FRIDAY

Literary Sketches
*by* EDMUND WILSON

Blood Money
*by* JOHN F. CARTER

FIFTEEN CENTS A COPY
FIVE DOLLARS A YEAR
VOL. XLI. NO. 525

**The New**
# REPUBLIC
*Published Weekly*
Wednesday June 12, 1929

British Labor's Victory
*by* H. N. BRAILSFORD
*(received by cable)*

Justice Holmes' Opinion in the
Case of Mrs. Schwimmer

The Spanish Students Fight On
*by* CARLETON BEALS

End of the Hoover Honeymoon
EDITORIAL

FIFTEEN CENTS A COPY
FIVE DOLLARS A YEAR
VOL. LIX. NO. 758

**The New**
# REPUBLIC
*Published Weekly*
Wednesday May 4, 1932

Literary Class War
*by* EDMUND WILSON

What Happened to Insull
*by* JOHN T. FLYNN

Mooney Stays in Jail
EDITORIAL

FIFTEEN CENTS A COPY
FIVE DOLLARS A YEAR
VOL. LXX. NO. 909

**The New**
# REPUBLIC
*Published Weekly*
Wednesday December 20, 1933

New England Is Waiting
*by* BRUCE BLIVEN

Maryland: Storm Warning - Gerald W. Johnson
Five Days in Decatur - - - Hamilton Basso
The Press Gets a Code - Chester T. Crowell

A Model for General Johnson
The Muddle of Repeal

FIFTEEN CENTS A COPY
FIVE DOLLARS A YEAR
VOL. LXXVII. NO. 994

*1924-1933*

*Its second decade found* The New Republic *floating a little desperately on a broad sea of business prosperity. The progressive enlightenment appeared over, and in its last flickering rays the United States had never seemed more parochial, philistine and absurd. The values of American society were materialistic, its methods were crass, its goals were sordid, and its business, as Calvin Coolidge and Sinclair Lewis joined in saying, was business. Its idols were the great tycoons; its hero worship, as* The New Republic *delighted in pointing out, went to visiting royalty—the Prince of Wales or Queen Marie of Rumania—and to aviators, like Charles A. Lindbergh. Its system of justice had become the creature of publicity and pressure—or so Professor Robert Morss Lovett plausibly reported of Chicago, the playwright Sidney Howard of California, the newspaperman Frank Kent (*The New Republic's *first T.R.B.) of Tennessee, Bruce Bliven, to be* New Republic *co-editor after Croly, of Massachusetts, and Margaret Sanger, the birth control crusader, of New York. And the nation continued to pride itself on its rejection of the arts, though the magazine gallantly continued its efforts to bring Americans the good news of Picasso (in a piece by Gertrude Stein's brother Leo), Brancusi and Marin (by Lewis Mumford), Joyce (by Padraic Colum), Isadora Duncan (by Shaemas O'Sheel) and Walter Damrosch (by Deems Taylor).*

*Yet, though America might seem spiritually and artistically bereft, the spirit of progressive idealism was not quite dead. Senators like George W. Norris of Nebraska and William E. Borah of Idaho labored valiantly to keep progressivism alive in Washington and received due appreciation from John W. Owens. Felix Frankfurter and Walter Lippmann debated where the progressive vote should go in 1924. Four years later Herbert Croly wrote perceptively about Al Smith (whom* The New Republic *eventually supported) and hopefully about Herbert Hoover. John Dewey analyzed the contributions of Justice Holmes and Robert Morss Lovett the contributions of John Dewey to the American liberal mind.*

*For the first half of* The New Republic's *second decade, the title of Owens' piece on Norris—"Norris, the Discouraged"—could have stood for American progressivism in general. Then the crash of 1929 shook the foundations of the national complacency and suddenly validated older progressive doubts about the infallibility of the system. The death of Croly in 1930 turned control of the magazine over to younger men.*

*A few social critics, as Lewis Mumford demonstrated in his essay on Thorstein Veblen in 1931, had already prepared the way for a new diagnosis of American society. Now, as unemployment spread, as the sense of national bafflement and impotence grew, as discouragement began to give way to despair,* The New Republic *began to express a new impatience and a rising radicalism. The progressive enlightenment was no longer enough: even Veblen seemed mild and academic; the idealists of the early thirties were moving on toward Marx. Edmund Wilson, the most brilliant of* The New Republic's *literary critics, thus responded to the pressures of the time by turning radical social reporter. His piece about the Scottsboro boys contains interesting premonitions of the contemporary South. John Dos Passos, who had been attracted by Marxism even before the depression, now provided a revolutionary's view of a 1931 hunger march on Washington and of the 1932 Democratic convention.*

*"Hoover or Roosevelt," Dos Passos concluded, "it'll be the same cops," and* The New Republic *confronted the New Deal with a similar skepticism. Still, even T.R.B. (no longer Mr. Kent) could not deny a new excitement in Washington, and writers like Ferner Nuhn wrote sympathetically of such New Deal personalities as Henry A. Wallace. A wonderful piece by Scott Fitzgerald on Ring Lardner was a reminder of the literary concerns of the twenties, but, like its author and its subject, it was out of fashion in the obligatory social consciousness of the thirties.*

*In a single decade business had fallen from its summit, the bottom appeared to have dropped out of American society, and the older progressives found their forecast of social strain and vulnerability overfulfilled. The change seemed to have left behind not only business complacency but even progressive idealism itself.* The New Republic, *faithful to the spirit of critical inquiry, now ventured into new and uncertain waters.*

ARTHUR M. SCHLESINGER, JR.

*April 23, 1924*

# PABLO PICASSO
by Leo Stein

Picasso came to Paris a badly educated young painter, but infinitely clever and facile. The first influence he felt was, I believe, that of the mordant illustrator Toulouse-Lautrec. Later, in the Blue period and in the Harlequin period, the illustrative interest remained obviously predominant. Picasso once explained the Blue period by the fact that Prussian blue was the cheapest color to be had. Doubtless that was an advantage, but the pictures of that period were blue in mood as well as in color. In the Harlequin period the temper is lighter, yet still sad and wistful. There is more flexibility in the line, and decidedly more alertness of observation and interest than in the Blue period. The Harlequin period was succeeded by the Pink period. It was during this time that Picasso began to move in the direction of "intellectual seriousness and pure expression."

It is necessary, if one would understand what was now about to happen, to consider the peculiar position of Picasso in the Paris art world. He was not French, but a Spaniard. There were, of course, many other Spaniards in Paris, most conspicuous among them Zuloaga. Picasso's extraordinary felicity and cleverness could easily have won him worldly success if that had been the kind of success that he desired, but he was really in revolt against the world. He had qualities of a solitary, though he was very fond of having people about him and had great personal charm. At his studio in the Rue Ravignon, where many habitually gathered—for Picasso characteristically had people come to him rather than go out to other people—he spoke little and yet was obviously the dominant personality. His comment on persons and things was commonly humorous and satirical, and he smoked his pipe and twinkled while others speculated and disputed. Occasionally he made caricatures and cartoons which were powerfully expressive as only a great caricaturist could make them. His dark, brilliant eyes were the most absorptive that I have ever seen, and I wondered at times, when he was looking at a drawing or an engraving, that anything should be left upon the paper.

The group of artists in which Picasso found himself was feeling more and more strongly the influence of Cézanne and tending more and more to regard as an end what to Cézanne had been a means— substantial form. Cézanne's personal ideal had two poles: to make of Impressionism something solid like Poussin, and to do over Poussin in

Impressionistic terms. His ideal, that is, was of a complete pictorial art. In fact, he rarely got as far as this, and was entangled to the end in the problem of means. Much of his work makes on me the painful impression as of a man tied up in a knot who is trying to undo himself. However, his concern with an essential problem, that of adequate expression in modern terms, made him the chief of the modern clan.

Picasso, the illustrator, had to come to terms with this. He was an outsider, not a Frenchman, and could not with the others accept Cézanne as a father—"*le père de nous tous,*" as Matisse once said. Instead, he regarded him as a rival. And here a peculiarity of Picasso's must be taken into account. Picasso never exhibited at the Salons or other collective shows. He stood apart. He at times explained this, but the explanations had not much value. The truth was that he felt as one apart, as one without companions or equals. He did not enter into rivalry. It was one of those complex cases where a man feels sure and yet evades the test. Exhibition was both a degradation and a risk. Picasso's confidence was good for much, but for no more.

There was, however, one rival who had to be met—Cézanne—and it is interesting to watch Picasso's course in the conflict. His drawing began to lose the nuances of the Harlequin period, and its curves grew larger, with marked opposition to straight lines. Deformation as a means of accent became more and more pronounced. The shapes were simplified and enlarged, but the quality of intrinsic form, in spite of all this, was not achieved. This seems indeed to be an inherent quality, and no painter, so far as I know, once without it, has ever acquired it. Nevertheless, since it was Picasso *contra mundum,* success was the only alternative to complete failure. Picasso unconsciously adopted a ruse. He overcame at length by avoiding the comparison entirely. When there were no longer common terms, he could believe what pleased him regarding his own work. The confrontation with Cézanne left him fancy free.

Picasso was not a great painter or a great master of composition, but in both directions he was capable. He had grace and felicity of a very rich kind, and he had endless ingenuity. He kept his type of cubism alive by his infinite inventiveness, by his success in devising new combinations. At bottom, however, there was very little to it all. As for his intellectuality, that is rubbish. His intellectual baggage is of the slightest, and the total output of intellect in his work is negligible. Picasso is thoroughly intelligent in the ordinary human way, and is ingenious to the last turn, but he is in no serious sense a thinker.

It should now be obvious enough that when his admirers shake their heads despondently over his painting of recognizable form and think that here he shows a weakness they would not have expected in him, it is time for them to look a little more closely into the work they believe superior. I think that if they do so they will find that there is no essential difference in quality between the cubist pictures and those recently exhibited in New York. In one case we have figure illustration, and in the other illustration of textures and shapes. Picasso fooled first himself and then all the world with solemn nonsense. Whenever he throws off the disguise he is found out.

The young artist who is quoted [in connection with a contemporary Picasso exhibit in New York] speaks of Picasso's romantic streak, and contrasts this with the intellectual character of the cubist pictures. In fact, the whole cubistic curve was a course of sheer romantic mystification, first of the artist by the artist, and then of everyone else.

Why then, it may be asked, is Picasso's cubist work better than that of others? The answer, of course, is that he has more talent. His talent is immense, but, to my thinking, it has been wasted on trivialities. Therefore this last work of his is immature and trivial, though often felicitous and successful.

Picasso was very human, with a keen appreciation of personal qualities. He had infinite gifts of expression. Like a Rembrandt or a Goya he would have grown to maturity of power by developing his native faculties. Instead, defects of character and inopportunity of circumstances led him to seek his realization in construction of pure form for which his talent was but slight. Realization cannot come through evasion. Picasso refused his real job as not good enough for him, and the result has been a wilderness of foolery and waste.

*May 28, 1924*

# WHY THEY LOVE BORAH
by John W. Owens

Senator William E. Borah, of Idaho, is one of the foremost men of public life, as very many of those in intimate touch with our public life believe, not because he is eloquent, there being many other eloquent men; not because he has a fine mind, there being many other fine minds; not because he is a patient, untiring student, there being many other patient, untiring students; not because he is courageous, there being many other courageous men, our frequent hasty judgments to the contrary notwithstanding—Senator Borah is a leading figure, in the opinions of many competent judges, because, beyond any other man in public life, he labors, unwearied and undiscouraged, to produce a supply of statecraft that will meet the demand of this nation and of the world.

Politically, the American people "keep coming on," discovering evils and seeking cures with few lapses into indifference (on that, skeptics and scoffers and the children of faith and light will agree!) and none is so quick to discover an evil and none so quick to seek a cure as Borah. Never does he lapse into the indifference that sometimes damns the mass. The maximum of the fervor of the mass is his minimum. Nearly two decades in the disillusioning, disheartening, deadening atmosphere of Washington have aged only his body. His spirit goes marching on, increasingly agile it seems, in the twin quest for evils and for cures; increasingly ardent in the conviction that it is worth while—that mankind can and will effect a net gain of cures over evils, however it may stumble and falter. He cannot be convinced that the demand for the good must forever exceed the supply.

Born in '65 in the yet new Illinois, whence he moved on to Kansas and on to the wilds of the Idaho of a generation ago, Senator Borah is of the breed that expects to tame the world and all therein—a surcharged specimen of the breed. Had Nature fashioned him for a materialist, he would have disemboweled the earth and harnessed its energies, or gone broke in the effort. But that was not her mood and intent in the hour of his fashioning. She sent him forth a preacher, and he must dig out the sins of organized society, and he must nourish, organize and direct the aspirations of men for the good. He is apart in the Senate, not alone because he has a craving for solitude and meditation that makes itself known to his associates, but because of this essential quality. . . .

Looking down on him from the gallery, noting that queerly emphatic apartness, the question bobs up:

Where would he be, if he were not there? To find a wholly satisfactory answer a century must be turned back. Put Borah on a lean horse, pull his hat down over his eyes, as he likes to have it, give him saddlebags containing a Bible and another shirt, start him over the hills of a new country as circuit-riding minister of the gospel. . . .

Thrust upon the stage of a world far different, mankind still is his prize to be sought with every energy. View him in the company of the whole group that defeated the League of Nations Covenant in the Senate. He is the one man of that group who felt an affirmative responsibility. Lodge, Reed, Johnson, Brandegee, Moses? Their work was done when the Covenant was rejected. They were through. It was enough that the country had been kept from making what they held to be a mistake. No obligation was upon them to be more than negative. But Borah, having denied the efficacy of the instrument made by Wilson, no sooner had made sure that the denial was consummated than he affirmed the necessity of an instrument for the same purpose, and proceeded indefatigably to search for it. As I recall, he was the first member of the Senate openly to denounce Wilson's proposal; and for three years he has occupied Wilson's old place as the apostle of peace.

He cannot think in impersonal terms of persons; he cannot think of France or Germany or Russia or England without seeing millions of human beings, happy or unhappy, comfortable or distressed. When a nation is hungry, he sees women and children, hands outstretched for food. When a nation is without fuel, he sees shivering babies.

He will go on, preaching peace and seeking the instrument to effectuate what he believes to be the will for peace. He can do no other. He will change his arguments and he will change his mind, probably, about instruments, but some argument and the search for some instrument will go on until his eyes are closed for the last time. That will be his unflagging contribution of supply to meet the world demand. Interspersed will be his contributions to meet the national demand. The railroad problem of today, and that of the year after next; the agrarian problem of today and that of the year after next; the problem of corrupt practices in politics, of top-heavy government at Washington, or what not—these problems will keep him sweating and striving as earnestly as though the solution of last year's problems had not immediately caused new ones.

Stop gathering a supply to meet the demand? Adjust the demand to the supply on hand? Ask what is the use of trying to make things better? Not so long as Borah is Borah. And so long as Borah is Borah, when he rings the bell, a large section of the American people will answer. For he and they are one.

*June 11, 1924 [George W. Norris]*

# NORRIS, THE DISCOURAGED
by John W. Owens

The saddest, heaviest-hearted man in the Senate—in the whole of Congress, for that matter—is George W. Norris, of Nebraska. Yet he has been, and he probably is today, the least laden of all members with that supreme travail: how to get back and how to stay on, and on, and on. To stay in Congress, particularly in the Senate, for ambition's sake, for pride's sake, for pleasure's sake, and, in some woeful instances, for bread-and-butter's sake, that is what darkens the days and makes fearful the nights of the run of Congress, who reached there by ruthless adherence to rule of devil take the hindmost and are subject to constant attack under the same merciless order.

But Norris's vitals never are torn by that. He behaves in a way that not even La Follette or Borah on the progressive end, or Brandegee on the conservative end, or Robinson on the Democratic end, would dare. Any time at all he tells the sovereign voters of Nebraska that he cares not three whoops in a gale of wind whether they send him back or not; rather hopes they will not; will not play ball with his own party at home, and it can go to the devil if it does not like his manners; and is perfectly willing to apply the recall to the nomination, election or anything else given him by the public.

What, then, causes his strange sadness? The same fact that, mainly, gives him the strange independence which would equal all human joy for ninety-nine in each hundred of the other members of Congress. His real interest, his profound concern is to do big and fine things for the common man; and he knows he will not, cannot, realize one per cent of his purpose.

These big and fine things do not constitute some elaborate and clearly formulated program for political, or social, or economic reconstruction. His purpose is to use government, so far as may be, to make daily life comfortable for the plain people, particularly the farmers of the Middle West, whom he knows and loves; to make the agencies of government decent and helpful. In the pursuit of that purpose, his instruments and immediate objectives vary from year to year, from condition to condition. Even so, he is as downhearted as though he had followed some brilliant, dazzling dream. After more than a score of years' unbroken service in Congress, he may be heard to say, time and again, when a test of strength is coming: "Oh, they [the old-line politicians of both parties] will be together to beat this idea."

Coming from an unsophisticated people, his urge to bring blessings upon mankind was not disciplined by reckoning the slow, almost infinitesimal steps by which progress is realized, and thus he has hurled himself unguardedly, times without number, against the enemy. Now, conscious that he is bruised and battered, he has the most realistic sense of the odds to be encountered. He goes on, it is true; he bares his breast and charges as bravely as in any earlier day. But the light of victory is not in his eye, and he will not repine when the order of honorable discharge is given him. He goes on, but it is because Nature gave him a heart that knows no other maneuver.

Senator Norris's disappointments and defeats in legislation which he has sought for the common weal have been the more emphatic and the more saddening, I believe, because of the quality of his mind, the way it operates. He thinks in terms of the particular, not of the general—which is perhaps natural in a man who came to maturity in the small world of the Nebraska of the Eighties and Nineties. When he sees something to be done, or to be undone, he sees that almost exclusively. Direct, regardless movement toward his objective inevitably has often involved possible and even patent dangers as grave or worse than those at which he aimed. Consequently, he has been made to endure opposition not only of old-line politicians, but of men at one with him in general purpose, such men as Borah and William S. Kenyon.

But though so often thwarted in his specific undertakings, he remains one of the men in Congress who thrill you. That is because he has had part in daring and dramatic enterprises, such as that of the little group of Republican insurgents in the House fourteen and fifteen years ago who went up against intrenched and seemingly impregnable Cannonism, and won in no-quarter, hand-to-hand fighting. It is because of the ways in which he manifests the independence that has been mentioned—for example, his leadership of the Senate fight against Ford's offer for Muscle Shoals, when his own crowd, the Middle West farmers, were as hot as the Southern farmers for acceptance.

And above all, it is because of the man himself. He has personality, individuality. Years ago, I read a vivid description of a peasant leader who arose in eastern Europe, a man who acquired education, position, power and contact with the great and famous, but remained rough-hewn, the possessor of homely virtues and the interpreter of the hopes of homely folk. There are no peasants in this country, city intellectuals to the contrary. Peasant stock is not bred from men touched with the argonaut spirit. But I never see Norris on the Senate floor—burly body; massive head and face; direct, candid, fearless speech—that I do not see that peasant of eastern Europe who lifted himself to mastery. Norris is the plain man in a fine and rare mold.

*June 25, 1924 [The Loeb-Leopold Case]*

# CRIME AND PUBLICITY

by Robert Morss Lovett

The recent kidnaping-murder in Chicago is pronounced by expert authority to be the greatest crime in the history of journalism. Wherever the connoisseurs of crime in its public aspect are gathered together, from cub police reporters to old-timers, there is but one opinion. De Quincey's account of the meeting of the Murder Club is pale beside these gatherings. The extraordinary collocation of exciting circumstances; the association of two capital offenses, kidnaping and murder, in one act; the suggestions of sexual perversion in the background; the baffling nature of the case at first, followed by the discovery of a clue, and the swift march of detection with the logical pattern and the dramatic incident of a Sherlock Holmes tale; and finally the social position of the two murderers, putting them above all ordinary temptation and leaving them as amateurs of crime for crime's sake—all these serve to throw the description of the story into clichés—unique, in a class by itself. Only one regret is heard on the lips of the connoisseurs: the lack of a woman in the case. But the public is scarcely conscious of this defect. In the height of the excitement a lady on trial for the murder of her husband, and hitherto known affectionately in the newspapers as the beautiful murderess, was quickly exiled from the front page and acquitted out of hand, apparently not so much because she was innocent as because she was a bore.

To summarize briefly: On Wednesday, May 21, Robert Franks disappeared on his way home from school; on the 22nd his father received a letter directing him to call at a certain drugstore to receive a telephone message with regard to the payment of ransom; on this same day, however, the naked body of the boy was found under a railroad culvert in the vacant land south of the city, killed by a blow on the head or by strangulation. Suspicion was directed to certain of the teachers in the school which the boy attended, and they were held for examination. So sure were the police of this lead that they held these teachers for six days without warrant, and subjected them to the third-degree methods of physical torture and menace of death, from which upper-class prisoners are usually exempt. Among names mentioned by one of these teachers was that of Nathan Leopold, a former pupil of the school, the son of a prominent merchant, and a law student of the University of Chicago. He was examined on

May 25 and dismissed. The day before, May 24, however, a pair of spectacles had been found near the culvert and later was traced through the optician to Leopold as one of three patients for whom the identical prescription had been filled. On Thursday, May 29, the police went to his residence and found with him his intimate friend, Richard Loeb, the son of another prominent Jewish family. Although no suspicion attached to Loeb, he was taken along with the idea that he might be useful in checking up on Nathan's whereabouts at the time of the crime. Both boys, examined separately, testified to having been together on the day of the murder, and set up an exact and circumstantial alibi, agreeing in material points. This alibi, however, involved the use of Leopold's car, and when his chauffeur testified that it had not been out of the garage on the day in question, both broke down and on May 31 made simultaneous confessions, identical except in the matter of the fatal blow. According to their statements, the crime had been planned for months, complicated arrangements for collecting the ransom had been made—only the victim was left to be selected at the last moment. . . .

The reason why this crime surpasses others in public appeal is that it is the work of young men who consciously appreciate the public point of view. In view of their bungling technique one can hardly call them craftsmen; but they are certainly of the artist class. They were both sons of rich men, with every want gratified. Clearly there was no sordid motive behind their crime. They were amateurs. They were both boys of unusual intellectual ability; Loeb graduated from college at eighteen, and Leopold was an even more brilliant student. They were gifted amateurs. Their scholastic success doubtless ministered to their egoism. They were both students of historical crime; Benvenuto Cellini and Cesare Borgia will certainly figure in their defense. Both were romantically bored by their luxurious bourgeois life, and they recognized in crime the most powerful means of escape, of setting the individual free from social bonds, of putting him *jenseits von Gut und Böse*. The same aesthetic motive for crime has appeared in literature—in *Crime and Punishment;* in Paul Bourget's *Le Disciple.* They resolved on committing a literary crime, murder for its own sake. They conceived of a masterpiece to be enjoyed by themselves and the public, for public appreciation was necessary to their own satisfaction. Their motive was something like that which Bojer makes his hero, in *The Prisoner Who Sang,* give for committing a robbery: "It was done to place my work before the severest of all critics, asking 'Is it alive? Do you believe in it? Does my art give a complete illusion? Is it true to life?' " Of course, escape from detection was necessary to their triumph, but their cool demeanor when first examined shows that in their rehearsal they had not overlooked the possibility of being suddenly faced by a development of their roles before the public.

Leopold in particular enjoyed his artistry. When first taken for examination by the police, he asked an officer named Johnson if he was George Johnson, one of the men wanted in the case. At police headquarters he delighted his questioners with a learned account of perversion in the Renaissance. In the days immediately after the discovery of the spectacles he was taking his examinations at the law school with complete *sang froid* and even called on one of his instructors for the purpose of discussing with him the case in detail. He was in the habit of taking a group of small lads out to study bird life. After the discovery of Robert Franks's body, instead of dismissing the group at a common point he escorted each one to his home, explaining to the mothers that he appreciated their anxiety and shared it. He had a moment of delighted triumph when he pointed out the amazing stupidity of the Illinois penal code in making it possible to commit two capital crimes for one penalty. Why kill? Why not, since kidnaping is punishable by death and killing makes it safer?

Richard Loeb was apparently a normal boy, good-natured, prepossessing, sharing the college youth's chief interest next to his studies, sports and girls. Leopold was a recluse and a cynic, devoted to his intellectual interests, but sullen and indifferent toward those who shared them. Leopold had gained great ascendancy over Loeb—the authority of a masterful mind. Whether or not sexual perversion played a part in their relation, there was something uncanny about it; it was a case of possession—of witchcraft. Doubtless this sense of power over his associate, of bending him to his will, was a source of Leopold's preliminary enjoyment of the crime—another literary motif.

An important phase of the relation between the two youths and the public is due to the fact that they both are of the privileged class. The populace has always taken a kindly interest in the scandalous exploits of its millionaires, from Claudius to Harry Thaw. And these young men are intensely class-conscious. They both asserted on their arrest that they feared no extreme penalty, and expressed quite simply their belief that money would pull them through the ordeal. Why should they not believe it? They know quite well that the rich break all laws, that they are not punished and no one expects them to be punished. Within recent months the President of the United States pardons a bootlegger; the Governor of Illinois is acquitted of embezzlement, by a jury accused of having been bribed; the directors of a mining company or a starch factory, who in defiance of law allow conditions which result in explosion and the death of scores of men, are not even reprimanded by the coroner. Why should they not expect to get away with murder? The parents have issued a statement promising that they will not seek by their wealth to defeat the ends of justice. No extraordinary sums for alienists' fees are to be paid, and the fees of the attorneys are to be fixed by a committee of the bar.

That the rich should deny themselves the use of their money to purchase justice is regarded as highly sportsmanlike, and approving comment in the press is general.

The trial will be largely one before public opinion, which will be represented by the jury. If Leopold and Loeb escape the extreme penalty it will be because society does not demand their death. And if it does not, this result will be because of the tragedy of two youths of its favored class suffering on the scaffold the grim fate which it meted out with no pity, rather with unctuous self-approval, to the anarchists, to the car-barn bandits, to thousands of poor men who in a very proper sense were its own victims.

*September 10, 1924 [Edward, Prince of Wales]*

# HE'S A PRINCE!
Editorial

The political campaigners have reason to be worried. They are not, but they ought to be. Here they go, from one end of the country to the other, trying to get themselves elected, pouring millions of words into ears visible and invisible, but if they were more sensitive they would realize that a great deal of static is sadly interfering with the attention of the voters.

The static all comes from the fact that a nice-looking young man in a well-fitting suit has stepped off a boat and is having a good time dancing and riding polo ponies. Lots of nice-looking young men wear well-fitting clothes and ride horses, but this particular young man happens to be a prince, the Prince of Wales, in fact; the son and heir of a well-known king. Now, unfortunately or otherwise, we have no king, not even a prince, of our own, and we seldom get a chance to see one belonging to somebody else. So those who can, rush to see him, and those who can't, rush to read about him. Columns and columns and columns. Common sense and monopoly and the Ku Klux and Defense Day are nowhere. It's all the Prince. If the words already printed about him were placed end to end they would form a double-track, standard-gauge access to the first King of England, whoever he was, with enough left over for a thousand extra copies of the *Social Register.*

If this nice young man isn't already wise to himself he can learn a lot of useful facts from reading the papers. If he doesn't know the color of his eyes one look in the *Daily Mirror* will tell him. If he doesn't realize that his coat is double- and not single-breasted, a million Wales fans will put him straight. If he is unaware that when interviewed he is nervous but will smile attractively just the same, a dozen lady reporters who asked him, "Will you marry an American girl," can describe his smile to him so he'll recognize it in a crowd next time.

If he only knew how much we cared about these little details he would surely multiply them. If he only knew what a throbbing interest is aroused by his two Oxford, rubber-heeled, high-polished shoes, he would try to wear three. If he only knew how many of our well-dressed young men want to hear about his waistcoat—which they know better than to call a vest—he would hire a statistician to count the buttons.

We're glad he doesn't know. We're glad he doesn't see all that we are given to read about him. He might think we were a rather silly crowd of people, and not realize that some go mad from thirst, some from starvation and others from not having had a king for well over a century. He is the first really square meal of nobility for years. No wonder we eat him alive.

No wonder we are told everything about him. Everything, everything. When he smiles he shows his teeth. When he raises his hat, his head is bare. A royal gesture. In the morning, he gets out of bed. In the evening, he gets back into it. It is not always the same bed, nor always the same hour. Sometimes he retires at eleven, sometimes at twelve, sometimes at one, sometimes at 2:17 (Daylight Saving). When he has breakfast (usually in the morning) he eats; and when he eats he chews. When he smokes, he lights the end of the cigarette which is not in his mouth. Does he get into his coat right arm or left arm first? Alas, we don't know yet—but give us time. At any rate, when he appears in public, his right arm is in his right sleeve, and his left arm is where it ought to be. When he goes out, his car (a high-powered Rolls-Royce) is driven by a chauffeur, on the right-hand side of the road. When he comes back, the car is still on the right-hand side of the road, but it is no longer the same side. Only princes can get away with this stuff.

This is common knowledge. There are other things about the Prince that only a few people know. They never hoard their knowledge. Sooner or later it all comes out in the papers.

"Yes, the Prince danced with me. I don't know why he singled me out. There were many girls just as attractive on board. We danced on Tuesday and again on Wednesday and Thursday. All the time he talked about his ranch in Canada. He's a perfect dancer."

"The Prince of Wales caught me on the jaw with a straight left. We were wearing twelve-ounce gloves. The barometer stood at $4.32 to the pound. The Prince wore a light-brown sweater. I said: 'Hit me again, Prince, like you did the first time.' He is a good boxer."

"H.R.H. shook my hand for thirteen seconds before going ashore. He has a good, firm grip. I've shaken a lot of hands in my time. He has five fingers, one of which I told him was called a thumb. He will make a good handshaker."

"The heir to the throne of Great Britain wears a four-in-hand tie of double-ply triple-X Nippon silk, purple and red in diagonal stripes. He told me he tied it himself. I think he has excellent taste."

"My Royal Rider mounted me from the port side just as the other ponies cantered on the field. He uses both stirrups. He pulled gently but firmly on the snaffle, leaving the curb disengaged. His touch with the whip was that of a gentleman and a sportsman. I don't believe all this about his falling off. He may have fallen with, but not off. 'Off' is not 'with.' When we got back to the stables the other ponies all asked why I hadn't got him to autograph the saddle. I said: 'Boys, there's a limit.' I think the Prince is a dandy horseman."

When this nice young man has gone home, he will leave behind him a large, but select, circle of people who met him, who handed him tea, who danced with him, who lent him their house, their car, their time, their dime, their cigars, who drew a laugh from him, or a bath for him. They should all band together into a great and imperishable society, united by a common vision, but decently separated as to social standing by some sort of formal degree. Thirty-second degree, the absent host; thirty-first, the young lady he danced with, and so on down from these Past Grand Masters and Exalted Ladies to the girl reporter who came near enough to see the invisible plaid in his suit, to the citizens of the county whose one mosquito bit him, to the young miss who saw him go by but was looking at the wrong automobile, to the post office clerk who canceled the stamp on H.R.H.'s letter but didn't know it until it was too late.

Young man, we're sorry for you. And please don't think us a bunch of snobs.

*October 8, 1924*

# OUR PROFESSIONAL PATRIOTS

by Sidney Howard

Spiritual suckers really get a run for their money in southern California: Los Angeles is the happy hunting ground of the spiritual grafter. You know the setting—the "garden spot of the world," where verdure is a whiskered, blighted deodar; where the modest violet blooms despairingly as the arid least it can do for the irrigation ditches which surround it; where every home is a bungalow and every bungalow a peanut-brittle defamation of the Mission Fathers; where Babbitt lives in retirement with a spare room for rent to Babbitt on a winter holiday; where meanness is made more hideous by bumptiousness and business depressions such as affect mortal communities are unknown or, at least, unadmitted; where racing cars and movie stars and faith healers and crystal-gazers and oil magnates vie with the oranges for biggerness and betterness; where, by publicly advertised command, you "bury your loved ones in the cemetery unusual." I contend that any city which boasts a "cemetery unusual" must be just the ideal spot for patriots, and so Los Angeles is. Also I trust that the spirit of hate in which this paragraph is written does not wholly escape the reader's attention.

The Better America Federation—a Los Angeles institution as ever was—stands abreast the livest standards of its native city and, in liveness and absurdity, stands above any other patriotic institution in the country. Its rousing offices leave the others of Ralph Easley and Company in the class of summer hotels during the winter season. The Better Americans display a whole floor of stenographers clicking out circular thrillers for the edification of not quite good enough Americans who have a timid streak and $10 to spare. There is a waiting room piled high with devastating literature, partly Better American and partly assorted with the American Defense Society generously represented, and there is a weekly newsletter with quotations from the *Federalist* and the daily press and such revolutionary playboys as the contributors to the *Worker* and *Industrial Solidarity*.

A wizened one, named Joplin (Jo. S.), sits there, high over the City of the Angels, and pounds his desk and compresses his lips and reads all the more dangerous radical publications (including this one) and tells you that "it is all part of the same game." And he is vicar, only, for the great beyond which is one Haldeman, who only shows himself to the elect. They are holy, these Better Americans: not even Ralph Easley himself is admitted to their company.

"Who is Ralph Easley's best friend?" Mr. Jo. S. Joplin asked me. "Sam Gompers is and that's enough for us!" Which isn't so surprising in Los Angeles.

They boast of their undercover agents, do the Better Americans, and set great store by their espionage reports, whereby hangs a little story not without its general bearing on militant patriotism. It is the story of a certain liberal preacher who is also a lecturer at the University of Southern California. This gentleman had occasion to make a speech in Pasadena. Having made the speech he was, in a manner, called to account for his utterances. An administrator of the university handed him a transcript to read of very wildly radical remarks attributed to him by the Better Americans and forwarded by them to his superiors with advice that appropriate action be taken. The lecturer read the transcript in considerable dismay and some horror. The administrator then handed him a second document, saying: "Here is the speech you really made. We had reason to believe that the Better Americans would be after you and we sent our own stenographer to protect both you and ourselves."

Like all good patriots they are simply hell on schools. I have a file of correspondence between them and Mr. Will C. Wood, the California superintendent of public instruction, for whose Communist patience my admiration knows no bounds. That he is a Communist tried and true there can be not the least doubt because he very effectively bucked the Better Americans in a plan to circulate their literature through the schools of the state. A pamphlet, "America Is Calling," was to be placed in every school child's hand, and a book, *Vanishing Landmarks,* in the hands of every teacher of school children, and there was to be a kind of Lusk law, to boot. The Lusk law failed to pass, and Mr. Wood bucked "America Is Calling," and as to *Vanishing Landmarks,* when the Better Americans set out to raise enough money for its free circulation, their campaign netted the exact sum of $5 each. Since that time they have been busy writing several thousand letters about a small boy who was given a copy of Mr. Upton Sinclair's novel *The Jungle.*

From one of the Better American letters, I quote:

. . . The parents of this state will appreciate knowing your position with reference to these two magazines, and again I ask—Do you approve of the Nation and the New Republic as magazines fit for circulation in the schools of this state? Is your board making the same effort to bar these magazines as it made to bar our pamphlet, America Is Calling?

The last I heard, *The New Republic* and *The Nation* were still

barred from the schools of Los Angeles if not from the unregenerate
schools of the rest of the state, and the Better Americans had just
uncovered a copy of one of Mr. Sinclair's books in a public library of
which, up to that moment, nobody had had a single Communistic
suspicion. As Mr. Jo. S. Joplin said, "I don't want you to think that
this is an innocuous organization. We are getting results all right."
Then there's the speakers' bureau. "Write early for your bookings
as we cannot accommodate everybody." California has always been
a little country by itself and the Better Americans undertake to do
everything for its orthodox patriotic welfare. Miss Hermine Schwed,
authoress of *Confessions of an Erstwhile Parlor Socialist,* was the
star speaker of last spring's triumphal tour. I have a report of one of
her best. It deals with boring-from-within as practiced by modern
novelists and playwrights. *Main Street,* for example, both the novel
and the motion picture, "created a distaste for the conventional good
life of the American!" Bad as it is, however, *Babbitt* is many times
worse, "as it is so poisonously subtle."

> Propaganda in the sense that we dislike it is the message that is gotten
> by between the lines and secretly. When Babbitt was a respectable citi-
> zen, true to his wife, a regular attendant at church, a member of the Rotary
> Club, the author made him out a smug, dull, colorless, uninteresting man.
> But as soon as he went philandering, became irreligious and broke loose
> from all civic pride as a Rotarian, the author painted him as a fascinating
> man.

Miss Schwed distributes her anathemas over several authors: Floyd
Dell, "rotten with delicately concealed radicalism"; George Bernard
Shaw, "particularly in *Heartbreak House";* H. G. Wells, "in all his
novels"; John Dewey and James Harvey Robinson, "the most dangerous
to young people." And of Communistic boring-from-within via the
stage, anathema to *Liliom, R.U.R., Anna Christie* and—oh, marvelous!
—*The Fool.* Then, to conclude, "Charlie Chaplin is the most dangerous
propagandist of Socialism in the motion-picture world."
But if I make the Better America Federation appear wholly innocuous, I defeat my own purpose as well as Mr. Jo. S. Joplin's, and I do
likewise misrepresent the facts of the case. For the facts are anything
but innocuous. During the past thirty years the business interests of
southern California have utilized the Merchants' and Manufacturers'
Association of Los Angeles to maintain the famous Los Angeles open
shop from which all blessings flow. Any employer who dared to sign
a union agreement found his credit cut off and himself denounced
as an enemy of industrial progress and of civic prosperity. The M. and
M., as it is affectionately called, found its hands full, what with its
antipicketing ordinances and all, and the Better America Federation
came out of its need for an aggressive propaganda agency in the

political publicity field. It was created as a southern California response to the Johnson progressivism which gave California a good many things that it needed.

A good many of those good things, the Better America Federation has, directly and indirectly, managed to undo. The Better America Federation, and various of its anomalous and anonymous subsidiary committees, have been credited with the control of twenty-two members of the state legislature. It is also credited with much of the pull which elected the present conservative administration on its economy program of abolition of as many as possible of the works of Johnson and his successor. It is further credited with the statement: "California was better off under the domination of the Southern Pacific Railroad than it has been since the progressives broke that domination." It is loud in denouncing those enemies of constitutional government, the initiative, referendum and recall. "Back to the Republic!" it cries, demonstrating the republic to be the golden mean between autocracy and democracy, between coercion and anarchy, between tyranny and demagogy.

The Better American gives his love of country widest expression in a little twelve-page booklet which he issued first some years ago as an attack upon the building ambitions of the Los Angeles Y.W.C.A. He has since reaffirmed the wisdom of that booklet. It is called "A Brief Outline of Arguments against the Program for Industrial Reforms Which Is Being Submitted to Various Social and Industrial Organizations"—a long title for twelve pages, but worthily descriptive.

The foreword is reprinted from Mr. Henry Harrison Lewis's magazine, *Industrial Progress* (Mr. Lewis is the same who discovered "Liberalism to be a new name for an old menace"):

> Certain religious, social and fraternal organizations are at the present time formulating and presenting with their endorsement plans for so-called industrial reconstruction . . . Business men, leaders in commerce who may be affected by these plans, are not consulted, but they are asked to contribute toward the up-keep of the organizations favoring them.

For example, again, Child Labor, as the Better Americans look at its pros and cons:

> . . . There is no practical wisdom in extending their school period . . . As a matter of fact it is unwise and results frequently in a handicap rather than an advantage to their future advance . . . This, of course, sounds heretical . . . But it can be demonstrated to be true.
>
> As to minors, no man or woman who loves his or her children, or who loves children of others, wants them compelled to work nights or any other time, for that matter, until they have passed the age of physical minority. Nor after that at nights if they work day times; and then only from the spur of poverty or distress.

I find that argument a little hard to follow and pass on to the Better American view of the minimum wage:

> This is largely an economic question. In practice, a minimum wage, as meant by organized labor, is really a maximum wage. The labor organizations recognize this, and it cannot possibly work in any other way where trade unionism prevails.

That too puzzles me. But I know that Los Angeles has nothing to fear, either from the minimum wage or from collective bargaining as per:

> They already have this right, that is fundamental, but what evidently is meant is the denial of the right of the employer to say who he will or will not recognize as representatives; and the denial of the right of the employer to refuse to bargain collectively if he chooses to do so.

The comment on the eight-hour law, the forty-four-hour week and the weekly day of rest is:

> This is an economic question. It is also a question of the "larger leisure." The question of the "larger leisure" is both a civic and a moral one . . . An investigation made in the large manufacturing districts in the East as to the manner in which the greater leisure operated, developed the fact that it was detrimental to the morals, efficiency and general morale, and was productive of the usual results of idle hours. Satan finds mischief still for idle hands to do, and, not merely mischief, but, unquestionably, evil . . . One day's rest in seven is right not only on physical but on moral grounds.

The little booklet served its initial purpose and the Y.W.C.A. never did get its new building. Afterward, when the Better Americans took the patriotic side in a fight to improve the Los Angeles school system, Dr. John R. Haynes, a regent of the State University, had the booklet reprinted and circulated at his own expense. It proved an effective weapon against the Better American stand but not quite effective enough to win the battle for the schools.

But I don't want you to think that Better Americans stop with propaganda, however effective. Said a director of the Federation:

> The biggest thing that the Better America Federation has done is to get the Criminal Syndicalist Act on the books and to keep it there against the efforts of those who are trying to repeal it . . . After the War we all took out bomb and riot insurance, but the best bomb and riot insurance is a membership in the Better America Federation.

I don't know how much you know about the Criminal Syndicalist Act in California, but this boast *is* a boast and if the Better Americans have won the criminal-syndicalist struggle single-handed they have quite a little to answer for to all other Americans except patriots. When I was last in California, one hundred men were serving indeterminate sentences of from four to fourteen years, convicted in batches, for violation of the Criminal Syndicalist Act by membership in the I.W.W. A majority of them are American-born, nonagitating workers, and more than half of them were convicted in Los Angeles. Not one of them was ever charged with any overt act such as sabotage or arson. Not one of them is even accused of inciting to violence. The process of convicting them was a process of proving their membership in an organization which does not conform to the Better American ideals of Americanism. The process of proving that the I.W.W. is "a conspiracy to violate the Criminal Syndicalist Act" amounts to just that. Other states have scrapped their criminal-syndicalist acts or given over enforcing them. San Francisco has always refused to invoke the act, but San Francisco has also refused to tolerate Better Americans.

Two gentlemen known as Dymond and Coutts, also known as stool pigeons, also known as *agents provocateurs,* have been the star witnesses of patriotism in these prosecutions. They joined the I.W.W. in 1917 (California's patriotic way while the inimitable Carlton Parker was keeping peace in the Northwest) and first disclosed themselves in 1918, when their testimony sent forty members of the I.W.W. to Leavenworth under the Espionage Act. The President has since pardoned those forty, but the hundred residents of the California penitentiaries remain in residence. During the whole six years since Coutts and Dymond gathered their evidence, they have been sent patriotically traipsing about the state, appearing here and there and gaining convictions for the patriotic cause with old testimony and old literature and a complete disregard of the reorganization and redirection of I.W.W.'ism. So complete and so successful has been this disregard that those two and their California patriot impellers will have almost all the credit for whatever revolutionary doctrine the I.W.W. may now or later promulgate. Most of the men convicted as members of the I.W.W. joined the organization since it abandoned its former sabotage program.

This, to my mind, constitutes the crowning, concrete infamy of the militant patriotism, and my real reason for giving these Better Americans these pages of publicity. I am glad, for the remainder of the country, that Los Angeles evoked and bred them. My sentiments toward Los Angeles may have been gathered during the course of this article. They cannot be shaken: I was there when the angels turned out to welcome Fatty Arbuckle home from envious cruelties of the San Franciscans who tried, through trying him, to defame their southern rivals. A people is best expressed in the institutions which embody its faith and Better America embodies the faith of Los Angeles.

In 1920 they voted Mr. Haldeman, the Better American president, the most useful citizen of the city for the year. They presented him with a gold watch.

*October 22, 1924 [Robert M. La Follette]*

# WHY I SHALL VOTE FOR LA FOLLETTE

by Felix Frankfurter

I belong to the increasing body of Americans who cannot forget that parties are instruments, because we are not tied to parties by bonds as obstinate and irrational as ties of church. For us, during the last two decades, each presidential election has brought with increasing emphasis the question: to what ends are the two old parties instruments? Bryce asked this question with his inveterate persistence. Listen to the answer:

> Neither party has, as a party, anything definite to say on these issues [which one hears discussed in the country as seriously involving its welfare]; neither party has any clean-cut principles, any distinctive tenets. Both have traditions. Both claim to have tendencies. Both have certainly war cries, organizations, interests enlisted in their support. But those interests are in the main the interests of getting or keeping the patronage of the government. Distinctive tenets and policies, points of political doctrine and points of political practice have all but vanished. They have not been thrown away, but have been stripped away by time and the progress of events, fulfilling some policies, blotting out others. All has been lost, except office or the hope of it.

No candid student of American politics would gainsay this picture except to paint it even darker than it was when Bryce wrote. As a believer in a two-party system I want two parties which will correspond to basic political realities which divide men, broadly speaking, into those who think things are substantially all right or fear to change them, and those who are greatly perturbed by the present-day economic and social tendencies of this country, and are eager for the high adventure of bringing society through slow, persistent, disciplined thinking and action nearer to what things ought to be.

The true principle of a free and popular government would seem to be so to construct it as to give to all, or at least to a very great majority, an interest in its preservation; to found it, as other things are founded, on men's interest . . . The freest government, if it could exist, would not be long acceptable, if the tendency of the laws was to create a rapid accumulation of property in few hands, and to render the great mass of the population dependent and penniless . . . Universal suffrage, for example, could not long exist in a community where there was great inequality of property.

So wrote Daniel Webster in 1820. A hundred years later "great inequality of property" is the most significant characteristic of our social-economic life. Its most devastating consequence is the permeation of the whole American life with material standards and material preoccupations. The federal statistics of income dryly tell the tale, but only partly, as figures do. Out of 6,787,481 who filed income-tax returns for 1922 (the last available year), 5,003,155 reported incomes below $3,000, and 6,193,270 incomes below $5,000; while 4,031 had incomes about $100,000, 1,860 over $150,000, 537 above $300,000, 228 above $500,000, and 67 above $1,000,000 per year. Beneath these quiet figures lie the most pulsating problems of American society.

I do not know the answers to these problems, but I do know there *are* answers. I also know that the indispensable step to the solution of a problem is the recognition that there is a problem. Neither, for instance, of the two parties, however, faces the issues. Neither has a conception of social aims through taxation. The Republican party is frankly stand-pat—things are all right. To the Democrats, also, things are all right, only those who administer them are not. What the country needs is "honest" Democrats and, doubtless, William J. Bryan would add, "deserving Democrats." The Republican and Democratic parties do not face the issues, because there are no differences in realities cutting across the two parties. They each represent unreal cohesions, because they are both organized appetites kept alive by the emotional warmth of past traditions. The "solid South" is thus the greatest immoral factor of American politics, and to the extent that Northerners help to perpetuate it they are accomplices in all the evils that flow from it. But with the rapid industrialization of the South, the increasing migration of Negroes to the North, with our new immigration policy and its inevitable repercussions upon politics and industry, one need not be foolish or fanciful to look for a realignment in political affairs which will, in Woodrow Wilson's phrase, "uncover realities."

At all events, one's duty is to make the effort and not wait to join the winning team. If it had not been for the Frémont campaign in 1856, there could have been no Lincoln in 1860. If it had not been for Keir Hardie and the work of the Fabians, there could have been no

British Labour party, but there might have been disastrous revolutionary interludes in England. The La Follette candidacy represents a determined effort to secure adequate attention for the great interests of the workers and of agriculture in those economic and social compromises which, in the last analysis, underlie all national action. "Different interests necessarily exist in different classes of citizens," the Fathers wrote in the *Federalist*, and the security of the state depends upon fair representation, as a basis of fair adjustment of the various interests. Labor and agriculture require more consideration and a better understanding, not because any class is to be coddled, but only because thus will national needs be satisfied. Adequate regard for the men and women who make up what we glibly call "labor" and "agriculture" and for the whole national economy that lies behind them does not at all mean amelioration through legislation. Much more important are the influences which will flow from educating public opinion, generally, to the claims and needs of labor and agriculture by recognizing their just position in the state. The greatest source of hope behind the La Follette candidacy is that, unlike the Progressive campaign of 1912, which was after all the reflex of a great personality, the present third-party movement was impelled by the insistencies of great bodies both of labor and of agriculture. It is rightly founded, as Webster put it, "on men's interest."

Foreign policies cannot be dissociated from the ideals and policies of a country at home. International relations mean international neighborliness. A national policy that will avoid the irritations, the injustices, the suspicions which create the atmosphere of hostility which breeds war is the surest international policy for peace. Both the Republican and the Democratic parties have failed in this respect because they have both pursued unworthy material interests in unworthy ways. Inevitably, the Democratic candidate has adopted "the silent treatment," to which he objects in the President, when it comes to our conduct toward Latin America, because both parties have an identic record of economic imperialism. This country under the guidance of both the Republican and Democratic parties has proven itself an exploiting neighbor, because of the false economic emphasis of our international policy. The Democratic candidate, who is silent about Mexico, Haiti and Santo Domingo, and oil in foreign parts, is greatly disturbed that "the English guns definitely outrange ours," and that our fleet is only as big as Japan's and smaller than the British! Did Mr. Davis learn something as ambassador to Great Britain that makes him want to arm us against her? Surely, we have here the revelation of a mind characteristically conventional. War with Great Britain will be avoided only if we are determined in the very marrow of our bones that war is an intolerable and therefore inadmissible mode for settling inevitable controversies. Is it seriously tenable that the hopes and the interests which are behind La Follette are, to put it mildly, less likely agencies for peace than those represented by the governing forces in the two old parties?

But what of La Follette himself? I am not voting for him for his sake. I do not regard him as a messiah. Belief in political messiahs is one of the greatest drawbacks to realizing that we ourselves, the man and woman in the street, must come to grips with our difficulties. But I welcome La Follette as a fit symbol of the movement which he leads. I do not believe in all his specifics; I am indifferent to others. But specifics by a party out of power are really unimportant, because necessarily they are somewhat academic and artificial. Behind such proposals is lacking the vivifying impact of responsibility. What matters in a statesman is his direction, his general emphasis and outlook. Senator La Follette's direction is revealed by forty years of public service. His aim has been consistently to give deeper meaning and scope to the masses of men, to make the commonwealth more secure and enduring by resting it on a broad basis of independent, trained and contented citizens. These are his aims. He has pursued them with unflagging devotion to the resources of reason. Nowhere does the university so permeate the life of a state as it does in Wisconsin. That is an achievement of which Senator La Follette was the guiding spirit. Probably no other man in public life today compares with La Follette in the extent of his reliance on disinterested expertness in the solution of economic and social questions.

Those of use who have no particular economic bias and who are least preoccupied with economic interests owe it most to bend our disinterestedness and our intellectual discipline to the solution of pressing economic-social problems. It is peculiarly up to us to supply the temper of good will and the courageous persistence of the inquirer. This election is important, more because of the forces in our national life that may permanently be encouraged or discouraged than because of any specific acts of the next administration. If clarification of American politics through the formation of a new party is required to make our politics more honest and more real, then all the talk of "throwing one's vote away" is the cowardly philosophy of the band wagon. Our duty is to help give cohesion and direction to the groping forces behind La Follette. The road ahead is long and steep; the goal is in the dim distance. When we attain it, others from there will start for a new goal.

*October 29, 1924 [John W. Davis]*

# WHY I SHALL VOTE FOR DAVIS

by Walter Lippmann

I shall vote for Mr. Davis because he is the only man who can be elected in place of Mr. Coolidge, and I do not wish directly or indirectly to give the present administration another term of power. I shall vote for Mr. Davis because it seems to me highly important that the next President should be willing to cooperate with Europe in organizing the peace of the world. I shall vote for him because it seems to me important that the next President should be neither bewildered, antipathetic nor obtuse in the face of the present sectional and class divisions. I shall vote for him because I believe that in this postwar world of fierce nationalisms his strong Jeffersonian bias against the concentration and exaggeration of government is more genuinely liberal than much that goes by the name of liberalism.

In short, I think it more important to vote so as to determine the character of the administration in the next four years than to vote for a new party system which may or may not be established in 1928 or in 1932. Perhaps the immediate consequences would not seem so much more real to me if I saw in the La Follette movement the materials and the ideals of a great liberalizing effort.

First, the practical politics of the La Follette movement. Here in the East its supporters, *The New Republic* among them, are arguing that the new party is to destroy and supplant the Democratic party as the opposition to conservative Republicanism. This seems to me impossible. The Democratic party is more or less indestructible because of the solid South. A party which enters every campaign with roughly half the electoral votes is not in my opinion going to disappear. It seems extremely unlikely that La Follette will break the solid South, and almost as unlikely that the Southern Democrats will coalesce, as *The New Republic* has suggested, with the Eastern Republicans. If the Democratic party survives, and if the Republican party survives, there is not under the presidential system of government any permanent future for a third party. I believe the La Follette movement is almost certain to be reabsorbed into the two old parties. It might dominate one of them for a time, as Bryan dominated the Democratic party, with one interval, from 1896 to 1912. But in the sense that it will make a new party system, intellectually distinct, emotionally honest, logical, clear-cut and free of cant, I do not believe in the promises made in its name.

I think the exponents of the new party have never really understood the federal character of the American party system, have never understood that we have in fact no national parties, but only national coalitions of state parties, and that as long as the President is not directly elected by a plurality of voters, the vitality of the party will remain in the state organizations. These state parties are independent bodies which come together every four years, as La Follette's Wisconsin and Lodge's Massachusetts used to come together. The national conventions set out to unite the state organizations on the basis of formulae which won't seriously divide them, and under the leadership of candidates who are popular in the dominant groups of states and acceptable to the others.

I shall not undertake here to argue whether this system is as absurd as it sounds, except to note in passing that it is the only political system we know under which a continental state has combined a strong central government with wide home rule. The British system of government is no analogy whatsoever, and even if it were, its comparative failure to deal successfully with Ireland and Ulster should be set beside the American success with half a dozen potential Irelands and Ulsters. In fact, I believe that the discerning historian will recognize more clearly than we can or perhaps need to do that the success of federalism in America has depended largely upon the sectional accommodations achieved through our flexible and unprincipled two-party system.

But whether or not the fundamental virtues of that system outweigh its obvious stupidities, its frequent venality and its intellectual sterility, it is so deeply imbedded in our social system that it will, I think, upset the plans of Mr. La Follette's supporters. I should feel less certain of this if it were not already apparent that the La Follette movement is yielding to the same conditions. It too is a coalition of local organizations, and this early in its career, it exhibits all the symptoms of that same equivocation which the unifying of diverse elements requires. On foreign policy, on the question of whether to break up monopoly or socialize it, on immigration, on Prohibition, even on the Supreme Court, the La Follette movement speaks with an uncertain voice or none at all. Why is that so? *The New Republic,* as I understand it, has argued that the La Follette movement was a gathering of the disfranchised and dissatisfied and that when they were gathered they would unite on a coherent platform. I am skeptical about this explanation. For I think Mr. La Follette was shrewd enough to know that his hope of uniting his followers lay in avoiding the issues that divide them. He acted as every political leader does, and for the same reasons and under the same compulsions. And when I see *The New Republic* making a virtue of Progressive ambiguities while it expends its scorn on Democratic and Republican ambiguities, I smell the old familiar business of rationalizing your partisanship.

I am prepared to admit, of course, that I am misreading the political situation and that in some way a significant and profound realignment of parties will result. But this possibility seems to me too remote and doubtful to overcome the feeling that it is very important not to give this administration four more years of power. I might vote for La Follette, nevertheless, if I felt that he was the exponent of a genuine liberal and progressive movement. For it might be worth while to ignore the character of the next administration for the sake of the educative effects of the La Follette movement.

But in many ways, and even though I warmly respect Mr. La Follette, I do not like the main drift of his preaching. His political program is almost violently nationalistic and centralizing; that seems to me reactionary and illiberal. His policy in respect to large corporations seems to me an illogical mixture of the individualism of 1890, as expressed in the Sherman Act, and prewar Socialism. His foreign policy seems to date about 1919 and to ignore all that has happened in Europe since the Treaty of Versailles was first published. The net effect of what he has to say about Europe is to combine American irresponsibility and isolation with provocative statements about the policies of France and England.

I feel that if I am to cast my vote for a candidate who cannot be elected, and by that vote to help elect the man I think ought not to be elected, then at least I ought to be able to vote for a man who is bravely and lucidly expounding what seems to me a liberal program. Mr. La Follette does not offer me that compensation. I shall therefore vote for Mr. Davis, because in foreign policy and in his attitude toward the sphere of government he seems to me to be on the right track, more nearly on the right track than either of the two other candidates. I shall vote for him, not only believing that he is headed in the right direction, but that in personal character and in experience of the postwar world he is the best-equipped man. And if the movement for a new party system has the vitality claimed for it, it will, I think, be helped rather than obstructed by the presence in the White House of a man able to understand it and resourceful enough to put it on its mettle.

*July 29, 1925 [The Scopes Trial]*

# ON THE DAYTON FIRING LINE
by Frank R. Kent

What's the sense of writing about the trial? The trial itself has been a trivial thing, full of humbuggery and hypocrisy, conducted by publicity-seeking lawyers, sensation-hungry correspondents, a bewildered judge, a befuddled jury, a popeyed crowd that has sweatingly packed the little courtroom and for the first time in history has torn a little American town up by the roots, uncovering its every small secret to a jeering world.

The real drama in Dayton was the people, not the trial. Not the conspicuous people who were tied up with the case one way or another, nor the motley throng of strangers who converged there for one purpose or another, nor even the unobtrusive prisoner at the bar, who was early backed into oblivion by the overpowering importance of his counsel. Not any of these, but the men and women born there, raised there, living there or thereabouts.

They were the real story. The more you saw of them, the further you dug below the surface, the stronger grew the realization of the depth and extent to which religion holds them. Religion—real religion, basic Bible religion—is the big thing in this country—the religion of the camp meeting, the revivals, prayer meetings and Sunday schools of the evangelical churches in the little towns, and of queer, violent, acrobatic sects, creeds and faiths, all based on literal Bible beliefs, in the more isolated districts. The whole region is saturated with religion. Nine tenths of the people are steeped in it. It is their mode of recreation as well as their means of redemption, their single emotional outlet, the one relief from the deadly drabness of a cut-off existence. In that part of the state there are almost no Jews, no Catholics and no Episcopalians. There are Methodists, Baptists, Disciples of Christ, Presbyterians, Seventh-day Adventists, Holy Rollers and Holy Jumpers. Of course, in the small towns, and even in the mountains, where the isolation and illiteracy are almost complete, there are plenty of exceptions; but it is the literal fact that so far as the great bulk of the people are concerned a religion, the rigidity of which it is difficult to exaggerate, absorbs all the thought they have aside from their work.

In Dayton—and Dayton is exactly like thousands of other places of its size—religion takes the place of golf, bridge, music, art, literature, theaters, dancing, tennis, clubs. It is the fundamental communal factor. Of the two thousand Dayton people, not more than fifty are without some touch or association with one or another of the nine evangelical churches. That proportion prevails in all the towns of Tennessee, in all that section of the country. It is not the life of the cities and it is not the life of the South, but it is the life of the small towns, the countrysides and mountain districts, not only in Tennessee but in Ohio, Utah, Georgia, Colorado, Iowa—in every state where people live in relative isolation.

For those in these places, take religion away and the desolation and distress would be pitiable to contemplate. Of course they take their religion in different ways, with different degrees of intensity, varying all the way from the lurid fanaticism of the hills where some twenty thousand Holy Rollers regularly gather at night under the torch-lit trees, driving themselves into dreadful convulsions through the unconscious practice of group hypnotism evoked by the weird writhings of their bodies and the wild rhythm of their chants and gestures, to the decent dignity of the better type of Dayton citizen who makes no public show of his religion, does not rant on the streets or argue with those who do not think as he does.

But deep down in his system he has it just the same. It is just as fundamental, although less emotional and more restrained than that of those who live primitively scattered about the lonely hills. In the Daytons of the country the interesting thing is that when men and women of an argumentative mind meet it is religion, not politics, about which they argue. They know no politics. Even the homely virtues of the impeccable Mr. Coolidge leave them cold. With those who read the metropolitan newspapers and go to the movies he is, of course, popular. But in the main they are not stirred by him or by any other political figure or by any political fact or issue.

When they argue about religion it is not whether the teachings of the Bible are right or wrong. They differ only upon interpretation of the Scriptures. They will dispute for hours as to whether it is better to say that Christ died to save sinners or that Christ lived to save sinners; whether regeneration, as the word is used in the New Testament, means the same as redemption; whether the Parables indicated one thing or another; whether St. Paul said this or St. John said that.

One night in Dayton I drove out two miles to a beautiful grove at the foot of the mountains where a hundred Holy Rollers for three hours prayed and sang violently until many of them were lying on the ground in a horrible state of physical exhaustion and mental collapse. When I got back to the town an evangelist meeting in the courthouse square was just ended. Instead of dispersing and going home, the well-behaved and mostly well-dressed crowd split up into groups and debated various points of Biblical interpretation until long after midnight. This was not an unusual meeting, it was a typical one; it was not due to the trial, it was the habit of the people, not only in Dayton but in ten thousand other Daytons.

To think seriously of convincing these people—either the relatively educated and intelligent church members of the Daytons, or the rougher and largely illiterate folks in the hills—of the soundness of the evolutionary theory as opposed to the Bible, is fantastic, futile, foolish. Scientific facts that clash with the Bible are to them mere ammunition for the Devil in his war against God. They not only cannot be convinced, they cannot be weakened. Evolutionary evidence serves to strengthen their belief, not dilute it. They see in it solely Satanic guile working through misguided or wicked men. They had rather—they say they had rather in pulpit and in private talk—that their children should never learn the alphabet at all than be taught that a single word in the Bible is to be doubted.

If during the trial a bolt of lightning from the sky had singled out Mr. Darrow for slaughter few would have been surprised. Many actually expected it. On the other hand, to thousands in this section it would have come as no surprise if Mr. Bryan, having gloriously defeated the forces of unrighteousness, were to be visited by an angel of the Lord who would whisk the old gentleman off to heaven in a chariot of fire.

*August 12, 1925*

# WILLIAM JENNINGS BRYAN
Editorial

The career of William J. Bryan was, in almost all its aspects, an unusually complete example of the futility of unenlightened and undisciplined good intentions. He brought to his work of popular tribune rare and abundant gifts. His heart was large and it beat strong. He had wide and lively sympathies with the point of view and the needs of the American people. He loved them and most ardently he willed their welfare. Being temperamentally an evangelist, he dedicated his life to persuading them to walk according to the light as he saw it. He obtained for a while considerable influence over them.

At his best he could sway a popular audience more successfully than any public speaker of his generation. His voice was a superbly flexible and full-toned instrument for his purpose. He used it artfully. He practiced all the tricks of the pulpit and the platform, but only for causes in which he devoutly believed. He was, of course, an ambitious man who wished to occupy the greatest office in the gift of his fellow countrymen, but he was also, in his own way, disinterested. He could sacrifice his personal interests and serve, if necessary, in a subordinate capacity as, for instance, Theodore Roosevelt could not. The episode of his career in which he appeared to the best advantage was the gallant and shrewd fight which he carried on against blind and reactionary influences in the Democratic Convention of 1912. It was his pugnacity which made Woodrow Wilson's nomination possible, and later it was his loyal cooperation which removed the most dangerous obstacles to the success of Mr. Wilson's first term. Throughout his whole relationship with his chief he behaved in a thoroughly creditable manner. There was a good deal that was second-rate about Mr. Bryan, but there was nothing petty, vindictive or sensitively egotistic. He did not cherish grudges and resentments and then save his self-respect by transfiguring them into divine judgments. He was incapable of self-righteous ill temper. He dealt fairly and even generously with friend and foe.

Probably his outstanding characteristic was a fluid and somewhat unsophisticated sincerity. By emphasizing his sincerity, we do not mean merely that he believed what he said. No man who preached as often, as easily and as ignorantly as he did could in any real sense believe what he said. He was intoxicated and betrayed by his own verbal facility and fluency, and sang many songs that passed out of existence with the occasion. By his sincerity we mean his disposition, despite ridicule and abuse, to translate his moral rhetoric into the only kind of action which he understood, viz., political action. It was characteristic of him always to run and jump toward an immediate political remedy for any real or supposed public misfortune or malady which deeply afflicted him, and to all the causes with which he was conspicuously associated most of his fellow countrymen were in the beginning more or less indifferent. He was urging progressive measures of one kind or another and protesting against the domination of big business many years before this brand of politics became popular. He deplored intemperance and believed in the possibility of its extermination by legal prohibition. He was a pacifist agitator and a prospective negotiator of arbitration treaties in the service of his Master, the Prince of Peace, at a time when most Americans could discover no relationship between the Gospel and the prevention of war. Late in life he suddenly realized that the salutary truths of religion, as he understood them, were being compromised by the spread of belief in materialistic account of the origin of the world and mankind, and as usual he invoked a political remedy. He called for laws which would prohibit the teaching of this impious doctrine in the public schools. In all these cases Bryan dared to rush in where angels feared to tread.

But notwithstanding his rare gifts of feeling and good will, he himself contributed little to the success of the causes which he had most at heart. His intelligence was not as robust as his good will, and his education was deplorably defective. He did not know the nature of scientific evidence and method. He did not understand what technical discipline is. The only art which he practiced was that of an orator, and his fluency and flexibility in addressing audiences confirmed the tendency which he derived from his education to confuse words with things and to depend upon utterances to save his fellow men and his own soul from perdition. He persistently agitated in favor of reforms without spending any time on methodical preparation. Indeed he deliberately disparaged expertise of all kinds. It seemed to him undemocratic. What he took to be the American way was to create armies out of minutemen, peace out of good will, science out of verbal analogies, religion out of inspired writings and evangelical enthusiasm, and a progressive society out of a marriage between aspiration and exhortation. He was occupied chiefly in improvising political hymns for audiences of small-town Americans and in moving them to sing and to vote in response to him.

In culture he was a cross between a nonconformist clergyman and a traditional Jacksonian Democrat; and both of these disciplines disqualified him for the world in which he lived. There was a time when most of the constructive American activities were improvisations which almost any good fellow could learn and which did not require on the part of those who followed them much methodical preparation. The good fellows who practiced these activities inevitably attached more importance to good nature and good will than to intelligence, and they inevitably disparaged the small minority of their fellow countrymen who measured the value of human achievement by exacting technical standards. Mr. Bryan belonged to this period. If he had flourished in a pioneer community before the Civil War he might have been a great and a successful popular leader. He could then have used his magnificent voice to exhort and beguile his fellow countrymen to respond to his appeals with a repetition of his own phrases and songs. But during the first quarter of the twentieth century a politician who was chiefly a good-hearted improviser of familiar rhythms like Mr. Bryan was certain in many important circumstances to be stricken with ineptitude and unsubstantiality. His quick sympathies detected the opportunities of leadership, but his obsolete equipment prevented him from seizing the occasions.

Once every four years when the Democratic party assembled in convention, Mr. Bryan's figure loomed large and effective. He expanded in an atmosphere of party contention and political rhetoric. But at other times and particularly in critical situations, when aggressive and specific action was required, he was powerless to precipitate himself into an effective incarnation. Prominent as he has been during the years of progressive agitation, he faded away during the succeeding years of progressive legislation. He could not realize a program. The leadership even of his own party passed to another man. The only important office which he occupied was that of Secretary of State, but he could not adapt himself to the requirements of the work and he emerged from the Cabinet a better, a sadder but a smaller man. During the turbulent years of the American crusade in Europe, he was for the most part invisible and even inarticulate. He was incapable of grasping what it was all about. It seemed almost as if he did not actually live unless he was improvising or haranguing from a pulpit or a platform on some traditional theme. His very sincerity evaporated when he ceased to sing and was obliged to meet the test of specific action. For a while his sermons and hymns were those of an evangelist; his behavior, when he had to choose, was usually that of a party politician.

His progressivism was accidental and devoid of leaven. His mind was nourished upon the sentimental social, moral and theological rhetoric which formed so large a part of American culture during the Middle Period. He believed profoundly in the literal inspiration, in the wholly salutary magic of his certain cherished words and scripts. He did not regard language as a vehicle of communication which derived its functional value from the interpretations attached to it by individual minds. His chosen words and in some measure all words possessed for him an essential potency analogous to the magical ferment which passes from the altar to the devout worshiper during the Catholic Mass. The Lord had strung them together into inspired histories and truths which it was impious to criticize or repudiate, and which it was salutary to believe, to repeat and if possible to translate into action. Mr. Bryan repeated them for the benefit of his own generation. He was the perfect example of the platform fundamentalist. He lived and loved to preach, and when he preached he envisaged his sermons as winged missals which carried the consolation and blessing of the revealed Word to the hungry and thirsty souls who welcomed them. But he was a fundamentalist who escaped the frequently harsh and unlovely traits of the sect. He was neither arrogant nor self-righteous. His fundamentalism was tempered by amiability. The net impression of him is that of a kind, a brave and an unselfish man who might have been a great power for good if only he had possessd in addition a circumspect and an inquisitive intelligence.

*October 20, 1926*

# MARIE OF RUMANIA

by Charles Merz

She is a queen, the mother of a queen, the author of a five-foot shelf of letters. When she was born, a tsar of Russia traveled fifteen hundred miles to see the christening. When she was married, her bridegroom built a glass-and-iron amphitheater to hold the crowd. When she was crowned, two and one-quarter miles of dinner guests sat down to banquet with her. It is of such stuff that royal lives are made. But more stuff than that is needed for a lady from the Balkans to win a reputation as far west as Idaho and Kansas. If Marie of Rumania is the most famous queen of Europe, and the toast of young democracies abroad, it is because she has a way with her. Fame is hers on her own merit. For she is something significantly new in queens, and it is a quite modern era which produced her.

She is called an English queen, Rumanian only by adoption. That is because she was born in England of England's royal family and lived in England as a child. She is, as her biographers have pointed out, no more English than she is Rumanian. She is a mixture of two strong races, Russian and German. Her mother was the only daughter of Alexander II, Tsar of Russia. Her father, the Duke of Edinburgh, was the second son of Queen Victoria and therefore German on both sides. Marie was born at Eastwell Park, the country seat of her father's family in Kent. As a child she was the delight of her grandfather when she visited him, because, it is said, she could play cribbage, and the idol of a large family of cousins. With several of these cousins there were young romances which are possibly the apocryphal inventions of the Continental press. It was, at any rate, no cousin whom she married, but a young man from the other end of Europe, a melancholy, high-flown young man with a lost heart and an adopted father. This happened when Marie was seventeen years old.

The young man was Ferdinand, Crown Prince of Rumania, but no more Rumanian than Marie herself. Ferdinand was a Hohenzollern. Not one of the wicked Hohenzollerns who became anathema from Maine to California, later on; but, for better or for worse, a Hohenzollern none the less, a young man who had become Crown Prince of Rumania in somewhat the same fashion as other men have become Vice-President of the United States: there being no heir apparent in Rumania, King Carol had offered the succession to Prince Leopold, who in turn had offered it to Prince William, who in turn had suggested

Ferdinand. Ferdinand was twenty-four when this occurred. He was twenty-eight when he was married, the marriage taking place, as chronicled above, in a Crystal Palace built for the occasion. This was in January 1893.

"I was tame enough in those days," writes Marie, "not the least like the modern girl. I suppose the modern girl would have called me an awful fool, and perhaps I was. . . . There were sad days, lonely ones, desperate ones, when I felt like running away. There was, I can tell you, more than one scuffle at the beginning." Some of the scuffling, one infers, was with old King Carol, who had a profound Rumanian conviction that woman's place was in the home. Certain differences of opinion also developed, it seems possible, concerning the future for Marie and Ferdinand himself. For out of health and out of heart (a prior love affair on Ferdinand's part had been broken off by royal edict) Ferdinand was more than once reported in these days to be ready to resign his claim upon the throne and retire to a garden.

One can imagine him broaching the subject to Marie, but one cannot imagine him laboring the point. Resign a throne? Give up a crown? Conceivably Ferdinand was invited to go try it. The granddaughter of a tsar of all the Russias was not made to be the wife of any gentlemanly rose farmer in the Danube. She was made to spread her fame into every land blessed with a daily press, and proved it.

One looks over the life that developed from these early years and tries to guess what it is that has made Marie the best-known queen in Europe, the most photographed queen who ever lived, the constant glory of the rotogravure sections, a celebrity from the boulevards of Paris to the farms of Texas, the prototype of all queen mothers in the movies, the subject of almost innumerable portrait sketches in the magazines, all written in a key of ecstasy.

She is beautiful? Yes, but there are other beautiful queens in Europe. She is a granddaughter of Queen Victoria? Yes, but the granddaughters of Queen Victoria are legion. She was the wartime queen of a small nation with its back against the wall? Yes, but so also were the Queens of Belgium and Greece, and neither of these ladies ever shared her glory. She is the mother of five handsome children? Other queens have handsome children. In behalf of these children she has raked Europe in a search for thrones? Yes, but that is the business of queen mothers. Nor has Marie's campaign been attended by success so glittering that we might have, here, an explanation of her fame. At one time there were three crowns in the royal family; now, as the result of a revolt in Athens and an amour in Bucharest, the number is reduced to one.

Certainly Marie's years on the throne (a dozen, now) have witnessed the striking of no great alliances abroad, no golden age at home. In these twelve years small progress has been made with two formidable and really menacing problems in Rumania, agrarian reform and the federation of racial minorities. These problems, to be sure, do not lie within the province of a queen. But if Marie's wide reputation is to be explained, it will not be easy to attempt it either on the ground of any political triumph she has scored or because of the happy fact that her reign has coincided with years of great peace and plenty for her people.

Marie's fame, one guesses, rests upon nothing intrinsic in her story, but rather upon something intrinsic in herself. She is a journalist, a thoroughly modern journalist, and the first queen-journalist in modern Europe. Over the story she has put the headlines.

Paris, in the first months of 1919, was the scene of a Peace Conference of statesmen dividing the spoils of war and drawing new boundary lines, Rumania's included. To Paris, in the first months of 1919, came Marie. Other queens had come to Paris, in these first days of peace. Other queens had ridden through the streets and bowed to the crowds and smirked and, overcome by the warmth of their reception, retired to their chambers. Marie, on arriving, wished to know: "Where are the reporters?"

She received them on March 7—not just a few of them, but all who cared to come, foreign and domestic, highbrow and lowbrow, Americans, Japanese and Siamese, asking no more than that they be reporters of the news, people who were telling other people (by the hundred thousand) what was happening in Paris to everybody's claims, Rumania's included. She received them—and of course she bowled them over. Next morning the press of twenty nations paid its tribute. In America the feature writers had a Roman holiday; even the Associated Press, which does its best to be unenthusiastic, spread itself upon this gracious, democratic lady "whose beauty enhances the charm of her forceful personality." Rumania's claims, languishing all winter, picked up suddenly in the news.

The incident is typical. In Marie's experience it has been duplicated more than once. It reflects an understanding of certain modern values which have much to do with fame: (1) the press is nothing for a queen either to snub or to fear; (2) it is all very well to sit on a throne, but one's subjects do not see the throne, they read the Sunday papers; (3) what is called public opinion consists largely of reflex action to newspaper headlines; (4) it is better to send en masse for the reporters than to let them come in ones or twos. One reason why Marie is the most famous queen in Europe is because she is the first queen in Europe to establish the press conference as a royal institution. The scepter is a pretty thing, but in 1926 the world is more often swayed by handouts.

Nor is this all. If Marie is aware of the press, and of the importance of the press to anyone whose business in life is the preservation of a wide renown, she is likewise aware of the vast army of headline-hungry readers behind the press, what interests them, and why. That is, she is not only a journalist by conviction, but instinctively a journalist in method; and for proof of that it is necessary to look no further than to Marie's own syndicate material. Twice within the last eighteen months she has set the pot aboiling. Once for the North American Newspaper Alliance, once for Mr. Hearst. Both times the writing and the selection of material have been her own, and not the work of a press agent. The choice of subjects is impressive. No dull Balkan politics, no peasant problems in Rumania, no genealogies, no dim and distant memories of a royal childhood, but live things which the souls of millions of shopgirls pant to read about: "My Experiences with Men," "Clothes and the Woman," "Can a Woman Make Herself Beautiful?" "Dreams Do Come True," "Beauty in Women," "Woman's Loss of Beauty," "What a Smile Can Do, "Making Marriage Durable." Here is no writing over people's heads but an instinct for the greatest common divisor of street-corner interest as sure as Mr. Hearst's, and a taste as catholic as Mr. Brisbane's. Here is sure-fire appeal for both the subway crowd and the farm-and-firesiders, served up by no less a personage than a reigning queen. Here is both the titillation of a bold idea and the profoundly moral undertone: for if Marie writes, under the head of "My Experiences with Men," that it is fun for beautiful women to play with fire, one always discovers, before the essay ends, that the gentle reader is advised against it, if attractive, and patted on the back, if plain. Here, in a word, is journalism at its modern best: a "news" subject, a dash of piquancy, but an anchor cast to windward, and a kind word for the also-ran: the journalism of those two most successful journalists—the inexhaustible Miss Fairfax and the eager Doctor Crane.

Fame? Is it any wonder that Marie is famous, when to ability such as this she adds the title Queen, and then goes on not only to interpret news, but to make it? For of course she makes it. As a queen, inevitably she is on the stage and not merely on the critic's bench; and on the stage she has shown that she possesses that sense of "timing" which lies behind the whole philosophy of what is and isn't news. There was an era, for example, when mere grandness was the only necessary attribute of famous and successful queens. Of no one's mere grandness did the world read more, in those days, than Marie's. "Room after room in her palace" (this is one of scores of similar accounts which might be clipped from the 1890s) "is a fairyland of rare tapestries, rich marbles, golden embroideries and white bearskins, the only rugs which she allows. . . . Robed in a trailing garment spangled with costly gems, her arms weighted down with barbaric bracelets," Marie would sit "in a golden room under a golden canopy" surrounded by many other golden things, including "a golden spinning wheel inlaid with precious stones." . . . Ah, the good old days, when a queen was a queen and a palace was a palace. Today, if one journeys with an ecstatic reporter through Marie's entourage one reads of pine rooms, plain and unadorned democracy and the simplicity of a queen who dotes on peasant costumes.

So it has been for twenty years, if you really wish to know what keeps Marie of Rumania in the news.

There was the day, some twenty years ago, when a dash of masculinity in fashion was just beginning to come in. Marie was in on that. Before Newport had abandoned the sidesaddle Marie was delighting the foreign correspondents with a riding costume of "crush hat, bolero and Cossack trousers."

There was the day, something less than twenty years ago, when "a business interest on the side" was becoming fashionable for ladies of society. Marie was in on that. She had a factory of her own, when a factory operated by a queen was news—"having seen the possibilities in a business venture of this sort," the New York press reported, "and with her own money establishing this unique industry [it happened to be the quill toothpick industry] in the land of her adoption."

Again, there was the day when it became the thing for royalty not only to tinker with a verse or two, but take up art in earnest. Marie has had a painting hung in a Brussels salon and a play produced in Paris. She is the author of four novels and a book of essays. About the time that the bedtime story began coming back (thanks to the radio) she wrote a bedtime story, too: about Stick-in-the-Mud and little Sootypootypuff, who teased him.

Styles change. It is the essence of Marie's far-flung fame that she changes just a bit in advance and so helps to set them.

Never is she behind the times. One might guess, even if one had not read of it in the papers, that in more recent days Marie would drive a locomotive fifty miles an hour, become an expert typist, and write an ad for Pond's Cold Cream.

Fame? Surely for Marie fame is no mere accident of time and space, but the plain reward of merit. For twenty years, with a verve of her own, a fascination for reporters and a sense of news values which cannot be matched on the continent of Europe, she has timed her activities so perfectly for the constant demands of a hungry modern press that she could have brought fame to a peasant's daughter, let alone a queen. She is coming, now, to a land whose inhabitants she has described as "gloriously generous," "terribly sincere" and "marvelously efficient"—all things which they had guessed themselves. She wishes to go as far west as Utah, to see Niagara Falls and the Yellowstone, "the cowboys and the Indians," the coal mines, police courts, slums and moving-picture magnates. She will see them all, and from each one of them she will extract copy enough to remain consistently on the front pages of a busy press—with two hundred gallant and desperately smitten news men ready to swear to it, if necessary, and if desired, that she has crossed Niagara on a wire.

One request she made when first she talked of this trip, and only one:

"I must plead with the American newspapers to be fair to me."

Fair to her? . . . God watch over young reporters on the road from Ambrose Light to Salt Lake City!

*December 15, 1926*

# BRANCUSI AND MARIN

by Lewis Mumford

*Marin at the Intimate Gallery:* The new Marins are, I think, among the finest fruits of our generation. They have the surface charm, many of them, of the earliest Marins, the charm of pure color, of eyes that seek and apprehend unexpected gems; they have the depth and strength, the inner feeling, of the later Marin, the pure lyricist, singing of the landscape and the ocean and the beauty of swift white sails, or baffled and hurt, yet still singing, in the midst of the soiled canyons of New York; and they have, incidentally, the marvelous technical range of an artist whose economies in expression intensify the swift, translucent quality of the medium itself. The fusion of the inner and the outer eye, focused unconsciously in the formula of design, puts Marin at the very summit of his art—and this means, at the present moment, of American art. Is it unreasonable to hope that the country which has harbored Marin might even produce a permanent anchorage for his pictures? What better nucleus could there be for a collection of American art, or what better pictures to represent modern America alongside the fine achievements of the past? Today we can find our Marins with Stieglitz. But where shall we find them tomorrow? What answer have our museums to make to this question?

*Brancusi at the Brummer Gallery:* "Intellectual passion drives out sensuality." This observation of Leonardo's came to me when I stood among the Brancusi sculptures. Brancusi, like more than one good man in our day, was one of Rodin's assistants; the work of the two artists, their technique, their feeling for form are in extreme contrast. Rodin is all surface: the surfaces are tactile; they catch the least quiver of light or shade, like bodies in movement: the structure, or the form implied through all these passages and undulations, is forgotten. The Musée Rodin is a magnificent carnival of sensual passion; desire—deep, anguished, volatile, thirsty, above all sensual—is transfixed in a hundred amazing attitudes, all personal in their conception. The Hand of God is Rodin's hand; the girl, the man, the embrace, the shudder, are drawn from the pockets of private experience. Rodin's marbles are a pageant of magnificent sensuality, like those Flemish feasts Taine once described.

In Brancusi, intellectual passion is dominant: it is a fine surgical knife that cuts bloodlessly into the innermost form. From the block of marble, from the trunk of riven oak, from a piece of granular stone, he extracts a form—its form—and the plastic medium becomes almost as refined as a concept. Here is a bird. It is not a bird that belongs to the jungle or the woods; it is that Golden Bird which is all birds—the highly polished marble whirling slenderly toward a point in utmost space is the character and activity of birds, their shape and their flight, wedded into a single form. Here is a block of marble, tapering slightly at its base; by the subtlest of transpositions, so subtle that they seem almost the work of the beholder's eye rather than the sculptor's hand, the marble becomes the virginal torso of a girl, and the torso is Chastity. Any other use of this block would seem a profanation. Or again, there is the trunk of a tree, with two inverted branches coming vigorously out of each side; the surfaces have been rounded, almost as if they had been put in a lathe; there is no hint of muscles or organs; and yet, in the unflinching strength of the conception there is no doubt of the character and sex of the figure—this is the idea of a young man. A solid cube of stone; a line down the center and the finest suggestion of a curve at the belly, divide the man from the woman. It is called "The Kiss"; the lips emphasize it; but the kiss is the kiss of perfect oneness; it has no beginning and no end; this solid block represents, unlike Rodin's kisses, not a man and a woman considered as separate beings, but their union. So one might go through each object in the Brancusi exhibition—the fish, reflected in the mirror on which they glide, are in their original medium, or the simple column of oak which might be set up in some park or wood to represent the reigning dryad. Carried to the utmost abstraction in line and surface, almost all of Brancusi's forms speak plainly for themselves: in only two cases, "Socrates" and the "Prodigal Son," did I feel unable to grasp the sculptor's intention. Almost alone among the artists of our time, Brancusi has been able to fuse together two important attitudes. One is the feeling for Nature, the renewal of the Pan impulse, which rose in the eighteenth century, dominated Turner and Corot, gave whatever gaiety and life belongs to the Impressionists, and swept through the annals of the natural sciences that dealt with the earth and organic life. The other is that belief in formal perfection, irrespective of time, place, history, which rose in modern times with Spinoza and the modern mathematicians, and which has carved a place in our daily life through the precise calibrations and inflexible logic of machinery; the pure forms of machines, with their elimination to the last degree of the human element, have prepared our minds to embrace the validity of "absolutes" in other departments of existence. Those who lack the sense of nature are sterile; their pure forms belong not to Plato's heaven but to the cemetery; their ultimate is the skeleton. Those who lack the sense of the absolute lack a belief in one of our highest capacities as human beings; for it is at the point where man can eliminate himself in favor of the object he beholds that he begins for the first time to understand the world in which he lives, and to the extent of his understanding, takes on the functions of godhead. In embodying plastically these two great conceptions of the universe, the organic and the mathematical, Brancusi's sculpture is intellectually unique; after the troubled tumult of Rodin and the realists, he is the lonely tree and the clear sky, one planted in the ground, the other overarching the universe.

*January 12, 1927 [Walter Damrosch]*

# A MISSIONARY RETIRES

by Deems Taylor

Those newspapermen who were bidden to meet at Walter Damrosch's house on an afternoon in December, to hear an announcement "of particular importance," went with interest and alacrity; for Damrosch not only knows news and wastes no journalist's time, but is likewise a famous host and allows no guest to depart unslaked. They got their refreshment and they got their news, which was that Damrosch was handing in his resignation as conductor of the New York Symphony Orchestra, a post that he had held continuously for forty-two years.

As one paper remarked the next day, it was as if the Statue of Liberty had resigned; for Damrosch has managed to identify himself with New York's musical activities to a degree that no living man has

approached. If you sing, play, or listen to music, you have probably
met him; if you hate music he has probably taken pains to meet you.
Few musicians have pursued so multifarious and unflagging a career.
When he succeeded his father, Leopold Damrosch, as conductor of
the New York Symphony in 1885, he succeeded him also as conductor
of the Oratorio Society and as assistant conductor of the lately founded
German Opera Company.

Nine years later he was head of an opera company bearing his own
name. He wrote a grand opera, *The Scarlet Letter,* and toured the
country with it. He has been, in the words of his *Who's Who* biography,
"devoted exclusively to the New York Symphony Orchestra, which he
organized into a permanent orchestra, since 1903." What he means
by "exclusively" may be inferred from the fact that since 1903 he has
managed to write another grand opera, *Cyrano de Bergerac,* incidental
music for Euripides' *Medea* and *Iphigenia in Tauris,* and Sophocles'
*Electra,* to start a school for bandmasters at Chaumont in 1918, at
Pershing's request, and to be one of the founders of the American Conservatory at Fontainebleau in 1921. For years past he has likewise
found time to deliver an annual series of lecture-recitals upon Wagner's
music dramas.

I have seen him referred to as a pioneer in American music. He is
not. His father, and his father's bitterest rival, Theodore Thomas, were
the men who cleared the ground. He has cultivated it. Or, to use a
more modern and urban metaphor, they dug up the prospects, he
closed the deal. He has been "selling" music to eastern America for
two generations, and with impressive success.

As a conductor he has had rather less than his due, I believe,
particularly from his less attentive and experienced listeners. For his
conducting is strictly for the orchestra. There are conductors who rally
the hearer to the music, whose gallant, inspiring backs suggest white
horses and flashing lances. Damrosch generally conveys the impression
that he would rather sit down. He does not draw pictures of the theme
with his right hand, nor manipulate invisible silken cords with his left.
His beat is a strict, graceless down-left-right-up that suggests nothing
beyond a man beating time.

But he knows his business. He does his drilling at rehearsals, and
his men admire him and respect him, and at suitably frequent intervals
play like angels for him. Even his bitterest detractor has never been
able satisfactorily to explain how he could have selected the magnificent
body of players with which he has surrounded himself, or stumbled
upon the extraordinarily beautiful and homogeneous tonal quality of
their ensemble.

The critics quarrel with his occasionally listless performances of the
classics—and rightly enough. He can sometimes make Tchaikovsky
dull and Beethoven unbearable. But I have never heard him miss a

cue, or allow wrong notes or sloppy attacks, and I have never heard him give a bad performance of difficult or unfamiliar music.

He never was a Karl Muck, and I don't believe he ever wanted to be one. He seems curiously impatient of ultrasubtle readings of the classics—an attitude possibly left over from his youthful days, when the conductor's task was not so much to interpret Brahms as to induce his audience to listen to Brahms at all. But give him something untried, something to coax his hearers into giving a hearing, something to challenge his own musicianship and the skill of his orchestra, and he brings to it not only enthusiasm and good intentions, but intelligence, imagination, and conducting technique. He has played more new music during the past quarter century, probably, than all his New York contemporaries put together; and as a rule has played it better. Find a modern orchestral work that has elements of permanent value, and you will usually find also that Damrosch gave it its first New York hearing.

American composers owe him an incalculable debt. I know of one American work that he accepted in ten minutes just after another conductor had returned it, without comment, after a year's perusal. He gave John Carpenter his first important New York hearing with the "Adventures in a Perambulator" suite. When George Gershwin began to loom large as America's first potential serious jazz composer, Damrosch promptly commissioned him to write a jazz piano concerto, and has played it all over the East. In the foreign field he has given first hearings to works by—among others—Stravinsky and Honegger, and has conducted them better than the composers' own countrymen have done. His first passion has always been music, more music, newer music. Musicians still remember Seidl's readings of Wagner; but they also remember that Damrosch gave the first performances of *Parsifal* ever heard in this country.

I am not sure, but I think he was the first American ever to conduct symphony concerts exclusively for children. He has been doing this for years. Even if you were allowed in to one of the Saturday morning children's concerts of the New York Symphony (which you would not be, unless you had a child with you), you would probably be unable to find a seat; for they are always crowded to the doors. A considerable proportion of his audience today must have been brought up by him, musically speaking.

"I wish to retire while I am still young enough not to have to give advancing years as the reason," he wrote in the letter announcing his resignation. So, reluctantly, they have given him what he calls leisure. This consists in continuing two series of children's concerts, remaining as guest conductor of the New York Symphony Orchestra, and broadcasting an extensive series of Wagner lectures and educational concerts over the radio. I am wondering when he will discover the Vitaphone.

*June 22, 1927 [Sacco and Vanzetti]*

# IN DEDHAM JAIL
by Bruce Bliven

The automobile slides through a pleasant green New England land-scape: parks and ponds and big houses set far back from the road, among Louisa Alcott's own lilacs. A sharp turn through the elms, a hundred feet down a side road, and here we are.

It does not look like a prison, this nondescript, rambling structure, painted white and gray, and, like the houses, set back in a lawn, with a curving driveway and wooden stables at one side. It looks like a private school—or do all private schools look like prisons? . . . The stables have been converted to garages, but even so, there is such an air of 1880 about them that involuntarily you lift your eyes to the gable for the galloping horse, silhouetted in iron, which should be there as weather vane. Up a flight of steps, through a door, and now we know where we are. Before us is another door, made of big vertical steel bars. A guard lets us in—an elderly, silver-haired New Englander, like a lobsterman come ashore. We are in a huge rectangular space, flooded with sunshine on this lovely June day. It is hardly a room. So much wall space has been removed and so many iron bars substituted that it is like a cage; and here come those it encloses. No ball and chain, no lockstep; but men in single file, heads bent, arms folded on their breasts. They look young and healthy, on the whole; there are some fine faces and well-modeled heads, and others which are less pleasing. These men wear trousers of gray stuff, uncouthly cylindrical—since they never have been pressed and never will be—and gray-and-white-striped shirts, cheap and coarse. They mount the stairs and pass along the balcony before the cell block, falling out of line one by one. The air resounds with the clash of metal, ringing harshly in our ears, as they lock themselves in. Every few minutes during the next half hour, another such file passes through, silhouetted against the bars and the lush green of grass and trees, climbs the stairs and breaks up as it enters the cells.

From the cell block they appear, these two most famous prisoners in all the world, walking briskly, side by side. No bars are interposed between them and their visitors; we are introduced, shake hands, sit down on a bench and some chairs, like so many delegates to a convention, meeting for the first time in a hotel lobby. They are in prison garb like the others; they look well, seem in good spirits. Both are of average height, both black-haired, both somewhat bald in front, a baldness which somehow gives them a mild domestic air. Vanzetti wears a big, bristling Italian mustache; Sacco is clean-shaven and his hair is clipped rather close on his round Southern skull. Vanzetti is expansive, a glowing friendly temperament, with bright eyes and an impressive face; Sacco is intelligent, too, but less emotional. He listens acutely, interjects a shrewd word or two at times. He judges men's specific acts, pessimistically, in the light of general principles, and usually for the purpose of deflating Vanzetti's too-generous view of human nature. What he says sounds true and sometimes profound as well. He is not sullen. Neither of them reveals to the casual visitor any trace of that warping of the faculties which the experts say has been produced in them.

Today is an anniversary of a sort, for these two. One month from today, or within the six days thereafter, they are to die. Unless the Governor of Massachusetts acts to stay the process of the law, these strong and healthy men, eager and full of life, will sit in the electric chair, their heads tonsured, their trouser legs split, for the electrodes, and say farewell to life. Thus the state will take its Old Testament revenge for a murder which someone committed seven years ago.

Well, perhaps Sacco and Vanzetti were members of the band which did that deed, though I know what I am talking about when I say that the chances against it are a thousand to one. But that they did not have a fair trial, there is no doubt whatever. No intelligent man has ever read the record of what happened in the courtroom, coming to the case with an open mind, without being convinced that these two were the haphazard victims of a blind hostility in the community, which was compounded of "patriotic" fervor, antiforeignism, and hatred of these men in particular because, as Professor Felix Frankfurter has summed it up, they denied the three things judge and jury held most dearly—God, country and property.

We try, sitting now on these hard chairs in Dedham jail, to speak of their plight, to offer the words of cheer which decency seems to dictate. They listen gravely, and we read in their eyes the disbelief which they are too courteous to put into words. When you have been under the shadow of death for seven years, you do not any longer clutch at straws of hope. "We'll be glad if you are right," says Vanzetti politely; but it is as though one said to a baby, "It will be nice, if you can reach the moon." They have long expected that their martyrdom, which has already been so incredibly cruel, will be completed, and that they will die in the chair.

They are willing to spend but a moment on their own case, however. Vanzetti's mind is full of something else, and now, impatiently, he pours it out. He is troubled about Tom Mooney, who is dying of a broken heart in a bleak, gray California prison by the Golden Gate. He looks at us appealingly, his words tumble out. God in Heaven! This man, who is to die in four weeks, is thinking only of another man three thousand miles away, victim of an injustice like his own. Could we do something, Vanzetti asks, for poor Tom Mooney? He himself has been doing all he can—writing, writing, letters to many people, especially some Austrian friends, urging them to keep up the fight. "I may not be able to help much longer," says Vanzetti, with a twisted little smile. "And he needs help, Tom Mooney. He's a sick man. If they don't look after him, he'll die."

Vanzetti's English, if not always idiomatically correct, is fluent and, on the whole, accurate. Sacco, perhaps, does not do quite so well; but it is fair to remember that most of the time they try to say things that are not too easy, even in one's mother tongue. You must not be deceived by an accent, or by the workingman's easy way they have of sitting on a hard bench as though they were used to it. These are book men. Their political faith is philosophic anarchism, and they know its literature from Kropotkin down. In this year's graduating class at Harvard, there will not be twenty men who, on their own initiative, have read as many difficult, abstruse works as these gray-clad prisoners.

Since today's visitors are in no mood for abstract controversy, the hosts, ever courteous, follow their lead. The homes of these two men in Italy are mentioned. Have we ever been there? We never have, but we have been not far away. Florence, we all agree, is charming. The polite Americans call it Firenze, the polite Italians give it the Anglicized form. And Naples! Ah, yes, lovely, is it not? And we go on to speak of a famous Italian wine; and one says, "When you are free, you will perhaps go back to Italy and drink again the Lachryma Christi?"

"When we are free . . ." says Vanzetti thoughtfully. Does he see against the bars a great clock which is ticking away his life and that of his companion?—"*Tick tock!* thirty-one days to live! *Tick tock!* thirty days to live!"

One does not know. He says nothing for a few minutes, and then speaks quietly of exercise. Lately they have been given an Italian lawn-bowling set, which they use during the hour and a half they are permitted to be out of doors. "It is good," says Sacco, and Vanzetti corroborates: "It makes you sweat." Besides this, every morning in his cell, Vanzetti takes setting-up exercises; he flexes his biceps to show you, lest his English may not have conveyed the idea. The prison food, he goes on, is not well selected, too much starch. Before they had the set of lawn bowls, Vanzetti had terrible indigestion much of the time. Now things are better. In their earlier years in prison, these men were treated with abominable cruelty. As their plight has become better known around the world, things have been made easier for them. Indeed, they have little to complain of, if you overlook their deadly peril of being victims of a foul judicial murder.

One of their visitors loses the thread of the conversation, thinking about that murder. One can understand a good hot-blooded killing; some day I shall commit one myself, if the organ grinder keeps on playing under my window. But to murder in blood that is seven years cold!—to assassinate men in order to bolster the prestige of an unbalanced judge . . . And now to find majority opinion in a great American community supporting that murder! . . .

He comes back from this bypath with a start, to hear Vanzetti speaking of his other trial, the one at Plymouth, which was even more brazen in its denial of common justice and common decency than the joint ordeal with Sacco. He remembers, Vanzetti does, with mild reproach, that some of the little fund which his friends—poor people, like himself—had raised to defend him was squandered. A man took money to get an automobile and interview possible defense witnesses. (Judge Thayer subsequently failed to take these witnesses seriously, on the ground that they were Italians and that their testimony, therefore, could not be important.) But this man who was given funds to get an automobile, instead of seeing witnesses, went joy-riding instead. Was that fair? Vanzetti asks.

He has a hatred of injustice, one sees that in him perhaps most clearly of all. With his philosophical and political ideas this writer does not happen to agree; and yet one must recognize that no other sect in the modern world comes as close to primitive Christianity as his. He is opposed equally to Mussolinism in Italy and Sovietism in Russia, and for the same reason: he is against any rule supported by force. They do not believe in force, these two men who (according to the state's official theory), after a lifetime of sober industry, on a given day suddenly turned murderers to get money "for the cause," when the cause didn't need it; planned a crime which bore every earmark of the expert professional, didn't get any of the money when it was over, and made no effort to hide or escape afterward.

And now they are to die in four weeks.

Four weeks! Our conversation has halted for a little; we all have things to think about. We learn now—by accident—that we are keeping our hosts from their dinner; if they are delayed much longer it will be cold, or they will get none. And so we stand up and shake hands and say goodbye. "Goodbye." "Goodbye." "You see my friend Mr. A—— in New York? You tell him I thank him so much. Perhaps you do something to help Tom Mooney?"

And they walk away toward the cell block, these three—Sacco and Vanzetti and the unseen gray-robed figure which is ever at their side; and we go out into the glorious June evening, to the car and the chauffeur and the road home.

*October 26, 1927 [Isadora Duncan]*

# ISADORA

by Shaemas O'Sheel

Europe will mourn her with a sharper grief and a more poignant realization of the void that is left by her going. French and Germans, Russians and Italians are all good Europeans in reverence for genius. To them Isadora was one with the glory that was Greece, one with the glory of all great art in all ages, one with Phidias and Michelangelo and Botticelli, one with great Ludwig and Glück and Chopin and Wagner; but our awareness of her as an artist was clouded by our habit of considering her good copy for sensational stories in the public prints. Yet in this morrow of the fantastic tragedy at Nice, it is we, most of all, who should mourn and remember and honor our own. For she was our own, and it seems to me that somehow no woman born of centuried Europe could have done what she did, and that somehow it was destined and appropriate that America should cradle the woman who re-created in our day the oldest of the arts.

Whether there is a kind of Platonic absolute of art is a question in dispute since the days of Lessing, but if the revelation of beauty and the sanction of wonder, the awaking of aspiration and the disquieting of thought and the release of energy for purposes beyond food and shelter, raiment and safety, are the ends for which all the arts alike assault the mind and soul by the several portals of the senses, it seems to me that Isadora Duncan was the greatest artist of our times; for it seems to me that, more than any other contemporary artist, she gave us, fused and incandescent, that revelation and sanction, that awakening and disquieting and release. It is necessary to say this now in justice to the generations who never can see her and who cannot be aware to what extent all the art they touch will bear her hidden impress; for every poet and musician and plastic artist of her generation sat at her feet, and she entered into sculpture and painting, music and poetry, her influence no more always to be traced than the rain that falls in the forest can be traced to the arbutus and the oak leaf that it nourishes. Alas, that her art, the most robust in facing the Moment, was the most fragile in the fingers of Time!—the price of its incomparable aliveness was its utter evanescence. Words must be summoned to preserve some memory of a thing that was as instant and perfect and beyond the power of words as the slant of an April shower in sunlight over green hills, or the toss of a branch of young leaves, or the arced flight of a marten, or the breaking of a white wave on dark waters. Words!—why did not some of the pompous promoters of this new "art" of the motion pictures ever think of devoting a trifling sum to making a record of Isadora's dancing? Why did she never think of it herself? At least some pale and imperfect image of her, paler and less perfect perhaps than the phonographic immortality of Caruso's voice, might have gone down to the generations to explain what I try and what abler others have tried to put in words.

When Isadora went to Munich, the dance as a great art did not exist. There was the lace-and-china-and-powder-puff prettiness of the ballet, and there was dramatic dancing, leaning heavily on properties and costumes, and striving to act out a story that was fundamentally a bit ridiculous to act out in a dance. But the dance as a great art, holding up its head among the hierarchies with the art of Palestrina and Beethoven and Wagner, with the art of the sculptor of the Sphinx and the painter of the bisons in the cave of Altamira, with Leonardo and Titian, Rembrandt and Rubens, Monticelli and Redon, with Homer, Petrarch, Chaucer, Coleridge, Shelley, Yeats—the dance as such an art did not exist. It had not existed for more centuries than man remembers. She re-created it from the same pregnant elements whose fiery substance has been seized and molded by all great artists—nature, the ancient mysteries and the old symbols, intelligence that is aware of wonder and sensitiveness that is aware of overtones and undertones, and genius, the shaping power that is not to be measured or understood.

Words are of little use to describe any good dancing, and of how little, therefore, to suggest hers! There was a bare stage, flooded with soft and tinted light, and a background of unfigured curtains whose heavy folds reached up into darkness. Bare of limb and splendid of limb she came and moved before us; like a curled leaf drifting over the grass. Plutarch wrote that music is audible dance and the dance is silent music. Say rather visible music, music translated for another sense, doubly alive. She danced only to great music, Beethoven's *Seventh Symphony*, and Chopin, and Glück, in whose ineffable melodies all passion and hope and despair are intensified to serenity; and this music she made visible with "majestic instancy."

Grace and sheer visual beauty were here in stirring splendor, but it was not these that moved us. There was something else. It was that Isadora's art was great *symbolic* art. The stage became the wind-drifted border between flowering meadow and sandy beach on the margin of some nameless sea where the horn of Poseidon faintly echoes, and Kypris, the World's Desire, might be born of any wandering wave. The folded curtain became the ancient trees that guard the vaporous cleft of the Pythoness in the forests of Delphi, and the towering crags of the Caucasus, at the end of the world, where Prometheus knows the vulture and remembers the love of man and the vengeance of gods. And she was the soul of man confronting nature and the enigmas of life, the brave and troubled soul of man among the mysteries. This was not drama. Others have given us dramatic dancing, and Isadora herself in her later period, or at least during her American tour of 1917, declined into dramatic dancing. But I speak of her art at its greatest. If it be denied that symbolic art is the supreme art, there is nothing to be said; but to the understanding I say that, more than any other we have known among us, she was companion and messenger of the rose and the sword, the rood and the poppy and the stars, and mystery, and wonder, and eternity.

That was why people wept when they watched her. People came out of the brisk stream of life flowing up Broadway, and sat in the Metropolitan Opera House or Carnegie Hall, a few feet away from the hard surfaces and pert hopes and immediate worries of that stream, and she tuned them like lutes and swept them with rhythms their forebears had forgotten ages ago, and the beauty and wonder of it called tears out of the core of their being. It was an emotion as far removed from sentimentality as her art was distant from prettiness. Any natural man, normally concerned with virile affairs, truck driver or president of a steel corporation, who might have come into her presence, would, after a brief orientation, have felt the power of her work, would have understood and been refreshed.

One of the newspapers, on the occasion of her death, said that her dances "came to be known, for some reason, as 'Greek.'" It is so that her work is usually thought of. She herself wrote that she went to nature as primitive man had done. She wrote that the dance was the earliest of the arts, and that primitive man had been inspired directly and immediately by the movements of wind and wave and bird and beast. She found the image and evidence of this in Greek sculpture and frescoes and the figures on vases. She overlooked the fact that many of these were made in a time of sophisticated and urban civilization, and pictured a dance that was not immediately from nature, but was part of centuried ritual. But there are works of Greek art that spring immediately from nature as the wave springs from the sea. Such are the *Wingless Victory* and the *Victory of Samothrace*. It is of these that she was sister. Isadora's brother, Raymond Duncan, was in fact a greater "Greek" dancer than she. He re-created with uncanny exactitude the gestures we see on the vases and reliefs; beautiful, angular, clearly ritualistic. He went to the vases and reliefs, to Greece; but she went to Niké Anapteros, to nature; Greece was merely on the way.

When I first wrote about Isadora, fifteen years ago, I predicted, as others did and as she did, that the dance as a great art was about to be re-established in the world, that many would arise to continue her work, that a great influence for beauty had been released. It was not long before I felt the heavy hand of a skepticism that still rests heavily upon me. I am not familiar enough with the art of the young women whom Isadora trained to know whether there is among them another Isadora; but it is not likely. Her sister Elizabeth Duncan is a greater teacher than she was; but it is unlikely that Elizabeth Duncan can turn out another Isadora. That she established an art of the dance is true. Because of her example, more than a few graceful and intelligent women and some men are dancing with the whole body and not only with mincing toes, and looking to Greece and to nature for inspiration. Her example and fame have evoked a very rash of "classical dancing" schools, and have made the lawns of every women's college and girls' school the scene of amazing antics by barelegged females clad in "three yards of cheesecloth." And precisely these results constitute the most striking proof that genius is the golden and priceless thing in the arts, and that nothing else matters very much. Numberless composers realized the truth of Wagner's methods, but there has been no second Wagner. It is easy to learn that the secrets of Duse were naturalness and inner intensity, but they will not make a Duse. You can photograph horses, but they will not be the horses of the Parthenon frieze. You can turn every young woman of the generation loose in "self-expression," but it will not produce an Isadora. That takes intelligence of the highest order. She had it. That takes a vital and brooding understanding of nature and life. She had it. That takes genius. She had it—more than any woman artist since Sappho.

*October 26, 1927 [Charles A. Lindbergh]*

# THE FLYING FOOL

by Bruce Bliven

I am one of those who protested that it was unfair to call him The Flying Fool. I went about explaining to all who would listen, and some who wouldn't, first, that the term did not connote opprobrium, being derived by analogy from The Riding Fool (i.e., one addicted to riding), and second, that, even thus explained, the phrase was unfair, since his Great Solo was the product of science, sheer science—all planned and studied in advance, as carefully as a June wedding. But now I have read his book (*We,* by Colonel Charles A. Lindbergh, G. P. Putnam's Sons, New York), the book which has already earned him $95,000 and is destined, I am told, to sell into the millions. And having read it, I am staggered.

The things in it which produce this effect, I should add, are obviously Lindbergh's own. I take it for granted that he had some assistance with the writing; here and there, a little of the slickness of the skillful "ghost" seems present. But on the whole, the narrative is unquestionably his. It sounds like him. It is simple, modest, businesslike.

Let me offer, in highly condensed form, those parts of his story which have inclined me to a changed view of him. He is not long in coming to the main theme. Ancestry, parentage, childhood, engage him for a total of three small pages of large type; and then, with an almost audible sigh of relief, he turns to aviation. "While I was attending the University" (of Wisconsin), he says, "I became intensely interested in aviation. Since I saw my first airplane near Washington, D. C., in 1912, I had been fascinated with flying, although up to the time I enrolled in a flying school in 1922 I had never been near enough a plane to touch it."

He had eight hours' flying instruction in that school, but made no flight alone. Before he had a chance to do so, he went off "barnstorming" as an airplane parachute jumper. The pilot for whom he worked, who was in turn hired by a series of county or state fairs to give the yokels a thrill, would take him aloft, and Lindbergh would step from the wing of the plane, wearing a parachute. Sometimes two parachutes are used in these stunts: the first opens and is cut away by the parachutist, who then falls again until the second one checks his descent. This gives the populace a double set of shivers. Lindbergh's very first drop was with two 'chutes, and came near to being his last:

> My first 'chute opened quickly, and after floating down for a few seconds, I cut it loose from the second expecting a similar performance. But I did not feel the comfortable tug of the risers which usually follows an exhibition jump. As I had never made a descent before, it did not occur to me that everything was not as it should be until several seconds had passed and I began to turn over and fall head-first. I looked around at the 'chute just in time to see it string out; then the harness jerked me into an upright position and the 'chute was open.

All this, during a total drop of 1,800 feet!

A few months later, in 1923, Lindbergh bought himself a plane, as another boy might buy a Ford. He saved up five hundred dollars and purchased for that sum at a government auction in Georgia (at a great bargain, of course) a "Jenny"—a wartime training plane. He had never flown alone; he had not been in a plane, even as a passenger, for six months; but he took thirty minutes' training in the unfamiliar type of ship and started off—alone and guided only by one small map of the United States—to fly from Georgia to Texas. His third night out, after landing in a strange cow pasture, he taxied head-on into a ditch and smashed his propeller. When the new one came, he began taking up passengers at five dollars each, and with the first of these, he tried to loop the loop, never, of course, having done any stunt flying:

I had, however, been in a plane during two loops and one tailspin.

He tried to begin his loop from a level flying position, which is impossible with a "Jenny." As soon as the nose pointed at the sky the plane began to fall backward, then rocked end for end and went into a nose dive. Lindbergh tried again, with the same result, and gave up "for that afternoon."

A little later, landing in another cow pasture in Kansas, he hit among some rocks, and broke a spar on one wing tip.

A few days afterward, as he made a forced landing in a Minnesota swamp, his ship "nosed over" and broke its propeller.

Soon after that, while he was flying in Nebraska, the water expansion tank exploded. He managed to land in a stubble field.

Flying in Florida, not long thereafter, his ship developed engine trouble, and he hit a hill which "wiped off my landing gear. One wheel went up through the front spar on the lower left wing, breaking it off."

He then started from Florida to California, but, while trying to take off in the street of a Texas town, he hit a telephone pole, which "swung the plane around and the nose crashed through the wall of a hardware store."

As soon as the ship was repaired, he started off again, but the next day, while trying to rise from sagebrush country, a Spanish-dagger plant perforated one wing.

Thereafter he became a cadet in the U. S. Flying School at Brooks Field, Texas, and presently participated in a collision in mid-air.

I felt a slight jolt followed by a crash. My head was thrown forward against the cowling and my plane seemed to turn around and hang nearly motionless for an instant. . . . Our ships were locked together with the fuselages approximately parallel. . . . The ships started to mill around and the wires began whistling.

Both aviators jumped with parachutes and landed successfully.

Within half an hour two planes with extra parachutes were sent to take us back to Kelly [Field]. About an hour after the crash, we had two new S. E. 5's and were back in the air again!

(The exclamation point is mine. Lindbergh never heard of any such punctuation mark.)

After graduating, he was for a short time a test pilot at Lambert Field, where he made another emergency jump, from a new plane, which had gone into a tail spin and refused to come out:

> I rolled over the right side of the cockpit and since I had jumped only about three hundred and fifty feet above the ground, I pulled the rip cord as soon as the stabilizer had passed. . . . On its next revolution the plane was headed directly toward the chute. How close it passed will never be known, for the risers leading up from my harness were twisted and swung me around as the ship passed.

Jumping from a height of three hundred and fifty feet is about equivalent to stepping out of a twenty-fifth-story window.

He next joined the U. S. Air Mail, where he soon made two more forced jumps. In both cases, a combination of night and fog caused him to lose his way, and he stepped overboard when his gasoline was nearly exhausted.

He was careful, though! While falling with the 'chute,

> I crossed my legs, to keep from straddling a branch or wire, guarded my face with my hands, and waited.

Once he lit in a cornfield, and once on a barbed-wire fence. Both times he summoned help and started at once to find his plane and get the pouches out. The mail must go on! . . . After a good deal of this sort of thing, he conceived the idea of that transatlantic flight which was to result in, among other things, his receiving 50,000 telegrams and 600,000 letters and postcards in a week. The story of the hop to Le Bourget need not be repeated here;. how safe the journey was is indicated by this summer's toll of some twenty-five deaths in other oceanic flights, most of them equally well planned . . . Lindbergh's narrative ends, practically speaking, with his descent from the sky into the arms of the ferocious, loving French mob. Another hand, in a lengthy addendum, enumerates the cheers.

Aviators tell me that his series of accidents is not especially unusual. Every flying man's life is full of adventures of the same sort, they say. Lindbergh himself is careful to point out that most of his crashes occurred long ago, in the prehistoric days of 1923 and 1924, and were due to lack of proper landing fields, adequately lighted. With today's better ships, fog-piercing lighthouses, radio beacons, marvelous new parachutes, flying has been made so safe that, you gather, he hardly feels it is any fun.

Yet we must come back, I think, to the phrase with which I began, merely adding that many of his brother fliers seem to come under the same category. Grant that he uses all the science there is; grant that he now takes no more chances than he can help (except by staying on the ground), still it is clear, I think, that this tall lad flies in answer to some deep-rooted demand of his inner nature, turns to the air as the moth to the candle, answers voices whose call his conscious mind does not even hear. He is The Flying Fool; a fact which the world instinctively recognized even through his hot denials—and loved him for it.

*January 11, 1928*

# JUSTICE HOLMES AND THE LIBERAL MIND

by John Dewey

When men have realized that time has upset many fighting beliefs, they may come to believe, even more than they believe the very foundations of their own conduct, that the ultimate good desired is better reached by free trade in ideas—that the best test of truth is the power of truth to get itself accepted in the market, and that truth is the only ground upon which their wishes can be carried out. That, at any rate, is the theory of our Constitution. It is an experiment, as all life is an experiment.*

Were I to select a single brief passage in which is summed up the intellectual temper of the most distinguished of the legal thinkers of our country, I think I should choose this one. It contains, in spite of its brevity, three outstanding ideas: belief in the conclusions of intelligence as the finally directive force in life; in freedom of thought and expression as a condition needed in order to realize this power of direction by thought; and in the experimental character of life and thought. These three ideas state the essence of one type, and, to my mind, the only enduring type, of liberal faith. This article proposes, then, to consider the identity of the liberal and the experimental mind as exemplified in the work of Justice Holmes.

* Quoted from a citation of Justice Holmes's dissenting opinion in the Abrams free-speech case in Felix Frankfurter's article on "Mr. Justice Holmes and the Constitution," the December 1927 number of the *Harvard Law Review*. I am glad to take this opportunity to express my indebtedness to this article. Such quotations in the present article as are not taken from it are drawn from the volume of the *Collected Legal Papers* of Justice Holmes.

If it were asserted that Justice Holmes has no social philosophy, the remark would lend itself to misconstruction and, in one sense, would not be true. But in another sense, and that in which the idea of a social philosophy is perhaps most often taken, it would be, I think, profoundly true. He has no social panacea to dole out, no fixed social program, no code of fixed ends to be realized. His social and legal philosophy derives from a philosophy of life and of thought as a part of life and can be understood only in this larger connection. As a social philosophy, "liberalism" runs the gamut of which a vague temper of mind—often called forward-looking—is one extreme, and a definite creed as to the purposes and methods of social action is the other. The first is too vague to afford any steady guide in conduct; the second is so specific and fixed as to result in dogma, and thus to end in an illiberal mind. Liberalism as a method of intelligence, prior to being a method of action, as a method of experimentation based on insight into both social desires and actual conditions, escapes the dilemma. It signifies the adoption of the scientific habit of mind in application to social affairs.

The fact that Justice Holmes has made the application, and done so knowingly and deliberately, as a judge, and in restriction to legal issues, does not affect the value of his work as a pattern of the liberal mind in operation. In his own words, "A man may live greatly in the law as well as elsewhere; there as well as elsewhere his thought may find its unity in an infinite perspective; there as well as elsewhere he may wreak himself upon life, may drink the bitter cup of heroism, may wear his heart out after the unattainable. All that life offers any man from which to start his thinking or his striving is a fact. And if this universe is one universe, if it is so far thinkable that you can pass in reason from one part of it to another, it does not matter very much what that fact is. . . . Your business as thinkers is to make plainer the way from something to the whole of things; to show the rational connection between your fact and the frame of the universe." Justice Holmes has shown fondness for the lines of George Herbert:

Who sweeps a room as for Thy laws,
Makes that and th' action fine.

But he takes it as having "an intellectual as well as a moral meaning. If the world is a subject for rational thought it is all of one piece; the same laws are found everywhere, and everything is connected with everything else; and if this is so, there is nothing mean, and nothing in which may not be seen the universal law." The field which Justice Holmes has tilled is a limited one, but since he has "lived greatly in it," his legal and social philosophy is great, not limited. It is an expression of the processes and issues of law seen in an infinite perspective; that of a universe in which all action is so experimental that it must needs be directed by a thought which is free, growing, ever learning, never giving up the battle for truth, or coming to rest in alleged certainties, or reposing on a formula in a slumber that means death.

"The Constitution is an experiment, as all life is an experiment." According to the framework of our social life, the community, the "people," is, through legislative action, the seat of social experiment stations. If Justice Holmes has favored giving legislative acts a broader and freer leeway than has, in repeated instances, commended itself to fellow judges, it has not been because he has always thought the specific measures enacted to be wise; it is not hard to see that in many cases he would not have voted in favor of them if he had been one of the legislators. Nor is his attitude due to a belief that the voice of the people is the voice of God, or to any idealization of popular judgment. It is because he believes that, within the limits set by the structure of social life (and *every* form of social life has a limiting structure), the organized community has a right to try experiments. And in his ken, this legal and political right is itself based upon the fact that experimentation is, in the long run, the only sure way to discover what is wisdom and in whom it resides. Intellectual conceit causes one to believe that his wisdom is the touchstone of that of social action. The intellectual humility of the scientific spirit recognizes that the test can only be found in consequences in the production of which large numbers engage. Time has upset so many instances of fighting private wisdom that, even when one's own wisdom is so mature and assured that for one's own self it is the very foundation of one's own conduct, one defers to the beliefs of others to the extent of permitting them a free competition in the open market of social life. Judicial decisions amply prove that it demands courage, as well as a generosity beyond the scope of lesser souls, to hold that "my agreement or disagreement has nothing to do with the rights of a majority to embody their opinions in law," and to declare that "constitutional law like other contrivances has to take some chances."

The faith that, within certain large limits, our social system is one of experimentation, subject to the ordeal of experienced consequences, is seen in Justice Holmes's impatience with the attempt to settle matters of social policy by dialectic reasoning from fixed concepts, by pressing "words to a dryly logical extreme." "There is nothing I more deprecate than the use of the Fourteenth Amendment beyond the absolute compulsion of its words to prevent the making of social experiments that an important part of the community desires." "It is important for this court to avoid extracting from the very general language of the Fourteenth Amendment a system of delusive exactness." It is impossible to state in any short space the full practical implications of Justice

Holmes's repeated warnings against "delusive exactness," where exactness consists only in fixing a concept by assigning a single definite meaning, which is then developed by formal logic, and where the delusion consists in supposing that the flux of life can be confined within logical forms. "The language of judicial decision is mainly the language of logic. And the logical method and form flatter that longing for certainty and repose which is in every human mind. But certainty generally is illusion, and repose is not the destiny of man. Behind the logical form lies a judgment as to the relative worth and importance of competing legislative grounds . . . You can give *any* conclusion a logical form. " "To rest upon a formula is a slumber that, prolonged, means death."

Yet nothing could be further from truth than to infer that Justice Holmes is indifferent to the claims of exact, explicit and consistent reasoning. In reality, it is not logic to which he takes exception, but the false logic involved in applying the classic system of fictitious fixed concepts, and demonstratively exact subsumptions under them, to the decision of social issues which arise out of a living conflict of desires. What he wants is a logic of probabilities. Such a logic involves distinctions of degree, consideration of the limitation placed upon an idea which represents the value of one type of desire by the presence of ideas which express neighboring but competing interests. These requirements can be met only by employing the method—borrowed, as far as possible, from science—of comparison by means of measuring and weighing. He objects to domination of law by classic logic in the interest of a logic in which precision is material or quantitative, not just formal. To rely on deduction from a formal concept of, say, liberty as applied to contract relations is but a way of hindering judges from making conscious, explicit, their reasons of social policy for favoring the execution of one kind of desire rather than another. Thus the formal logic becomes a cover, a disguise. The judgment, the choice, which lies behind the logical form is left "inarticulate and unconscious . . . and yet it is very root and nerve of the whole proceeding." "I think the judges themselves have failed adequately to recognize their duty of weighing considerations of social advantage. The duty is inevitable, and the result of the often proclaimed aversion to deal with such considerations is simply to leave the very ground and foundation of judgments inarticulate and unconscious." Formal logic has become a mask for concealing unavowed economic beliefs concerning the causes and impact of social advantage which judges happen to hold. It is hard to imagine anything more *illogical* than leaving the real premises for a conclusion inarticulate, unstated, unless it be the practice of assigning reasons which are not those which actually govern the conclusion.

Upon the positive side, Justice Holmes has left us in no doubt as to the logical method he desires to have followed. "The growth of education is an increase in the knowledge of measure. . . . It is a substitution of quantitative for qualitative judgments. . . . In the law we only occasionally can reach an absolutely final and quantitative determination, because the worth of the competing social ends which respectively solicit a judgment for the plaintiff or the defendant cannot be reduced to number and accurately fixed. . . . But it is of the essence of improvement that we should be as accurate as we can." In deprecating the undue share which study of history of the law has come to play, he says that he looks "forward to a time when the part played by history in the explanation of a dogma shall be very small, and instead of ingenious research we shall spend our energy on the study of ends to be attained and the reasons for desiring them." More important than either a formal logical systematization of rules of law or a historical study of them is "the establishment of its postulate, from within, upon *accurately measured* social desires instead of tradition." And so he says in another address: "For the rational study of the law the black-letter man may be the man of the present, but the man of the future is the man of statistics and the master of economics." Summing it all up: "I have had in mind an ultimate dependence of law [upon science] because it is ultimately for science to determine, as far as it can, the relative worth of our different social ends. . . . Very likely it may be with all the help that statistics and every modern appliance can bring us there will never be a commonwealth in which science is everywhere supreme. But it is an ideal, and without ideals what is life worth?"

There is a definitely realistic strain in the thinking of Justice Holmes, as there must be in any working liberalism, any liberalism which is other than a vague and windy hope. It is expressed in his warning against the delusive certainty of formal logic, against taking words and formulas for facts, and in his caution to weigh costs in the ways of goods foregone and disadvantages incurred in projecting any scheme of "social reform." It is found in his belief that intelligent morals consist in making clear to ourselves what we want and what we must pay to get it; in his conception of truth as that which we cannot help believing, or the system of our intellectual limitations. It is seen in his idea of a rule of law as a prediction where social force will eventually impinge in the case of any adopted course of conduct. At times, his realism seems almost to amount to a belief that whatever wins out in fair combat, in the struggle for existence, is therefore the fit, the good and the true.

But all such remarks have to be understood in the light of his abiding faith that, when all is said and done, intelligence and ideas are the supreme force in the settlement of social issues. Speaking in commemoration of the work of Justice Marshall, he remarked: "We live by symbols. . . . This day marks the fact that all thought is social, is on its way to action; that, to borrow the expression of a French writer, every idea tends to become first a catechism and then a code; and that according to its worth an unhelped meditation may one day mount a throne, and . . . may shoot across the world the electric despotism of an unresisted power." Again and again he says that the world is today governed more by Descartes or Kant than by Napoleon. "Even for practical purposes theory generally turns out the most important thing in the end." Just because facts are mighty, *knowledge* of facts, of what they point to and may be made to realize, is mightier still.

We live in a time of what is called disillusionment as to the power of ideas and ideals. The seeming eclipse of liberalism is part of this distrust. To believe in mind as power, even in the midst of a world which has been made what it is by thought devoted to physical matters, is said to evince an incredible naïveté. To those whose faith is failing, the work of Justice Holmes is a tonic. His ideas have usually been at least a generation ahead of the day in which they were uttered; many of his most impressive statements have been set forth in dissenting opinions. But patience, as well as courage—if there be any difference between them—is a necessary mark of the liberal mind. I do not doubt that the day will come when the principles set forth by Justice Holmes, even in minority dissent, will be accepted commonplaces, and when the result of his own teachings will afford an illustration of the justice of his faith in the power of ideas. When that day comes, the spirit of Justice Holmes will be the first to remind us that life is still going on, is still an experiment, and that then, as now, to repose on any formula is to invite death.

*February 22, 1928 [Alfred E. Smith]*

# SMITH OF NEW YORK
by Herbert Croly

Al Smith had the advantage, for a political leader, of being born and educated in a well-developed, self-contained and, in a sense, homogeneous community. I do not mean New York City, which is as far as possible from being in any but a legal sense a community. I mean

Tammany Hall. It is usually unfortunate for a man or a woman with political gifts and ambitions to be born in New York or any other large American city. New York, Philadelphia and Chicago are political and social hodgepodges, composed of many ill-adjusted interests, many undomesticated racial groups and many divided and suspicious economic classes. The official spokesmen of American city electorates either represent nothing at all, except a dominant special interest, or they build up for their own benefit some artificial combination of interests without direction, endurance or vitality. Tammany Hall, on the other hand, is the most suggestive example of the growth in the social tissue of a sprawling modern American city of a peculiarly political community. It exists in order to govern for the benefit of its members an unwieldy and haphazard collection of racial and economic groups. It provides a fireside, a refuge, a leadership and a kind of political education for the poorer citizens of foreign birth. They pay with their votes, which enable Tammany to distribute among the faithful the emoluments, the immunities, and often the corrupt or semicorrupt opportunities of political power.

In 1873, when Al Smith was born, Tammany Hall had more or less continuously governed New York for many years. After the Civil War the educated and well-to-do gradually acquired the habit of bitterly attacking it; at one time or another they exposed practices on its part which presumably should have disqualified its candidates for popular confidence. But revelations of scandalous official malpractice could not impair the vitality of its social institutions and tribal loyalties. Tammany took care of its own voters and their families as scrupulously as the most benevolent social democracy could have done, and more artfully. They were the kind of people which needed to be cared for. Consisting as they did of the poorer workers, usually of foreign birth or parentage, who as immigrants had felt lonely, forlorn and insecure in a foreign country, they asked for steady work, amusements, kindness, understanding, and a helping hand in the perplexities and calamities of life. In the beginning they were chiefly Irish Catholics, but later, as the tide of Slavic and Jewish immigration rose, Tammany extended its grateful shelter to the newcomers of other nationalities. The leader of every district dispensed to his particular people favors, licenses, charity, counsel and human sympathy. His followers repaid him with the kind of devotion which the half-helpless members of a savage tribe cherish for a victorious chief. His was the power to make or unmake their lives. He soothed their psychological sore of alien inferiority and helped them to secrete a sense of collective importance.

Al Smith started in life as a typical member of this society. His relatives were hard-working, respectable Irish people, poor without being impoverished. His father died during his boyhood, and he was obliged to go to work early in order to save himself from being a burden on his mother. His education was confined to a few years at a parochial school. He worked for a while as a clerk in a fish store and at other minor jobs, but whenever he showed any ability he was destined to exercise it in public service. In spite of the humble circumstances of his family, he was born, be it remembered, into the ruling class of New York. . . .

He is a superb actor in conventional plays which belong to a provincial political stage. Like all natural actors, he can seize dramatic opportunities and improvise the words, the attitudes and the byplay which the situation calls for, and he can provoke and maintain in his audience an attitude of breathless attention and expectation. He creates a kind of interest in his performance which overflows automatically into confidence in him as a man. Playing, as he does, one part in a series of episodes, his performance amounts to a dramatization of his personality for his people. He imposes himself on the popular imagination very much as a successful clergyman might impose himself on his congregation, but with much more effect. His vehicle is not the monologue, but the deed, the public combat, hard hitting for worthy purposes, and dextrous triumph over opponents.

In calling him a political actor I am far from implying that he is not also a diligent political businessman, or that in his performance he is making believe to himself and his public. Successful political leaders are all actors—more or less. They must play a part. They may play it well or ill, cynically or sincerely, in a routine manner or with entertaining variations. Al Smith is distinguished from other political actors by the sincerity, the invention, the ease and the vivacity which he puts into his rendering of his public role. The unusual success happens in his case to be an extraordinary personal tour de force. Although born, in a sense, on the political stage, he was entered on the books for only inferior parts. Entirely by his own efforts he has become a great star whom the multitudes acclaim. He could not have succeeded at all without a natural gift for putting up an appearance, but he could not have achieved such a great success unless he had backed up the pretensions of his career with the emotional energy of the whole man. His success is the best possible testimony of a rare personal integrity, which derived from an alliance between a lively intelligence, abundant good will and a large generosity of impulse.

They call him the Lincoln of Little Old New York. A little of this comparison will go a long way, but it is valid in one important respect. Both men achieved by self-education an exclusive and high level of personal activity and at the same time carried on a fruitful correspondence with common-or-garden people. They both refused to give themselves credit for personal distinction. Al Smith acts on assumptions and motives similar to those of his followers. He combines a gift for popularity with an incapacity for demagogy. He is not troubled by criticism and scruples. His mental and moral background is and has remained thoroughly conventional. He is a loyal Catholic, a steadfast Tammany politician and, in spite of the Hamiltonian analogies of his own work, a traditional Democrat. He could not have permitted himself misgivings and scruples without hurting his correspondence with his audience and without also dividing his intelligence from his good will. That is why there is nothing pretentious, highbrow, high-hat or upper-class about him. He is just Al Smith of New York—a good fellow, a two-handed fighter, a hard worker, a shrewd politician, an expert executive and most of all the well-loved hero of the melodrama of New York politics.

His lack of intellectualism and ideas helps to explain his success, but it is also associated with his serious limitations. He knows the East Side and Broadway, but does not know Greenwich Village or Columbia Heights, or Washington or Kansas, or China or Europe. In New York he has played with brilliant success the star part in a play whose successive acts were dictated by the circumstances and experiences of his own life. This performance is rapidly coming to an end, and he must either retire or assume a more exacting role in a new drama on a larger political stage. The very sincerity and prosperity of his past performance, limited as it has been, may prove to be his undoing in the new role. It is a question whether Al Smith of the East Side, New York, can become Alfred Smith of Washington and points south and west. Outside of New York he is no longer to the manner born. His special political community has never given birth to a national political leader. Unless much modified, it probably never will. Smith's people are less typical and generally American than Lincoln's, and he has to pay a higher price for complete correspondence with them. On the new stage he has lost his self-assurance, his free and easy carriage and the certainty of his touch. Thus far he has tried to be President of the United States, not by showing himself off and letting people into his confidence, but by sitting tight around a table and hugging his hand.

The stage of national politics does not furnish familiar situations and characters which prompt him to happy and appropriate improvisations. His self-education has not prepared him for the ambitious work of writing a scenario for a national political career. A secure base in New York City, a thorough knowledge of the state government and the opportunity, which his experience equipped him to seize, of performing an obvious public service, all conspired to make him a successful governor. The Republicans could contest only the details of his program, not its principle and general tendency. But as a candidate for President, his former advantages are transformed, at least in part, into handicaps. His opponents are more formidable and occupy a better strategic position. The framing of an effective program is a task whose intrinsic difficulty is only equaled by its unavoidable risk. His own knoweldge and experience are not in this connection instructive. His advisers, like all advisers, disagree. He lacks intellectual curiosity and imagination. He needs ideas. He has never cultivated them. He needs to talk with people from other parts of the country or with New Yorkers whose experience, interests and outlook are different from his own. He does not do it. He is still surrounded by the same little clique of friends, who, intelligent and disinterested though they be, are incapable of supplementing his own deficiencies. That is why, in this critical moment of his career, instead of dramatizing his personality for a national audience, he falls back on his Tammany inheritance and plays poker.

The difficulty is, I suspect, that Al Smith, as a nursling both of Tammany and the Catholic Church, is accustomed to depend too much on authority. He can move around with perfect assurance and address within ascertained and permitted limits, but outside those limits he does not know what to do with his fine intelligence. The limits in his case are established by the accidents of his surroundings. His intelligence has served him well as the handmaid of this accidental personality, but now that he needs its help in order to increase the scope and range of his habitual activities, he finds himself intellectually muscle-bound. He is accustomed to taking for granted much more than he can afford to take for granted as a presidential candidate. His inheritance, which accounts for so much of his success, is now deserting him. In order to rise above the handicap he would have to be indeed a great man. Perhaps if by some freak of fortune he could be nominated and elected President, he could eventually infuse into his new work some of the superb assurance of his career in New York. But the assurance would have to come at the end of a period of probation by some process of trial and error, and not, as is now necessary, by a process of intellectual elasticity and imaginative projection.

The work of projection which confronts him is more difficult than that of Bryan in 1896 or Roosevelt in 1904. The Democratic party, on which he ought to be able to count, supplies only obstacles, deficiencies and traps. Its leaders will nominate him, if at all, as a magnet for votes. . . . Al Smith cannot do anything without this mechanics of a party, and he cannot do anything with it. Once installed in the White House, he might force life into it by some exploit in reconstructive surgery, but as a presidential candidate, his hands are tied. He can only make use of its machinery, endure the involuntary malice of its component parts, arrange to carry its dead weight and pull the string which will move the dummy to sit up and shout, "I'm for Jefferson and Al Smith" just as if it were alive. . . .

In so far as this sketch of Al Smith's personality and qualifications is true, we can understand why hitherto he has disappointed so many of us as a presidential candidate. He is not sure what to do. If he takes an aggressive line and tries to connect the Democratic party or his own foreign following to a questionable program, he probably could not be nominated. If he sits tight and plays poker, he probably can be nominated, but he cannot be elected. The dilemma is not of his making, and if the nomination is within reach, he can hardly be blamed for clutching at the accessible prize and postponing until later the bother of being elected. In that event he will be nominated by playing poker, and the most disastrous mistake he can make is to assume that he can elect himself by the same means. His chances are poor at best, and they will not be increased by angling for little schools of voters. If he is to win, he is obliged to bet that the American people are ready for a revolt against Republicanism. Let him consequently reveal himself to them, as he has revealed himself to the voters of New York, in the part of a valiant soldier and an adroit general in the warfare against Republicanism. Let him insist upon creating a real issue between the Republican nominee and himself. As long as he is likely to lose, he will find it more satisfactory to lose after a brave and significant fight than after a feeble and petty fight. It would be a great pity for a man who has behaved so handsomely as governor of New York to behave shabbily as a candidate for the presidency.

*June 27, 1928 [Herbert Hoover]*

# HOW IS HOOVER?
by Herbert Croly

The nomination by the Republican party of Herbert Hoover for President, like the nomination of Theodore Roosevelt in 1904, is a signal of the influence of novel factors in American politics. Mr. Hoover is an engineer who is also a businessman. The methods which he represents as a businessman are determined by training and experience as an engineer; and the purposes which inform his activities as an engineer are determined by his outlook as a businessman. As a combination of engineer and businessman he is a startling apparition in American politics. Although several men with engineering training have received the nomination for President by one party or the other, they were picked, not because they were engineers, but because they were generals. Never before in the history of the United States has any man been nominated for the presidency who was an engineer but not a general, or who was a businessman. Yet his success is not an accident. If he had not the qualities which are natural to an engineer-businessman, it is doubtful whether he would ever have triumphed over his more political competitors. That is why his nomination advertises the intrusion of new motives and actors into the stale American political drama.

In the past, a preoccupation with business or the training and experience of an engineer would, except in very rare instances, practically disqualify a man for high, and particularly for the highest, political position. American business or engineering has aimed at a mastery of processes or affairs, with human beings as incidental to them, while politics has consisted in maneuvering and cajoling human beings, but taking processes for granted. American political leaders have usually been sanguine, self-assertive, unsystematic, persuasive, loquacious and sympathetic men who specialized in personal relationships and who were experts in circulating the verbal and emotional currency of political intercourse. They might or might not have a talent for reaching decisions and the management of affairs, but their political activity concerned itself with words rather than with physical processes, and with life in its dramatic and human rather than its technical aspects. A businessman like Mark Hanna, who became during the last generation a considerable power in American politics, happened to possess a negotiable political personality, whose virtues he enhanced late in life, but very few businessmen are capable of this kind of flexibility. Those American political leaders who have qualified for the presidency have usually been lawyers with a long and varied experience of political traffic, who specialized in expressing themselves in customary political terms to their fellow countrymen and in looking and playing the part of statesman. During the period of progressive agitation they were transformed into exhorters and preachers like Bryan, Roosevelt, La Follette and Wilson, but they depended for success no less on words, and they were still essentially actors in a conversational political drama. They had created in their own minds an image of what the American people were and wanted. Their political lives consisted in cutting verbal and other capers in celebration of this image.

Mr. Hoover is devoid of these conventional political qualities and habits of mind. He is not loquacious in public; he is not affable; he is not sympathetic; he is not adaptable; he is not playing the part of a popular moral leader or conventional statesman. He has never been elected to any office in the gift of the American people; and he has never, in order to get elected, bowed and scraped and smiled and flattered his fellow countrymen. The old-style politicians are instinctively opposed to him. He does not conduct himself in the accommodating way which they like. He is a poor public speaker and a pedestrian and undistinguished writer. While he likes to talk and talks well and with a complete grasp of his subject, his conversation is adapted to only small audiences. He arouses lively enthusiasm and personal loyalty among individual intimates and particular groups, but he cannot communicate anything vital from himself to a crowd. It would be difficult to imagine a less political and popularly ingratiating personality than that of this round, sedentary, factual-minded man who seems incapable of pretending to be anything that he does not know himself to be. Politics is not a stage for him, and he is incapable of playing a part even in the service of his imagination. To his mind it is a workshop in which there are certain results to be achieved by those who are capable of understanding and utilizing the actual and usually the measurable conditions of achievement. He is a statesman in his own way, but he is a statesman who is preoccupied with understanding and governing economic and technical processes rather than all kinds of foolish, irrelevant, suggestible and insubordinate people.

His nomination calls, consequently, for a good deal of explanation. It is a triumph not of agitation and campaigning, but of political engineering. He has not captured for himself a place in the imagination of the American people. His personality did not contribute to his success except in its proper and powerful effect on his intimates. His program and outlook must have been negligible, for he refused to reveal them. He was opposed by a powerful conspiracy of state Republican bosses, by the great majority of Republican politicians who foresaw the unwelcome prospect in him of another independent and masterful President, and by large financial and business interests which do not consider him, from their point of view, sufficiently amenable. Finally, the whole agricultural interest in its political manifestation regarded him with suspicion and dislike. How, then, was his nomination brought about? What were the positive influences in his favor which were sufficient to overcome such a formidable array of enemies and obstacles?

Numerous and formidable as his opponents were, they were poorly equipped to play their common game effectively. There was no alternative candidate upon whom the unplacated politicians, the suspicious big-business men and the aggrieved agrarians could agree. This was partly the fault of Mr. Coolidge. The President's whole performance since he announced last August his choice not to run is psychologically puzzling and is open to several interpretations. Its effect in the beginning was to harm Mr. Hoover, but, as time went on and he repeated the expression of his choice, it began to work in Hoover's favor. For, while he continued to produce some uncertainty among Mr. Hoover's friends, he produced more among his enemies. He helped to prevent them from uniting on anyone else by keeping the possibility open that he might consent to be drafted. But Mr. Coolidge's influence was not in this respect decisive. He could have prevented Mr. Hoover's nomination, but wouldn't. Hoover's enemies would have prevented it, but couldn't. Mr. Hoover in some way nominated himself. As soon as Mr. Hughes counted himself out, his enemies were unable to produce a candidate with any real momentum to his pretensions. If Mr. Coolidge had intended by his behavior to expose the bankruptcy of old-style Republican political leadership, he could not have adopted a course which was better calculated to accomplish his object. The only candidates which Mr. Hoover's many enemies could produce to contest his nomination were sectional leaders and petty state bosses who happened to be Senators. Not one of them measured up to the job. Not one of them could produce the necessary qualifications for national leadership. The Republican party has for a long time been too disorganized to develop a genuinely national leader. Harding was, of course, a pitiable failure, and Coolidge has been a garrulous apology for the absence of leadership whom the Republican party would have liked to renominate in order to disguise its poverty in dynamic ideas and personalities.

Mr. Hoover's qualities enabled him to take advantage of the sterility of the older American politics. His positive strength derived in part from the enthusiasm which he inspires in a few people of ability and energy, but chiefly from the confidence which the large body of small businessmen throughout the country have come to feel in him. The trade papers were all enthusiastically for him, and so were the chambers of commerce. The effectiveness of their support proved the existence of a new power in American politics. They recognized in him the practical, nonpolitical point of view of a businessman, combined with the methods of a technician and with the experience of managing large human as well as large business enterprises. Eight years ago it was his work as relief and food administrator which recruited supporters for him as a presidential candidate. Today it is chiefly his work as Secretary of Commerce which accounts for his success. He has placed himself as a candidate at the head of the most aggressive and influential class in the United States, and if elected as President, he will increase their political consciousness and reveal by his successes and failures how far a businessman and engineer who may also be a statesman can dispense with the old art of politics.

Thus, Mr. Hoover's nomination is really symptomatic of the triumph of business over traditional American politics. The predatory business which the progressives fought based its political calculations upon an alliance with the Old Guard, but the more successful business which Mr. Hoover represents repudiates the alliance. It is prompted by motives and determined by methods which the Old Guard—the Curtises, the Watsons, the Hilleses, the Willises—do not share and cannot understand. They cannot conceive of politics or government as a workshop. It means for them a comedy of intrigue and pretense, of which the solemn clown is the hero and the successful barker the appropriate intermediary with the public. Mr. Hoover, on the other hand, has introduced into politics engineering method, and he has achieved thereby at least one brilliant and well-earned success. In nominating himself he has not tried to play the popular favorite. He has merely maneuvered shrewdly to take advantage of the poverty of his enemies and of an increasing craving on the part of American business for a more trustworthy vehicle of political expression.

But if Mr. Hoover, in nominating himself, has dispensed with the cheaper manifestations of American political art, he has also, in his capacity as engineer, businessman and statesman, neglected a good deal that was good in the older tradition. Politics, even though it has much to gain from a technical mastery of physical processes, must remain to a very considerable extent the art of integrating or conciliating perverse, foolish, aggrieved and socially undernourished human beings. The Republican administration and convention have combined their consent to Mr. Hoover's nomination with a rough repudiation of the demands of the organized political agrarianism of the country. No doubt there was abundant justification for refusing to the commodity farmers the privileges which they demanded, but it leaves them, nevertheless, with a righteous grievance. They can allege with justice that industry fattens upon a rich diet of privileges while agriculture grows lean upon the husks of immaculate economic theory. The engineer's and businessman's government which Mr. Hoover embodies will have to overcome a lively sense of injustice on the part of one of the largest economic classes in the community, which may obtain one of several dangerous political expressions. Moreover, this farmer's sense of wrong will fit in neatly with the revenge which the older politics will try to take on Mr. Hoover for its defeat at his hands. This older politics consisted fundamentally of the somewhat base arts which the political agents of the successful classes had to use in order to neutralize the sense of inferiority and social unimportance from which the great majority of the unsuccessful suffered. It exploited the overflowing hearts of the millions whose pockets and whose heads were relatively empty. Mr. Hoover can be nominated as a competent and incorruptible engineer-businessman who knows how to do things and who disdains the sentimentalism of the old politics, but can he be elected in this incarnation? His opponent will be the most seductive political personality in the United States of today, who by inheritance and experience is peculiarly skillful in pulling the heartstrings of the easily moved populous class of the underdog.

In another respect, also, Mr. Hoover has hitherto ignored something which was good but degenerate in the older politics. He has ignored any appeal to moving ideas. From the point of view of the older politics, ideas and convictions dwindled usually into empty shams and shibboleths, but these intellectual pretenses were at bottom the shoddy tribute which the strivers for political power were obliged to pay to an alleged public opinion. Mr. Hoover's campaign did not attribute any importance to the influence which activity of intelligence may exert on political behavior. One of its major assumptions was that public opinion was apathetic and that it was the kind of sleeping dog which should be left to lie. He merely took Coolidgism for granted and paraded it now and then as a perfect creed for government by the engineer-businessman. As a matter of fact, this addiction to Coolidgism was a necessary but none the less a sorry pretense. He will be obliged to stick to it during the campaign, but it is not a genuine expression of his personal philosophy, and it is not a sufficient creed for the kind of government which he would like to furnish to the American people. Mr. Hoover is a theoretical individualist, a conservative and a believer in government subordinated to business, but he is not a standpatter. His own personality is restless, alert, progressive and dynamic, and he is interested primarily in giving reality, if not to bigger and better ideas, at least to different and better methods of doing the business of the world. As President he will not be like Mr. Coolidge, a sedative; he will be a ferment. His chance of election would be increased if he could capitalize politically the leaven that is in him. But during the campaign he will remain handcuffed to Coolidgism, from which he cannot emancipate himself until and unless he is elected.

*May 1, 1929 [Policewoman]*

# THE BIRTH-CONTROL RAID
by Margaret Sanger

"This is *my* party!" shouted Policewoman Mary Sullivan, in the midst of her personally conducted raid on the Birth Control Clinical Research Bureau in New York City, last week. Subsequent developments have demonstrated that this boast was as premature as it was untruthful. For Policewoman Sullivan's little raiding party, carried out with a vigor that swept aside as unnecessary such things as common courtesy and ordinary good manners, has proved to be of vital interest to every thinking member of this community. And the end is not yet in sight. As I write these indignant words, the announcement comes that Chief Magistrate William McAdoo now admits that the police, in seizing the case histories of our patients, had exceeded the scope of the search warrant he had issued authorizing this raid—an act on their part which constitutes a misdemeanor.

After you have spent some fifteen years, slowly and with infinite pains and patience, working for the right to test the value of contraceptive practice in a scientific and hygienic—and lawful—manner, without interfering with the habits or the morals of those who disagree with you, it is indeed difficult to submit with equanimity to such brutal indignities as were gratuitously thrust upon us at the clinic a week ago. Compensations there have been, of course—mainly in the enlightened attitude of such dailies as the New York *Herald Tribune* and others, and the generous offers of aid from distinguished physicians. But even these can scarcely counterbalance the evidence of the sinister and secret power of our enemies.

As in the breaking up of the birth-control meeting in Town Hall in 1921, the raid on the Birth Control Research Bureau gives us a glimpse of the animus which may direct the action of the police. In their futile efforts to annihilate a social agency which had already been given a clean bill of health by the health department of the municipality, by the state board of charities, and by the Academy of Medicine, our hypocritical antagonists have not the courage to fight us squarely, in the open, but adopt the cowardly subterfuge of utilizing minor and crassly ignorant members of the police force. Our research bureau has been functioning since 1923, operating within the law, and cooperating with recognized charitable institutions.

From whatever point of view it is analyzed, Policewoman Sullivan's "party" was a deplorable failure. A failure, first of all, because it has exposed a complete lack of intelligence in those who conducted it, and a woeful lack of coordination in the Police Department itself. It is not enough for Grover Whalen or District Attorney Banton to disclaim all foreknowledge of the raid. Modest as may be the headquarters of the research bureau, it is highly significant and important. Therefore, to permit minor members of the police force, or hostile assistants in the office of the District Attorney, to pass judgment upon its fate denotes either a lack of coordination of powers, or a bland carelessness in directing them. Certainly no official of the city government, cognizant of awakened public opinion concerning the social value of contraception, and aware, moreover, of the searching criticism to which the Police Department of New York City is now subjected, would ever have chosen the present moment as one psychologically suited to inaugurate a brutal raid upon a modest unadvertised clinic which was functioning quietly and successfully in an obscure side street, minding its own business and hoping that its powerful ecclesiastical neighbors would mind theirs. At a time when the criminal elements of the city—racketeers, gangsters, gunmen and hijackers—are so active and successful, it would seem to a bystander that all the intelligence, skill, and brawn of the force should be mobilized and focused upon "crime control."

Even the thrill of satisfaction we have had in the offers of distinguished doctors to testify in our behalf, in the letters to the press and the courageous, outspoken editorials, cannot obliterate the memory of Policewoman Sullivan standing in the clinic and shouting vigorously and victoriously, "This is *my* party!" I would rather forget that here was a woman fighting against other women who were devoting their lives to succor and to save their fellow women. By trickery and hypocrisy she had obtained her "evidence," and now she triumphantly commanded the doctors and nurses into the waiting patrol wagons.

Whatever the outcome of this raiding party, I hereby call upon the citizens of New York to find out for themselves how and where it originated, and why it was carried out. I ask them to recall the breaking up by the police of the birth-control meeting in Town Hall, with the subsequent revelation that this illegal action was instigated by Roman Catholic ecclesiastical authorities. We are paying, and paying heavily, for the support of a great police force. It is our right and duty to insist that it shall function in an efficient, legal, and socially effective manner. Policewoman Sullivan's "party" exposes it as operating in a manner which suggests the gratification of private prejudices and unreasoning emotion, rather than the evenhanded administration of justice and the law.

*October 23, 1929*

# JOHN DEWEY AT SEVENTY

by Robert Morss Lovett

The celebration of John Dewey's seventieth birthday is properly the occasion for considering in detail his contributions to the several departments of thought and action in which he has been engaged. It would be impossible to attempt in this article even a summary of these activities, but it may be pointed out that they all are referable to a single principle. Doctor Dewey is a humanist in the modern sense. His pragmatism is an expression of the realistic attitude which limits the consideration of mankind to the elements and functions of human nature itself, and finds its field of investigation in human experience. Constantly in his writings we find reference to these terms of final authority—human nature and human experience. In departure from the traditional procedure of philosophy, he treats reason and the moral and aesthetic senses as functions, not as independent entities. He puts the query, "If reason is independent of empirically verifiable realities of human nature, such as instincts and organized habits, why should there not also exist a moral or practical reason independent of natural operations?" And the answer is found in his attack upon the notion that "morality is distinct in its origin, working and destiny from the natural structure and career of human nature." In regard to art he declares the same alternative. "Either art is a continuation, by means of intelligent selection and arrangement, of natural tendencies or natural events; or art is a peculiar addition to nature, springing from something dwelling exclusively in the heart of man." In dealing with society he warns us: "Whenever we are concerned with understanding social transition and flux, or with projects of reform, personal and collective, our study must go to analysis of native tendencies." And finally, of experience he tells us, "We need a word like experience to remind us that the world which is lived, suffered and enjoyed, as well as thought of, has the last word in all human inquiries and surmises."

This trust in human nature is not only the basis of Doctor Dewey's philosophy. It determines his thought and colors his mood in every field of endeavor—education, politics, art. It finds its working devices in two corollary principles—freedom and cooperation. Dewey's early reputation was made as an educator in the Elementary School of the University of Chicago. There the characterizing features of his method were to give the child the utmost possible freedom of initiative, to make the child's experience in dealing with the world about him the basis of his learning, and to encourage him to work easily and happily with others. Dewey's influence in higher education has been in the same direction—to set the individual free by training his capacities. He has realized that the public schools, instead of ministering to this result, are made vehicles of propaganda for vested interests, and instruments of standardization. No one has spoken out more boldly on this theme than Dewey.

> Our schooling does not educate, if by education be meant a trained habit of discriminating inquiry and discriminating belief. . . . We dupe ourselves and others because we have not that inward protection against sensation, excitement, credulity and conventionally stereoptyped opinion which is found only in a trained mind. This fact determines the fundamental criticism to be leveled against current schooling, against what passes as an educational system. It not only does little to make discriminating intelligence a safeguard against surrender to the invasion of bunk, especially in its most dangerous form—social and political bunk—but it does much to favor susceptibility to a welcoming reception of it.

Furthermore, Dewey has realized that freedom on the part of the pupils can be inculcated only by teachers who are themselves free from political and class control, and that this freedom of teaching can be secured only by organization. Accordingly, he has been for years an active member of the New York local of the Federation of Teachers.

It has often been objected to this gospel of freedom in the school that its practice leaves the pupil recalcitrant and willful, unstable and indisposed to sustained effort. In place of routine authority, however, Dewey has a source of discipline in the second principle to which I have referred, that of cooperation. Man by virtue of his human nature is an associative animal. He finds his chief happiness in communication and cooperation with others. This is the theme of an eloquent chapter in *Experience and Nature*, in which Dewey considers language the most fundamental of social functions. He holds with the behaviorists that we should not have talked with ourselves unless we had first talked with others. "Language," he says, "is cooperation in an activity in which there are partners." "Communication is an immediate enhancement of life, enjoyed for its own sake." And language makes possible the pooling of activity and interest which is the strongest social force. "Shared experience is the greatest of human goods." "There is no mode of action as fulfilling and as rewarding as is concerted consensus of action." Thus the impulse toward freedom, which in its free play results in anarchy, finds in the tendency toward association its restraining and corrective principle.

In the human instincts of freedom and cooperation Dewey finds the basis of democracy; and here as elsewhere his faith in human nature is a lively faith, though he admits that it is on trial. After being accepted in the nineteenth century as almost axiomatic, democracy has experienced a serious check in the twentieth. Not only is its present failure to meet the necessities of the industrial world a matter of criticism, but it is subject to the competition of other forms of organization, Fascism in Italy, Communism in Russia, which have certain immediate advantages in the way of efficiency. In the face of the antidemocratic tendencies of political thought since the war, Doctor Dewey has stood firmly for the primitive faith. In his little book *The Public and Its Problems,* he exposes the reasons why the principle of democracy has been so little effective in spheres in which the public interest clearly outweighs the private. He points out that the revolution which changed the face of society took place as the result of the application of science and technology in a world where there were no forms of public control fitted to cope with the new conditions. Peoples gained the right to select their representatives, but the precedents of government were still those of privilege and private interest, and to elected, as to dynastic, rulers, the immediate consideration was their own continuance in power. To this end they sought alliance with the strongest economic force, and the protection of private property remained the chief function of government. In this welter of inherited habits and new thought, democracy was forced to create its institutions. It is little wonder that "the new age of social relationships has no political agencies worthy of it," and that "the democratic public is still largely inchoate and unorganized." From the application of the known principles of human nature, it appears that "this inchoate public is capable of organization only when indirect consequences are perceived, and when it is possible to project agencies which order their occurrence." Such perception and projection are the functions of social science. Dewey points out that the hope of discovering the means by which a "scattered, mobile and manifold public may so recognize itself as to define and express its interests" gains plausibility from the analogy of the development of natural science. This progressed only after the *a priori* method was abandoned in favor of observation and experiment—"the analysis of what is going on and why it goes on." Such a proceeding is only beginning, with respect to social phenomena.

As social philosopher as well as educator, Dewey relies on the two principles of freedom and cooperation. There must be freedom both of social inquiry and of distribution of its results, for "there can be no public without full publicity with respect to all consequences which concern it." To say that we have such freedom at present is absurd. Even where legal restrictions have been diminished, "there is a social pathology which works powerfully against effective inquiry into social institutions and conditions." The initiation of a scientific plan of social inquiry and its persistent exercise in contemporary matters, the extension of the experimental method under its guidance to human affairs, and the correlation of all social studies in its support—these are the means available for the organization of the public.

I have tried to outline the underlying principles which give unity to Dewey's work and account in no small degree for the position which he tolds today. There would be a conspicuous lack in this process if it failed to take account of his own personality. For Dewey constitutes still another exception to the conventional idea of the philosopher, in that he lives his philosophy. In deducing his conclusions from the facts of human nature, he has had a peculiarly favorable example of that material to draw upon. No one can be long in his company, can observe the rugged, earnest features, gaze into the deep-set eyes with their look of furtive trust (as someone said of Emerson's), hear that even voice with its calm, neutral tones, without feeling that we have here a man of extraordinary simplicity and sincerity. He is his own best argument for trusting human nature. Dewey is not enthusiastic. He is quiet, candid, patient. When you talk to him he gives complete attention, and when he speaks it is with the assurance of understanding. His writing has the quality of his behavior—it is, above all, honest. He uses words with a full sense of responsibility, and his sentences, if occasionally contorted with the violence of his struggle to speak the truth, have often the clean thrust of aphorism or epigram. Dewey is rather retiring than expansive, more at home in the study than on the platform, yet he has not held himself above the melee. He has not been afraid of controversy. When his principles have been challenged in the case of obscure individuals, he has fought for them. Recently, as a member of the Teachers' Federation he espoused the cause of his colleagues in New York City subjected to discrimination because of liberal opinions. When the A.F. of L. repudiated the liberal view of labor education held at Brookwood, he struck boldly at Matthew Woll, the head of the reactionary forces. He has defied the Civic Federation in setting forth a sane view of the civilization of Soviet Russia, and he is at the head of the organization to develop cultural relations with that country. He has lately accepted the presidency of a League of Independent Political Action, whose work is to bring to articulate organization in its own interests the public that is so inchoate, so supine, so indifferent. It cannot be said that Dewey fails to show his faith by his words. His faith in human nature, in its capacity for development through education, for collective action through democracy, for making the world a different place in which to live, through art, is a cause of faith in others, as his works are examples to them. In the presence of John Dewey the most timid is ashamed to flinch, the least hopeful, to despair.

*April 30, 1930 [Efficiency Experts]*

# LOOM DANCE

by Sherwood Anderson

They had brought a "minute-man" into one of the Southern cotton-mill towns. A doctor told me this story. The minute-men come from the North. They are efficiency experts. The North, as everyone knows, is the old home of efficiency. The minute-man comes into a mill with a watch in his hand. He stands about. He is one of the fathers of the "stretch-out" system. The idea is like this:

There is a woman here who works at the looms. She is a weaver. She is taking care, let us say, of thirty looms. The question is—is she doing all she can?

It is put up to her. "If you can take care of more looms you can make more money." The workers are all paid by the piece-work system.

"I will stand here with this watch in my hand. You go ahead and work. Be natural. Work as you always did.

"I will watch every movement you make. I will coordinate your movements.

"Now, you see you have stopped to gossip with another woman, another weaver.

"That time you talked for four minutes.

"Time is money, my dear.

"And you have gone to the toilet. You stayed in there seven minutes. Was that necessary? Could you not have done everything necessary in three minutes?

"Three minutes here, four minutes there. Minutes, you see, make hours and hours make cloth."

I said it was put up to her, the weaver. Well, you know how such things are put up to employees in any factory. "I am going to try this," he says, "do you approve?"

"Sure."

What else is to be said?

There are plenty of people out of work, God knows.

You don't want to lose your job, do you?

(The boss speaking.)

"Well, I asked them about it. They all approved.

"Why, I had several of them into my office. 'Is everything all right?' I asked. 'Are you perfectly satisfied about everything?'

" 'Sure,' they all said."

It should be understood, if you do not understand, that the weaver in the modern cotton mill does not run his loom. He does not pull levers. The loom runs on and on. It is so arranged that if one of the threads among many thousand breaks, the loom automatically stops.

It is the weaver's job to spring forward. The broken thread must be found. Down inside the loom there are little steel fingers that grasp the threads. The ends of the broken thread must be found and passed through the finger that is to hold just that thread. The weaver's knot must be tied. It is a swiftly made, hard little knot. It will not show in the finished cloth. The loom may run for a long time and no thread break, and then, in a minute, threads may break in several looms.

The looms in the weaving rooms are arranged in long rows. The weaver passes up and down. Nowadays, in modern mills, she does not have to change the bobbins. The bobbins are automatically fed into the loom. When a bobbin has become empty it falls out and a new one takes its place. A full cylinder of bobbins is up there, atop the loom. The full bobbins fall into their places as loaded cartridges fall into place when a revolver is fired.

So there is the weaver. All she, or he, has to do is to walk up and down. Let us say that twenty or thirty looms are to be watched. The looms are of about the breadth of an ordinary writing desk or the chest of drawers standing in your bedroom.

You walk past twenty or thirty of them, keeping your eyes open. They are all in rapid motion, dancing. You must be on the alert. You are like a schoolteacher watching a group of children.

But these looms, these children of the weaver, do not stand still. They dance in their places. There is a play of light from the factory windows and from the white cloth against the dark frames of the looms.

Belts are flying. Wheels are turning.

The threads—often hundreds to the inch—lie closely in the loom, a little steel finger holding each thread. The bobbin flies across, putting in the cross threads. It flies so rapidly the eye cannot see it.

That is a dance, too.

The loom itself seems to jump off the floor. There is a quick, jerky movement, a clatter. The loom is setting each cross thread firmly in place, making firm, smooth cloth.

The dance of the looms is a crazy dance. It is jerky, abrupt, mechanical. It would be interesting to see some dancer do a loom dance on the stage. A new kind of music would have to be found for it.

There are fifteen looms dancing, twenty, thirty, forty. Lights are dancing over the looms. There is always, day in, day out, this strange jerky movement, infinitely complex. The noise in the room is terrific.

The job of the minute-man is to watch the operator. This woman makes too many false movements. "Do it like this."

The thing is to study the movements, not only of the weavers but of the machines. The thing is to more perfectly coordinate the two.

It is called by the weavers the "stretch-out."

It is possible by careful study, by watching an operator (a weaver) hour after hour, standing with watch in hand, following the weaver up and down, to increase the efficiency by as much as 100 per cent. It has been done.

Instead of thirty-six looms, let us say seventy-two. Something gained, eh? Every other operator replaced.

Let us say a woman weaver makes twelve dollars a week. Let her make sixteen. That will be better for her.

You still have eight dollars gained.

What about the operator replaced? What of her?

But you cannot think too much of that if you are to follow modern industry. To every factory new machines are coming. They all throw workmen out of work. That is the whole point. The best brains in America are engaged in that. They are making more and more complex, strange and wonderful machines that throw people out of work.

They don't do it for that reason. The millowner doesn't buy for that reason. To think of millowners as brutes is just nonsense. They have about as much chance to stop what is going on as you have.

What is going on is the most exciting thing in modern life. Modern industry is a river in flood, it is a flow of refined power.

It is a dance.

The minute-man the doctor told me about made a mistake. He was holding his watch on the wrong woman.

She had been compelled to go to the toilet and he followed her to the door and stood there, watch in hand.

It happened that the woman had a husband, also a weaver, working in the same room.

He stood watching the man who was holding the watch on his wife in there. His looms were dancing—the loom dance.

And then suddenly he began to dance. He hopped up and down in an absurd, jerky way. Cries, queer, seemingly meaningless cries, came from his throat.

He danced for a moment like that and then he sprang forward. He knocked the minute-man down. Other weavers, men and women, came running. Now they were all dancing up and down. Cries were coming from many throats.

The weaver who was the husband of the woman back of the door had knocked the minute-man down, and now was dancing upon his body. He kept making queer sounds. He may have been trying to make the music for the new loom dance.

The minute-man from the North was not a large man. He was slender and had blue eyes and light, curly hair and wore glasses.

The glasses had fallen on the floor.

His watch had fallen on the floor.

All the looms in the room kept running.

Lights danced in the room.

The looms kept dancing.

A weaver was dancing on a minute-man's watch.

A weaver was dancing on a minute-man's glasses.

Other weavers kept coming.

They came running. Men and women came from the spinning room.

There were more cries.

There was music in the mill.

And really you must get into your picture the woman—in there.

We can't leave her out.

She would be trying, nervously, to arrange her clothes. She would have heard her husband's cries.

She would be dancing, grotesquely, in a confined place.

In all the mills, the women and girls hate more than anything else being watched when they go to the toilet.

They speak of that among themselves. They hate it more than they hate long hours and low wages.

There is a kind of deep humiliation in that.

There is this secret part of me, this secret function, the waste of my body being eliminated. We do not speak of that. It is done secretly.

We must all do it and all know we must do it. Rightly seen it is but a part of our relations with nature.

But we civilized people are no longer a part of nature. We live in houses. We go into factories.

These may be a part of nature, too. We are trying to adjust ourselves. Give us time.

You—do not stand outside of this door to this little room, holding a watch in your hand, when I go in here.

There are some things in this world, even in our modern mass-production world, not permitted.

There are things that will make a weaver dance the crazy dance of the looms.

There was a minute-man who wanted to coordinate the movements of weavers to the movements of machines.

He did it.

The legs of weavers became hard and stiff like legs of looms. There was an intense up-and-down movement. Cries arose from many throats. They blended strangely with the clatter of looms.

As for the minute-man, some other men, foremen, superintendents and the like, got him out of there. They dragged him out at a side door and into a mill yard. The yard became filled with dancing, shouting men, women and girls. They got him into another machine, an automobile, and hurried him away. They patched him up. The doctor who patched him up told me the story.

He had some ribs broken and was badly bruised, but he lived all right. He did not go back into the mill.

The "stretch-out" system was dropped in that mill in the South. The loom dance of the weavers stopped it that time.

*May 14, 1930*

# JANE ADDAMS AT HULL HOUSE

by Robert Morss Lovett

On September 14, 1889, Jane Addams and Ellen Gates Starr took up their residence in the old Hull Mansion, at 800 South Halsted Street, Chicago, an event which Hull House will celebrate on May 9, 10 and 11 of this year. By Miss Addams's desire, the celebration will be limited to a reunion of those who at various times have joined her and Miss Starr in residence, and to the usual spring exhibition of the various activities of the House. Among the former residents are not a few whose presence will testify to a significance in the occasion beyond the merely local. The Premier of Canada, Parliament permitting, will be present as an old resident, with Miss Julia Lathrop, Mrs. Florence Kelley, Gerard Swope, W. L. Chenery, and, as a trustee, Professor John Dewey. But it will be remembered always that Hull House is an institution belonging peculiarly to Chicago, one through which, among others, the city has shown its pioneering spirit, and of which it is justly proud.

The beginning of Miss Addams's and Miss Starr's residence among the poor of Chicago marks the beginning of the modern social movement in the United States. The distinct characteristic of that movement is the recognition of the great tragedy of modern society in class separation; and the determination to deal with it by understanding, sympathy, and the establishment of social justice. Far back in the nineteenth century, Disraeli had proclaimed the existence of "two nations . . . who are as ignorant of each other's habits, thoughts and feelings as if they were dwellers in different zones or inhabitants of different planets; who are formed by a different breeding, are fed by a different food, are ordered by different manners, and are not governed by the same laws—the Rich and the Poor." Later Karl Marx discovered the class war. In England Ruskin proclaimed: "I will put up with this state of things, passively, not an hour longer. . . . I simply cannot paint, nor read, nor look at minerals, nor do anything else that I like, and the very light of the morning sky . . . has become hateful to me, because of the misery that I know of and see signs of where I know it not, which no imagination can interpret too bitterly." In Russia, Tolstoy examined the situation more specifically and learned what to do:

> Without prejudice I looked at our own mode of life, and became aware that it was not by chance that closer intercourse with the poor is difficult for us, but that we ourselves are intentionally ordering our lives in such a way as to make this intercourse impossible. And not only this, but on looking at our lives, or the lives of rich people, from without, I saw that all that is considered as the *summum bonum* of these lives consists in being separated as much as possible from the poor, or is in some way or other connected with this desired separation. It was only when I repented—that is, left off considering myself to be a peculiar man and began to consider myself to be like *all* other men—it was then that my way became clear to me.

Hull House was in America the expression of this world-wide movement. Ruskin's teaching at Oxford resulted in the founding of Toynbee Hall in East London, and Toynbee Hall was the progenitor of Hull House by only a few months. Hull House was followed by similar social settlements all over the country; there are forty-four listed in the telephone directory of Chicago alone. It is easy to point out the limitations of this type of social effort. Merezhkovsky has demonstrated that Tolstoy did not really succeed in becoming a peasant. It is true that the existence of the residents at Hull House is unspeakably secure and comfortable compared with that of their neighbors. Moreover, it is clear today that the oppressed and exploited will win their cause only by their own effort—as Shaw says, only the poor can abolish poverty. Yet the settlement is a symbol. It means that neighborhood between men and women of different classes is possible; that they can speak the same language and learn to know each other's habits, thoughts and feelings, and not be repelled by their different manners. Above all, the residents of the settlement can see for themselves that the poor are not governed by the same laws, or by laws with the same interpretation, as the rich. They can bear witness to wrongs which they cannot abolish. A signal evidence of the position which Hull House has won is the fact that so many victims of so-called justice hasten thither for help. In the long struggle of the needleworkers with their employers, when their pickets were being beaten by the police, it was Miss Starr's presence on the picket line, in the patrol wagon, in court for trial and sentence, that aroused public opinion to the issue of freedom versus slavery. In the ghastly misery of Palmer's Red raids, it was to Jane Addams rather than to any other citizen of Chicago that the innocent sufferers turned for help.

It is doubtless true that the contact between Hull House and its neighborhood was closer and more intimate in the early years than it is today. Of this Miss Addams's *Twenty Years at Hull House* is evidence, as are Miss Starr's racy oral reminiscences. For one thing, the group of residents was smaller and division of function not so exact. Hull House has paid the penalty of its success. It has seen activities in which it was a pioneer, which were once part of the immediate service of its residents, taken over by institutions. The playgrounds which it initiated have become the city's small parks; the classes, except those in English and citizenship for adults, have been replaced by the Board of Education's evening schools. The Immigrants' Protective League, the Juvenile Protective Association are independent organizations, with headquarters within Hull House walls. There are a nursery school, a music school, an art school, a boys' club and gymnasium, classes in cookery and pottery, clubs for dancing and drama, all conducted by experts. But it should be said at once that all these enterprises issue out of and lead into human associations and relations.

One of the chief functions of Hull House has been that now represented by the Immigrants' Protective League, to welcome the foreigner and enable him to secure such hospitality as this country affords. How many thousands of how many races have found welcome and help there is beyond computation. The population maps which hang in the octagon room record the ebb and flow of racial tides in the district. The map made in the early 'nineties is beautifully variegated in many colors; the last of the series shows largely dark-blue and black, representing Italians and Greeks. These maps remind us that Miss Addams has seen nearly all the migrant races of the world pass by her doorstep, and has lived as a neighbor among them. She has entered into their psychology, seen their point of view and appreciated their racial contribution to our national life, and ours to them. With a certain sad humor she tells of a meeting with leading Italians of the neighborhood to discuss a miniature race riot in which a Negro boy was killed. She pointed out that there was no racial antagonism between Italians and Negroes, no excuse for this outrage, to which the Italian doctor replied, "You must remember, Miss Addams, that our people are becoming Americanized."

It was doubtless the trust and affection with which Miss Addams had inspired so many Europeans, visitors to Chicago as well as humble neighbors, and the recognition of her knowledge of psychological and social conditions in Europe, which led to the invitation extended to her to become president of the International Congress of Women, which was summoned to meet at The Hague in the spring of 1915. She was our leading internationalist. It is interesting in the light of later events to read the resolutions of this conference, and see how they anticipate the wise terms of peace offered by Wilson in his Fourteen Points and disgracefully abandoned after Germany had surrendered to them. After the adjournment of the conference, Miss Addams visited the courts and chancelleries of both warring and neutral countries to promote the idea of a conference of neutrals which should offer continuous mediation to the belligerents. After the Armistice, she visited Germany with Dr. Alice Hamilton to take account of the conditions of starvation resulting from the maintenance of the food blockade by the Allies. Another distinguished service rendered by Miss Addams was her participation in the investigation by an American committee of the situation in Ireland under the Black and Tans. She has steadily given her influence and support to all movements and institutions directed to the reconstruction of a world shaken to pieces by the war and badly patched together at Versailles. She has been in favor of the League of Nations, the World Court, disarmament, and education for peace. As president of the Woman's International League for Peace and Freedom she welcomed the foreign delegates to the convention in this country in 1924, and by her tact and skill carried off a situation rendered difficult by the outbreak of fanatical nationalism with which they were received. She was the representative of the honor, dignity and courtesy which should mark the intercourse of a great nation with foreigners. . . .

But it is Jane Addams of Hull House that we remember gratefully this week. In spite of differences of opinion in regard to the most controversial of all subjects, war and peace, her fellow citizens of Chicago are proud of her and of her work. Hull House is in a peculiar sense symbolic of the best things of Chicago, its democracy, its sense of cooperation and shared activity, its toleration. And to those who know it intimately, those of the family numbering seventy or more who inhabit "the block," it seems under Jane Addams's gracious guidance to symbolize some of the best things in humanity. The unique value of a settlement depends on the personality of its members, and of the settlement personality Miss Addams is a perfect type. She enjoys telling a story of Paul Jones when he was Bishop of Utah. A fellow ecclesiastic complained to Miss Addams that the Bishop was given to consorting with certain of the baser sort, including Wobblies and such, and Miss Addams, always charitably eager to put the best interpretation on things, suggested that perhaps the Bishop went among these people to convert them. "Oh, no," responded the ecclesiastic, "he goes with them because he likes them." Miss Addams tells this with her usual gentle humor, never suspecting, I am sure, that she herself is the cream of the jest.

*April 8, 1931 [Society Reporter]*

# MAKING BOLSHEVISTS AT PALM BEACH
by Inez Callaway Robb

Whenever I hear persons discussing the current depression and suffering and want, I simply smile bitterly. They have heard of such things, but I am in a community where I can see them with my own eyes. Here in Palm Beach, once vulgarly nicknamed the "gold coast" of Florida, I have seen privation that is privation!

For several years the newspaper for which I am society reporter has sent me to Palm Beach during the winter to study social conditions. Every day during the season it has been my privilege to telegraph my paper little pleasantries about Mrs. Busk dining at the Bath and Tennis Club, that Mr. Melornah was seen on the Everglades links and that Mr. and Mrs. Archibald Cheddinghamm dined at home with friends.

But this winter it is all changed and I do not have nearly so much to write about, on account of the Bolsheviks. In the past, I used to telegraph two columns of luncheons and dinners and teas to my paper every day, but now I am doing well if I have more than half a column of social notes. There are just about as many parties as ever, but people don't want their names in the paper as giving or attending such frivolous affairs, because it makes more Reds.

Mr. Hamilton Fish, Jr., of New York, who is a Congressman and a member of the House Foreign Affairs Committee, and who knows so much about the Red Menace, came down here recently and explained to the colonists about the Bolsheviks.

Mr. Fish is but one of two lecturers who have been here to urge the colony to think better of its ways. Mr. Billy Sunday, the well-known evangelist, was the other speaker. But while Mr. Sunday made God seem very eminent, Mr. Fish made the Bolsheviks seem very, very imminent.

And this latter fact was a great shock to a colony as rich and sensitive as Palm Beach. Everyone's nerves were already jumpy from the depression, for it is enough to make anyone morbid and alarmed when really Important Hostesses start serving watered champagne and domestic caviar.

So, one can understand that Mr. Fish had a melancholy group to deal with when he came here recently to discuss "Russian Activities" before the most socially select and wealthy audience in the nation. And what Mr. Fish didn't say about the Bolsheviks! Well, people were afraid to go home and open closet doors or look under beds.

The audience's reaction was immediate. It will no longer be possible to point the finger of scorn at society folk and accuse them of callousness and indifference. Less than twenty-four hours after Mr. Fish had frightened everyone so, Mr. Manee Mints, one of the richest men in the United States, called up all the members of the press assembled in Palm Beach and commanded an audience at his palatial home.

The little press gathering in Mr. Mints's library was composed of five ladies and a gentleman, and between us we represented *The New York Times,* the New York *Herald Tribune,* the New York *Evening Post,* the New York *Sun,* the New York *Evening World,* the Chicago *Tribune* and the Philadelphia *Public Ledger.*

Of course, a big man of affairs such as Mr. Mints, with Bolsheviks on his mind (for it turned out that they were what he had on his mind), had no time to say "Good day" to us, but we had scarcely hoped for so much anyway. As Mr. Mints has a great deal of leisure to handle down here, he has no time to waste, and he went at once to the heart of the matter without any preliminary amenities.

The newspapers, he said, were simply dreadful, almost unbearable, and made life very hard for persons like himself, because the press went about making Bolsheviks. And the papers make Bolsheviks, because we society reporters wired them whenever Mr. Mints and his beautiful and popular wife had a few friends in for a bite of lunch or supper.

The press, Mr. Mints pointed out, did a very great deal of harm, a very great deal indeed, when it might just as easily do a little good occasionally. But the press didn't seem to want to do good, and it took the heart right out of Mr. Mints.

Well, one can imagine how surprised we were, because none of us ever dreamed that Mr. Mints was bothering his head about the press, except to see that his name was spelled correctly. It hadn't seemed possible that he had time to worry about us when he had so many banks and corporations to merge and so many coupons to clip.

But that's where we were mistaken, for Mr. Mints confided that he had even spoken to Mr. Joseph Pulitzer—or was it Mr. Ralph Pulitzer?—about what a menace the newspapers were and how foul their influence had become. But evidently Mr. Pulitzer had been unable to do anything about it, because the papers hadn't improved.

Mr. Mints said the newspapers didn't even print the news correctly. He had taken particular note of this situation the week before Mr. Fish came to Palm Beach. Mr. and Mrs. Mints had spent that particular week in going through the 1930 accumulation of press clippings. There were three thousand clippings and not a single one had been altogether accurate!

It was his opinion, Mr. Mints added, that the press didn't want to tell the truth, because he had had a bitter experience with the New York papers when one of his corporations had merged with another corporation. The metropolitan papers wouldn't accept Mr. Mints's own typewritten statement about the merger, but made up a version of their own out of whole cloth.

But, Mr. Mints declared, we society reporters were as guilty as our papers, and if we did not stop telling the public that he and Mrs. Mints and other members of the winter colony gave teas and dinners, we could expect the lower classes to march on Washington.

One of the newspaper girls (always a forward young thing) suggested that our papers might discharge us if we stopped reporting the teas and dances and that it would be embarrassing to starve.

But Mr. Mints just ignored her and went right on telling us about the breadline he helps to maintain in New York. He feeds four thousand persons a day, and they would certainly feel badly, if not plain antagonistic and Red, if they saw in the papers that Mr. Mints was giving parties in Palm Beach. He said those men actually picked newspapers out of garbage cans!

Mr. Mints's conclusion was much more drastic than we had expected. He positively forbade us to use his name or that of his beautiful and popular wife in our newspapers ever again. Or at least until the depression ended.

Of course, this was a bitter, bitter blow to us newspaper people. The rotogravure editor of my paper wired me at once, saying he could not imagine what he would do without Mr. and Mrs. Mints's pictures. But I telegraphed back to remind him that this is a time when we must all be brave.

*May 13, 1931*

# A PORTRAIT OF JAMES JOYCE

by Padraic Colum

It is teatime at the Joyces'. Mrs. Joyce gives us the best tea and the nicest cakes that are to be had in any house in Paris. The children are here, now a young man and a young woman: George, a singer; Lucia, charming and retiring. Mrs. Joyce, with her rich personality, her sincere and steadfast character, is an ideal companion for a man who has to do Joyce's work. She talks about Galway to me, and the old rain-soaked town comes before me as she talks about the square, the churches, the convent in which were passed many of her years. Some close friends, Irish, English, French, American, are here for tea. It is Joyce's birthday—his forty-seventh—the second of February.

This particular day is worth noting in Irish intellectual history. In the first place it is Saint Brighid's Day, the first day of spring, when, according to Irish-speaking people, the sun "takes a cock's step forward." Saint Brighid was the patron of poets. James Stephens' birthday is on the second of February; Thomas MacDonagh's also fell on the same date. The fact that James Stephens and he have the same birthday is of enormous interest to Joyce. I do not know that he has any belief in any system of astrology, but I know that he is very much influenced by correspondences which seem to disclose something significant in man's life. The whole of *Ulysses* is a vast system of correspondences. "Signatures of all things I am here to read," Stephen Daedalus muses as he walks along the strand, "seaspawn and seawrack, the nearing tide, that rusty boot." The "signatures" are to be read, not only in the still life along the seashore, but in all sorts of occurrences. The fact that he and James Stephens have the same first name, that they both have two children, a boy and a girl, and that the hero of *Portrait of the Artist as a Young Man*, who is also a figure in *Ulysses*, is named Stephen, is not only of great interest but of extreme importance in Joyce's mind.

James Joyce, because of the state of his eyes, reads very little nowadays, and so it is a surprise to find that the conversation has turned to literature. He speaks of Henry James, who he thinks has influenced Proust's *Remembrance of Things Past*. He praises *Portrait of a Lady*, dwelling with much delight on the presentation of Isabel Archer. He says that he has taken up *Madame Bovary* again recently, but found the narrative part tedious. For Yeats's poetry he has a high regard, and mentions that, in collaboration with an Italian poet, he did a translation into Italian of "The Countess Cathleen" (it will be remembered that it was the lyrics in this play that possessed the mind of young Stephen Daedalus at a sorrowful time of his life). And having spoken of Yeats he goes on to speak of some other Irish writers. George Moore gave him one of his recent books; Joyce was sorry that the book was not *Esther Waters,* which he likes. I thought that as a Dublin man he would have a share in that city's veneration for Swift. He has nothing of it. "He made a mess of two women's lives," he says. I speak of the intensity that is in passages of Swift's writing. "There is more intensity," Joyce says, "in a single stanza of Mangan's than in all Swift's writing." Then I remember that the earliest prose of Joyce's which I read was an essay on Mangan; it had appeared in the college magazine while Joyce was a student. I am delighted to hear this European master praise a poet who is so little known outside Ireland. He does not think that the patriotic anthem "Dark Rosaleen" is Mangan at his best. He praises "Kathleen-ni-Holohan." "The Lament for Sir Maurice Fitzgerald," "Siberia," and two less-known poems which are described as translations—the epigram that begins "Veil not thy mirror, sweet Amine," and a poem of exile that has for a beginning "Morn and eve a star invites me, One imploring silver star." He praises Goldsmith, too, especially the Goldsmith of "Retaliation," quoting with great delight the lines upon Burke

> whose genius was such
> We scarcely can praise it, or blame it too much;
> Who born for the universe, narrowed his mind,
> And to party gave up what was meant for mankind.
> Though fraught with all learning, yet straining his
> throat
> To persuade Tommy Townshend to lend him a vote.

He praises Goldsmith for his human qualities. "He was unassuming," he says. For Joyce thinks it is a virtue in a man to make no disturbance about what he does or the life he has to live. "What is so courteous and so patient as a great faith?" he asks in his youthful essay on Mangan, and perhaps it is because they are indications of this great faith that he praises modesty and courtesy in certain men.

In the evening I see James Joyce again: it is at a dinner which is a birthday celebration. His appearance, his manner, his hospitality have a quality which is courtly. I am reminded of an old-fashioned grace that was in a few Dublin houses of the old days where gentlemanliness was evident in appearance and discourse. James Joyce's family is here and some close friends of the family: Miss Sylvia Beach, the American woman who published *Ulysses*; and Sullivan, the Franco-Irish tenor who is singing at the Paris Opera. The waiter brings a special wine, which Joyce recommends to us very earnestly, though he does not drink it himself as it is red. It is Clos Saint Patrice, 1920, and it is from the part of France where Saint Patrick sojourned after he had made escape from his Irish captivity. Joyce will not have it that Patrick was from the Island of Britain—he was a Gaul. He notes how the Tannhäuser legend in its earliest form is attached to Saint Patrick. When he crossed the river and planted his staff, the staff flowered, and where it flowered are the vineyards of today. "He is the only saint whom a man can get drunk in honor of," Joyce says, praising Patrick in this way. We laugh, but he insists that this is high praise. He vaunts Patrick above all the other saints in the calendar. Some of us mention Saint Francis, but Joyce is no Franciscan, and he dismisses the Poor Man. We think that he may have more sympathy with the intellectual saints, the great Doctors of the Church; he declares he takes little interest in Augustine. Aquinas, then, whose aesthetic Stephen Daedalus, in *Portrait of the Artist as a Young Man*, accepts? But Joyce does not seem to have the veneration for Aquinas that he once had. I think he may put Ignatius Loyola high, on account of the noble praise he has given to the Jesuit order in *Portrait of the Artist*. But he does not praise Loyola—the only saint he will praise is Saint Patrick, and we are convinced by his argument as we drink the Clos Saint Patrice. And then we hear Joyce saying very earnestly, "He was modest and he was sincere," and this is praise indeed from Joyce, and he adds, alluding to Patrick's confession, "He waited too long to write his 'Portrait of the Artist as an Old Man.'"

This evening I have an instance of his genuine dismay at any suggestion that people whom he knows may be involved in anything violent. I had mentioned that after the kidnaping of a Russian general, the house I was living in had been watched by the police, for many Russians had apartments in it. I even had gone on to say that I thought the attic I had rented to do some work in was being searched for papers. Joyce was disturbed. Now he asks me about the affair, and I tell him that nothing is happening—there is no search going on now. Joyce is actually relieved to hear this. He has led the most heroic life of any writer living today; what he has accomplished could only have been done through the confrontation every day of obstacles which would have made another despair or turn back. And so when he speaks of his aversion to aggressiveness, turbulence, violence of any kind, his words are impressive. "Birth and death are sufficiently violent for me," he says. The state for which he has the highest esteem was the old Hapsburg Empire. "They called it a ramshackle empire," he says; "I wish there were more such ramshackle empires in the world." What he liked about old Austria was not only the mellowness of life there, but the fact that the state tried to impose so little upon its own or upon other people. It was not warlike, it was not efficient, and its bureaucracy was not strict; it was the country for a peaceful man. Crime does not fascinate James Joyce as it fascinates the rest of us—the suggestion of crime dismays him. He tells me that one of his handicaps in writing *Work in Progress* is that he has no interest in crime of any kind, and he feels that this book which deals with the night life of humanity should have reference to that which is associated with the night life of cities—crime. But he cannot get criminal action into the work. With his dislike of violence goes another dislike—the dislike of any sentimental relation. Violence in the physical life, sentimentality in the emotional life are to him equally distressing. The sentimental part of Swift's life repels him as much as the violence of some of his writing.

For Sullivan he shows the most brotherly regard. It seems to me that he sees in this tenor the singer he might have been. They are men of the same age, each has won European recognition in the country where recognition in their particular art is hardest to obtain and most worth while—Joyce in France with his writing, Sullivan in Italy with his singing. Joyce might have had his appearance in opera or on the concert platform. When he was a student in the university and sang at one of the Feis Ceoil competitions, he was awarded a silver medal; the director of the Academy of Music sent for him and offered him free training. Later on, when he was in Trieste and had the manuscripts of *Dubliners* and *Portrait of the Artist as a Young Man* coming back to him, he had the temptation to forsake literature and make his career that of a singer. What wasted life these ten years in Trieste were, teaching languages, receiving no encouragement as a writer, no acknowledgment! I know by the way he speaks about those days that the temptation to turn to another career must have been a bitter one.

In Paris he goes to the Opera; he goes every night on which Sullivan has a leading role. He thinks Sullivan is phenomenal in *William Tell*. "There are eight hundred top notes in it, including seventy of the highest register between B flat and C sharp." It is characteristic of Joyce that he should have made this estimate. He ranks Rossini with the very great composers and puts *William Tell* with the greatest of the operas. He discerns in it the theme which he himself has worked out in *Ulysses*—the father's search for the son, the son's search for the father. Ostensibly the opera is about the relation of men to their fatherland; into it comes the old patriot's relation to his son Arnold, and Arnold's love for Mathilde, whose father is the oppressor of the fatherland, and the fugitive who is pursued by the imperial forces because he has protected his daughter from their molestation. All this Joyce makes clear to us as we sit with him at this pleasant celebration.

We drink more of the Clos Saint Patrice. What of Joyce's relation to the country to which Patrick returned after his sojourn in France? He does not speak of it. And yet he says that he should like to live in a city that was not one of the great cities of the earth—one that has a population of about 300,000. "I go to forge a new conscience for my race," Stephen Daedalus said as he left the city that has about that population. We have no speeches on this birthday: no one tells James Joyce (although a few of his fellow countrymen are present) that the creator of Stephen Daedalus has not failed in the labor of creating that new conscience. We know that he has not failed although we keep silence about it.

In the apartment to which we return there is jollity. George Joyce sings; Sullivan sings; James Joyce sings. He is persuaded to sing a humorous Irish ballad, "Mollie Branagan," and he renders it with gusto; the phrasing, the intonation, are as an old ballad singer would have them. And then he sings a tragic and sorrowful country song which I have never come across in any collection nor heard from anyone else except James Joyce. It is about a man who has given his life to a stranger—he may be from Fairyland or he may be Death himself. It has for burden "O love of my heart" and "O the brown and the yellow ale," and these refrains in Joyce's voice have more loss in them than ever I heard expressed. He had said to me when we were at the Opera together, "A voice is like a woman—you respond or you do not; its appeal is direct," and he said this to show that what was sung transcended in appeal everything that was written. His own voice in the humorous and the sorrowful song was unforgettable.

And now we sit at the table, two of us, and drink out of the great flagon of white wine that is there, and talk about Dublin days and scenes and people. All memories are sorrowful, and Joyce, who remembers more than any other man, has much to be sorrowful about. He faces suffering in operations on his eyes—ten already. But his thought is never personal; he thinks of friends, he plans how to serve them. Some words are said about writing. "What goes on in an ordinary house like this house in an ordinary day or night—that is what should be written about," he says. "Getting up, dressing, saying ordinary words, doing ordinary business, eating, sleeping, all that we take for granted, not leaving out the digestive processes." For writers who are prophetic Joyce has little regard. "It would be a great impertinence for me to think that I could tell the world what to believe or how to behave." I think of a passage in this early essay of his on Mangan, a passage that is significant because Joyce's mind has not changed in the time between youth and prime. "It must be asked concerning every artist how he is in relation to the highest knowledge and to those laws which do not take holiday because men and times forget them. This is not to look for a message but to approach the temper which has made the work, an old woman praying, or a young man fastening his shoe, and to see what is there well done and how much it signifies." He thinks that too much fuss has been made about the work of

recent Irish writers. "If we lift up the back-skirts of English literature
we will find there everything we have been trying to do." Every shade
of meaning that any writer might want to find can be found in the
English language, he says. I feel that only a man who is sustained
by some great faith can speak as simply as he speaks. "In those vast
courses which enfold us and in that great memory which is greater
and more generous than our memory, no life, no moment of exaltation
is ever lost; and all those who have written nobly have not written in
vain, though the desperate and weary have never heard the silver
laughter of wisdom." So he wrote in this youthful essay which I have
quoted from before, and perhaps these words hold his faith.

*August 5, 1931*

# THORSTEIN VEBLEN

by Lewis Mumford

Just two years ago Thorstein Veblen died. About a year ago I went
through the economic and sociological journals to see whether anyone
had been tempted to add to the rather perfunctory appreciations of
him that appeared soon after his death, but I could not find a word
about him. The reason for this neglect was at first obscure to me; but a
sympathetic economist explained that Veblen's economics had been
displaced by the detailed analysis of the so-called statistical school,
and his theories were out of the current because they did not account
for the actual prosperity that had come about under unrestricted mass
production after 1921.

The deflation of this "prosperity" will undoubtedly have a favorable
effect upon Veblen's reputation; in fact, the signs of his recovery are
beginning to multiply. At Columbia, a student of economics is at work
on his biography; in *The New Freeman*, a little while ago, Mr. Max
Lerner wrote a generous appreciation of Veblen's work. The statistical
economists may even eventually discover that the difference between
their confidence in the New Capitalism and his distrust of "business
sabotage" was the difference between gullibility and insight.

But perhaps the chief reason for Thorstein Veblen's neglect among

the economists was the fact that he was so much more than an economic theorist. He was one of the half-dozen important figures in
scholarship that America had produced since the Civil War, certainly
in the social sciences; when one has added Lewis Morgan, Henry
Adams, William James and Charles Peirce, one has almost completed
the roster of decisive and original minds. His early academic training
was in philosophy; and he cooled his heels for many a year whilst
he waited for an apointment in this department. When he finally
approached economics, he carried into the subject a relentless eye, a
withering contempt for the fake problems and solutions of marginal
economics, and—however he picked it up—a remarkable grasp of the
actual industrial processes.

Veblen was not naïve and ignorant enough to think, with the current
historians of industry, that the industrial revolution began with the
steam engine and the power loom; he traced the psychological disposi-
tions favorable to disciplined industry back to neolithic times, and its
actual institution to the invention of machine tools. Veblen broke down
the conventional divisions between economics, ethnology, anthropol-
ogy, psychology and the physical sciences: in both subject matter
and methodology he divorced himself from his contemporaries, for
he had the synthetic mind of the genuine sociologist. Needless to say,
Veblen had pupils in abundance; but none of them was quite the man
to carry Veblen's load of scholarship, scientific penetration, philosophic
detachment and human insight. It was easier for them to proclaim the
virtues of walking in bare feet than to try to step into Veblen's boots.

Sooner or later someone will do justice to Veblen the sociologist;
but there are still other phases of him that call for appreciation. For
Veblen was a satirist and a man of letters; and if his scientific confreres
did not seize the occasion of his death to do him justice, one might
have thought that our literary critics, in search of a promising subject,
would somehow have stumbled upon Veblen's trail. Curiously enough,
the only person who ever thought of considering Veblen's contributions
as literature was Mr. H. L. Mencken, and for some odd reason he
failed to understand Veblen's massive satire, or to recognize the exquisite aim of his literary style. I had the good fortune to see Veblen
frequently in 1919, when he was one of the editors of *The Dial;* and
though I cannot pretend to have fathomed this infinitely remote and
complex personality, I at least learned something about his aims and
methods.

Thorstein Veblen was a humorist whom Miss Constance Rourke
might well have added to her galaxy in *American Humor,* for he had
the American mechanism of the impassive face and the solemn exaggeration. His sentences were as elaborately wrought as Henry James's;
his desperately accurate circumlocutions, his perfectly elephantine
means of expressing a platitude in such a way as to show its fatuous-

ness, his use of polysyllabic jargon, after the worst fashion of the young Ph.D.—all these characteristics were part of the mechanism of his humor. When he was obscure, he did not fall into obscurity by accident: it was rather the summit of a delicate effort, and he enjoyed the effect he sought to produce on the reader who must be astute enough to follow him. Veblen was careful about the last detail of his writing, being even jealous of any changes that were made in his copy to make it conform to those rules of punctuation and capitalization which most magazines—foolishly, it now seems to me—insist upon. The following instance will serve for a dozen others. In one of his *Dial* articles Veblen had characterized Samuel Gompers as the sexton beetle of the American labor movement. In preparing the MS. for the printer, one of the editors had automatically changed this over to sexton beadle, in order to make sense. Veblen was furious: his white ashen face was more ashen than ever with anger—such anger as seemed especially terrible in the mild and reticent person that Veblen always was. He wanted to know if the unknown dunderhead who had mutilated his copy did not realize that a sexton beetle was an insect that spent its life in storing up and covering over dead things? Besides, there was an overtone in the allusion: Gompers looked more like a beetle. (Veblen was right: I never saw Gompers after that without recalling the insect.)

But this is only one side of Veblen. He was one of the foremost critics of art and culture; his comments on art, in his first book, *The Theory of the Leisure Class*, make him the first conscious exponent of the *Neue Sachlichkeit* in the arts, and his analysis of leisure-class culture must be put alongside Tolstoy's malicious descriptions in *What Is Art?* I cannot forbear to quote one or two passages from Veblen which will show how completely out of the style of his own period (1899) his thinking on these subjects was. Consider this:

> The requirements of pecuniary reputability and those of beauty in the naïve sense do not in any appreciable degree coincide. The elimination from our surroundings of the pecuniarily unfit, therefore, results in a more or less thorough elimination of that considerable range of elements of beauty which do not happen to conform to the pecuniary requirement. The underlying norms of taste are of very ancient growth, probably far antedating the advent of the pecuniary institutions that are here under discussion. Consequently, by force of the past selective adaptation of men's habits of thought, it happens that the requirements of beauty, simply, are for the most part best satisfied by inexpensive contrivances and structures which in a straightforward manner suggest both the office which they are to perform and the method of serving their end. . . . On this ground, among objects of use the simple unadorned article is aesthetically the best. But since the pecuniary canon of reputability rejects the inexpensive in articles appropriate to individual consumption, the

satisfaction of our craving for beautiful things must be sought by way of compromise. The canons of beauty must be circumvented by some contrivance which will give evidence of a reputably wasteful expenditure, at the same time that it meets the demands of our critical sense of the useful and the beautiful, or at least meets the demand of some habit which has come to do duty in place of that sense. Such an auxiliary sense of taste is the sense of novelty.

Veblen's application of this insight to a specific situation is no less pertinent than the generalization itself:

> The canon of beauty requires expression of the generic. The "novelty" due to the demands of conspicuous waste traverses this canon of beauty, in that it results in making the physiognomy of our objects to taste a congeries of idiosyncrasies; and the idiosyncrasies are, moreover, under the selective surveillance of the canon of expensiveness. This process of selective adaptation of designs to the end of conspicuous waste, and the substitution of pecuniary beauty for aesthetic beauty have been especially effective in the development of architecture. It would be extremely difficult to find a modern civilized residence or public building which can claim anything better than relative inoffensiveness in the eyes of anyone who will dissociate the elements of beauty from those of honorific waste. The endless variety of front presented by the better class of tenements and apartment houses in our cities is an endless variety of architectural distress and of suggestions of expensive discomfort. Considered as objects of beauty, the dead walls of the sides and back of these structures, left untouched by the hands of the artist, are commonly the best feature of the building.

I will not spoil such criticism by underlining its point and validity; but it is obvious that the almost complete ignorance of Veblen's work, among those who are critically interested in the arts in America, is a disgrace to our intellectual culture, and a sign of the great hiatus that still exists between learning and life. The only thinker who could compare with Veblen for scholarship and acumen was Karl Buecher, and his classic work, *Arbeit und Rhythmus*, is still untranslated into English. Veblen's thought should not be confined to economic circles: it should be filtering through and penetrating every pore of our intellectual life. In that process, its solecisms would be discovered and thrown aside, and its great original contributions would become fundamental commonplaces. Under the last item, I would include the distinction between the pecuniary and the technical processes of industry, his analysis of the replacement of magic by matter of fact, his discrimination between the canons of conspicuous waste and the canons of economy and his appraisal of leisure-class ritual.

But I cannot leave Veblen without a word or two about his personality. His visible self was one with his works. Even his most commonplace conversation had a grimly whimsical touch, and he was capable of such a massive practical joke as writing a report on the activities of the Wobblies in the Northwest, when he was a government investigator during the war, in which he painted an engaging portrait of their character, pointed out the justice of their grievances and the wisdom of their demands, and urged the government's wholehearted acceptance of their program. It was all good common sense; but I can picture the silent chuckle with which he must have placed that report upon the desk of his superior.

Veblen had this, too, in common with the traditional satirist: underneath that remote, impassive exterior was an extremely sensitive and tender man, and there was some proportion between his aloof style and savage satire on one hand, and the warm hopes that they concealed. Miss Helen Marot relates that Jacques Loeb once bitterly reproached Veblen for being too detached. Loeb, who for most of us would be the image of the rigorous scientist, complained that Veblen dealt with human problems and human beings as if he were merely handling inert physical objects! But one did not have to know Veblen very intimately to realize that the mask, however elaborate, was still a mask. During the Reconstruction Period, when revolution was sweeping rapidly over Europe and seemed ready to descend on America, Veblen occasionally forgot the Olympian ironist and showed where his hopes and sympathies lay. For a time, he looked toward an immediate revolution which would wipe out the kept classes, as he called them so punctiliously; he was in favor of turning the productive machinery over into the hands of disinterested technicians, who would serve the common weal.

But in this, Veblen's hopes outran his judgment. During the spiritual debacle of 1919 he also suffered from a severe attack of influenza, and this completed his enfeeblement; for he had long been an invalid, and he was then past sixty. Presently, the fashionable ladies who had in a brief spell of poplarity listened to his lectures at the New School for Social Research left him; then the engineers fell away; and finally, he wandered off, a deserted and lonely man, feeble, ill, pale, wistful, demonic, proud. There was a touch of Don Quixote about his figure. The likeness was accentuated at one time because one of his intimates was a heavy, squat little man, an economist, who did excellently in the role of Sancho Panza; and Veblen, tall, slender, with a pointed beard and cold, sad eyes, was surely a Knight of the Rueful Countenance: that sobriquet fitted well, too.

But the monsters Thorstein Veblen essayed to fight were real monsters—class egotism, the callousness of riches, the pomp of possession, the disregard of humanity in favor of property and privilege—and he did this by the most effective of weapons, description that was itself satire, and satire that never had the need to depart from description!

No one except Tolstoy was Veblen's superior in restating some common human custom or habit in such a way as to bring out its essential barbarity or folly. The author of *The Theory of the Leisure Class, The Theory of Business Enterprise, The Higher Learning* and *The Nature of Peace* will come eventually, I think, to be numbered with those kings of satire who wage contention with their times' decay and who will outlast even the tenacious institutions they seek to destroy.

*August 26, 1931 [The Scottsboro Boys]*

# THE FREIGHT-CAR CASE

by Edmund Wilson

Chattanooga, Tennessee: old low sordid Southern brick buildings, among which a few hotels, insurance companies and banks have expanded into big modern bulks, as if by sporadic effort; business streets that suddenly lapse into nigger cabins; a surrounding wilderness of mills that manufacture some 1,500 different articles, from locomotives to coffins and snuff; and a vast smudge of nigger dwellings—almost a third of the population are Negroes. "Hell's Half-Acre" in the mill district is a place where people don't dare go at night: the saying is that among the niggers there is an average of a murder a day. In Chattanooga, the manufacturers, enslaving the Negro almost as completely as the planters did before the Civil War, have kept him in his African squalor and produced a new type of squalor: Southern slackness mixed with factory grime.

The night of last March 24, two white girls from Huntsville, Alabama, came into Chattanooga in a boxcar—according to the testimony of one of them, in the company of several boys. Both had been workers in the old Huntsville cotton mills, and both had apparently from an early age been practicing prostitution to make a little money on the side. They are alleged to have lived indifferently among Negroes and whites, and one of them is said to have been arrested for "hugging" a Negro on the street. Victoria Price, the older girl, said she had been married twice; Ruby Bates, the younger one, said she had never been married. Both of them "dipped snuff."

According to the girls' story, they had spent that night in Chattanooga at the house of a woman they knew. They left the next morning at about 10:45 on a freight train bound for Memphis, traveling in a low roofless car of the kind that is known as a "gondola." The gondola was about two-thirds full of gravel. The girls had bobbed hair and wore overalls. Riding in the same car were about half a dozen white boys.

At Stevenson, Alabama, just across the state line, about twenty colored boys got in and scattered themselves through the train. They were a miscellaneous lot of hoboes—representing, like the white boys and girls, the bottom layer of that far-Southern society. Only one of the nine afterward arrested was able even to write his name. Certain of these Negro boys said that they were on their way to Memphis to look for jobs on the docks. In some cases, they were friends who were traveling together; in others, they did not know one another.

What happened on the train is uncertain. But apparently one of the white boys, walking along the top of a boxcar, stumbled over one of the Negroes and threatened to throw him off the train. At any rate, ill feeling was roused, and presently the colored boys came trooping down into the gondola. One of them had a gun and another a knife, and the white boys were outnumbered. Some kind of fight evidently took place, and the white boys either jumped off or were put off the train—all except one, who slipped down between the cars and was rescued by one of the Negroes.

The group who had been put off were furious, and one of them had a cut head. This boy went to the nearest railroad station and told the telegrapher there that the niggers had tried to murder them; and the telegrapher, very indignant, telephoned ahead along the line to have the Negroes taken off the train.

So when the train arrived at Paint Rock, it was boarded by the sheriff with his deputies, and nine of the boys were arrested. The others had disappeared. The Negroes supposed at first that they were being arrested for bumming a ride. One boy was found in an empty car, where he said he had been riding by himself ever since the train left Chattanooga. Four others had been traveling on an oil car and said that there had been a disturbance but they hadn't known what it was about. It seems reasonable to assume that, if violence had taken place, the boys responsible had escaped. The one with the pistol was never found; beyond the cut head of the boy who had complained, no evidence of foul play was discovered.

But there were the two white girls alone on the train with a gang of niggers. The authorities demanded of the girls whether the niggers hadn't attacked them. This the girls at first denied; but under pressure of repeated questioning, accompanied by a certain amount of prompting, they confessed that they had both been raped. The doctor who examined the girls found proof that they had been having sexual intercourse but no reason to conclude that they had been roughly handled, except for a small bruise on one of them which might well have been caused by riding on gravel.

The boys were put in jail at Paint Rock, but when a mob gathered and threatened to lynch them, they were removed to the town of Gadsden. In their cells, they went mad with fury—yelled wildly and beat on the doors and tore up their beds and bedding. They told their lawyers that they had been led from their cells at Gadsden by a lieutenant of the National Guard, then handcuffed together in pairs and systematically clubbed by people brought in from the streets. On April 6, they were put on trial at Scottsboro, Alabama, the county seat of Jackson County.

Scottsboro is a small town, and the people there have little excitement: it was a long time since anything had come their way so sensational as nine niggers accused of rape. The day of the trial was a festival: it happened also to be fair day and horse-trading day. Though the normal population of Scottsboro is only about 1,500, there were at least 10,000 people in town. The poor whites had come in with their guns, prepared to slaughter the boys then and there, and they might very well have done so if the Alabama branch of the Commission on Interracial Cooperation had not persuaded the Governor to send out the state militia, who guarded the trials with fixed bayonets, machine guns and tear-gas bombs. What with the bugle music of changing guard, *The Star-Spangled Banner* and *Dixie* played by a band from the hosiery mill and a parade of twenty-eight Ford trucks, with a phonograph and amplifier, organized by an enterprising Ford agent who had taken advantage of the occasion to try to pick up his slackening sales, the town was in a delirium of gaiety.

In the meantime, inside the courthouse, Ruby Bates and Victoria Price were testifying that the colored boys had held them down in the gondola and raped them; each had been raped by exactly six. Ruby Bates could not identify her assailants, but Victoria Price rose to the occasion better. She turned out to enjoy the limelight, developed a sense of her role and—very much to Ruby's resentment—played the younger girl off the stage. Spurred on by the prosecutor's insistence, she got to the point, at one of the trials, of undertaking to identify the boys in the order in which they had attacked her. "Yonder he sits! Yonder he sits!" she would declare, as the State's attorney went through the half dozen—though at other times she admitted she wasn't sure. At any rate, the crowd roared: the hammering of the judge couldn't quiet them.

Three of the Negro boys testified that they had seen other Negroes attack the girls—though they afterward told the lawyers that they had been induced to do this by the court officials, who had promised to shoot them in the courtroom if they didn't, but to have them let off if they did. The white boy who had remained on the train had testified

before the grand jury that he had seen the Negro boys having intercourse with the girls, but was not called by the State at the trials because—as the prosecutor is said to have complained—he couldn't be
persuaded to say that he had seen the girls "raped." The other white
boys had either fled or been told to disappear: at any rate, they were
never produced. The doctor in that Southern courtroom was asked
whether the semen he had found in the girls had been that of a colored
or a white man.

Eight of the boys were immediately found guilty and sentenced to
death in the electric chair. At the announcement of the first two verdicts, the brass band struck up outside, and the crowd enthusiastically
applauded: the jury had sat through the trials with the crowd in full
view through the windows. Only the youngest boy—fourteen (the oldest was only twenty)—got off with a mistrial. The prosecutor, on account of his youth, had asked only for life imprisonment. Yet,
notwithstanding this clemency of the State, eight of the jury, in this
case, too, demanded electrocution. One of the other boys had also said
originally that he was only fourteen, but he later asserted he was nineteen. Pressure had been brought to bear: it had been feared that he
would get off with the penitentiary.

It had, of course, been exceedingly difficult to find anyone to defend
the boys. Each of the seven lawyers who composed the Scottsboro bar
had in turn been assigned to the defendants, and all except one had
got out of it. One of these lawyers, attorney for the Alabama Power
Company, is said to have remarked that the Power Company had juice
enough to burn all nine of the defendants. The only man who was willing to take their case—even for formal decency—was Mr. Milo C.
Moody. Mr. Moody is, from all reports, by way of being the town
heretic. He has always made something of a practice of taking up unpopular positions, but he is old now and, in competition with the brass
band and the Ford agent's amplifier, was not able to do much for his
clients.

In the meantime, however, the Scottsboro case had been attracting
the attention of an intelligent Negro physician in Chattanooga, Dr. P.
A. Stephens. Dr. Stephens brought it to the attention of the Inter-
denominational Alliance of Colored Ministers, and they raised the
inadequate sum of $50.08 and appealed to Mr. Stephen R. Roddy, a
Chattanooga attorney, to undertake the defense of the boys. Mr. Roddy
is young and conventional; yet not so conventional that he would not
consent—for little remuneration—to make a trip down to Scottsboro and
see whether anything could be done. As soon as he appeared in the
courtroom, Judge Hawkins hastened to announce that if Mr. Roddy
would conduct the defense, the Scottsboro bar would be released. Mr.
Roddy replied, however, that he had been sent merely to observe.

Fresh from getting through the crowd and the guard and with the music of the brass band in his ears, he decided that there was no hope for a postponement, and, a member of the Tennessee bar, he was unfamiliar with Alabama procedure. He asked to be associated with Mr. Moody; and he put on the stand, at the end of the trials, the commander of the National Guard and one of the court officials, and had them testify that the cheering of the crowd outside which followed the announcement of the first two verdicts had been so loud that the jurors could not have failed to hear it.

But Dr. Stephens and the colored ministers were not the only people interested in the Scottsboro case. The Communists had recently been active in Chattanooga, and on February 10, three of them had been arrested for an attempt to hold a street demonstration. They were tried during the last week of March and all found guilty of violating the Sedition Statute, a law which, dating originally from 1715, had never before been applied, construed or noticed during the whole hundred and thirty-six years of Tennessee's history. A motion for a new trial, however, was made, and on April 18, Judge Lusk of the criminal court, in an opinion which—though handed down in the state that had declared illegal the teaching of the theory of evolution—might serve as a model to other courts, set aside the verdict of the jury and granted the defendants a new trial. He pointed out that these latter had been arrested before they had had a chance to make any subversive speeches, and that in any case "membership in the Communist party and adherence to its principles" had been "recognized as lawful" by the admission of its candidates to the Tennessee ballots. "This case," Judge Lusk concluded, "has given the Court much concern. As a lover of the institutions of this state and nation, I look with deep concern upon the activities of subversive agitators of every sort. But, in meeting these movements, we must demonstrate our superiority to them by keeping, ourselves, within the law. The best way, in my judgment, to combat Communism, or any other movement inimical to our institutions, is to show, if we can, that the injustices which they charge against us are, in fact, nonexistent."

In the meantime, the Communists in Chattanooga had heard about the arrest of the nine Negroes and had gone down to Scottsboro the day of the trial. One of their principal aims at the present time is to enlist the support of the Southern Negroes—to whom they have been preaching the doctrine, arrived at from analogy with the Ukraine and completely unrealistic in America, of "self-determination for the Black Belt."

The Communists assigned to Chattanooga, therefore, seized upon the Scottsboro case as an opening wedge for realizing this long-range program. Their first step was to have their defense organization, the International Labor Defense, send Judge Hawkins a telegram which amazed him and made him angry: this message described the cases against the Negroes as a "frame-up" and a "legal lynching" and said that the ILD would hold the judge personally responsible. After the trial, Mr. Roddy says he was visited by ILD representatives and asked to conduct a spectacular defense. According to Mr. Roddy, they went through all the gestures of taking him up into a high place and showing him the kingdoms of the earth. They told him he had the chance to make a national reputation, to become a second Clarence Darrow—a dream, one gathers, entirely alien to Mr. Roddy's ambitions. He asked how they proposed to pay him. They explained that they would raise the money by holding meetings among the Negroes and getting them to contribute to a defense fund. This idea seemed distasteful to Mr. Roddy. He and the ILD did not inspire one another with confidence.

The ILD went next to the attorney who had so efficiently defended the arrested Communists. Mr. George W. Chamlee is quite a different type from Mr. Roddy. A shrewd lawyer and a clever man, humorous, worldly-wise, deep in the politics of the state and able to see every side of every question, he is by way of being a local character; he works by himself, forms his own opinions and pursues his own ends, and is not infrequently found in opposition to the conventional elements of the community. Some years ago, he made himself conspicuous by defending streetcar strikers; and he has represented both Negroes and radicals in cases which it would perhaps have been impossible to get any other Chattanooga lawyer to take. It is true that, as a candidate for office, he has undoubtedly derived political support both from the Negroes and from organized labor. And, on the other hand, he once scored an equal triumph by getting off a group of Tennesseans convicted of lynching, whose cases had been appealed to the Supreme Court. At the recent trial of the Communist agitators, when the prosecutor attempted to make much of the fact that the defendants were avowedly in favor of the overthrow of the government and had forsworn loyalty to the American flag, Mr. Chamlee reminded his opponent that both their grandfathers, when they had fought in the Civil War, had repudiated the Federal government and professed allegiance to another flag.

Mr. Chamlee, at home and in the Communist press, is given the title of "General"; but this means merely that he once held the office of attorney general of Hamilton County. In the last Democratic primaries, he ran for renomination against Mr. Roddy, the Democratic county chairman. Both were defeated by a third candidate, but Mr. Roddy got more votes than Mr. Chamlee—and it may be that political rivalries have contributed to the antagonisms which have developed in the course of the Scottsboro case.

At any rate, the situation has been complicated by still another element. Dr. Stephens had been approached by the International Labor Defense, and at first he had cooperated with them. But their obvious tone of propaganda had strongly aroused his suspicions, and he and the colored ministers had broken off relations with them. Dr. Stephens had written for advice to the headquarters in New York of the National Association for the Advancement of Colored People, and the result was two defense campaigns not merely separate but mutually hostile.

Precisely what is the history of the split between the ILD and the NAACP is difficult to find out. But its underlying causes are plain. The National Association for the Advancement of Colored People is a non-political organization, which, under the leadership of Mr. Walter White, has in many cases been admirably successful in protecting the legal rights of Negroes. In the Arkansas riot cases of 1925, in which seventy-nine Negro sharecroppers and tenant farmers, who had attempted to sue their landlords for money due them, had been charged with insurrection and sentenced either to long prison terms or to death, the NAACP fought the verdicts and caused the Supreme Court to reverse its decision (handed down in the Leo Frank case) and to hold that if it could be shown that a trial had been dominated by the fear of a mob, the conviction could be overruled. The NAACP works quietly and by conventional methods. Its general tendency is to encourage the Negroes to approximate to white respectability, in order that they may compete in the same fields and claim the same rights as white citizens. The aims of the Communists have been indicated. The rupture between the two organizations was inevitable by their very nature, as seems always to be the case when Communists and bourgeois liberals attempt to work together. Whatever the immediate occasion of the break, the result is that the liberals end by accusing the Communists of disingenuous or Jesuitical tactics, of diverting money raised for special defense funds to Communist propaganda, of prejudicing their particular causes by waving the red flag too openly and of being willing and even eager to make martyrs for their atrocity-mongering press, which aims to awake the class consciousness of its readers; while the Communists, on their side, accuse the liberals of insincerity or timidity, of sacrificing the success of their causes by sticking too closely to the conventional machinery and trusting to the fair play of capitalist courts, of being unwilling to deal with fundamentals for fear of antagonizing the rich persons or foundations who subsidize them and of attempting to mislead the proletariat as to the latter's genuine interests in order to safeguard their own bourgeois positions. In this particular case, the NAACP pointed out that it was not the "bosses" but the white working class who had forced the issue at Scottsboro, as it had been not white bourgeois but workers who had lynched Negroes in Alabama, persecuted Negro peons in Arkansas, stolen the Negro school funds in South Carolina and in general excluded the Negroes from their unions, with the result that, later on, at the time when white wages were being raised and white working conditions bettered, the Negroes were left out in the cold; whereas higher education for Negroes had been made possible only by the power trust and the steel trust, Standard Oil, the mail order chain stores and the capitalist Christian Church. To this the Communists retorted that the capitalists of these organizations did not give a damn about the Negroes; that what they were aiming at was to exploit them as strikebreakers and underpaid labor, and to make sure that the educated Negro leaders were conservatives who would stick on their side.

Walter White and William Pickens, the secretary of the NAACP, went to Scottsboro and Chattanooga and took steps to engage new counsel. A ludicrous and pathetic contest began between the Communists and the NAACP to get the parents of the sentenced boys to endorse their respective organizations and to authorize their lawyers to defend them. The NAACP accused the Communists of having carried off certain members of the families of the defendants and of keeping them incommunicado; and the Communists charged the NAACP with having induced certain of the Negroes to sign statements which they could not read and which had never been read to them. Before the motion for a new trial had been made, the bewildered prisoners and their relatives had been persuaded to sign and repudiate a variety of documents. The Communists have had some success in exploiting the mothers of the boys, whom they produce at their money-raising meetings, and, according to the NAACP, have resorted to bogus mothers when they were not able to get the real ones. One of the genuine mothers, returning to Chattanooga, wrote as follows to her entertainers—I quote from the *Daily Worker:*

"Well I sure miss you all but I was just homesick. I'm sorry I was that way, but after all I love the Reds. I can't be treated any better than the Reds has treated me. And I am a Red too. I tell the white and I tell the black I am not getting back of nothing else. I mean to be with you all as long as I live. . . . Well, I am looking for you to come to see me like you said. You can't realize how highly I appreciate the kindness you all did for me. . . . I hope next time I be to see you all I will be less worried. I never stayed away from my family that long for I think my children don't get along without me. . . . Give all the Reds my love for I love them all. . . .

"From one of the Reds, Janie Patterson."

Another wrote as follows:

"My dear friend, organ of the League of Struggle for Negro Rights. This is Azie Powell's mother. I was away from home at the time those men was out to see me. I was out trying to collect some money what a man owes me to defend for my boy. . . .

"From birth I has work hard plowing, farming by myself for a living for my children. Have had no help supporting them. So sorry, deeply sorry to my heart that my boy was framed up in this. I am almost crazy, can't eat, can't sleep, just want to work all the time, so weak I don't see how I can stand much longer. Living on the will of the Lord. . . .

"Azie was raised on a farm, he was born on a farm, got one little girl, seven years of age already has heart trouble. Have two boys, two girls in all with no father assisting. Poor me, poor me, so burdened down with trouble, if I could only see my baby Azie once more. Lord have mercy on my poor boy in Birmingham. My boy is only fourteen, will be fifteen November 10.

"Poor me, worked hard every day of my life, can't make a living hardly to save my life. . . .

"From Josephine Powell, Atlanta, Ga.

"P.S.—Not knowing what to say or what to do for the best."

The Communists held parades and mass meetings, broke up meetings of the NAACP, themselves had a demonstration in Harlem broken up by the police, made indignant protests to the President, sent a hundred telegrams to the Governor and organized an "All-Southern Conference," at which the organizers were arrested.

Two parties appeared among the Negroes: those who were persuaded by the arguments of the Communists or were excited by Communism as a new form of revivalism (the meetings were often held in churches); and those who, from conservatism, caution or willingness to mind their place, were opposed to the agitation. In one case, a married woman named Bessy Ball attended a Communist meeting and was elected a delegate to the All-Southern Conference. Her husband had been listening to the counsels of the respectable Negro preachers, and when she got home, he beat her up. It was true she had gone to the meeting with the man who lived next door. When their daughter had Ball arrested, he was congratulated on his conduct by the judge, who advised him to use a shotgun on the Reds if they gave him any trouble. Bessy Ball was fined $10. The house next door was raided, and her friend and his mother were arrested, but eventually released. They went home and were immediately visited by their neighbor, Mr. Ball, who had been given carte blanche by the Court to wage a private war on the Reds. Finding a copy of the *Liberator*, the Negro Communist paper, he proceeded to tear it up; and when the Communist mother protested, he hit her on the head with a wooden block. Later, he shot at the son with the shotgun prescribed by the judge. Both he and the son were arrested on charges of assault with intent to kill. Mr. Ball was soon released, but the Communist was kept in jail.

The more docile Negroes were scared. It is reported that since the Scottsboro trials there have been practically no Negroes riding Southern freight trains, and at the time when feeling was running high, the white people in Scottsboro say they almost had to shake hands with their servants every morning to convince them that they meant them no harm. The white Southerners, of course, resented both the Communists and the NAACP as impertinent meddling from the North. On one occasion, the *Jackson County Sentinel* announced that it would "have no editorial this week on the 'Negro Trial' matter. We just couldn't do one without getting mad as hell." "The International Labor Defense of New Yawk and Rusha" had told them that they "must have Negro jurors on any jury trying the blacks if they were to get 'their rights.' A Negro juror in Jackson County would be a curiosity—and some curiosities are embalmed, you know." And the International Labor Defense received the following telegram from the Alabama Ku Klux Klan: "You Negroes are invited to Alabama. We want your scalp along with the nine we already have. And we'll get you as well as anyone else who is a party to the telegram sent South in behalf of the nine Negroes to burn. Read this to your entire body."

A change of venue to another county was first promised by the Court, then denied. A hearing on motions for new trials was set for June 5. Mr. Roddy, Mr. Chamlee and Mr. Joseph Brodsky, an ILD attorney, all appeared in court. Some of the jurors were cross-examined with a view to making them admit that they had been aware, during the trials, of the brass band and the demonstration, and Mr. Chamlee filed a motion for new trials, asserting that the indictments were vague and mentioned no exact facts or dates; that bias had been present in the case; that the defendants had had no chance to employ counsel; that the jury had been prejudiced and had included no Negroes; that the defense were in possession of newly discovered evidence; that it had been impossible at the trials to question Victoria Price as to whether or not she practiced prostitution; that the Negroes at the time they were arrested had displayed no consciousness of guilt; that the State had failed to produce the white boys; that there must have been on the train from fifteen to eighteen colored boys, and that if any crime had been committed, there was no certainty it had not been committed by the boys who got away; that the ride from Stevenson to Paint Rock could only have lasted forty or fifty minutes and that it would hardly have been possible for a fight and twelve rapes to have taken place within so short a time.

The hearing was the occasion in Scottsboro for another popular demonstration. Mr. Chamlee, when he went to the courthouse, brought a bodyguard along, and Mr. Brodsky was made to stay in the building till two or three hours after the hearing was over, by which time the crowd had gone home. Judge Hawkins, who, for re-election, has to depend on the Jackson County voters, has denied the motions for new trials.

The defense will appeal the case to the Supreme Court of Alabama, and if they are unsuccessful there, will appeal it to the Supreme Court of the United States.

In the meantime, the Communists in Alabama have continued to work at their program. In the Southern states, the Negro sharecroppers are held in a state of peonage which differs little from their original state of slavery. The Communists have stimulated them to organize, and on July 16, under Communist tutelage, in a church at Camp Hill, a Sharecroppers' Union held a meeting of which one of the objects announced was to protest over the Scottsboro case. A white posse came to break it up, and as a result the sheriff was shot, a Negro picket was shot and killed, four Negroes disappeared—presumably lynched—and thirty-four Negroes were arrested.

*December 23, 1931 [The Hunger Marchers]*

# RED DAY ON CAPITOL HILL

by John Dos Passos

Washington has a drowsy look in the early December sunlight. The Greco-Roman porticoes loom among the bare trees, as vaguely portentous as phrases about democracy in the mouth of a Southern Senator. The Monument, a finger of light cut against a lavender sky, punctuates the antiquated rhetoric of the Treasury and the White House. On the hill, above its tall foundation banked with magnolia trees, the dome of the Capitol bulges smugly. At nine o'clock groups of sleepy-looking cops in well-brushed uniforms and shiny-visored caps are straggling up the hill. At the corner of Pennsylvania Avenue and John Marshall Place a few hunger marchers stand around the trucks they came in. They looked tired and frowzy from the long ride. Some of them are strolling up and down the avenue. That end of the avenue, with its gimcrack stores, boarded-up burlesque shows, Chinese restaurants and flophouses, still has a little of the jerkwater, out-in-the-sticks look it must have had when Lincoln drove up it in a barouche through the deep mud or Jefferson rode to his inauguration on his own quiet nag.

Two elderly laboring men are looking out of a cigar-store door at a bunch of Reds, young Jewish boys from New York or Chicago, with the white armbands of the hunger marchers. "Won't get nutten that a-way," one of them says. "Whose payin' for it anyway, hirin' them trucks and the gasoline. . . . Somebody's payin' for it," barks the clerk indignantly from behind the cash register. "Better'd spent it on grub or to buy 'emselves overcoats," says the older man. The man who first spoke shakes his head sadly. "Never won't get nutten that a-way." Out along the avenue a few Washingtonians look at the trucks and old moving vans with *Daily Worker* cartoons pasted on their sides. They stand a good way off, as if they were afraid the trucks would explode; they are obviously swallowing their unfavorable comments for fear some of the marchers might hear them. Tough eggs, these Reds.

At ten o'clock the leaders start calling to their men to fall in. Some tall cops appear and bawl out drivers of cars that get into the streets reserved for the marchers to form up in. The marchers form in a column of fours. They don't look as if they'd had much of a night's rest. They look quiet and serious and anxious to do the right thing. Leaders, mostly bareheaded youngsters, run up and down, hoarse and nervous, keeping everybody in line. Most of them look like city dwellers, men and women from the needle trades, restaurant workers, bakery or laundry employees. There's a good sprinkling of Negroes among them. Here and there the thick shoulders and light hair of a truck driver or farm hand stand out. Motorcycle cops begin to cluster around the edges. The marchers are receiving as much attention as distinguished foreign officials.

Up on the hill, cordons of cops are everywhere, making a fine showing in the late-fall sunshine. There's a considerable crowd standing around; it's years since Washington has been interested in the opening of Congress. They are roping off the route for the hunger marchers. They stop a taxicab that is discovered to contain a small white-haired Senator. He curses the cops out roundly and is hurriedly escorted under the portals.

Inside the Capitol things are very different. The light is amber and greenish, as in an aquarium. Elderly clerks white as termites move sluggishly along the corridors, as if beginning to stir after a long hibernation. The elevator boy is very pale. "Here comes the army of the unfed," he says, pointing spitefully out of the window. "And they're carrying banners, though Charlie Curtis said they couldn't." A sound of music comes faintly in. Led by a band with silvery instruments like Christmas-tree ornaments that look cheerful in the bright sunlight, the hunger marchers have started up Capitol Hill. Just time to peep down into the Senate Chamber where elderly parties and pasty-faced pages are beginning to gather. Ever seen a section of a termite nest under glass?

There's a big crowd in the square between the Capitol and the Congressional Library. On the huge ramps of the steps that lead to the central portico the metropolitan police have placed some additional statuary; tastefully arranged groups of cops with rifles, riot guns and brand-new tear-gas pistols that look as if they'd just come from Sears,

Roebuck. People whisper "machine-gun nests," but nobody seems to know where they are. There's a crowd on the roof around the base of the dome, faces are packed in all the windows. Everybody looks cheerful, as if a circus had come to town, anxious to be shown. The marchers fill the broad semicircle in front of the Capitol, each group taking up its position in perfect order, as if the show had been rehearsed. The band, playing "Solidarity Forever" (which a newspaper woman beside me recognizes as "Onward Christian Soldiers"), steps out in front. It's a curious little band, made up of martini-horns, drums, cymbals and a lyre that goes tinkle, tinkle. It plays cheerfully and well, led by a drum major with a red tasseled banner on the end of his staff, and repeats again and again "The Red Flag," "Solidarity," and other tunes variously identified by people in the crowd. Above the heads of the marchers are banners with slogans printed out: IN THE LAST WAR WE FOUGHT FOR THE BOSSES: IN THE NEXT WAR WE'LL FIGHT FOR THE WORKERS . . . $150 CASH . . . FULL PAY FOR UNEMPLOYMENT RELIEF. The squad commanders stand out in front like cheerleaders at a football game and direct the chanting: "We Demand—Unemployed Insurance, We Demand—Unemployed Insurance, WE DEMAND—UNEMPLOYED INSURANCE."

A deep-throated echo comes back from the Capitol façade a few beats later than each shout. It's as if the statues and the classical-revival republican ornaments in the pediment were shouting too.

A small group leaves the ranks and advances across the open space toward the Senate side. All the tall cops drawn up in such fine order opposite the hunger marchers stick out their chests. Now it's coming. A tremor goes over the groups of statuary so tastefully arranged on the steps. The tear-gas pistols glint in the sun. The marchers stand in absolute silence.

Under the portal at the Senate entrance the swinging doors are protected by two solid walls of blue serge. Cameramen and reporters converge with a run. Three men are advancing with the demands of the hunger marchers written out. They are the center of a big group of inspectors, sergeants, gold and silver braid of the Capitol and metropolitan police. A young fellow with a camera is hanging from the wall by the door. "Move the officer out of the way," he yells. "Thank you. . . . A little back, please, lady, I can't see his face. . . . Now hand him the petition."

"We're not handing petitions, we're making demands," says the leader of the hunger marchers. Considerable waiting around. The Sergeant at Arms sends word they can't be let in. Somebody starts to jostle, the cops get tough, cop voices snarl. The committee goes back to report while the band plays the "Internationale" on martini-horns and lyre. . . .

*July 13, 1932 [Franklin D. Roosevelt]*

## OUT OF THE RED WITH ROOSEVELT

by John Dos Passos

They came out of the Stadium with a stale taste in their mouths. Down West Madison Street, walking between lanes of cops and a scattering of bums, the crowds from the galleries found the proud, suave voice of the National Broadcasting Company still filling their jaded ears from every loudspeaker, enumerating the technical agencies that had worked together to obtain the superb hookup through which they broadcast the proceedings of the Democratic Convention of 1932. Well, they did their part: the two big white disks above the speakers' platform (the ears of the radio audience) delicately caught every intonation of the oratory, the dragged-out "gre-eats" when the "great Senator from the great state of . . ." was introduced, the deep "stalwart" always prefixed to "Democrat" when a candidate was being nominated, the indignant rumble in the voice when the present administration was "branded" as having induced "an orgy of crime and a saturnalia of corruption"; the page with the portable microphone in his buttonhole had invariably been on hand when a delegate was recognized from the floor; the managers for the N.B.C. had been there all the time, stage-managing, moving quietly and deftly around the platform, with the expression and gestures of old-fashioned photographers, coaxing the speakers into poses from which they could be heard; telegrams had been read giving the minute-to-minute position of the nominee's plane speeding west; the radio voice of Wally Butterworth had whooped things up describing the adverse flying conditions, the plane's arrival at the airport, the cheering throngs, the jolly ride from Buffalo, the Governor's nice smile.

But when Franklin D. Roosevelt (in person) walked to the front of the rostrum on his son's arm while the organ played "The Star-Spangled Banner" and an irrepressible young lady from Texas waved a bouquet of red, white and blue flowers over his head, to greet with a plain, sensible and unassuming speech the crowd that had yelled itself hoarse for an hour for Al Smith three days before, that had gone delirious over the Wet plank and applauded every phrase in the party platform, and sat with eager patience through the week-long vaudeville show—nothing happened. Courteous applause, but no feeling. The crowd in the huge hall sat blank, blinking in the glare of the lights. Neither delegates nor the public seemed to be able to keep their minds on what the candidate, whom they had nominated after such long sessions and such frantic trading and bickering downtown in their hotel rooms, had to say. As he talked, the faces in the galleries and boxes melted away, leaving red blocks of seats; even the delegates on the floor slunk out in twos and threes.

Starting on Monday with "The Star-Spangled Banner" and an inaugural address of Thomas Jefferson's, read by a stout gentleman with a white gardenia in his buttonhole; through the Senator from Kentucky's keynote speech, during which he so dexterously caught his glasses every time they fell from his nose when he jerked his head to one side and up to emphasize a point; through Wednesday's all-star variety show that offered Clarence Darrow, Will Rogers, Amos 'n' Andy, and Father Coughlin "the radio priest" (who, by the way, advised the convention to put Jesus Christ in the White House), all on one bill; through the joyful reading of the platform with its promise of beer now and a quietus by and by on Prohibition snoopers and bootleggers; through the all-night cabaret on Thursday, with its smoke and sweaty shirts and fatigue and watered Coca-Cola and putty sandwiches and the cockeyed idiocy of the demonstrations—Governor Byrd's band in plumes and rabbit's fur (which he kindly loaned to Ritchie and to Alfalfa Bill when their turn came) and the pigeons and the young women who kept climbing up on the platform and bathing in the klieg lights like people under a warm shower, and the sleepy little Oklahoma girls in their kilties—and the grim balloting while the sky outside the windows went blue and then pink until at last the sun rose and sent long, frightening, bright horizontal shafts through the cigar smoke and the spotlights and the huddled group of worn-out politicans; through the nominating speeches, and the seconding speeches and the reseconding speeches, and the old-time tunes, "The Old Gray Mare," "A Hot Time in the Old Town Tonight," "I've Been Working on the Railroad"—

Through all the convention week and flicker of flashlight bulbs and the roar of voices there had been built up a myth, as incongruous to this age as the myth of the keen-eyed pilot at the helm of the ship of state that the Republicans tried to revitalize three weeks ago; the myth of the young American working his way by honesty and brawn, from Log Cabin to President. This stalwart Democrat was to rise in his might, wrench the government out of the hands of the old bogey Republicans, Wall Street, Privilege, Graft and Corruption, return it to the People and thus in some mystic way give jobs to the jobless, relieve the farmers of their mortgages, save the money the little fellow had deposited in the tottering banks, restore business to the the small storekeeper and producer and thereby bring the would-be Democratic officeholders massed on the floor back to the fleshpots of power. A powerful myth and an old myth. But when, largely through the backstage efforts of Mr. McAdoo, the myth took flesh in the crippled boy and unassuming speech of the actual Governor of New York, the illusion crashed. Too late.

You come out of the Stadium and walk down the street. It's West Madison Street, the home address of migratory workers and hoboes and jobless men all over the Middle West. Gradually the din of speeches fades out of your ears, you forget the taste of the cigar you were smoking, the cracks and gossip of the press gallery. Nobody on the street knows about the convention that's deciding who shall run their government—or cares. The convention is the sirens of police motorcycles, a new set of scare headlines, a new sensation over the radio. There are six-day bicycle races and battles of the century and eucharistic congresses and big-league games and political conventions; and a man has got a job, or else he hasn't got a job, he's got jack in his pocket, or else he's broke, he's got a business, or else he's a bum. Way off some place, headline events happen. Even if they're right on West Madison Street, they're way off. Roosevelt or Hoover? It'll be the same cops.

You walk on down, across the great train yards and the river to the Loop, out onto Michigan Avenue where Chicago is raising every year a more imposing front of skyscrapers, into the clean wind of the lake. Shiny store fronts, doormen, smartly dressed girls, taxis, buses taking shoppers, clerks, businessmen home to the South Side and North Side. In Grant Park more jobless men lying under the bushes, beyond them sails in the harbor, a white steamboat putting out into the lake. Overhead, pursuit planes fly in formation advertising the military show at Soldier Field. To get their ominous buzz out of your ears, you go down a flight of steps, into the darkness feebly lit by ranks of dusty red electric lights of the roadway under Michigan Avenue. The fine smart marble and plate-glass front of the city peels off as you walk down the steps. Down here the air, drenched with the exhaust from the grinding motors of trucks, is full of dust and grit and the roar of the heavy traffic that hauls the city's freight. When your eyes get used to the darkness, you discover that, like the world upstairs of store fronts and hotel lobbies and battles of the century and political conventions, this world too has its leisure class. They lie in rows along the ledges above the roadway, huddled in grimed newspapers, gray sag-faced men in worn-out clothes, discards, men who have nothing left but their stiff hungry grimy bodies, men who have lost the power to want. Try to tell one of them that the *gre-eat* Franklin D. Roosevelt, Governor of the *gre-eat* state of New York, has been nominated by the *gre-eat* Democratic party as its candidate for President, and you'll get what the galleries at the convention gave Mr. McAdoo when they discovered that he had the votes of Texas and California in his pocket

and was about to shovel them into the Roosevelt band wagon, a prolonged and enthusiastic *Boooo.* Hoover or Roosevelt, it'll be the same
cops.

*August 10, 1932*

# NORMAN THOMAS: THE ENRAPTURED SOCIALIST

by Matthew Josephson

In the Connecticut village where I happen to reside, the editor of the
weekly gazette is an old-fashioned American Socialist, who is tolerated
by the shrewd native shopkeepers much as village atheists have always
been tolerated in this country. When Norman Thomas was unanimously
chosen, last May, to lead the Socialist campaign, this good man threw
his hat in the air and wrote exultantly:

> Norman Thomas, who has been nominated for President by the Socialist
> party, is a graduate of Princeton and was formerly assistant to Dr. Henry
> Van Dyke, rector of the Brick Presbyterian Church in Fifth Avenue, New
> York. He is not one of your wild-eyed Reds. . . .

No, not a "wild-eyed Red," but one of the finer flowers of our liberal
American Protestantism, an enlightened son of our vast lower middle
class. I allude to his petty-bourgeois origin and background, not
invidiously, since they are in no sense his fault, but because, in thinking upon the Socialist nominee for President in 1932, one is tempted to
use the Marxian yardstick. By this, Thomas's leadership of Socialism
in America has aspects of novelty and flies in the face of tradition.

The traditional line of socialism, even in this long-immunized country, always took its point of departure from the ideas that the truly
social character of large-scale capitalism, plus the injustice it inevitably
dealt labor, would, by a process of historic materialism, tend to weaken
capitalism, increasing at the same time the solidarity and the strategic
industrial power of labor. In the predestined social revolution labor
would conquer government. The driving power for revolt would come

from the proletariat, once it was conscious of its dominant economic role. But Norman Thomas was not himself driven to socialism, as slaves are driven to revolt. Nothing in his past or his early education, as he himself declares, explains his socialism. He came to this of his own free will, out of an abundance of nice moral scruples, out of the sympathy of a bighearted social worker, and because he was a sincere, latter-day Christian who had lost hope in organized religion. He is, in short, a preacher who, it has been observed, underwent a new religious conversion and began some time ago "to deliver sermons in the street, instead of from the pulpit. In the front pews of his outdoor economic church there are some listeners; but the gallery seems almost empty."

This enraptured Socialist seeks by persuasion to produce in great numbers of other people the same conversion experienced by himself; and his tendency must unconsciously be to make his appeal to a mildly rebellious section of the middle class from which he himself springs, and which he understands. For the laboring masses, whose language he speaks but haltingly, his appeal will be weaker—although realistic thinkers see in the failure of radicals to effect technical and political reorganization of labor the one great bar to profound social change. This is the character of Socialist leadership in 1932.

If Norman Thomas were selfishly in pursuit of power, he could easily go elsewhere, as other "independents" or radicals have done. But his ruling ambition in recent years has been to revitalize the Socialist movement in America, to rally the millions of potentially radical Americans to its banner. Did not the elder La Follette in 1924, a year of "normalcy," gather up 4,800,000 votes? Thomas is intelligent, senses the new chances of his party today, understands the obstacles within and without, to right and left. He knows also the melancholy record of the old S.P. during the past twenty years (since Debs won a million votes), and before the national convention he spoke thus:

"I feel convinced that there is the possibility of a powerful political force in our party. But I also feel terribly the need for drastic reorganization, which I shall urge at the presidential convention. Candidly, our party has been *glacially slow*; it has been in a fearful state during the last four years. . . .

"What we need is an adequate labor program," Thomas commented, coming to the heart of the problem. "None has been worked out as yet; *and this must be done in the most clear-cut terms.*" True enough. For what good was a Socialist party which aimed at socializing the means of production and did not have the support of the working masses? If the Socialists would do nothing, then there was danger, increasingly evident, that the Republicans or Democrats would inaugurate socialism in some form. (One of Mr. Hoover's aides has recently alluded to the Republican administration, in private talk, as "our socialist government.") And on the left there was danger of the Communists. Logically they sought to destroy the Socialist party. Full of dogmatic passion and, at times, fanatical energy, they might go far, despite their weaknesses and present blunders. They at least were working along the labor front. Wherever a labor situation developed—such as Socialists under De Leon and Debs would exploit for the class war—it was the Communists who "pre-empt those situations," Thomas himself freely admitted.

"At any rate, we have a social philosophy which the two large political parties lack," Thomas concluded earnestly. "What we need is boldness, audacity. We need the flaming passion of a Mazzini."

Will Thomas be the Mazzini of American socialism? . . .

For some fifteen years, Norman Thomas's record has been one of perpetual, energetic crusading for civil liberties, for strike relief, for municipal reform, for world peace. But rebelling or crusading, he has nearly always retained the respectful tolerance of his most conservative contemporaries.

Why? Because there is something naïve in the bighearted social worker who espouses the cause of reform. His type is perfectly familiar in our history: that of the "Goo-Goos," or Good Government Boys, whom Lincoln Steffens describes so well in his autobiography; and opponents have learned not to fear this type.

By preference or by natural disposition, Norman Thomas is less concerned with the reform of labor and its preparation for the conquest of power than he is with the moral need for socialism. The notes of moral censure of our civilization are strongest in him; and we have no doubt merited his reproaches.

> Never yet has any civilization endured with no philosophy but a superficial pragmatism. . . . Success is our God, measured in terms of money. . . . We have no moral standards to which to appeal in our warfare against the underworld.
>
> What is it that socialism offers? In the first place a philosophy, a social vision, a loyalty adequate to the realities of the interdependent world which the machine age has imposed upon us. . . . Not a detailed program, important as it is, but a new faith . . . is the answer to our bewilderment, apathy or despair.
>
> Once there is a collective will for action, once men care enough for some social ideal, a lot of impossibilities melt away. By this flaming ideal of national unity Mazzini melted away the barriers which divided Italy and forged its nationalism.

In 1919, while helping to lead the Paterson textile workers' strike, Norman Thomas made a speech to the workers to cheer them on in their fight. Suddenly the police entered the hall and cut off all the lights. Not only was crusading forbidden, but the authorities, it appears, sought to hamper the strikers' activities and prevent their meeting by plunging the place in darkness. Norman Thomas may have been surprised or indignant, as no economic determinist would have permitted himself to be. (He would be indignant again in 1929, when ballots cast for him were stolen by Tammany agents in New York.) The trouble, to his mind of an ardent uplifter, was the darkness: the darkness brought violence, and injustice; besides, it was plainly unconstitutional. (A Marx or a Lenin would have inferred more logically that entrenched economic injustice ordained darkness.) Thomas longed to bring light, to persuade the wicked authorities to behave, to recall them to the spirit in which our fathers conceived this government of liberty, equality and the rights of private property. Boldly arming himself with a candle, by its guttering light he read to the strikers as well as to the police officers present the Declaration of Independence. The strike, one recalls, was beaten; but Norman Thomas has been carrying a candle all about the country ever since.

*March 15, 1933 [Henry A. Wallace]*

# WALLACE OF IOWA
by Ferner Nuhn

A favorite remark of the new Secretary of Agriculture is that as correlations may be worked out for almost everything in the world, from the number of petals on daisies to the mental alertness of men, nowhere in nature is there anything comparable to the enormous variability in the incomes of human beings.

I mention this remark because it expresses Henry A. Wallace's two chief characteristics: a scientific habit of mind, and a strong sense of social justice. And perhaps the combination of these two major characteristics has produced Wallace's dominating conviction that in the realm of economics social justice can be defined, that it can be measured, and that it can eventually be realized if human beings will put their minds and hearts to the task.

It is natural, of course, that the particular aspect of social justice in which Wallace has been most interested is the farmer and his livelihood. Wallace, who has lived among farmers all his life, is preoccupied with their economic problems. For in Iowa, where he was reared, agriculture is the basic industry. The towns and cities, with their heterogeneous architecture, their chambers of commerce, their pseudoindustrial, Hooverized Republican tendencies, seem hollow and unreal in comparison. But beyond the cities, things take on a life that seems authentic. The pattern of windbreak and farm cluster, the shapes of barn and silo, the design of fields, impress one immediately as the basic and fundamental expression of the state. Moreover, it is the farmers who have been interested most in social change. It was they who voted the Republicans out and it was the more rural counties, even, which gave Thomas the better proportion of support, whereas the people of the towns and cities supported the old regime of laissez-faire and rugged individualism. And it is also the farmers, with their solidarity, their faith in mass action, their courage in the face of violence and arrest, who have supplied us with one of the few hopeful signs in the depression.

Wallace stands firmly behind the farmers, and they return his support with a loyalty which few other farm leaders can inspire. It is not because he is a "good fellow" among them—he is not that type. On the contrary, he is reserved and studious. He makes no attempt to ingratiate himself with his audience, he tells no funny stories, he is not eloquent, he simply loads his speeches with ideas and cold facts. The farmers respect his disinterestedness and his authority, and they have had to agree with him, as he is constantly insisting in his journal, that the two major elements in all social progress are sympathy and knowledge.

Wallace, whose thick, wiry hair, gray-blue eyes and slight figure make him look younger than forty-four, did not develop his strong sense of social justice uninfluenced by his surroundings and his upbringing. His forebears were of Scotch-Irish stock, deeply religious people, who before moving into Iowa lived in Pennsylvania and New England. His grandfather, besides being a farmer and editor, was also a minister. *Wallace's Farmer*, which he founded, reflects in its slogan—"Good Farming, Clear Thinking, Right Living"—something of the atmosphere in which Henry Wallace grew up. His father was Secretary of Agriculture under Harding. Though less liberal than his son, he saw the necessity of agricultural reform and particularly of cooperation among the farmers.

As a young man, Wallace, in that spirit of scientific research which has dominated much of his career, began to experiment with the breeding of corn, an experiment in which he is still interested. He familiarized himself with all the current theories concerning high-production corn and finally succeeded in producing a seed corn with its strains definitely fixed and refixed each year. It has proved its worth, yielding four to ten bushels per acre more than the common variety. With the same practical and scientific methods which he had employed to develop his "Hi-bred" corn, he turned to the field of economics.

In those days he developed a statistical method to a high degree of utility and employed it in the correlation of weather cycles and crop production, and the monthly charting of the relative returns of hog-fed corn and corn sold as grain.

His peculiar gift for prophecy made it possible for him to anticipate many phases of the depression long before it began. Hardly had the war ended when Wallace was investigating its probable aftereffects. As early as January 1919, in an article on the farming depression in England following the Napoleonic Wars, he discussed the collapse of inflated prices and the persistence of high fixed charges which resulted in a profound agricultural depression. He concluded that the World War had created an almost identical economic situation and that the reconstruction period would be a repetition of that following the Napoleonic Wars. In 1920, true to his prophecy, came the first agricultural collapse. It was also during these years toward the end of the war, when prices were still high, that Wallace was constantly dinning into his readers' ears the advice that now was the time to pay off debts. Moreover, Wallace at the same time was pointing out the significant fact that this nation had changed from debtor to creditor and that our foreign trade was in danger. He asserted that our hope of preserving the export market was by removing the tariff in order that foreign countries might trade with us, by lending money abroad so that foreign nations could buy our goods, and finally by canceling the war debts.

At present Wallace is supporting three types of farm-relief legislation—the refinancing of indebtedness, the liberalization of the money standard, and the domestic-allotment plan. Wallace has no illusions about the permanent effectiveness of the last measure, but he supports it because he is convinced that if there is to be protection, agriculture must share in it equally with industry. He believes that this plan offers a method of reducing crop acreage—an insoluble problem under a laissez-faire policy—but his main reason for supporting it is his belief that, crude though it may be, it represents that social and economic planning which we must increasingly develop to preserve civilization. Indeed, Wallace has a fond hope that if planned cooperation can be proved workable in agriculture the example may lead men to abandon competition throughout the entire economic structure. He does not believe, however, that there will be any final security unless there is national planning and international cooperation.

Today he is less of the cloistered scientist than he formerly was. His editorials have assumed more warmth and more directness; he has been doing more and more public speaking. Nevertheless, the new Secretary of Agriculture still remains an ascetic. It is characteristic of him that he is a vegetarian even in a state which leads in the production of hogs.

Primarily, he is a disinterested spirit, motivated by a sense of justice and by scientific method. In his new position he will be tried in ways that are new to him. Though he is far from being unversed in the problems of the general world, in which the machinery of a definite program tends so regularly to wear away the original texture of principle, it is yet to be seen how greatly his sense of strategy will protect him from accepting mutilated programs as a substitution for fundamental ones. But there is little doubt that in Henry A. Wallace the Middle West contributes to national affairs an authentic figure, not out of place in the line of George W. Norris and the elder La Follette.

*March 22, 1933 [F.D.R.]*

# WASHINGTON NOTES
by T.R.B.

The speed with which the government of the United States has moved from democracy toward dictatorship has more or less stunned the statesmen on the Hill, but it apparently has pleased nearly everyone else. As things stand today, Mr. Roosevelt has, in some respects, more power than any other President under our Constitution ever had, except perhaps Mr. Wilson in wartime, and while some thoughtful men here are disturbed over what they call a surrender of its constitutional rights by Congress, the shadow of the national emergency stills their protest and controls their vote. And when the facts are considered it seems clear that nothing else could be done.

The two messages of the President, one on banking and the other on economy, evoked an extraordinary popular response. So far as the first is concerned, I think, the people, though eager to get over the immediate crisis, are even more eager for a complete reorganization of the whole rotten banking system with which we have been afflicted. The note struck in the new President's inaugural address, in a general way, seemed a promise that this would be done. The completeness of the collapse, the National City Bank revelations that preceded it and the dictatorial powers now lodged in the federal government offer the opportunity for this reform and a chance to establish the banking business on sound foundations.

Whether Mr. Roosevelt has it in him to take full advantage of this opportunity remains to be seen. In the enunciation of broad general principles he is at his best. His words are encouraging. Both his messages and his inaugural have been commended generally for their "outspoken boldness" and "refreshing courage." But this job of banking reorganization requires much more than oratorical adequacy. It means a sound and concrete plan, backed by the whole driving force of the presidency. Mr. Roosevelt has a sufficient number of capable men to form the plan, but however meek and cowed the New York banking group seem at the moment, there is still a lot of fight in them and they are not without formidable Senate support.

Under the economy measure, Mr. Roosevelt is given power practically to remake or remold the whole administrative section of the government. The extent of his authority is hard to exaggerate. In normal times, of course, it would be unthinkable. Under existing conditions, however, there is no doubt of the popular desire that he be invested with this authority, just as there is not the slightest doubt that Mr. Roosevelt planned as far back as last January to ask for it. It is what he has wanted from the start, what he told his intimates in New York and again at Warm Springs he intended to ask for.

It is inconceivable that having now obtained what he desired and intended to request of Congress long before the banking collapse occurred, he will not use it for the purpose planned. It is obvious that his main purpose is to reduce the veteran-compensation load by $400,000,000, for on a cut of that size hinges the whole administration financial program. Even with that amount sliced out, it is going to be no easy job to come within an approximate budget balance before the ratification of the new amendment to the Constitution.

To fall short of that figure means that the thing cannot be done. The new Director of the Budget, Mr. Douglas, an exceedingly competent man, will do the work and the recommendation will go in. But anyone who thinks this does not mean a real fight does not know the power of the lobby that operates here for the veterans, nor does he appreciate the fear inspired in the Congressional bosom by the organized minorities in state and district. Let the crisis pass and the public indignation evaporate, as it always does, and a different picture will be presented. Soon or late Mr. Roosevelt has got to fight with all there is in him, and when that time comes it will be possible to pass a real judgment on him. It is not possible now. . . .

*October 11, 1933 [Ring Lardner]*

# RING

## by F. Scott Fitzgerald

For a year and a half, the writer of this appreciation was Ring Lardner's most familiar companion; after that, geography made separations and our contacts were rare. When we last saw him in 1931 he looked already like a man on his deathbed—it was terribly sad to see that six feet three inches of kindness stretched out ineffectual in the hospital room; his fingers trembled with a match, the tight skin on his handsome skull was marked as a mask of misery and nervous pain.

He gave a very different impression when I first saw him in 1921—he seemed to have an abundance of quiet vitality that would enable him to outlast anyone, to take himself for long spurts of work or play that would ruin an ordinary constitution. He had recently convulsed the country with the famous kitten-and-coat saga (it had to do with a World's Series bet and with the impending conversion of some kittens into fur), and the evidence, a beautiful sable, was worn by his wife at the time. In those days he was interested in people, sports, bridge, music, the stage, the newspapers, the magazines, the books. But though I did not know it, the change in him had already begun—the impenetrable despair that dogged him for a dozen years to his death.

He had practically given up sleeping, save on short vacations deliberately consecrated to simple pleasures, most frequently golf with his friends, Grantland Rice or John Wheeler. Many a night we talked over a case of Canadian ale until bright dawn when Ring would rise and yawn.

"Well, I guess the children have left for school by this time—I might as well go home."

The woes of many people haunted him—for example, the doctor's death sentence pronounced upon Tad, the cartoonist (who, in fact, nearly outlived Ring)—it was as if he believed he could and ought to do something about it. And as he struggled to fulfill his contracts, one of which, a comic strip based on the character of "the busher," was a terror indeed, it was obvious that he felt his work to be directionless, merely "copy." So he was inclined to turn his cosmic sense of responsibility into the channel of solving other people's problems—finding someone an introduction to a manager, placing a friend in a job, maneuvering a man into a golf club. The effort made was often out of proportion to the situation; the truth back of it was that Ring was getting off—he was a faithful and conscientious workman to the end, but he had stopped finding any fun in his work ten years before he died.

About that time (1922) a publisher undertook to reissue his old books and collect his recent stories, and this gave him a sense of existing in the literary world as well as with the public, and he got some satisfaction from the reiterated statements of Mencken and F.P.A. as to his true stature as a writer. But I don't think he cared then—it is hard to understand, but I don't think he really gave a damn about anything except his personal relations with people. A case in point was his attitude to those imitators who lifted everything except the shirt off his back—only Hemingway has been so thoroughly frisked—it worried the imitators more than it worried Ring. His attitude was that if they got stuck in the process he'd help them over any tough place.

Throughout this period of huge earnings and an increasingly solid reputation on top and below, there were two ambitions more important to Ring than the work by which he will be remembered: he wanted to be a musician—sometimes he dramatized himself ironically as a thwarted composer—and he wanted to write shows. His dealings with managers would make a whole story: they were always commissioning him to do work, which they promptly forgot they had ordered, and accepting librettos that they never produced. Only with the aid of the practical George Kaufman did he achieve his ambition, and by then he was too far gone in illness to get a proper satisfaction from it.

The point of these paragraphs is that whatever Ring's achievement was, it fell short of the achievement he was capable of, and this because of a cynical attitude toward his work. How far back did that attitude go—back to his youth in a Michigan village? Certainly back to his days with the Cubs. During those years, when most men of promise achieve an adult education, if only in the school of war, Ring moved in the company of a few dozen illiterates playing a boy's game. A boy's game, with no more possibilities in it than a boy could master, a game bounded by walls which kept out novelty or danger, change or adventure. This material, the observation of it under such circumstances, was the text of Ring's schooling during the most formative period of the mind. A writer can spin on about his adventures after thirty, after forty, after fifty, but the criteria by which these adventures are weighed and valued are irrevocably settled at the age of twenty-five. However deeply Ring might cut into it, his cake had the diameter of Frank Chance's diamond.

Here was his artistic problem, and it promised future trouble. So long as he wrote within that inclosure the result was magnificent: within it he heard and recorded the voice of a continent. But when, inevitably, he outgrew his interest in it, what was Ring left with?

He was left with his fine etymological technique—and he was left rather helpless in those few acres. He had been formed by the very world on which his hilarious irony had released itself. He had fought his way through to knowing what people's motives are and what means they are likely to resort to in order to attain their goals. He was up with the best of them, but now there was a new problem—what to do about it. He went on seeing, and the sights traveled back the optic nerve, but no longer to be thrown off in fiction, because they were no longer sights that could be weighed and valued by the old criteria. It was never that he was completely sold on athletic virtuosity as the be-all and end-all of problems; the trouble was that he could find nothing finer. Imagine life conceived as a business of beautiful muscular organization—an arising, an effort, a good break, a sweat, a bath, a meal, a sleep—imagine it achieved; then imagine trying to apply that standard to the horribly complicated mess of living where nothing, even the greatest conceptions and workings and achievements, is else but messy, spotty, tortuous—and then one can imagine the confusion that Ring faced coming out of the ball park.

He kept on recording, but he no longer projected, and this accumulation, which he has taken with him to the grave, crippled his spirit in the latter years. It was not the fear of Niles, Michigan, that hampered him—it was the habit of silence formed in the presence of the "ivory" with which he lived and worked. Remember it was not humble ivory—Ring has demonstrated that—it was arrogant, imperative, often megalomaniacal ivory. He got a habit of silence, then the habit of repression that finally took the form of his odd little crusade in *The New Yorker* against pornographic songs. He had agreed with himself to speak only a small portion of his mind.

The present writer once suggested to him that he organize some *cadre* on which he could adequately display his talents, suggesting that it should be something deeply personal, and something on which Ring could take his time, but he dismissed the idea lightly; he was a disillusioned idealist but he had served his goddess well, and no other could be casually created for him—"This is something that can be printed," he reasoned, "this, however, must join that accumulated mass of reflections that can never be written."

He covered himself in such cases with protests of his inability to bring off anything big, but this was specious, for he was a proud man and had no reason to rate his abilities cheaply. He refused to "tell all," because in a crucial period of his life he had formed the habit of not doing it—and this he had elevated gradually into a standard of taste. It never satisfied him by a damn sight.

So one is haunted not only by a sense of personal loss but by a conviction that Ring got less percentage of himself on paper than any other American author of the first flight. There is *You Know Me, Al*, and there are about a dozen wonderful short stories (My God! he hadn't even saved them—the material of *How to Write Short Stories* was obtained by photographing old issues of magazines in the public library!) and there is some of the most uproarious and inspired nonsense since Lewis Carroll—the latter yet to be properly examined and edited. Most of the rest is mediocre stuff, with flashes, and I would do Ring a disservice to suggest it should be set upon an altar and worshiped, as have been the most casual relics of Mark Twain. God knows, those three volumes should seem enough—to everyone who didn't know Ring. But I venture that no one who knew him but will agree that the personality of the man overlapped it. Proud, shy, solemn, shrewd, polite, brave, kind, merciful, honorable—with the affection these qualities aroused he created in addition a certain awe in people. His intentions, his will, once in motion were formidable factors in dealing with him—he always did every single thing he said he would do. Frequently he was the melancholy Jacques, and sad company indeed, but under any conditions a noble dignity flowed from him, so that time in his company always seemed well spent.

On my desk, at the moment, I have the letters that Ring wrote to us; here is a letter one thousand words long, here is one of two thousand words—theatrical gossip, literary shop talk, flashes of wit but not much wit, for he was feeling thin and saving the best of that for his work, anecdotes of his activities. I reprint the most typical one I can find:

> The Dutch Treat show was a week ago Friday night. Grant Rice and I had reserved a table, and a table holds ten people and no more. Well, I had invited, as one guest, Jerry Kern, but he telephoned at the last moment that he couldn't come. I then consulted with Grant Rice, who said he had no substitute in mind, but that it was a shame to waste our extra ticket when tickets were at a premium. So I called up Jones, and Jones said yes, and would it be all right for him to bring along a former Senator who was a pal of his and had been good to him in Washington. I said I was sorry, but our table was filled and besides, we didn't have an extra ticket. "Maybe I could dig up another ticket somewhere," said Jones. "I don't believe so," I said, "but anyway the point is that we haven't room at our table." "Well," said Jones, "I could have the Senator eat somewhere else and join us in time for the show." "Yes," I said, "but we have no ticket for him." Well, what he thought up was to bring himself and the Senator and I had a hell of a time getting an extra ticket and shoving the Senator in at another table where he wasn't wanted, and later in the evening, the Senator thanked Jones and said he was the greatest fella in the world and all I got was goodnight. Well, I must close and nibble on a carrot. R.W.L.

Even in a telegram Ring could compress a lot of himself. Here is one:

WHEN ARE YOU COMING BACK AND WHY PLEASE ANSWER.
RING LARDNER

This is not the moment to recollect Ring's convivial aspects, especially as he had, long before his death, ceased to find amusement in dissipation, or indeed in the whole range of what is called entertainment—save for his perennial interest in songs. By grace of the radio and of the many musicians who, drawn by his enormous magnetism, made pilgrimages to his bedside, he had a consolation in the last days, and he made the most of it, hilariously rewriting Cole Porter's lyrics in *The New Yorker*. But it would be an evasion for the present writer not to say that when he was Ring's neighbor a decade ago, they tucked a lot under their belts in many weathers, and spent many words on many men and things. At no time did I feel that I had known him enough, or that anyone knew him—it was not the feeling that there was more stuff in him and that it should come out, it was rather a qualitative difference, it was rather as though, due to some inadequacy in one's self, one had not penetrated to something unsolved, new and unsaid. That is why one wishes that Ring had written down a larger proportion of what was in his mind and heart. It would have saved him longer for us, and that in itself would be something. But I would like to know what it was, and now I will go on wishing—what did Ring want, how did he want things to be, how did he think things were?

A great and good American is dead. Let us not obscure him by the flowers, but walk up and look at that fine medallion, all torn by sorrows that perhaps we are not equipped to understand. Ring made no enemies, because he was kind, and to many millions he gave release and delight.

*November 1, 1933 [Russian Bureaucrats]*

# RUSSIA AND WORLD REVOLUTION
by Leon Trotsky

Much water has gone under the bridge since the time when the ideas of Lenin and his closest co-workers were the definitive ideas of the Soviet republic and the Comintern. Circumstances have changed, people have changed; the ruling stratum of the U.S.S.R. has been renovated completely; the old ideas and slogans have been ousted by new ones. What had formerly composed the essence has now become transformed into a harmless ritual. But instead, there remain preserved intentionally the convictions of some statesmen of the West, based on recollections, as to the indissoluble tie between the Soviet government and the Comintern. It is time this view was revised! In the present-day world, so torn by contradictions, there are far too many real bases for enmity to seek artificial reasons for fanning it. It is time to understand that despite the ritualistic phrases employed on holiday occasions, the Soviet government and the Comintern now inhabit different planes. Not only are the present leaders of the U.S.S.R. prepared to make no national sacrifices for the sake of the German and, in general, the world revolution, but also they do not hesitate for a moment to take such actions and make such pronouncements as deal the heaviest blows to the Comintern, and the workers' movements as a whole. The more the U.S.S.R. strengthens its international position, the deeper becomes the rift between the Soviet government and the international revolutionary struggle. . . .

Lenin considered that the historical character of a war is determined by those social forces which oppose each other on the battlefield and by the political goals they pursue. The present Soviet diplomacy springs completely from the conservative principle of maintaining the status quo. Its attitude toward war and the warring sides is determined not by a revolutionary criterion, but by the legalistic criterion: which one crosses the foreign boundaries first. Thus the Soviet formula sanctions the defense of national territory against aggression for capitalist nations as well. We shall not discuss how good or bad this is. In general, the purpose of this article is not to criticize the policies of the present Kremlin, but to show the profoundly altered principles of the entire international orientation of the Soviet government, in order thus to eliminate those fictitious barriers which are in the way of the recognition of the U.S.S.R.

The plan for building socialism in one country alone is in no wise an empty phrase; it is a practical program, embracing in equal degrees economy, internal policies and diplomacy. The more decisively the Soviet bureaucracy has intrenched itself in its position as to national socialism, the more the questions of international revolution, and with them the Comintern, have been relegated to the background. Every new revolution is an equation with many unknowns, and hence it includes in itself an element of major political risk. The present Soviet government seeks, with might and main, to ensure its internal security against risk connected not only with wars but with revolutions. Its international policies have been transformed from international-revolutionary policies into those which are conservative.

True, the Soviet leadership cannot openly avow the facts as they are, either to its own workers or those of other countries. It is shackled by the ideological heritage of the October Revolution, which forms the reservoir for its authority with the working masses. But while the shell of the tradition remains, the content has evaporated. . . .

# DECADE THREE
# 1934-1943

**The New**
# REPUBLIC
*Published Weekly*

Wednesday September 11, 1935

H. N. BRAILSFORD
## Mussolini Goes to War

*Neutrality and Oil*
### U. S. A. vs U. S. S. R.

### Soaking the Poor
by DAYTON D. McKEAN

FIFTEEN CENTS A COPY
FIVE DOLLARS A YEAR
VOL. LXXXIV, NO. 1084

**The New**
# REPUBLIC
*Published Weekly*

Wednesday October 14, 1936

*Five Dollars for a Landon Man*
## Anarchists Burn a Church
by RALPH BATES

## How I Am Voting
Carl Sandburg, Archibald MacLeish, John A. Ryan
George Jean Nathan, Ferdinand Lundberg *and others*

## John Lewis: Giant Killer
by JONATHAN MITCHELL

*Landon on Social Security*

FIFTEEN CENTS A COPY
FIVE DOLLARS A YEAR
VOL. LXXXVIII, NO. 1141

**The New**
# REPUBLIC

November 23, 1938

### Let the Jews Come In!
*Editorial*

We Built the Nazi Air Force . . *M. M. Fagen*
What the Election Means . . . . . *Editorial*
Catholic Church in Politics: II . *L. H. Lehmann*
Power Is What You Make It . . . *Max Lerner*
A Brain-Truster Explains . . . . *John T. Flynn*
Mr. Dooley on Mr. Dewey . *John Chamberlain*

FIFTEEN CENTS

**The New**
# REPUBLIC

May 5, 1941

## ALL OUT NOW!
*Americans must shake off their creeping paralysis*
*of the will or the Battle for the World will be lost*

### Where Hitler Will Strike Next
*by Max Werner*

### Germany Executes Her "Unfit"
*by Michael Straight*

FIFTEEN CENTS

*1934-1943*

The New Republic *began its third decade in the sixth winter of the great depression. But the sense of acute crisis had begun to fade; and, though the magazine was not quite prepared to accept the pragmatism of the New Deal as a substitute for basic social reconstruction, its editors were recovering their poise. The magazine could turn once again to social phenomena without feeling the compulsion to underline a sociological moral—thus Jonathan Mitchell, the T.R.B. of the moment, on the Louis-Baer fight; Otis Ferguson, the brilliant film critic, on Jimmy Durante; David Low, the English cartoonist, on Walt Disney.*

*So, too, literature began to escape from the Marxist operating table. Lionel Trilling would doubtless write differently about Eugene O'Neill today, but as a young critic nearly thirty years ago he still saw him in broad and humane moral perspective. No two writers were less in the fashion of the thirties than Amy Lowell and Scott Fitzgerald; but* The New Republic *ran a discerning piece on Miss Lowell by Van Wyck Brooks, even though John O'Hara was excessively patronizing on Fitzgerald (as Max Eastman was on Freud). In 1943 Henry Miller gloomily predicted that his fellow countrymen would never be permitted to read his book, not anticipating the day (to be recorded by Stanley Kauffmann in Part V) when* Tropic of Cancer *would be found in every drugstore.*

*Yet politics necessarily remained the dominant preoccupation. For a season,* The New Republic *flirted with collectivism. But by the mid-thirties, the New Deal was beginning to demonstrate that reform and recovery might be possible within the existing system; and Roosevelt, as Marquis Childs showed in a famous piece in 1936, was earning the hatred of the American rich. All this induced, in Roosevelt's second term, a new tolerance toward what was going on in Washington—a tolerance that soon turned into enthusiastic support. By the late thirties the magazine was vigorously in the Roosevelt camp. Among Roosevelt's rivals, John L. Lewis received a sardonic portrait at the hands of Jonathan Mitchell, and Wendell Willkie a sympathetic one from William Allen White.*

*Developments abroad reinforced the impulse to rally behind Roosevelt. Thomas Wolfe's anguished sketch of an episode in Nazi Germany foreshadowed the terror to come. The great debate between isolationism and intervention had its reflection in the pages of* The New Republic. *Then, in 1940 as a generation before, the magazine surrendered its perfectionism to its sense of international responsibility. Pearl Harbor ushered in a new phase. The magazine, like the nation, committed itself to a new time of total war.*

—ARTHUR M. SCHLESINGER, JR.

*September 26, 1934 [Adolf Hitler]*

# EDITORIAL

If ridicule could kill, Adolf Hitler's prophecy at the National Socialist Party congress at Nuremberg of a thousand years of Nazi rule would have laughed Germany's dictator out of office. But the humorlessness of latter-day Germany has been one of its great tragedies. Instead, the German press, under the gentle ministrations of its ruler Goebbels, overflows with enthusiastic commentaries on the Fuehrer's prophecy. They must have exceeded even that gentleman's expectations. In the Third Reich, personal sycophancy and political stupidity go hand in hand. In this respect, the Nuremberg performance exceeded all previous demonstrations of Nazi debasement. Hitler assured two thousand women politicians of his party that the preoccupation of their sex with political problems is a "product of Jewish intellectualism," and was rewarded with boisterous applause. Enthusiasm rose to still greater heights when he declared that "the Nazi program for women has but one point: the child."

There was more fancy than fact, however, in his declaration that the Storm Troopers are "regarded by me as the main buttress of the Third Reich." The practical measures adopted by the Fuehrer and his lieutenants against the Brown Shirt troopers on this occasion told another —and truer—story. "Though the Storm Troops were given a good position in the huge stadium," reports William Shirer, Universal Service correspondent, "Hitler's own bodyguard of Black Shirts was drawn up in front of the rostrum separating him from the mass of Brown Shirts." The much-discussed appointment of a new Vice-Chancellor and of an heir presumptive to Hitler's throne in the event of the Chancellor's incapacity or death has not yet materialized, showing that the fight for supremacy among Hitler's aides is not yet decided. Disappointment awaits those, also, who were credulous enough to hope for a change in the party's policy on the Jewish and trade-union questions. Hitler cannot afford to sacrifice these important stage props in the Nazi scenery, lest he lose his still widespread popularity among the younger element and the thoughtless masses.

*October 9, 1935*

# JOE LOUIS NEVER SMILES
by Jonathan Mitchell

These people are here, 95,000 of them, because they have money. Down there on the field, men have paid $150 and more for a pair of tickets. Twenty thousand seats were stamped "ringside," and the customers out beyond third base were bilked. They should have known that Mike Jacobs, who is running this fight, is a smart man. No one can do anything to him, because he has the support of Hearst.

It feels good to have money again. Everyone in this crowd has money. The people who were swindled by Jacobs can afford it. Happy days are here again. Of course, things aren't so good, with twenty millions on relief. A man can be fired, and next morning there are ten men in line waiting for his job. But the unemployed have been around for a long time. No one can expect us to sit home and be sympathetic indefinitely.

It is a cold, clear night. The Stadium rises steeply around one half of the field. The floodlights on its upper edge are directed on the field and the bleachers, and the Stadium itself is black except for a steady row of red exit signs. Almost the whole of the immense field is covered with chairs. Jacobs has pushed the customers so closely together that all that can be seen of them, under the floodlights, is their microscopic, bright faces. They form neat rows, divided into plots by the aisles, like commercial Dutch tulip beds. There are acres of them, shining pinkly. Men in white, with high cardboard signs in their caps, move gravely about selling pop, like gardeners. The ring is at second base, and the movie operators' metal cage, high on a pole, that you used to see at fights is missing. The only movement comes from white tobacco smoke, rising in heavy waves. Through it you can see the American flags along the top of the Stadium, after the fashion of the opening verse of "The Star-Spangled Banner."

Near at hand the crowd is a respectable, bridge-playing one. About a fifth are Negroes, more carefully dressed and more mannerly than the whites. The little drunk with the long woolen muffler is certainly a Bronx dentist. He thinks correctly that the preliminary match now going on is poor, and keeps screaming, "Lousy." He brandishes a handful of crumpled bills and will give odds to anyone. There seems to be something painful in his past that he would like to explain, but the woolen muffler keeps blowing in his face, and communication between him and us is eternally frustrated.

There is a stirring in the aisles near the ring. The people who amount to something, and who are bowed through the police lines outside the Stadium, are entering. There are five state governors, the Republican National Committee, important business figures, and a large number of people whose press agents made them come so that their names would be in tomorrow's papers. Max Baer and his attendants are now at home plate. A dozen little pushing figures open up the crowd for him, and another dozen follow behind. Baer wears a white bathrobe, and has his hands on the shoulders of the state trooper in front of him. He nods to his many friends. Joe Louis, with another state trooper and other attendants, pushes in from third base. We learn afterward that his bride, Marva Trotter, is in the first row in a bright-green dress and orchids. Louis seems to see no one.

The floodlights are extinguished. Nothing exists except the brightly glowing ring. That is old Joe Humphries being lifted through the ropes, the man who announced fights before the depression. Since then he has been sick, and had a bad time. We have all been having a bad time, for that matter. Jack Dempsey squats in Baer's corner, but no one notices him. Humphries's assistant is bawling into the microphones: "Although Joe Louis is colored, he is a great fighter, in the class of Jack Johnson and the giants of the past." His voice fades away, and returns. "American sportsmanship, without regard to race, creed or color, is the talk of the world. Behave like gentlemen, whoever wins." Nearly two thousand police at the entrances of the Stadium are there to break up a possible race riot.

Baer has stripped. He has made a lot of money, Baer has. From all reports, he has spent a lot. He has played Broadway, Miami, and the other hot spots. Why shouldn't he have done so? Joe Louis takes off his flashing silk bathrobe, blue with a vermilion lining. It is the only extravagant gesture he makes. For all his youth, he is thick under the jaws, thick around the waist. His face is earnest, thoughtful, unsmiling.

Max Baer hasn't been, I suppose, what you would call a good boy. Joe Louis has, though. This is his greatest advantage. He once was taken to a night club, and it is reported that within ten minutes he wanted to go home. He said he was sleepy. He is supposed to have saved his money. Louis's father died when he was only two years old, down in Alabama. Until she married again, his mother had a hard struggle to support the children, and they were very dear to her. Louis is fond of his mother. She is a Lily of the Valley at her church in Detroit, where the family now lives. The Lilies are having a supper, or some such event, in a few days. She wants him there, and he is going with his new wife.

We are too far away to hear the gong. They are out in the middle of the ring, with a stubby little man in a white sweater moving softly around them. Baer holds both hands, open, clumsily in front of him.

Look at Joe Louis. He is leading with a straight left arm, his right hand before his face ready to block, and his right elbow tucked in to his ribs. That is scientific. That is what they teach in correspondence courses, or the night gymnasium classes of the Y.M.C.A. In the first thirty seconds, you can tell that he reeks of study, practice, study. Any romantic white person who believes that the Negro possesses a distinctive quality ought to see Louis. He suggests a gorilla or a jungle lion about as much as would an assistant professor at the Massachusetts Institute of Technology.

Baer stands flat-footed, with his great death-dealing right fist doubled by his side. He swings, and you can almost count three while the fist sails through the air. Louis moves sidewise and back, because he has been taught that if you move with a blow it can never hurt you. Baer's glove slides up the side of Louis' head harmlessly. He swings again and again, and, carefully and unhurriedly, Louis slips away. Look! Louis at last is going in. A left, a right and another left in close. Louis has pulled in his head, and with both arms up before him, he looks like a brown crayfish. All you can see is the twitching of his shoulders. So incredibly fast he is that the blows themselves are almost invisible. His hands cannot possibly move more than a few inches. Look! Baer is backing into a neutral corner. Louis is raining down blows. Baer's nose spurts blood, his lower lip bleeds, his face is red pulp.

Baer must have meant something to many people. He made wisecracks and went to parties and was a harbinger of the return of the old days. He was Broadway, he was California and Florida, he represented the possession of money once more and spending it. This saddle-colored, dour-faced, tongue-tied, studious youth, who is punishing Baer, punishing him more cruelly than human flesh and bones can endure, what does he represent? Baer stands with his hands hanging at his sides. He is helpless. He cannot hit the dissolving form before him, and he has never learned to protect himself. He holds his fine head, with its sweep of tightly curled hair and its great, brooding nose, high above his torturer. Pride alone keeps his head up, pride that has no tangible justification whatever. It was the same pride that kept Colonel Baratieri at Adowa, twenty years before Joe Louis was born.

It is the first round, and the fight is as good as over. Maybe it was foolish to spend money going to a fight. There must be many people, even down there in the ringside seats, who couldn't afford to spend what they did on tickets. No one can be sure of his job with twenty millions on relief. This is a crazy country, with people handing out a million dollars to Mike Jacobs and Hearst, while families right here in New York City are without enough to eat.

Round one is ended. Jack Dempsey vaults into the ring in a single, startling leap. Perhaps it is a trick. He must have vaulted from the ground to the edge of the ring platform, and from there into the ring itself. But from a distance, it seems one motion, and it is beautiful. Beside the man that Dempsey was, Baer and Louis and Schmeling are phonies. Nowadays everything, including men, is somehow different. The next three rounds are slaughter. In the second, Baer makes a wild, swinging, purposeless attack. For probably fifteen seconds, he appears formidable, but his attack has no substance inside it. With the third round, he is beaten, but Louis does not rush in, as Dempsey would have, to kill. Deliberately he circles Baer, with his earnest, thoughtful face, seeking an opening through which to strike without possible risk of injury. He takes no chance of a last, desperate fling of Baer's prodigious right hand. He is a planner. He is a person who studies the basic aspects of a problem and formulates a program. Apparently his studies are satisfactory, for he carefully steps up and knocks Baer down twice. Baer is on the canvas when time is called. Dempsey slides across the ring, picks Baer up like a mother, fusses over him until the fourth, and final, round. Baer once more is down. When the stubby referee, swinging his arm, reaches seven he tries to rouse himself. This turns out later to have been a fortunate gesture. The customers who suspected the honesty of the fight, and were unconvinced that a man could be half killed by fifty blows full on the jaw, were reassured as they watched Baer struggling to his feet. Had he been trying to throw the fight, they reasoned, he would have lain still. At the count of ten, Baer is on one knee, his swollen face wearing a comical expression of surprise.

The floodlights return us to time and space. Near at hand, there is remarkably little cheering, even from Negroes. They act as if, despite the police, they think it more prudent to restrain their feelings. There in the ring, placing his hand on Baer's shoulder in a stiff gesture, is the best fighter living, and the first Negro whose backers and trainer are men of his race. No white man shares in Louis' winnings. If the whites of the Boxing Commission will permit the match, he will be champion of the world.

All across the Stadium, the neat tulip beds are being broken up as tiny figures push into the aisles and toward the exits. A man with a small blond mustache is sobbing: "Maxie, why didn't you hit him?" Downtown in the Forties and Fifties, redecorated speakeasies will quickly be crammed to the doors and customers turned away. In Lenox Avenue in Harlem, Negroes will be tap-dancing from curb to curb, and singing: "The Baer goes over the mountain," and "Who won the fight?" Tomorrow the financial sections of the newspapers will report that business leaders regard the fight as final proof that the country's economic worries are past and a comfortable and prosperous future is assured.

*September 23, 1936*

# EUGENE O'NEILL
by Lionel Trilling

Whatever is unclear about Eugene O'Neill, one thing is certainly clear —his genius. We do not like the word nowadays, feeling that it is one of the blurb words of criticism. We demand that literature be a guide to life, and when we do that we put genius into a second place, for genius assures us of nothing but itself. Yet, when we stress the actionable conclusions of an artist's work, we are too likely to forget the power of genius itself, quite apart from its conclusions. The spectacle of the human mind in action is vivifying; the explorer need discover nothing so long as he has adventured. Energy, scope, courage—these may be admirable in themselves. And in the end these are often what endure best. The ideas expressed by works of the imagination may be built into the social fabric and taken for granted; or they may be rejected; or they may be outgrown. But the force of their utterance comes to us over millennia. We do not read Sophocles or Aeschylus for the right answer; we read them for the force with which they represent life and attack its moral complexity. In O'Neill, despite the many failures of his art and thought, this force is inescapable.

But a writer's contemporary audience is inevitably more interested in the truth of his content than in the force of its expression; and O'Neill himself has always been ready to declare his own ideological preoccupation. His early admirers—and their lack of seriousness is a reproach to American criticism—were inclined to insist that O'Neill's content was unimportant as compared to his purely literary interest and that he injured his art when he tried to think. But the appearance of *Days Without End* has made perfectly clear the existence of an organic and progressive unity of thought in all O'Neill's work and has brought it into the critical range of the two groups whose own thought is most sharply formulated, the Catholic and the Communist. Both discovered what O'Neill had frequently announced, the religious nature of all his effort.

Not only has O'Neill tried to encompass more of life than most American writers of his time but, almost alone among them, he has persistently tried to *solve* it. When we understand this, we understand that his stage devices are no fortuitous technique; his masks and abstractions, his double personalities, his drumbeats and engine rhythms are the integral and necessary expression of his temper of mind and the task it set itself. Realism is uncongenial to that mind and that task;

and it is not in realistic plays like *Anna Christie* and *The Straw*, but rather in such plays as *The Hairy Ape, Lazarus Laughed* and *The Great God Brown*, where he is explaining the world in parable, symbol and myth, that O'Neill is most creative. Not the minutiae of life, not its feel and color and smell, not its nuance and humor, but its "great inscrutable forces" are his interest. He is always moving toward the finality which philosophy sometimes, and religion always, promises. Life and death, good and evil, spirit and flesh, male and female, the all and the one, Anthony and Dionysus—O'Neill's is a world of these antithetical absolutes such as religion rather than philosophy conceives, a world of pluses and minuses; and his literary effort is an algebraic attempt to solve the equations.

In one of O'Neill's earliest one-act plays, the now unprocurable *Fog*, a Poet, a Business Man, and a Woman with a Dead Child, shipwrecked and adrift in an open boat, have made fast to an iceberg. When they hear the whistle of a steamer, the Business Man's impulse is to call for help, but the Poet prevents him lest the steamer be wrecked on the fog-hidden berg. But a searching party picks up the castaways, and the rescuers explain that they had been guided to the spot by a child's cries; the child, however, has been dead a whole day. This little play is a crude sketch of the moral world that O'Neill is to exploit. He is to give an ever-increasing importance to the mystical implications of the Dead Child, but his earliest concern is with the struggle between the Poet and the Business Man.

It is, of course, a struggle as old as morality, especially interesting to Europe all through its industrial nineteenth century, and it was engaging America in the second decade of its twentieth. A conscious artistic movement had raised its head to declare irreconcilable strife between the creative and the possessive ideal. O'Neill was an integral part—indeed, he became the very symbol—of that Provincetown group which represented the growing rebellion of the American intellectual against a business civilization. In 1914 his revolt was simple and socialistic; in a poem in *The Call* he urged the workers of the world not to fight, asking them if they wished to "bleed and groan—for Guggenheim" and "give your lives—for Standard Oil." By 1917 his feeling against business had become symbolized and personal. "My soul is a submarine," he said in a poem in *The Masses*:

My aspirations are torpedoes.
I will hide unseen
Beneath the surface of life
Watching for ships,
Dull, heavy-laden merchant ships,
Rust-eaten, grimy galleons of commerce
Wallowing with obese assurance,
Too sluggish to fear or wonder,

Mocked by the laughter of the waves
And the spit of disdainful spray.

I will destroy them
Because the sea is beautiful.

The ships against which O'Neill directed his torpedoes were the cultural keels laid in the yards of American business, and their hulls were first to be torn by artistic realism. Although we now see the often gross sentimentality of the *S.S. Glencairn* plays and remember with O'Neill's own misgiving the vaudeville success of *In the Zone*, we cannot forget that, at the time, the showing of a forecastle on the American stage was indeed something of a torpedo. Not, it is true, into the sides of Guggenheim and Standard Oil, but of the little people who wallowed complacently in their wake.

But O'Neill, not content with staggering middle-class complacency by a representation of how the other half lives, undertook to scrutinize the moral life of the middle class and dramatized the actual struggle between Poet and Business Man. In his first long play, *Beyond the Horizon*, the dreamer destroys his life by sacrificing his dream to domesticity; and the practical creator, the farmer, destroys his by turning from wheat-raising to wheat-gambling. It is a conflict O'Neill is to exploit again and again. Sometimes, as in *Ile* or *Gold*, the lust for gain transcends itself and becomes almost a creative ideal, but always its sordid origin makes it destructive. To O'Neill the acquisitive man, kindly and insensitive, practical and immature, became a danger to life and one that he never left off attacking.

But it developed, strangely, that the American middle class had no strong objection to being attacked and torpedoed; it seemed willing to be sunk for the insurance that was paid in a new strange coin. The middle class found that it consisted of two halves, bourgeoisie and booboisie. The booboisie might remain on the ship but the bourgeoisie could, if it would, take refuge on the submarine. Mencken and Nathan, who sponsored the O'Neill torpedoes, never attacked the middle class but only its boobyhood. Boobish and sophisticated: these were the two categories of art; spiritual freedom could be bought at the price of finding *Jurgen* profound. And so, while the booboisie prosecuted *Desire under the Elms*, the bourgeoisie swelled the subscription lists of the Provincetown Playhouse and helped the Washington Square Players to grow into the Theatre Guild. An increasingly respectable audience awarded O'Neill no less than three Pulitzer prizes, the medal of the American Academy of Arts and Sciences and a Yale Doctorate of Letters.

O'Neill did not win his worldly success by the slightest compromise of sincerity. Indeed, his charm consisted in his very integrity and hieratic earnestness. His position changed, not absolutely, but relatively to his audience, which was now the literate middle class caught up with the intellectual middle class. O'Neill was no longer a submarine; he had become a physician of souls. Beneath his iconoclasm his audience sensed reassurance.

The middle class is now in such literary disrepute that a writer's ability to please it is taken as the visible mark of an internal rottenness. But the middle class is people; prick them and they bleed, and whoever speaks sincerely to and for flesh and blood deserves respect. O'Neill's force derives in large part from the force of the moral and psychical upheaval of the middle class; it wanted certain of its taboos broken and O'Neill broke them.

Whoever writes sincerely about the middle class must consider the nature and the danger of the morality of "ideals," those phosphorescent remnants of a dead religion with which the middle class meets the world. This had been Ibsen's great theme, and now O'Neill undertook to investigate for America the destructive power of the ideal—not merely the sordid ideal of the Business Man but even the "idealistic" ideal of the Poet. The Freudian psychology was being discussed, and O'Neill dramatized its simpler aspects in *Diff'rent*, to show the effects of the repression of life. Let the ideal of chastity repress the vital forces, he was saying, and from this fine girl you will get a filthy harridan. The modern life of false ideals crushes the affirmative and creative nature of man; Pan, forbidden the light and warmth of the sun, grows "sensitive and self-conscious and proud and revengeful"—becomes the sneering Mephistophelean mask of Dion.

The important word is *self-conscious*, for "ideals" are part of the "cheating gestures which constitute the vanity of personality." "Life is all right if you let it alone," says Cybel, the Earth Mother of *The Great God Brown*. But the poet of *Welded* cannot let it alone; he and his wife, the stage directions tell us, move in circles of light that represent "auras of egotism," and the high ideals of their marriage are but ways each ego uses to get possession of the other. O'Neill had his answer to this problem of the possessive, discrete personality. Egotism and idealism, he tells us, are twin evils growing from man's suspicion of his life, and the remedy is the laughter of Lazarus—"a triumphant, blood-stirring call to that ultimate attainment in which all prepossession with self is lost in an ecstatic affirmation of Life." The ecstatic affirmation of Life, pure and simple, is salvation. In the face of death and pain, man must reply with the answer of Kublai Khan in *Marco Millions:* "Be proud of life! Know in your heart that the living of life can be noble! Be exalted by life! Be inspired by death! Be humbly proud! Be proudly grateful!"

It may be that the individual life is not noble and that it is full of pain and defeat; it would seem that Eileen Carmody, in *The Straw*, and Anna Christie are betrayed by life. But no. The "straw" is the knowledge that life is a "hopeless hope"—but still a hope. And nothing matters if you can conceive the whole of life. "Fog, fog, fog all bloody time" is the chord of resolution of *Anna Christie.* "You can't see vhere you vas going, no. Only dat ole davil, sea—she knows." The individual does not know, but life—the sea—knows.

To affirm that life exists and is somehow good—this, then, became O'Neill's quasi-religious poetic function, nor is it difficult to see why the middle class welcomed it. "Brown will still need me," says Dion, "to reassure him he's alive." What to do with life O'Neill cannot say, but there it is. For Ponce de Leon it is the Fountain of Eternity, "the Eternal Becoming which is Beauty." There it is, somehow glorious, somehow meaningless. In the face of despair one remembers that "Always spring comes again bearing life! Always forever again. Spring again! Life again!" To this cycle, even to the personal annihilation in it, the individual must say "Yes." Man inhabits a naturalistic universe, and his glory lies in his recognition of its nature and assenting to it; man's soul, no less than the stars and the dust, is part of the Whole and is willing to be absorbed by it. In short, O'Neill solves the problem of evil by making explicit what men have always found to be the essence of tragedy—the courageous affirmation of life in the face of individual defeat.

But neither a naturalistic view of the universe nor a rapt assent to life constitutes a complete philosophic answer. Naturalism is the noble and realistic attitude that prepares the way for an answer; the tragic affirmation is the emotional crown of a philosophy. Spinoza—with whom O'Neill at this stage of his thought has an obvious affinity—placed between the two an ethic that arranged human values and made the world possible to live in. But O'Neill, faced with a tragic universe, unable to go beyond the febrilely passionate declaration, "Life is," finds the world impossible to live in. The naturalistic universe becomes too heavy a burden for him; its spirituality vanishes; it becomes a universe of cruelly blind matter. "Teach me to be resigned to be an atom," cries Darrell, the frustrated scientist of *Strange Interlude;* and for Nina life is but "a strange dark interlude in the electrical display of God the father"—who is a God deaf, dumb and blind. O'Neill, unable now merely to accept the tragic universe and unable to support it with man's whole strength—his intellect and emotion—prepares to support it with man's weakness: his blind faith.

For the non-Catholic reader O'Neill's explicitly religious solution is likely to be not only insupportable but incomprehensible. Neither Saint Francis nor Saint Thomas can tell us much about it; it is neither a mystical ecstasy nor the reasoned proof of assumptions. But Pascal can tell us a great deal, for O'Neill's faith, like Pascal's, is a poetic utilitarianism: he needs it and *will* have it. O'Neill rejects naturalism and materialism as Pascal had rejected Descartes and all science. He too is frightened by "the eternal silence of the infinite spaces." Like Pascal, to whom the details of life and the variety and flux of the human mind were repugnant, O'Neill feels that life is empty—having emptied it—and can fill it only by faith in a loving God. The existence of such a God, Pascal knew, cannot be proved save by the heart's need, but this seemed sufficient and he stood ready to stupefy his reason to maintain his faith. O'Neill will do no less. It is, perhaps, the inevitable way of modern Catholicism in a hostile world.

O'Neill's rejection of materialism involved the familiar pulpit confusion of philosophical materialism with "crass" materialism, that is, with the preference of physical to moral well-being. It is, therefore, natural that *Dynamo*, the play in which he makes explicit his anti-materialism, should present characters who are mean and little—that, though it contains an Earth Mother, she is not the wise and tragic Cybel but the fat and silly Mrs. Fife, the bovine wife of the atheist dynamo-tender. She, like other characters in the play, allies herself with the Dynamo-God, embodiment both of the materialistic universe and of modern man's sense of his own power. But this new god can only frustrate the forces of life, however much it at first seems life's ally against the Protestant denials, and those who worship it become contemptible and murderous.

And the contempt for humanity which pervades *Dynamo* continues in *Mourning Becomes Electra*, creating, in a sense, the utter hopelessness of that tragedy. Aeschylus had ended his Atreus trilogy on a note of social reconciliation—after the bloody deeds and the awful pursuit of the Furies, society confers its forgiveness, the Furies are tamed to deities of hearth and field: "This day there is a new Order born"; but O'Neill's version has no touch of this resolution. There is no forgiveness in *Mourning Becomes Electra*, because, while there is as yet no forgiving God in O'Neill's cosmos, there is no society either, only a vague chorus of contemptible townspeople. "There's no one left to punish me," says Lavinia. "I've got to punish myself."

It is the ultimate of individual arrogance, the final statement of a universe in which society has no part. For O'Neill, since as far back as *The Hairy Ape*, there has been only the individual and the universe. The social organism has meant nothing. His Mannons, unlike the Atreides, are not monarchs with a relation to the humanity about them, a humanity that can forgive because it can condemn. They act their crimes on the stage of the infinite. The mention of human law bringing them punishment is startlingly incongruous and it is inevitable that O'Neill, looking for a law, should turn to a divine law.

Forgiveness comes in *Ah, Wilderness!*, the satyr play that follows the tragedy, and it is significant that O'Neill should have interrupted the composition of *Days Without End* to write it. With the religious answer of the more serious play firm in his mind, with its establishment of the divine law, O'Neill can, for the first time, render the sense and feel of common life, can actually be humorous. Now the family is no longer destructively possessive as he has always represented it, but creatively sympathetic. The revolt of the young son—his devotion to rebels and hedonists, to Shaw, Ibsen and Swinburne—is but the mark of adolescence and in the warm round of forgiving life he will become wisely acquiescent to a world that is not in the least terrible.

But the idyllic life of *Ah, Wilderness!*, for all its warmth, is essentially ironical, almost cynical. For it is only when all magnitude has been removed from humanity by the religious answer and placed in the Church and its God that life can be seen as simple and good. The pluses and minuses of man must be made to cancel out as nearly as possible, the equation must be solved to equal nearly zero, before peace may be found. The hero of *Days Without End* has lived for years in a torturing struggle with the rationalistic, questioning "half" of himself which has led him away from piety to atheism, thence to socialism, next to unchastity and finally to the oblique attempt to murder his beloved wife. It is not until he makes an act of submissive faith at the foot of the Cross and thus annihilates the doubting mind, the root of all evil, that he can find peace.

But the annihilation of the questioning mind also annihilates the multitudinous world. *Days Without End*, perhaps O'Neill's weakest play, is cold and bleak; life is banished from it by the vision of the Life Eternal. Its religious content is expressed not so much by the hero's priestly uncle, wise, tolerant, humorous in the familiar literary convention of modern Catholicism, as by the hero's wife, a humorless, puritanical woman who lives on the pietistic-romantic love she bears her husband and on her sordid ideal of his absolute chastity. She is the very embodiment of all the warping, bullying idealism that O'Neill had once attacked. Now, however, he gives credence to this plaster-saintliness, for it represents for him the spiritual life of absolutes. Now for the first time he is explicit in his rejection of all merely human bulwarks against the pain and confusion of life—finds in the attack upon capitalism almost an attack upon God, scorns socialism and is disgusted with the weakness of those who are disgusted with social individualism. The peace of the absolute can be bought only at the cost of blindness to the actual.

The philosophic position would seem to be a final one: O'Neill has crept into the dark womb of Mother Church and pulled the universe in with him. Perhaps the very violence of the gesture with which he has taken the position of passivity should remind us of his force and of what such force may yet do even in that static and simple dark. Yet it is scarcely a likely place for O'Neill to remember Dion Anthony's warning: "It isn't enough to be [life's] creature. You've got to create her or she requests you to destroy yourself."

*October 14, 1936 [John L. Lewis]*

# JOHN THE GIANT-KILLER
by Jonathan Mitchell

John Llewellyn Lewis is not easy to explain. He is so complex, indeed, that a number of quarreling schools of thought have sprung up around him, as they have around the time-space concept, or the origin of the American Indian. Mr. Lewis is a labor leader of more than twenty years' standing, the president of the United Mine Workers and, until recently, the single most powerful individual in the A.F. of L. At the moment, however, he is at the head of a fast, smashing attempt to unionize the ten million workers of the country's mass industries, as perilous a challenge as labor has ever made to the employing class. The problem is to reconcile this with Mr. Lewis's past.

An old-time A.F. of L. leader like Mr. Lewis ought to be a conservative. It seems unnatural to find the president of an A.F. of L. union risking his own position, and his union's resources, in what is likely to be a desperate struggle with the employers of steel, automobiles, rubber, radio and glass. The great organizing campaigns in the past have usually been led by left-wing labor militants—someone, for example, like Mr. William Z. Foster in 1919. Professor John R. Commons and other students of the American labor movement long ago split labor leaders into two types, the business type, exemplified by Mr. Samuel Gompers, and the agitational type, of which the greatest was perhaps Mr. Eugene V. Debs. Seemingly these two types are joined in Mr. Lewis, making him a white blackbird in labor history.

For that matter, it makes him a comparative rarity among human beings. The fact that most labor leaders, once they attain well-paid jobs, power and dignity, tend to grow conservative proves no more than that they are like the rest of us.

One of the current explanations of Mr. Lewis seeks to minimize his extraordinary quality—unsuccessfully, in my opinion. Mr. Lewis is portrayed as belonging to the business type of labor leader, and his present militancy is ascribed chiefly to the fact that he has been cursed, or blessed, by an extremely able, intelligent opposition within the United Mine Workers. Many of these oppositionists have been Socialists, or men with Socialist backgrounds, and for a number of years Mr. Lewis fought them with great ruthlessness. However—so this explanation runs—the increasing sickness of the coal industry and the dwindling membership of the union during the postwar decade compelled him to recognize the inadequacy of traditional A.F. of L. policies. Under the goading of the oppositionists, he reluctantly became convinced of the necessity, first of government intervention in the coal industry, and second of at least some degree of social planning in the industrial system.

This explanation, then, attempts to show that Mr. Lewis's militancy has been forced on him, against his will, by the anarchy of coal and the pressure of the left-wingers in his union. In support of this theory, it is argued that as late as 1925, when Mr. Lewis published his only book, *Miners' Fight for American Standards,* he apparently had implicit faith in the workings of free capitalism. By 1928, however, after continuous intra-union wrangling, he abruptly sponsored a bill in Congress for the rationalization of coal under federal auspices—which was the precise action that the oppositionists had been advocating.

This readiness to accept government intervention in industry, a shift entailing a clear break with the Gompers tradition of the A.F. of L., can also be shown to have been the chief factor leading to Mr. Lewis's present national leadership. It enabled him to sense the full potentialities for labor of the N.R.A., and made him sympathetic to the aims of the New Deal. In return, Mr. Roosevelt adopted him as the principal spokesman for labor, and entrusted him with far-reaching official duties. During the last three and a half years, he has become only a little less celebrated than figures like Shirley Temple and Joe Louis. To the millions of unorganized workers in the mass industries, he has come to stand as their natural champion.

All of this is true, but, at least in my opinion, it is not the whole story. Mr. Lewis learned a great deal of fundamental economics and labor philosophy from the oppositionists, but he did not learn to become a militant. Certainly it is misleading to suggest that Mr. Lewis is being driven, either by events or his associates, into the steel-organizing campaign. He is going into it like an Andalusian bull—head down and eyes open.

There is a second explanation of Mr. Lewis, offered by his enemies, of whom he has a notable collection. It is that he is power-crazy. With cynical unanimity, Mr. Lewis's recent colleagues of the A.F. of L.'s executive council and the officers of the American Iron and Steel Institute profess to see no other possible motive in his present course. This seems to me vicious nonsense. Mr. Lewis has a very just appreciation of the value of power and has fought titanic fights to keep the headship of the United Mine Workers. In these fights he used violent and dictatorial tactics that some of his radical opponents cannot forget. But about the last thing that a man solely concerned with power would do would be to take the desperate risks Mr. Lewis is now taking. The steel-organizing campaign is no setup. Presumably the steel companies cannot defy their employees and the conscience of the country indefinitely, but anyone who supposes that Mr. Eugene Grace, Mr. Ernest

Weir or Mr. Tom Girdler mean to surrender without a fight, in which they will exert the last ounce of their immense resources, is deluding himself. Mr. Lewis might perhaps be convicted of being a magnificent gambler, but not of having a miserly lust for power.

There is a final explanation of Mr. Lewis, given by the intimate group around him. It is simply that he is an idealist, a man whose life is dedicated to the struggle of the working class. This is a fairly roseate image of Mr. Lewis. He is no Eugene V. Debs, giving away his overcoat to shelterless men on wintry nights and declaring that always he would stand with the most despised. Nevertheless, I believe it has an important element of truth.

The most obvious fact about Mr. Lewis is that he is a coal miner, and the son of a coal miner. It seems to me equally obvious that the miners, all over the world, occupy a special place in the labor movement—so special, in fact, that the ordinary categories of conservative and radical, into which most of us can be dropped, hardly apply to them. There are many reasons why this should be so, one of which is that mining requires a recklessness and fortitude needed in no other industry. The nature of mining seems to act automatically to sift out the most militant individuals of the working class, much as screens set up at the foot of tipples sift out the best grades of coal. Whether or not this is true, it is a demonstrable fact that the miners are at once the most responsible and the most militant group in the labor movements of many countries.

Unionism in the Welsh and Scottish coal-mining areas has a special quality that is part of Mr. Lewis's heritage. It has always been hopelessly tangled up with evangelical religion. Possibly the horrors of the early Welsh coal mines, where half-naked mothers acted as draft animals in the black, suffocating galleries, served to identify unionism with the path to Heaven.

John L. Lewis is himself as American as a flung pop bottle at a baseball game. But this religious bias, the feeling that heaven is a place where angels all carry union cards, is a part of his birthright. Nearly every formal speech made by Mr. Lewis is studded with Biblical quotations. For example, at the meeting of the state chairmen of Labor's Non-Partisan League in Washington, he wished to describe the disaster to labor that would follow Mr. Roosevelt's defeat. Under a Republican administration, he said, "the voice of labor, like that of Rachel in the wilderness, rising in wails and lamentations and pleas for succor, will be unanswered." This is preacher's talk. Continually there pops up in his speeches an identification between the tribes of the Bible, persecuted but beloved by God, and the men and women of the working class.

Mr. Lewis is class-conscious to a degree relatively uncommon in America. It is something that a child growing up in a coal miner's home must have absorbed intuitively, in the same way that it learned to talk. Because his father took part in a strike and was afterward blacklisted by the coal operators, the lesson was terribly underscored for John Lewis. When in 1933 he became a member of the N.R.A.'s Labor Advisory Board, he was thrown for the first time in his life into daily, intimate contact with the heads of American industry. They readily accepted him as a man of astonishing energy and exceptional practical wisdom. They endeavored to make him feel that he was one of themselves. Under this friendliness, Mr. Lewis grew increasingly restive. An eyewitness tells of a conference at the N.R.A. headquarters at which Mr. Lewis abruptly got up from his chair and began to explain, in the slightly ponderous manner he affects for important occasions, the gulf between the businessmen around him and himself. He was not angry, but he wanted to make clear that all they stood for was wrong, that he had fought against them in the past and intended to do so in the future. When this had had time to sink in, the conference was resumed.

This coal-miner background of Mr. Lewis needs to be considered in deciding whether he belongs to the business or agitational type of labor leader, whether he is a conservative or a militant. He has never been a conservative in the sense that Mr. Gompers was, or that Messrs. Hutcheson, Wharton, Frey, and the rest of the majority faction of the A.F. of L. are today. In the postwar decade, Mr. Lewis on a number of occasions made peace with the coal operators north of the Ohio River on terms that were disadvantageous to his followers, and was bitterly criticized by the oppositionists in his union for doing so. But the record shows, I think, that these were strategic truces made necessary by the desperate warfare in progress on other fronts, primarily with the non-union operators of West Virginia, Tennessee and Alabama. Whenever there has been a reasonable chance of making gains for his men, he has fought the mineowners, and fought with a grim, intolerant joy.

Mr. Lewis became president of his union in 1919, when he was thirty-nine. Within two years the coal industry had started on its long, catastrophic slide to bankruptcy, and from then on he was fighting savagely and brilliantly, against union operators, against nonunion operators, against reactionary rivals in the union like Mr. Frank Farrington, against radicals like Mr. Alexander Howat and the Progressive Miners' group. During this period, not merely the oppositionists within the union, but almost everyone else in the country, gave him advice. The coal industry was investigated by the government, by scientific bodies, by church foundations and social-work groups. Only the German war guilt has as extensive a modern literature as coal. It can be argued, as the oppositionists argue, that Mr. Lewis moved toward government intervention only after the need for it had been painfully beaten into his head. It can also be argued that he moved the first instant that public opinion had been sufficiently aroused to justify it.

In 1933, with the New Deal and the triumphant success of the United Mine Workers' organizing campaign in the nonunion coal fields, Mr. Lewis found himself for the first time in years without a fight on his hands. Almost at once, he plunged into the task of organizing the workers of the mass industries. It is not necessary to ascribe this to his earlier ambition. He was a member of the N.R.A.'s Labor Advisory Board, and the unions springing up spontaneously in the mass industries turned inevitably to him for help. The rank-and-file steel committee of 1934, and the automobile workers of Detroit, became his special charges. Step by step he was led to his break with the A.F. of L. and the inauguration of the C.I.O.

Probably no true radical of the labor movement could be head of a strong, rich union like the United Mine Workers. Mr. Lewis lives like a conservative labor leader, dresses like one except for his white hat— and most of the time behaves like one. Nevertheless, unlike the rest of us, he cannot easily be crowded into either radical or conservative compartments. He is a coal miner, and a man of more than natural size.

*March 24, 1937 [Fellow Passenger]*

# I HAVE A THING TO TELL YOU
by Thomas Wolfe

It is astonishing how short a time it takes to get acquainted on a journey. As we made our way a second time along the corridors of the speeding train I reflected that already Stefanowski and I were as accustomed to each other as if we had been friends for many years. As to the new-found friends in our compartment, we were delighted with them all. In the most extraordinary way, and in the space of fifteen minutes' time, we seemed to have entered into the lives of all these people and they in ours. Now we were not only immensely interested in the information they had given us about themselves; we were as warmly, eagerly concerned with the problems that confronted them as if their troubles were our own.

During a long and sumptuous meal—a meal that began with brandy, proceeded over a fine bottle of Bernkasteler and wound up over coffee and more brandy and a good cigar, a meal on which we were both exuberantly determined to spend the remainder of our German money, we discussed our companions again. The little woman, we agreed, was charming. And the young man, although diffident and shy, was very nice. We even had a word of praise for Fuss-And-Fidget now. After we had cracked his crusty shell the old codger was not bad. He really was quite friendly underneath.

"And it does show," said Stefanowski quietly, "how good people really are, how easy it is to get along with one another in this world, how people really like each other—if only—"

"—if only—" I said, and nodded.

"These damned politicians," Stefanowski said.

At length we called for our bill and paid it. Stefanowski dumped his marks upon the table, counted them. "You'll have to help me out," he said. "How many have you got?"

I dumped mine out. We had enough to pay the bill, to give the waiter something extra. And there was enough left over for a double jolt of brandy and a good cigar.

So, grinning with satisfaction, in which our waiter joined amiably as he read our purpose, we paid the bill, ordered the brandy and cigars, and, full of food, of drink, and of the pleasant knowledge of a job well done, we puffed contentedly on our cigars.

We were now running through the great industrial region of western Germany. The pleasant landscape had been darkened by the grime and smoke of enormous works. Now it was grim with the skeletons of enormous smelting and refining plants, disfigured with great heaps of slag, with mountainous dumps. It was a new portion of the land, one of the few I had not seen before. It was brutal, smoky, dense with life, the grimy warrens of industrial towns. But it had the brutal fascination of these places too, the thrilling power of raw, enormous works.

Stefanowski informed me that we were already almost at the border and that, since our own coach went directly through to Paris, we should have no additional need of money for porter's fees.

This made us remember the difficulties of our fellow travelers, who were Germans. We agreed that the existing law which permitted native citizens to take only ten marks from the country was, for people in the business circumstances of our little blond companion and old Fuss-And-Fidget, a very trying one.

At this moment Stefanowski had a brilliant inspiration, the result of his own generous impulse. "But why," he said, "why can't we help them?"

"How? In what way can we help them?"

"Why," he said, "I have here a permit that allows me to take twenty-three marks out of the country. You have no permit, but everyone is allowed—"

"To take ten marks," I said and nodded. "So you mean then," I concluded, "that since each of us has spent his German money—"

"But can still take as much as is allowed out of the country—yes," he said. "So we could suggest it to them—" he went on.

"—that they give us some of their marks to keep, you mean?"

He nodded. "Yes. It is not much, of course. But it might help."

No sooner said than seized upon. We were almost jubilantly elated at this opportunity of doing some slight service for these people to whom we had taken such a liking. At this moment, even while we were smiling confirmation at each other, a man in uniform came through the car, paused at our table—which was the only one that was now occupied—and quietly but authoritatively informed us that the Pass-Control had come upon the train and that we must return at once to our compartment to await examination. We rose, knowing now we had no time to lose, hastened back along the coaches of the swaying train, entered our compartment again and immediately told our fellows that the inspection would soon begin and that the officials were on the train.

There was a flurry of excitement. Everyone began to get ready. The blond lady took out her purse and passport and with a worried look began to count her money. Stefanowski watched her quietly for a moment and then, taking out his own certificate and showing it, remarked that he was officially allowed possession of the sum of twenty-three marks, that he had had the sum in his possession, but now had spent it. I took this as my cue and remarked that I too had spent the ten marks that the law allowed me.

Our little blond companion looked eagerly at both of us and read the friendship of our meaning.

"Then you mean?" she said, and gleefully—"but it would be wonderful, of course, if you would!"

"Have you as much as twenty-three marks?" said Stefanowski.

"Yes," she nodded quickly, with a worried look, "I have more than that. But if you would take the twenty-three and keep them until we are past the frontier—"

He stretched out his hand. "Give them to me," he said quietly. The transfer was completed, the money in his pocket, in the wink of an eye.

In another moment Fuss-And-Fidget had taken ten marks from his pocket and without a word passed them across to me. I thrust the money in my pocket, and we all sat back, a little flushed, excited but triumphant, trying to look composed.

A few minutes later an official opened the compartment door, saluted and asked for our passports. He inspected Stefanowski's first, found everything in order, took his certificate, saw his twenty-three marks, stamped the passport and returned it to him.

Then he turned to me. I gave him my passport and the various papers certifying my possession of American currency. He thumbed through the pages of the passport, which were now almost completely covered with stamps and entries, and finally smiled quite kindly, and returned my passport to me. Then he inspected the passports of the little blond lady, her companion and Fuss-And-Fidget. Everything, apparently, was in order, save that the lady had confessed to the possession of more than twenty marks, and the official regretfully informed her that he must take from her anything in excess of ten. It would be held at the frontier and restored to her, of course, when she returned. She smiled ruefully, shrugged her shoulders, and gave the man twelve marks. All other matters were evidently now in order, for the man saluted and withdrew.

So it was over then! We all drew a deep breath of relief, and commiserated our charming lady friend upon her loss. But I think we were all quietly jubilant, too, to know her loss had been no greater, that we had been able in some degree to lessen it. I asked Fuss-And-Fidget if I should return his money now or later on. He told me to wait until we had crossed the frontier into Belgium. At the same time, he made some casual explanation, to which none of us paid any serious attention at the time, to the effect that his ticket was good only to the frontier, and that he would utilize the fifteen minutes of our wait at Aachen, the frontier town, to buy a ticket for the remainder of the trip to Paris.

We were now, in fact, approaching Aachen. The train was slackening speed. We were going through a pleasant countryside, a smiling landscape of green fields and gentle hills, unobtrusively, mildly, somehow unmistakably European. The seared and blasted districts of the mines and factories were behind us. We were entering the outskirts of a pleasant town.

This was Aachen. In another moment the train was slowing to a halt before the station. We had reached the frontier. There was to be a wait of fifteen minutes and a change of engines. All of us got out— Fuss-And-Fidget to get a ticket, the others to stretch their legs and get a breath of air.

My Polish friend and I got out and walked forward along the platform to inspect the locomotive. The German locomotive which would here be supplanted by its Belgian successor was a magnificent machine, which bore in every line the evidence of the tremendous engineering talent that had created it.

Knowing how vivid, swift and fugitive are those poignant first impressions that come at the moment when we change from one country to another, I waited with an almost feverish interest for the approach of the Belgian locomotive. I knew in advance it would not be so good as the German one, because the energy, the intelligence, the strength and the integrity which produced it were inferior, but I was eagerly sensitized to observe the exact degree and quality of these differences between the powerful, solid and indomitable race that I was leaving and the little people I would now encounter.

Presently we walked back along the platform, found our little blond-haired lady and, flanking her on either side, began to stroll up and down beside the train. At length, observing the station clock and seeing that the moment scheduled for departure had already come, we moved quickly back toward our own coach and our own compartment.

As we approached, it was evident that something had happened. There were no signs of departure. The conductor and the station guard stood together on the platform. No warning signal had been given. And, moreover, there was now evident a kind of subdued tension, a sense of crisis that made my pulse beat quicker as I approached.

I have often observed this phenomenon in life; its manifestations under certain conditions are nearly always identical. A man has leaped or fallen, for example, from a high building to the pavement of a city street. Or a man has been shot, or beaten. He has been struck by a motorcar; or again, a man is dying quietly on the street before the eyes of other men. But always, the manifestation of the crowd is just the same. Even before you see the faces of the people, when you see their backs, their posture, the position of the head and shoulders, you know what has happened.

You do not know, of course, the precise circumstance, but what you sense immediately is the final stage of tragedy. You know that someone has just died or is dying, and in the terrible eloquence of backs and shoulders, the *feeding* silence of the watching men, you sense a tragedy that is even deeper. It is the tragedy of man's cruelty and his lust for pain, the tragic weakness that corrupts him, that he loathes but that he cannot cure.

And always the manifestation of this tragedy is just the same. Even before one arrives one knows from this silent eloquence of shoulders, backs and heads that something ruinous and horrible has happened. I knew the signs too well. And now, as I hastened along beside the train and saw the people gathered in the corridor in that same feeding posture, waiting, watching, in that deadly fascinated silence, I was sure that once again in life I was about to witness death.

That was the first thing that came to me—and I believe to all of us— that someone had died. And what stunned us, what stopped us short, appalled, was that death had come to our compartment. The shades were tightly drawn, the door closed, the whole place sealed in-penetrably. We had started to get on the train when this thing burst upon us. And now we saw our lady's young companion standing at the window in the corridor. He motioned quickly to us, a gesture warning us to remain where we were. And as he did, it flashed over all of us that the subject of this tragic visitation was the nervous little man who had been the companion of our voyage since morning.

The stillness of the scene, the shuttered blankness of that closed compartment, were horrible. Even as we stared, appalled and horror-stricken, at that fatal curtained closet, which had so short a time ago housed the lives of all of us, and which had now become the tenement of death, the curtained door of the compartment was opened and closed quickly, and a man came out.

He was an official, a burly-looking fellow, with a visored cap, a jacket of olive green. He was a man of forty-five or more, a Germanic type with high blunt cheekbones, a florid face and tawny mustaches, combed out sprouting, in the Kaiser Wilhelm way. His head was shaven, and there were thick creases at the base of the skull and across his fleshy neck. He came out, climbed down clumsily to the platform, signaled excitedly to another officer and climbed back into the train again.

It was a familiar type, one that I had seen and smiled at often, but one that now became, under these ominous circumstances, sinisterly unpleasant. Even the man's physical weight and clumsiness, the awkward way he got down from the train, the awkward way he climbed up again, the thickness of his waist, the unpleasant width and coarseness of his clumsy buttocks, the way his sprouting mustaches seemed to quiver with passion and authority, the sound of his guttural voice, raised coarsely, somewhat phlegmily, as he shouted to his fellow officer, the sense that he was fairly panting with an inflamed authority —all these symptoms had now become, under the ominous prescience of the moment, loathsome, sinsister, repellent.

All of a sudden, without knowing why, I felt myself trembling with a murderous and incomprehensible anger. I wanted to smash that fat neck with the creases in it. I wanted to pound that inflamed and blunted face into a jelly. I wanted to kick square and hard, bury my foot, dead center in the obscene fleshiness of those clumsy buttocks. And I knew that I was helpless, that all of us were. Like all Americans, I had never liked the police or the kind of personal authority that it sanctifies. But this feeling, this intensity, with its murderously helpless rage, was different. I felt impotent, shackled, unable to stir against the walls of an obscene but unshakable authority.

The official with the sprouting mustaches, accompanied now by his colleagues, opened the curtained doors of the compartment again, and now I saw that they were not alone. Two other officials were in the compartment and our nervous little companion—no, he was not dead!—he sat there *huddled*, facing them. He sat looking up at them as they bent over him. His face was white and pasty. It looked greasy, as if it were covered with a salve of cold fat sweat. Under his long nose his mouth was trembling in a horrible attempt at a smile. In the very posture of the men as they bent over him there was something revolting and unclean.

But the official with the thick creased neck had now filled the door and blotted out the picture. He went in, followed by a smaller colleague, the door was closed again behind him, and again there was that vicious and ill-omened secrecy.

All of this had happened in a moment while we had looked on with stupefied surprise. Now the people gathered in the corridor began to whisper to one another. In a moment our little blond lady went over, whispered to the young man at the window and then came back, took Stefanowski and myself by the arm, and led us away, out of hearing.

Then, as both of us whispered "What is it?" she looked around cautiously again and said with lowered voice: "That man—the one in our compartment—was trying to get out of the country and they've caught him."

"But why?—What for?—What has he done?" we asked, bewildered.

Again she glanced back cautiously and then, drawing us toward her till our three heads were almost touching, she said, in an awed and almost frightened tone, "They say he is a Jew. They searched his baggage—he was taking money out."

"How much?" said Stefanowski.

"I don't know," she whispered. "A great deal, I think. Several thousand marks. They found it."

"But how—" I began. "I thought everything was finished. I thought they were done with all of us when they went through the train."

"Yes," she said, "but don't you remember he said something about not having a ticket the whole way? He got off the train to get one. And I think that's when they caught him," she whispered. "I think they had their eye on him. That's why they did not question him when they came through the train"—as indeed, I now remembered, "they" had not—"And they caught him here," she went on. "They asked him where he was going and he said to Paris. They asked him how much money he was taking out; he said ten marks. Then they asked him how long he was going to remain in Paris, and for what purpose, and he said he was going to be there for a week and that he was attending this congress of lawyers that he spoke about. They asked him then how he proposed to stay in Paris for a week and attend this congress if all he had was ten marks. And I think," she whispered, "he got frightened then. He began to lose his head. He said he had forgotten, that he had twenty marks besides, which he had put into another pocket. And then, of course, they had him. They searched him. They searched his baggage, and they found more," she whispered in an awed tone. "Much, much more."

For a moment we all stared at one another, too stunned to say a word. Then the little woman laughed in a low, almost frightened, sort of way, a little uncertain "o-hoh-hoh-hoh-hoh" ending on a note of incredulity.

"This man," she whispered again, "this little Jew—"

"I didn't know he was a Jew," I said. "I should not have thought so."

"But he is," she whispered, and looked stealthily around again to see if we were being overheard. "And he was doing what so many of the others have done—he was trying to get out with his money." And again she laughed, the uncertain little "hoh-hoh-hoh" that mounted on a note of incredulous amazement. And yet, I saw, her eyes were troubled, too.

All of a sudden I felt sick, empty, nauseated. That money, those accursed ten marks, were beginning to burn a hole in my pocket. I put my hand into my vest pocket and the coins felt greasy, as if they were covered with sweat. I took them out and closed them in my fist and started to cross the platform toward the train.

The woman seized me by the arm. "Where are you going?" she gasped. "What are you going to do?"

"I'm going to give that man his money. I can't keep it now."

Her face went white. "Are you mad?" she whispered. "Don't you know that that will do no good? You'll only get yourself arrested and, as for him—he's in trouble enough already. You'll only make it so much worse for him. And besides," she faltered, as the full consequences came to her, "God knows what he has done, what he has said already. If he has told that we have transferred money to one another—we may all be in for it!"

We had not thought of this. But now we did. And as we saw the possible consequence of our act we just stood there and stared helplessly at one another. We just stood there, three abreast, feeling dazed and weak and hollow. We just stood there and prayed.

And now they were coming out of the compartment. The fellow with the sprouting mustache came out first, carrying the little man's valise. He looked around. It seemed to me he glared at us. We just stood still and prayed. We expected now to see all of our baggage come out. We thought that we were in for it.

But in a moment the other three officials came out of the compartment, with the little man between them. They marched him right along the platform, white as a sheet, greasy-looking, protesting volubly, in a voice that had a kind of anguished lilt. He came right by us. I made a movement with my arms. The greasy money sweated in my hand and I did not know what to do. I started to speak to him. And at the same time I was praying that he would not speak. I tried to look away from him, but I could not look away. He came toward us, still protesting volubly that everything could be explained, that all of it was an absurd mistake. And just for a moment as he passed us, he stopped talking, glanced at us, white-faced, smiling pitiably, his eyes rested on us for a moment, and then, without a sign of further recognition, he went on by.

I heard the little blond woman at my side sigh faintly and I felt her body slump against me. We all felt pretty weak and hollow. In a moment we went on across the platform and got up into the train. The evil tension had been snapped. People were now talking feverishly, still in a low tone but with obvious released excitement. Our little blond companion leaned from the window of the corridor and spoke to the fellow with the sprouting mustache who was still standing there. "Are—are you going to keep him here?" she said in a low tone. "You're not going to let him go?"

He looked at her stolidly for a moment. Then an intolerable smile broke deliberately across his brutal features. He nodded his head, slowly, with the finality of a gluttonous satisfaction. "*Nein,*" he said. "*Er bleibt.*" And, shaking his heavy head ever so slightly from side to side, "*Geht nicht!*"

They had him. Far down the platform we heard the sudden fifing shrill of the engine whistle. The guard cried warning; all up and down the platform doors were slammed. Slowly the train moved from the station. We rolled right past him. He stood among them, protesting volubly, talking with his hands now, insisting all could be explained. And they said nothing. They had him. They just stood and watched him, each with the faint suggestion of that intolerable slow smile upon his face. They raised their eyes, unspeaking, looked at us as we rolled past, with the obscene communication of their glance and of their smile.

And he—he too paused once from his voluble and feverish discourse as we passed him. He lifted his eyes to us, his pasty face, and he was silent for a moment. And we looked at him for the last time, and he at us—this time, more direct and steadfastly. And in that glance there was all the silence of man's mortal anguish. And we were all somehow naked and ashamed, and somehow guilty. We all felt somehow that we were saying farewell, not to a man but to humanity; not to some nameless little cipher out of life, but to the fading image of a brother's face. We lost him then. The train swept out and gathered speed—and so farewell.

I turned and looked at Stefanowski. He, too, was silent for a moment. Then he spoke.

"Well, then," he said, "I think that this is a sad ending to our trip."

And we? We went back in and took our former seats in our compartment. But it seemed strange and empty now. The ghost of absence sat there ruinously. He had left his coat and hat; in his anguish he had forgotten them. Stefanowski rose and took them, and would have given them to the conductor. But the woman said, "You'd better look into the pockets first. Perhaps there's something in them. Perhaps"—quickly, eagerly, as the idea took her—"perhaps he has left money there."

Stefanowski searched the pockets. There was nothing there. He shook his head. The woman began to search the cushions of the seats, thrusting her hands down around the sides. "It might just be, you know," she said, "that he hid money here." She laughed excitedly, almost gleefully. "Perhaps we'll all be rich."

The young Pole shook his head. "I think they would have found it if he had," he said—and here he paused suddenly, peered out the window, and thrust his hand into his pocket. "I suppose we're in Belgium now. Here's your money." And he returned to her the money she had given him.

She took it and put it in her purse. I still had the ten marks in my hand and was looking at them. The woman looked up, saw my face, then said quickly, warmly, "But you're upset about this thing! You look so troubled."

I put the money back and in a moment said: *"Ich fühle gerade als ob ich Blutgeld in meiner Tasche hätte."*

She leaned over smiling, and put her hand reassuringly upon my arm. *"Nein, nicht Blutgeld—Judgeld!"* she whispered. "Don't worry about it. He had plenty more!"

My eyes met those of Stefanowski for a moment, and his too were grave. "This is a sad ending to our trip," he said again.

And she—our little blond companion—she tried to laugh and joke, but her eyes were also full of trouble. She tried to talk us out of it, to talk herself into forgetfulness.

"These Jews!" she cried. "These things would never happen if it were not for them! They make all the trouble. Germany has had to protect herself. The Jews were taking all the money from the country —thousands of them escaped, taking millions of marks with them. And now, when it is too late, we wake up to it! It is too bad that foreigners must see these things, that they've got to go through these painful experiences—it makes a bad impression. They do not understand the reason. But it is the Jews!" she whispered.

We said nothing and the woman went on talking, eagerly, excitedly, earnestly, persuasively, but really as if she were trying to convince herself, as if every instinct of race and loyalty was now being used in an effort to justify something that had filled her with a sense of shame and sorrow. But even as she talked her clear blue eyes were full of trouble. And at length she stopped. There was silence for a moment. Then gravely, quietly, the woman said, "He must have wanted very badly to escape."

We remembered then all he had said and done throughout the journey. And now every act and gesture, every word became invested with a new and terrible meaning. We recalled how nervous he had been, how he kept getting up to pace up and down along the corridor. We recalled how he kept peering around at us suspiciously, how eagerly he had asked Stefanowski if he would change places with him when the Pole had got up to go into the dining car with me. We recalled his explanations about having to buy passage from the frontier to Paris, the explanations he had given to the conductor. And all these things which at the time we had dismissed as irascible ill temper or trivial explanation, now were revealed in a sequence of terrible significance.

"But the ten marks!" the woman cried at length. "In God's name, since he had all this other money, why did he give ten marks to you? It is so stupid!"

And we could find no reason, except that he had done it because he thought it might alleviate any suspicion in our minds about his true intent; or, what was even likelier, I thought, that he was in such an inner state of nervous frenzy that he had acted blindly, wildly, on the impulse of the moment.

We did not know. We never would find out the answer now. We discussed the money he had given me. The young Pole remarked that I had given the man my name and my address and that if he was later on allowed to complete his journey, he could write to me. But we all knew I would never hear from him again.

Late afternoon had come. The country had closed in, the train was winding through a pleasant, romantic landscape of hills and woods. There was a sense of forest dusk, cool darkling waters, the slant of evening and the wane of light. We knew somehow that we had entered another land. Our little blond companion peered anxiously out the window and then asked if we were really now in Belgium. The conductor assured us that we were. We gave the man our late companion's hat and coat and explained the reason for them. He nodded, took them, and departed.

The woman had her hand upon her breast, and now when the man had gone I heard her sigh slowly, with relief.

In a moment she said quietly and simply: "Do not misunderstand. I am a German and I love my country. But—I feel as if a weight has lifted from me *here*"—she put her hand upon her breast again. "You cannot understand perhaps just how it feels to us but—" and for a moment she was silent as if painfully meditating what she wished to say. Then quickly, quietly: "We are so happy to be—*out!*"

*Out?* I too was "out." And suddenly I knew just how she felt. I too was "out," who was a stranger in it. I too was "out" of that great land whose image had been engraved upon my spirit in my childhood and my youth, before I had ever seen it. I too was "out" from that land which had been so much more to me than land, which had been for me so much more than place. It was a geography of heart's desire. It was a soul's dark wonder, the haunting beauty of the magic land. It had been burning there forever, like the dark Helen burning in man's blood. And now, like the dark Helen, it was lost to me. I had spoken the language of its spirit before I ever came to it. I had spoken the accents of its speech most brokenly from the hour when I first entered it, yet never with a moment's strangeness. I had been at home in it and it in me. It seemed I had been born in it and it in me. I had known wonder in it, truth and magic in it, sorrow, loneliness and pain in it. I had known love in it, and for the first time in my life I had tasted there the bright delusive sacraments of fame.

Therefore, it was no foreign land to me. It was the other half of my heart's home. It was the dark lost Helen I had found, it was the dark found Helen I had lost—and now I knew, as I had never known before, the countless measure of my loss—the countless measure of my gain—the way that now would be forever closed to me—the way of exile and of no return—and another way that I had found. For I knew that I was "out." And that I had now found my way.

To that old master, now, to wizard Faust, old father of the ancient and swarm-haunted mind of man, to that old German land with all the measure of its truth, its glory, beauty, magic and its ruin—to that dark land, to that old ancient earth that I had loved so long—I said farewell.

I have a thing to tell you:

Something has spoken to me in the night, burning the tapers of the waning year; something has spoken in the night, and told me I shall die, I know not where. Losing the earth we know for greater knowing, losing the life we have for greater life, and leaving friends we loved for greater loving, men find a land more kind than home, more large than earth.

Whereon the pillars of this earth are founded, toward which the spirits of the nations draw, toward which the conscience of the world is tending—a wind is rising, and the rivers flow.

*September 29, 1937 [Dorothy Thompson]*

# THE RIGHT PEOPLE
by Heywood Broun

The case of poor Miss Thompson is of quite a different order. She is a victim of galloping nascence. Most of her newspaper training was received abroad where she was an active if not particularly profound foreign correspondent. Returning to her native land, she is suddenly filled with the same fervor of discovery as "stout Cortez" or Columbus. Such a mood has many advantages. The old *Sun* in New York favored lads from Kansas or the Coast on the theory that it wanted reporters who would gape at the Flatiron Building rather than homebodies who would take it in their stride. Indeed, if Miss Thompson had served an adequate apprenticeship in a city room she might have become a competent reporter in the course of the years. Unfortunately she sprang Minerva-like out of the head of Jove. Before the ship had passed Ellis Island, Miss Thompson began to see all, hear all and say all. In fact she had been on the *Herald Tribune* no more than a couple of weeks when she undertook to contradict Walter Lippmann.

In all fairness to a very vigorous young lady, she did make contacts with one or two old trappers in an effort to learn the nature of the country, but not one of them was a guide sufficiently forceful to inter-rupt upon occasion and say, "This time I'm telling you." Miss Thompson's very vigor is a handicap to her emulating Henry Adams and getting an education. If all the speeches she has made in the past twelve months were laid end to end they would constitute a bridge of platitudes sufficient to reach from the *Herald Tribune's* editorial rooms to the cold caverns of the moon. And Miss Thompson the orator bobs up in the most curious places. Never since its inception had the Union League Club permitted a woman to enter its portals, much less address the members, and then one evening, suddenly there was Dorothy Thompson stampeding the old gentlemen into riotous enthusiasm with the ringing declaration that she purposed to support the capitalist system. A fashionable physician told me that the next day he felt compelled to warn no less than six of his patients that if the Union League Club was to pull any more such heady stuff he would be obliged to forbid them permission to sit in the lounge and watch the buses go by.

Within a week Miss Thompson had shattered another precedent by speaking at the Harvard Club, and the Colgate alumni of New York were next to give way. Dorothy Thompson is greater than Eliza, because not only does she cross the ice but breaks it as she goes. Moreover, she is her own bloodhound. A facial cream has got her now, and she will be a regular on the air as well as in politics. Possibly I speak out of a certain prejudice. Some months ago I had an engagement to talk at the New School for Social Research and was unable to appear, on account of illness. I ran into a man who went, and I asked him who took my place. "Who do you think?" he said. "Dorothy Thompson." And so, of late I always sit tense and worried in that interval at Episcopalian weddings where the minister pauses and asks if anybody has anything to say, and I look around furtively to see if by any chance Miss Thompson is among the congregation.

But again in the interests of fair play, a sport for which I am quite an enthusiast, I must admit that Dorothy Thompson has upon occasion written out of a passionate fervor for good causes. I have in mind a column of rejoicing that she did when the Committee for Industrial Organization won its peaceful victory in Big Steel. Miss Thompson is sounder in her emotions than in her reasoning. She is unfortunately an Indian giver, and since the first outburst she has had no good word for CIO. Instead, her criticism has all been against labor's use of pressure and power. Seemingly she feels that the victory in Big Steel was all done with mirrors.

Of late, disquieting news has reached me from an inside source. An old newspaper associate of Miss Thompson informs me that she asked him to suggest some book she might read to familiarize herself with American history. He gave her *The Federalist*. Now that Dorothy Thompson is reading a book I'm afraid there will be no holding her. . . .

*September 14, 1938 [F.D.R.]*

# THEY STILL HATE ROOSEVELT
by Marquis Childs

No phenomenon of the times is more disturbing than the persistent hatred of President Roosevelt which finds a more and more poisonous expression among a considerable section of the American people. No slander is too vile, no canard too preposterous, to find voice among those who regard the President as their mortal enemy. And what is more, not a little of this slander finds its way into print. This is not new, of course, but within the past year it has taken on a more menacing and violent tone. . . .

The truth has no relation to the deep-seated prejudices and fears out of which the Roosevelt phobia has grown. Slander and malice descend to the most childish trivialities, or they would be trivialities if they were not so inherently mean and vicious. Grown men and women accept in all seriousness the most fantastic tales. A good example is the postage-stamp story which was current coin at parties in New York and Washington this spring. The President, the story goes, has a friend who knew one of the nation's foremost stamp collectors. At the President's suggestion the mutual friend sends the collector to the White House with some of his most valued specimens. Mr. Roosevelt gets out some of his prizes and the two men are comparing notes when the visitor is called to the long-distance telephone. Shortly afterward he leaves the White House, taking his stamp books with him, of course. Later he discovers that his most valuable specimens are missing. (The value grew in the telling, needless to say.) He complains bitterly to the mutual friend who arranged the White House visit, and a few days later is asked to meet the President's wife in New York. At their meeting Mrs. Roosevelt asks him the value of the missing stamps and then sits down and writes out a check for the amount.

There was a time when even the most ardent Roosevelt-haters had somewhat lost their ardor for this sort of thing. Something of bewilderment, something of hurt resentment, was discernible in their attitude. It was unfair, it was contrary to nature, it was against all the rules. Here this man had been beaten a half-dozen times in Congress and he had run into a major depression. But what happened? Nothing at all. He kept right on being just as popular as ever. A kind of defeatism set in; there was nothing you could do about a man like that except to let him wear himself out.

But that is over now. In the "purge" there is a new incentive for attack. All the old bogies are being trotted out again, with the same arrogant indifference to the realities that are involved. That the President has spoken, mildly enough, in three or four instances for liberal as opposed to conservative Senators is taken as an attempt to destroy the "American system," an attempt to abolish representative government. The President is compared to Caesar and Mussolini. The fact that formal party lines are so blurred as to be almost nonexistent means nothing to these critics. By any conceivable standard, as the *New York Post* pointed out, Senator Tydings might run more logically as a Republican than a Democrat. But that is irrelevant. What has happened is a sufficient excuse to set the whole pack to baying again.

Then there is the threat of a third term. While no one professes to know what is in the President's mind, it has nevertheless loomed larger as a possibility in recent weeks. If the so-called purge were not a sufficient irritant, the suggestion that four more years of Roosevelt are possible, perhaps even probable, would touch off the passions of those who look on the President as altogether vile. White House advisers have suggested that if Mr. Roosevelt runs again it will be because he has been forced to do so by implacable opposition to his program. There is a definite logic in this. At any rate, from the point of view of practical politics it would serve as an excellent text for Mr. Roosevelt's 1940 campaign. The attack on the President has been so violent and so crude that this line would carry no little weight.

No incident is too petty, no device too mean, to serve the Roosevelt phobia. For years stories have been circulated about the fabulous sums that James Roosevelt, the President's son, had made by selling insurance to firms that wanted "protection." The facts as disclosed show that these stories were gross distortions. Roosevelt-haters have taken a kind of sadistic satisfaction from the fact that Father Divine has established a heaven on an estate across the Hudson from Hyde Park; that was what the so-and-so deserved. Fitzpatrick in the St. Louis *Post-Dispatch* had the perfect commentary on this latest incident. The yacht *Exquisite*, home port Newport, is bound down the Hudson, on one bank a large sign marking Father Divine's heaven; a lady standing in the stern is staring up at the opposite bank with a pair of field glasses. To the man seated beside her she is saying, "Think of something else, Cartwright; he doesn't seem to mind."

This is one of the most remarkable things about Mr. Roosevelt. He doesn't seem to mind. In fact, one suspects that the President may welcome this hatred from his class. He said so at Madison Square Garden at the end of the 1936 campaign. Certainly it has been an invaluable political asset. (I once heard a very shrewd and tough Democratic politician, now an anti-New Dealer, say that the campaign of 1936 began and ended with the Liberty League dinner in February; the Democrats needed nothing more than that.) But more important, perhaps, is the President's realization of what this class hatred may mean with reference to his place in history. For it is a phenomenon that will not go unnoticed by the historians. And it is a fairly safe prediction that, whatever happens to the New Deal, Roosevelt will stand as a symbolic figure at the end of one era and the beginning of another. That realization, it is barely possible, may be one of the reasons why the President has drawn down upon himself the hatred of the cushioned and the comfortable.

One thing, and one thing alone, could bring about a shift in the attitude of the hating class and that, of course, is a war. It happened with Woodrow Wilson, and I see no reason to believe that it would be otherwise with Franklin Roosevelt. Reform would inevitably be suspended, and those who now hold the economic controls would come to Washington with resounding proffers of cooperation and pledges of patriotism. In the face of a war, or perhaps even the threat of a war, this cooperation would under the present organization of production be essential. It is no accident that those who rail most violently against the Roosevelt domestic policies speak with grudging approval of the President's foreign policy.

*March 1, 1939 [Jimmy Durante]*

# THE GREAT DURANTE
by Otis Ferguson

We will never know how good or bad J. P. McEvoy's book for *Stars in Your Eyes* may actually be, because its scenes are constantly exploding into Jimmy Durante. It is the (by now) old plot about the young hopeful among the stars and garters of Hollywood life, and it holds together and gets into more naturally funny situations than most musicals. The staging is good (sets by Jo Mielziner), and the show is elegantly turned out in John Hambleton's costumes. Music and lyrics by Schwartz and Fields, adequate enough but nothing catchy; and a good cast.

Ethel Merman is better than usual (another singer who can put over a song without singing much) and has worked out a fine comedy part for herself by the end, getting her lines off enough to drive them through an oak block. Richard Carlson did a nice quiet job of avoiding the sappy; Mildred Natwick almost rates equal billing with Merman for her grace and dry wit; and the stage was full of people like Clinton Sundberg, Ted Gary, etc. The only sour note was Tamara Toumanova, who is one of those Lupe Velez types with less ability than perpetual motion, getting in your hair like a comb. Her dancing is her fortune, but what thumps she gave the stage here I could willingly give up to keep her out of the story. (The dancing in general was all right, no more, and there was less of it thrown at you than usual, happy days.)

These are the credits, but the show is still Jimmy Durante's. Everybody knows the Durante character now: The hat, always the hat. In the last number this time he has a Russian shako that is white and mangy and about two feet tall, but he could work just as hard with a beret, and I estimate he has dusted off more acres of stage than any five comedy tumblers in the business. The sandpaper voice, the face in general, nose and eyes in particular; the smile and that wall-eyed sidewise take. The ripping motion, back and forth and around with the clear angry intention of getting there ahead of himself, whirls, half-turn jerks, and the quality of stopping as though he had been bumped into by a brick wall. As for his stage character, there is of course the intellectualized malaprop in which he delights ("It's exacerbating, that's what it is!"). After that, there are the passions, few, but running strong: rage and a determination in everything that makes everything else seem like rage ("Am I mortified! Am I humialated!"); and love. And in everything a deliberate humor of contrasts: the silver tenor and that old-crow delivery; the long words and the quick ability to misapprehend any idea you could name; the great lover and that face and figure—a slab of asbestos blazing with desire.

The energy is another thing, and in Jimmy's case terrific; but energy can only help the natural clown, it can't make him funny. He is spontaneous, naturally; in coming up the hard way he had to rely on spontaneity before he could ever rely on being a national act or character. He ad-libs out of good spirits and for the advancement of laughter, and a show simply cannot die once he is out of his dressing room.

Nobody but the people in a cast could tell you how many times Jimmy has taken up the slack of deceleration or driven the tempo up to a new briskness; his showmanship is the shrewd and weather-beaten result of working in singles and teams in any fleabag that would have him, all the way from the bottom to pretty near the top, and if you say you ever saw him miss planting a line by fractions of a second, in all the audience and stage and orchestra hubbub of one of his knock-down shows, why please send back the ring and my photograph and what is left of the half-pound Fanny Farmer's: it is over.

Jimmy is so constant in strange motions that he always has you going at a simmer of smiling and still feeling weak, so that when his punch line comes, the house is ready to lift. Yet the big belt this time is hardly among theatrical rarities: Jimmy is singing as usual (the voice has a frog in it as big as a lily pad, but really good pitch), kidding the number as usual, but giving it all, and finally climbing to the high note of which he is proud and which the band builds up to hold, and holds. Well, Jimmy lasts about three bars on this and then suddenly whangs his hat halfway through the floor, coming down to the trumpets as though he'd kick them back into their throats. "When the hell do I BREATHE around here?" Jimmy Durante says, brushing the warp out of his coat sleeves and breathing all over the place. Then he picks up the hat and is immediately putting his heart into the music as though it wouldn't stay if it weren't walloped.

In another number he suddenly breaks without warning in the

middle of a phrase to announce with the fierce resolve of human nature and all patience driven past the limits: "I'm going out for an EIGHT. BAR. REST!" The band vamps quietly, Jimmy charges out at the wings as though he'd break his legs off at the shoulder, charges back center in the same bad state of balance, muttering and fanning himself with the hat ("It's too much, that's what it is!"). By the downbeat of the ninth bar he has become aware of the audience again and is in there putting a torch to the music.

Apart from a few ideas like this you can see more plainly than ever that what is funny is not the situation, not the words; that since the gestures are known and predictable they cannot be funny all night; that funny costumes are good for one yokel guffaw (no more) unless what we really laugh at is the attitude of the man in under the funny hat, his seriousness in it and pride in it, his unselfconscious furiousness and importance. What you wouldn't believe until you have seen it was the Durante-Merman number before the finale. The two of them simply stand offside sort of giving each other significant looks not to miss the music cue, and then, when the band hits it, coming front and center like the courier in a Civil War movie, to stand there and sing about "It's All Yours." A fire alarm would ring in the wings, and Jimmy would stomp back to the telephone on the piano and "Hello, hello" and some kind of gag—any gag—and front and center again for a finish; and then on some fine rousing chords from the pit the two of them would go off in a sort of glorified trucking step. Applause, and then the routine over again and then applause and so on.

I don't know how many times they did it, with few variations—except that Jimmy took to throwing this tremendous shako at the leader in the pit, with goose feathers coming out of it like a broken pillow, and it was so heavy the leader would throw it in the air half a rod, and it molting every inch, and it still wouldn't make the stage. Well, it was just that, and the crowd would not let them off, and yet the routine went on and the impromptu phone gags went as low as, "Hello, is this the meat market? Well meet my wife." And the crowd would not let them off, and Durante was killing himself and laughing, and tearing around keeping up the bad jokes and pillow fight, and it was the best shambles for the least cause I ever saw.

The conception of this business was good, if simple, but that must wear out quickly, and after a while it comes down to Durante, picking up a houseful of widely assorted people as a magnet picks up iron filings. It is something in him essentially comic, something that never lets down, a constant perfection of eye in picking out the absurd and unexpected from all situations. He is funny because he is funny. If you could go any farther than that, except to smoke up the place with words, you would know what humor is and be able to practice it (by the way, how funny *are* you actually?).

But when you come out on the street and begin to breathe normally again, you will notice something that was not billed in the program or featured in the show, never stressed, and naturally buried in the noise and bustle. A conniver, a seller-outer and crazy man in his stage part, Jimmy Durante somehow retains for himself, the man under the stage character and funny hat, the absurd reassurance of rough-and-ready but sweet human kindness which enlists you behind him, tempering all that harsh outward violence with a mutual good faith between him and you and the extra he makes a great kick at, telling him get the hell out of here. His character off stage, as a matter of fact, is not terrific or Ritz Brothers. Unmistakably Durante, he is quiet, a man who works hard and is weary, and protected from the rude shoving, autograph hunters and flashlight bulbs perhaps by his very air of not seeking them but going about his business as though no better and no worse than all the other citizens wrapped in their average clothes and own business. So he can poke along Broadway and be buttonholed by any acquaintance and introduced to anybody on the sidewalk, and use the easy language of the street and country to say, friendly and brief, that much and no more, "Hiya, pal."

There is a kind of humor that nickers in the air when a man takes a bad fall or a loss in human dignity; and this, observed and charted by the philosophers, has become mistaken for the risible instinct itself. Whereas true comedy requires as much participation and hope of the good, true and beautiful as high tragedy—those elaborating the thesis that laughter comes from the feeling of superiority and enjoyment of other men's discomfiture are supplying us with a personal dossier sadder than it is funny. Those who do not have to write books about it know that a good part of the fun of watching a man like Durante is in the way we're with him and love him, the way we spot him for a good and happy guy. This is not any one man or group of men out for an audience laugh and damn all. It is rather as though we were all gathered there for the purposes of a humor as tempered with mercy as the humor we can muster, without forcing, for any joke perpetrated on ourselves.

*June 17, 1940*

# WENDELL WILLKIE
by William Allen White

Take it by and large, Wendell Willkie is the best prospect for the Republican presidential nomination. And by that token, as these lines are written in late May, it looks as though Wendell Willkie would not have a Chinaman's chance to win it. His two heavy handicaps are: first, the fact that he was a registered Indiana Democrat until five years ago; and second, that on the whole his outgivings, since his backers began to groom him as a dark horse, have been too candid and too decent.

His record as a public-utility magnate would not necessarily bar him as a Republican candidate. Nor would the charge, which is backed with some evidence, (a) that the Commonwealth and Southern, of which he is president, squelched an opposition newspaper in Chattanooga, Tennessee, and (b) that his corporation contributed to the political delinquency of a state senator in Michigan. (All this he denies quite convincingly.)

The thing that will bother the Republican politicians is that Wendell Willkie refuses to use their language, apparently scorns their inner-temple ritual, and delights to make a record which knocks galley-west their cat-footed strategy for this campaign. For instance, he was an outspoken supporter of the Hull treaties. The Republicans in the House and Senate this spring have made a record against those treaties. Again, he is a believer in supporting the President's foreign policy, particularly in Roosevelt's malevolent neutrality to Hitler. The Republican leadership this spring is loaded down with an isolationist record in the vote in Congress to defeat the embargo provisions of the Neutrality Act last fall, and the Republican convention will be filled with snorting patriots whose only political aim is to get That Man.

Sadly enough, Wendell Willkie is not a desk pounder when he refers to Mr. Roosevelt. The president of the Commonwealth and Southern has had his own personal hand-to-hand grapple with Mr. Roosevelt in the sale of certain Willkie properties in the South to the T.V.A. Mr. Willkie knows the President's prowess. And most likely the President respects Willkie's sparring, boxing and toe work. It was a drawn fight. Mr. Willkie, for five years since he quit voting the Democratic national ticket, has been a bitter critic of the President. But since Mr. Willkie has been groomed in the paddock as a Republican presidential entry he has had horse sense enough to temper his criticism with some courtesy. Evidently he realizes that no Republican can win (barring a revulsion in October on the President's war policy) without the independent vote. And Mr. Willkie, who is sharp and shrewd, with a business rather than a political mind, realized instinctively that the independent vote was turning from Roosevelt more in sorrow than in anger. Mr. Willkie knows full well what no Republican politician can get into his head and what few Democrats sense—that every time the plutocratic fist bangs the desk or beats a palpitating breast about the President, the independent voter who has been drifting away from Roosevelt is tempted to sneak back to the Old Smiler.

The thing that puzzles open-minded citizens about Wendell Willkie is this: Is he just a pretty smooth guy or has he really got something on the ball? By which I mean specifically: Is all this brutal candor, all this smart attitude toward the liberal vote, all this strategy which makes Mr. Willkie plug for civil liberties, stand for internationalism, and plunk hard for an economic solution of peace problems through reciprocal trade treaties—is all this the approach of a smooth bond salesman? Or does it represent the rugged honesty of a man whose association with politicians has been such that he despises them and rejects their tricks?

I can hardly qualify as an expert witness in testifying for Mr. Willkie. I have seen him just three times. I have talked with him for perhaps half an hour. I have watched him in action at short range, a matter of ten or twelve feet away, and have heard him speak off the record two or three times. And I like him. I am satisfied that his independence is genuine. I had read several pounds of the propaganda stuff about him that is being sent out from Wall Street and points west. I am prepared to say it is by all odds the slickest literary goose grease that I have taken out of the second-class mail for a long time. The appeal of this stuff is the Willkie appeal. His propaganda is aimed at the average fairly independent voter, and it is a swell sales talk.

The Willkie propaganda stresses the very virtues which Willkie is displaying in his sample case: business experience; the businessman's scorn of political expediency; a frankness that is a kind of intransigent don't-give-a-damnitiveness about political traditions and conventions; a general political attack which represents a nice balance between Andrew Jackson with his "to the victor belong the spoils," and old Commodore Vanderbilt—"the public be damned!" To me this seems genuine chiefly because Willkie was once an unreconstructed hickoryshirt-and-blue-jeans Democrat. The Willkie creed apparently is that to business belong the spoils. In Kansas City he sounded a keynote:

I became president of Commonwealth and Southern about the same time Mr. Roosevelt became President of the United States. My company was charging 5½ cents a kilowatt hour then and the average annual consumption per consumer was 600 kilowatts. Today the charge is 2.9 cents and the average consumption is 1,230 kilowatts. It is the lowest average rate and highest average consumption of any power company in the country. . . . I doubt that Mr. Roosevelt has done as well with the government.

Probably, if the President's supporters should ask What about the garroting of the Tennessee newspaper and the charge against the Michigan senator, Mr. Willkie would reply What about Frank Hague in New Jersey, what about the Kelly-Nash machine that slaughtered the workers on Memorial Day, what about Jim Curley and the various wreckers of civil liberties who are your friends, supporters and allies today?

For the American people are tired of the smoothy in politics—even if he is honest. They don't like the oleaginous weasel words with which so many politicians grease their way back when they venture upon a dangerous salient of honesty. But alas, the politicians don't know how weary the people are of buncombe. So it seems to me that Wendell Willkie hasn't a look-in at the Republican Convention unless the Republicans are scared within an inch of their lives. Yet on their ticket he might make a better race against Mr. Roosevelt than any of the present probable Republican nominees.

Granted all the charges made against Wendell Willkie are true, what do they prove except that he rationalizes the kind of conduct which the other candidates, if they were in the White House, would ignore or condone? Moreover, his record as a young lawyer defending civil liberty, his intelligent views upon the tariff and our relations with Europe either at war or in peace are so well known that he could not equivocate in the campaign or sidestep his duty under pressure if he were in the White House. All of which does not prove that Wendell Willkie is God's perfect child in politics. Far from it. But in this hour his faults are not those which would scar, spot or blemish him unless he happened to be running against a paragon.

Now, what sort of a man personally is this unknown dark horse who is being groomed in the Augean stables of our plutocracy? Closing my eyes, I can see him clearly. For he is spiritually most photogenic. Behold a big man, six feet two inches maybe, not fat, not logy, but dominant. He has slightly, only slightly, stooped shoulders, a leonine head, large features, a shock of black hair which he waves like a mane —a challenging banner—when he charges oratorically upon an enemy. His skin is good, clear, youthful; his smile develops a coy dimple and shows even, strong teeth. His voice is normally low, indeed repressed. But he can increase it to the blare of a slide trombone. His kindly, twinkling eyes in moment of combat blaze uncomfortably upon his opponents. He has the kind of information and erudition that are typical of a well-educated American; his speeches reveal the conspicuous fact that he is from a Western high school and a state university. In some way his mental makeup, his Midwestern accent, his eager enthusiasm are a flaunting rebuke to the detachment of Groton and Harvard, to the suavity of Lawrenceville and Princeton, to the smugness of Hotchkiss and Yale. He calls wah "war" and fahmehs "farmers," and flourishes his flat *a* with a wallop. He grins easily, but I never heard him give a belly laugh. He chuckles. But don't be fooled by that coy dimple. Don't let that adolescent smile deceive you, for it rhymes with guile and he has got plenty of it. He makes quick and final decisions and does a big day's work in a six-hour day.

He is a new species in politics. If he is not soured by defeat at Philadelphia, Wendell Willkie may emerge a first-class figure in American life after the confusion and possible party chaos which may end this year's campaign. But he will have to take the veil, renounce Commonwealth and Southern and all its works and, far from the hurly burly of Wall Street in the shaded cloister of the Statue of Limitations, lead a chaste and monkish life.

*August 5, 1940*

# AMY LOWELL
by Van Wyck Brooks

Amy Lowell's force of will, the secret of her success and failure, was her most markedly racial characteristic. For this was the Yankee will, and she won her victories by it, and she largely failed by this will in her life as a poet. Too much of her poetry sprang from the will, not the poet. But there was no doubt about the will. She was a Lowell and a Lawrence, and she liked to run things, whether fleets of clipper ships or colleges or towns; and, having the taste, she had the capacity, as dozens of the Lowells had. She ran right well whatever she chose to run. She was a born promoter, as masterful as her forebears were, and the shrewdest of salesmen also, like the old China traders; and, seeing that America was giving birth to a first-rate product, she put her shoulder to the wheel and pushed it on the market. The product was American poetry, which was plainly on the rise again and which she

handled like any other "big business." Was it good, bad, or indifferent?
What did it matter? It was good in bulk, and that was the point. It
was another form of Standard Oil; and Miss Lowell set out to put it
"on the map," as others had put salvation or woman's suffrage. Agassiz,
in just this wholesale fashion, had put natural science on the American
map; and this required perception, in his case as in hers. For Miss
Lowell had perception. What scorn she felt for those who did not have
it!—for the "caged warblers" and "phonograph" poets who thought they
still lived in Victorian times, for those whose work was not their own
but echoes, for those who cowered in ivory towers and never looked
out of the window, for those who praised the glories of old New
England and could not see the genius of Masters and Sandburg. She
scorned Henry James and other "traitors." * She scorned the lady-
painters and performers of Chopin, with their "ghastly nights on cracked
hotel-pianos." She was arrogant enough to impress occasional English
observers, who were full of admiration for her because she reminded
them of their own dear betters. She ran ocean liners and terrorized
their orchestras by telling them to stop their outrageous noise; and
she whizzed over the face of the earth in her claret-colored motor,
reorganizing hotels where she spent the night. Like Eliot's Cousin
Nancy, she "strode across the hills and broke them"; and, if she was
not bearded, she was full of oaths; and her bed had eighteen pillows,
and she had ten thousand black cigars and seven megatherian sheep-
dogs that mauled and all but murdered her visitors. This Daniela
Webster was also an actress, whose earliest idol was Duse, and all her
dramatic flair, with her verve and her gusto, went into the great
pitched battle that she waged for the poets. She fought in the front
rank, when occasion called for her, or, as less often happened, behind
the lines, where she mustered her majors and colonels, her generals
and lieutenants.

For literary soldiership, or literary statesmanship, America had never
seen Miss Lowell's equal. Literary politicians had always abounded,
but she was the prime minister of the republic of poets; and under her
control this republic rose from the status of Haiti and became an
imperial republic of the caliber of France. The poets had reason to
thank their stars that they had a Lowell behind them, for whom editors
and publishers were factory hands and office boys. Her telephone
had the force of a dozen Big Berthas; and God might have picked
up the fragments of those who opposed her—there was little left of
them for men to bury. One could hear the guns go off at the other
end of Texas. But the Texans and Nebraskans and the people of St.
Paul crowded the window ledges of their halls to hear her; and the

* See her portraits of T. S. Eliot and Ezra Pound in *A Critical Fable.* Amy
Lowell felt that Henry James made a great mistake in detaching himself from
his countrypeople.

map on which she had put poetry started and trembled under her feet—the map of poetry blossomed in purple and red. She touched a fuse wherever she went, and fireworks rose in the air; and there were no set pieces more brilliant than hers, no Catherine wheels or girandoles or fountains. There was no still, small voice in Amy Lowell. Her bombs exploded with a bang and came down in a shower of stars; and she whizzed and she whirred, and she rustled and rumbled, and she glistened and sparkled and blazed and blared. If, at the end, it seemed like the Fourth of July, it was a famous victory, none the less, though the fields and the trees were littered with the sticks and the debris, with charred frames and burnt-out cases.

Besides, much more was left than people felt on the morning after. Miss Lowell was a pyrotechnist, but some of her scenic effects were permanent; and when she was not permanent she was salutary. Her theory of "externality" was undoubtedly fallacious, and much of her work was factitious, the fruit of the will. As if poetry could ever be "external"! Yet her actual externality was good for the moment. It was a challenge to internality at a time when the "internal" poets were so often sentimental, derivative and soft. When the *fond* was so corrupt and weak, the way to sting it into life was to assert that nothing was important but the *forme*; and all the new poets made much of tech-nique—they sometimes talked as if nothing else mattered. And what, in the end, did this matter?—though the end perhaps might be long in coming. The poets of the further future were to gain by this immediate future, in which the false remnants of the past were trampled out of sight and in which all manner of new forms were placed at their dis-posal when they developed the *fond* that was equally worthy. The world could always wait for its poets, and this was a time for tuning the instruments; and the free verse and polyphonic prose which Miss Lowell adapted and popularized provided a whole new orchestra for the poets who were coming.

How good this audacity was, after so much futile indirectness! After so much weltering in borrowed souls, how good it was to "live in the eye alone"! How good was imagism to sharpen the perceptions, and all this zest for seeing, reporting, recording, this joy in the visible world, this picture making, after so much wreathing and writhing and fainting in coils. How good this "religion of art," the note of the epoch, after so many woolly abstractions and impotent emotions, so many blurred conceptions and moldy morals! This technical virtuosity, so clean and fresh, this feeling for orchestral color and verbal music, and this all but morbid fear of the obvious also! These poets reacted against bad technique by making technique an end in itself. What of it! The poets of the future would redress the balance. And they rightly threw out of the window the old New England classics, with all their Miltonic ideals and all their Victorian nature worship. No need to fear that they would not come back. Were the Yankees really in danger of losing their ethos? If the classics went out by the window, they were sure to return by the door when the noble mind had outlived the abuse of its virtues. The new generation started with Poe, the first favorite of Frost as of Robinson, with Emily Dickinson's novel perceptions and Whitman, who had discarded the past. The new generation was also redressing a balance.

As a writer as well as a propagandist, Miss Lowell was part of all this movement, so similar in France and England in its causes and effects. For the whole Western world was undergoing the same changes, and Boston was a center of this world—as it had been in the eighteen forties. It had never ceased to be a center, despite the croakers and despite the dry rot; and in the darkest hour of Boston and Cambridge, world influences had emanated from these twin cities in the persons of William James and Mrs. Eddy. For all the reactionary forces that opposed new culture, they were still hungry for new culture; and Amy Lowell was as hungry for the culture of this morning as an Omaha woman's club was hungry for the culture of the day before last. She made the Omaha woman's club hungry for it—and she begged it and borrowed it, stole it, invented it, like all the writer-conquerors, with a high hand and a high heart and the enterprise of a merchant-adventurer. No doubt, her externality reflected her own extroversion.

It was an escape as well from a troubled psyche; for Miss Lowell's inner life knew no repose. She had solved none of her vital problems, and she remained the conventional child that expressed itself in the first of her volumes of poems.* Indeed, she was never a poet, properly speaking—the poet in her never struggled through—so she seized on the outsides of things as her only chance of effectuality, and her dramatic instinct achieved the rest. She had awakened suddenly to modern painting and music, and she pillaged them as she pillaged the Boston museums where she had played as a child. Among her *objets d'art* she was always the child, a Gargantuan child with the reach of a khan or a brigand; and she pillaged books—she tore the entrails out of them—and she used in the composition of her rockets and pinwheels the *alchimie du verbe* of Rimbaud, Verhaeren, Mallarmé, and heaven knew how many others. She wrote free verse after Debussy's piano pieces; she stole the show at aquariums, with their "swirling, looping patterns of fish"; and every place she read about and every place she visited—whether Mexico, China, Peru, St. Louis or Charleston—left in her hand some scrap of a rhythm or a picture.

---

* *A Dome of Many Colored Glass,* 1912. This book was a curious revelation of Amy Lowell's equipment as a poet in the proper sense. It represented her work up to the age of thirty-eight, after which she developed her "external" method. Conventional and weak in thought and feeling, it was on the level of the writing of most of the current New England poetasters.

She found a mine in Keats, whom she admired for his fearlessness, straightforwardness, directness, for all he had in common with herself; but everything served her purpose that gave her a little gold or brass, a beam of sandalwood or a bolt of silk, a flag, a trumpet, a tuba or a box of spices. And she toiled over her poems from midnight till dawn, not as one to whom the muses whispered, but as one who had to wrestle with them and force them to their knees in the sweat of her brow.

Well, was it all for show? Was it merely a night of the Fourth of July? Was it only a parade and swagger of Boston fashion? There was surely enough of the material in Miss Lowell's talent, too much noise, too much excitement; and yet how much remained that was new and crisp, what vividness of color, what joy of action! One could say much for externals that enlivened the senses; and, when one had given up to time the bric-a-brac, the petals of Chinese flowers whose roots were somewhere else around the planet, one came back to Miss Lowell's storytelling. She was a storyteller, if not a poet, who had studied her art in Chaucer, in Keats and in Browning, and who, in some of her best tales, followed Miss Jewett and Miss Wilkins, when she was not touched by Robert Frost. Perhaps this deep Yankee in her was to live the longest, the Yankee whose tales in *East Wind* and the ballad of *Evelyn Ray* refurbished this old New England genre with a note of her own that was wholly fresh. Her colors here were browns and grays, but some of her blues and reds were fast; and, among other pieces, *Can Grande's Castle*, with its cinematographic style, remained her most characteristic. Perhaps its excess of vivacity wore one out. It was charged with enough electricity to burn one's hand off; it was like a third rail, it was like a power line, and one had to touch the wires with circumspection. But there Amy Lowell exulted in her strength; and her feeling for ships and battles, for barbarism and heroism, for pageantry, pomp, dash and fanfaronade, for the theater of history and the clash of peoples boiled up and bubbled over with a splendid *brio*. She was Lady Hamilton, she was Nelson, she was Commodore Perry in Japan, with his sailor chanteys; and no New England historian since the great days of Prescott and Motley had given the world such brilliant historical scenes.

*March 3, 1941*

# IN MEMORY OF SCOTT FITZGERALD

by John O'Hara

It is granted that Scott Fitzgerald was not a lovable man, but most of the time he was a friendly one, and that characteristic, in a man of his professional standing, is as much as anyone can ask. I always warmed to Scott, was always glad to see him, always. But then if you saw him too long a time his intelligence, about which he was almost overconscientious, would go to work, and he would let you bore him. He would almost encourage you to bore him. He let you go right ahead, being banal and uninteresting, and knowing how much you were embarrassed yourself by your ordinariness. At the same time he was professionally one of the most generous artists I've ever known. Dorothy Parker pointed that out to me one time when I had some reason to be irritated with Scott, and though Dorothy Parker has said many true things, she has said nothing truer than that. I guess the loneliness of his private hells was so enormous that he really would have got no great relief by sharing a little of it—in other words, by letting you know him better—and so he figured to keep it all for himself. Well, that was his business, and thus he kept his integrity, which I won't attempt to define, simply because everyone who knew him knew he had it.

And he kept it in death. I read the *Herald Tribune* obit, and I understand the *Times* one was just as bad. The curious hostility of those pieces may be attributed to that integrity coming through, even to people who didn't know Scott, who probably hadn't even read him (I am reliably informed that the piece in *Time* was written by a man who until he was assigned to do the piece never had read anything of Scott's). The integrity, the aloofness, came through and annoyed some people, and so they just went ahead and wrote their angry little pieces, saving their wit and tolerance for some spectacular Bowery bum or deputy chief inspector of police.

F. Scott Fitzgerald was a *right* writer, and it's going to be a damned shame if the generation after mine (I am thirty-six) and the one after that don't get to know him. I had the good luck to read *This Side of Paradise* when it first came out, twenty years ago, and I've read it practically annually since then. He was the first novelist to make me say, "Hot dog! Some writer, I'll say." I was younger than his people in *This Side of Paradise*, but I was precocious. Amory Blaine's mother's maiden name was Beatrice O'Hara, and I was in love with a girl named

Beatrice then, a coincidence that became less important page by page. The people were right, the talk was right, the clothes, the cars were real, and the mysticism was a kind of challenge. By the time *The Beautiful and Damned* and *The Great Gatsby* appeared, the man could do no wrong. In a burst of enthusiasm I once said to Dorothy Parker, "The guy just can't write a bad piece." And again she was right. She said, "No. He can write a bad piece, but he can't write badly." He sent me the page proofs of *Tender Is the Night*, which was a major honor in my life. I read it three times then, but only twice since, for that fine book is not to be read just any time. It's a dangerous book to encounter during some of the moods that come over you after you're thirty. You don't like to think of yourself, lone, wandering and lost, like Richard Diver, going from town to town in bleak upstate New York, with All That behind you.

And then a year ago Scott invited us out to his house in the San Fernando Valley for Sunday lunch. It was going to be a big thing, though a small party. He was going to have Norma Shearer and Loretta Young, and I wish I had told him that if I were choosing people to lunch with I would not pick either Norma Shearer and/or Loretta Young. Anyway, they weren't there. There were only my wife and I. The food was good and there was a lot to drink, but I was on the wagon and Scott was not. He was terribly nervous, disappearing for five and ten minutes at a time, once to get a plaid tie to give my wife because she was wearing a Glen plaid suit. Once to get a volume of Thackeray because I'd never read Thackeray, another time to get some tome about Julius Caesar which he assured me was scholarly but readable—but which he knew I would never read. Then we went out and took some pictures, and when we finished that he suddenly said, "Would you like to read what I've written, but first promise you won't tell anyone about it. Don't tell them anything. Don't tell them what it's about, or anything about the people. I'd like it better if you didn't even tell anyone I'm writing another novel." So we went back to the house and I read what he had written. He saw that I was comfortable, with pillows, cigarettes, ash trays, a Coke. And sat there tortured, trying to be casual, but unhappy because he did not know that my dead pan was partly due to my being an extremely slow reader of good writing, and partly because this *was* such good writing that I was reading. When I had read it I said, "Scott, don't take any more movie jobs till you've finished this. You work so slowly and this is so good, you've got to finish it. It's real Fitzgerald." Then, of course, he became blasphemous and abusive, and asked me if I wanted to fight. I saw him a few times after that day, and once when I asked him how the book was coming he only said, "You've kept your promise? You haven't spoken to anyone about it?"

*May 19, 1941*

# A SIGNIFICANT MEMORY OF FREUD
by Max Eastman

Berggasse 19 was a big roomy house full of books and pictures, the whole mezzanine floor padded with those thick rich rugs in which your feet sank like a camel's in the sand. I was not surprised to see hanging beside Rembrandt's "Anatomy Class," without which no doctor's office would be recognizable, a picture of "The Night Mare"—a horrid monster with a semievil laugh or leer, squatting upon a sleeping maiden's naked breast. Freud's early specialty had been anatomy, and he had in him the hard scientific curiosity suggested by Rembrandt's picture. But he had too, in my belief, a streak of something closely akin to medieval superstition. He liked to talk about *"The* Unconscious," personifying the mere absence of a quality—and that the quality of awareness—and making it into a scheming demon for which anatomy certainly finds no place. Freud's discovery that impulses suppressed out of our thoughts can continue to control those thoughts, both waking and sleeping, and also our actions and bodily conditions, was certainly a major event in the history of science. But what a lot of purely literary mythology he built around it! Mental healing always did and always will run off into magic.

With such thoughts I sat there whetting my curiosity until the door opened and he came in.

Well—he was smaller than I thought, and slender-limbed, and more feminine. I have been surprised at the feminineness of all the great men I have met, including the Commander of the Red Army. Genius is a nervous phenomenon and, except for the steam-roller variety that struts the boards just now, it involves delicacy. Freud's nose was flatter than I expected, too, and more one-sided. It looked as if somebody with brass knuckles had given him a poke in the snoot. It made him, when he threw his head clear back and laughed softly, as he frequently did, seem quaint and gnomelike. His voice was gentle too, gentle and a little thin, as though he were purposely holding back half his breath in order to be mischievous.

"What did you want?" he said in perfect English as we shook hands.

"Not a thing," I said. "I just wanted to look you over."

"You want to quote my commendation of your book. But why should I support you? Can't you stand up on your own legs?"

"I'm trying to," I said. "And that isn't what brought me here at all.

Still, I do wonder why, if you think I got it right about you and Marx, you want to make a secret of it."

He made no answer, and was not troubled by the silence this caused. It was a hard silence, a sort of weapon in his hand, and I made it worse by saying:

"There *is* one thing I always wanted to ask you. I don't see why you talk about unconsciousness as though it were a thing. The only *thing* there, when we are unconscious, is our brain and body. Wouldn't it clarify matters if you stopped using the noun and stuck to the adjective—instead of saying '*the* Unconscious,' say 'unconscious brain-states'?"

"Well, haven't you read our literature?" he said tartly. "The Unconscious is not a thing, but a concept. It is a concept that we find indispensable in the clinic."

"It is a dangerous concept," I said, "because people inevitably think of it as a thing."

"Well, then, let them correct their thinking!"

It wasn't very pleasant, and I tried to say with a smile: "You're perfectly sure you're not resurrecting the soul?"

"No, there's no soul," he said. "There's only a concept, which those of us engaged in practical work find indispensable."

"Perhaps you're a Behaviorist," he went on. "According to your John B. Watson, even consciousness doesn't exist. But that's just silly. That's nonsense. Consciousness exists quite obviously and everywhere —except perhaps in America."

He enjoyed that crack at America so much that he began to laugh and be genial. In fact, he began to lecture me in a fatherly way about the relations between the psychic and the physical. He talked fluently, and I am a good listener, and we were soon very friendly.

"You mustn't confuse the word *psychic* with the word *conscious*," he said. "My old psychology teacher here in Vienna, Theodor Lipps, used to warn us against that. Psychic entities are not necessarily conscious."

My answer, of course, was: "Then the Unconscious is not merely a concept after all, but a thing, an 'entity,' just as I thought!"

However, I did not make this answer until I got home and was putting down our conversation in a notebook. I was too far on the under side of my inferiority complex to catch a great man up like that. Perhaps it is just as well, for the contradiction, left standing, is very neat and pretty. It shows Freud in the very act of being both a scientist and a demonologist. Freud would not let his discoveries be a contribution to psychology. They had to be psychology—"Freud's psychology." And there had to be quite a little of the infallibility of the Pope in his pronunciamentos.

He had now become so genial, however, that he even said a good word for America—namely, that she had produced John Dewey. "John

Dewey is one of the few men in the world," he said, "for whom I have a high regard."

I said that I had taught and studied under Dewey at Columbia and thought very highly of him too, though the World War had divided us. "The war was a watershed in America."

That remark interested him, and he kept returning to it afterward. Indeed, he had a way of calling the conversation back to where it was going, not letting it get lost, that reminded me of Plato's Socrates. For instance, I said that the war was a watershed in America, dividing radicals from liberals, but not in Europe, because in Europe everybody was in it whether he wanted to be or not.

"Officially," he put in with a sly inflection. And then he exclaimed: "You should not have gone into the war at all. Your Woodrow Wilson was the silliest fool of the century, if not of all centuries."

He paused for my answer, which got stuck accidentally in my throat.

"And he was also probably one of the biggest criminals—unconsciously, I am quite sure."

I remarked that Woodrow Wilson's literary style was a perfect instrument of self-deception, and that delighted him. He asked me if I had read *The Story of a Style*, a psychoanalytic character-reading of Wilson on the basis of the relative predominance of certain words in his speeches. I said I had, and we agreed in praising the book. We got a long way off from my remark about the watershed, but Freud called me back to it.

"I would like you to say some more about that watershed business," he said.

"Well, take Dewey, for instance. He went over on the war side and wrote a book against Germany, and it seemed for a time to change his whole way of thinking. Most of our intellectual leaders who did that stopped thinking altogether."

"Why?" Freud asked.

"You know why people stop thinking," I said. "It's because their thoughts would lead them where they don't want to go."

That amused him again, and the whole of his gentleness came back, including the delighted little crinkles at the corners of his eyes. He put his head way back finally and laughed like a child. Sometimes a child at play reminds you of an odd little old man; there was something of that odd little old man in Freud's ways. He waggled his head and hands about all the time, looking up at the ceiling and closing his eyes, or making funny little pouts and wry faces, when he was trying to think of a word or an idea. I never ceased feeling that underneath it all was an obdurate, hard, cranky streak, but I also never ceased feeling its great charm. He was curious about the support I gave to the Russian Bolsheviks.

"You believe in liberty," he said, "and there you get just the opposite."

I gave him our glib explanation: The class dictatorship is transitional —a method of moving toward a more real and universal liberty.

He made gestures like a man fighting with cobwebs or doing the Australian crawl.

"That is all up in the air," he said. "People who are going to produce liberty some time in the future are just the same for me as people who are going to have it ready for you in the celestial paradise. I live in this real world right here. This is the only world I am interested in."

I told him the very thing I admired about Lenin was his way of taking the real world exactly as it is, and yet trying to do something with it. "The Bolsheviks," I said, "have a hypothesis and they're trying it out."

That appealed to the scientist in him and he became both serious and mild. "It *is* an intensely interesting experiment," he said. "Really, it's all *terra incognita* to me. I don't know anything about it."

"What are you politically?" I asked.

"Politically I am just nothing."

He settled down in his chair and squinted at me. "What are you going to do when you get back to that America of yours?" he asked.

"What makes you hate America so?" I queried.

"Hate America?" he said. "I don't hate America, I regret it!"

He threw back his head again and laughed hilariously. "I regret that Columbus ever discovered it!"

I laughed with him, and rather egged him on, no doubt, for I am not touchy about our national faults.

"America," he went on, "is a bad experiment conducted by Providence. At least I think it must have been Providence. I, at least, should hate to be held responsible for it."

More laughter, and then I asked, "In what way bad?"

"Oh, the prudery, the hypocrisy, the national lack of independence! There is no independent thinking in America, is there?"

I said there was a new and very lively spirit among young people.

"Mostly among Jews, isn't it?"

"The Jews are not so free from prudery and hypocrisy," I replied.

He seemed to change the subject. "You didn't answer my question. What you are going to do when you get home? Have you any definite plans?"

"None except that I am going to write."

"I'll tell you what I want you to do. I want you to go home and write a book on America, and I'll tell you what to call it. *Misgeburt*—what is that word in English?"

"Abortion?"

"No, not abortion."

"Monster?"

"Well, that will do. You write a book about the monstrous thing that America turned out to be . . ." He paused. "The word is *miscarriage*. 'The Miscarriage of American Civilization'—that shall be the title of your book. You will find out the causes and tell the truth about the whole awful catastrophe."

He was standing up now. "That book will make you immortal. You may not be able to live in America any more, but you could go and live very happily somewhere else!"

I had risen too, and he extended his hand.

"Now I want to see that next book of yours without fail. So please remember to send it to me, and I'll read it with very happy memories of this conversation. . . ."

A very gracious dismissal. How suave and charming!—And, wrapped up in it, what a wallop! . . .

Are those, I thought, the European life-forms? Is Freud a little vain and cranky with too much peering into other people's complexes? Is it perhaps our rather hardheaded skepticism about the more mythological of his discoveries in "the Unconscious" that caused this extreme feeling? His great friend Dr. Brill tells me that this feeling dated back to his visit to this country in 1909, and the meager recognition he received from scientific circles then. I do not know. . . .

*December 15, 1941 [Pearl Harbor]*

# EDITORIAL

The week began at 2:26 P.M., Eastern Standard Time, Sunday, December 7, when WOR interrupted a broadcast of the Giants-Brooklyn football game in New York City to say that Japan had struck at Hawaii. National broadcasts were made at 2:30.

For many months members of Congress and their constituents had tried, most of them with great sincerity, to decide whether this particular act or that one was, in a favorite word of Congressional debaters, "tantamount" to war. There was great division of opinion about the width of the oceans which border the North American continent.

There was a nationwide hope that war, which all saw as inevitable, could be qualified by a phrase or a word or a reservation of some kind. The echo of the bombs that exploded on United States soil at Pearl Harbor silenced the qualifying word. The continents closed. The argument ended. It was war.

The Senate recognized the fact of war unanimously, 82 to 0. Absentee members concurred. The House voted the declaration 399 to 1, Miss Rankin of Montana, one of the two present members of the House who opposed the declaration of war against Germany in 1917, again being unable to overcome her scruples against fighting. There were hisses in the gallery but most Americans respected her. President Roosevelt signed the joint resolution at 4:10.

Individual Americans responded according to their natures, which are various. General Robert E. Wood said, "Of course the America First Committee will support the war." This apparently was the end of the Committee. Senator Wheeler said, "Everyone, regardless of party affiliations, must back up the administration." Senator Nye observed bitterly that "the United States has done its utmost to provoke a quarrel with Japan." Charles A. Lindbergh belatedly advocated support of the government.

The New York *Daily News* went on worrying about whether elections would be held and said that we must "fight for America first for a change. . . . If the Philippines, Hong Kong, Singapore and Dutch East Indies can cash in on our defense of ourselves, fine; but if they cannot —well, our first duty is to ourselves." The oceans on the big globe on the first floor of the Daily News Building looked as wide as ever, from Colonel Patterson's editorial rooms. But the *News* withdrew an antiwar cartoon, in its later editions. The Chicago *Tribune* said: "Recriminations are useless . . . all of us, from this day forth, have but one task."

Westbrook Pegler chewed nails and wrote: "In a brawl with Adolf Hitler who is, after all, the principal enemy, it is well to have a man in the White House who will not bother to break clean or keep his punches up." Dorothy Thompson kept her eye on the ball: "The only logical answer to Japan's declaration of war against us is to reply with a declaration of war against the Axis. . . . As sure as God made little green apples, Germany is going to declare war on us when it pleases her to do so."

The fact of the week was that the diverse American people, who form a democracy, had become a united people. There had been no coercion.

*January 5, 1942 [Walt Disney]*

# LEONARDO DA DISNEY

by David Low

Artists are commonly supposed to work by inspiration rather than by the conscious use of their intelligence. It is not always profitable to refute this insulting assumption, for the subtleties of a creative process are hard to communicate; and the tendency of the ignorant to surround the arts with the dignity of mystery has its advantages. But if it were necessary to prove that occasionally artists use their brains one could always produce Leonardo da Vinci and Walt Disney. The man Leonardo was an adventurous mind, fond of wheels, an engineer. As an artist he was an innovator constantly experimenting to widen the domain of art. He was (so far as I can make out) the first to go after painting round instead of flat, so that he produced an effect, new in his time, of the figures standing out from the background. Before that artists, judging color and outline more important than light and shade, had been satisfied with figures that seemed merely to be superimposed. Leonardo added to the capacity of expression the power to give depth of atmosphere. ("La Gioconda," by the way, is not a good example of the point, for it has been tinkered with too often. Perhaps the "Virgin and Child" in the Louvre is a better one.)

Leonardo's philosophy was that will was the energy of life. He was all for energy. Muscular movement and the dynamics of anatomy were favorite studies of his. The sketches for his famous equestrian bronze of Francisco Sforza show that he worked out that horse in a whole range of movement, galloping, rearing up, and still. Just like the drafts for what we call a "film cartoon." Incidentally, though Leonardo, by an unaccountable oversight, neglected to invent the cinema for himself and therefore had not its possibilities to play with, he was more than a bit of a cartoonist in our modern sense. Ordinary shapes bored him. He liked strange blobs and angles and burlesque outlines; he often drew allegorical sketches, moral and social satires and fables.

As to the other one: Disney, I think, has the grave disadvantage of not having been dead five hundred years. His generation appreciates his works, of course, but not, I fear, in the right way. Cinema audiences can hardly be expected to perceive his true significance. They are too preoccupied with sound accompaniment and idea content. Put on one side, please, the music and noise. Throw out Donald Duck. Forget "film cartoons." Consider moving drawings.

The first moving drawings made for screen projection by that old

Frenchman (whose name I forget) in 1877 (or was it 1885?) were elementary. The drawing was poor. They moved. That was as much as you could say. There followed a procession, mostly of Americans, including Winsor McKay, with his delightful but crudely moving *Trained Dinosaur, Gertie*; J. R. Bray and the magnificent *Colonel Heeza Liar*; Earl Hurd and *Bobby Bump*; Bud Fisher, who animated his newspaper comic strip *Mutt and Jeff*; Sidney Smith; Wallace Carlson and *Dreamy Dud*; Paul Terry and *Farmer Al Falfa*; and Paul Felton and *Hodge Podge*. Not all of these black-and-white comics crossed the Atlantic for British inspection.

About fifteen years ago, so far as Britain was concerned, film-cartooning was topped by Max Fleischer's *Koko, the Clown* and Pat Sullivan's *Felix the Cat*, both of which had regular runs in our cinemas. With Fleischer the animation was too conventional to be artistically interesting, obviously just a trick of drawing over photographs. With Sullivan, it was evident that collective fertility in original tricks of draftsmanship and novel mechanical devices had enabled the whole art form to be advanced a couple of miles or so.

The movement, improving slowly, had up till then been confined to the simplest actions from the easiest angles, in profile mostly, tiresome in repetition. Sullivan's animation was not yet subtle, but it was "all-round." His figures moved from all angles, sometimes a bit painfully, and they had the beginnings of perspective and individual character. Then along comes Disney.

Pat Sullivan and his predecessors were, so to speak, penny-comic. Disney organized the experts and with specialized animators, better draftsmanship, color and multiplication of the number of drawings per foot soon pushed the art first to tuppenny-comic, and then to threepenny. Now, by gosh! he has made it sixpenny, no, shilling! His last three features, *Snow White, Pinocchio* and *Fantasia*, have been each an advance upon the last in artistry and extension of range. They reveal a growing understanding of the meaning of observed movement and therefore greatly increased powers of creating imagined movement. Compare the play of human expression in the face of Snow White with that in the faces of the Centaurettes in *Fantasia* and mark the striking improvement. Subtlety is now possible.

Now here's the point. It was perfectly clear donkeys' years ago that graphic Art (with a capital A), hit by the mechanical age, needed a new idea. Heaven knows, it hasn't had one since somebody two thousand years ago thought of painting pictures to frame and hang on the wall as a change from carpets. The improving quality of facsimile reproduction probably means sooner or later a consequent reassertion of *real* values in art as opposed to rarity and other artificial commercial values. The painting of pictures to hang on walls threatens to become an increasingly precarious profession except for the few best artists. Admire the new "schools" and "movements" as much as you like or as much as they deserve; their merits are irrelevant here. All the cubes, abstracts and surrealists' ironmongery haven't really saved the situation.

It was perfectly clear also that as the machinery for representing movement improved, some intelligent lad would drop to it that the new idea was here, that the means were present for opening a new and exciting vista of possibility in graphic Art (with a capital A). At present your conventional artist who wishes to represent the beauty and character of, say, a woman or a landscape discovers the emotional elements of shape and color in the subject, and, following principles of selection and emphasis, puts them down in clarified form. But the woman moves with charm, the trees bend in the breeze. There are also emotional elements in the movements to be discovered, selected, emphasized and represented in heightened form. Why not?

National Galleries and Historical Museums are at present stuffed with portraits of the Great Men of the Past, painted looking out of their frames frozen in moments of time. It is obvious that, as records at least, these portraits are sadly deficient, for true character is not displayed in a man's physical shell but in his individual *use* of it. A row of dead men don't look so very unlike one another; but Roosevelt has his characteristically restless eye and sudden smile, Churchill his jutting forward of chin. We have many portraits which are great pieces of paint, so far as they go; but if, without losing their present excellent qualities, they gave us also with equal artistry in actual animation characteristic movements of the originals, a shrug of shoulder, curl of nostril, turn of head, they would be great, both as art and as truth. Yes? No?

I do not know precisely how much Disney has to do with the making of his own films. Much of the modern technique of making animated drawings is not, of course, his creation. (Bray and Earl Hurd, I am told, had most to do with that.) I do not know whether he draws a line himself. I hear that at his studios he employs hundreds of artists to do the work. But I assume that his is the direction, the constant aiming after improvement in the new expression, the tackling of its problems in an ascending scale and seemingly with aspirations over and above mere commercial success. It is the direction of a real artist. It makes Disney, not as a draftsman but as an artist who uses his brains, the most significant figure in graphic art since Leonardo. In *Fantasia* he lifts the art of drawing movement right out of the "comic" and essays for the first time serious studies of a higher plane. Walpurgis Night (*Night on Bald Mountain*) and the prehistoric sequences (*Rite of Spring*) drive right to the foothills of the New Art of the Future.

Your stick-in-the-muds will scoff, no doubt. But I know what

Leonardo would be up to if he were alive today. He would be in his back room inventing simplifications of animating processes and projection devices.

*December 6, 1943*

# ANOTHER OPEN LETTER
by Henry Miller

I hope it will not seem picayune on my part to pass comment on the introductory remarks accompanying the excerpts from my "Open Letter" recently (November 8) printed in your pages. If you wish to help me, and I take it that was the motive in broadcasting my appeal, then allow me please to expatiate a bit. But before I proceed, let me express my gratitude for printing even a part of that "Open Letter." Already, in the space of a few days, I have received the most warming letters from your readers, in addition to money, clothes and art materials. I have thanked these individuals privately and I now wish to thank them again publicly.

What I have to say, in making some slight rectification of your editorial comments, concerns not only myself but other unfortunate American writers, painters and musicians. It is seldom any of us has a chance to get the attention of the American public; yours is a liberal organ, as I understand it, and what I relate may be of some importance to your readers.

In the first place, in addition to the four books you credit me with, I have also written the following published works: *Tropic of Capricorn* (Vol. 1), *Black Spring, Aller Retour New York, The World of Sex, Hamlet* (2 vols.) in collaboration with Michael Fraenkel, and a brochure entitled "Money and How It Gets That Way." A book on America, called *The Air-Conditioned Nightmare*, is to be published in England in the spring of 1944; fragments of it have already appeared in various English and American reviews.

In the second place it is hardly correct to say, as you do, that "his frankness about sex made it necessary for one of his books to be published abroad, and has presumably restricted the circulation of other works of his." *All* my books were being printed in Paris—first, because I had taken up residence there; and second, because only in

Paris was I able to find a publisher courageous enough to print my work. It is true it took him three years to make up his mind to publish the first book, *Tropic of Cancer*, and then only after I had found someone to guarantee him against financial loss or imprisonment. All the books published in Paris were written in Paris, whither I had fled in desperation, being unable to obtain recognition in my own country. For ten years I wrote without a line of my work appearing in print— in America. Having found Jack Kahane of the Obelisk Press, Paris, I made no attempt to seek an American publisher for my work. I intended to remain in Europe for the rest of my life. The day war was declared my publisher died, and in 1940 I was forced home from Greece because of the war, my passport being invalidated for travel to any new country. About 1938 or '39 James Laughlin IV, of New Directions, began to make it known that he would bring out in unexpurgated form an American edition of the books published by the Obelisk Press, Paris. To date nothing of the kind has happened. A great many people think him to be my champion and benefactor. Nothing could be further from the truth.

To be specific, it was not simply "my frankness about sex" which made American publication impossible, but the use of perhaps a half-dozen words which in this country and in England too, of course, are still taboo, despite the fact that the great majority of English-speaking people use them daily in speech, despite the fact that the great masters of the English language also made liberal use of them in their books. Sex has been handled quite frankly by a number of English and American writers, but owing to the fact that they did not have recourse to these half-dozen frightening words their works have escaped censorship. (In a place like Boston, to be sure, it is not necessary to use these words in order to have the police on your neck.) As we all know, exception has been made of Joyce's *Ulysses*, but oddly enough not of *Lady Chatterley's Lover*. I have been informed by eminent jurists, who are sympathetic toward my work, that the decision in the *Ulysses* case does not establish a precedent for my work. Why? Because *Ulysses* will be read only by an elect few and is therefore unlikely to undermine the morals of the great community. An admission, it seems to me, that the decision, though based on sound logic, is highly unethical.

Had the war not intervened, these very books of mine which English and American censors label "unfit to read" (though I found from personal experience that these same censors enjoyed the reading of them immensely) would have been published in at least a half-dozen European countries. All of these countries are our present allies, except two, and even these are hardly to be classed among the backward nations. Just before the outbreak of war, negotiations were under way for translation and publication of these notorious works in the following languages: French, German, Norwegian, Dutch, Italian,

Spanish, Greek and Chinese. *More*—after writing for almost twenty years without recognition or remuneration I was just on the eve of receiving from my Paris publisher a modest monthly stipend. I mention this because those who see only the sensational and buffoonish aspects of my sporadic appeals for help, or who like my American publisher pretend that I drink up what is given me, perhaps do not realize that in Europe I was offered the opportunity to live like a normal human being, that I would not have had to battle with a hostile public, or fear to be thrown in jail for expressing myself freely.

I have a certain amount of guilt about receiving money as a painter when I know that there are painters of real talent who are in an even more unfortunate position than myself. I have been asked why I do not take a job, as other men do. I want to answer that question once and for all. Yes, I have been offered jobs, at a good salary too. All sorts of jobs. I could, for instance, work in the movie studios out here—the door is wide open. Why don't I do as other men, other writers? Because I am different, for one thing. And because I know that if I work eight hours a day at something which I am totally disinterested in I shall have no desire to write the kind of books I am now engaged, and have been engaged, in writing. I intend to do nothing but write and paint as I please. I consider that I am the best judge of how to spend my time, energy and talent. Writing scripts for the movies, writing copy for advertising agents, writing gags for the radio, writing appealing stories for paying magazines with nationwide circulation, writing for the newspapers—all these outlets for a writer I regard as nothing more than high-class prostitution. It may be possible now and then for a good prostitute to turn out a work of art, but it seems to me the chances are slim. Besides, I don't like prostitution, especially the intellectual sort. I have more respect—indeed, I often have both pity and admiration—for the streetwalker than for the artist who prostitutes his talent. And this country is full of intellectual prostitutes.

Some people say: "Why don't you take a job in the movies for a few months, then you can do as you please for a year or two." My answer to that is: "Why don't you send your daughter into the streets for a little while before marriage so that she can bring in a little much-needed change? Once she's married, nobody will know the difference."

We are supposed to be fighting for the four freedoms. Aside from the freedom to starve, the only freedom I know of in this country is the freedom to think. I have never in this country known freedom from want or freedom from fear. And there are millions of others like me, quite exclusive of Negroes, Chinese, Mexicans, Filipinos or other "undesirables." We too have our Untouchables, but we are also more hypocritical than our Hindu friends.

On my trip around America, which I undertook with my friend Abraham Rattner, the painter, we discussed at great length ways and means of giving the American artist security. We demonstrated to our own satisfaction the feasibility of supporting *all* the artists (who needed support) in this country without burden to the community. We proved by facts and figures that it could be done even in a capitalistic country such as ours. There is absolutely no reason why in a supposedly prosperous country such as America the artist should starve or else prostitute himself, no reason why he should struggle hopelessly to have his works brought to the attention of the public. A book such as *Lust for Life* creates a run on Van Gogh, but the living Van Goghs still suffer the same fate. We speculate on dead authors, dead painters, dead art products. We are practical in everything but that which concerns us vitally. We are at the peak of efficiency when it comes to destruction.

What matter if we win the war? The four freedoms will still remain a mirage. When the next war comes, other remote intangibles will be dangled before our eyes. Between wars we shall always be too busy repairing the damages of the last war to ever begin practicing the ideals we allowed our youths to be slaughtered for. There has been a great deal of talk over the radio about the new-model airplanes, the new-model automobiles, washing machines, vacuum cleaners, and so forth, which will be put on the market once the war is over. I have yet to hear a word about a new-model plan of life for the artist in this country. I don't say that the artist should be treated exceptionally, though there are excellent reasons to support this view. I do think, though, that a living artist should get as good a break as, if not better than, a dead one, that if anything he should have as good a life (materially) as a bricklayer. The life of a people resides in its artists, its men of vision, its creators. Our policy, so it seems to me, is to reward the nitwits and the halfwits, the charlatans, the mountebanks, the prostitutes.

This may seem like quite a tirade, and I sincerely beg your indulgence. I have tried—more, perhaps, than any other living writer—to tell the truth about myself, as a lone individual, in these trying times of ours. I don't say that I have succeeded; but I have tried. And I should like to be recognized for an effort which, believe me, was made not without great cost. It seems so ironical that I, who "by common consent of the critics" should be considered "one of the most interesting figures on the American literary scene," am obliged to call attention to myself as a water colorist. Here I sit in Beverly Glen making water colors, doing the best I can—and O how poor is my best!—while all the time what I really wish to do is to go on writing, giving of my best, giving of my real talent. It may seem sentimental to say that such a condition is a sad one, yet so it is. And there is no one to blame for it. The type I represent is out of joint with the times, perhaps that is all. And yet, if tomorrow by a decision of the Supreme Court those half-dozen terrifying words were restored to currency, if I, like the great English writers of the past, were permitted to use them, I should undoubtedly be sitting in clover. I might be the most widely read author in all America—*now while I am still alive*. But, unless I am vastly mistaken, not all the King's horses nor all the King's men can bring about such a miracle. We are not afraid to kill, by the million if our honor is at stake, but we are deathly afraid of a few good old Anglo-Saxon words—*in print. Alors, tant pis pour moi!*

# DECADE FOUR
# 1944-1953

*1944-1953*

As The New Republic *quietly marked its thirtieth anniversary in November 1944, the Second World War was reaching its climax. Six months later Germany surrendered, and the world began to grasp the full enormity of the Nazi purpose. R. H. S. Crossman's account of Buchenwald described the horrible fulfillment of the process of political regression which Thomas Wolfe had seen a decade earlier. In the meantime, Franklin Roosevelt had died; and two years after that tragic April of 1945, Henry Wallace, now* The New Republic's *editor (in an aberrant moment both for himself and for the magazine), wrote a thoughtful recollection of his former leader.*

*Much of the past persisted in the postwar world, asserting itself with violence against the grain of the time, as Harold Ickes and Robert S. Allen suggested in their scornful attacks on General Mac-Arthur and Senators McCarran and McKellar. But the postwar world was bringing with it a new cast of characters and a new constellation of issues. As the wartime coalition broke up, American foreign policy faced the perplexing and versatile challenge of an expanding communism. At the same time, the revolution of nationalism in the under-developed world was discharging unpredictable new forces into international affairs. Vincent Sheean's friendly portrait of Nehru indicated the new dimensions which American policy had now to take into account.*

*At home, American liberalism confronted the problem of defining its own relations with a communism which seemed now less benign than some liberals had supposed it in the thirties. Such episodes as the Hiss trial, vividly described here by Alistair Cooke, and the rise of Senator McCarthy and primitive anti-communism made the confrontation more difficult for some than it should have been: to contend that an entire generation stood in the dock with Alger Hiss surely only muddied the issue. Soon the nation began to tear itself apart in recriminations over history.*

*In 1952, two new men appeared in American politics, each holding out in his own way the promise of carrying the nation beyond the sterile postwar controversies and healing the wounds in the body politic. But Eisenhower, as Irving Brant argued in a prophetic piece before the election, had betrayed much of his opportunity even before he began (though the result was not the "stark and limitless" disaster that Brant feared). Adlai Stevenson may have lost the election, but he nonetheless restored the progressive morale. John Steinbeck spoke eloquently for the liberals of the early fifties in urging on Stevenson the continuing burdens of progressive leadership in another conservative age.*

*And so, as its fourth decade drew to an end,* The New Republic *found itself isolated from the national majority, as it had been in the twenties. Once again its role was to preserve standards and press analysis, to raise insurrections in men's minds in preparation for a new progressive revival.*

—ARTHUR M. SCHLESINGER, JR.

March 27, 1944

# DOWN UNDER IN HARLEM
by Langston Hughes

If you are white and are reading this vignette, don't take it for granted that all Harlem is a slum. It isn't. There are big apartment houses up on the hill, Sugar Hill, and up by City College—nice high-rent houses with elevators and doormen, where Canada Lee lives, and W. C. Handy and the George S. Schuylers and the Walter Whites, where colored families send their babies to private kindergartens and their youngsters to Ethical Culture School. And, please, white people, don't think that all Negroes are the same. They aren't.

Last year's Harlem riots demonstrated this clearly. Most of the people on Sugar Hill were just as indignant about the riots as was Mayor LaGuardia. Some of them even said the riots put the Negro race back fifty years. But the people who live in the riot area don't make enough money really to afford the high rents and the high prices merchants and landlords charge in Harlem, and most of them are not acquainted personally—as are many Sugar Hillites—with liberals like Pearl Buck and John Haynes Holmes. They have not attended civic banquets at the Astor, or had luncheon with emancipated movie stars at Sardi's. Indeed, the average Harlemite's impression of white folks, democracy, and life in general is rather bad.

Naturally, if you live on nice, tree-lined, quiet Convent Avenue, even though you are colored, it would never occur to you to riot and break windows. When some of the colored leaders whose names are often in the white newspapers came out of their elevator houses and down into Harlem during the riots, to urge, with the best intentions in the world, that the mobs stop breaking windows and go home, lots of the rioters did not even know who they were. And others of them said, "Boo-oo-o! Go home yourself."

It is, I should imagine, nice to be smart enough and lucky enough to be among Dr. DuBois's "talented tenth" and be a race leader and go to the symphony concerts and live on that attractive rise of bluff and parkway along upper Edgecombe Avenue overlooking the Polo Grounds, where the plumbing really works and the ceilings are high and airy. For just a few thousands a year one can live very well on Sugar Hill, in a house with a white-tiled hall.

But under the hill on Eighth Avenue, on Lenox, and on Fifth, there are places like this—dark, unpleasant houses with steep stairs and narrow halls, where the rooms are too small, the ceilings too low and the rents too high. There are apartments with a dozen names over each bell. The house is full of roomers. Papa and mama sleep in the living room, the kids in the dining room, lodgers in every alcove, and everything but the kitchen is rented out for sleeping. Cooking and meals are rotated in the kitchen.

In vast sections below the hill, neighborhood amusement centers after dark are gin mills, candy stores that sell King Kong (and maybe reefers), drugstores that sell geronimoes—dope tablets—to juveniles for pepping up Cokes, pool halls where gambling is wide open and barbecue stands that book numbers. Sometimes even the grocery stores have their little side rackets without the law. White men, more often than Negroes, own these immoral places, where kids as well as grown-ups come.

The kids and the grownups are not criminal or low by nature. Poverty, however, and frustration have made some of them too desperate to be decent. Some of them don't try any more. Slum-shocked, I reckon.

One Saturday night last winter, I went into a barbecue stand where the jukebox was loud and the air thick with smoke. At the tables there were mostly young folks—nice, not-very-pretty girls dressed in their best, with young men who had cleaned up after work. Some of the young men still wore their last spring's artificial camel's-hair coats—a top coat in winter, with the snow outside—but they were trying to look nice, to be nice in the Harlem slums.

A half-dozen teen-age boys came in and stood around listening to the records on the jukebox. Shortly, a quarrel began among them. Almost immediately knives were drawn and switch-blades flashed, and one youngster let a blackjack a foot long slide out of his sleeve.

The woman at the counter who served my sandwich said, "Somebody ought to call the cops." (As though cops could solve the problems of poverty and delinquency in Harlem.) The white proprietor behind the beer bar paid no attention to the turmoil. Short of murder or destruction, white proprietors in Harlem seldom mix in Negro squabbles—just as they never belong to neighborhood committees to improve conditions, either.

"I just don't want 'em to fight in here," the woman said, "that's all!"

The boys didn't fight. They simply milled around, showed their weapons, bluffed and cursed each other. But their language frightened some of the quiet, not-very-pretty girls at the tables with the young men in their thin near-camel's-hair coats, out on a Saturday night trying to look nice and have a nice quiet time.

Louis Jordan on the jukebox, loud. Over the music the woman behind the counter said, "This time of night, all these young boys ought to be home."

"That's right," I said.

Home. A dozen names on the bell. Roomers all over the house. No place for a kid to bring his friends. Only the pool halls open, the candy stores that bootleg liquor, the barbecue stands where you can listen to the jukebox even if you're broke and don't want to buy anything, and long Harlem streets outside dimmed out because Hitler might send his planes overhead some dark night.

Should the planes come, their bombs most certainly would be louder than the jukeboxes, and their flying fragments of metal sharper than the cheap steel of drugstore switch-blades in the hands of kids who have no homes where they can bring their friends. A piece of bomb can hit harder than a boy with a blackjack up his sleeve.

Hitler in Berlin. Bad kids in Harlem. Indignation in the Mayor's office. Also on Sugar Hill. Louis Jordan's records:

I'm gonna move . . .
. . . outskirts of town . . .

Barbecued ribs, a quarter. Sign:

DON'T ASK FOR CREDIT—HE'S DEAD!!!

Riots. Long discussions downtown about forming more committees to make more surveys for more reports for more detailed study by more politicians before taking action on conditions in Harlem.

Sign over the barbecue counter:

WE CAN'T PAY OUR BILLS WITH TRUST!
CAN YOU?

That sign, of course, is in reference to credit for sandwiches. It has nothing to do with the democratic system. It simply means that if you haven't got a quarter, you don't eat. There has been a sort of permanent scarcity of quarters in Harlem, so that sign might very well serve the committees as a motto for their surveys.

*August 21, 1944 [Mae West]*

# WHAT MAISIE KNOWS
by Stark Young

Miss Mae West, as her habit is, is again, after an absence much too long, presenting herself in a play of her own composition. *Catherine Was Great* glows with quite a lot of glowing, you might say, endless costumes, musical noises, and a cast of innumerable persons. The costumes into which Mr. Michael Todd, the producer of the play, expands are lavish in cost and variety, and must count up to far above a hundred; though very few of them have any genuine style, and almost none of them is worn well, thanks to the lack of a certain training among our actors by which the sense of wearing stage costume—especially historical—may be acquired.

The acting that surrounds Miss West's performance is fairly nondescript; to criticize most of these players would only be lacking in humor. This is partly because few of them would be any good in any part, much less as eighteenth-century Russians. It is also, however, partly because of the fact that the player does not know exactly what to do around Miss West. The style of acting, however much or little, that he has acquired, he cannot fit into the occasion. This is because the acting he practices is of the representational kind; it is representational, photographic, journalistic, plain prose, everyday, just folks or, if you like, natural. Whereas Miss West's acting is strictly presentational. Which means that she frankly presents herself and the dramatic moment as herself, as theater, as a show. She both represents and presents. High or low as may be the plane on which she, we might say, operates, she is the real thing. She is a challenge to what you know of the theater art. The point is not whether you like her or not, or admire her or not; it does not turn on what your final judgment of her may be. The point is that your approach to her is a giveaway with respect to your theater comprehension, theory and dialectic.

*Catherine Was Great*, as a play, is called no play at all by those who concern themselves over that question, or perhaps thought it might be a play. It is a succession of episodes in which the Empress of All the Russias proves to be irresistible for every sort of man, of every degree, her beauty incomparable, and her subtlety and her libido of a high, equal supremacy. To this is added a dash of historical allusion, something, for example, of democratic concern about the serfs, and a concluding ceremony in which the great savior of her country is richly honored, et cetera. None of it matters; Miss West keeps putting on new costumes, trains, furs, jewels, amid different settings unblushingly and expensively concocted by Mr. Howard Bay. The writing of the scenes is nothing to speak of, the history thrown in is mere baggage. It should be a dull evening. I did not find it so at all. Instead of being annoyed, I just kept hoping Miss West would get a good scene at last or have some lines that really came off with a bang—which never happened—and I felt pleased and chuckling and lively that she should be on the stage most of the time.

One of the chief sources of Miss West's interest for us is the extent to which the element of the abstract, as it were, clings about her. She is a performer of great canniness and of incredible, though well-disguised, energy, dogged labor, and an almost insolent amount of skill. But basically she is as abstract as Harlequin, or Pierrot, or the Charlie Chaplin in the films, or Sarah Bernhardt, or one of the pattern-figures out of history, like Julius Caesar, stern, martial, conquering hero, who —see Quintilian and elsewhere—when he was a young man, painted his nails and rouged his cheeks and was known as the Queen of Bithynia, because of his relations with its monarch; or like Cleopatra, seductress, wanton, serpent of the Nile, but who, we read, spoke five languages and nine dialects, and was so temperate in her wine that the pious Roman frauds writing their Augustan chronicles had to invent a magic ring supposed to keep the numberless cups from going to her head. So much just here about other people is out of proportion, no doubt, but it is fun and it will serve; for we can come back now to Mae West, a step that is always easy even for those who profess to be bored or horrified. She is, to repeat, as abstract as the figures I have mentioned; or as a song, good or bad; or as the circus.

And one of Miss West's secrets, though whether she knows it is thus and keeps it so I have no idea, is what, outside of business of course, she herself thinks of it all and of herself. How beautiful does she think she is, how brilliant, how dramatic? But no matter what she thinks, there must be few indeed who take this lady for a raving beauty, all curves and damask roses, the serpent of the Hudson, East River and Long Island Sound, the bird of Fire Island. Nobody believes that she has passed from one romance or passionate episode to another, or would care if she had.

Nobody would say she had great glamour, allure, et cetera—who else in the theater has, these days? But she does have something to hold your attention, she does create a howling, diverting mythology of glamour; you watch her as you watch an animal in a cage, tigress or cinnamon bear. Her cultural motifs and her ideas go round in a circle; they all come to one conclusion in fact, which seems to be that every woman has the lure and that every man can be had, and which seems dumb and flat only when she fails to insist on it as bold and true and as a theme to be accompanied by her special sway of knees and hips, her pauses, her unerring delivery and her tone—as a Frenchman once called out at the Paris opera, that nose has a remarkably fine voice. The result of all this at its best is riotous and is theater, take it or leave it. The humor is healthy and masculine, more barroom than glandular. With capital showmanship—the best on Broadway—it ultimately, as Lucian would say, invites your incredulity. For one example —Miss West may or may not be pleased to hear so—but when Potemkin rushes into her chamber, booted and spurred, and they hurry to bed, putting out the lights as they go, and his various garments are flung on to the forestage, the effect on the pulse is about the same as that we got from the stern lady some years ago, when we were trying to control it evidently, passing out leaflets on birth control at the entrance to Grand Central Station. This, of course, is the fun of the West occasion. This is a perfect case of where Miss West's fun is all male and wholesome. And what, to pick out a single instance, could be better corrective for the silly adhesive muck that Miss Bergner brings to the original fun intended for *The Two Mrs. Carrolls* than the whole Mae West sex fable?

Practically speaking, it would be only friendly to urge Miss West as a dramatist to stick somewhat closer to this very showmanship of hers. The motivations of her play need more distinctness and more variety, and the scenes themselves some cutting down or out. And if, for example, Rabelais is to be mentioned as being taken to bed by the Czarina, there is need, for Broadway audiences, of some greater explanation as to what this Rabelais is and why his book is chosen above one of Voltaire's. As for Miss West's Voltaire—not without echoes of Shaw's Monsieur Voltaire, friend and mentor of Catherine's—some persuasive citation or quotation of his might well be included. For instance, they speak of Catherine's plays being performed at court. Well, there is that remark of Voltaire's when he said that the theater was the most delightful of pastimes known to men and women when more than two of them are met together.

*July 30, 1945*

# BUCHENWALD

by R. H. S. Crossman

I was desperately busy on the morning when the interrogator brought K—— into my office. To get rid of them, I asked them both to dinner, conscious that I was almost certainly in for a wasted evening. We had seen too many "concentration-camp prisoners"—pathetic broken creatures—most of them homeless and stateless. When one had heard their story through, there always came the moment when one had to explain that we could not provide them with visas for England or the States; they must return to a Displaced Persons' Center and wait.

But the moment we met in the mess it was obvious that K—— was different. Fair-haired, slim, about thirty-four, with neat, gold-rimmed glasses and a pleasant Austrian accent, he looked as though his borrowed gray-flannel suit belonged to him. In spite of eight years in Buchenwald, he had been able to discard, along with the grotesque gray-and-white prisoner's clothes, the prisoner's mentality. K—— was not only liberated: he was free.

We started dinner at seven and finished at 3:30 A.M. We talked Buchenwald; and what follows is only a fragment of what K—— had to tell.

As a young Austrian Catholic, K—— had had a tough time at first. When he got there in 1938, Buchenwald was composed of criminals, who held all the key positions under the SS; some two thousand German Communists—the cream of the party; Jews; Gypsies and homosexuals. Each group was distinguished by its own badge, green for criminals, red for politicals, yellow for Jews and pink for homosexuals. As a political, K—— was grouped with the Communists, who did not see any particular reason why they should help an Austrian "crypto-fascist."

Somehow K—— managed to come to terms with three or four Communist intellectuals. "We had one thing in common—a will to survive. Mine was based on religion, theirs on Marxism. All of us realized there was one thing we could not afford—pity. I remember getting up early one morning to have ten minutes alone. I was sleeping in a three-tiered bunk less than three feet wide with four men on each tier. Privacy was a little difficult. I walked outside the barracks and there were rambler roses in full bloom festooned up the wall. It was five o'clock and dawn was breaking. I wasn't looking where I was going and I stumbled against a body swinging from the wall and bumping the roses. It was a Gypsy, who had hung himself by his braces. And do you know, there was a cigarette end drooping from the corner of his mouth.

"Yes, one lived by the will to survive. You remember the winter of 1940? It was our worst winter, because they allowed us no parcels. We were beaten if we went to bed in anything except our underclothes. One day we stood for nineteen hours on end at attention on the parade ground because one prisoner was missing. I saw nineteen people fall dead. The SS counted and recounted—and the funny thing was that in the end the silly swine found that no one was missing.

"I had done well. As an intellectual I had no special skill which would give me a soft job in the jeweler's workshop or the bookbinder's or the shop where the model Viking ships were made for the SS to give as Christmas presents. I was due for the quarries until a Communist offered me a job in the smithy a hundred yards away. I knew nothing about it, but there was a fire there, and he told me to stand beside it and pull bolts out of a rusty bar and put them back again. I could see the Jews in the quarry through the windows.

"One day I looked up and saw a Jew crawling on hands and knees toward the smithy. I watched him. It took him over an hour to do the hundred yards. I knew what was coming. Finally I heard the scratching on the door. I moved involuntarily to the door and opened it a foot. I saw him lying there outside. His nails were bleeding. The next thing I knew, I was lying on the floor by the fire and my comrade was standing over me saying, 'You bloody fool.' We picked up the body on our way home from work and carried it back to the camp.

"You ask me how I, as a Catholic, can tell you that: Because we had to reserve our pity for useful things—for helping the comrades when we could really help. I learned some hard lessons. I hated the Communists' contempt for the upper-class prisoners. But mostly it was justified. There were high-grade civil servants, important businessmen and dignitaries there. In the camp we were all on a level, all dressed the same. Most people's morale is supported by the corset of their social prestige and rank and status. Strip those corsets off and they sag. They lose all self-respect and the proletarians look at them with contempt. You want examples? Well, the SS gave us a brothel in 1942, fourteen girls from another camp. The secret camp committee decided to put it out of bounds for all politicals, but some of the upper-class people paid their two marks and soon they were fighting for the girls and stealing in order to give them presents. It was the same with the two hundred Polish boys. That was the sort of thing which made the proletarians say that the bourgeoisie have no self-respect when you take off their corsets.

"How were we organized inside the camp? When the SS got rid of Commandant Koch—the one whose wife liked men with tattoos, selected them for her pleasures, and then had them skinned to use the

tattooed breast-skins as parchment for lampshades—the new commandant was easier to deal with. The Communists got themselves into
all the key positions which had been held by the criminals. There was
a Communist block leader in charge of each block; Communists ran
the hospital, the canteen, the kitchen, and, most important of all, the
Labor Office, which decided on the movement of prisoners from camp
to camp and the composition of the work commandos. The SS had to
leave most of this work to the German inmates, especially when the
camp grew in size and thousands of foreigners were brought in. The
choice was whether the criminals should have this power or the po·
liticals. Of course, anyone who had it had power of life and death,
yes, of life and death. As more and more foreigners came in, the Communists naturally tended to select foreign Communists to head up the
barracks. They had an iron discipline. They did many hard things, but
they saved the camp from total extermination.

"It was funny to see the SS power ebbing away. Partly it was just
fatty degeneration. The SS men were shirking military service and
were making a good thing out of the camp. They got corrupted by
power, emotionally exhausted by beating and killing, and they knew
they were losing the war. You won't believe it, but on the day of
liberation the Communists and the Russian soldiers were walking
about in brand-new SS boots and wind-jackets and many of the SS
had only shoes. And all the time the SS were torturing or beating us to
death.

"I got a job as secretary to the doctor in charge of the typhus experimental station. I worked in closely with the Communists in the
key jobs in the hospital. We were in a strong position, because the
ordinary SS were terrified of coming near either of our buildings for
fear of infection. The two doctors were the only staff provided, and
we worked on them pretty successfully. In my section a great deal of
experimental work was carried out on the inmates. We produced one
good antityphus serum, but we reserved that for the inmates and sent
one out to the SS divisions at the front consisting mostly of water.

"It was through our positions in the hospital and experimental stations that we were able to save many people from execution. A party
of some fifty British, for instance, was brought in one day, mostly para-
chutists from the Maquis. Their morale was O.K. They formed a national group like the Russians and got in contact with the German
comrades. One day we got wind that they were all to be executed in
a week's time. I talked it over with a Communist in the hospital and
we agreed that we might be able to save four. So they held a meeting
and selected the four. The rest knew they were for it.

"The most difficult problem was the British commanding officer, because he was so well known in the camp. The only way to save him
was to substitute him for a dying man in the hospital and let him take

the dying man's papers. Unfortunately, the only foreign language he knew was French, and he was very tall. And there were no Frenchmen in the hospital. By luck a transport of Frenchmen arrived two or three days before the execution date, many of them down with typhus. But there was only one who would do.

"I shall never forget that time. The Communist who had agreed to do the job kept on saying to me, 'One little injection will do the trick. If your man is worth saving we can't be squeamish.' But the Englishman and I decided we couldn't murder the man and we hung on till the Frenchman really was dying. That was the day before the execution.

"After the execution we both got the feeling that perhaps the man hadn't been dying after all, and that we really had polished him off. So we've got the address of the Frenchman's wife and we're trying to find her, to explain what happened and to offer her compensation.

"Anyway, it all went off all right. After a week in hospital, posing as the dead Frenchman, the Englishman was moved out to a camp where he was less well known. We kept contact with him until liberation. You're surprised that one had scruples about little things like waiting for a man to be really dying before injecting him. But it was those little things which were the faith that kept me going. The Communists, of course, didn't mind about them. For them the end justified the means, and there is no doubt it was Communist discipline which saved the camp. In the end we had enough arms in the camp to take over before the Americans arrived.

"It's a queer thing, but in Buchenwald we didn't waste much time hating the SS. They beat us, they butchered us, they exploited us; but our hatred (and our love, too) was reserved for the comrades inside. It was the stool pigeons and the informers and the men who had let us down whom we really hated. The SS was an act of God. You didn't hate it, you just accepted it as the established order; or, if you were clever, you worked on it and corrupted it to make life bearable.

"I can see that you still wonder why one troubled to survive. Of course, a lot didn't, especially the nonpoliticals. But a concentration camp is just another form of human existence. After the first shock one accepts it, just as one accepts the front line or the slum. And if you decide to survive and adapt yourself, you live just as fully in Buchenwald as anywhere else; though the chances of death are a good deal higher.

"Like normal people, we had our escapes. We were allowed to receive books. Heavens, how I read in the half hour available! I shall never read so greedily again. We got the world news from the commandos, who mixed with the Germans outside, and I think we were the best-informed people in Germany. We used to send directives to comrades outside on propaganda. Then there was the cinema. We had it twice a week, mostly nonpolitical stuff. The SS had a sense of humor. They put the screen in the room where the beating block was kept. We used to watch films of people eating and drinking and sitting in armchairs, with the beating block just there behind. But on the whole it helped."

I shall never forget that dinner party. K——, with his neat gold-rimmed glasses, his boyish enjoyment of a good story, seemed not only to have survived Buchenwald, but to have developed out of it a new, steely, ironical philosophy. Perhaps, I thought, as I listened to him, the fraternity and internecine struggle of Buchenwald, the mixture of idealism and conspiracy, of self-sacrifice and self-assertion, are a microcosm of the moral and political struggle which will face all of us in the postwar world.

*January 7, 1946 [Reuther versus G.M.]*

# WASHINGTON NOTES: EDITORIAL

Walter Reuther is talking. He is presenting the case of strikers walking the picket line in Detroit as the new year begins, in zero weather. He is addressing the President's three-man fact-finding board, across the table from white-haired Charles E. Wilson, head of General Motors, while fifty reporters watch the scene with bated breath.

Reuther is thirty-eight, his salary $7,000. White-haired Wilson, flanked by respectable dignitaries of G.M., is sixty-five, his remuneration last year, in salary and bonuses, $459,000. General Motors has 426,000 stockholders. But they merely own the company. They have little to do with its management. Even provided they sympathized with Reuther's workers, which they probably don't, there is almost no way for them to intervene against the du Pont minority, but controlling, interest.

The room is a government chamber, a green-and-gold affair with 40-foot ceilings; I laid my coat and hat on a gilt piano on my way in. At one end sits the three-man panel, ruddy-faced, balding chairman Lloyd K. Garrison; Milton Eisenhower, Kansas college president, a spectacled, strong-jawed younger version of his brother; bow-tied Judge Stacy, Chief Justice of the North Carolina Supreme Court, deep-voiced, reflective, head thrust forward in a peering look. They are the jury in this strange case.

Walter Reuther is talking. Your first impression is of youth. He has brownish-red hair, almost pitch-black eyes. His voice is high and loud, he is speaking easily and excitedly. His hands are in action . . . or else hooked into his vest pockets . . . or else thrust into his trousers. This is no lawyer working for a fee, his voice has fervor and emotion; his answers to panel questions are needle-sharp. "Our boys are walking the streets in zero weather," he is saying, "for they know that everything that's good and decent, somebody had to fight for." His eyes are narrow, like a plainsman's. He is self-confident, young and sure of himself; he is talking extemporaneously, without notes; he sounds like all the New Deal economists who helped Franklin Roosevelt in the past twelve years. And that is the point your mind finally fixes on. This is a new kind of strike, a new kind of leader.

Reuther is emphasizing again and again the concept that workers have got to have high pay to buy the goods they produce. In the midst of this strike he has set his ideological sights far and away beyond those of any past leader of a big labor group. The Communists oppose Reuther; he isn't their kind. Reuther took three years off and worked in Germany, Russia and the Orient. He came back more of a native product than ever, with a remarkable comprehension of domestic and world issues. What he is saying and what he implies is that this isn't a strike, it's a crusade; furthermore, whatever happens here, it's just a beginning. Something new has happened in the labor movement.

Walter Gordon Merritt rises to give G.M.'s rejoinder. G.M. head Wilson, with his $459,000, doesn't trust himself to do the talking. He has brought down this New York attorney, specialist in labor cases. What a contrast! Walter Gordon Merritt is sixty-five, old enough to be this whippersnapper's father. His voice is bland, suave, sensible. He wears a double-breasted black suit, might be a respectable undertaker, but he has taken care of that, too—there is a single splash of orange in his black tie. He belongs to the New York Harvard Club ('o1); his experience with antiunion cases goes right back to the Danbury Hatters, that classic of injunctive repression. He is the very picture of rectitude, soundness, probity. His tone is carefully couched to contrast with Reuther's impetuosity; it is a quiet, conversational voice, better adapted to his immediate audience. He engages in a little courteous byplay about his young antagonist; he takes the three-man panel into his confidence; his voice is that of an indulgent parent talking to equals about some difficult neighborhood boy. He emphasizes the words "radical" and "revolutionary." And he tells the panel baldly that giant General Motors does not want the government messing around with its books. "If the fact-finding board rules otherwise," he says, "General Motors will withdraw from the proceedings . . ."

Now, even as he is talking, President Truman calls his bluff. He tells the panel to go ahead; look into G.M.'s data on prices and profits. Chairman Garrison reads the President's statement aloud as a messenger rushes it to him, and all the faces on labor's side break into grins. And G.M. decides not to withdraw—not for the time anyway. Not, perhaps, until it can think up some more good full-page advertisements for the newspapers. . . .

Well, folks, there you are. To me it was a pretty impressive performance. I have known Reuther before, but have never seen him in action like this. This present strike may make him, or break him, in the labor world. But I have an idea we are going to see a lot more of him, and young men of his type, in the next generation or two. And I had another queer feeling as I watched: the sense that here in the room something was being born, something pretty important was happening: that a man and a time were coming together, that an Idea was finding a Leader. . . .

*April 14, 1947 [Franklin Delano Roosevelt]*

# THE MAN WE REMEMBER
by Henry A. Wallace

Now, two years after Franklin D. Roosevelt's death, there keeps returning to me the memory of those great qualities which he had in so large a measure and which today are so lacking in our national leadership. He had, first of all, a surpassing talent for improvisation, an ability to call forth genius to flesh out his dreams. He had, secondly, an overwhelmingly infectious humanity, a quality of affection that radiated from him to his countrymen and was returned with the same intensity. He had, lastly, that huge sense of destiny which grew and grew over the years until it almost completely obscured his human faults and failings and made him, while he still lived, part of the American legend.

Roosevelt was a masterful improviser. He caught at ideas like an artist, absorbed them, implemented them, rejected them as soon as his imagination caught a fresher note that served his broad purposes better. He came to Washington in the spring of 1933, to a city paralyzed by the dead hand of custom and habit. He destroyed the paralysis by rejecting all the patterns of convention and throwing the doors of

Washington open to the men whom the "practical" world called crackpots. He arrived with no inflexible code of ideas; within a month he had made our capital the most powerful center of fresh thought in the Western world. Dreamers and planners, schemers and politicians, poured in, all of them magnetized by the man in the White House, whose eyes sparkled when he heard them talk.

My first conversation with Roosevelt was in the summer of 1932, when he first broached the shelter-belt idea to me. Roosevelt was a great lover of trees; the concept of a belt of trees stretching across the continent and sheltering the arid plains had long intrigued him. He thought the shelter belt might even change the climate of the continent. Though experts disagreed with him on his concept of climatology, it bothered Roosevelt but little. He wanted a continental shelter belt, and a year later men were planting it. His detailed planning, his mastery of the hard facts that went into grand schemes were sometimes faulty—but the grand schemes themselves were his domain. In a city of small-minded men, he collected them like a connoisseur. . . .

All ideas were grist for Roosevelt's mind—reciprocal-trade pacts, youth programs, conservation camps, labor-relations boards, agricultural-assistance schemes. As the Supreme Court would invalidate them or as they became outmoded by the passage of a crisis, Franklin Roosevelt would pass on to more dynamic concepts. His enthusiasm for ideas continued to the very end. He delighted in the term "United Nations," which he coined. He zestfully discussed with Winston Churchill the creation of a new world currency, the unit of which was to be a "dimo."

There was a radiant warmth about Roosevelt's personality. It touched all who worked with him directly, and reached further to touch the millions who voted for him term after term. He conducted his Cabinet meetings with a spirit of joy and irreverence; sometimes I wonder what they would have been like without Madame Secretary.

The Roosevelt charm was a tool of which he was fully aware; he used it consciously. He believed he could talk any man into loyalty, into continuing to work for him despite the bitterness of outside attacks. Sometimes he failed; more often he succeeded. In January 1945, Madame Perkins was ready to resign her post as Secretary of Labor; she had cleaned out her desk and wound up her affairs. But on inauguration day Franklin Roosevelt turned the full charm of his personality on her and she stayed.

He absorbed his ideas usually in conversation, for he loved good talk. At the end of a day he delighted to sit down with a drink, surrounded by sparkling talkers, and let conversation ripple around him. He loved to ramble himself—about his boyhood, about his travels abroad in his youth, about personal adventures and speculations. From the talk of others Roosevelt would pick choice nuggets of information, well-turned phrases, novel suggestions that he would incorporate into his own speeches and thinking.

His mind, like a curiosity shop, stored up odd items—of fact, history and folklore. Its diversity astonished some of the more plodding and pedestrian politicians, who would stand rapt, in wonder, while Roosevelt aired his enormous fund of accumulated knowledge.

His geniality and warmth knew no self-consciousness. I remember accompanying him on a trip to the drought area in 1936. His entourage would stop its inspections from time to time to talk to the stricken farmers, and Roosevelt would speak to them in his polished Harvard accent. Never for a moment did he seem to suspect that this was not the authentic idiom of the plains, nor was there ever a hint of patronizing or a trace of self-consciousness. And the farmers loved him for it.

Perhaps the most startling of all the intimate qualities of his mind was his spectacular spatial memory. He could remember strange streets, bays, oceans, harbors, countrysides, with almost total visual recall. During the war his knowledge of maps, distances and physical barriers was invaluable. (Usually, he was right, but sometimes he was wrong.) He remembered the depths of waters on marine charts, the heights of mountains, the quality of roads and highways. He loved to draw plans of buildings; he drew rough ones for the construction and placing of many a new building in Washington. Some he loved; others, like the Pentagon, he loathed.

This quality he extended to his vision of America, as a country. No man saw the nation more clearly as a geographic whole than Roosevelt did. He thought of it in terms of watersheds and rivers rather than in terms of states. He could catch great geophysical ideas quicker than any other man with whom I worked in the government. I remember bringing to him the original program of the soil-conservation districts. He grasped the idea instantly and the next day we had his letter, setting forth our ideas as to a state law, on its way to each of the forty-eight governors.

Roosevelt always had with him, too, the special conviction of destiny —that his was a great age of history, and that he was born to act in and dominate these times.

The world beyond America closed on Roosevelt gradually. For years he toyed with the idea that Italy was friendly, that the fascists in Europe did not mean to fight for keeps. It was only by degrees that the conviction grew on him that this was a struggle which must eventually strike at American security and American destiny. And as the conviction entered his thinking, it gradually stole from him his light-heartedness.

It was not until the spring of 1938 and the Austrian crisis that Roosevelt realized that this was a time of war that might sweep America with it. From then on, with the conviction of struggle to come,

Roosevelt maneuvered deftly to make ready his people. Hitler and Mussolini were mad dogs susceptible to force alone, but the American people were unaware of it. It was true that Roosevelt did not force through appropriations heavy enough to meet the dangers that were clearly developing, that he did not stockpile sufficient materials to meet inescapable demands. But Roosevelt had the politician's master sense of what was possible. He stood between the reality of the outside world, whose dangers he understood, and a people who lived in blithe ignorance of all these dangers. His great consideration was to create a public opinion that would tolerate even a minimum of preparedness.

The war itself oppressed him. He disliked the easy bandying about of the word "victory" in government drives. At times he seemed moved by a feeling that America might possibly fail in her goals. "This is going to take everything we've got, and even then we may not win," he said soon after the war broke out.

Perhaps not even during the war did Roosevelt evolve a complete philosophy. He played by ear, conscious of all the conflicting elements he led, seeking to reconcile them in each new crisis by new ideas and fresh thinking. I believe that any other approach to the problems of his times would probably have failed. His unending search for an ever new equilibrium in men and affairs beyond the confines of a doctrinaire philosophy may, I think, in itself have been the approach to a philosophy for free men in a free society.

*May 10, 1948 [Henry L. Stimson]*

# GROWTH OF A STATESMAN
by William Harlan Hale

In the summer of 1885, young Henry Stimson, a New York physician's son who had just finished his freshman year at Yale, went out to the Rocky Mountains to see what was then still Indian frontier country and half-mapped wilderness. In the summer of 1945, almost two generations later, the same Henry Stimson journeyed to Potsdam as Secretary of War of the world's most powerful nation, to confer amid the ruins of the German Reich which he had helped destroy. And while he was there he received the secret flash that his War Department's first atomic bomb had gone off successfully in New Mexico—thus closing one cycle of history and opening another.

Those sixty years saw America's full emergence from parochialism and isolation. Henry Stimson materially helped it emerge. Serving in the Cabinets of four Presidents, he left a major imprint upon each. Setting forth as a protégé of that stanch Hamiltonian, Elihu Root, upon whom he sought to pattern his career, he retired on the verge of eighty as a close admirer and partial legatee of Franklin D. Roosevelt.

A personal chronicle covering so broad a span of thought and action could hardly fail to be interesting. But Stimson's memoirs (*On Active Service*: Harper's, $5) are even more than interesting. As set down by his collaborator, McGeorge Bundy, on the basis of diaries, papers, and recollections of key ideas and salient men, they constitute a central document of our times.

In his public career as well as in his private law practice, Stimson was a conspicuous success. What is more, he grew. Not that the man who had started out in Root's stiffly Republican downtown law office became transformed into a whole-souled democrat under the second Roosevelt. On the contrary, he candidly says that he "never posed as an egalitarian." He seems to have stuck throughout his life to the point of view which he expressed back in 1910 to his second great friend and mentor, Theodore Roosevelt: "The Republican Party, which contains, generally speaking, the richer and more intelligent citizens of the country, should take the lead in reform."

Nevertheless, he grew. He was like both the presidential Roosevelts in that he climbed out of satisfied and rather stuffy beginnings to view ever wider horizons. But unlike the first Roosevelt, he did not spill over into flag-waving effervescence and then dry up in incoherent frustration. Like the second Roosevelt, whom he cherished even though he could not go along with his New Deal, he caught the clear vision of world-wide cooperation, and when he faced President Truman as one of Roosevelt's closest survivors he proposed what might have been the most revolutionary foreign-policy measure in our history—to renounce voluntarily the use of the atom bomb and relinquish our control of it in the interest of reaching immediate understanding with Russia.

Summarizing the world between two wars, Stimson writes, "The besetting sin of the nations was nationalism; that of the statesmen was timidity." He appears to have looked on the great powers somewhat as he did on his fellow Republicans—those "richer and more intelligent citizens" who should therefore "lead in reform." Only by bold moves on their part could the disordered world be held together. And Stimson was bold.

Back in 1915, while Woodrow Wilson was still trying to persuade himself that America could stay out of the war and yet affect its outcome, Stimson had decided for himself that there could be no neutrality in the face of aggression. In the 1920s, when it was treason for Republicans to do so, he argued that we must lower our tariffs to aid world recovery. By 1931, when America was still blindly trying to collect the uncollectible war debts, he reached the prophetic position that "debts incurred in a common struggle should never be repaid."

Next year, convinced that Japan had fallen into the hands of "mad dogs," he startled a complacent world by refusing as Secretary of State to recognize her grab of Manchuria; and then, barely giving his countrymen time to accustom themselves to his new moral stand against aggression, he began to argue (much against the pacifist inclinations of his somewhat frightened chief, President Hoover) that words were not enough and that if Japan persisted in her course, we must impose economic sanctions.

Stimson confesses that for a short time, at the start of the 1930s, he was bemused by such characters as Mussolini, Hindenburg and Laval, and underestimated the rising force of fascism and dictatorship; but by 1935 he had become convinced that the Nazi-Japanese threat was heading our way, and by 1939 (at a time when most good Americans were coming to the aid of the isolationist party) he had decided that it would be our duty to pitch in to prevent a fascist victory.

All told, one might say that Stimson was America's most radical traditionalist. He rarely let stock patterns and prejudices ensnare him; new challenges called for new answers, and he had a knack for tackling first things first. Thus, he did not let his own Republicanism stand in the way of joining up in 1940 with Franklin D. Roosevelt, in whom he recognized the leader of the internationalist cause. Neither did his personal conservatism inhibit his keenness to collaborate wholeheartedly with wartime Russia. Here and there, to be sure, old-line prejudices appear in his memoirs, as when he belabors home critics of our deal with Darlan for their "ideological naïveté" and shows annoyance at those who objected to high wartime arms-industry profits. But then, again, Stimson proudly recalls such things as his championship of General Stilwell against both the American and Chinese pals of Chiang Kai-shek (for whose regime he has little or no use); and when he comes up to Marshall Plan Europe, he shows a broad tolerance of its socialist movements and insists that "we cannot ask that Europe be rebuilt in the American image."

His memoirs run to nearly seven hundred pages; yet they strike one as curiously hard-bitten and condensed. Personal impressions, physical descriptions, anecdotes and high-level gossip play almost no part in the book; it is austere in narrative, reserved in criticism (save when it deals with the Washington admirals of World War II, who were Stimson's special bane), generous in praise (perhaps to a fault when it comes to President Hoover), and Olympian in its concentration on larger issues.

It isn't easy to read—just as Stimson wasn't always an easy man to follow. But in spite of its self-discipline and dryness, it gives an impression of unusual candor. It is a book of ideas, by a man whose strategy was ideas. Stimson emerges in it as a hardheaded, driving, abstemious and yet spacious personality, strong on self-improvement, Protestant morality, "gentlemanly" leadership, and the code of *noblesse oblige*, while somewhat short of that external warmth which builds up political sex appeal. He was also, by his own admission, a man who took time (sometimes too much time, according to columnists like Drew Pearson, who sniffed at his long rests and vacations) to think. But the thinking that resulted was broad, humane and firm, and Americans of all parties may long ponder this statesman and the lessons he has left.

*January 24, 1949*

# HARRY TRUMAN ON HIS OWN NOW

by Michael Straight

The inaugural oath which Harry Truman has taken is perhaps the greatest commitment that any man can accept. The presidential tasks, of administration, initiation and inspiration, are far beyond one man's capacity. And yet the power of the President is so great that the years of his service may be identified with his personality. Just as the New Deal expressed the exuberant and adventurous spirit of Franklin Roosevelt, so the Fair Deal will express the character and ambitions of Harry Truman.

No two personalities could be farther apart. And yet the program which Truman has laid before America carries forward the New Deal in proposals as bold as Roosevelt ever made. Those who remember the Truman of 1946 and 1947 are asking: Is this another program for the record, or does it correspond to the real convictions of a President who at sixty-four is developing into a new personality?

We believe that Truman has not greatly changed in office, but that the impact of his character on today's problems will make the Fair Deal a memorable time in American social progress.

Truman is not a man to lead a crusade. Unlike Roosevelt, he cannot easily conceive or dramatize new ideas. He has a continuing dislike for "professional liberals" and their passion for changing America. If he changes the face of America it will not be according to any book he has read or any doctrine; it will correspond to the human needs that he has felt.

A onetime dirt farmer, born of pioneer parents; a business failure along with millions of other Americans; a Democrat by tradition, because there were no Republicans around; a hero of Battery D; convenient for Tom Pendergast's machine; a county politician in Washington Township, south of Tom's town, Kansas City; friendly with every businessman; known to every barber; Lion, Eagle, Moose and Elk; member of the Legion, the V.F.W., the Regular Veterans Association, the order of Ahepa, the Society for the Preservation of Barbershop Singing, 33rd Degree Mason—President Truman, as Frank Gervasi says, is the square root of America.

The big cities over which Roosevelt presided are still big cities to him; the faraway lands which lay at Roosevelt's fingertips are still far away. His liberal friends distrust New York liberals; his Jewish friends distrust New York Jews. He is more at home in a clubhouse than in a union hall; happier playing poker than debating with intellectuals. He swears freely in the presence of men, and never before ladies. Without eloquence or command of speech, he lights fires among crowds, who sense that Roosevelt was for them and that Truman is of them. He knows, because he shares the hopes and fears of millions of Americans who half admire, half resent those who shove them around.

He doesn't *sympathize* with the millions of Americans who get shoved around; he *participates* in their experiences, because he has been shoved around. Roosevelt's strength was his compassion; Truman's strength is his experience.

He knows the need for federal aid to education, because he and his mother scraped dimes together to buy his schoolbooks. He wants stronger civil-rights statutes, because he has lived under the Klan and seen blood shed in race riots. He knows what inflation means, because boom and bust after the last war broke Truman and Jacobson, men's outfitters, of 12th Street in Kansas City. Frank Gervasi points out that it took Truman twenty years to pay off debts he had voluntarily assumed and that just three years before he became President of a $250-billion-a-year nation, Truman paid off the last remaining debt on his haberdashery store.

Yet many men, exploited all their lives, have entered politics to serve the exploiters.

Truman in politics was always an organization man. He built a good record in the Senate, because he was part of a good organization. Suddenly he found himself head of the organization. If anything, his task was harder than Roosevelt's. As President, Roosevelt lifted the performance of our government and the awareness of our people to the level of America's new tasks. Yet, save for a few months between

Munich and Dunkirk, the liberal movement which flowed through him knew where it was going. In Truman's term, the compulsion to one world and the breaking into two worlds left liberals uncertain of their ends, and set as tasks of leadership the re-evaluation of a great world movement and the determination of objectives as well as tactics and strategy.

Reaction was in the ascendant and anticipated its assumption of full power. Roosevelt at such a time might have gone down with all flags flying. Truman, governed by innate caution and a sense of inadequacy, followed liberal principles and conservative policies. Pulling back his lines, he found himself, in 1947 and 1948, little better than a constitutional monarch with responsibility and no authority and with not much time to prepare himself and to grow.

Of course, Truman has grown in administrative ability and in understanding, although his capacity for growth is not unusual. He lacked at first a judicial approach in the determination of the problems that mounted on his desk. He was quickly convinced by a persuasive argument; he made snap decisions; he often burned his fingers. He learned to listen; to bring both sides into any conference; to end by saying, "I want time to think this over," and to assign his staff to investigate quietly before making up his mind.

He lacked also a comprehensive approach to government. From Roosevelt he inherited a coalition. So from his first day he was involved in a continuing conflict between liberals and conservatives within the administration. Generally the liberals were outnumbered. They held the staff posts and lost the command posts. They prepared speeches and programs; the conservatives made the appointments and ran the government. Truman relied on his old friends, who were mostly untrained, although the federal government demanded more specialized ability than any industry. Consequently the government gained a reputation not only for conservatism, but for incompetence and mediocrity. In the major postwar problems of reconversion, inflation, labor relations and peace, the government shared much of the responsibility for mismanagement and failure.

So, Truman's ties to labor and to his own party leaders weakened until, early in 1948, the Democratic Left split three ways: some groups supporting Truman for renomination; some seeking to build a new party on the prewar, people's-front pattern; some, including the *New Republic*, searching for a new standard bearer for the Democratic Party. All three groups joined in one conviction, that Truman could not win.

Truman in 1948 reached a decisive turning point. His own staff was largely liberal. And, beset by Dixiecrats, Progressives and rebellious Democrats, he debated their wisdom. It was clear to him that he would run, and that the Eightieth Congress would be his campaign target.

But a major battle was fought and won before he decided to make his fight also on an affirmative liberal platform. With that decision made, the Democratic platform, except for details in the civil-rights plank, was Truman's platform.

Militant liberalism won for Truman and so re-established itself in government. The challenging programs outlined in the State of the Union message, the budget and the Economic Report are not the unwitting commitments of a man without comprehension of their significance or of the opposition they will arouse. When he read to the Cabinet paragraph eight of the anti-inflation program of the State of the Union message, all hell broke loose. The conservatives fought first to eliminate the entire paragraph, which referred to expansion of capacity, then to omit the reference to the steel industry. Truman yielded momentarily on the second point, reconsidered, and put the reference back in.

Roosevelt knew the things he would not trade; ruthlessly he traded everything else, to get what he wanted. He ran Congress; his leaders resented taking orders, but they took them. Now the same men—Rayburn, McCormack and Barkley—will seek to run the nation. They may well conflict with the administration. It will not be a conflict of liberalism and conservatism. But the Fair Deal may be shaped by what they think Congress will accept.

A new President takes office in the spirit of a honeymoon. Within six months, if he moves ahead, he makes so many enemies that the rest of his term may consist of compromises. The New Deal, despite Roosevelt's continuing vitality, had almost died three years after his first election. For Truman, the next six months are all-important. If he engages at once in major battles his casualties will be costly. If he waits, his popular following may fall away and his opportunity be lost.

Some of his friends are now busy weaving a myth of Truman, the invincible leader, the second Lincoln. This seems to us to be dangerous and a little grotesque. He is a typical American whose strength is his averageness. His record has still to be made. It may be given to Truman to accomplish more than all but a handful of Presidents could accomplish. He still may fail.

We are sure that Truman, win or lose, will not fit into any of the niches of history which we may prepare for him. He will never really trust the New Dealers or the trade-union leaders, and they will never really understand him. The climate of intellectual restlessness and economic militancy in which they thrive will never completely blend with the air of small-town complacency in which Truman lives. Yet, if he accomplishes a significant part of his present objectives, Truman will be remembered as one of the major figures in American liberalism. And, since he dislikes all labels, no one would recoil more from this thought than Harry S Truman.

*July 4, 1949 [The Alger Hiss Case]*

# A GENERATION ON TRIAL
by Alistair Cooke

It is never easy on the conscience, and an assault on what we call our sense of reality, to come out of a trial into the daylight and the world of sunlight, business, gossip and friendship. To come out of the paneled courtroom in New York where they are trying Hiss and limp into Foley Square is to exchange two worlds any decent citizen is meant to accept as one: a world in which every casual memory and date is screened for perjury, and a world in which dates are heedlessly made, truth is the "I said to her" of the couple on the bench, and a drunken bum failing to filch a cigarette calls you a son-of-a-bitch and staggers off, free as the dust and the smell of chicory. Then you have a soda and a sandwich and hear more headlong perjury at your elbow in a half hour than a Lloyd Paul Stryker will expose in a lifetime.

No wonder you can only give a dusty answer to friends who seize you in the evenings and the weekends and ask which is the liar, which is the guilty one? You only wish they would come into the courtroom and see terror and comedy putting on a medieval ritual. It is one of the great, and perhaps inevitable, misfortunes of this trial that it asks twelve human beings, twelve of Chesterton's "ordinary men looking on," to interpret the friendships and beliefs of the mid-1930s in the political climate of 1949. In this sense, it is not only Alger Hiss who is on trial. It is a whole generation. And whatever the verdict, there is a historical tragedy latent in the lives and careers of Hiss, Chambers and Henry Julian Wadleigh of the same kind, and not so secular at that, as in the trial of Saint Joan.

To see just where this tragedy applies, you have first to be careful to separate the courtroom procedures and traditions that shock the layman, unused to trials, especially if he is an idealist, or a nonreligious liberal, who wants to make the courts more heroic than they can ever be; who assumes they are the guardians of a man's faith and of a way of life. Two of these procedures that hurt the sensitive are the requirements of a witness not to make assumptions or deductions but to give positive answers, and the whole tradition of cross-examination.

Charles F. Darlington, an assistant chief of the trade-agreements section of the State Department, was the most conspicuous victim of the first procedure, only because he is a lawyer himself and meant to appear a very smooth article. He was asked to say what he "observed" about Wadleigh's "behavior" when he asked questions. This naturally provokes opinions. But opinions are not evidence. Has he any independent recollection of a certain document "remaining on top of the desk"? He says he thinks "it would be normal . . ." and Thomas F. Murphy, the government counsel, groans, "Will you please direct the witness, Your Honor, to answer questions?

A layman assumes that "to tell the truth, the whole truth, and nothing but the truth" is a good and practicable oath. But as a moral command, it is clearly an impossibility. And the pathos creeps in when you see in the flesh a witness whose notion of a truthful memory is even more scrupulous than that of somebody else who possesses the legal knack of being "a good witness."

For example, Mrs. Chambers' memories of where the Hisses lived in Washington happen to be essential to the second indictment—the charge that Hiss lied before the grand jury in saying he had never seen Chambers after January 1, 1937. She first said she and her husband had gone to a New Year's Eve party at the Hisses' when they were living at Volta Place, on December 31, 1937. It has been established that the Hisses did not move to this address until the very end of December of that year. Under ordeal by Stryker, Mrs. Chambers amended her testimony to put the date a year earlier. Then she started to wrestle with her uncertain memory of three parties—a housewarming, a wedding anniversary and the New Year's Eve party. After long silence, she says, almost to herself, that the Volta Place party "must have been the housewarming." Stryker whisks around. "You were at the Thirtieth Street House, not Volta Place, then, on December 31, 1937. Is that your testimony now?"

Another long pause. Mrs. Chambers' eyes go to the ceiling and she drums her housewife's fingers on the rail, like a woman checking the figures on a grocery bill. She says, hopelessly, "I am trying to recall," and wanders off into the dark underground of her memory. She has been said by the press, indeed on her own confession, to be "not very good on dates." But this is only because her replies seem to spring from a premise in her own mind that the law cannot allow for. It is that, somewhere deep in her memory, if only she can concentrate her digging in the right place, the truth and the recollection will be found to run in overlapping seams. But every time she tries, she discovers to her obvious alarm that the memory is a poor miner and that the deep recesses of truth are guarded by jesting Pilate.

A little later, Stryker was trying to find out when she had decided to include Alger Hiss on a jaunt Mrs. Hiss is supposed to have made to drop some children's things off at the Chamberses' apartment in New York. When did she have her memory refreshed? She thought it was when the F.B.I. spoke to her.

"Was there any sort of leading question on the part of the F.B.I. to suggest Mr. Hiss might have been there?"

She answered at once, quietly and with much dignity, "You are insulting, sir."

Murphy came snorting to his feet and the judge's head bobbed over the bench and his pink face reddened. "Mrs. Chambers," he lectured, "from the standpoint of both the government and the defendant this is a most serious case. Mrs. Chambers, I tell you again not to indulge suggestions of that kind."

You have to be a lawyer to sense the correct direction from which righteous indignation is likely to come. Anywhere outside a court, Stryker would have seemed to get what was coming to him. But sarcasm and invective are the counsel's monopoly and the witness must swallow his emotion and say yes and no. It is doubtful whether the American jurists who have cherished this inheritance from English common law ever anticipated the explosion on the legal scene of Lloyd Paul Stryker. For he prowls the shadowy fence between truth and untruth like a tomcat howling at the neighborhood to come and join in the obviously hopeless search for an honest man.

These, then, are the conventions that put any trial in a certain emotional frame and make it, I should say, even harder for the jury to eschew emotion, prejudice, bias, sympathy and all the other admonitions that, if faithfully sworn to, would produce not twelve jurymen but a dozen saints.

What is there in this trial, more than any other, that reflects an inevitable personal tragedy which the court cannot appease or resolve? It is, I think, the fact which constantly emerges through this disheveled stockpile of memory that the main characters were idealists at a time when the nature of loyalty—to the state, to one's beliefs, to one's family and fellow men—was undergoing one of those historic and permanent changes. In the Western world, loyalty has simmered down to a negative assumption that a man is bound first to his family, then to his country's policies, and between these poles his yearnings toward reform swing freely within the limits of Christian charity.

The positive religious impulse of our time has been the Soviet assertion of another integrity, whose ghastly vitality the sentimental liberal has learned about only since he has come to see that Hitler produced in the Third Reich an inverted parody of the Communist state. This "integrity" is like the priest's in denying the prior loyalty of the family and the state. It is a dedication (as I think, a pathological one) to the omnipotence of the revolutionary clique, which transcends the loyalties of human love, of family and of state. Up to now we have heard about it as a monster Displaced Person at large over Eastern Europe. We have seen our own tradition debauched by it in the figure of Rubashev, in *Darkness at Noon*. Before that, we saw it as a monstrous figure of fiction in Conrad's *Under Western Eyes*.

To be such a character, we are told, takes demoniac guile and the

guts of a martyr. It is still next to impossible to watch Gromyko and
Malik out at Lake Success and grant that they, in their Sears, Roebuck
suits, can really be such men.

And the fascination of the Hiss trial, the weird sense of a ghoul
invading a clambake, is the possibility that this sensitive editor and
Maryland farmer, and the handsome young lawyer in the Brooks
Brothers suit, might both some time have made that dedication.

*October 10, 1949*

# PRIME MINISTER NEHRU

by Vincent Sheean

The Prime Minister of India, who is to arrive in the United States
for the first time on October 11, is one of the remarkable personalities
of the century. His country is the largest political unit, in numbers of
persons governed, now existing; it is at a crucial intersection both of
geography and of the flow of ideas; it is the largest holder of sterling
balances; it is the land mass which most requires development and
promises most return from such development. Quite aside from India's
contributions in the past, these strictly practical contemporary considerations would give enormous importance to a visit from its Prime
Minister.

But Jawaharlal Nehru, who has been Prime Minister for two years
and a half, has been a remarkable personality for decades. Readers
in this country know, from his autobiography and from the later work
called *The Discovery of India*, that his mind has an altogether different
quality from that usually found among holders of even very high
office. Newspaper readers for thirty years have followed from afar,
sometimes with incomprehension but usually with sympathy, the
events of his long struggle as a leader of the masses for the independence of India. It has been possible to discern an evolution in his
mode of thought and action which should be instructive to men at all
times and places, from the fiery vehemence of the 1920s to the controlled and responsible conduct of government today. The fires are
still there, without a doubt, but they are ruled by an intelligence which

appreciates to the full how much all Indian life (including such things as the supplies of basic food) must in this phase depend upon the acts, the words and even the attitudes of men in power.

The central themes of Nehru's thinking are clear. They are to be read in his books, his public speeches and his deeds. He has at all times opposed colonial imperialism, as he does today, and it can hardly be questioned that he has played a great part in bringing it to the last gasp not only in India but throughout Asia.

In this respect he stands as a champion of all the Asian peoples, and even those with whom he is embroiled in dispute at present (such as the Pakistan leaders) would not deny it. At times in the past—less sharply at present—he has blended his anti-imperialism with a social program hardly to be distinguished from straight socialism. His late opponent, Mohammed Ali Jinnah, used to say that he was "from Benares by way of Moscow." This was, of course, a forensic exaggeration; Nehru has little indeed to do with Benares, and it is twenty years and more since he visited Moscow.

The kernel of truth contained in the exaggeration is this: Nehru, although completely emancipated, was born a Brahmin, and there is something unconsciously, irrepressibly, irretrievably aristocratic about his personality. His Western education and his sense of justice have led him, for years past, into beliefs involving the broadest kind of social democracy, which naturally brought him (1927) to visit Moscow. Not to be interested in what the Bolsheviks were doing, in the 1920s as now, would be imbecilic on the part of any public man. But his socialism (which is in any case his own and not that of the Indian National Congress) has never fallen under Communist domination or even influence. At the present moment he has not hesitated to imprison some thousands of Communists in India, not for their ideas or beliefs, but because they tried to disrupt the railroad system and imperil the food supply of hundreds of millions of people.

Nehru is thus, by most standards, a "man of the Left" in just about the same sense that Franklin Roosevelt was a man of the Left. In government he has followed the principle Roosevelt so insisted upon, that first things should come first, and in the case of India the very first of all things is food for the masses. This has not interfered with the formulation of great schemes for flood control, water power, land reclamation and universal education, upon which beginnings have been made. The new Indian government has, in the two and a half years of existence, had grueling difficulties, of which the greatest and most persistent has been the dislocation of many millions (about ten in all) of the population—Hindus from Pakistan taking refuge in India, Moslems from India taking refuge in Pakistan. Against this terrible situation Nehru's long-term solution has been kept steadily in mind, and that is the creation of a secular state in which these differences will not be recognized. Again in this case (as with electrification, education, etc.), long-term objectives sometimes are obscured by short-term necessities, but they are never forgotten.

The American public is familiar with Nehru's appearance through innumerable photographs published here for three decades—the fine, sensitive face, the white cap of the Indian National Congress (the "Gandhi cap"), the uplifted head and hand. Most of the photographs seen here seem to have been taken in characteristic attitudes while Nehru was speaking to a public audience. He is, so far as I know, about the most indefatigable public speaker in existence. I followed him through one crowded day on his visit to Calcutta last January, and he made nine speeches between breakfast and dinner. In India he uses English or Hindi, depending on his audience, and sometimes in the same speech he uses first one and then the other. The language problem in India is such that in almost any audience there will be some persons —in some areas a majority—who understand English considerably better than they do Hindi. . . .

Readers of Nehru's books know how forbearing he always has been toward those whom history had placed in the position of enemies to the Indian National Congress, i.e., the British. It was, of course, a leading Gandhian principle that the enemy should be treated with courtesy at all times, always being notified in advance of moves to be taken, and to be conciliated with friendliness whenever possible. In Nehru's own case, since his formative years had been spent in England, actual bitterness was probably impossible because he understood the British too well. They kept him in jail, off and on, for a matter of nine years, and it requires a certain largeness of spirit on the part of any man to overlook this, but he did overlook it. In fact, he is sometimes quoted as saying that he got more work done, in the way of reading and writing, in jail than anywhere else. It was in jail that he learned (out of a book) those few simple physical exercises which he still performs every day, which have helped his body to withstand the stresses and fatigues of his extraordinary position.

And it is extraordinary. Nehru is not only Prime Minister; in a very real sense he is the essential strength, the apex of the popular pyramid, in the Indian government. He has able assistance from the Deputy Prime Minister, Sardar Patel, with whom he probably does not see eye to eye in social and economic matters; between them they make a strong combination. But it is Nehru who possesses the capacity, even in a phase of anticlimax, of arousing the enthusiasm of the masses so that grievances are forgotten and political differences obliterated. It is done partly by personality, partly by legend, and in great part by the gift of unconscious bravery. He apparently thinks nothing of exposing himself in an open car in the midst of ungovernable millions of people up and down the streets of Calcutta, the most disaffected and turbulent great city (as it always has been) in India. The security police are in a constant state of agitation about him, but he seems long ago to have abandoned any worries about his own safety.

There is one further aspect of Nehru's historic activity which has not yet fully come into the public consciousness, but which I believe to be on the eve of fulfillment. That is, what he can do for the world of which India is a part. As is well known, he is the political heir of Gandhi, and in spite of the great and obvious differences between them as personalities, this heritage is not to be taken lightly. It seems likely to me that the conditions now obtaining—not only materially but psychologically—in this gathering twilight have, independently of human volition, placed India in a central place. It is now a kind of heartland, as its geographical shape, oddly enough, prefigures. Its future involves the future of the whole body. I believe Nehru knows this—I am only guessing; he has never said so to me—and that he is prepared to do whatever he can. There is a sort of valiant and determined synthesis in his conduct of public affairs, which is matched by a sort of intellectual scorn for the sterility of logical excess.

It would be easy to show—as the Pakistan leaders have shown—that the principle of "accession to India," which governs Nehru's formal statements on Kashmir, would have led to exactly opposite results in the cases of Hyderabad and Junagadh. This accession principle is, of course, merely formal; if you proceed to the reality underlying all such legal arguments, the fact is that no modern state could long endure the existence of a hostile, medieval autocracy like Hyderabad in its very middle. Equally, no modern state, especially in a time of exacerbated emotion, could sit idly by while its nationals were murdered and despoiled by tribal raiders on its very borders. It is true that formal logic cannot equalize these three actions (Kashmir, Hyderabad, Junagadh), but it is also true that the stern necessities of holding a newborn state together could not permit such disintegration to proceed.

The same sense of reality limits Nehru's international activity to what, at a given time and in front of a given situation, he can actually do. The Delhi Conference of the independent countries of Asia, last January, is a case in point: it caused great apprehension in the foreign offices, but it was so skillfully managed, and indeed circumscribed, that it achieved its objective without unduly rocking the boat.

Such skill and sensitivity to the currents of feeling are rare. When they are accompanied by what I believe to be Nehru's supreme desire for peace in the world, there exists the possibility of peace. Blessed are the peacemakers, especially when they know what can and cannot be done.

324

December 25, 1950 [Douglas MacArthur]

# MACARTHUR HOME FOR CHRISTMAS
by Harold L. Ickes

Abraham Lincoln constantly exchanged worse generals for better ones during the Civil War. Otherwise, he would have failed in his duty to the people. He reshuffled until, in Ulysses S. Grant, he found a man equal to the task of restoring peace. What was Lincoln's duty is President Truman's. General MacArthur, all things considered, has failed in Korea. The heroic soldiers and marines who chased the MacArthur *ignis fatuus* to the border of Manchuria should not pay the entire cost.

There was no absurd Stassen or Knowland to demand, after McClellan had been routed at Bull Run, that Lincoln should recognize him as the supreme commander. Yet, today, these and other political and newspaper hysterics are shouting to President Truman to abandon his authority and give General MacArthur *carte blanche* to determine foreign and military policy in the Far East. Could asininity go further? Behind the smoke screen of the pro-MacArthur newspaper chains of Hearst, Roy Howard and Bertie McCormick, nondescripts in and out of Congress are demanding that the President violate the Constitution by delegating nondelegable powers to the man who failed in the Philippines, who was badly informed—if informed at all—when South Korea was invaded, and who is responsible for the worst defeat in American military history. At tremendous human sacrifice he attempted to surround the Chinese Communist hosts in North Korea; instead, they surrounded his armies and sent them plunging back over the roads which they had but recently trod as triumphant victors. To be sure, there was one brilliant interlude for which MacArthur has already been given high credit. But that one stroke which drove the North Koreans out of Pyongyang was more than matched by the rout of the UN armies with terrific casualties. United States prestige has been damaged to an extent that will be difficult to rebuild.

It is an immutable law of life, and a just one, that he who makes a mistake, even if honestly, shall pay the penalty. MacArthur's grievous fault should be expiated, at least in part, by himself. The total debt should not be imposed upon bereaved widows and orphans and parents to pay in the cruel coinage of war—death and mutilation and torture in prison stockades. This is especially true since MacArthur ignored warnings by apprehensive superiors that what, if successful, might be a glorious adventure, might, if unsuccessful, be an inglorious defeat except as it might be relieved by the deathless heroism of UN

soldiers battering their way out of the entrapment in which Mac-
Arthur's orders snared them. Even the British and the French governments unofficially suggested the dangers involved to ennuied State
Department officials. If these cautions were forwarded to MacArthur,
they, too, were given no heed. As usual, MacArthur was all-knowing.

MacArthur might have defended Korea. He chose to attack. Greater
glory might lie that way. He committed the colossal blunder of dividing
his forces in half, sending one army northeast and the other northwest,
with a wide gap of difficult but undefended terrain between. It was
through this inviting gap that the Chinese struck, with great power and
in overwhelming numbers. The tragic and precipitate katabasis of the
UN troops is still being written in blood and tears and tragic sufferings.

MacArthur refused to listen to doubts raised by the C.I.A., based
upon information that that organization had and which MacArthur
apparently neither had nor cared about. His Chief of Intelligence, upon
whom he implicitly relied because he was first and foremost a Mac-
Arthur idolator, was Major General Charles A. Willoughby, who, significantly, was also MacArthur's reservoir of knowledge and fount of
military wisdom during the unfortunate Philippines campaign immediately following Pearl Harbor. It was because he relied upon General
Willoughby's misinformation and his own godlike qualities when the
North Koreans invaded South Korea that MacArthur was so unready
there—as unready, in fact, as were the Departments of State and of
Defense in Washington. At this early stage of the war, we narrowly
escaped annihilation because MacArthur's "Chief of Intelligence" had
no intelligence of which he could be chief. However, General Willoughby could be, and was, second only to MacArthur in arrogance
and self-importance. Yet, to this same Willoughby was entrusted the
duty, to the contemptuous exclusion of all others, of keeping Mac-
Arthur informed on what the Chinese Communists were doing or
might attempt. This pretentious general, to whom history will doubtless assign his proper niche, should also feel the weight of the righteous
anger of President Truman.

General MacArthur boasted that he would have American soldiers
home by Christmas. It is to be hoped that, in any event, President
Truman will bring MacArthur and Willoughby home by Christmas.
And they should stay here until some appropriate Congressional committee can make a full and objective investigation, not only of the
events leading up to the Korean debacle, but of the reasons for the
failure of MacArthur in the Philippines.

September 17, 1951 [McKellar and McCarran]

# "TWO OLD MEN" OF THE SENATE

by Robert S. Allen

It takes a mighty rugged constitution to be a State Department official these days. Besides undergoing frequent public sluggings by Senator Joe McCarthy, there is also the little-known ordeal of being privately browbeaten and threatened by the "two old men" of the Senate Appropriations Committee.

They are Senator Kenneth McKellar, eighty-two-year-old Tennessean, chairman of the committee, and Senator Pat McCarran, seventy-five-year-old Nevadan, who heads three committees—Judiciary, Internal Security and the Appropriations Subcommittee in charge of the budgets of the State, Commerce and Justice Departments. McKellar has been on the government payroll, as a member of Congress, for forty years; McCarran, for twenty-two years.

A graphic illustration of the kind of performance they stage behind the locked doors of their committee is the experience of three young State Department executives, each an outstanding success in his profession and each working in Washington at considerable personal sacrifice. They are Deputy Undersecretary Carlisle H. Humelsine, Assistant Secretary Edward W. Barrett, and Foy D. Kohler, chief of the broadcasting of the Voice of America. Each was subjected to a ferocious hazing, during the course of which they were ordered, under dire threats, to violate the executive order issued by President Truman last year forbidding agencies to divulge the individual security records of employees without express White House approval. McKellar and McCarran demanded that this official regulation be disregarded.

The full story of what happened to these three young officials is recorded in the unpublished proceedings of the Senate Appropriations Committee. It explains why government leaders are finding it so difficult to prevail on promising youths to take responsible public jobs.

Humelsine was the first to "get the works." McCarran lashed into him with, "Will you give this committee the loyalty reports on every State Department employee connected with the Voice of America program? I want a yes or no answer."

"Senator, I have no individual discretion in that matter," replied Humelsine. "I am under the same restriction as everyone else in the State Department on this executive order. Only the President can release those confidential records. We don't have the power to do that."

"In other words," snapped McCarran, "we can't get those records."

"Not unless the President of the United States personally authorizes your having them," said Humelsine. "It is entirely up to him."

"Let me give you a little advice right here," broke in McKellar. "You had better tell the President to instruct you to give these things to this committee. If you don't, you're going to be in one hell of a fix. Is that clear to you?"

"And I want to add," declared McCarran, "that before I get finished I am going to show that there are people in your program who shouldn't be there. I'm going to have you all up before my Internal Security Committee for investigation."

"We welcome any investigation," interjected Barrett, head of the Voice of America.

Barrett's remark promptly brought the "two old men" down on his head. "I would like very much to have your background and loyalty record," cried McCarran. "I'd like to know all about you."

"That's easy," retorted Barrett. "My life is an open book."

"All right," shouted McCarran, "then answer this question. Are you connected with any socialistic or communistic institutions?"

"Of course not," said Barrett. "I am not now and never have been. I have never belonged to any organization listed on any subversive list. During the war, I was deputy chief of psychological warfare in the Mediterranean theater, and later I became editorial director of *Newsweek* magazine."

"What are your views on Socialism and Communism?" demanded McKellar. "What about fellow travelers; are you for them or against them?"

"The reason I came to Washington at considerable personal sacrifice," answered Barrett, "was to fight Communism. If I hadn't felt so deeply about that, I wouldn't be here today."

"All right," said McCarran, "you are against Communism. Now turn over those loyalty files to us."

"Yes, give them to us," thundered McKellar. "We pay you, and we're entitled to this information. This order by someone else against doing that doesn't go very well with us. I want to warn you that you're hurting your own case when you refuse to give that information to this committee."

"We explained why we can't do that," said Barrett. "The President issued an executive order forbidding those records to be made public without his permission. We can't violate a regulation like that. We are wholeheartedly fighting Communism, but we can't defy the President of the United States and disobey an official order that he has issued."

"I'm not afraid of Communists in Russia," cried McKellar, "but I am afraid of Communists in America. I don't see a thing that your organization has done to fight Communists in America. That's what I'm interested in. By the way, are you a churchman?"

"Yes, sir."

"Are you a Presbyterian?"

"Yes, I happen to be a Presbyterian."

"Well," said McKellar, "nobody's going to change your religion, and you and your Voice of America aren't going to change anything either."

"And there is one thing you want to remember," concluded Mc-Carran. "There is no compromise between Communism and democracy. Nothing can stop the Reds except war. That is my view and the view of many of us. I hold that view very, very seriously. Nothing will stop them except bullets, and the sword and the bayonet." (Neither McCarran nor McKellar, of course, has ever held a bayonet, let alone faced one. Humelsine and Barrett, in contrast, made brilliant records in the last war.)

Kohler was startled by McCarran demanding of him, "Whom do you know in the Russian government?"

"Did you say Russian government?" asked Kohler.

"That's what I said," retorted McCarran. "Whom do you know personally in the Russian government?"

"I have no friends in the Russian government," said Kohler. "I have met some Russian officials in the line of duty, such as Molotov, Gromyko, Vishinsky and Malik. But I have never met anyone in the Russian government on an unofficial basis."

"This committee wants the names of Russians who have defected from the Communists," demanded McKellar.

"I will give you a list of names if we are assured you won't make them public," said Kohler. "But we can't give you names for publication because the lives of these people and their relatives in Russia would be placed in immediate jeopardy."

"That's no valid reason for not making them public," argued Mc-Kellar. "I don't know why you don't reveal those names to the world."

"Surely you wouldn't want us to jeopardize the welfare and possibly the lives of these people?" asked Kohler.

"I don't know about that," said McCarran. "I can't see your point of view on this matter."

"Let's subpoena all of them," McKellar concluded. "We'll show you who's boss around here."

*November 3, 1952*

# THE TRAGEDY OF EISENHOWER

by Irving Brant

Win or lose, Dwight Eisenhower today is one of the most tragic figures in American history.

Applauded by all the world as a professional soldier and military hero, he stepped five months ago into the alien field of politics and from that day has gone steadily down in the esteem of those who once admired him most.

Starting as one who would accept but not seek the office of President, he has sought it through all the demoralizing compromises that come from excessive desire to win.

Dependent on others for a swift briefing in civil affairs, he has steadily learned the wrong things from the wrong people.

Counted on to rescue the Republican Party from its discredited Old Guard, he has made himself the hapless prisoner of the faction he defeated.

Saying "I am not a politician," he has proved it by embracing political hacks and blatherskites.

Lifted to eminence by General Marshall, he has taken the hands and endorsed the candidacies of men who called Marshall a front for traitors and a living lie.

Saying that in working against Communism there must be no unfairness, he has called on the voters to re-elect character assassins and deniers of civil rights.

First helping, as a soldier, to create and execute an enlightened world policy, he has kicked it into the alleys of partisan vituperation and isolationist discord.

Promising to make the country secure and solvent, he has talked of tax reductions impossible to attain without making it insecure or insolvent.

After proclaiming, in 1945, his belief that Russia was peaceable and friendly, he has denounced political decisions made then by civilians who shared his error.

After joining, as Army Chief of Staff, in the unanimous advice of the Joint Chiefs to remove American troops from Korea in 1947, he has blamed the State Department for an invasion which that withdrawal made possible.

After telling the country that he had no recipe for ending the Korean conflict, he has denounced the government for having none and has made harrowing appeals to the parents and wives of American soldiers.

Famed as an organizer of international defenses, he has scoffed at his own handiwork, insulted the people of France, bid for the votes of Polish and Czech Americans by inciting their relatives to suicidal revolt, and sent a wave of fear through free Europe by reckless attacks on the moderation of American policy.

Promising to end corruption in the federal government, he has helped his colleague, Richard Nixon, to falsify the facts and deceive the voters about his $18,000 subsidy from real-estate and oil millionaires.

Declaring himself deeply suspicious of compulsion by any side in labor disputes—"by union leaders, by employers, or by a government"—he has endorsed the Taft-Hartley Act, under which there is compulsion of the workers, for the employers, by the government.

Seeking votes by running on the *Democratic* farm plank, he is tied up with Banker-Farmer Allan Kline, chief opponent of the Democratic platform and his reputed choice for Secretary of Agriculture.

Praising and endorsing the *completed* T.V.A., he has called the *proposed* (and similar) Columbia River Authority a product of the "whole-hog mentality" of federal bureaucrats striving for monopolistic power.

Endorsing federal aid to education, which Democrats would finance from offshore oil deposits, he has promised to sign a bill which would give that oil to three states, and thereby deliver it to oil companies whose Congressional campaign contributions constitute the greatest uninvestigated scandal of the past ten years.

Ignoring the destruction of price and rent controls by Republican Congressmen, he has accused the administration of a deliberate policy of price inflation.

Charging the federal government with pushing its "long nose further and further into the people's business," he has adopted the language of those who would despoil the public domain by destroying its timber, denuding its watersheds and grazing lands, obliterating its wildlife, grasping its resources and ruining its places of transcendent beauty.

That is the downhill side of Eisenhower's candidacy. On the upward slant there is an expedient call for expansion of social security, supplanting the General's famous remark, in derogation of that system, that the way to find security is to go into a penitentiary for life.

Beyond this, Eisenhower has the same friendly personality as ever, but it shines dimly in a campaign marked by platitudinous generalities, avoidance of living issues and party records, substitution of emotion for reason, and nostalgic references to a Kansas boyhood which seems to be all that is left of "the real Eisenhower."

How has this amazing debacle come about? Nobody would charge the General with being the planner of all the subtle maneuvers against the public welfare that have come from him. Neither can it be said that he is the innocent victim of shrewd political schemers.

Part of the answer, but not all, lies in the organic structure of his campaign. It can be seen in the answer given San Francisco reporters who asked what the General was going to talk about in that city. "The speech is being written in New York, and Ike won't know until he gets his copy about four o'clock on Friday." And when one of Eisenhower's speech writers was needled about the candidate's latest vacillation on tidelands oil, the ghost writer blurted out: "But I didn't write that speech. It was written in Texas."

Five batteries of speech writers have produced the public utterances which, teletyped to Eisenhower's train, have converted him from the Ike of yesteryear into the composite personality that dismays the thinking people of America. Each one has done his part in filling those speeches with the doctrines and non-doctrines which have made a majority of the people distrust the Republican Party.

Ghost writers are small fry. They could do little if Eisenhower were not surrounded by advisers who represent the same reactionary elements, the same resort to trickery in place of square and honest debate.

Finally, Eisenhower would not deliver the speeches furnished to him if there were any real gulf between him and the reactionaries who have helped to bring him down. When a candidate is handed a speech referring to the whole-hog mentality of men devoted to public power development, he does not deliver that speech unless (a) he agrees with it, or (b) he abandons his principles in order to win votes, or (c) he knows too little about politics and policies to be capable of avoiding the worst in both.

So, too, in the case of Eisenhower's embrace of McCarthy, Jenner and Cain and his kowtowing to Senator Taft. He may tell himself that he abandoned General Marshall only in appearance, or that politics is a dirty game and one must learn to play it. But does anybody believe that Marshall would have done the same to him? This was a situation in which a man needed to be ready to lose the Presidency rather than sacrifice his self-respect. Had Eisenhower acted on that principle, he would be nearer the Presidency than he is today, and thoughtful people would contemplate the possibility of his election with less foreboding.

The tragedy of it is that what Eisenhower has surrendered he never can regain. On the ABC radio program *Crossfire* a couple of weeks ago, one of Eisenhower's top supporters predicted that their candidate would veer away from Taft, McCarthy and Jenner and let the people hear "the real Eisenhower." The maneuver was accomplished. It was unconvincing.

The notion that a synthetic Eisenhower could suddenly be replaced by the real Eisenhower, like a shift from cold to hot water, could only emanate from public-relations experts. Has "the real Eisenhower" canceled the Taft mortgage? Has he insisted that Nixon be honest about his finances? From him has come the cruel hoax of a promise to go personally to Korea to seek an end of the war. (Will Stalin meet him there?) Grievous though it is to say it, a man who does not realize what has been done to him, or what he has done to himself, does not contain the raw materials of a President.

Never in all our history have the people of the United States faced such a test as they do today. Owing to the failure of the American press to do its duty, owing to the wealth of one political party and the poverty of the other, there is an absence of equalizing factors in a campaign made unequal at first by the military fame of the one nominee and the initial obscurity of the other.

There are virtually no newspapers to tell the people that this campaign is between a machine and a man—between a spurious Goliath and a genuine David—none to tell them that Adlai Stevenson is such a blend of courage, honesty and political genius as the country has not known in generations. Voters must find that out for themselves, over the deafening din of the opposing claque.

Overhanging all this is the unprecedented danger that lies in error —danger to the nation's future, to the peace of the world, to the welfare and safety of every American family. Inevitably one thinks of our last military President, General Grant. The Eisenhower pattern is all too similar—honesty, good intentions, inexperience, a farm boy's outlook perpetuated through Army isolation, and a dense surrounding circle of powerful men who know what they are after. But the world is not the same, the country is not the same, the consequences of failure will not be the same. Disaster, stark and limitless, can be the result of a wrong choice on November 4.

*January 5, 1953 [Adlai Stevenson]*

# THE "STEVENSON SPIRIT"

by John Steinbeck

A friend of mine used to tell a story about his grandmother and the Lincoln letter. No one had ever seen the Lincoln letter, but it was well known that it lay in a certain black, locked box along with other family treasures. The old lady used the Lincoln letter as a threat, sometimes saying that she would will it to a museum, now offering to will it to one member of the family and now to another.

As the children grew older, their interest in the Lincoln letter grew sharper, and still they had never seen it. It was the family treasure. When, in the fullness of time, the old lady died, some of the sadness was mitigated by the knowledge that at last they would see the Lincoln letter.

The family opened the locked black box with some ceremony immediately on their return from the cemetery, and there, on top of a pile of trinkets, was the Lincoln letter. But it was not from Lincoln. It was to Lincoln, written by their grandmother in 1863. It criticized him for past actions and encouraged him for the future. Their grandmother had never mailed the Lincoln letter, but had kept it all those years.

And with that, I think I have precedent to call this The Stevenson Letter.

Governor Stevenson, by now you will have had literally millions of letters from the people who voted for you and from men who voted against you in the last election. It is not likely that I will say anything new to you, nor would I want to. I want merely to add my voice to the chorus.

The last election was unique insofar as I know. I remember no instance in the history of our nation or of any other nation where a defeated candidate emerged with his followers doubly dedicated to him. The exact opposite has usually been true. We all know the picture of the despised and deserted loser, loaded with blame for losing.

Mr. Stevenson, during the campaign I came in contact with many people working for your election. Girls who gave up their lunch hours to work at switchboards, actors who abandoned their one day with their families, men and women who stood in line for the privilege of carrying posters, or licking envelopes, or ringing doorbells. None of them had any remote chance or desire of personal gain. When the election was lost, these people—and I among them—suffered deep shock and then, within a very few days, there we were again, saying, "What can we do now?"—refusing to accept defeat, eager to put in four years of work and to try again.

Do you know of anything like this in our political history? I don't. I've wondered about it a good deal.

I think that politics—the word, the practice—had become disreputable to the point where politics and crime were confused in many minds. The career of a politician was for the greedy, the unscrupulous. Men of ideals and conscience avoided politics as an arena where wolves tore at the body of the nation and snapped and snarled at each other. Having a brother in politics was quite a bit like having a sister in a brothel. Then, in a few short months, you, àn unknown man to the great body of the people, changed that picture. You made it seem possible for politics to be as it once had been, an honorable, virtuous and creative business. You let light into a dark and musty room. You made political campaigning an excitement, an adventure, a road of hope.

I think that's why those girls who worked at the switchboards want to go on working. They have a sense of selfless fulfillment. They have a direction and an end they can be proud of. And since you started this process in them and in me, quite naturally we want you to continue.

Many of us think it may have been a salutary thing to have lost the election. We think that we who consider ourselves liberals have grown flabby. We have considered the social gains of the last twenty years as permanent beyond need of defense. Some of us have been cowardly—have edged toward reaction in the face of the hysterical shrieks from both Left and Right. We may have become a fat-calf cult, preening ourselves over old or fancied victories. Meanwhile, the Democratic Party, to which we gave our loyalty, has grown soft too, and, as is inevitable, corrupt men have crept in and made themselves secure. Further, to hold the party together and to make it effective electionwise, the strangest of bedfellows tried to get under a too-narrow blanket. The gamblers and heelers, the scavengers and the big-city machines were there, the traders in votes for patronage, and who cares how you get the votes; the medieval Democrats whose affiliation with the party was due to geographic or ethnic accident— men who no more believe in democracy than they do in the Bill of Rights which supports it.

We do not think or say the party was all rotten, but we know that there are brown spots in it and that decay is eating toward the core.

And finally there were the flabby liberals, greasy with virtue—the same breed who lost Czechoslovakia to the Kremlin and Germany to Hitler. I include myself among these, and I think we may have been more dangerous to the party and to the nation than the machine crooks or the geographic anachronisms.

If you had been elected, Mr. Stevenson, you would have had to carry all this muck along with you, whether you wanted to or not. I imagine that nearly every letter you get tells you what to do and how to conduct yourself, and I imagine further that every letter boiled down is a plea not to leave the scene—not to abandon the bright new hope you raised. You should see the eyes of the volunteers—how they brighten when your name is mentioned—how they have memorized paragraphs, even whole sections, of your speeches—how they pin their hopes of the future on you. I should think this might be at once the most wonderful and the most horrible thing that could happen to a man.

I have heard every kind of excited suggestion about your future, but the main one is that you should go on television periodically to comment on the Republican administration and on your own party— in a word, to become a kind of loyal opposition with a stinger. I have heard that you should get your club and lionskin and stroll toward the Augean barn—a ridiculous figure, but not a bad idea. In the main, the cry is Lead! Lead! Don't for a moment give up your leadership.

Mr. Stevenson, I have read your speeches, listened to you speak. As a professional writer, I know that no amount of skilled words can cover a lie or hypocrisy for very long. I know beyond all doubt that you believe in and love democracy. This being so, you must fear the principle of leadership; you must be terrified to have too much faith, too much hope and trust and responsibility placed in your hands. We have seen what terrible directions this process can take. I do not think you can refuse leadership, however. That seems to have been forced on you from within yourself, as well as from without. And you must have gone over and over the kind of leadership that is good and healthful for a democracy. That is the leadership which imposes responsibility on the electorate, which makes the leadership, so that there is no surrender of power by the people, but rather, a resumption of power through participation.

Surely you will have a cleansing job to do on the Democratic Party, and some of it will of necessity be painful and some deadly, but to a great extent, the cleaning process will be automatic, if you will act as spokesman. If you will, as you have in the past, set down and say and repeat those principles and that direction which our evolutionary democracy must follow—if you will do this during the next four years and make it so clear as to be impossible of more than one right, sharp intepretation, I believe the dissidents, the reactionaries, the hustlers, main-chancers will fall away to join a party where their gifts, talents and visions are more acceptable.

You have given us a look at truth as a weapon, at reason as a tool, at humor as a method, and at democracy as a practical way of life. We would be crazy if we let you go.

I don't see how you can refuse, even though you know probably better than any of us the nature of our gift to you. We offer you the highest gift of the people—work beyond your strength, responsibility beyond your endurance, loneliness to freeze you, and despair and vilification. Quite contentedly, we propose to take from you most of the sweet things of a man's life—privacy and companionship, leisure and gaiety and rest. We offer to cut your heart out and serve it up for the good of the nation. And the terrible thing is—I don't think you can refuse. Your greatness is the property of the nation, but to you it is a prison.

# DECADE FIVE
# 1954-1964

**THE New Republic**

Alexander Kendrick:
Moscow's Courtship
of "Comrade Tito"

PAGE 14

Can the Republicans
Pull Themselves Together?

JANUARY 10, 1955     20c

**THE New Republic**

This Doodling
Do-Little Congress
*An Editorial*

Pages 3-5

## Why Adlai Stevenson
## Haunts the Democrats

BY REP. STEWART L. UDALL

Faith of a University. . . . . . . *Robert E. Fitch*
Portrait of Little Rock . . . *Patrick O'Donovan*
The Regulatory Agencies . . . *Anthony Lewis*

HERBERT HOOVER'S HERO
*A Review by David Cushman Coyle*

MAY 19, 1958     25 cents

# THE NEW
# REPUBLIC

## Let Us Begin

"Now the trumpet summons us again – not as a
call to bear arms, though arms we need – not as
a call to battle – though embattled we are – but
a call to bear the burden of a long twilight
struggle year in and year out, 'rejoicing in hope,
patient in tribulation' – a struggle against the
common enemies of man: tyranny, poverty,
disease and war itself. . . . I do not shrink from
this responsibility. I welcome it."

JOHN F. KENNEDY
January 30, 1961

January 30, 1961, 25 cents

**Three Poems** *Robert Graves*

# THE NEW
April 11, 1964, 35 cents
# REPUBLIC

## The Mild Mr. Rusk
*Alex Campbell*

*Books and the Arts*

Murray Kempton   Marquis W. Childs
J. K. Galbraith   Robert Brustein
Gertrude Himmelfarb   Frank Getlein
Benjamin Schwartz   Albert Goldman
Stanley Kauffmann

*1954-1964*

*Its fifth decade found* The New Republic *in the mood and predicament of thirty years earlier. In the days of Theodore Roosevelt and Wilson, and later of Franklin Roosevelt and Truman, it had enjoyed a relationship, however intermittent and conditional, to power. Now, as in the nineteen-twenties, the country had entered a time of contentment, with power apparently predisposed against ideas, against intellectuals and against all rockers of the boat. Passion appeared reserved for the dissenters from the official consensus. The task of the magazine was to work underground and help organize the resistance.*

*In the beginning of* The New Republic's *fortieth year Senator McCarthy had already passed his zenith: Willard Straight's son Michael superbly reported his crisis and decline in the series "Trial by Television." As McCarthyism faded, the magazine could give more attention, as it had in the twenties after the end of the Red scare, to literature and the arts. It was a lively season of criticism, ranging from Mary McCarthy on Voltaire, Robert Graves on T. E. Lawrence, Malcolm Cowley on Thomas Wolfe, Richard Rovere on Orwell, Malcolm Muggeridge on Evelyn Waugh, to Delmore Schwartz's pieces on films.*

*As in the twenties, the literary and artistic ferment seemed to be a prelude to political change. America seemed destined for something more than the man whom Joseph Harsch called "Eisenhower the Good" sought or than "Nixon's World" was prepared to offer. The New Republic's decision to support John F. Kennedy for the Democratic nomination in 1960 disappointed faithful Stevensonians like Gerald W. Johnson. But Kennedy as President fulfilled the magazine's best expectations, and to an astonishing degree, in the brief time permitted to him, renewed the atmosphere of the progressive enlightenment of half a century earlier. Once again,* The New Republic *was read in the White House.*

*If John F. Kennedy's life nobly embodied reason in politics, his death was a terrible reminder of the frailty of human nature, of the thinness of the membrane of civilization, of the impulses of unreason, violence and hate in modern man's repressed depths. So, too, the world itself was poised between science and disaster, living under the shadow of nuclear holocaust and striving to master its own death wish. But if human resources were not omnipotent, nonetheless man had within him the possibility of immense decency and civility, intelligence and courage. John Kennedy had demonstrated this; so too had Eleanor Roosebelt, as movingly described by Donald Meyer; so too had Robert Frost in Adlai Stevenson's fine eulogy; so too had Learned Hand, so sensitively remembered by Francis Biddle.*

*In such evocations, in such images, in such memories,* The New Republic *summoned up its own best guidance for the future. It had been a bitter half-century since those innocent days when Willard Straight first asked Herbert Croly to edit a new magazine—fifty years of trial and torment which the men of the progressive enlightenment could not have foreseen, yet years so often redeemed by reason and courage in the face of catastrophe. At the end of the half-century, the abyss still stretched out before mankind, and no one could predict what was to come. But in a world of unreason, as Walter Lippmann noted on the occasion of* The New Republic's *fiftieth birthday, there would be need of a journal of "unopinionated opinion—one that would be informed, disinterested, compassionate and brave," and one "of which the touchstone is the civilized tradition itself."*

—ARTHUR M. SCHLESINGER, JR.

*May 10, 1954*

# JOSEPH N. WELCH
by T.R.B.

Joseph N. Welch is an elderly pixie from Boston, with a huge nose, and we love him. He is the trial lawyer with the permanently surprised eyebrows whom the Army called in to handle its case with McCarthy. At first we mistook him and his balding head and big beak for a dull old codger; he seemed to be just another of Secretary Stevens' mistakes. But the quizzical lines round his long upper lip should have told us. He is a pixie. He can put a polished dart, poisoned with humor, into McCarthy's hide every time the latter rushes at him. He is a New England Puck looking at Caliban with suave interested contempt. He holds the taut audience in his hand and makes it shout with laughter; he waits, with parted lips and the innocence of a trusting child, for witness's answer and then makes the dry, lethal and hilarious comment. Here is a figure who is a match for McCarthy at last; who knows the use of ridicule and who bides his time to put McCarthy on the witness stand, under oath, and shorn of Congressional immunity. Will that happen? No; we can't believe it. Every instinct of the four G.O.P. Senators on the subcommittee and of the Administration, whose appeasement policy is really the culprit in the dock, is to call the fratricidal Republican battle off. McCarthy plans to keep Stevens on the witness stand indefinitely until his terms are met.

Fascinated disgust draws us to the hearings, where the McCarthy staff strikes us as being as repellent a crew as you could find. We have watched them for years, and it is a comfort to know the nation is seeing them now, too. We don't hope for a direct or definitive verdict from the Mundt Committee in this nightmare show, but at least the public can now see for itself what things are like around here. . . .

Through all this, Eisenhower appears in the background, a blurred figure, going or coming from golfing vacations, appealing to the Publishers' Association for newspapers to print more unifying news; bitter now against McCarthy but not actually breaking with him by name nor coming to the aid of his assistant Stevens, who carried out the President's own appeasement policies.

*June 28, 1954*

# THE FANATICISM OF JOSEPH MCCARTHY
by Michael Straight

Joseph McCarthy has a genius for creating turmoil in the hearts and minds of this country, and the reason may be that since early childhood a terrible turmoil has raged in his own mind and heart.

That mind and heart in turmoil was well described by Eric Hoffer in *The True Believer*. "Only the individual who has come to terms with his self," writes Hoffer, "can have a dispassionate attitude toward the world. Once the harmony with the self is upset and a man is impelled to reject, renounce, distrust or forget his self he turns into a highly reactive entity." Hoffer continues:

> The fanatic is perpetually incomplete and insecure. He cannot generate self-assurance out of his individual resources—out of his rejected self—but finds it only by clinging passionately to whatever support he happens to embrace. This passionate attachment is the essence of his blind devotion and religiosity and he sees in it the source of all virtue and strength. . . . The fanatic is not really a stickler to principles. He embraces a cause not primarily because of its justness and holiness but because of his desperate need for something to hold on to. Often indeed it is his need for passionate attachment which turns every cause he embraces into a holy cause.
>
> The fanatic cannot be weaned away from his cause by an appeal to his reason or moral sense. He fears compromise and cannot be persuaded to qualify the certitude and righteousness of his holy cause. But he finds no difficulty in swinging suddenly and wildly from one holy cause to another. . . .
>
> Though they seem at opposite poles, fanatics of all kinds are actually crowded together at one end. . . . They hate each other with the hatreds of brothers. They are as far apart and close together as Saul and Paul.

"The fanatic . . . finds no difficulty in swinging suddenly and wildly from one holy cause to another. . . ." In July 1949, a newcomer arose on the floor of the Senate to make a passionate defense of the belief that all men are innocent until proved guilty by due process of law. He denounced that group of nationalists who would "attempt to call up all the emotions of war hatred." He scorned those who would "wave the flag and speak of the white crosses over the graves of the American dead." He condemned those who "ask in self-righteous phrases why

. . . the Government of the United States of America should concern itself with applying decent rules of justice to vicious criminals." He cried:

> Mr. President, America came into Europe with clean hands. The people of the world had come to respect not only America's great military and economic power but also to respect and admire her conception of decency and fair play and above all her judicial system which gave to every man, no matter how much in the minority, his day in court. This vast wealth of good will which had been built up over the years is being dissipated by a few men of little minds who, unfortunately, in the eyes of the world represent the American people.

This enemy of McCarthyism was Joseph McCarthy, speaking in defense of the rights of German soldiers tried and sentenced for the Malmédy massacre.

"Passionate attachment," says Hoffer, is the essence of the fanatic's "blind devotion." McCarthy was not a fanatic in his beliefs at first. He came late and a stranger to the cause of anti-Communism. His mood, on returning to Wisconsin from Wheeling, West Virginia, was one of amazement and delight at the political diamond mine into which he had stumbled. He was not then a fanatic in any cause but McCarthy. But gradually he came to believe his tirades.

The fanatic is egocentric. And so McCarthy in the hearings saw all issues and conditions in terms of himself. Moreover, to McCarthy, everything he said, every point of order was always "extremely important." If the chairman or anyone else turned away as he spoke, McCarthy was enraged. He wanted deeply to be liked by everyone, but it was more important to him to be hated than to be ignored. In turn, his hatred was directed impartially to men of either party who threatened to take from him the center of the stage.

"The fanatics of various hues . . ." writes Hoffer, "hate each other with the hatreds of brothers." So McCarthy, laying forth his beliefs, said of the conflict with Communism: "There is no remote possibility of this war—and it's a war . . .—ending except by victory or by death for this civilization."

The fanatic stands above the law and above duly constituted authority. He disdains authority as part of the society he rejects. He scorns the law as the instrument of the order he is sworn to overthrow. So McCarthy claimed that he spoke for the Army, rather than the responsible officials appointed by the President. He stated: "I just will not abide by any secrecy directive of anyone."

The fanatic seeks to destroy real and imagined enemies who stand in his way. So, in the present conflict, the fanaticism of McCarthy stood forth in his original brief of countercharges. The Army brief attributed a minor and rather moderate role to McCarthy. His was the reply of a man verging on paranoia. With the narrow vision of one preoccupied with persecution he affirmed "we must look for motive." He uncovered it in the supposedly criminal acts of Mr. Struve Hensel. Late in the hearings, when his brief had lain for five weeks before the public, he conceded that he had no evidence whatever linking Mr. Hensel to the Army report. He had simply read the report, remembered old charges against Mr. Hensel, and then "put two and two together." McCarthy was never more emotional than when he cried that Carr and Cohn had been "smeared." Yet, Hensel swore that on May 3 McCarthy told him that in attacking him he was just following the advice of an old farm hand, Indian Charlie, who had told McCarthy that "if one was ever approached by another person in a not completely friendly fashion one should start kicking at the other person as fast as possible below the belt until the other person was rendered helpless."

The fanatic rejects objective truth in dedication to the truth of his own creation. Hoffer quotes the view of Ernest Renan that self-contempt produces in man "the most unjust and criminal passions imaginable, for he conceives a mortal hatred against truth, which blames him and convinces him of his faults." So the record of the hearings is replete with evidence of McCarthy's disregard for truth. His assertions are rarely outright lies. But the impression they are intended to leave is untrue. Thus on the first day McCarthy charged that Samuel Reber, Deputy High Commissioner in Germany, had appointed a man to shadow Cohn and Schine through Europe, had made repeated attacks upon them, and was subsequently forced to resign as a security risk. The facts were these: the "shadow" was an official from the Visitors Bureau sent at the request of the two boys to make arrangements; the "attacks" were nothing more than Reber's private refusal to accede to the demand of the boys that he publicly denounce a subordinate official whom they marked out for destruction; and Reber resigned three years after his retirement was due, while no charges of any kind were pending against him.

Yet, with the stubborn devotion of the fanatic, McCarthy clung to his untruths. He said of Symington, for example, "The only time I hear him raise his voice at this table is when we appear to be hurting those that defend Communism." This demonstrably false charge was one of McCarthy's Big Lies. It was indignantly repudiated, but following the manner of his teacher, he repeated it over and over and over, until in many untrained minds a part of it stuck.

To the fanatic, morality is that which advances his cause. McCarthy upbraided Symington for using Communist methods. And yet Struve Hensel swore, and the Senator did not deny, that two of McCarthy's agents falsely told a woman that her daughter had been involved in a hit-and-run accident, simply to gain her son-in-law's address.

The fanatics of the extreme Left, the Communists, rarely speak in moral terms, treating morality as a by-product of the class structure. McCarthy also appeared indifferent to conventional codes of moral conduct. He seemed to be insensitive to the suffering he inflicted on others. He was plainly surprised when Mr. Welch declined to embrace him on the day after his attack on Frederick Fisher. Once in the hearing, when the role of the White House was exposed, McCarthy showed a glimmer of conscience. "I fear," he said, "I may have done an injustice to Mr. Hensel and John Adams." But if McCarthy was otherwise incapable of immorality, his enemies were not. To McCarthy the attack upon himself by Senator Flanders was "vicious" and "dishonest." The witnesses who critized him were "grossly dishonest." The monitoring of telephone calls, which he had practiced, was "the most dishonest and indecent thing I have heard in years." Over and over he begged Symington "in common decency, in common honesty" to testify, as McCarthy had done. All this suggested the impact of the Church upon McCarthy. It had taught him to employ its verbal symbols, even while ignoring much of the content of its teaching.

The adjectives that McCarthy used commanded an automatic allegiance among moral men. So they were rational words for him to employ. But perhaps their use rose also from realms beyond reason. They were the same words that some might use in condemning McCarthy, that some part of McCarthy might use to condemn himself.

Day and night McCarthy lunged at real and imagined enemies. Only one seemed beyond his reach—the enemy within. It emerged on the afternoon of June 9 and struck at Welch with instruments of mental torture. Later, McCarthy reported that when the outraged Welch struck back he felt knots in his throat. He knew that it was his one great error in the hearings, for which he had only the enemy within to blame.

Joseph McCarthy was remorseful on the following day; not because he had hurt himself. He was at times fearful. Yet he had nothing to fear from Ray Jenkins. Speaking of Robert Stevens he turned to Shakespeare. The misquotation was not surprising from one who found spelling difficult; but no passage could have been more revealing. To his wife, Macbeth declared:

> For mine own good
> All causes shall give way: I am in blood
> Steep'd in so far, that, should I wade no more
> Returning were as tedious as go o'er.

Was this in the deeper sense an allusion to himself? Macbeth was noble in origin, haunted by conscience, free of vulgarity, sublime in defeat. McCarthy was none of these, yet they had much in common.

The great Shakespearean scholar, Bradley, said of Macbeth "he has never . . . accepted as the principle of his own conduct the morality which takes shape in his imaginative fears."

Did McCarthy doubt and despise himself at moments? Outside the room admirers were waiting to reassure him—women to shower their adulation, men to shake his hand, nuns to whisper shyly that they were praying for him, children to ask his autograph—and he made a particular point of appearing tender to children. He smiled. The forces of freedom were closing around McCarthy. But not yet was Birnam forest come to Dunsinane.

*March 21, 1955 [T. E. Lawrence]*

# LAWRENCE VINDICATED
by Robert Graves

There is no doubt that the Lawrence legend needs investigation after the lapse of twenty years—as when the credentials of a candidate for sainthood are officially laid before a court of high ecclesiastics and a counsel is appointed to challenge them in fullest detail. This lawyer, popularly known as the "Devil's Advocate," faces an honorable but hardly pleasant task. He must inquire whether the saint's humility was not perhaps a form of servility; his abstinence a lack of appetite; his miracle-making a mere hypnotic trick; and whether the witnesses have been biased in his favor by local ambition or some other even less creditable motive. But the Devil's Advocate is not authorized to invent scandalous and unsupported charges against the dead man, misquote documents, or needlessly rattle skeletons in his family closet; and ears would burn on the Vatican Hill should a Devil's Advocate remark unblushingly, as Mr. Aldington does here: "If I have been guilty of bad taste, well, I have been!"

Personally, I cannot read this book [*Lawrence of Arabia: A Biographical Enquiry*, by Richard Aldington] without revulsion. Instead of a carefully considered portrait of Lawrence, I find the self-portrait of a bitter, bedridden, leering, asthmatic, elderly hang-man-of-letters—the live dog who thinks himself better than the dead lion because he can at least scratch himself and snarl. Granted, I may not be a proper person to review this book, because I knew Lawrence intimately and never had a more generous friend. But Mr. Aldington was equally not a proper person to write it, because he did not know Lawrence at all and has made little attempt to understand him, or even to consult those who did—although in his approach to public sources of information he has untruly represented himself as acting "on behalf of the executors and the family."

First of all, the skeleton in the closet. With his friends, T. E. Lawrence made no secret of his birth. Sir Thomas Chapman, an unhappily married Irish baronet, fell in love some seventy years ago with the gifted daughter of a Scottish engineer and persuaded her to accompany him to France, where—a divorce being impossible—they lived as man and wife. He adopted the name Lawrence, and they continued as a devoted couple until his death. She bore him five sons. The eldest became a missionary in China; T. E. was the second; the third and fourth were killed in the First World War; the fifth is now one of our leading archaeologists.

Mr. Aldington's bad taste and bad judgment are nowhere seen to worse advantage than in the suggestion that the main psychological urge behind Lawrence's adventures in Arabia was a revolt against his mother. Granted, she had an inflexible will, and so had he; but they respected and loved each other the more deeply for recognizing this tie. Mrs. Lawrence is still alive, and in full possession of her mental faculties. She had already reached her nineties three or four years ago when she broke a leg, but made light of it and was soon about again. I have never met a woman of greater energy, nobility, and forthrightness, or of stronger religious fervor.

Both parents firmly believed in a united family and wanted the parental impress, not that of any public school, to be set on the boys' characters. In the recently published *Home Letters*, written by the three who were killed, Thomas Lawrence is almost always mentioned in the connection with sport, which was his department, as hers was religion; he seems to have been courteous, gentle and simple-minded, and died in the great influenza epidemic of 1919. Now, Mr. Aldington, playing the part of a social psychologist, remarks that Mrs. Lawrence was "not an equal mate for a gentleman"—which would be comic were it not so shocking. As Eric Kennington writes: "Sarah Lawrence has always been a natural queen." The extraordinary courage and endurance she showed in Central China among bandits and pirates at the age of seventy should earn her a mention in any decent dictionary of heroines. Robert Lawrence, the missionary son, describes how a Chinese soldier pointed a rifle at her and ordered her away from a ferry; she stamped her foot and shouted "Boo!"—which drove him off in terror. When pirates came aboard the mission boat on the Yangtse and one of them grabbed her fur muffler, she took it back, saying simply: "You have no use for this!"

Mrs. Lawrence did not encourage her sons to bring girl friends home to tea. She told me once in her broad Scottish: "We had no use for girls in our house." Since she had just given my wife a much-traveled tin bathtub for our children, I asked gently: "But aren't they useful sometimes for bathing their youngest brothers?" "Nonsense, boys are just as good, and make far less fuss about it. Ned [T.E.] always used to scrub little Arnie for me, in this very bath, and take him for walks too, and tell him long stories."

The literary atmosphere at 2, Polstead Road, Oxford, a late-Victorian brick house, severely furnished, was a strange compound of evangelism, adventure and medieval romance. The clue to Ned, who differed from his elder brother in never feeling any call to become a missionary, is Sir Galahad, or Sir Guy de Tabarie, who taught Saladin the Rule of Chivalry—pure-heartedness, love for a chosen lady, and the righting of wrong. He always remained loyal to this code.

I hear a loud guffaw at this point. A heckler springs up to say: "Galahad my left foot! Tell me, Mr. Graves, can any fair-minded person read this exhaustive and well-documented book without being convinced that Lawrence was an impostor and a psychopathic liar? That he imposed the legend of military feats which he had never performed, and of honors that had never been awarded him, on credulous fools—including yourself as his biographer? That he was also grasping, insanely ambitious and probably a homosexual pervert?"

Yes, heckler, I certainly agree that there is no limit to what fair-minded readers can be persuaded to accept, when a book is lurid enough and comes provided with so formidable a critical apparatus of source references. Who will be bothered to check them? But what of the spoken and written testimonies of all ranks who fought with Lawrence in the desert, from private soldiers to senior officers? In 1927 I questioned a dozen or so of these veterans, who unanimously found Lawrence the bravest and most resourceful man they had ever met. And there was no mistaking the deep sincerity of Field Marshal Allenby's gratitude to Lawrence for securing his right flank and making possible the 1918 break-through in Palestine. He told me: "Colonel Lawrence would have been an impossible divisional general, but a first-class commander in chief." Even Mr. Aldington would hardly suggest that Lawrence's paid claque included the terrible Allenby and the redoubtable Sir Winston Churchill, who has spoken more highly of Lawrence than of any other man of our generation.

Facts are Mr. Aldington's weakest allies, sneers his strongest. He has not hesitated to tamper with the text of Lawrence's letters, changing:

I came to know Syria like a book, much of North Mesopotamia, Asia Minor, Egypt and Greece.

to:

I came to know like a book Syria, North Mesopotamia, Asia Minor, Egypt and Greece.

and then commenting: "Wild exaggerations!"

He makes out that Lawrence lied in claiming to have been offered the post of High Commissioner of Egypt, and that Sir Winston Churchill made an "emphatic disavowal of this offer." "No" was certainly the answer of Sir Winston's secretary to a misleadingly framed question of Mr. Aldington's; but Sir Winston Churchill has himself since written:

> I am sure that the post was never offered *officially* to Col. Lawrence, but I think it very likely that I talked over the possibility of his being offered it and asked him how he felt about it. It is very likely also that his not welcoming the idea played its part in my not pressing it any further.

Since Lawrence mentioned the offer in a contemporary letter to his mother, I cannot but believe that it was made.

Elsewhere, Mr. Aldington writes:

> This habit of attributing imaginary grandeurs to himself rather grew on Lawrence, as the time for his first discharge from the R.A.F. grew nearer. It is true that he was offered by a banker, and refused, a position in the City of London, where at one time he had reserved for himself the position of night watchman at the Bank of England.

This "job in the City," as Lawrence called it, was no less than the Secretaryship of the Bank of England offered him by Sir Montague Norman, the Governor, as has now been officially revealed. Lawrence, in fact, was always more likely to understate than to overstate the honors pressed on him. And since we are on the subject of understatement: Mr. Aldington mentions that, while Lawrence was working in the Cairo map department at the beginning of the war, he "went for an official Cook's tour to Kut el Amara." Cook's tour, indeed! It was a dangerous and delicate mission behind the Turkish lines with which he and Aubrey Herbert M.P. had been entrusted by the War Office: they were ordered to restrain the Turkish commander by bribes from pressing the siege of General Townsend's forces. But since the commander was unfortunately both rich and patriotic, they succeeded only in arranging an exchange of a thousand British sick against an equal number of Turks.

Mr. Aldington continues:

These things were mixed up with such fantasies as Lawrence's telling his neighbor, ex-Sergeant Knowles, that he might again be asked to undertake the reorganization of Home Defense. . . . The distinguished persons who were asked about the Egypt myth also brushed aside the idea that Lawrence had ever been offered "Home Defense."

The "distinguished persons" in this context, namely Mr. Amery and the second Lord Lloyd, have now stated that neither were they questioned, nor would they have known about the offer, had it been made. And Sir Winston Churchill has answered: "I certainly hoped that Colonel Lawrence would play such a part." And Lord Winterton, a Cabinet Minister and one of Lawrence's fellow soldiers in Arabia, writes in his memoirs that "just prior to Lawrence's death, Mr. Churchill held the view that he should be appointed Minister of Defense." Furthermore, Captain Liddell Hart states that Lawrence was approached by emissaries of the then Prime Minister, Lord Baldwin, to cooperate in the defense side of the Rearmament Program.

Mr. Aldington's sneers at the story that Lawrence "arranged the surrender of Erzeroum" are most disingenuous. Lawrence claimed merely that he enabled the War Office to put the Russian commander in touch with certain disaffected Arab officers serving in the Turkish garrison. Mr. Aldington triumphantly records that General Wavell does not mention this fact in his *Encyclopaedia Britannica* article on the surrender, "though then military attaché on that front," and it therefore must be a lie; General Wavell, however, was serving in France at the time, as can he checked from the *Army List*. He has also pounced on a passage in my *Lawrence and the Arabian Adventure* (1928), where, by a failure to correct proofs, I made out that he had "read in three years every book in the Oxford Union Library, 50,000 volumes probably, at the rate of six volumes a day." It must have been clear to Mr. Aldington from the biographical material which I subsequently published, and from which he quotes, that the words "which interested him" had dropped out after "book." Then there was Lawrence's claim to have ridden in 1906 on a bicycle made for him at Oxford by Mr. Morris—later Lord Nuffield—which Mr. Aldington thinks he has disproved by a note from Morris Motors to the effect that Mr. Morris made no more bicycles after 1900. Yet in the *Home Letters*, Lawrence is found writing about his broken "Morris bike" to his father, who had bought it for him: so, presumably, it *was* a Morris bike.

I grant that Lawrence's inherited Irish imagination tempted him to coax stories into a more artistic shape than he found them; but at the same time an inherited Scottish conscience always restrained him from wanton lying for his own glorification. I also grant that he was a confirmed leg-puller; I hope that I am not indiscreet in saying that this was a family failing—which accounts for the account in Lowell Thomas's book, of Lawrence's alleged Far Eastern adventures, supplied by the younger brother. And I grant that he would often hide the truth in a misleading statement. He records, for instance, that he "lost the first draft of his *Seven Pillars of Wisdom* while changing trains at Reading in December 1919." We are meant to believe that a thief had stolen the bag containing the manuscript from a bench where he had laid it down. But I have come to the conclusion that it was "lost" in the colloquial sense only: Lawrence was dissatisfied with the book and wanted to rewrite it completely, instead of correcting the draft. Since, therefore, two or three thousand foolscap pages would have been difficult to incinerate in his All Souls' College grate, he alighted at Reading on his way back to Oxford from London, dropped the bag in the Thames, and caught the next train—after which, having by now destroyed his original documents, he sat down to rewrite it from memory at the rate of four or five thousand words a day, trusting that memory would be creatively selective. But why Reading, not London? I remember now that he told me, some time later, how he had once thought of "pitching the book into the Thames"; and then he mentioned Dante Gabriel Rossetti's attempt to "lose" some books in the Thames at Chiswick, forgetting that it was tidal water; long-shoremen brought them back next day muddied but complete.

I find it intolerable that Mr. Aldington suspects Lawrence of homosexual perversity and an insane hatred of the female sex. It is true that he "kept a film of oil," as he once wrote to me, between himself and young attractive women; yet when the one to whom he specifically referred broke her back, he spent most of his weekend leave from camp sitting by her bedside in the public ward of a hospital. The homosexuality is just a bad guess! If Mr. Aldington had written to me, I would have put him right on the point.

The true, hidden horror of Lawrence's later life is hinted at in *The Seven Pillars*, when he writes of the personal motives which sustained him during the Arab Campaign—in the course of which he received no less than thirty-two wounds. He mentions patriotism, pugnacity, love of adventure and so on, but

. . . the strongest motive throughout has been a personal one, not mentioned here, but present, I think, every hour of these two years. Active pains and joys might fling up, like towers, among my days; but refluent as air this hidden urge re-formed, to be the persisting element of life, till near the end. It was dead, before we reached Damascus.

The dedicatory poem of *The Seven Pillars* is to "S.A.":

I loved you, so I drew these tides of men into my hands
and wrote my will across the sky in stars
To earn your Freedom, the seven pillared worthy house,
That your eyes might be shining for me when we came . . .

He goes on to describe how Death had taken her "apart into his quietness." The identity of "S.A." is unknown—to all, I suppose, except "S.A." herself, if she still lives. But she was without doubt the only woman in his life, and he had kept himself sexually chaste for her sake. Lawrence revealed to me in a letter (1921) that "S.A. still exists, but out of my reach because I have changed."

I once accidentally, and greatly to my embarrassment, read two or three lines of a long letter she had written him after the war; her handwriting was neat, strong and imaginative. She signed herself "Jehanne"—the name of the captive heroine in Maurice Hewlett's romantic novel of the Crusades, *Richard Yea and Nay*, which Lawrence once insisted on my reading, without explaining why. It is my guess that "S.A." was of Syrian nationality, but English education, living in Damascus behind the Turkish lines, and that he paid his secret visit there, in June 1917, as much to see her as for political and military reasons. Ten years later, when I was writing his biography, he wrote to me:

> You may make public, if you like, the fact that my reticence upon this northward raid is deliberate and based on private reasons: and record your opinion that I have found mystification and perhaps statements deliberately misleading or contradictory, the best way to hide the truth of what really occurred, if anything did occur.

"Because I have changed" does not imply an emotional or spiritual change in Lawrence: it refers to a typical incapacity. On his return ride, while reconnoitering the Turkish camp at Deraa, disguised as a Circassian recruit, he unluckily caught the eye of the battalion commander. Taken to headquarters, he was flogged into permanent impotence when resisting a sexual assault, yet managed to escape next day. Lawrence put it obliquely to me once in a letter: "I lost my nerve at Deraa." "Nerve" must here be read as the Latin *nervus*, since he never lost his courage or presence of mind, which lasted him to the end. He writes, somewhat more openly, in *The Seven Pillars*, at the close of his chapter about the flogging:

> A raiding party of Wuld Ali . . . [showed us] unexpected generosity [which] . . . momently stayed me to carry the burden, whose certainty the passing days confirmed: how in Deraa that night the citadel of my integrity had been irrecoverably lost.

Lawrence seems to have now felt in honor bound to cut "S.A." out of his life, since he could never give her children. The emotional frustration and spiritual torture to which this condition subjected him would have turned any lesser man to madness or suicide and explain his subsequent vagaries and abnormalities. Not only the personal part he took (though one of the most tenderhearted men I have ever met) in massacring the survivors of the Deraa police battalion during the rout of the Turkish army a year later ("by my order we took no prisoners for the first time in the war"); not only the cloak of mystery that he cast around himself, though the truth was far more startling; not only his grandiose ambitions as a literary artist, and the unnecessary purple patches inserted into *The Seven Pillars*, which in its original draft had been simply and movingly written; not only his decision, in default of marriage, to enlist in "a lay monastery," the R.A.F., where he gladly accepted the moral and physical humiliation of the "toughening process" dealt out to the newly enlisted; but the quasi-sexual delight—"the lustfulness of moving swiftly"—which he found in riding a high-powered motorcycle of his design over the English countryside at eighty miles an hour. He was killed on it, shortly after his honorable discharge from the R.A.F., swerving to avoid two errand boys on bicycles.

Mr. Aldington's comment on the Deraa incident, which in better days would have earned him the horsewhip, is: "This catastrophe was a punishment for his . . . insolence and contempt for his enemies . . . whom he frequently called stupid. Who was stupid *this* time?" He then goes on to identify "S.A." with "a handsome Arab donkey boy"!

Old Mrs. Lawrence has not read the book, because she has lost her sight. But she made Eric Kennington give her a report on it, listened without a hint of disturbance or passion, and then said in mild astonishment: "But for my game leg, I'd go out to France and ask him: 'Why are you doing this?'"

I should have liked to go with her and watch the effect of a Boo! and a stamp of her still sound foot.

*June 6, 1955 [Mary Pickford]*

# THE LITTLE GIRL IN CURLS

by Delmore Schwartz

Mary Pickford's autobiography, *Sunshine and Shadow*, is fascinating and valuable in a variety of important ways. It is full of material for the historian, the sociologist, the psychologist, and the student of American civilization and popular culture. And in another kind of review it would be possible to deal at length with Miss Pickford's friendships, her travels, her relationships with David Belasco, Mack Sennett, Samuel Goldwyn, D. W. Griffith, Ernst Lubitsch, her meetings with Rudolph Valentino, Woodrow Wilson, Einstein, George Bernard Shaw, Eisenstein, and particularly her friendship with Charlie Chaplin. What Miss Pickford omits is at times almost as important as what she includes: she says nothing of having written a novel, and almost nothing about her two books of personal philosophy which indicated how little fulfillment she found in fame. She scarcely speaks of other female stars, except for Pearl White and a passing reference to Clare Boothe, whom she identifies in a characteristic way as "later to become a famous playwright and ambassador"; and it is equally characteristic that when she tells of her meeting with Shaw she should remember two objects on his desk: a bust of Shakespeare and an Academy Award Oscar. So, too, a paragraph about how "I raised $5,000,000 in one afternoon and evening in Pittsburgh during the Liberty Bond Drive" is immediately followed by "another child's role that I played when I was an adult was Sarah Crewe of *The Little Princess*." There is an unintended precision here, for in both instances Miss Pickford was playing a starring part before an enthralled audience.

What is most valuable for the purpose of understanding the motion pictures is Miss Pickford's experience of stardom and its overwhelming effect upon her attitude toward herself. The fabulous identity of the star continues to be the most powerful and tyrannical of influences in determining the quality of a film; as Miss Pickford shows, the star's identity intervenes not only in her private life, but in the choice of scripts, the character of the direction, the camera work, the acting and the attention given to other players until, sooner or later, the star becomes the prisoner of her own stardom forever.

Miss Pickford had to continue to play the part of America's sweetheart through most of her career, as Greta Garbo had to play the part, in all her films, of an imaginary being named Greta Garbo, and as Marilyn Monroe will be Marilyn Monroe in all her films. In fact, at

one point Miss Pickford says: "If reincarnation should prove to be true
and I had to come back as one of my roles, I suppose that some
avenging fate would return me to earth as Pollyanna, 'the glad girl' ";
and this is only one instance of Miss Pickford's strong sense of stardom
as destiny.

Cecil B. de Mille's foreword to Miss Pickford's book shows a like
attitude. Mr. de Mille either failed to read Miss Pickford's book to the
end or forgot what he read: but it does not matter at all; the meaning-
fulness of his remarks remains important enough to quote at length:

> I do not know who first called Mary Pickford America's sweetheart
> [Miss Pickford provides a detailed account], but whoever it was put in
> two words the most remarkable personal achievement in the history of
> motion pictures. . . . Mary Pickford [has] on the screen the absolutely
> unique position which no actress can challenge . . . she was one of the
> . . . handful in any generation who fire the imagination of millions
> because, somehow, they respond to something very deep in the hearts
> of their contemporaries . . . the explanation of her enduring career [is
> that she] typified, more than anyone else in motion pictures, the kind of
> person we all want to love.

This suggests what the scripts of Miss Pickford's films bear out, that
the kind of person we all want to love is out of reach, except upon
the screen. And Mr. de Mille's sensitivity is such that, fearing his
reference to Miss Pickford on the screen may be misunderstood or
understood in a privative sense, he immediately hastens to add that
those who have known Miss Pickford personally know that "the public's
image of her is a true one." And then Mr. de Mille speaks of an
occasion in 1953, twenty years after Miss Pickford's last film was released, when he appeared with Miss Pickford on radio and TV and he
spoke of how long he had been a friend of hers:

> She seemed a little dismayed . . . perhaps it was ungallant of me
> not to explain to the vast audience that when Mary and I first played
> together on the New York stage, Mary had the part of my very much
> younger sister. But Mary should not be worried about anyone's counting
> the years. It will be a good many years before she is as old as I am
> now: but even then she will still be the image of childhood.

Thus Mr. de Mille's attitude matches Miss Pickford's view of
reincarnation: both ascertain the notion that the universe may be
casting the stars their parts for eternity. Whatever Mr. de Mille's
literal belief, it is unimportant compared with his desire to say what
he does say and his sense that what he asserts is desirable. For it is
not immortality, but an immortal childhood which he confers upon
Miss Pickford. It is possible to identify his sentiment with the mode

of being which Keats praises in "Ode on a Grecian Urn"; but it is also possible to see its kinship with the timeless, changeless and deathless existence of human beings in comic strips; his distressing assumption that an immortal childhood is entirely desirable is unquestionable, and there is the implication, which Mr. de Mille naturally disregards, that if America's sweetheart must always be a child who never reaches puberty, then she may also be America's spiritual jailbait, or something worse.

Exaggeration: unless one looks at the photographs which throng Miss Pickford's book, this will seem an unjustified interpretation of the extent to which Miss Pickford concentrated upon being the image of a child on the screen and in person. The photographs drawn from Miss Pickford's films show her becoming younger and younger from 1914 to 1922, and some of the photographs drawn from private life intensify this impression by suggesting that Miss Pickford's screen identity was devouring the rest of her being; there is one photograph taken in 1926 of Miss Pickford with her husband Douglas Fairbanks in which the latter looks twenty-three years of age and his wife looks like his nine-year-old kid sister. The image of America's sweetheart is that of a child before puberty; it is a vivid, visual and physical image of a dear cunning child who is presexual, asexual and even at times unbiological; to judge by the choice of attire, this effect can hardly have been wholly unconscious or unwilled; but it was the public, not the star, who was guilty of morbidity of some sort.

The degree to which some powerful sexual undercurrent and identification made Miss Pickford powerful shows itself most clearly in the tendencies which came to the fore when her popularity began to decline in 1922: for example, Miss Pickford's immediate successor was Clara Bow. Clearly the It girl could hardly have supplanted America's sweetheart without the collaboration of many things which go far beyond the compass of Hollywood. Yet, at the same time this exhibits Hollywood's sensitivity to national moods and the quickness with which it responds. Hollywood responded to the advent of the flapper and the Jazz Age by making films in which sex became comparatively respectable, and the new vogue was introduced by none other than Cecil de Mille, who remarked at the time that "the ruined woman is as out of style as the Victorian who used to faint." Miss Pickford, bewildered, attempted after a time to gain a new identity, and by playing the part of a flirtatious grown woman to establish a more overt connection with that Id whence, with the help of Elinor Glyn and Freud, Miss Bow's It derived its strength. But Miss Pickford's effort was wholly in vain. She remained as much a captive of her own image upon the screen as she had been when her films were most successful.

It was at the height of her fame that she enjoyed, she says in retrospect, her happiest years as America's sweetheart; she was one of Adolph Zukor's Four Famous Players, and she is certain that the happiness of those years depended upon her relationship with Mr. Zukor. She became, in her own words, one of his three children—the other two were begotten in marriage—and if it was as a father that he supervised her public and private life, it was as a daughter that she obeyed. This is illustrated very well by the occasion when Mr. Zukor, Miss Pickford and her mother journeyed by train to Boston. As they boarded the train, Miss Pickford caught a glimpse of Pearl White in the club car, looking like an empress in a large picture hat, surrounded by admirers, lighting a cigarette and lifting a highball to her lips "in the presence of all those men." "I requested permission to sit in the club car," to which Mr. Zukor answered, "Mary, are you out of your mind?" and then departed for the club car himself.

The peril of Pearl White should indicate what a prolonged and soul-searching ordeal Miss Pickford's desire to divorce her first husband and marry Douglas Fairbanks must have been. It was not only the club car which Miss Pickford had to renounce as America's sweetheart, but also the large sums offered her to lend her name to advertisements of evening gowns and cosmetics; and "with complete sincerity" she solemnly promised newspaper reporters that she would not marry for a year after she secured her divorce. Now, some thirty-five years after, she still feels the necessity of justifying the breach of her promise to the press, which occurred, after much hesitation, as a result of Fairbanks's pleading. And she feels, still, some guilt about the divorce itself, as her characterization of her first husband shows; and she also feels some consolation in the fact that when she went with her mother and her attorney to Nevada to get the divorce, everyone seemed to think that it was either her mother or her attorney who was getting the divorce: "They never suspected that this creature with the flat-heeled shoes and the blond curls hanging down her back was married." Her pleasure in the visual image can hardly be dismissed; and it involves her blond curls and freedom from the stigma of marriage. A sweetheart is not a wife, nor does she look like one; in most films, romance ends with marriage; hence, a married woman can come no closer to being a real sweetheart than adultery.

Fairbanks and Miss Pickford were warned that "our pictures might be total failures at the box office, that our hard-won prestige would be buried under an avalanche of malignant gossip and denunciation," and Miss Pickford felt strongly an obligation to the public "to sustain the special picture which the roles portrayed on the screen built up in the world's eyes." The result was a period of severe tension and anxiety; Miss Pickford was troubled enough to ask Fairbanks if their love could survive the loss of their careers. His answer, which is in subtitles like much of the dialogue reported by Miss Pickford, was:

"I can't speak for you, Mary, but my feeling for you is not of the moment. It has nothing to do with your career or your fame, or how other people feel about you. I love you for yourself."

Miss Pickford disregards or is unaware that this avowal says nothing of Fairbanks's loss of his own career. As it happened, both careers declined but survived their love. And Miss Pickford's account disregards also the unexpected outcome; after a period of unfortunate publicity, the possibility that Miss Pickford's divorce would be invalidated transformed the newly wedded couple from sinners to victims in the mind of the public.

This very real drama is literally no more intense nor important, in Miss Pickford's account, than the occasion, years after, when she decided to cut the curls to which she has referred again and again. It was an event comparable only to the cutting of the Gordian knot: Miss Pickford describes the hairdresser as "a pathetic picture of stifled rebellion and indecision," and "as he gripped the shears I had the feeling he needed aromatic spirits of ammonia more than I did. I closed my eyes when he applied the scissors." Elsewhere Miss Pickford has described her feelings before the event as a nightmare in which she believed she would become "almost as Samson after his unfortunate meeting with Delilah." And the consummation itself requires italics: "*it was the first time scissors had touched my head!*"

The piety of the hairdresser left six curls intact: "two of these are now in the Museum of San Diego, two in Los Angeles," and Miss Pickford kept two for herself. When she returned home shorn with all six, Douglas Fairbanks turned pale, fell into a chair and cried " 'O no, no, no!' " as great tears came into his eyes. Seeing how upset she herself was, he expressed the hope that it was for the best and was silent as she placed the curls "gently side by side." But soon after, "an avalanche of criticism overwhelmed me. You would have thought that I had murdered someone and perhaps I had . . . but it was very sad to be made to feel that my success depended, solely or at least in large part, on a head of hair." Yet Miss Pickford did not resent this dependence until her popularity had diminished a great deal. She felt misgivings about "how as the years went by and I continued to play child's roles it would worry me that I was becoming a personality instead of an actress. I would suddenly resent the fact that I had allowed myself to be hypnotized by the public into remaining a little girl." But Miss Pickford neither made her irrevocable visit to the hairdresser, nor, save for two instances, attempted any other kind of role until the public was no longer hypnotized. Yet she is right to make as much as she does of her curls, for they were essential to the visual image which made her America's sweetheart.

It is not until her last chapter that Miss Pickford deals directly with the title which identified her, and before describing its origin, she tells of how, on a sleepless night, she made an inventory of all her nicknames and titles, "appalled by their number." The number is large to begin with, and it becomes even larger because the names she was called in private life and the names of the characters she played in films are equally real. Hence, it may not be their quantity that is appalling, but their passing: "I wonder whether with the going of each name there had also gone the particular identity." This is a recognition of what is implicit throughout: Miss Pickford's intense feeling that the reality of selfhood was given to her by the parts she played; appearance is the supreme reality, and the actuality of the individual merely the nondescript soil out of which it has grown. Miss Pickford was born Gladys Smith—which displeased her even in childhood—and it was David Belasco who bestowed Mary Pickford upon her, a name which, she rejoices to think, has been used by only two others, a great aunt killed by a tram in London at the age of seven, and an Eskimo boy, aged three. Among other nicknames, she mentions with pride and pleasure one which is not literally a title or a nickname at all: "Marion Davies always introduces me as 'my illegitimate daughter by Calvin Coolidge,' a title which she first bestowed on me when that blameless gentleman was still in the White House."

Miss Davies may or may not have been thinking of Warren G. Harding. But given Miss Pickford's intense and persistent solicitude about moral propriety in every other connection, and above all her indignation that the newspapers voiced "cowardly and disgusting" suggestions that Miss Pickford had married Fairbanks in haste because a baby, who might be illegitimate, was on the way, her willingness to accept the title of the President's daughter is extraordinary and becoming; the stigma of the bar sinister is clearly annulled by the radiance of the White House: this is the attitude of a queen, and precisely the attitude communicated by King Alfonso of Spain when they met and he inquired about Fatty Arbuckle and, on being told of the scandal that had overtaken Arbuckle, expressed sympathy and sent regards. It was again with the dignity of a queen that Miss Pickford responded when a Hollywood producer asked her to "relinquish the title of America's sweetheart in favor of a young protégée of his. . . . I answered that the title was not mine to give, that, in fact, I had never accepted it, but that, such as it was, it had been conferred on me as a gesture of love by an old and honored friend."

The drama of this incident and the perfection of Miss Pickford's reply permit no comment. It should be said, however, that the old friend was not Uncle Sam; it was Pop Grauman who first used the phrase in 1914, on the marquee of a theater, spelled out in electric lights.

Miss Pickford's final paragraph is an overwhelming coda:

Almost twenty-five years later I was back in Toronto as guest of honor to 800 young World War II aviation cadets. Everything was all right until they began singing "Let Me Call You Sweetheart." . . . It was more than I could bear. Despite my firm resolution and the overgenerous mascara the tears started rolling down my cheeks. . . . I can only say in all humility that it is good to have lived to know that after so many years off the screen these young men, soldiers soon to embark, perhaps on their last voyage, could still pay me the sweetest, most gallant compliment of all, to ask to be called their collective sweetheart.

The stills of her most famous films make one certain that Miss Pickford will live forever in the hush, the darkness, and the immortality of her silent pictures, worthy of Keats's words:

> Bold lover, never, never can'st thou kiss,
> Though winning near the goal—yet do not grieve
> She cannot fade, though thou hast not thy bliss,
> Forever wilt thou love and she be fair
> . . . Forever panting and forever young.

*August 8, 1955*

# ON MARILYN MONROE
by Delmore Schwartz

Miss Monroe, like the true Hollywood beauties of old who preceded her as daughters of Venus, is a national phenomenon, like Buffalo Bill, the Mack Sennett bathing beauty, crossword puzzles, Coca-Cola, Babe Ruth, and chewing gum. She can be understood only from one point of view, that of beauty, which is its own excuse for being, a truth which, as Emerson was but one among the first to recognize, must be pointed out to the American public time and again. Nothing that Miss Monroe says in any role can be quite as meaningful as the ways in which she sways; her poise and carriage have a true innocence, have a spontaneity, an unself-consciousness which are the extreme antithesis to the calculated sex of the strip tease and other forms of the propagation of prurience.

As an image and symbol, Miss Monroe represents an advance—or a regress, depending upon one's point of view—but in any case something new and different from her predecessors as screen sirens and queens. Most of them made sexual attractiveness quite as exciting as Miss Monroe does, but scarcely ever without making sexual beauty inseparable from evil, ruin, destruction, and all the stigmas imposed by Puritanism—the screen siren was a deadly vamp like Theda Bara, a honky-tonk Medusa like Marlene Dietrich, an unattainable Valkyrie who suggested Nirvana with a Swedish accent like Garbo, or a platinum blonde who suggested, like Jean Harlow, the blank and fatal beauty of an iceberg; but whatever her incarnation, she united love and death, beauty and evil, passion and demoralization as cause and effect.

Miss Monroe, however, is either beyond good and evil or prior to it. Sex is naughty, in a way, but very nice; it is naughty only as eating candy between meals might be, or getting a tan on the beach: it's not going to kill anyone, wreck a man's life, cause Anthony to lose the Roman Empire, inspire Nelson to win the Battle of Trafalgar; nor will it either precipitate or prevent another world war. Miss Monroe's attitude toward herself precludes such unnecessary overcomplications: she likes herself, she likes her body, she likes men, and she is having a wonderful time.

To speak thus of Miss Monroe as an image and a symbol and a "sign of the times" is to risk seeming pompous, or jocose. The literal seriousness of the point can be made clear by citing two very different witnesses: women's clubs all over the nation protested when, two years ago, Miss Monroe appeared in *Niagara*, a film in which the Falls seemed less of a natural force than Miss Monroe; and in the preface to a recent· pocketbook of photographs of the film production itself, George Axelrod, enchanted enough to disregard the disappearance of his comedy, says, "Marilyn Monroe doesn't just play The Girl, she *is* The Girl." But clearly the whole truth belongs to the future and future social historians: the most one can say now is that Puritanism is no longer alive enough to inspire defiance; and the new attitude which Miss Monroe embodies with such natural and joyous ebullience first began to emerge in the lyric which Celeste Holm sang in *Oklahoma!* in which she expressed much mock distress at being just a girl who can't say no.

*December 26, 1955 [Estes Kefauver]*

# KEFAUVER JOINS THE RACE
by Michael Straight

The millions of Americans who watched the press conference on their television screens on the night of December 16 saw a soft-spoken, dignified man. He was less tense, more sure of himself than the man who opened his 1952 campaign by challenging and humiliating Harry Truman in New Hamspshire; who went next to Florida which custom decreed was Richard Russell's political preserve; and who moved on to Nebraska to insure that the dollars poured out on behalf of Senator Robert Kerr were spent for nothing. And yet the self-assured, familiar figure of December 16 was at heart still an outsider, gambling at long odds on his own endurance and power to work political miracles, and refusing obstinately to listen to the warnings of his closest friends.

Paul Douglas, his closest ally in the Senate since 1949, and his champion in the struggle for the nomination in 1952, was the first to tell Kefauver that in 1956 he would work wholeheartedly for Stevenson. Hubert Humphrey, another close friend, all but sealed up Minnesota against him, in the course of assuming the leadership for Stevenson throughout the Midwest. Michael DiSalle, who offered to manage his campaign, told Kefauver, after checking in all parts of the country, that an open and all-out contest with Stevenson would be ruinous, and so passed out of the picture. And at the November meeting of the Democratic National Committee, men and women who labored with the dedication of fanatics for Kefauver in 1952 came to remind him that in those days Stevenson was unknown. "Whom have you turned to when you were in trouble on Capitol Hill?" Kefauver asked the leaders of the A.F.L. and C.I.O. "We know," they answered, "but our choice is made."

In terms of the political principles he stands for and the political services he has rendered, Kefauver's claims to leadership are powerful if not unique. He bucked the veterans' lobbies, the nationalists and the isolationists in endorsing a union of Western democracies. He spoke out in favor of antilynching legislation, and for cloture to end the filibusters that block the enactment of laws for civil rights. He fought the McCarran Immigration Act, and followed up an earlier record of voting against the Un-American Activities Committee in the House of Representatives by opposing passage in the Senate of the Internal Security Act. When Humphrey in 1954 undertook to outbid the Republicans by outlawing the Communist Party, Kefauver alone voted against a bill which many Senators conceded in private was wretchedly conceived and poorly drawn. And when the Democratic leaders in the House and Senate courted war by granting Eisenhower a blanket endorsement for his rash and ambiguous commitments on the Chinese coastal islands, Kefauver once again stood almost alone in advocating a course of wisdom and restraint.

Moreover, in terms of service to the party, Kefauver more than any legislator has drawn the vital lines between Democrats and Republicans over the past three years. Speaker Sam Rayburn and others have made forays against the Administration on matters such as the $20 tax cut. Kefauver, isolated as he has been by the Senate Democrats, pointed out with tenacity and skill the worst aspect of the President's commitment to narrow pressure groups rather than to the great majority, and his choice of doctrine over need in the campaign to undermine the T.V.A.

In spite of all these claims upon his party, however, Kefauver remains the outsider looking in. The stop-Kefauver movement may have shrunk, as Kefauver believes, to the doubtful figure of Scott Lucas. And yet the Democratic citadels of the South and the Northeast remain almost unassailable to Kefauver's assaults. The Senate Democrats resent Kefauver's preoccupation with his own career. The Southern leaders scorn him as one who has crossed the line to judge matters of life and death for Southern whites in national terms. Southerners assume that Stevenson, being a Northerner, will stop short when they warn him that bloodshed in the South will be the price of further reforms. Kefauver they really fear as a spokesman for civil rights. For he is a Southerner, and he can't be intimidated by bluff.

Reasons far more obscure than these lead the independents, the reporters, the commentators, the intellectuals, and some former officials of the New Deal and the Fair Deal to discount Kefauver's claims. They grant that courage and vigor are demanded of a President and that Kefauver has rare courage and vigor. They add that executive capacity, a sense of priorities, and the ability to summon outstanding men to public service are the further requirements of a President, and they sense that Kefauver lacks these qualities. They suspect further that Kefauver's intense interest in people and his warmth and his obvious honesty are not deep-seated traits of personality, but the outward features of a chosen political image. More important, of course, these groups have heard a voice in American politics unequaled for intellectual clarity since Wilson's time, and for as long as Stevenson is willing they are committed to him.

There remains the Democratic rank and file. Kefauver believes that these people are not committed to Stevenson and that given the opportunity they will reaffirm their faith in him. The opportunity is present in the primaries.

Eighteen states held primary elections in 1952. In fifteen of these Kefauver won his party's endorsement. Next year there will be primary elections in nineteen states. Of these, less than half are binding on the delegates sent to the Democratic convention. And because these primaries, in Pennsylvania, Illinois, New York and New Jersey, among other states, require as much effort as contests that are meaningful, Kefauver plans now to ignore them where he can. So far he is committed only to California. But before long it seems certain that he will announce his entrance into the primaries in New Hampshire, Florida, Wisconsin and Oregon. In Nebraska, Minnesota, Ohio and Maryland, all states that he won in 1952, he will wait and watch Stevenson.

Kefauver and Stevenson will first collide in Florida, and that is very much to Kefauver's liking. He attaches little importance to the warm welcome Stevenson received there two weeks ago. He believes that he is still far better known. He relies upon the indifference of the politicians pledged to Stevenson in Northern Florida, whose preoccupation in the primaries really lies in the races for sheriffs and county judges. In Southern Florida, where the majority of the votes lies, Kefauver believes that his views on Middle East politics will score.

In Oregon, where Stevenson may be entered against his wishes, and in California, Kefauver foresees further success. In terms of issues, he believes that Democrats will move from Stevenson's brand of conservatism to his own militancy.

In terms of personalities, he welcomes Stevenson's apparent decision to make the contest one of shaking hands. For he believes that Stevenson in person will not overwhelm the voters, and that no one can shake as many hands as Estes Kefauver.

Nancy Kefauver may dread the months ahead. Her husband does not. He will not listen to the advice of men who beg him to pull out of the race, for he has been alone all his life and learned to trust his own judgment alone. He will not give up, even if he suffers initial defeat, for as he worked his way through law school and fought during every adult hour, one objective made his sacrifices worth while and is built too deeply into his being to be discarded now. He will not tire. He has endured this test before and knows he can survive it; he doubts if Stevenson is as strong. He has the rugged determination of the outsider. The professional rank-and-filer, and in turn the multitudes throughout the country who pride themselves as being rank-and-filers, feel kinship for him, and will work for him as a few volunteers will work for Stevenson. The kinship of the outsiders is cemented every time that Kefauver and a voter shake hands. The handshake with Stevenson creates no such binding force.

For the present Kefauver is far behind. But he was far behind in 1947 when he defied Mr. Crump and ran for the Senate; and he was far behind again when he started out in 1952. Some who grant his appeal have worked to forestall a primary battle by securing agreement now on a Stevenson-Kefauver ticket for 1956. But the opportunity for such an agreement, if it ever existed, has been passed over by both men, and will not occur again until after the second ballot at Chicago. There remains the task of preventing the kind of all-out contest that could undermine the Democratic Party's chances next November. Here the outlook is uncertain. The contest will enliven the party and capture the nation's attention while Republicans languish. It will also require heavy expenditures and engender bitterness and division among Democrats. The two contenders are unlikely to personally attack each other. Their supporters cannot refrain from these attacks. "In California," remarked one Kefauver supporter, "you can't elect a dog catcher without getting into a dogfight."

*September 10, 1956*

# GEORGE ORWELL

by Richard H. Rovere

By 1949, when *Nineteen Eighty-Four* appeared, George Orwell was by no means a lonely prophet; by then the wilderness was full of voices. But Orwell's had a stunning clarity and edge. Anyone could see the flower of totalitarianism in Stalin's Russia or Stalin's Poland or Stalin's Czechoslovakia. It took Orwell to uncover the living roots of totalitarianism in contemporary thought and speech, in the puritanism of civic virtue, in our slackening of ties with the usable past, in cravenness before the gods of security, in mass entertainment's deadening of impulses. He put "newspeak" and "doublethink" into the language, and our habits of speech and thought are the better for this.

*Nineteen Eighty-Four* was a dazzling illumination, and I suppose that for most people it will always be the first thing to spring to mind whenever Orwell's name is mentioned—just as most of us, in free association, would respond to "Swift" with *Gulliver's Travels*. It was not Orwell's first illumination but his last. Years earlier, even before *Animal Farm* had won him his first really wide circle of readers, he had exerted a liberating and strengthening influence on a whole generation of writers and intellectuals. That generation, of which I am a member, knew him first as a journalist. It was not Orwell's view of any particular question that made his work as a journalist so exciting and his example as a writer so bracing to his colleagues. Nor was it merely the verve and acuity of his writing, though this was indeed part of it—quite apart from any special tendencies of his thinking, he was a magnificent performer. But the important and stirring thing was the way he coupled contempt for all the "smelly little orthodoxies" of his time with a continuing interest in ideas and a decent respect for the opinions of mankind. He was free, on the one hand, of pieties of any sort and, on the other hand, of flippancy. He was at once responsible and absolutely independent, and this in a day when responsibility and independence were customarily disjoined. He fused a moral commitment with a fiercely critical mind and spirit, and if today there are more writers who approach this ideal than there were twenty years ago, it is largely because they have profited by his precepts and have been moved by the magnificent gesture of his career.

The thrust of his moral imagination has been felt by all those who read *Nineteen Eighty-Four*, but that was by no means the end of it, nor was it the beginning. Though *Nineteen Eighty-Four* was no doubt his most important book, that work of apocalyptic fury did not provide the most impressive display of his gifts. The reader of *Burmese Days* and *Coming Up for Air*, which seem to me the two most successful of his early novels, will discover that his imagination was more than moral. He could deal superbly with the individual consciousness and with the intercourse of character. He could be wonderfully evocative of moods and times and scenes and conditions of life. No one who has seen anything of England or encountered any members of the British lower middle class can miss the verisimilitude of *Coming Up for Air*. We have it on excellent authority that *Burmese Days* is as sensitive a rendering of Indian and Anglo-Indian life; in any case, it could scarcely be more memorable. I would rank *Down and Out in Paris and London* with these two novels if I did not think it too directly autobiographical and reportorial a work to be described as a novel at all; whatever its category, it is a matchlessly vivid description of the life of poverty and unemployment and squalor. It is impossible to read the *plongeur* passages without having the sensation of gray soapy water sloshing about the arms up to the elbow. Though Orwell's bent was for such description and for a manner that is ironical, astringent and detached, he could on occasion be lyrical and quite astonishingly tender, as one may learn from the sections on Tubby Bowling's boyhood in *Coming*

*Up for Air,* or from the haunting and pathetic scenes between Julia and Winston in *Nineteen Eighty-Four.*

In all of his novels, including those that might, on balance, be described as failure, one feels oneself always in the presence of a writer who is fully alive and has eyes and an intellect and a vibrant character of his own. The conventions of criticism demand, I suppose, that he be placed as a "minor" novelist. He was not in any crucial sense an innovator, and he did not penetrate the mysteries to the depths reached by Dostoevski or Conrad. He did not people a world as Balzac did—though one has the feeling that something like this would have been within his powers if he had devoted himself entirely to fiction or if he had lived and written longer. He was of the second rank, but he was never second-rate, and to my mind and taste the distinction is anything but invidious.

John Atkins, the author of a useful critical study of Orwell, has said that "his uniqueness lay in his having the mind of an intellectual and the feelings of a common man." I cannot quite accept this, for I recognize no sentient state that can be described as "the feelings of a common man." As for "the mind of an intellectual," that is what every intellectual has. Still, I think Mr. Atkins is reaching for a central truth about Orwell and one that is not easy to grasp. Perhaps one could say that his uniqueness lay to some degree in his almost studied avoidance of the unique. The experience he chose to deal with was the kind of experience known to large numbers of people, to whole social classes, to entire nations. He did not often concern himself with the single instance. As a novelist, he was rather old-fashioned in the sense that he did not explore the extremes of behavior. In fact, the most obvious and persistent of his faults was an intolerance of eccentricity and neurosis.

He set great store by normality. This is not to say he despised the extraordinary or placed no value on the uncommon or superior. He was an extraordinary person himself, he detested conformity, and he never celebrated mediocrity. "The average sensual man is out of fashion," he wrote, and he proposed to restore him, giving him "the power of speech, like Balaam's ass" and uncovering his genius. Because we know that he believed there was a great deal in a name, we can assume that in *Nineteen Eighty-Four* he did not settle lightly on one for the central character, Winston Smith, who linked the memory of a most uncommon Englishman with the commonest of English patronymics. What Orwell cared about most deeply was the general quality of human exeprience in his time. The virtues he honored were the universally accessible ones—candor, courage, love, common sense, integrity, decency, charity. The tyrannies he anatomized were those that could hurt us all.

Orwell, who was fascinated by the English class structure and enjoyed drawing fine distinctions of status, spoke of his own family as members of the "upper lower middle class." His father was in the Opium Department of the Indian Civil Service and was at Motihari when Orwell was born. Orwell was one of three children; his home life, he said, was drab, and he felt "isolated and undervalued." It is safe to assume that he changed his name because he disliked the memory of the years in which he had borne it. If his home life was dreary, it was also brief. "I barely saw my father before I was eight," he wrote. And at eight he was sent to a boarding school on the South Coast, the inferior place he calls Crossgates in "Such, Such Were the Joys," an essay full of that anguishing vividness he scarcely ever failed to achieve. At Crossgates, Orwell did what was expected of him and won a scholarship to Eton. He finished Eton and acknowledged in later life that he had rather liked the place, but he did not go on to a university. He thought it better to see something of "real life." He went back to India and served five years in Burma as a member of the Indian Imperial Police. He was to some extent, at least, the Flory of *Burmese Days,* a guilt-ridden servant and beneficiary of the Raj.

In the essay "Why I Write," Orwell says that he had known his vocation from the age of five or six but that from the age of seventeen to twenty-four, a period that included all the Burma years, he had sought to escape it, "with the consciousness that I was outraging my true nature." So far as I know, he never explained why he sought to flee what he regarded as his destiny or whether he had in mind some other fulfillment. As a matter of fact, it is difficult to find one's way about in the years between Eric Blair's adolescence and the emergence of George Orwell in 1934, when he was thirty-one. His own writings are vague as to dates and sequences in this period. I think it is quite clear, though, that he was a young man who suffered a good many torments of mind and spirit. His attempt to avoid writing could have resulted from an admixture of insecurity, or fear of failure, and self-denial. There are traces of Calvinist asceticism all through his work. At any rate, not long after his return from Burma, he entered upon the mortification of the flesh that provided him with the materials for *Down and Out in Paris and London.* He sought out poverty, whether to write about it or merely to suffer it we cannot tell. "What I profoundly wanted at that time," he wrote several years later, in *The Road to Wigan Pier,* "was to find some way of getting out of the respectable world altogether." But why did he seek out misery? Why did he embrace poverty instead of Bohemia? John Atkins has said that the moment Orwell thought of anything beyond endurance, he put himself to the test of enduring it. I think there is something to this. It was compulsive behavior, almost masochistic in character, and it makes Orwell's retention of independence and cool judgment all the more interesting and all the more impressive. The most powerful

critic of fanaticism in our times was a man who had a good many
fanatical impulses.

At some point between 1928 and 1934, he taught school for a while,
and at another time he worked as a clerk in a bookshop. After 1933,
there are few uncertainties. In that year, his first journalism began to
appear—articles and reviews under the name of Eric Blair in *Adelphi*
and other magazines. *Down and Out* was published in 1933 and
*Burmese Days* in 1934, when he became Orwell. His surrender to
destiny was now complete. He did a book a year for several years, in
addition to the newspaper and magazine work that kept him alive.
After *Burmese Days*, there were three more books dealing with
poverty. A *Clergyman's Daughter*, published in 1935, and *Keep the
Aspidistra Flying*, published in 1936, are novels of English life. They
have their particular distinctions—the Trafalgar Square scene from
*A Clergyman's Daughter* may well be the finest thing of Orwell's
fiction—but they are not his best work. In them, however, one can
trace his growing concern with politics and his drift toward socialism.
He was a socialist by the time he did the fourth of his books on
poverty, *The Road to Wigan Pier*, which was published in England in
1937 and has not yet been published in this country, doubtless because,
being largely a factual report of the mining communities of South
Wales in the worst part of the depression, it has been thought to
have too antiquarian a flavor. But then, the bubonic plague of which
Defoe and Pepys wrote had lost a good deal of its topicality, and
Orwell on life in Swansea and Wigan and Newcastle in 1936 seems
to me fully the peer of Defoe and Pepys on London in 1664.

*The Road to Wigan Pier* is a masterpiece. It is also a basic document
in the intellectual history of this century. The book had been commissioned by Victor Gollancz, the publisher, on behalf of the Left
Book Club, an organization whose tendency is evident in its title, as
a study of human misery in an exploitative social order. The first half
is exactly that. Orwell was never more brilliant as a journalist. The
second part is an examination of socialism as a remedy. It was perhaps
the most rigorous examination that any doctrine has ever received at
the hands of an adherent. It was so tough, so disrespectful, so rich in
heresies that Mr. Gollancz, who, as proprietor of the Left Book Club,
was the shepherd of a flock that scandalized as easily as any Wesleyan
congregation, published the book only after writing an introduction
that could not have been more strained and apologetic if he had
actually been a Wesleyan minister who for some improbable reason
found himself the sponsor of a lecture by George Bernard Shaw
on the Articles of Religion.

In discomfiting his fellow socialists as he did, Orwell performed, for
the first time, what was to become his characteristic service to his
generation. In 1956, I find it rather awkward—indeed, I find it down-

right embarrassing—to have the responsibility of explaining exactly what this service was. For it was really nothing more or less than clearing minds of cant, and the service should never have been necessary in the first place. It has to be understood that the typical intellectual of the Thirties was a man so shocked by social injustice and the ghastly spectacle of fascism that his brain was easily addled by anyone who proposed a quick and drastic remedy. The humanistic mind in those days was poorly equipped to deal with social and political ideas, and grappled with them almost as awkwardly as in recent years it has grappled with the problems of nuclear physics. We tend now to recall Communism as the only brain-addler of the period, but there were others. Non-Communist liberalism had a way of stiffening into illiberal orthodoxies, as did pacifism. Fascism itself won over a few essentially humanistic intelligences, and so did extreme conservatism. Almost at the onset of social and political consciousness, intellectuals surrendered their critical faculties. Many of them thought they had excellent reasons for doing so. It was perfectly obvious, they would argue, that the conditions that cried out for change would not be changed by individuals. Still less would they be changed by acts of cerebration. They would be changed only by the action of large numbers of people—by parties, by armies, by collectives of one sort or another. Parties and armies require discipline. Discipline necessarily calls for a ceding of rights and privileges. Ergo, for the benefit of mankind, for the prisoners of starvation, for the greatest good of the greatest number, for the Cause, it is necessary to give up the right to be critics, iconoclasts, Bohemians, individualists.

It can be objected, I know, that I am only describing a species of conformity and that conformity continues to be quite a problem. Certainly it does, and that is one of the reasons why Orwell is needed today. But today's conformity is one of assent, and I am talking about a conformity of dissent, which is in many ways a more terrible thing. Twenty years ago, it was the critics of society who allowed their critical powers to atrophy; it was the independent-minded who threw away their independence. W. H. Auden, the poet of the decade, wrote the apologia in a quatrain that stands as the dedication to Erika Mann in On This Island, published in 1937:

Since the external disorder, and extravagant lies
The baroque frontiers, the surrealist police
What can truth treasure, heart bless,
But a narrow strictness?

To some of us, then, it seemed a compelling and quite lovely bit of poet's logic. To Orwell, it was a non sequitur—illogical and unlovely.

Orwell arrived on the scene in the middle Thirties and proceeded to fire the camps of the orthodox wherever he found them. How he came to this role is, I think, quite a mystery. His acquaintance with social and political ideas and practices was, if anything, even slighter than that of most of his contemporaries, and there were, as I have suggested, aspects of his temperament that seemed to make him rather a promising candidate for fanaticism. Nevertheless, he stood almost alone in his generation as a man of consistent good judgment and as one who never for a moment doubted that it was possible to be at once humanistic and tough-minded, to make commitments and avoid the perils of commitment. He was no less shocked by social injustice and fascism than the next man. He had known poverty and had written four books on it, at least two of which, *Down and Out* and *The Road to Wigan Pier*, are classics. He saw the point about parties and armies and took more than his share of responsibilities. For all his heresies as a socialist, he was no stranger to the grubbiest of political chores, and in 1936 he went to Spain and bore arms against fascism—an experience that led to another classic, *Homage to Catalonia*. He was not, of course, alone in seeing the perils of commitment, but most of the others who saw the perils either withdrew their commitments or made silly countercommitments. Orwell did neither. He felt that withdrawal was out of the question "unless you are armored by old age or stupidity or hypocrisy." But of the committed writer he said, "His writings, insofar as they are to have any value, will always be the product of the saner self that stands aside, records the things that are done and admits their necessity, but refuses to be deceived as to their true nature."

He was becoming established as a critic and journalist when he went to Spain. He was wounded in the neck and hospitalized in Lérida; he had joined the POUM, which opposed the Communists and was critical of the Popular Front government from a more or less Trotskyist point of view, and he left Spain with some difficulty and with a price on his head. He published *Homage to Catalonia* in 1938; though it was a passionately Loyalist book, it gave as great offense to the passionate Loyalists as *The Road to Wigan Pier* had given to socialists and Communists, and by the time of his death had sold only 900 copies. From 1938 to the middle years of World War II, he had a difficult time of it; he was held in great admiration by people whose admiration was worth having, but partly because of his political views and partly because of the general dislocations of the period he had little work and little sense of function. He wanted to join the Army, but the Army would not have him. In 1939, he published *Coming Up for Air*, and in 1941 *The Lion and the Unicorn*, but these did little to help keep him alive or relieve his sense of frustration. He served in the Home Guard, did occasional scripts for the British Broadcasting Corporation, and wrote brilliantly from London for the *Partisan Review* in New York. It was not until fairly well along in the war that he attracted a sizable British audience for his periodical writing, most of which appeared in the Labourite *Tribune*. His tuberculosis, which he never seems to have done much about, had progressed during the war; it was in an advanced and incurable state by 1945, so that for the short period in which he had a large number of readers, from the publication of *Animal Farm* until his death in a sanatorium a few months after the publication of *Nineteen Eighty-Four*, life held many agonies and few rewards. He once said that *Nineteen Eighty-Four* would have been a less bleak and bitter book if he had not been a dying man when he wrote it.

There is not much to do with Orwell's novels except read them. Nor is there much to be said about his style. It was colloquial in diction and sinewy in construction; it aimed at clarity and unobtrusiveness and achieved both. Cyril Connolly once performed an experiment by scrambling some sentences of Orwell's with some of Ernest Hemingway's and some of Christopher Isherwood's. He defied the reader to tell the writers one from another and argued that, since identification was impossible, all writers who strive for the colloquial throw away a good part of their heritage as writers. He felt that those who worked in a Mandarin Dialect—those, that is, who strove for elegance of phrase and exquisiteness of texture—were at least using all the resources of their language, while those who worked in what he called the New Vernacular needlessly confined themselves to a narrow range of rhythms and tones. I think Connolly was wrong in saying that his three novelists could not be told apart and wrong in his dispraise of colloquialism. But beyond saying that Orwell's was simply the style most commonly used in modern English and American writing and that Orwell employed it with great vigor, there is really not a great deal for a critic to say.

In consequence, there has been a search for the sources of Orwell's strength in Orwell's character. No doubt that is where the sources are to be found; *le style est l'homme même*, and so forth. But it cannot be said that the search has been very productive. What nearly everyone seems to find in Orwell is rectitude and more rectitude. Lionel Trilling has said that the profoundest statement he ever heard about Orwell came from a college student who said: "He was a virtuous man." John Atkins has said, "The common element in all George Orwell's writing was a sense of decency." Mr. Atkins also calls him a "social saint." Irving Howe, poking fun at the "old maids of criticism hunting for stray bits of morality as if they were pieces of tatting left in the parlor," and pointing out that Orwell himself had said that "sainthood is a thing human beings must avoid," has ventured the opinion that Orwell was a "revolutionary personality." But what is that except another term, one with secular and socialist overtones, for a saint? A "revolutionary personality" is what the Ethical Culturist calls Jesus Christ.

What is probably behind the use of these terms is a confusion of the prophet and the saint—that and an appreciation of the fact that Orwell saw through all the pretenses of his time and never made a fool of himself. None of this really has much to do with personal "goodness." On the contrary, there is often a rather direct and visible relationship between folly and purity of spirit. "The surrendering and humbling of the self breed pride and arrogance," Eric Hoffer has written, and, of course, pride and arrogance breed folly. The obverse of this is the old set-a-thief-to-catch-a-thief principle. It takes a certain amount of wickedness to understand the mechanics of wickedness as Orwell did and to perceive that "the essence of being human is that one does not seek perfection, that one *is* sometimes willing to commit sins for the sake of loyalty, that one does not push asceticism to the point where it makes friendly intercourse impossible, and that one is prepared in the end to be defeated and broken up by life, which is the inevitable price of fastening one's love upon other individuals."

In any event, Orwell had his share of wickedness. He could say cruel things and his fairness of judgment did not always extend to individuals. He called Kipling a "gutter patriot" and W. H. Auden a "gutless Kipling." (He could be remorseful, too; he publicly apologized for this characterization of Auden.) His judgments were not always as charitable as they were sound; there was a bit more to be said for the radical intellectuals of the Thirties than he could find it in his heart to say. I do not see how, on logical grounds alone, he could be as indulgent as he was toward P. G. Wodehouse and at the same time as bitter about the liberals and radicals, to whom he had a way of referring as "the pansy left." Standing alone, his plea for Wodehouse would have seemed an act of generosity and understanding. But it seems only fair that if one is going to excuse Wodehouse for allowing himself to be exploited by the Nazis, one should be approximately as forgiving to those who allowed themselves to be exploited by the Communists. Orwell was quite frequently unfair in this way, but his unfairness flowed not, I think, from self-righteousness but from ill temper, from his passion for the truth, and, part of the time, from his use of overstatement as a device of rhetoric. His choler and intemperance had something in common with that of Dr. Johnson and with that of the author of *Gulliver's Travels*, of whom he once wrote: "Politically, Swift was one of those people who are driven into a sort of perverse Toryism by the follies of the progressive party of the moment." It was Orwell's distinction that the follies of his friends never drove him to abandon them.

*November 12, 1956 [Louis D. Brandeis]*

# PASSION AND PATIENCE

by Alexander M. Bickel

Despite the pervasive importance of the Supreme Court's work, very few of its members have ever become household names. Very few were accompanied through their careers by the sort of popular image of themselves, constituted of fact merging into legend, which is the shadow of great men in other walks of public life. An exception to this generalization which springs instantly to mind is Holmes. Another is Louis D. Brandeis, born in Louisville, Kentucky, one hundred years ago this month, who was a Justice of the Supreme Court from June 1916 till his retirement in February 1939. Brandeis—Isaiah, as he was sometimes spoken of by the many high-placed personages who sat at his feet—died on October 5, 1941, full of years and of honors, both of which he had carried lightly and with grace.

It seems that there was a bumper crop in 1856. One hundred years later we remember the births of Freud, of Shaw, of Woodrow Wilson and of Louis D. Brandeis. This is a goodly and a varied company. And it is one in which Brandeis is not misplaced.

The first two names are, of course, writ large. And Wilson was the President who led America to assume the world. Brandeis's fame is less, and his signature is not as boldy stamped on the good that he did us. But his service was of the first rank. His life spanned the near-century of enormous change and upheaval from the beginning of the American Civil War to the beginning of World War II. In the midst of this social revolution, working in the lawyer's characteristically episodic and pragmatic fashion, Brandeis strove effectively, with the capacity of genius for taking infinite pains and with unsurpassed inventiveness and courage, to shape a new society, adjusted and adjustable to changing material conditions and yet founded on the bedrock of ancient and immutable values. He is counted one of those who, in the disordered and perilous switchyard of recent history, among the collisions and derailing and the carnage, had the purpose and the creative powers to make fast the coupling of the nineteenth century to the runaway twentieth. And who is to say that the maintenance of this continuity without the loss of forward motion is not the central problem of government in our time?

Brandeis was not a political leader, and we do not know him as the initiator of large events or the father of institutions. He was one judge on a nine-man court, and he was a private practitioner of the public profession of the law, as it has been proudly called, who, aside from his Justiceship and a brief, *ad hoc* tenure as special counsel to the Interstate Commerce Commission, occupied no official position. Nor was Brandeis a professional philosopher or an academic teacher, and he left us no systematized body of social and economic thought. Yet his great work was that of a teacher, a unique sort of teacher to the public, combining in himself the powers and methods of an Old Testament prophet and Anglo-American common-lawyer. He taught mainly by the case method. He analyzed and solved certain pressing social and economic problems. But he could devote himself fully to only a few, picked relatively at random out of the welter of other ones. He gave us, therefore, not comprehensive or universal or eternally valid solutions to our problems, but the fact of the solution of a few, and the indication of a fruitful way to go about dealing with the other ones and with the same ones again.

Brandeis also preached, of course; but never at large, never out of the hard, confining and yet enlarging context of actual situations. He preached facts, understanding, responsibility, self-reliance, freedom, courage, dignity, the fulfillment of the individual as the overriding purpose of society. He preached, therefore, hospitality to social and economic change and experimentation, decentralization of governmental and economic power, and the supreme importance of maintaining inviolate what the English common law knew as the liberties of the subject.

It has been justly said that these ideas—they are our legitimate national heritage—were in the air. But that is not where Brandeis got them, nor where he left them. They were, for him, rooted in his own unified view of the human situation. He found and articulated them in terms of the concrete problems to which he applied himself in his practice at the bar and in his career on the bench. Brandeis's temperament, his morality, his conception of man's lot in life inclined him toward the ideals of our libertarian beginnings. But in his keeping, these ideals of a homogeneous, simple nineteenth-century community were made to do the hard work of solving the problems of the burgeoning, heterogeneous industrial society of his own day. Without trivializing them—indeed, he enhanced their majesty with the eloquence of workaday allegiance and application—he made of these ideals operative rules of modern social conduct.

Brandeis's greatness does not lie in success. He was one of the influential figures of the century; but not because he prevailed in all essentials; not because all his remedies for social ills, or even all his diagnoses, have been accepted. In many respects—what he called the curse of bigness is an example—his goals remain to be attained. Brandeis's achievement is that he gave new content to old ideals, a content immediately and creatively relevant in a society in which, as he himself said, "the only abiding thing is change." For this reason, to the extent that we survive in freedom and well-being, he is a builder of the commonwealth we are building.

I have mentioned Brandeis's phrase, "the curse of bigness." It alludes to a problem—that of the elephantiasis of industry, government and other institutions—which occupied Brandeis more intensely perhaps than any other, and which is still with us. Because Brandeis's views on bigness illustrate most aptly the nature and the sources of his thought, it is fitting to single them out for closer attention. Perhaps as good a brief statement as any of Brandeis's position is found in a hitherto unpublished letter to Harold J. Laski, dated September 21, 1921. Brandeis commented on our lack of "study and care in developing and adjusting," and our lack of "both patience and persistence in applying," social-political inventions. Hence, he said, few of our inventions have had a fair test. "But," he continued, "the most potent causes of our failures have been our unbounded faith in the efficacy of machinery and our worship of the false god, Bigness." Then:

> I hope you will develop further the cult of the unit of greatest efficiency and spread further the truth that progress must proceed from the aggregate of the performances of individual men—and that each is a wee thing, despite the aids and habiliments with which science, invention and organization have surrounded him. When once these truths are widely recognized we shall, I believe, have vision, wisdom and ingenuity enough to adjust our institutions to the wee size of man and thus render possible his growth and development.

Brandeis saw in exaggerated size the danger of irresponsible political and social power being wielded from the overly impregnable bastion of economic concentration; the loss of a healthy diversification of effort and achievement in a country as large and complex as ours; and the sheer diminishing of returns bred by all indiscriminate mass efforts. But, as the passage quoted above suggests, that was not all. There was a moral problem as well. The twentieth century, Paul A. Freund has written,

> is an era of mass movements of the separation of ownership from control; of impersonal and anonymous corporate acts, obscuring responsibility and shielding individuals from the consequences of their failing. . . . To him [Brandeis] the rise of giantism and the moral dilemmas it has posed—the curse of bigness, as he was not ashamed to describe it—was lamentable, corrupting man's character. . . .

Brandeis, who was not ashamed to speak of the curse of bigness, might not have been ashamed either to define man's goal on earth as being "to strive, to seek, to find and not to yield." The curse of bigness was that it crushed the will to strive and to seek, because it made it exceedingly difficult for the individual to find and to know that he has found; and it made it often impossible not to yield. Bigness crushed the human spirit. It was, of course, not the only feature of our society which could tend to do so. Certain restrictions on freedom of speech and thought had the same effect and were to be resisted for precisely the same reason. It was in a free-speech case that Brandeis wrote: "Those who won our independence believed that the final end of the state was to make men free to develop their faculties. . . ." And the same danger arose from invasions of privacy. "The makers of our Constitution," Brandeis said in asserting a constitutional right against wiretapping, "undertook to secure conditions favorable to the pursuit of happiness. They recognized the significance of man's spiritual nature, of his feelings and of his intellect. They knew that only part of the pain, pleasure and satisfactions of life are to be found in material things." Giantism, however, epitomized the problem for Brandeis.

There went along, to be sure, with Brandeis's unremitting distrust of the growth of his own day a loving regard for things and men as they had once been. In this, no doubt, there was a romantic strain. Brandeis's enthusiasm, for example, for the enterprise and self-reliance of early New England seamen, of which he read in Samuel Eliot Morison's *Maritime History of Massachusetts*, was touched with nostalgia and surely some idealization. (No doubt it was, at least in part, of a like admiration for the pioneer spirit that Brandeis's Zionism was born.) There is the touch of idealization also in Brandeis's descriptions, in judicial opinions, of early American industrial development, which he contrasts with modern bigness in terms of a loss of virtue. But the idealizing backward glance of the romantic was only an occasional indulgence with Brandeis. He had no illusions about the hazards, the cruelties, the failures which could visit the efforts of the brave and self-reliant. Indeed, the hazards and the failures formed the backdrop against which the effort attained nobility. Certainly Brandeis had compassion, and he was grieved by, and would try mightily to remedy, wanton man-made cruelty. But hardship as such did not appall him. Helplessness, dependence, irresponsibility did.

Such were the sources of Brandeis's concern with bigness. His battle against institutional elephantiasis—at the bar and on the bench—was lifelong, and far from uniformly successful. But no setback ever deterred him from pressing the fight. He believed that the trend to bigness was not irreversible, and that it could be arrested, slowly but effectively, by education and by the steady application of measures each of which taken alone might seem peripheral. It may appear that there was something gallantly quixotic in this belief. But it sprang from the same deep source as Brandeis's distrust of bigness itself, and it was just as central to his thought.

Man, Brandeis wrote Laski, is a wee thing. "Man," he wrote in one of his most celebrated dissents, "is weak and his judgment is at best fallible." Yet he held also that man's judgment, properly informed, has an immense potential, and that man is able to command circumstances and to shape the conditions of his life to a rational and satisfactory pattern. Man must, therefore, never give up. Man's greatest limitation was his failure to understand his own limitations and to pace himself and his efforts accordingly. Otherwise, all was possible. This paradox of limited man and his limitless potential was at the core of Brandeis's faith, and it gave him his unique combination of passion and patience. And this combination constitutes perhaps that feature of "the Brandeis way" which we might most meaningfully take to heart in our time. For, in some measure, it is indispensable to the steadfast and effective pursuit of any social goal.

It is interesting to note that in May 1939 Harold Laski, whom Brandeis had exhorted in 1921 to "develop further the cult of the unit of greatest efficiency," wrote an article in this magazine entitled, "The Obsolescence of Federalism." The "unity which giant capitalism postulates in the economic sphere," Laski wrote, "postulates a corresponding unity in the conference of political powers upon the federal government. There is no other way. . . ." And the reason there was no other way was that otherwise it would take fifty years to obtain the "necessary uniformities." "Not even the resiliency of American democracy can afford to wait so long." Thus passion without patience, having lost a battle, declines to continue the war and admits total defeat by changing its objective. It behooves us to remember—because we face at home and abroad so many vast tasks, because we pursue such elusive ultimate objectives, and because it is in the nature of our urgent, energetic national character to expect results—it behooves us to remember Brandeis, a passionate fighter who had also the patience necessary for significant victories.

*November 19, 1956*

# THE LIFE AND DEATH OF THOMAS WOLFE

by Malcolm Cowley

Wolfe was determined to be a great writer, like a thousand other boys of his age, but his determination was more ardent or obsessive and was based on a special sort of emotional need. It also led to a special program, which is most clearly announced not in this volume [*The Letters of Thomas Wolfe*], but in one of the early letters to his mother. The letter started calmly, with news of the play he had written for Professor Baker's 47 Workshop, at Harvard, and a hint that Baker thought he would have a brilliant future. Then, growing excited as he wrote, Wolfe spoke of his plans. "I know there is nothing so commonplace, so dull," he said, "that is not touched with nobility and dignity. And I intend to wreak out my soul on paper and express it all. This is what my life means to me: I am at the mercy of this thing and I will do it or die."

The next sentence revealed the nature of the "all" that he was going to express at the risk of his life. "I never forget," he said, "I have never forgotten. I have tried to make myself conscious of the whole of my life since first the baby in the basket became conscious of the warm sunlight on the porch, and saw his sister go up the hill to the girl's school on the corner (the first thing I remember)." That happened when Tom was eighteen months old, and one finds it recorded in *Look Homeward, Angel*: ". . . the second spring, one warm day, he saw Daisy go off to the school up the hill; it was the end of the noon recess, she had been home for lunch." And so it was with the many other memories recorded in that tumultuous letter to his mother. If the remembered events took place before he left North Carolina, they would reappear in *Look Homeward, Angel*; if afterward, they went into *Of Time and the River*. Neither book was a novel in the ordinary sense; both were taken from an immense store of conscious memories, with more to follow.

"This is why I think I'm going to be an artist," he said at the end of the letter, after setting down his catalogue of impressions. "The things that really mattered sunk in and left their mark." Then came the program he would follow at any cost, even that of shortening his life. "I will go everywhere and do everything. I will meet all the people I can. I will think all the thoughts, feel all the emotions I am able, and I will write, write, write."

He was starting with an unusual equipment for carrying out such a program. His ambition was matched by a sort of unflagging energy that is a talent in itself, indispensable for his type of writing, and the energy was supported by a strong physical constitution. He had the build of an All-American center; he was six and a half feet tall, long-armed and barrel-chested, with a powerful heart. He could endure hunger, cold, and sleeplessness like an Arctic explorer, could gorge himself on meat like an Eskimo, and could withstand savage doses of coffee, tobacco, and alcohol.

He had a good mind, in the conventional use of the term, that is; he made high marks at school and college, which he finished before he was twenty, and later at the Harvard Graduate School. He reasoned clearly and—a curious point about an author who would depend so much on sensation—he won special distinction in a course in logic. More important is the fact that his mental operations were almost completely verbalized, so that he seldom groped for a word. Many of his letters dashed off at top speed are careless masterpieces of eloquence.

He was a teachable person, in the sense that he had a rather un-common capacity for being helped by his elders. There were four of these, outside the family, who played a decisive part in his career. The first was Mrs. Margaret Roberts, who, with her husband, ran the boys' school that Tom attended in Asheville. In one of his letters he addresses her as "you mother of my spirit who fed me with light." The second was a father figure, George Pierce Baker of the 47 Work-shop, who believed in the integrity of Wolfe's talent and kept telling him, "Write! Write! Do nothing else." The third was Aline Bernstein, whom he met on a boat returning from Europe in the summer of 1925; she was a successful stage designer, kind and practical, who was nineteen years older than Wolfe. She kept watch over him while he was writing Look Homeward, Angel.

Maxwell Evarts Perkins, his editor at Scribner's, was the last and closest of these elder friends. Wolfe regarded him as a spiritual father, while Perkins—who had five children, all daughters—treated Wolfe as an only son. At last the son broke away from the father, in a letter of twelve thousand words—most of Wolfe's decisive steps were taken by writing letters—but he continued to depend on Perkins and express his gratitude. Indeed, he was grateful to all his foster parents, even when he quarreled with them, and before the end he was reconciled with all of them except Baker, who had died too soon.

But more than he relied on his capacity for learning from others (and the lessons had to be those he wanted to learn), more than he relied on his energy or strength or intelligence, Wolfe relied on his memory, or rather on a peculiar quality of his memory. He says in that fascinating little book, The Story of a Novel:

The quality of my memory is characterized, I believe, in more than ordinary degree by the intensity of its sense impressions, its power to evoke and bring back the odors, sounds, colors, shapes, and feel of things with concrete vividness. . . . I would be sitting, for example, on the terrace of a café watching the flash and play of life before me on the Avenue de l'Opéra and suddenly I would remember the iron railing that goes along the boardwalk at Atlantic City. I could see it instantly just the way it was, the heavy iron pipe; its raw, galvanized look; the way the joints were fitted together. . . . Or again it would be a bridge, the look of an old iron bridge across an American river, the sound the train makes as it goes across it; the spoke-and-hollow rumble of the ties below . . . or it would be, most lonely and haunting of all the sounds I know, the sound of a milk wagon as it enters an American street just at the first gray of the morning, the slow and lonely clopping of the hoof upon the street, the jink of bottles, the sudden rattle of a battered old milk can, the swift and hurried footsteps of the milkman, and again the jink of bottles, a low word spoken to his horse, and then the great slow, clopping hoof receding into silence.

Besides the intensity and exactness of such impressions, there was another feature of Wolfe's memory, or rather of the experiences preserved in it, that gave an urgent force to his writing. Many of the experiences had a background and color that had never been portrayed in literature. There were tender-minded persons at the time who believed that events had to reach a certain order of dignity or seemliness before they were worthy of being treated in drama or fiction. Wolfe had quite a different feeling. "There is nothing so commonplace, so dull," he had told his mother, "that is not touched with nobility and dignity."

He knew that his mother would understand, because he had been talking about events in their own household. They belonged to a family of "good people," in the Southern phrase, which means hardworking people, self-respecting and without pretensions. The name Wolfe was Pennsylvania German, and Tom's father was a stonecutter born near Gettysburg. The Westalls, his mother's family, were Scotch-Irish from the Carolina mountains. On both sides they were eloquent talkers, but they had never tried to preserve their talk on paper. Tom was the first writer among them, or in the town where they lived, and his voice had more power because he was conscious of speaking for the silent generations and of giving them a sort of posthumous nobility. Like Dreiser in this respect, he was a new man, speaking for a new order of society, in a country that was still new in literature.

He had his ambition, this equipment, and this opportunity, but he had very little time—only a dozen years from the summer day in 1926 when he started *Look Homeward, Angel.* During those years he worked like a man possessed—"like a fiend," he kept saying in his letters—always with the feeling that time was the enemy he had to outwit. He was trying, as Proust had done, to rescue his whole experience from time and give it a permanent meaning. . . .

*December 17, 1956 [Voltaire]*

# THE REFORM OF DR. PANGLOSS
by Mary McCarthy

Was it a good idea to try to turn *Candide* into a comic operetta? Many people thought so; I confess I did myself. The materials seemed to be there: a gay, quite dirty story with exotic settings and a sufficiently improbable plot. A satire on optimism, moreover, could be expected to have a certain topicality. Leibnitz's monads are no longer an issue, if they ever really were to the general public, but it is not hard to imagine Candide and Pangloss as a pair of Point Four administrators or running a U.S.I.S. library in Bangkok or broadcasting for Radio Free Europe. A philosophy which gasses out of existence all unpleasant realities is official American doctrine, and if nobody actually believes that the American "way of life" represents the best of all possible worlds, few, including Pangloss, actually believed in *his* doctrine. As Voltaire put it, "he continued to maintain it without believing in it," which is our own situation.

What went wrong, then, with the musical *Candide?* Four authors, all of them prominent, worked for a year with a prominent composer and a prominent scene designer to translate to the stage a tale that Voltaire wrote in three days, and the result is a sad fizzle which is more like a high-school pageant than a social satire. The gaiety is gone; the dirt is gone; the negativism is gone. This is an uplift *Candide,* with a ringing message at the end. Candide and Cunegonde and the Old Woman and Pangloss all reform in the final scene and start to build a new life in a rugged pioneer setting that looks rather like Valley Forge in an American history textbook. "We'll build our house and chop our trees and make our garden grow." The curtain goes down on a burst of radiant affirmation.

In Voltaire, Candide's garden, located in the soft clime of the Propontis, provides the little band with a diet of candied citrons and pistachios; even so, they remain perfectly unregenerate. Candide grows bored and decamps, to be inducted into a life of luxurious pederasty by an Arab. Voltaire was decidedly pessimistic about the rewards of virtue, even in a warm climate. But there is no pessimism in this musical, no pederasty either. Miss Hellman and her collaborators have elected to play it safe. Anything in the original that could give offense to anyone—Jews, Arabs, or Holy Church—has been removed.

What the present authors have forgotten or failed to see is that *Candide* is a   dangerous work. It is really and truly subversive. A fuse burns in it; that is why it is exciting. There are many things wrong with the present production—costumes, scenery, music—but the chief and essential failure is a failure of nerve. One cannot blame the authors for hesitating, say, to attack the Church openly. The production would doubtless have been banned if they had or if they had followed Voltaire one tenth of the way in sexual frankness. Yet a *Candide* without daredeviltry, without that element of risk that makes the spectator catch his breath, is not worth doing. If Voltaire's *Candide* could not be produced with most of its episodes intact under modern conditions, then the whole idea was a poor one. We must simply face the fact that we, or our stage, are not up to Voltaire. A bowdlerized *Candide*, a *Candide* that cannot afford to be candid is a contradiction in terms.

Voltaire's tale, precisely, is about facing facts. Obstinate nature is set up against a denatured official doctrine. The two philosophers, Pangloss and his pupil, Candide, are confronted with a series of object lessons in fires, floods, earthquakes, pestilence, from which they learn absolutely nothing. They are exposed to man's "unnatural" behavior in the sexual sphere, to his insensate money greed and religious bigotry, all seen by Voltaire, in this work, as unalterable—customs of the country which have the iron force of natural laws. That a custom or an institution (such as war or the bastinado) should seem as infrangible as a natural law to those who practice it is one of the absurdities of the universe explored by Candide in his enforced travels, but so it is, and there appears to be no hope of change or reform; escape is the only recourse, and the new fate is often worse than the last. In the end, Candide settles down, though not with Cunegonde, who has become his implacable enemy, and not in a garden, to live by the sweat of his brow, but very comfortably, in an aristocratic house, as a "nobleman of distinction," whose wife has furnished him with a false pedigree. The pair live "as happily as it is possible to live," the degree of this being left to the measurement of the reader.

Candide is a permanent recruit; when he is finally mustered out, he has got the rudiments of an education; that is all. As for Pangloss, he

never reforms; the very idea is unthinkable. Toward the end of his
career, Candide comes upon an old man expiring in a hospital and recognizes in his enfeebled philosophizing the style of Pangloss:

"No man in the world," said Candide, "but Dr. Pangloss could maintain optimism in such a deplorable situation, where every other mortal
would preach pess—"
"Do not pronounce that detestable word," said the poor old man. "I
am that very Pangloss. Wretch, let me die in peace; all things are good;
everything is best."

These words cost him his last tooth and, shortly after, he dies. The
obstinacy of Nature is matched by the obstinacy of doctrine. The
ideas of Pangloss are unkillable, just as Pangloss himself, up to this
point, has proved to be. Pure survival is the hero of the tale; the
characters have a persistent life that is like the persistence of a
fixed delusion; they can be stabbed, burned, drowned, disemboweled,
and yet they keep turning up again, with the same speeches in their
mouths. The old woman who has been left with only one buttock,
Candide, who has lost a leg, Cunegonde, her brother, the Jesuit, the
immortal Pangloss are prodigies of survival, absurd, magnificent Jack-
in-the-boxes who cannot be kept down; the only important character
who lacks this ineffable power is the virtuous Anabaptist, who drowns
once and for all in the shipwreck off Lisbon; he is shown, significantly,
as a selfless man—the word perhaps has two senses.

The best moments of the musical Candide are those that dramatize
this power of survival. It was a happy notion to have the optimistic
Pangloss and the pessimistic Brother Martin played by the same actor,
the English revue star Max Adrian, doing a series of quick changes.
Voltaire would have been pleased to have thought of it himself. When
Brother Martin is swallowed by a shark and reappears, a moment later,
pulled up by Candide on the other side of the raft in the form
of Pangloss, there is a genuine laugh, the only unforced one in the
production. The sharklike spirit of Voltaire seems to grin, for an
instant, from the deep.

But that is the best that can be said. The fate of sex in this
production is typical of the whole. As the curtain goes up, Candide
and Cunegonde are about to be married; their wedding is interrupted
by the outbreak of war, which is seen as the cause of their troubles.
The real Candide's troubles sprang from quite another source: he
was caught with Cunegonde by her father behind a screen in the
castle and summarily kicked out. It was Nature in Candide making its
first assertion, the old Adam popping up in the earthly paradise of
Westphalia.

Throughout the tale, the old Adam in Candide continues to rise to every sexual opportunity; this natural behavior sometimes earns him a beating and sometimes saves his life—that is the way the world goes. Candide is simple, and one token of his simplicity is his candid readiness to make love or have love made to him, if necessity decrees it. This promptitude in rising to the occasion is a kind of natural wisdom that saves him from being an utter fool; the inveteracy of the "lower" appetites, morever, is only another form of that obstinate resilience manifested by the characters who refuse to die when they are killed. The Jack-in-the-box is a penis. It gets you into trouble and gets you out of it. That is Voltaire's only affirmation.

The musical Candide, however, remains a virgin from first to last; a good bourgeois, he respects Cunegonde too much to tamper with her. Like any other sentimental operetta hero, he is an official stencil of virtue. This virtue allows him to denounce the other characters in an angry editorializing style, to "tell off" poor old Pangloss like a crusading progressive ramming *real truths* down the throats of deluded humanity. There are no *real truths* in Voltaire, only sad facts that must be faced gaily and politely.

*April 29, 1957 [Scott McLeod]*

# DOOLEY REDIVIVUS
Editorial

"Did ye see in th' papers," said Mr. Hennessy, "how they're sindin' Scott McLeod to be ambassadure to Ireland?"

" 'Tis funny ye should mention that," replied Mr. Dooley, "just when I'm standin' here thryin' to recall whether 'twas a poet or a secur-rity officer who made the famous remark: 'I care not who makes the laws iv a nation, if I can sarve on the investigatin' committees.' But ye mustn't think they're sindin' McLeod to Dublin out iv malice, Hinnissy. Very like, it just came up in a casual conversation, d'ye know. The President happens to notice one day that his Sicrety iv State is back in town, an' he takes him to wan side an' says, 'While ye're here, Foster,' he says, 'ye might just tell me how the wurrld is gettin' along.'

" 'Oh, times is lookin' up,' says the Sicrety iv State. 'Our relations with

England haven't been annywhere near so plisint since the Rayvelu-
tionary War,' he says, 'an' that's nothin' to our relations with France
an' Israel,' he says. 'To the oppressed peoples in the satellites,' he says,
'I just sint kind regards an' the hope iv a speedy an' complete liberation,' he says, 'but not so speedy as to worry the Rooshians about
losin' their empire,' he says. 'I told them,' he says, 'if they needed anny
help, just say the wurrud,' he says, 'an' we will give them every assistance, short iv helpin' them,' he says. 'In short,' he says, 'by exertin'
a stiddy moral pressure,' he says, 'we're bound to win some sort iv
moral victory.'

"'Well, you take care iv it, Foster,' says the President. 'Dwight D.
Eisenhower is not the man to stand in ye'er way.'

"'Speakin' iv people in me way,' says the Sicrety iv State, 'I do belave
I've found the place for Scott McLeod.'

"'Is that a fact?' says the President. 'An' where is that, now?'

"'Well,' says the Sicrety, 'I thought to meself, what sort iv appint-
ment wud prove that we are on such terms with McLeod as wud plaze
the Old Guard, but not on anny such terms as wud make anny modhren
Raypublican think we was on anny such terms as we ought not to be.
Then I remembered we had a job open in Dublin, an' I says to meself,
well, Foster, me lad, 'tis not as good as sindin' him to th' moon, but
still, 'tis better than a poke in th' eye with a sharp stick.'

"'It is that,' says the President, 'but d'ye think the Irish will like it?'

"'I dunnaw,' says the Sicrety. 'They're a hard lot to plaze. They
didn't like the Black and Tans ayther, till they got used to them.'

"'Well,' says the President, 'you always had a livvil head, Foster,
an' if ye think it's a good idea, it suits me right up to th' handle.
Where do I sign?'

"And that, Hinnissy, is how 'twas done."

"But d'ye not think," asked Mr. Hennessy, "that th' Congress might
tell th' Sicrety to sind up another boy?"

"I do not," said Mr. Dooley. " 'Tis a foolish man, Hinnissy, who
stands behind his own plate-glass window an' makes faces at th'
fellow with a brick in his pocket. Th' Congress don't dare turn down
McLeod and the Sicrety knows it."

"An' why is that, now?" asked Mr. Hennessy.

"Sure, an' how else wud they get him out iv the counthry?" answered
Mr. Dooley.

*November 18, 1957*

# JUSTICE FRANKFURTER AT SEVENTY-FIVE

by Alexander M. Bickel

During the Twenties and early Thirties, when the Justice [Frankfurter] was Byrne Professor of Administrative Law at Harvard, a majority on the Supreme Court of the United States frequently ignored, it is fair to say, "the ethical foundations of the law" and the Court's role in seeking and promoting them. The Court's intellectual processes were often shoddy. Finally, the Court almost consistently set its course in blithe disregard of the functions of other institutions of government and in defiance of deep-seated popular desires. Opposition within the Court came resoundingly from Holmes and Brandeis, later from Cardozo and Stone, and occasionally from Chief Justice Hughes. On the outside, the leading voice was that of Professor Frankfurter.

Seldom in our history has solidly founded private scholarship been so responsibly and effectively brought to bear on public issues as it was in this period through the writings of Professor Frankfurter. There were numerous articles in professional publications. There were series of lectures, among which those published as *The Commerce Clause under Marshall, Taney and Waite* deserve special mention for the lucidity which made them accessible to the general reader. *The Labor Injunction,* written with Nathan Greene, was a critique of the Court's disastrous stewardship of labor relations. It resulted, shortly after publication, in passage of the Norris-LaGuardia Act; and its philosophy and documentation had much to do with the new departure made in the Wagner National Labor Relations Act, the basic policies of which are still law. Other writings, including many that appeared in this journal, were addressed beyond the professional audience. A representative collection of them was edited by Archibald MacLeish and Edward F. Prichard, Jr., and issued under the title, *Law and Politics.*

But this catalogue of writings tells only a partial story. It will be many biographies of many men from now before we can know (and then so much will remain intangible) the full extent of Felix Frankfurter's influence. Countless leading figures of the time felt directly, and not only through his published works, the force and attraction of Mr. Frankfurter's mind and personality. The impact on events was, we may be sure, appreciable. Mr. Justice Brandeis was referring to this fact when, writing to Harold J. Laski in 1928, he made an estimate that needs no elaboration: "He [Frankfurter] seems to me clearly the most useful lawyer in the United States."

Nor is this all. Mr. Frankfurter was, of course, a teacher, and he was a great teacher. To him were drawn, year after year, the best minds and most venturesome spirits among Harvard law students. Such a teacher multiplies himself in his students. Justice Brandeis—as he would—saw what was happening and understood the consequences earlier than most. In 1952, he wrote, also to Harold J. Laski: "The year has been for Felix, also, one of happy usefulness, with an ever-widening appreciation of his rare qualities. His students are becoming teachers. Given another 20 years of such activity, and he will have profoundly affected American life."

Justice Frankfurter's interest in his students did not end with their graduation, and it was not always necessary to enroll in the Harvard Law School to become a student of his. Nor has he stopped having pupils since his elevation to the bench. His generation has always been the next one. He brings quick and generous understanding to the young. He is never disrespectful of them on the score of mere youth. He is always ready to allow his abundant resources of enthusiasm to be tapped. And there is a special quality to the sustenance he has provided to younger men. The profession of the law has a tendency to seal itself off, or to permit itself to be sealed off. This is a tendency that the Justice, a man of catholic intellectual tastes, has never shared. For lawyers, he has always held invitingly open the door to the wide world of the mind and the spirit. And he has kindled in many who were immersed in other disciplines an appreciation of the law. "So many authors have expressed their gratitude to Mr. Justice Frankfurter," Mark DeWolfe Howe has written in the foreword to the first volume of his biography of Justice Holmes, "that it is becoming almost a ritual of scholarship to acknowledge the indebtedness." A ritual not only—not, by far, only—of legal scholarship pursued in the traditional ways.

I have spoken of the abundance of the Justice's enthusiasms, for this is one of the splendors of his temperament, and a source of many of his good works. But he is endowed also with a glorious capacity for indignation. Out of this capacity, out of his awareness of the ethical foundations of law and his consequent passionate attachment to the integrity of the processes of criminal justice, and out of the breadth of his conception of the private lawyer as a public servant—out of these sources sprang his defense of Sacco and Vanzetti in a celebrated article first published in the *Atlantic Monthly* and later expanded in book form. There can be no pretense of even suggesting the role played by Mr. Frankfurter in the Twenties and Thirties without mention of this episode.

Mr. Justice Frankfurter took his seat on the Supreme Court of the United States by appointment of President Roosevelt (it was Mr. Roosevelt's third appointment) in January 1939. This was for the Court the time, one might say, of the great spring cleaning. The debris of twenty years or so of judicial wrongheadedness had to be swept away. The Social Statics of Mr. Herbert Spencer had to be read out of the Due Process Clause of the Constitution, and appalling vacuums of power ordained by the old Court's construction of the Commerce Clause had to be filled in. This was the work of vindicating the essence of the dissenting views of Holmes and of Brandeis, and in this work Mr. Justice Frankfurter strove mightily. And had he not been there, his writings and his teaching would have played their role in this inevitable development—in this development which his writings and his teaching helped to render inevitable.

To clear away the debris was not, however, to clear away the problems. New questions arose, of course. They were perhaps only the old questions in new aspects—the old sheep in new wolves' clothing. But they required new answers. There were those who sought to evolve techniques for mechanizing the judicial process, so that abuses such as those chargeable to the old Court might be forever avoided. In order that the likes of Herbert Spencer might never find their way into the Due Process Clause again, let us so define that clause, it was said, as to bind posterity to our views. And let us find new utility in other, seemingly less imprecise clauses of the Constitution, and by applying them achieve our ends. This, as Justice Frankfurter saw, was illusion and wish-fulfillment. Assurance that the Court's values were the right ones could not be derived from mechanical formulas of any sort. There were no labels and no devices that would serve this end; only the integrity of the intellectual process; only candor in recognizing and facing the task. The old complicated rectitudes—duty to sustain what must endure, deference to the electorally responsible institutions—could not be simplified.

The life and work of Mr. Justice Frankfurter is a creative unity—a life and work of great courage and candor. He does not mask, from himself or from us, what he has called "a judge's perplexities." (The phrase appears in his very important address, "John Marshall and the Constitution," which was delivered in 1955 and appears in *Of Law and Men*, a collection of his papers and addresses edited by Philip Elman.) No other judge, not even Brandeis, has had a subtler appreciation of the institutional capabilities and infirmities of the Court, and of their bearing on tasks it should and should not assume. No other judge has faced the essential task with greater valor or (the word is used with the image of Mr. Stimson in mind) greater rectitude. Let the evidence of the Justice's own words in a concurring opinion at the last term of Court speak to this. The case was *Sweezy v. New Hampshire*:

> To be sure, this is a conclusion based on a judicial judgment in balancing two contending principles—the right of a citizen to political privacy,

as protected by the Fourteenth Amendment, and the right of a State to self-protection. And striking the balance implies the exercise of judgment. This is the inescapable judicial task. . . . It must not be an exercise of whim or will. It must be an overriding judgment founded on something much deeper and more justifiable than personal preference. As far as it lies within human limitations, it must be an impersonal judgment. It must rest on fundamental presuppositions rooted in history to which widespread acceptance may fairly be attributed. Such a judgment must be arrived at in a spirit of humility. . . . But, in the end, judgment cannot be escaped—the judgment of this Court.

*June 30, 1958*

# SHERMAN ADAMS

by T.R.B.

We watched Sherman Adams last week sit ramrod-stiff for his public humiliation in the great cream-yellow barn of a House caucus room as big as an airplane hangar. Here was the mysterious, rarely seen Adams— small, white-haired, ascetic; muscular, proud face, a gnomelike man with a square jaw. He came prepared to admit that he had been "a little imprudent," and he was prepared to die, apparently, before he would go an inch beyond that. We are inclined to believe he is sincere in this attitude, too, for it is his extraordinary insensitivity rather than his deeds that tell the story.

Curiously enough, the mood of the affair was sad, poignant, transcending politics, transcending Sherman Adams even. For who can see pride humbled without a tear or watch mistakes exposed without being himself in the dock? There was an odd kindness about the committee— the kindness of the death call. The great moment came when Representative John Moss (D., Cal.)—not tauntingly, and almost as though it were driven out of him unwillingly—recalled to Adams the "whiplash" of the Republicans' smug charges in the 1952 campaign against the Democrats.

Adams sounded crisp and cool and almost plausible. But consider these additional facts: (1) Adams professed to tell the whole story in his public statement June 12, and Press Secretary Hagerty next day announced that he had given "all the facts"—subsequent to which came word of the $2,400 Oriental rug, the vicuña coat, and, even in the very committee room, of hospitality at the Waldorf-Astoria! (2) Adams said the rug was a "loan" from Goldfine; an interview in the *Washington Star*, December 28, 1954, with Mrs. Adams, told of the "immense" Oriental rug she had "just purchased." (3) Adams's explanation that he thought the shifting Boston hotel suites were rented permanently by Goldfine became ridiculous when the New York hotel suite was added. (4) And how can anyone believe—or believe Adams believes—that his telephone calls to regulatory agencies (many of whose members he selected) would not have "influence," or that his securing of information (in violation of rules) would not benefit his client? (Hagerty says Goldfine already *had* the information; in that case, why ask Adams to get it?)

The scene shifts to the Eisenhower press conference and the heartfelt comment, "I need him." When all else is forgotten of this Administration that poignant cry may be remembered. It summarizes all the desolate story of delegated powers, lack of leadership, and inadequacy.

Administration defenders are raising the *tu quoque* red herring that Congressmen also exert pressure and take junkets. Obviously Congressmen should mend their ways, but the analogy falls on its face. Congressmen are elected; Adams is not. They don't appoint regulatory commissioners; Adams does. They don't throw moral thunderbolts from Eisenhower's elbow; Adams does. They don't take sanctuary from the press in the White House; Adams does.

*October 6, 1958*

# ELEANOR ROOSEVELT
by Donald Meyer

What we have to do with here is a very fine mind. Its quality is not in a conventional mold, so it can be mistaken for something else: sensitivity, a liberal and generous spirit, woman's intuition. Mrs. Roosevelt has these, certainly, but she also has what these do not normally imply, a penetrating, powerful and persistent realism. *On My Own* [the third volume of her autobiography] has much to do with politics and politicians of course—the United Nations, American foreign policy, the Democratic Party, Adlai Stevenson, Tito, Khrushchev. As she talks of such men and matters, one gradually realizes two important things: Mrs. Roosevelt speaks without rhetoric, and she speaks with precision. . . . In an age hardly able to think for itself, let alone communicate, except in the clichés of organized power, the resources of such a mind ought to be comprehended.

Mrs. Roosevelt's narrative not only of her experiences but of her tactics during her years in the UN is in effect a formulation of the gyroscopic balance between inflated illusion and narrow gamesmanship, a balance implacably demanded of anyone who really wants to be responsible in the largest affairs of our time. In the course of her telling, she succeeds, amazingly, in making of the methods of the UN—that tediously pedantic object of maddeningly loose hopes—something vital. She knows the difference between action and those imitations of action flaunted in the grandiose jargon of our ideology-cursed era: "free world versus slave world," "the principles of freedom," "atheistic Communism," and the like. She simply does not need such rhetoric in order to project her understanding.

As a consequence, Mrs. Roosevelt is the perfect anti-Communist. "I think I should die if I had to live in Soviet Russia," she says, and she knows why. At the same time, she knows that two hundred million people do live in Soviet Russia, and five hundred million in Red China, and she knows that her reasons for finding Communism deadening are not the reasons several hundred million other people in the world are going to have if—and she knows it is an "if"—they do not give themselves to Communist rule. Mrs. Roosevelt is not bemused by that marvelous egocentricity which imagines that if only the American Way of Life can be "sold" to aspiring millions all will be well. . . . [She] recalls to one's mind the tradition of our best liberal leaders, who knew that politics—not even liberal politics—is not fine ideals, but patient application to things as they are. All else is adolescence—fantasy without responsibility.

The poise and power of Mrs. Roosevelt's mind are fruits of a long struggle for personal identity. And here, it seems to me, one can find her realism united to her experience as a woman.

It has nothing to do with genes, chromosomes, the "eternal woman," or anything constitutional, but with something social and as old as our civilization: the assumption that heroes of abstract thought should be men, with women left to tend the particular. This may someday be felt to have been a tragic split, for it has helped allow men to pervert the powers of abstract imagination into romantic, fanatic political ideologies, and women, excluded from the glorious affairs of abstract principle, to languish in a few realms where politics has not usually invaded—home, boudoir, Sunday school. Mrs. Roosevelt has not escaped such restrictions by learning the tricks of abstract imagination, by becoming, that is, more like a man. Rather, she has extended her own imagination, shaped by her experiences as a woman, into male domains. Despite every reason in her early life to do so, and despite every reason in her middle life to do so, she never lost her sense of being someone different from the patterns expected of her by others. Her father, her parentless youth, the patterns of New York "society," mother-in-law, children, stricken husband, governor and President— they all dominated her. "I was lost somewhere deep down inside myself," she said, in *This I Remember*, quite objectively, without complaint. Nor did she, in the manner of the "emancipated woman," ever rebel. What she did, over years and years, first in New York City, then in New York State, then in the nation, was to find her identity gradually not in some pattern all her own, but precisely in the process of comprehending other people's patterns.

We are all alerted to the falseness of public images. In Mrs. Roosevelt's case, the answer is that there is no answer. Her pattern is to exhibit in herself how the conflict, complexity and passion of other patterns can be accommodated in the reach of a single mind. The result of her long search for herself appears to be that, in the ordinary sense, she has no self. Instead, she is now freely what she always was, a kind of synthesis provided for others. Visiting a primitive Ettu village in Japan, where the people were doomed to "the lowest and most degrading work," she learned, she says, "how important it is to recognize that there is a bond among all peoples." That is what Mrs. Roosevelt's life has been—the recognition of bond.

*January 12, 1959*

# ALDOUS HUXLEY — ROMANTIC PESSIMIST

by C. P. Snow

It is always wrong to deny or forget one's gratitude, as a wise radical friend of mine said, warning himself as well as me, just after we had listened to one of Churchill's speeches in 1940. It would be wrong for any Englishman of my age, ten years or so younger than Aldous

Huxley, to deny the gratitude we owed him in the Twenties. No one has set us thinking about so many different things; no one sharpened our wits or widened our sensibilities so much. That happened, and it's on the literary record for good and all.

Having said that, I now want to say that I am profoundly out of sympathy with *Brave New World Revisited* and with *Brave New World* and, I fancy, with any further attempts of his to rationalize his views on the social condition of men. I never like literary Utopians much: I like literary anti-Utopians even less. Both Orwell's *1984* and Huxley's two *Brave New Worlds* seem to me likely to do much more harm than good. They are neither art nor life, but essays at just that kind of abstraction which most distorts the truth. They are quite different in kind and intention from books which Huxley refers to with approval, such as *The Power Elite* and *The Organization Man*. Those admirable works are written within the grain of society; they are part of the real social world just as a direct realistic novel is; we can learn from them some of the price we have to pay for advanced industrial security, without losing contact with its immense gains. Immense gains, I said, for the sooner intellectuals in the United States and Western Europe realize that industrialization is the one hope of the poor, the sooner we shall get hold of a social purpose again.

In both of Huxley's anti-Utopians there is one basic fact. It is that in organized societies men can be deprived of their free minds: the power-bosses in Communist countries, the concealed power-bosses in capitalist societies, can use various kinds of technique, sheer force, propaganda, subliminal advertising, drugs, and so on, to make the "masses" go contentedly, unresistantly, and even happily to whatever actions the power-bosses decide on for them. The trouble with statements of that kind—and it is the trouble with two thirds of this new book—is they are neither true nor untrue. Of course, in advanced industrial society (let's call it "a.i.s.") a very large amount of power seems to be concentrated in a few hands and sometimes is. Of course, by the nature of a.i.s. and the scientific revolution which brought it about, new sorts of persuasion, manipulation, coercion and control can be used on a larger proportion of the population more immediately than ever in the past. So far, so bad.

But that that this is transforming the texture of individual life now or in the foreseeable future seems an entirely romantic view. In fact, one is left wondering what romantic conception of the free mind is hallucinating Huxley—how does he imagine it operating in, say, a peasant in medieval England or in Tsarist Russia? And in what ways are these operations preferable to those of an unfree mind in a factory in Lancaster, Pennsylvania, which has been exposed to subliminal advertising or even tranquilizers? And in what senses does he imagine

the unfree mind in Lancaster really demonstrates its individual un-
freedom, as opposed to a similar mind about twenty years ago, before
a.i.s. got fully into its swing? How long is it since he talked dis-
interestedly and intelligently to people fully within the grip of a.i.s.
not seeing it, as he is bound to see it, from outside and with distaste?

He appears to have become—perhaps he was always so—more
pessimistic about the individual condition. Probably the combination
of social pessimism and individual romanticism is more common than
we think. It is a serious disqualification for social thinking, for a
rather curious reason. It means that one is constantly trying to think,
to idealize, the individual into a nonsocial context. Huxley has always
been tempted to this. He has never had any feeling for the social
plasma in which we, as human beings, really live our lives. The social
plasma is incomparably more important to our destinies than tranquilizers, mescalin, hidden persuaders, the whole bag of sophisticated
horrors.

*January 26, 1959 [Evelyn Waugh]*

# MY FAIR GENTLEMAN
by Malcolm Muggeridge

The dust jacket of Mr. F. J. Stopp's study of Evelyn Waugh shows his
subject, dressed in check tweeds, a large, unlighted cigar in his hand,
and leaning over a gate inscribed: *"Entrée Interdite aux Promeneurs."*
This portrait is by Cecil Beaton, who specializes in photographic
studies of the royal family. It conveys the whole irony and poignancy
of Mr. Waugh's life out of which his writings have come—the notice
in French on the gate of what is supposed to be an English country
house, itself, along with Mr. Waugh's singular fancy dress, serving to
draw attention to him when, according to Mr. Stopp's and his own
account, one of his major objects in life is to avoid being intruded
upon or noticed.

My own acquaintance with Mr. Waugh is slight. The last time I
saw him was at a wedding. I am no expert on wedding attire, but
his seemed unusual. A tall black hat, I thought funereal in character,
provided an additional bizarre touch. He made considerable play
with an old-fashioned Victorian ear trumpet, though whether for use

or ostentation I cannot say. Occasionally he seemed to head in my direction, almost to orbit round me, but no trace of recognition appeared on his large, rubicund countenance. I felt no particular desire to be recognized by him, but these strange gyrations struck me as odd. In any case, on the few occasions that I have been on speaking terms with Mr. Waugh, I have formed the impression that he does not like me.

Usually, such antagonisms are mutual. I cannot, however, say that I reciprocate Mr. Waugh's dislike. There is, to me, something oddly sympathetic about this professional eccentric. I admire the bizarre, though nonetheless often highly effective, protests he has made against the times in which we both live. I once saw him at Brighton, on this occasion attired in an enormous overcoat and gray bowler hat. He was making his way alone on to the pier. I was tempted to follow him and see whether it was the machines—"What the Butler Saw," or some other—which attracted him thither, or whether he just went to the end to stare for a while out to sea. Despite his bulk and peculiar accouterments, he had, I thought, an air almost of sanctity. The fool who persists in his folly becomes wise, Blake wrote. In this sense at least, Mr. Waugh may be accounted wise. Most of us, in the pursuit of folly, at a certain point prudently draw back. Mr. Waugh has persisted to the end. He has fought the good fight, if only with bladders and in the setting of a harlequinade.

Mr. Stopp's study is painstaking, sympathetic and occasionally illuminating. He suffers, however, under the disability that he has only felt able to offer serious criticism in the words of others. His own attitude is too uniformly approving to be interesting. Also, alas, he notably lacks Mr. Waugh's gift for the terse ironical phrase, the sharp, icy comment. He is deeply serious, if not solemn, and has that curious convoluted way of writing which life at a university (in his case, Cambridge) seems so often to inculcate. Mr. Waugh has long passed the time when he needs an apologist. He has, in any case, been most ardently his own. And, in his last work, *The Ordeal of Gilbert Pinfold*, a discerning reader may find out a great deal more about him than most authors have disclosed about themselves. Mr. Stopp could scarcely have hoped to add to this.

His *Evelyn Waugh* is divided into two parts, the first biographical, the second an analysis of Mr. Waugh's works. The biographical section takes us rather sketchily from Mr. Waugh's childhood in a prosperous London suburb, Golder's Green, the son of Arthur Waugh, for many years head of the publishing firm of Chapman and Hall, to his time at Lancing, where he began to emerge as a "character" and distinguished himself at the school debating society. Mr. Stopp adds, rather naïvely, that the Headmasters' House, at which Mr. Waugh was, had special connections with Eton, and that this may account for Mr.

Waugh's subsequent large acquaintanceship with Etonians. I can think of other explanations.

Mr. Waugh went on to Hertford College, Oxford, where he obtained a history scholarship, and there became an eminent figure among the group of aesthetes whose leader and chronicler was Harold Acton. A portrait by Henry Lamb belonging to this period bears out Harold Acton's description of him as

> a prancing faun, thinly disguised by conventional attire. His wide-apart eyes, always ready to be startled under raised eyebrows, the curved sensual lips, the hyacinthine locks of hair, I had seen in marble and bronze at Naples, in the Vatican Museum, and on fountainheads all over Italy.

He neglected to take his degree, though he obtained a third-class in his finals. After Oxford, he was at a loose end, did a bit of preparatory-school teaching (resulting later in *Decline and Fall*), tried his hand at carpentry, and, after his first marriage, began to write. His marriage was a failure, and he spent most of the remaining years before the outbreak of the 1939–45 war in traveling and writing travel books.

With great gallantry and persistence, although by this time thirty-seven, he managed to become a combatant soldier, and was with the Royal Marine Commandos in North Africa. Then he transferred to the Blues (the Royal Horse Guards) and, by one of life's little ironies, was given indefinite leave of absence to write a book—*Brideshead Revisited*. From this compulsory retirement, he was rescued by Mr. Randolph Churchill, with whom he joined Fitzroy Maclean's Military Mission in Yugoslavia. It was during this period that he first elaborated his interesting theory that Marshal Tito is, in fact, a woman. I caught a glimpse of him in the war, in Algiers, at a picnic party given by the Duff Coopers. He seemed, I thought, somewhat bemused and melancholy. His uniform, though exact, somehow gave the impression of not quite belonging to him. He looked, I decided, like a letter delivered to the wrong address.

In 1930, he had been received into the Roman Catholic Church, and after the war married into a delightful family of that faith, the Herberts. Thenceforth, he settled down to elaborate his impersonation of a crusty old country gentleman, collecting the requisite properties, both personal and household, and occasionally appearing in London in this role. Mr. J. B. Priestley and others have complained about the impersonation on the ground that the writer has been suffocated by the elaborate superstructure it has required. This seems to me absurd for two reasons: firstly, that Mr. Waugh remains an excellent writer, probably the most accomplished today in the English language; and, secondly, that his impersonation of a country gentleman is as integral a part of his writing as was George Orwell's equally absurd converse impersonation of a down-and-out.

An interesting comparison could be made between these two. Whereas Mr. Waugh considers it "common" to pile plates after a meal, Orwell thought it "unproletarian" to drink in a saloon bar; whereas Mr. Waugh's wardrobe is based on sporting prints of the late nineteenth century, Orwell's followed the general lines of a workman in *Punch* jokes of the same period. If Orwell had not been able to convince himself that he was once down and out in Paris, and to dress and play the part, however imperfectly, the probability is that he would never have written *Animal Farm* or *1984*. In the same way, Mr. Waugh's masquerade has been essential to his work. Without it we might well have lacked his delightful comedies, in the Wodehouse manner (though Wodehouse with a decided dash of vinegar), that little masterpiece, *The Loved One*, as well as *Brideshead Revisited*, his books on the war, and, finally, *Pinfold*.

Precisely the same comment may be made on Mr. Waugh's occasional political attitudes, which some have found offensive. Peppery old gentlemen living in the country, and needing ear trumpets to hear what is said to them, are naturally pretty antediluvian in their ideas. *The Times* is too Red for them, modern Toryism is little better than Bolshevism, and if they have occasionally heard the radio playing in the servants' hall, television is something they just do not know about. So it must be with Mr. Waugh, though, according to Mr. Stopp, acute boredom often induces him to go off to the local cinema in the afternoon. Again, it is an infinitely touching picture—the gray bowler perched on the large head, the defiantly "loud" country suit, the pony trap harnessed and whip cracked. But to go where? To the local Odeon to see Gary Cooper. "World, World; Oh! World," as Lear remarked in not wholly dissimilar circumstances.

Mr. Waugh would, in any case, accept what he supposed to be the political attitudes which went with his Roman Catholicism. For instance, he would feel bound to approve of Franco quite irrespective of any private distaste he might have for the Franco régime. He has labored hard to make himself into a conformist, though his conformism is a do-it-yourself brand of his own. Thus, as a wartime soldier, his object was to submerge himself in smart regimental life. The novelist and gentleman. This, of course, did not make for popularity in the mess. His fellow officers wanted to be diverted by the author of *Vile Bodies*, not confronted with a slightly grotesque, aging version of themselves. They expected him to be funny and unusual, not taciturn and sullenly laboring to be usual. As is clear from his two novels *Man at Arms* and *Officers and Gentlemen*, the Pinfold voices told Mr. Waugh this at the time—which must have made his suffering all the greater. He bore it, as always, with fortitude.

Mr. Stopp is puzzled by the great popularity of Mr. Waugh's novels —especially, of *Brideshead Revisited*—in the United States. This is the only book by Mr. Waugh I have never been able to get through. It seems to me to be tedious and rather foolish. On the other hand, I find no difficulty in understanding why its American edition should have sold 700,000 copies. Its success, surely, is exactly comparable with that of *My Fair Lady*. Indeed, it might well have been called *My Fair Gentleman*. It sustains the illusion, especially dear nowadays to many Americans, that the old familiar social landmarks are still extant in England. How amusing that yesterday's *Chicago Tribune* target should be today's solace! It is the kind of situation with which Mr. Waugh in his young days would have been particularly fitted to deal. Indeed, up to a point (Lord Copper) he does deal with it in the first part of *The Loved One*. That he should have benefited from it financially is, therefore, right and proper.

The side of Waugh which is most admirable, as Mr. Stopp clearly shows, is his unpretentious dedication to the craft of letters. He has refused to be sidetracked into all those ancillary activities upon which the rest of us have, uselessly and often shamefully, expended so much spirit. He decided to be a writer instead of a carpenter, and thenceforth devoted himself wholeheartedly and conscientiously to this pursuit. How few in our time have managed to do this! Even the terrible Pinfold experience (equivalent, in the context of his life, to Scott Fitzgerald's crack-up) was coolly, neatly, expertly recorded. So rare a devotion deserves at least the Order of Merit. I should love to see it round his neck even though he still looked at me across it with those angry, explosive eyes of his.

*April 20, 1959 [Graham Greene]*

# THE LIFE AND SOUL OF THE PARTY
by Honor Tracy

To entertain his fellow men is one of the kindest things an author can do; and as an entertainer Mr. Graham Greene has few rivals in the English field. For sheer readability—a mysterious attribute having no connection with either beauty or truth and indeed well-nigh absent from some of the world's greatest literature—he comes perhaps second only to Mr. Somerset Maugham. From the fact that he divides his work into Novels and Entertainments, however, it may be doubted if he is content with this. In the distinction there is something self-conscious, even something arbitrary: we cannot but wonder what Mr. Greene has in mind. Although he might not thank us for a suggestion that the Novels are not entertaining, or that the Entertainments are not novels, the implication of a difference in genre is clear. It would make quite a sticky last point for a radio quiz:

Which is *The Quiet American?*
—Novel.
Which is *Our Man in Havana?*
—Entertainment.
Quite right (*studio applause*)

And thousands and thousands of dollars would change hands.

We live in a popular age, and the first care in arranging literary quizzes must be to avoid deleterious strains to the mind, and excessive claims on the knowledge, of competitor and audience. The prize might be less easily won if the aspirant had to explain the reasons of the author. What has that quiet American specifically got that our man in Havana hasn't, it might be asked, to justify his place in the higher category? The honest fellow does not even offer us a message, except Mr. Greene's personal one as to the futility of messages. Pyle is young and earnest, "impregnably armoured by his good intentions and his ignorance"; in the name of what he calls democracy he brings suffering and death to the Indochinese people he assumes he is helping; when the bomb laid by his democratic Third Force explodes in the Place Garnier, "a man without his legs lay twitching at the edge of the ornamental gardens," saved from Communism and French Imperialism alike. Wormold in Havana is middle-aged, disillusioned and frivolous, except in what concerns his daughter; to get money for her finishing school and her dowry he accepts the post of British secret agent, writing imaginary reports, cooking expense sheets and recruiting a phantom staff among names haphazardly picked out, which in the police state of Cuba inevitably leads to the death of their flesh-and-blood owners.

Evil results arising from intentions not in themselves blameworthy, held by people neither good nor bad, are the theme in both cases. Why, then, is the greater weight given in the first? Certainly, the author has taken more pains with it, it is better worked out and written, the story is more probable, the characters less mechanical; but there is no essential difference. Indeed, the implied deprecation of the second sounds like an appeal to the public. "Don't be hard on me," Mr. Greene seems to say, "I wasn't really trying." Or can it be that, because Pyle is American, because Pyle stands for wealth and material power, because there are so many Pyles, because anti-imperialist Pyle is not yet hep to the fact of his own imperialism, he ranks by sheer portentousness? Has Mr. Greene succumbed so far to the present-day fallacy of mass, of quantity, to the notion that ten Pyles are worse, a hundred deaths more terrible, than one?

The question is interesting because of a widespread belief that Mr. Greene, when not deliberately playing down to us, is a very serious and, above all, a very Catholic writer—a puzzling belief, since the mental climate of his books is so unmistakably, so fashionably pagan. Obsession with aspects of the doctrine and practice, an artful decoration of text with the vocabulary, does not make a "Catholic" novel any more than does a quotation from Péguy, placed with a flourish at the head of Chapter One. Undoubtedly one of the themes in *The Power and the Glory*, that the sacraments are valid even though the priest administering them is a coward and a soak, may be described; but we do not read and reread the novel for the sake of this simple, and to many of us familiar, truth but for the terror of it, the suspense, the heat, dust and smell of Mexican town and village, the flight through the rain, the deliberate rejection of safety by the hunted priest—in a word, for the story. Even less does *The Heart of the Matter* grip us by the force of Scobie's religious dilemma, if that is the word for presumption so enormous. It is by the sense, wonderfully conveyed, of empire in decay, of the seediness of colonial life delivered up to suburbia, to the Bungaloids, of the despair in loveless, childless marriage, of the terrible African heat that smothers the good impulses and brings on the rest like weeds; and, Heaven forgive us, we may be more anxious to know if Scobie was promoted after all, or how he got the money for his wife's passage to South Africa, than whether he damned his immortal soul.

It is, then, the storyteller and not the thinker or moralist who compels our admiration. Mr. Greene is a dazzling showman who functions on different levels with, we cannot help thinking, a similar fundamental purpose at each. Like the Fat Boy, he wants to make our flesh creep; he wants to make us sit up and cry *Oh!* The dictionary says that to "entertain" is to "amuse, agreeably hold the attention of" and it is perhaps worth noting that our author's ingredients for achieving this are murder, lust, lunacy, failure, poverty, disgrace. Even *Loser Takes All*, his one attempt at pure comedy, has to be brightened up with a broken marriage. This does not deter him from offering any number of rueful asides on the degenerate times in which we are fated to live: having created his joyless world, Mr. Greene thoroughly disapproves of it; having looked upon his work and seen that it was bad, he reviles it like any puritan. The aging Fowler speaks to his native mistress: "'Phuong,' I said—which means Phoenix, but nothing nowadays is fabulous and nothing rises from its ashes," a remark meaningless enough to satisfy the most incorrigibly middlebrow reader and one of a kind that runs unabashed through all the books, whether Novel or Entertainment. Again, "A picture postcard is a symptom of loneliness," Mr. Wormold somewhere avers; statements of this sort encourage the library reader to think that he or she is getting value for money, and rather recall Mr. Thurber's Dr. Bisch, who together with his large following believed that an automobile bearing down on him was a symbol of sex. It took, we may remember, the luminous mind of a Thurber to perceive that in fact it was an automobile. The flow of Mr. Greene's wry, facile comment helps to establish him as a philosopher among the unphilosophical without interrupting the fun; fresh or difficult truths would stand up from it like rocks, demanding respect and attention.

But if Mr. Greene is not a philosopher, he is a psychologist: he knows just what, deplorably enough, we all like. A mere list of his villains will show how aware he is of the vestigial Neanderthaler lying doggo in the bosoms of the readership. And how full-blooded the villains of the earlier period were! Dr. Forester, the fiendish German spy and psychoanalyst of *The Ministry of Fear* into whose "nursing home" prominent anti-Nazis vanish for "treatment," might well have come from "Sapper"; so might the harelipped Simon Raven in *This Gun for Hire*, estranged from humanity by his disfigurement, ready for murder at a glance; and Mr. Cholmondley too, fat, white, smooth and unctuous, with his great emerald ring and his passion for sweet things, who paid the assassin with stolen banknotes.

A cut above them is Acky, the unfrocked clergyman, endlessly overflowing in letters of remonstrance to the Bishop and in Latin obscenities, with his slut of a wife, his murderousness: a truly sinister creation that might have figured in a prize-winning French film, or even in a novel by Wilkie Collins. And with the Boy in *Brighton Rock*, Mr. Greene hits the jackpot in repulsiveness. It is not that this little monster is more depraved or more sadistic than so many luminaries of the "tough" American novels that were poured out at the time, to which indeed—since it is unrelated to English life—*Brighton Rock* may well have been a spirited English reply. It is the fact of his being an adolescent, almost a child. When the book appeared baby gangsters and murderers were less familiar in both life and literature than they afterward became, and Mr. Greene scores heavily with this device; and not content with that he gives an occasional turn to the screw by emphasizing the traits of immaturity in the creature, such as the dread of sexual failure and of the girl's possible contempt or ridicule, or the lack of ease *vis-à-vis* his middle-aged gangster rival. This destroys, of course, any belief we may have had in him as the leader of grown, hard men, but Mr. Greene is always willing to sacrifice the general effect for a particular one. And finally there is the knockout when the Boy's widow, the depressed little slavey whom he married to prevent her being called to give evidence against him, goes to play over the message he had recorded for her one day on the pier. She expects words of tenderness, uttered in a beloved voice she will never hear again; but we know she is going to receive the coarsest, most cruel abuse. Strange to say, this piece of brilliant Grand Guignol is included among the Novels.

It is no great wonder if the children of Adam find their attention agreeably held by such matters: they interest us more than any others, as every news editor will confirm. Where Mr. Greene excels, where indeed he approaches wizardry, is in the power of holding it also by descriptions of the most squalid of people, the drabbest of milieux. Gray little commercial travelers, bad journalists, private detectives, slatternly waitresses, priests without a vocation, humbugs of every sort, suffering from indigestion, body odor, decayed teeth or sheer chronic futility, bob up in their seedy environments, the seaside promenade or boardinghouse, the colonial Nissen hut, the genteel villa or the dusty office, and keep us as enthralled as would the most glittering assembly in the land. No English novelist but Dickens has written as vividly of the failed, the come down, of all that in life we incline to turn away from; but where Dickens transfigures it by the warmth of his humanity and the magic of his genius, Mr. Greene simply treats it as exotic. His eye is original, if his mind is not; the masterly, film-director's eye that in Africa, Indochina, Mexico picks out infallibly the one detail to bring the character, the landscape, before the reader's own achieves in playing on the familiar and the dreary, an even greater triumph.

With this eye, and an ear no less acute, with a prodigious knack of description, dialogue and narrative, Mr. Greene is incapable of being dull; and only the most ungrateful wretch alive would harp on the fact that the verities of God and man ask for something more.

404

*September 28, 1959 [Nikita Khrushchev]*

# FOLLOWING MR. K

by T.R.B.

To be candid about it, traveling with Nikita Khrushchev produces a galling sense of irritation. He is a fascinating figure, compounded of such bizarre contrasts as Mayor Fiorello La Guardia, W. C. Fields, Jimmy Hoffa and—oddly enough—Winston Churchill. He is comical as a clown and tough as nails. The unspoken source of his confidence is the very fact of his being here. Six months ago the administration said, "Put down your gun or we won't play!" Well, the gun is still pointed—and Mr. Khrushchev is here.

He began lecturing the United States shortly after the wheels of his turbo-jet airliner smoked their rubber at Andrews Airport. He played with his hat at the welcome of an ill-at-ease Eisenhower and stole the show. This was amusing enough, but thereafter his rough-tough lines grew more conspicuous. There is some evidence that he has misjudged the temper of the country and believes that he can bully a soft adversary.

At the National Press Club, Mr. Khrushchev sounded his principal themes: coexistence, peace and more trade. A couple of brutal questions were thrown at him which, for American self-respect, had to be put sooner or later along the route—about Hungary, and his personal relations with Stalin. Suddenly those who had seen only his quizzical drollery got a revelation. Here was a man of ruthless force and will. Saturation TV coverage carried the subsequent story.

Khrushchev let himself go next day before the Economic Club of New York. A polite question on Soviet censorship and radio jamming brought it about. Mr. K did not bother to be diplomatic. He treated the audience like one at home. His voice rose to a shout. He had come on the President's invitation, he said; he was not going to brook opposition, "to beg"; the issue of censorship was a domestic affair. Besides that, we had refused a passport to Paul Robeson. The chairman of the meeting tried to end with a pleasantry. But nobody could forget the scene.

Mr. K's proposal to end armaments was as simple as a minister's proposal to end sin. Just end it. Two thirds of his speech at the UN could have been given by Eisenhower. He told of the horrors of war and the joys of turning arms expenses to peaceful pursuits. But Mr. K assigned every virtue to Communists, every vice to the West.

It was a tremendous scene in the great modernistic hall of the UN as he presented his hour-and-a-half speech under spotlights, with spectators all wearing earphones, in a building that rises to a soaring dome and looks like part conservatory, part cathedral, and part wigwam.

Only a psychiatrist could tell how much Wilsonian idealism and how much cold cynicism was in Khrushchev's mind. "Four years to Utopia!" ejaculated one reporter. For the simplehearted, the Communists had once again grabbed the peace football.

A nation which has Eisenhowers gets Khrushchevs. Mr. K gives to this reporter the impression of contemptuous self-confidence. Repeatedly he mentions that the Soviet is turning out three engineers to one in America. He arrived in Washington with the moon in his pocket. Mr. K emphasizes that the Soviet has a sense of mission, of knowing where it is going. Under the tranquilizers of Washington, America lacks what Lippmann calls a sense of national purpose. Perhaps even Khrushchev cannot arouse the country.

*October 5, 1959*

He's left, but it won't ever be quite the same again. And who will ever forget those thirteen incredible days! I can see him now, acting out in pantomime the can-can dance he saw at Hollywood, giving his heavy posterior a wriggling imitation, and roaring with laughter. Or holding the squawking duck against his paunch at the Beltsville Agricultural Station, chuckling with glee. Or solicitously inquiring of the unfortunate Henry Cabot Lodge—whom he used as a straight man for his jokes (after deflating him almost overnight from a Truth Squad into a cloying guidebook—"How is my Capitalist holding up?"

Or I can see those little fat eyes narrowed to angry slits and looking out ruthlessly on us—a competitor nation that might be laughing at him and his peasant origin (you could never be sure!)—or worse still, laughing at Little Mother Russia.

There are other memories of that amazing trip, with 350 reporters and cameramen, twice across the United States; the hurried, perfunctory visit to Roosevelt's grave at Hyde Park, where he had no time to eat but came out waving a seeded roll, shouting in gleeful English, "One for the road; one for the road!" (And Mrs. Roosevelt's quiet remark: "No, he was not interested in me. That gentleman is interested only in power.") Or I can see him coming, with Lodge and bodyguards and cameramen, down the aisle of the rolling fourteen-car special train that carried him up between the blue Pacific and velvet mountains on a spectacular trip from Los Angeles to San Francisco; coming up in his queer walk (halfway between an amble and a waddle) in a floating press conference and shaking hands with each newsman . . . and the strong grip of those short, iron fingers.

Oh, well, there is only one story like that in a century, I suppose, and we won't have another like it until Chou En-lai comes over. Television and radio coverage reached saturation, and the enormous accompanying press party included gray-flannel English correspondents ("Well done, old boy!"), toothy Japanese cameramen (in Tokyo everyone carries a ladder), agile representatives of Paris *Match* and German *Quick*, rough-hewn Russians with a suspicious look, who knew English but wouldn't talk it, and everyone else down to the Syracuse *Herald-Journal*.

When this typewriter is rusted and the writer forgotten, stories will still be told in the National Press Club of the Khrushchev party swinging into the supermarket in San Francisco like a California flash flood that brought a near-riot and scenes which even yet I don't believe, though I saw them happen. I watched a cameraman scale a mound of glass coffee jars ("special for the day") which collapsed noisily after a shot or two, with fragments and grounds all over the place. An attendant came up and fussily tried to clean them up with two pieces of cardboard, oblivious of the pandemonium around him. One cameraman rolled on the floor with a butcher, with few to interfere or care. "What did he fight you for?" we asked at the hotel later. "Nothing, nothing at all!" he explained; "I was just standing in his meat."

And whether apocryphal or not, another story expressed the grim humor of the affair. Two cameramen on the supermarket floor: "She's fainted," said one. "Either that or she's on sale," said the other cameraman.

Nikita Khrushchev stands five-feet-five and weighs more than two hundred pounds, and at San Francisco the hotel got out a special news release quoting the chef as saying he was on a salt-free diet. That means high blood pressure and certain temperamental characteristics of interest to diplomats, just as Mr. K's overweight is presumably of interest to his physicians. He eats with gusto, putting his head down close to the plate. And just when you think of him as a comical clown with his peasant origin written all over him, he rises to his feet for a speech which, even through the translator, is moving and menacing and compelling. It may be sacrilege to some but I found his frank acknowledgment, as an atheist, of the knowledge of the precepts of Christ, and of his identification of some of them with his own visions for Russia, of deep interest. This man, and do not doubt it, believes in his own propaganda.

*March 7, 1960 [Akira Kurosawa]*

# THE FACT OF MORTALITY

by Stanley Kauffmann

> Iván Ilych's life had been most simple and most ordinary and therefore most terrible.
> —From *The Death of Iván,* by Leo Tolstoy

Tolstoy's entire novella might well be reprinted here, for, in a sense, it is the best possible comment on the Japanese film under discussion. The picture is *Ikiru* (in English *To Live*), and the themes of the two works are the same: the realization of the approach of death; the bewilderment and anger at the course of one's past life; the shame of fear; the knowledge that the world has already discarded you, that you merely make others uncomfortable; the inescapable holiness of your last days because you are already in touch with great secrets or the absence of them; and the revelation that only dying is death, that once a man dies, death is finished and all that remains is the man's life —as it was—now unalterable and complete.

The picture begins, stunningly simply, with an X ray; a narrator tells us that this is the stomach of the hero, who will die in some months of gastric cancer. Then we see the man Watanabe sitting at his paper-laden desk in the city hall, unaware of his fate, a minor middle-aged bureaucrat in a hive of jealous underlings. He sits there endlessly stamping approval on endless papers and forms, and at once we want to shout: "For God's sake, get out. You've wasted enough time. Get out and draw a few free breaths before it's too late."

We go with him to the hospital, where, in spite of doctors' euphemisms, he perceives the truth. We see the initial paralyzing shock, and through quick, beautifully economical flashbacks, done with the understatement of Japanese painting, we see his past life, widowhood, loving care for his son. Then Watanabe arouses from his shock to do something: to use his last months somehow. The first impulse is the frantic one. He withdraws half his savings and, with the aid of a bohemian whom he meets, he tries to go on a spree. But he can't eat the food, the liquor sickens him, the trollops don't really answer his needs.

Then he encounters a bright, vital girl who used to be a clerk in his section and, only for the sake of her company, begins to spend time with her; but she is soon bored with him because all he does is sit and look at her. When she threatens to stop seeing him, he becomes panicky and tells her of his sickness, why he needs her, that just once before he dies, he wants to touch life warmly, fully, and that he wants her—the seeming wellspring of it—to teach him how.

But she, in splendid ignorance, replies that she doesn't understand him; she simply loves living and enjoys her new job—in a toy factory—because the toys give pleasure to thousands she will never see. The naïveté and obviousness of this do not prevent it from answering his question. He moves into a third phase. He returns to the office and takes up a petition of some mothers who have long pleaded to have a swampy lot in their slum neighborhood converted into a playground. Against massive bureaucratic resistance, Watanabe sets out to further their cause.

Here, alas, the film goes into an unduly long coda. When the doomed man begins his mission, we jump ahead to a wake held for him after his death. Various speeches are made at his funeral feast, there are numerous flashbacks filling us in on what happened between the last time we saw him alive and this occasion: how he fought the delays of office to realize his small ambition. This section is much too fully explored. If the wake had shown us the Deputy Mayor patronizing the dead man but claiming credit for the playground and had then shown us the policeman bringing in the dead man's hat (he dies in the playground alone at night), that would have been sufficient. The last scene should have been that of the man sitting alone in a playground swing in the midnight snow, dying happily—if it is ever unobscene to couple those two words.

This is a film rooted in the most universal of truths, the one that cuts across all cultural barriers, all concepts of love, success, God: the fact of mortality. It confronts that fact with honesty and a touching eagerness. Takashi Shimura, who (under the same director) was the woodcutter in *Rashomon* and the leader in *The Seven Samurai*, is magnificent as Watanabe: an actor who creates fiercely the indignity and helplessness and groveling fear of the man newly sentenced, along with the ravening hunger for sensual pleasure, then for spiritual refreshment, then for a crumb of achievement to be his immortality.

Excepting the slack editorial hand toward the end, it would be hard to overpraise Akira Kurosawa's direction. He clearly has all the resources of film technique at his command and, confident of his knowledge, is not constrained to display it. Fancy montages, whirling effects, bizarre angles are not for him. It is his purpose to make life seem to occur and, like a true artist, he does this by showing less than would occur in life. He selects his elements perfectly, never lets the emotional scenes stray past sentiment to sentimentality, and with unmelodramatic juxtaposition weaves the elements in his story, letting the rhythm as well as the content flick away at our sensibilities with gentle, telling strokes.

As for the wake, which seems discursive, since the ceremonial itself is more meaningful to a Japanese than it could be to us, the irony of its treatment here is bound to be somewhat ineffectual. The purely human elements in the film are placeless; ritual, both in life and art, is parochial.

The only film comparable to this that I can remember is de Sica's *Umberto D.*, which too treats of the failing of the light, but *Ikiru* is, for me, more powerful. (Incidentally, it is a strong refutation of one aspect of neorealism, which *Umberto D.* represents. Kurosawa's fine cast, especially Shimura, is more creditable and affecting than any carefully coached group of "real" people could possibly be.) Moreover, it is not an exercise in gloom. Because it faces and penetrates and diminishes true horror, the film achieves a measure of Tolstoy's effect: it shrives and strengthens.

*May 2, 1960*

# THE NEW, IDEAL HARVARD MAN
by Christopher Jencks

Perhaps Harvard University is the only American institution of higher learning sufficiently complacent about its virtues to be realistic about its vices. Among all the official "self-studies" which have poured from the university presses in the last decade, Harvard's have been almost unique in transcending the usual platitudes about "difficult problems," "dedicated efforts" and "dynamic solutions." Certainly, the college's recent report on the combustible issue of freshman admissions policy is a model of critical realism, even if the revolution it portrays and advocates is in some ways alarming.

In the years before Pearl Harbor, Harvard students were selected largely by social and economic criteria. Since scholarship funds were limited to a handful of exceptionally talented applicants, most students had to come from families with five thousand dollars to spend for the four years. Furthermore, most public schools did not offer adequate academic preparation for the entrance exams, or for freshman year, and so the average applicant had to come from a family with enough money to finance at least a couple of years of private schooling.

Family counted in other ways as well. If your father had been to Harvard you were virtually assured of admission. Lacking such qualifications, you could redeem yourself by persuading your father to become a member of the Harvard faculty, or by moving him to Nevada and thus capitalizing on the search for "geographic distribution" which began in the Thirties under President Conant.

The results of this admissions policy were predictable. The students were no brighter than the national average, according to College Board scores, and the great majority acquired only the veneer of culture required to maintain a "Gentlemen's C." A study of American scientists who went to college in those years show that on a per-capita basis Harvard was not even among the top fifty colleges in the country. Yet, studies of national income show Harvard alumni of this era are second only to Yale's, and analysis of Who's Who suggests that as a social training ground Harvard was surpassed by none.

Since 1945 all this has changed. Like other "elite" institutions, Harvard has gone academic, and while it is still easier to get into Harvard if you come from the "right" family, you must also be among the top tenth of the nation in scholastic aptitude. The new recruits have new ambitions. Business careers now attract only a handful of mediocre students, and while many gifted graduates still enter law, medicine and even the arts, the most talented are increasingly lured into the academic profession. On a per-capita basis, Harvard is now one of America's top ten feeders of Ph.D. mills, with about one alumnus in six headed for a scholarly career.

Harvard's admissions report approves and encourages this trend. The ideal freshman class, the report says, would be composed of 1,200 students who "show exceptional promise of some creative achievement." And, according to this faculty committee, a creative achievement is a scholarly achievement. Admittedly, 1,200 gifted future scholars cannot be found even among Harvard's nearly 5,000 applicants, and so the college must accept other students "who are not destined to win Nobel prizes and who will not accomplish 'breakthroughs' in any field of scholarship, but who nevertheless exhibit strengths which can make them important contributors to the life of their country and their time." This second-rate group of nonscholars would presumably include such alumni as Franklin D. Roosevelt, Learned Hand, and perhaps Harvard's President Pusey. That, however, is not the company today's Harvard faculty is most eager to recruit; the new breed will follow in the footsteps of such alumni as Percy Bridgman, David Riesman, or perhaps T. S. Eliot.

In some measure the new scholarly emphasis at Harvard and a few dozen other "highly selective" colleges reflects the requirements of the age. Better secondary schools, both public and private, have taken over the Ivy League's traditional role of civilizing the young. Authors like Freud, Marx and Eliot, who were once regarded as material only for college upper-classmen, now appear on high-school seniors' reading lists. Paperbacks, television and the upper-middlebrow press have introduced college applicants to culture, and Harvard must now rise to a more difficult task. By general consensus, inside and outside the universities, that task is to provide intellectual training.

There would be few to quarrel if the Harvard report merely urged the primacy of intellectual ability and training. But the faculty report on admissions goes on to more controversial assumptions. First, it suggests that Harvard College can make its greatest contribution to the nation by training scholars and scientists (rather than artists, politicians, doctors, lawyers, journalists, businessmen, ministers or philanthropists). Perhaps so, although the roster of the Harvard Alumni Association would hardly suggest that this has been its principal contribution in the past. The second assumption of the report is even more disturbing. The primary criteria for evaluating every applicant is his predicted undergraduate point average. While it is only natural for professors to seek students who write the kinds of examinations and papers of which professors approve, it is by no means established that such mark-hounds are the ones who "show exceptional promise of some creative achievement," either in scholarship or in any other field of endeavor.

A few years ago an insouciant admissions officer tried to illustrate the dangers of current policies by resurrecting the Harvard application of a now Harvard professor. The name and date were changed, and the application joined 4,000 others for admission to the class of '61. The professor was rejected. His high-school record did not show sufficient "promise." We suspect that if this experiment were repeated on a large scale, a substantial portion of currently eminent Harvard alumni would be told that they were not sufficiently talented and should apply elsewhere. No doubt such students can get a good education elsewhere; many eminent men have emerged from obscure colleges, or from no college at all. But there is considerable evidence that the highly selective colleges such as Harvard offer a unique and valuable experience, not available in many more accessible institutions. To make this experience available only to men who promise to win Nobel prizes or achieve break-throughs in some academic discipline may make Harvard a more congenial place for the professors who run it, but what is good for Harvard is not necessarily good for the country.

America needs not only a "brain trust," but men of action who can employ such resources. As we discovered in 1929, and may rediscover in 1960, it does little good to raise up a generation of intellectuals if you then put a Hoover or an Eisenhower in charge of the country. Franklin Roosevelt may not have been Harvard's brightest alumnus, but without such men the university's brain-power would have much less leverage on the national life. Only by continuing to select such candidates for admission as Mr. Roosevelt and, yes, Jack Kennedy is the college going to assure vital and continued contact with the outside world.

*June 23, 1960*

# THE WORLD OF LYNDON B. JOHNSON
by Selig S. Harrison

The most striking discovery one makes in examining the Johnson history is how little he has changed. Unlike Kennedy—whose political coloration is not at all what it was ten years ago—Johnson seems to have been from the beginning more or less what he is today. He took his seat in the House in 1937 as a protégé of Franklin Roosevelt. . . . He was a young political natural on the make who had nailed his flag squarely to the mast of the national government then in power.

Arriving in Washington as secretary to a Texas Congressman in 1931, Johnson found in the Roosevelt Administration the patronage base on which he was to build his later career. As Texas Administrator for the National Youth Administration (1935–37) he had 30,000 jobs and scholarships to hand out. His political baptism came at a time when nearly the whole Texas Democratic Establishment was pro-Roosevelt and pro-New Deal. In the middle Thirties Texas was still an agricultural state with an old-fashioned Populist distrust of Wall Street. High interest, profiteering in freight and utilities rates, and high tariffs that got in the way of the overseas cotton trade, were all part of a demonology the Texans in Washington shared in common with more cerebral New Dealers—former Interior Undersecretary Abe Fortas or Justice William O. Douglas—who remain Lyndon Johnson's good friends today.

Sam Rayburn cosponsored the first R.E.A. legislation with George Norris, and Johnson fought hard to get public power into his impoverished Tenth District. But Johnson's commitment to the New Deal was never much more than the commitment of a "public-power liberal" whose social conscience was stung by the needs of his home-state constituents. Nor has he pretended otherwise. William S. White, then of *The New York Times*, found Johnson literally in tears in a Capitol corridor on the day after Roosevelt's death. Describing him as "a typical representative of a hundred formerly obscure men whose leap into national prominence had been immeasurably aided by the President's paternal coaching," he quoted fulsome tributes, which were conspicuously personal—"He was just like a daddy to me always"; and, "The only test he had was this: Was it good for the folks?"

Interviewed on April 23, 1947, Johnson told an Associated Press reporter that "the term 'New Dealer' is a misnomer. I believed then and I still believe in many of the causes Roosevelt backed. That includes development of water power and other natural resources. I believe in the R.E.A. and think all-weather roads should be built to every farmhouse. But I believe in free enterprise and I don't believe in the government doing anything that the people can do privately."

Reviewing Johnson's record, one finds that he has voted the Democratic Party line on international issues, even, at times, when this has been fiercely unpopular in Texas. He has insisted that Congress should not harass the Executive in the conduct of foreign policy and has accordingly supported both Truman and, as Majority Leader, Eisenhower, remaining silent when many Senate Democrats felt that Administration policy blunders cried for a public airing.

Johnson is no isolationist. His public utterances have never had a suggestion of America go-it-alone. At the same time, they have invariably stopped short of any specific description or characterization of the outside world. In general he has appeared concerned to keep the onus on the Russians for any breakdown in communications and diplomatic exchange. When the 1957 *Face the Nation* interview with Khrushchev prompted some charges that CBS had let itself be used as a propaganda forum, Johnson declared that "we should welcome this example of direct argument," calling on the Administration to press for reciprocal privileges in the Soviet. In this same "Open Curtain" speech he urged U.S. initiative on a five-phased disarmament program tending to support the Administration proposals then being pursued by Harold Stassen in London.

It is perhaps too much to say, as his partisans do, that Johnson set in motion the official thinking which led to the U.S.–U.S.S.R. cultural-exchange pact in late 1957. But the record does suggest that for all of his single-minded interest in preparedness, Johnson would probably carry over his Senate mode of operation—"always keep your lines of communication open"—into something of an effort to negotiate with the Russians. How effective Johnson's overpowering style in personal encounters would be in the protocol-conscious world of diplomacy defies prediction. His only meetings with Khrushchev have been in groups when he has had little to say. Johnson was one of twenty-five ranking Senators who spent two hours with the Soviet Premier on September 16, 1959, and met him briefly at a White House dinner the night before ("He said he had read all my speeches and didn't like any of them"). When Johnson was asked on a TV panel what he would have said to him in the U-2 aftermath, he responded that "I would talk to Mr. Khrushchev . . . about their action in suppressing the people of Hungary, about their promise to have free elections for fifteen years and then denying them. About their capturing our prisoners and never turning them loose. About their own spy activities. . . . If Mr. Khrushchev wanted to talk about anything of that kind, I would give it to him fast and furious."

Johnson gave V. K. Krishna Menon of India what must have been one of his more uncomfortable and perplexing moments when, following Johnson's statement on outer space to the UN Political Committee on November 18, 1958, Menon engaged in some characteristic needling. "That was a very impressive presentation," announced Menon, confronting Johnson as he stepped down from the dais. "I wish that your country would give as much time to disarming as you give to preparations for arming." Where others have trailed off in exasperated silence or risen to the bait with wild abandon, Johnson, as those present recall it, brushed him off with an unruffled and vaguely sarcastic smile. "Well now, Mr. Ambassador, we're ready. We'll disarm tomorrow. Can you deliver the disarmament of the Communist bloc? I don't know much about this building but let's get a room and we'll do it right now."

Johnson's appearance at the UN was part of an attempt—his Mexican visit was also in the fall of 1958—to get increased exposure as a world statesman. Taking hold of the space issue in the post-Sputnik months, Johnson had referred, in his personal January 8, 1958, "State of the Union" message before the Democratic caucus, to the need to "win and hold" what he called the "ultimate position—from which total control of the earth may be exercised . . . Whoever gains that ultimate position gains control, total control, over the earth." *The New York Times* pointedly commented on the next day that "if ever anything was a matter for international cooperation and coordination, this is it."

Within a week Johnson had picked up the cue and asked that the U.S. take the initiative before the UN in inviting all member nations to help "join in this adventure into outer space together." His appearance before the UN to testify to a bipartisan dedication to peaceful U.S. intentions in outer space logically followed. The world press was fascinated. "TEXAS 'COUNTRY BOY' JOHNSON LEAVES MANY AT UN BEWILDERED" was the headline on the report from the St. Louis *Post-Dispatch* UN correspondent Donald Grant. "A country boy from Texas come to howdy and shake" was, it seems, Johnson's opening gambit at a news conference of some sixty correspondents

from Asia, Africa, Europe and Latin America. "The diplomatic correspondent of a newspaper in Amsterdam leaned over to ask exactly
what was meant by 'howdy and shake'," wrote Grant, "but there was
no time for an answer. . . . 'Come with us, arm in arm, united, and let
us explore this joint adventure together in the hope that we can consign
our antagonisms to the ash can.' 'I suppose,' whispered the young man
from Reuters, just out from London, 'that by ash can he means
dustbin.' "

He would have too much native good sense, one concludes, to take
the United States on any wild adventures. He conveys steadiness and
looks every inch the strong President.

One area in which Johnson seems to have worked out in his mind
the beginnings of definition is aid and trade policy. He commits himself in broad humanitarian terms to a U.S. role in aiding the under-
developed countries. He would broaden what is now a "closed
corporation" of alliances, and seems to think in terms of regional-aid
machinery set up by such indigenous figures as Lopez Mateos, of
Mexico, in Latin America. He would organize "a central authority
to coordinate trade and aid activities in this field of total competition
with the Soviets. The last new trade idea that's been advocated was
Cordell Hull's reciprocal-trade program."

He has not felt called on, thus far, to seek much foreign-policy
advice, and one can only speculate on who these advisers would be or
how he would use them. Talking with Johnson and those close to him,
one is given the names of certain men whose foreign-policy expertise
he is said to "respect"—men such as former Undersecretary of State
Will Clayton; Justice Douglas; Dean Acheson; Benjamin V. Cohen;
Charles "Chip" Bohlen; Fulbright; *Denver Post* publisher Palmer
Hoyt, and former Assistant Secretary of State George C. McGhee. But
it is the Brain Truster, not Johnson, who does the initiating; Dean
Acheson will send a memo to idea men George Reedy or Gerald
Siegel on Johnson's staff (both mainly trained in domestic affairs),
or he will talk with Johnson when they meet socially at the home of a
mutual friend. Most of these men have to stop and think to recall an
occasion when they have talked more than a few moments with
Johnson on a matter of foreign policy.

*July 11, 1960*

# I'M FOR ADLAI STEVENSON
by Gerald W. Johnson

*The New Republic's* invitation to switch to Kennedy is doubtless all right for those who are liberals first and eggheads afterward, but some people are so peculiarly constituted that they are the other way around. For one, I believe that for the past seven years the country has suffered less from lack of liberalism than from lack of realism—if, indeed, there is a difference. I am accordingly persuaded that our most urgent need is a leader who not only knows what is going on in the world, but has a pretty shrewd idea of what it means.

Without prejudice to Senator Kennedy, I believe that Adlai Stevenson's grasp of the essentials of our present situation, at home and abroad, is firmer than that of any other man in public life in either party. And I believe, considering what we have been through recently, that this qualification is more important than any other that a candidate might possess in 1960.

The Republican Party, thanks to superior organization and more money, has frequently won with a second-rater or worse; but the Democratic Party has never achieved a signal success except when it put up its very best man. Truman? He was not only the best, he was the only man who could have beaten Dewey in 1948. Truman was no egghead, but at that he had more brain-power than a majority of his critics and—which is the supremely important thing—what he had he used.

At this moment it is worth remembering that every really damaging criticism aimed at Truman was based on his judgment not of measures, but of men. When great issues were presented he was right with astonishing consistency; but some of his appointees let him down lamentably. I think he is wrong again in his judgment of the man Stevenson. Truman calls him indecisive; but four years ago Stevenson decided not to make any effort to obtain the nomination in 1960, and he has been adamant on that point despite more pressure than has been brought upon any potential candidate since Teddy Roosevelt in 1912. Having made up his mind, he has been harder to shake than Woodrow Wilson.

But all that he has ever said is that he will not seek the nomination, not that he would not accept it with pleasure if it were offered. That is to say, he has not attempted to use his position as titular leader of the party to throw obstacles in the way of any other candidate. They have had a fair field to show what they can do. If Kennedy runs away with the nomination on the first ballot Stevenson can and will support him heartily; but he has not sunk the knife into either Johnson or Symington. Therefore, if Kennedy can't make it, Stevenson would be the logical compromise because nobody has cause to feel aggrieved by him.

So much for his position. That of the Stevenson men, however, is a little different. Some, no doubt, are more afraid of a reactionary Democrat than they are of Nixon, and in view of the odds against Stevenson's nomination they may be justified in switching. But there are some who feel that Stevenson's two campaigns, although he lost, did far more to introduce common sense into national politics than the winner did. Hence they can contemplate a third experience of the kind with tranquillity; Stevenson might lose, but the country would gain.

This is a bit ruthless as regards the candidate. It is, in fact, using him as a whipping boy. But it is emphatically not to his discredit. On the contrary, it is the last full measure of confidence, implying that to lose with Stevenson is a more valuable public service than to win with a lesser man. In any event, Jim Doyle is not the only man who feels that way, not by many thousands. It may be bad politics, but it is the way the genuine eggheads are made. When they descry in the offing a man who was built by nature to cope with just such a situation as now exists, they are for him and they will remain for him whether he can be nominated or not.

The Battle Hymn of the boys of North Carolina includes the defiant pronunciamento:

I'm Tarheel born, and I'm Tarheel bred,
And when I die, I'll be Tarheel dead.

A similar spirit informs the embattled eggheads. I was a Stevenson man in 1952. I was a Stevenson man in 1956. I am a Stevenson man in 1960. And I suspect that when what Dr. Samuel Johnson called "lapidary inscriptions" are in order an appropriate epitaph on my tombstone would be, "He voted for Stevenson till the cows came home."

No, I don't know that he can be nominated. No, I don't know that if nominated he can be elected. But I do know that he would make a good President, and I am immovably persuaded that he would make a great one. Therefore I am for him, forward, backward, and starting in the middle and going both ways at once. And with that my duty is done.

October 17, 1960 [Richard M. Nixon]

# NIXON'S WORLD
Editorial

At no moment so far in this campaign has Mr. Nixon by a gesture, a phrase, an expression, given us to feel that he has within him those "deep anxieties, long sensed" (the words are those of Mr. Eisenhower's former speech writer, Emmet Hughes) which darken the thoughts of serious students of world events. As James Reston of *The New York Times* commented the morning after the second TV debate, "Mr. Nixon . . . is presenting a picture of the nation's position that is definitely not supported by most well-informed observers either in this capital or in the United Nations."

Contrast the Vice-President's bold assertion last week, that "at the present time Communist prestige in the world is at an all-time low and American prestige is at an all-time high," with the world as it was that week. At the UN, the new African members lined up solidly with the rest of the Afro-Asians against the United States and the West (the Communist bloc abstaining) on a resolution urging renewed contact between the President and Mr. Khrushchev. In that week, a majority of the votes at the British Labour Party Conference were cast for a policy of military disengagement from the United States and unilateral disarmament. In that week General De Gaulle demanded a veto right for France over the use of nuclear weapons anywhere by the West; Mr. Khrushchev delivered a new ultimatum on Berlin and a new attack on the UN Secretariat; the Algerian War was no nearer an end, with all of the menacing implications that conflict has for the future of relationships between Africa and Europe; hemispheric solidarity was shaken not only by the sight of the Cuban-Soviet entente in New York, but by rumblings of trouble in Ecuador and by a deepening reluctance everywhere in Latin America to be, or to be thought to be, too faithful a disciple of Uncle Sam. Prime Minister Nehru left the United States "disappointed" at the West's brusque repudiation of his initiatives in the UN. It can be reported on excellent authority that non-Communist national leaders in Manhattan were alarmed at the inertia and shortsightedness of United States diplomacy, and even more alarmed at Khrushchev's privately expressed contempt for the inner strength and will of this country. Chalmers Roberts of the *Washington Post* summed it up: "The heart of the matter is simply that the whole American approach to this extraordinary gathering has been just about 180 degrees opposite to what it should have been."

And elsewhere? South Korea, for whose independence Americans died and into which billions of dollars have been poured since the Korean War, remains on its feet only because it is propped up by a continuing United States subsidy. Much the same sad story is true of Iran. And last week, Washington abruptly cut off all defense support to Laos—80 per cent of whose national budget has been underwritten by the United States, the situation being too uncertain for further investment now.

Mr. Nixon's response to all this is a mild acknowledgment that one can always do better, and a sanctimonious observation that "it isn't necessary to run America down in order to build her up."

If that were all Nixon was saying, however, it could be passed off as campaign oratory: one can't expect the Vice-President not to flatter his audience or appeal to its desire to be comforted. But in his TV debate with Senator Kennedy last Friday, Mr. Nixon went far beyond that self-deception that believes the lie and brought forth a new and alarming doctrine. Senator Kennedy had said that "if you're going to get into war for the defense of Formosa it ought to be on a clearly defined line," and that that line ought not to include small islands lying from six to fifteen miles off the coast of Communist China. The Vice-President's response was immediate and demagogic. He contrived to suggest that Kennedy's endorsement of drawing a line this side of Quemoy and Matsu was comparable to Dean Acheson's failure to draw a clear defense line prior to the outbreak of the Korean War. He went on to say that the defense of these offshore islands is necessary bcause of "the principle involved."

"Principle" is a solemn word, and the voters had better be clear what this principle would mean if applied. The practical result of the new Nixon Doctrine is United States involvement in a war with Communist China at any time the Communists launch an all-out attack on these offshore islands. In such a war, it can be predicted with almost absolute certainty that the United States would fight without Asian allies and very little support from any other quarter. One can be sure also that an attempt to implement this doctrine would destroy, probably for all time, the slim remaining possibility that Formosan independence could be established by separating the future status of that island from that of Quemoy and Matsu.

What Mr. Nixon said perfectly illustrates how dimly he comprehends the character of a responsible foreign policy, a policy described in these pages some weeks ago by Louis J. Halle: "We must be the opposite of weak and provocative; strong and conciliatory. The simplicity of such a policy (of which Theodore Roosevelt was a famous exponent) should not be confused with naïveté, for it is no less sophisticated than it is simple. In fact, its implementation requires a sophisticated discrimination between what is *strong* and what is *provocative*, a discrimination that we have failed to cultivate in the recent past."

Mr. Nixon is no isolationist—no isolationist would pledge himself in advance to go to war with Communist China over Quemoy and Matsu—and yet what he has just said about the offshore islands ought to send the public back for another look at other parts of the Vice-President's record on international affairs. His overvaluation of what is accomplished by kitchen debates is sophomoric. But there is the fact too that in January of 1950 he opposed a sixty-million-dollar authorization for Korean aid, though a month later he turned about and approved the same proposal. When he ran for Vice-President the first time, Mr. Nixon made much of General Eisenhower's pledge to seek an armistice in Korea. But a year earlier he had attacked Truman's firing of General MacArthur and introduced a resolution demanding that MacArthur be restored to his post; though the point of that controversy was disagreement between the President, who was fighting a limited war of containment, and General MacArthur, who advocated a "hot pursuit" that would have pushed the war into China.

Mr. Nixon has generally taken a liberal trade position, but he voted to kill the Trade Agreements Act of 1949. He has associated himself with the President's opposition to the Bricker Amendment, but he was one of the original sponsors of that Amendment in 1952. He defended President Eisenhower's unilateral suspension of nuclear tests, but when this proposal was advanced by Adlai Stevenson, he denounced it by saying that "Mr. Stevenson's brand of peace seems to amount to achieving peace through weakness." Up to a week ago, the Vice-President favored repealing the restrictive Connally Amendment under which the United States reserves the right to determine which cases come under the jurisdiction of the World Court. Now, under pressure from Senator Goldwater, he has just reversed himself.

Many of these switches are explicable in terms of party loyalty. And that requires us to examine with some caution the Vice-President's downgrading of parties in this campaign. What of his proposition that "it isn't the label that [Senator Kennedy] wears or that I wear that counts"? Our two parties are not sharply divided by ideology, coalitions form and fade, but Mr. Nixon knows that the President is not only the spokesman for the whole nation but also the leader of and in some ways the instrument of a party. The President is pledged to carry out the platform of his party; he is obliged to work intimately with leaders of that party in Congress; his appointments are, in the main, party appointments. He runs with his party, not against it.

And what distinguishes this party whose ticket Mr. Nixon heads is its lack of sympathy for and understanding of those forces of change that have burst upon the world since 1945 and that will keep the world in a state of peril for decades ahead. Mr. Nixon's party feels in its bones that if you are rude enough to Khrushchev, if you shout your anti-Communism loud enough and can muster enough votes to keep Communist China out of the UN (as Mr. Lodge blithely assures us can be done), if you don't let the budget get too high and if you give free enterprise its head, we'll not only be all right, but we'll be better than anyone. Unfortunately, there is almost nothing in common between this way of looking at things and that of the Nkrumahs, the Nehrus, all these young leaders in Africa and Asia with their anticolonial and more or less socialist attitudes, or even the enlightened statesmen of Western Europe.

It is in part because Senator Kennedy has a progressive domestic program that he is better qualified to speak for America abroad. It is because he sees the significance of Khrushchev's remark that Russia's position in the world will not be determined by UN votes "but by the economy of the Soviet Union" that Kennedy is qualified to lead. He understands the correlation between power and diplomacy ("I don't confuse words with strength"). And he respects intelligence. (Who, one wonders, would be Nixon's counterparts to such foreign-policy advisers as Adlai Stevenson, Chester Bowles, Walt Rostow, David Lilienthal, Richard Gardner, Ernest Gross, Benjamin Cohen, Paul Nitze and Harlan Cleveland?)

Just before the election of 1956, *The New Republic* in endorsing Adlai Stevenson said that "foreign policy is the issue." It still is. The dangers to freedom are greater now than then, and the opportunities fewer—which is the principal reason why in our judgment a victory for Senator Kennedy and all progressive Democrats is so important this year.

*December 12, 1960*

# EISENHOWER THE GOOD

by Joseph C. Harsch

In former times kings and princes acquired popular descriptive labels which have clung to them ever since. There were Charles "the Bald," Charles "the Bold," and Charles "the Great," Edward "the Confessor," "Saint" Louis, Richard "the Lionhearted," John "Lackland," and "Bloody" Mary. One obscure Anglo-Saxon king has come down to us as "the Unready," although this may be a language corruption rather than a reflection on his military behavior.

It is interesting that none was ever popularly known as both "good" and "great."

It is, of course, premature to pass judgment on the career of Dwight D. Eisenhower, but as the third of his three public careers comes to its appointed end the presumption is permissible that by medieval standards of nomenclature he would be known as Eisenhower the Good, rather than Eisenhower the Great.

He has been popular with, and trusted and respected by, the people. This is attested by the fact that they twice elected him to their highest magisterial office and presumably would have been happy to do so a third time had the opportunity been constitutionally available. Similarly, popular princes were in times past usually given the title of "Good."

The title "Great" has been reserved for princes of massive authority and spectacular successes. The specific deeds of those who achieved it were frequently anything but "good" either by our standards or by even those of their own times. Perhaps it is to Mr. Eisenhower's credit that future historians are unlikely to refer to him as "great." His reputation for goodness is challenged only by a few known incidents such as his hesitation to dispense with the services of Sherman Adams after that gentleman's indiscretions with Mr. Goldfine. And that, after all, could be put down to loyalty to a faithful courtier and loyalty is a "good" quality, although to admit it here would be to admit it also for Harry Truman's more frequent loyalties to questionably deserving associates.

There are three flaws in Dwight Eisenhower's title to greatness which future historians are more likely to notice than do his contemporaries. One belongs to each of his three careers, as soldier, politician, and statesman. In each case the flaw can measure the difference between a distinguished career and a truly great career.

Eisenhower the Soldier led, or presided over, an enormous, complex and decisively successful military operation which began on the shores of North Africa and ended with the German surrender at Rheims. But there is a question whether he ranks with the great military commanders of history. The question arises out of the conviction of many who served in high rank under his command that he missed the one great opportunity to exercise the essential and decisive quality of command at the moment when the exercise of it could have shortened the war by six months and produced victory for the Western Allies well before the Russian armies had broken into central Europe.

After the successful Normandy landing and the spectacular sweep across France, Hitler's western armies were broken and scattered. Had the momentum of the Allied advance been maintained, Eisenhower's armies would certainly have swept across the Rhine and deep into Germany. There was no organized defense at the Siegfried Line or behind the Rhine ready to contest the Allied advance. It came to a halt in the mud of the Rhineland, and the Second World War dragged on into the following spring.

At the time of the halt Eisenhower possessed in Patton and Montgomery two of the great field commanders of all time. Each believed that he could maintain his advance across the Rhine and sweep on into Germany if given all available support. There wasn't enough fuel or ammunition reaching the front at that time to keep both going. Each wanted to keep on and each clamored for the supplies and the permission. They were passionately jealous and fiercely competitive rivals.

Eisenhower did not make a choice between Patton and Montgomery. He divided his supplies between them and ordered them to advance in step along a "broad front." The decision was presented at the time, and defended since, as the prudent course of action. It also avoided the prickly problem of making the choice between Patton and Montgomery. One was American and the other British. National pride would have been bitterly hurt had the one been favored over the other. Also, while both were magnificent battle leaders and fighters, they were also both prima donnas. It was probably politically impossible to hobble and starve the one and release the other. But it might conceivably have been possible to cajole or coerce the two into working as a team.

Montgomery was probably bluffing when he offered to serve, if necessary, under Patton. Yet it was a bluff which might have been called. There were other possible devices, such as the alternating command system which worked so successfully with Spruance and Halsey in the far Pacific. One can't help feeling that a Marlborough, a Wellington or a Napoleon would have found the solution to the problem. Dwight Eisenhower did not find it, and the Russians reached

Berlin, Prague and Vienna before the armies of the West. Much sorrow has flowed from that sequence.

Eisenhower the Politician led, or presided over, two enormously successful presidential election campaigns for the Republican Party. Events proved beyond doubt that there was never the slightest question about the outcome of the first campaign. There wasn't much serious question at the time. Yet, when his more timorous advisers urged him to avoid offending Senator Joseph McCarthy, Eisenhower put away a passage he had prepared for a speech in which he paid his respects to his former commanding officer, General Marshall.

George Marshall had for many years been Dwight Eisenhower's friend, patron and supporter. It was Marshall who picked Eisenhower for the North African campaign, who defended Eisenhower in Washington after the first failure at Kasserine Pass and during the tempest over the Darlan–de Gaulle affair, and who gave Eisenhower the Normandy invasion command. Eisenhower would probably have ended the war as an obscure division commander had it not been for George Marshall. There were other debts which are not yet on the public record.

McCarthy had attacked Marshall, brutally and wickedly. Eisenhower's impulse and intention was to speak in Marshall's defense. He owed Marshall far more than he owed any other living man. For the sake of an alleged few votes, he allowed himself to be persuaded to keep silent. So far as we know today, George Marshall never discussed the incident with anyone. He died, in silence. Eisenhower's debt to Marshall stands unpaid.

Eisenhower the Statesman led, or presided over, a phase of what appeared to be gradually improving relations between the United States and the Soviet Union. The trend of events through the meeting at Camp David seemed to be moving in a promising direction.

On the first of May in 1960, when Eisenhower's Presidency still had nine months to go, an American reconnaissance aircraft was brought down inside the Soviet Union. Eisenhower was scheduled to meet Nikita Khrushchev in Paris two weeks later. Eisenhower's record as a peacemaker and a statesman depended on the outcome of that meeting in Paris.

It is official Washington doctrine that Nikita Khrushchev intended to wreck the Summit before he reached it. What is not known is the date on which the decision was taken in Moscow to wreck the Summit. There is interesting and impressive evidence the decision was taken only at the last minute, and only after Mr. Eisenhower had personally and publicly claimed responsibility for the U-2 mission and publicly asserted that the flights would continue.

It is also contended that the Summit was a foregone failure and that the West ended up ahead of the game because it never took place.

This is possible. The fact is, however, that until the time of his assumption of personal responsibility for the U-2 flight Dwight Eisenhower was an influential force in world affairs. Whether he might have been able to use his influence for good during the remaining months of his term of office is problematical, but it was a respected influence. It disappeared from world affairs at the moment that he assumed personal responsibility.

That action ended Eisenhower's influence with his allies as suddenly as it did in Moscow. The allies were aghast—not of course at the reconnaissance flights, in which they had participated and which their governments entirely approved, but at the Eisenhower assumption of personal responsibility for them, which violated all standard procedure in such cases and which certainly provided Khrushchev with the perfect weapon for wrecking the Summit even if it did not necessarily cause the wrecking.

There are several explanations offered for the Eisenhower role in the U-2 affair. The most plausible, and the one backed by the most impressive evidence, is that Mr. Eisenhower's political advisers told him that it would be bad domestic politics for him to make the conventional disclaimer, that the Democrats would accuse him of being on the golf course when he should have been minding the store. The Democrats undoubtedly would have done so.

It probably was good domestic politics for the President to assert a personal knowledge of the specific flight, which apparently he did not have, and also to assert that the flights would be continued, which they were not. But was it good foreign policy to end abruptly and for all time Mr. Eisenhower's capacity to play a role in foreign affairs? The postscript on his personal influence as a statesman was written in Bonn six months later in the twilight of his Presidency when he sent his emissaries to the Germans asking for help to stanch the flow of gold from the American Treasury. For Dwight Eisenhower the Germans did not have a penny to spare.

The soldier did not harness Patton and Montgomery.

The politician did not defend his greatest benefactor.

The statesman did not survive the U-2 incident to play out his role to the end.

For other reasons he will long be remembered in the hearts of his people as Eisenhower the Good.

For these reasons it is unlikely that future historians will refer to him as Eisenhower the Great.

*February 13, 1961 [Richard Wright]*

# A WORD OF FAREWELL
by Irving Howe

When Wright's first novel, *Native Son*, appeared in the Thirties, it seemed important, both as an example of literary naturalism and an outcry of Negro protest. A few years later came *Black Boy*, the story of Wright's boyhood and youth in the deep South and perhaps his single best piece of work. Here, one felt, was the American Negro novelist who would speak without hesitation, who for the first time would tell the truth not only about the familiar sufferings of his people but about their buried responses, those inner feelings of anger and hatred which no white man could reach. And this, I think, Wright did succeed in doing. He told us the one thing even the most liberal and well-disposed whites preferred not to hear: that Negroes were far from patient or forgiving, that they were scarred by fear, that they hated every moment of their humiliation even when seeming most acquiescent, and that often enough they hated *us*, the decent and cultivated white men who, from complicity or neglect, shared in the responsibility for their plight. No Negro writer had ever quite said this before, certainly not with so much force or bluntness, and if such younger Negro novelists as James Baldwin and Ralph Ellison were to move beyond Wright's harsh naturalism and toward more subtle modes of fiction, that was possible only because Wright had been there first, courageous enough to release the full weight of his anger.

Before the implications of this fact, it seemed not very important that his image of Negro life in America was becoming historically dated (which is true) or that he occasionally succumbed to black nationalism (also true) or that he wrote badly (sometimes true). The bitterness and rage that poured out of Wright's books form one of the great American testaments, a crushing necessity to our moral life, forever to remind us that moderate analyses of injustice are finally lies.

And now, after fourteen years of voluntary exile in Paris, chosen, as he once told me, because he could no longer bear to live in the United States and see his children suffer the blows of race hatred, Richard Wright is dead. His life was incomplete, as it had to be, and at the end his work as tentative and fumbling as at the beginning. His later years were difficult, for he neither made a true home in Paris nor kept in imaginative touch with the changing life of the

United States. He was a writer in limbo, and his best fiction, such as the novelette *The Man Who Lived Underground,* is a projection of that condition. His work, so far as I can tell, is hardly read today by serious literary persons; his name barely known by the young.

*Eight Men,* Wright's most recent and apparently last book, is a collection of stories written over the last twenty-five years. Though they fail to yield any clear line of chronological development, these stories do give evidence of Wright's literary restlessness, his wish to keep learning and experimenting, his often clumsy efforts to break out of the naturalism which was his first and, I think, necessary mode of expression. The unevenness of his writing is extremely disturbing: one finds it hard to understand how the same man, from paragraph to paragraph, can be at once so brilliant and inept—though the student of American literature soon learns to measure the price which the talented autodidact pays for getting his education too late. Time after time the narrative texture of the stories is broken by a passage of jargon borrowed from sociology or psychology: perhaps the later Wright read too much, tried too hard, failed to remain sufficiently loyal to the limits of his talent.

The best stories are marked by a strong feeling for the compactness of the story as a form, so that even when the language is scraggly or leaden there is a sharply articulated pattern of event. Some of the stories, such as "Big Black Good Man," are enlivened by Wright's sardonic humor, the humor of a man who has known and released the full measure of his despair but finds that neither knowledge nor release matters in a world of despair. In *The Man Who Lived Underground* Wright shows a sense of narrative rhythm, a gift for shaping the links between sentences so as to create a chain of expectation, which is superior to anything in his full-length novels and evidence of the seriousness with which he kept working.

The main literary problem that troubled Wright in recent years was that of rendering his naturalism a more supple and terse instrument. I think he went astray whenever he abandoned naturalism entirely; there are a few embarrassingly bad experiments with stories written entirely in dialogue or self-consciously employing Freudian symbolism. Wright needed the accumulated material of circumstance which naturalistic detail provided his fiction; it was as essential to his ultimate effect of shock and bruise as dialogue to Hemingway's ultimate effect of irony and loss. But Wright was correct in thinking that the problem of detail is the most vexing technical problem the naturalist writer must face, since the accumulation of detail that makes for depth and solidity can also create a pall of tedium. In *The Man Who Lived Underground* Wright came close to solving this problem, for here the naturalistic detail is put at the service of a radical projective image—a Negro trapped in a sewer—and despite some flaws, the story is satisfying both for its tense surface and its elasticity of suggestion.

For some readers, the obsession with violence they detected in Wright's work was more disturbing than any of his technical faults. As Alfred Kazin has written, "If he chose to write the story of Bigger Thomas (in *Native Son*) as a grotesque crime story, it is because his own indignation and the sickness of the age combined to make him dependent on violence and shock, to astonish the reader by torrential scenes of cruelty, hunger, rape, murder, and flight. . . ." Apart from the fact that something very similar and quite as damning could be said about the author of *Crime and Punishment*, this judgment rests on the assumption that a critic can readily distinguish between the genuine need of a contemporary writer to cope with ugly realities and the damaging effects these realities may have upon him.

The reality pressing upon all of Wright's work is a nightmare of remembrance, and without the terror of that nightmare it would be impossible to render the truth of the reality—not the only, perhaps not even the deepest truth about American Negroes, but a primary and inescapable one. Both truth and terror depend upon a gross fact which Wright faced more courageously than any American writer: that for the Negro violence forms an inescapable part of his existence.

In a sense, then, Wright was justified in not paying attention to the changes that have been occurring in the South these past few decades. When Negro liberals write that despite the prevalence of bias there has been an improvement in the life of their people down South, such statements are reasonable and necessary. But what have they to do with the way Negroes feel, with the power of the memories they must surely retain? About this we know very little and would be well advised not to nourish preconceptions, for it may well be that their feelings are quite close to Wright's rasping outbursts. Wright *remembered*, and what he remembered other Negroes must also have remembered. Perhaps by now the terror and humiliation that fill his pages are things of the past, even in Mississippi; but men whose lives have been torn by suffering must live with their past, so that it too becomes part of the present reality. And by remembering, Wright kept faith with the experience of the boy who had fought his way out of the depths to speak for those who remained there.

The present moment is not a good one for attempting a judicious estimate of Wright's achievement as a novelist. It is hard to suppose that he will ever be regarded as a writer of the first rank, for his faults are grave and obvious. Together with Farrell and Dos Passos, he has suffered from the changes of literary taste which occurred during his lifetime: the naturalist novel is little read these days, though often mocked, and the very idea of a "protest novel" has become a target for graduate students to demolish. The dominant school of criticism has little interest in the kind of work Wright did, and it rejects him less from a particular examination than from a theoretic preconception—or, to be more precise, from an inability to realize that the kind of linguistic scrutiny to which it submits lyric poetry has only a limited value in the criticism of fiction.

Now, I would not pretend to be writing from any established superiority to current taste, for I too find the murk and awkwardness of most naturalist fiction hard to bear. But I believe that any view of twentieth-century American literature which surmounts critical sectarianism will have to give Wright an honored place, and that any estimate of his role in our cultural life will have to stress his importance as the pioneer Negro writer who in the fullness of his anger made it less possible for American society to continue deceiving itself.

Anger and violence may be present in his work, but the Richard Wright I knew, slightly in person and somewhat more through letters, was a singularly goodhearted and sweet man. When I met him in Paris a few years ago, he was open, vigorous and animated, full of shrewd, if not always just, estimates of the younger writers, actively concerned with the intellectual life of the African students who clustered about him, and, at a time when it was far from fashionable, still interested in the politics of the democratic Left.

Richard Wright died at fifty-two, full of hopes and projects. Like many of us, he had somewhat lost his intellectual way during recent years, but he kept struggling toward a comprehension of the strange and unexpected world coming into birth. In the most fundamental sense, however, he had done his work: he had told his contemporaries a truth so bitter that they paid him the tribute of striving to forget it.

*May 15, 1961 [Adolf Eichmann]*

# REFLECTIONS ON THE EICHMANN TRIAL

by Patrick O'Donovan

JERUSALEM—The first obsessive interest in the trial of Adolf Eichmann has died a natural death. This death has been hastened by satiety and by the fact that Eichmann is so illusive and so unsatisfying a protagonist, by the slow dignity of the court and its preoccupations with the law, by the fact that you can only sup on a limited amount of horror.

Like many others, I came to Israel doubtful of the morality of this trial. It seemed to be contrary to the spirit of the Rule of Law, to smack of hot vengeance rather than of impartial justice. This is perhaps an overly British reaction. But then, too, there was the widely accepted theory that this was a trial ordained by Ben-Gurion, born out of an illegal act and made to suit several political purposes. There could have been at least four of these. The desire to hold the trial could have been part of his messianic zeal to press the moral claims of Israel upon the Diaspora. Dr. Gideon Hausner, the Israeli Attorney General, made just such a point when he said that wherever Jews are hurt, the hurt was felt first and hardest in Israel.

The trial could have been held to refresh the memories of his own people. Old men forget, but young men cannot be bothered to learn. Israel has a young population, and almost half of it now consists of Asian and African Jews. None of these have experienced the suffering of their Continental brethren that made the creation of Israel, to Ben-Gurion and his like, an immediate and imperative necessity.

Then, again, the trial would serve to remind the United States and the United Kingdom of their duties toward Israel. Several times already, though so far only in passing, the idea has been put forward that a vast amount of the tragedy of the Final Solution to the Jewish Problem could have been avoided if these nations had helped in the extraction and acceptance of threatened Jews. Roosevelt shilly-shallied. Britain presented a blank and bureaucratic No. Permits for émigrés were few. Émigré ships trailed hopelessly across the seas looking for a place that would take them in. There is a lot more of this still to come, and much of it will probably be brought out by the defense. It is just possible that this is the reason that Britain and America, alone of the responsible powers, have sent no official observers to this trial. The trial, therefore, may serve to avoid a second betrayal. (It must be remembered that Israel is a country that lives under the perpetual threat of war.)

The trial could also serve to confute the right-wing Herut Party, which is rabidly anti-German and has accused Ben-Gurion of selling out to the enemy, even in accepting German reparations. No one can call this trial pro-German; it is certainly not an act of international tact. It was conceived, and in advance defended here, in terms of reasons that were essentially Israeli.

These arguments, widely credited to Ben-Gurion outside Israel, do not appear a proper basis for any trial in Western law. For a people's court, yes; for human vengeance, yes; for justice under the law, no.

But in Jerusalem these doubts have melted. If anyone had these intentions, they are quite incidental. The trial itself has no political airs. Justice is being done and is seen to be done. Among the Israelis there is no doubt of their right to try this man, and all the observers that I have met agree in this. . . .

All this time, every day and at every session, there sat that lay figure, Eichmann, all but expressionless, straight-backed, never scratching himself. Almost every journalist worth his old carbon paper has had a shot at describing him. There was a Frenchman—and the French press is used to headier if less decorous state trials—who wrote that he could see a gas chamber in each of his eyes. Most took the easy way out, which was to describe him as some version of a mean bureaucrat or as a little clerk of a man. Most, again, have included some allusion to a trade in describing him—milkman, footman, dentist, customs inspector, tout or a small-town collector of taxes—which was rough on honorable trades, but it is possible to see for what the baffled press was groping.

Now, after weeks of being watched and of regaining at least a sort of public importance, Eichmann is changing. There is certainly no sign of the quiet factory hand from the Argentine. He looks more and more like what he was—a Nazi of insufferable and unjustified vanity, a man of great vulgarity of intellect, a man of cold mind who is totally insensitive to his fellow men. He seems a person who is at once despicable and frightening, and from his "confession" it is clear that there is more than a trace of cowardice in him. It is not in Jerusalem, even now, possible to think of him as a lonely underdog. He repels pity as a lonely underdog. He repels pity as a duck's back repels water.

The evidence for the prosecution is being called. It is a combination of documents and of witnesses. Few if any of the documents are new, and the witnesses told the sort of stories that anyone who is over thirty knows only too well. The stories are appalling. Jewish spectators press their hands to their faces to keep themselves from crying out loud. Witnesses struggle for self-control. Witnesses ramble and digress, because they want to tell it all. And only occasionally do their stories directly touch Eichmann. At times he seems almost to retire as the accused. He leaves this crucifying trial and sits in his glass box, scribbling notes, arranging files, checking documents. The prosecution has proved, and indeed to a reasonable man has proved, by documents in fact, that Eichmann was in at the start—in September 1939 —when the Plans for Polish Jewry were laid. They are proving that he even disobeyed Himmler's later orders to lay off. They are proving that he was a frequent, if fastidious, spectator of the concentration camp operations. And—God save us all—they have a witness to testify that he killed a Jewish boy himself, with his own hands, by beating, whom he caught stealing a peach in his Budapest garden.

There is a secondary purpose in the careful documentation of the conspiracy against the Jews. For the Israelis, the Nuremberg Trials

were not quite enough. The fate of the Jews was only an item—
though an essential one—in the indictment and condemnation. Here
the prosecution is concentrating on the fate of their brethren, and
in doing so they are rewriting as well as recalling the vast fate of the
European Jews.

If in this trial Dr. Hausner is the accusing voice of the Jews—
disciplined, calm, and inexorable—this is still not a vengeance trial.
Only once so far has there been a call for the bloody man's blood from
the gallery and that was and would be definitely forgivable—even
in the Old Bailey. The spectators are quiet in their tears. The three
judges are still the quiet voices of Western justice. The presiding
judge checks extravagance or excess in the witnesses or prosecuting
counsels and he goes out of his way to help the aging defense counsel,
Dr. Servatius from Germany. Despite the vast press apparatus attached
to the court, this is still a court of traditional and—dare I say it—
Christian justice. The court is a new sort of Israeli triumph and it compels a new sort of respect.

Any trial that may end in the death of a man or in his punishment
now perturbs a conscious Christian, a civilized and a liberal man. I
felt more perturbed at the trial of the five spies in the Old Bailey
(No. 1 Court) in the city of London than I do now in this District
Court of Jerusalem. And I do not believe that Adolf Eichmann could
have got a fairer trial anywhere in the world today.

*July 10, 1961 [Henry Miller]*

# AN OLD SHOCKER COMES HOME
by Stanley Kauffmann

Henry Miller's *Tropic of Cancer* is now published in this country
in an unlavish edition of 318 pages set in big type, at a price of $7.50—
and this in spite of a large first printing. The interest of the price
is that here it relates to the content of the book—not, as is usual, to
its length or format. The publisher knows that the public knows the
book's reputation and is willing to pay much more than is currently
charged for books of similar production cost. This gives, from the
start, a different atmosphere to its publication. Rather than call it

cashing in on prurience, let us say that the publisher is asking the purchaser to make a contribution to a defense fund in case of legal prosecution, although no provision is made for refunding, say, three dollars per copy if the publisher is unmolested.

The book itself, first issued in 1934 in Paris (in English), is an autobiographical first novel recounting the experiences, sensations, thoughts of Miller, a penniless American in the Paris of the early Thirties. It is not so much a novel as an intense journal, written daily about what was happening to him daily, full of emotion recollected in proximity, as he scrounged for food, devoured books, conversed volubly, and flung himself into numerous beds. It is formless, in the sense that it could have continued indefinitely, but then Miller is an enemy of form. He writes of a Ravel composition:

> Suddenly it all died down. It was as if [Ravel] rememebered, in the midst of his antics, that he had on a cutaway suit. He arrested himself. A great mistake, in my humble opinion. Art consists in going the full length. If you start with the drums you have to end with the dynamite, or TNT. Ravel sacrificed something for form, for a vegetable that people must digest before going to bed.

The "full length" is Miller's ideal. Frankness of fact and devotion to truth are not always concurrent, but Miller has, within his powers, both of these. He says on an early page: "There is only one thing which interests me vitally now, and that is the recording of all that which is omitted in books."

He had been a husband and a hireling in various jobs in New York and elsewhere, always a hungry reader with literary ambitions, when at thirty-nine he broke loose and, without money, went.alone to Paris to write. He swore he would never take a job again. In fact, he takes two in this book—as a proofreader on the Paris *Tribune* and as an English teacher in Dijon. But the point was made—he had broken away.

Essentially that is what the book is: a mirror-image of the testimony which is given at revival meetings. There you can hear about men who got right with God; this man got right with art and sex and the use of his brain and time. Like all converts, he is on fire. Like all converts, he simply will not leave your lapels alone. Thus he is a bit tedious. Because he came fairly late in life to a personally valid ethic, he cannot believe that anyone he talks to has ever done it before him.

The book is a fierce celebration of his enlightened freedom, which is to say his acceptance of real responsibilities instead of merely respectable ones. But in the course of this paean he exhorts us mercilessly with such discoveries as: sex can be fun; America is commercialized and doomed; civilization must refurbish its values or perish.

(Edmund Wilson has called the book "an epitaph for the whole generation that migrated to Europe after the war.") All this now suffers, of course, from the passage of time. These burning messages have been the commonplaces of novelists, most of them inferior to Miller, for at least a couple of decades. But could these views have been startling even in 1934? This was eight years after the publication of a much more widely read novel of Americans in Paris, *The Sun Also Rises*. Hemingway is as unlike Miller as is imaginable in temperament, but surely the new liberty and the dark apocalypse are in his book.

How Miller rages at us. And what is his chief complaint? That we are not like him, living like him, desiring and perceiving like him. A prime function of art is criticism, and if the artist in question has merit, he certainly is a superior person, and modest coughs are out of order. But the smuggest bourgeois has no smugness like that of the self-consciously liberated bohemian. It tainted Gauguin and D. H. Lawrence; it infects Miller.

He is often compared to Whitman, which must please him, because he thinks Whitman "that one lone figure which America has produced in the course of her brief life" (despite the fact that he began by worshiping Dreiser). There is considerable basis for the comparison, especially in attitude. Miller sees no democratic vistas and certainly does *not* hear America singing, but he too is a buddy of the universe and privy to its secrets, calling on the rest of us to be as open-shirted and breeze-breasting as himself. Also there is in Miller, although on a much lower level than in Whitman, a feeling of settled iconoclasm, of artistic revolt made stock in trade. There are attempts at bardic sweep, some of them successful, and there is Whitmanesque rejoicing in the smack of wine and flesh.

Sometimes Miller uses language stupidly (he calls Paris "more eternal" than Rome). Sometimes, as in the rhapsody on Matisse, he writes a symbolist poem with a heat that carries us across its weaker passages. Or he can transmute sensation into images that propagate like guppies. For example, one day, broke and hungry, he finds a concert ticket and uses it.

> My mind is curiously alert; it's as though my skull had a thousand mirrors inside it. My nerves are taut, vibrant! the notes are like glass balls dancing on a million jets of water. I've never been to a concert before on such an empty belly. Nothing escapes me, not even the tiniest pin falling. It's as though I had no clothes on and every pore of my body was a window and all the windows open and the light flooding my gizzards. I can feel the light curving under the vault of my ribs and my ribs hang there over a hollow nave trembling with reverberations. How long this lasts I have no idea; I have lost all sense of time and place. After what seems like an eternity there follows an interval of semiconsciousness balanced by such a calm that I feel a great lake

inside me, a lake of iridescent sheen, cool as jelly; and over this lake, rising in great swooping spirals, there emerge flocks of birds of passage with long slim legs and brilliant plumage. Flock after flock surge up from the cool, still surface of the lake and, passing under my clavicles, lose themselves in the white sea of space. And then slowly, very slowly, as if an old woman in a white cap were going the rounds of my body, slowly the windows are closed and my organs drop back into place.

I have quoted this at length because it is a good cross section of his style. "The tiniest pin" and "after what seems an eternity" are careless spewing; but the "old woman in a white cap" is orphic.

This is Miller. Narrative is not his forte; his characterizations are sketchy; his philosophy is jejune. It is in pressing his whole existence against the warm wax of his prose and leaving there its complete imprint that he is at his best—in following every quiver of sentience to its source or destination with phrases that sometimes add up to a gorgeous fabric. Karl Shapiro, in an introductory essay streaked with gibberish, says that "everything [Miller] has written is a poem in the best as well as in the broadest sense of the word." This is a sentimental and foolishly inclusive judgment, but it points in the right direction.

Shapiro says that Miller writes with "complete ease and naturalness" about sex, as Lawrence and Joyce did not. To me, there is (speaking only of this book) much less sex than bravado. As far as specific language is concerned, Lawrence thought there was something thaumaturgic in four-letter words and had Mellors speak them therapeutically. Joyce wrote down the words that his miraculous surgery of the psyche revealed. Miller employs them—mostly *outside* of dialogue—to demonstrate somewhat ostentatious emancipation and contempt for slaves of convention.

Anyway, to talk about complete naturalness in the use of those words by a member of our society is arrant nonsense. The only person who could use them completely naturally would be a mental defective unaware of taboos. The foulest-mouthed longshoreman knows that he is using naughty words and is wallowing in them. Miller uses them in an exultation very much like that of a college boy away from home for the first time.

Proof of his lack of naturalness about it lies in his avoidance of earthy language when he talks about his great love, Mona. Virtually every other girl in the book, well or lightly regarded, is referred to at some time or other as a c--t. Making Mona an exception seems to show not only some residual puritanism but exhibitionism in the other cases. In fact, before one is far along in the book, the plentiful four-letter words become either irritating or tiresome. I thought of Robert Graves' remark that in the British Army the adjective "f---ing" has come to mean only a signal that a noun is approaching.

Lawrence Durrell, no more reluctant than numerous other foreigners to tell Americans what their best works are, says that "American literature today begins and ends with the meaning of what [Miller] has done." Further: "To read *Tropic of Cancer* is to understand how shockingly romantic all European writing after Rousseau has become." (Durrell, of all artists, must know that "romantic" is a qualitative, not a pejorative, term.) These statements are typical of the—to me— inflated praise that this book has evoked. I hazard a couple of guesses at extrinsic reasons for this. First, when a gifted man writes a prosecutable book, it is often overlauded as a tactical move by those interested in the freedom of letters—especially those who hold that sex is Beautiful, not sexy. Second, possibly these statements are, as much as anything else, a tribute to Miller's purity of commitment, to his abhorrence of the pietisms of Literature and the proprieties of the Literary Life, to his willingness—if not downright eagerness—to suffer for the right to live and write as he chooses. His is no small spirit; it is just not as large as some have told us.

Here, then, is his first novel, available (*pro tem*, at least) in his own country twenty-seven years after its publication abroad. Durrell believes that this place is next to *Moby Dick*, which seems to me a hurtful thing to say about a frisky minnow of a book that ought not to be compared with leviathans. Far from being "the jewel and nonpareil" of American literature (Durrell again), Miller cannot be put near such twentieth-century novelists as Dreiser, Fitzgerald, early Dos Passos, early Hemingway—let alone Faulkner—without unfair diminution.

This book belongs, modestly but securely, in the American tradition of profundity-through-deliberate-simplicities that has its intellectual roots in Thoreau and continues through such men as Whitman and Sherwood Anderson until, in a changed time, it thinks it needs to go abroad to breathe. Miller stands under his Paris street lamp, defiantly but genially drunk, trolling his catch mixed of beauty and banality and recurrent bawdry—a little pathetic because he thinks he is a discoverer and doesn't realize that he is only a tourist on a well-marked tour. We see him at last as an appealingly zestful, voracious, talented hick.

*August 7, 1961*

# THE WORLD OF GEORGE KENNAN
by Louis J. Halle

For most of two years after Stalin's death, the State Department experts were taking the line that no real change had ensued; Russia under Stalin's successors, they said, was essentially what it had been under Stalin, its drive and direction unaltered. Consequently, when the fact of change became unmistakable, a shifting of kremlinological personnel had to take place.

Before October 1956, the experts maintained that Moscow was able, without any extraordinary difficulty, to keep the satellite populations under absolute control—so much so that, even in case it invaded Western Europe, it would not have to worry about its lines of communication across the satellite territories. Since the Polish and Hungarian uprisings, no one maintains any more that this is true.

From the outset, the experts committed thmselves to the view that no dissension within the Communist ranks was possible. Even the break between Russia and Yugoslavia seemed not to affect their thinking. They went right on to insist that no real difference of opinion between the Soviet Union and Red China (which, one recalls, was regarded as just another satellite) could be expected. They committed themselves so firmly to this that, when the inevitable dissension began to come into the open, their embarrassment was conspicuous. Forced by the fact to retreat from their extreme position, they have today taken their stand on the dogma that the present dissension is in the nature of a family quarrel only, that it cannot lead to any real break, because the factors that unite the two Communist powers outweigh the issues that divide them by such large margin.

In pointing out the limitations of the inside experts, I would not have it thought that we could do without them. They represent an element of discipline to wishful thinking and a necessary check on the unorthodox; and they are quite indispensable for producing technical and topical estimates, whether of Soviet military doctrine, of Soviet economic policies, or of personnel shifts inside the Soviet bureaucracy. It is only the large final judgments for which they tend to be disqualified. What is needed for such judgments is a sense of how history moves, an understanding of the constant elements in human society, and a perspective that shows every particular thing in its relation to the whole. No specialist, in his capacity as such, has these qualifications.

All this is by way of introduction to the phenomenon that is George Kennan. Kennan represents the distinction of an individual mind that thinks for itself, that goes its own way. Consequently, the "unsoundness" of George Kennan has for years been a staple of conversation in the academic departments of Russian studies. No doubt he has sometimes been wrong, and when wrong he has suffered from the vulnerability of one who is wrong alone, as opposed to the invulnerability of those who are wrong all together. I am impressed, however, by the fact that, standing independent of intellectual fashion and orthodoxy, he has tended to be right in what counts. He has not been like the expert of the definition, who avoids all small errors as he makes his way on to the one grand fallacy.

Reading Mr. Kennan's latest book [*Russia and the West under Lenin and Stalin*], which has been largely put together from lectures given at Oxford and Harvard, I was struck by the degree to which his personal vision of the world is integrated and whole. A complete study of that vision, of the world of George Kennan, would require a monograph, but some of its elements may be identified here.

The world of that vision is, in the first place, a world of good and evil. The good is represented by a conventional propriety that applies to the conduct of personal relations and relations among sovereign states alike. Superficially, this may appear simply as a matter of good manners, but in its hidden roots it is civilization itself, with all its ideals and (to use a key word in the Kennanite vocabulary) its hopefulness. The failure of the Russian governments, after 1917, to accept this conventional propriety as a basis for their relations with the rest of the world has been a profound evil. It represents an abnormality, and nothing hopeful in a lasting sense will come about except as the development of civilization in Russia makes for a return to the civilized norm in the conduct of international relations. This gives to all of Kennan's views a basis of conviction. Part of the reason why he writes so movingly is that, in a deep and quiet way, he believes so strongly in the legitimacy of our challenged civilization.

Again, while he does not tell us this in so many words, he obviously does not share the delusions of the unsophisticated about the role and significance of ideology in human affairs. In his vision, those who constitute the government in Moscow are people first and Communists second. It never occurs to him, therefore, to explain the behavior of the Chicherins and Litvinovs, the Stalins and Khrushchevs, simply by the maxims of Marx or the sayings of Lenin. These persons represent live, unreconstructed humanity rather than some theoretical abstraction called Marxian Man. In this vision, Stalin appears as a good deal closer to Ivan the Terrible than to any doctrinaire concept of what the representative of the workers of the world should be. Gibbon explains him better than Marx.

Inevitably, the view of Stalin as an evil tyrant rather than as Marxian Man leads to an interpretation of the events of his reign that is different from the conventional interpretation. Take, for example, the following passage:

> From the bourgeois world, as from his political entourage in the world of Communism, Stalin wanted only one thing: weakness. This was not at all identical with revolution. Unless other states were very small, and contiguous to Russia's borders, so that there were good prospects for controlling them by the same concealed police methods he employed in Russia, Stalin did not want other states to be Communist.

Or again:

> . . . universal world dominion is a technical impossibility, and . . . the effectiveness of the power radiated from any one national center decreases in proportion to the distance involved, and to the degree of cultural disparity. It was this reality that Stalin, in a very incipient way, was up against in his encounter with Chinese Communism and the Kuomintang in 1927.

One of the elements in Kennan's realism, as it seems to me, is that "Stalinism" appears in some senses to be a more significant term to him than "Communism." "Communism," after all, may be so many different things that one can hardly generalize usefully about it, but "Stalinism" is tied to the personality and the policy of one man who, in the Kennanite world, represented the quintessence of human evil. When Stalin at last died, therefore, Kennan saw possibilities for hope that did not appear to those who thought of Russia as being under the government, not of mortal men, but of a body of immutable ideological doctrine. (One is tempted to recall a remark of Jimmy Walker when a censorship bill was up for consideration in the New York Legislature. He said he had heard of girls being "ruined," but never by a book.)

This is not to say that ideology has no significant place in the world of George Kennan. He sees the implacable hostility of successive Soviet governments to the bourgeois world as one consequence of an ideological training that emphasizes hatred and distrust, and that closes the channels of fruitful communication. Here, however, as in other instances, the role of ideology, though great, is something quite different from its pretensions. Marxist doctrine has powerfully influenced the men who have governed in Moscow, but not in the way the Marxist fathers intended.

Finally, Kennan appears to see what few who have not profited from long experience inside government can see as vividly, that governments do not always know what they are doing. Simple people without experience are prone to believe that the men in Washington act with deliberation on the basis of an insight denied to the rest of us; and people have always tended to assume that, however feckless they might themselves be, their enemies plotted every move with a fiendish and elaborate purposefulness that was more than human. We were familiar, in Stalin's day, with the view that his every move represented the farsightedness of the master chess player, and we still have those among us who believe that Khrushchev never sneezes except in accordance with a Master Plan left by Lenin. In the world of George Kennan, however, the record is largely one of blindness and blundering on both sides, in the West and in Moscow alike.

This is the basis for the sense of tragedy that pervades Kennan's historical writing. It is, perhaps, not quite grand tragedy in the Greek or Shakespearean senses, since one finds a sort of desperate insistence that the blindness and blundering are not necessary, hence not inevitable. What is tragic is that the world is repeatedly condemned to horror quite unnecessarily. If the statesmen had been up to what we have a right to expect of them, neither of the two world wars would have occurred, the revolutionary extremist would not have triumphed over the revolutionary moderates in post-Tsarist Russia, and the Weimar Republic would not have succumbed to Hitler. In fact, one repeatedly sees these great issues as turning on a hair. Thus, if the German people in 1933 had had only a little more patience with the Brüning government, which was on the verge of solving the economic crisis when it was dismissed, the Nazis might never have come to power. "The fault, dear Brutus, is not in our stars, but in ourselves. . . ." Thucydides had much the same view.

When it comes to the account of the military interventions in Russia by the Western allies, from 1918 to 1920, Kennan is virtually compelled to adopt the pen of a Voltaire to do justice to the element of comedy in the tragedy. At the great crisis in Russian affairs of March 1918, when the Congress of Soviets was about to ratify the Brest-Litovsk Treaty, our American military attaché in Russia, who occupied the post in consequence of having had his name confused with another's by the War Department, put an important telegram to Washington into his pocket and forgot to send it. The American and British interventions took place without any purpose related to the actualities of the situation. They took place against the wills of Woodrow Wilson and Lloyd George, who were simply too busy with other matters to address themselves effectively to Russian policy. But these interventions were so decisive in their effect, says Kennan, "that I think it may well be questioned whether Bolshevism would ever have prevailed throughout Russia had the Western governments not aided its progress to power by this ill-conceived interference." (These words were written before they could have any application to our Cuban intervention of April 1961.)

This kind of tragic nonsense, Kennan seems to be telling us, is quite unnecessary, and we ought to stop it this minute. There is no reason why we can't begin to behave sensibly at last, and all hope depends on this.

I can best sum up the world of George Kennan by noting that, unlike the world of so many technical specialists, it is a world of humanity—more specifically, a world of human beings who seem constantly to be under their own curse. It is this, rather than a world of statistics, abstract principles, and dogmas. And because it is this, Kennan views it all with a deep compassion. There are no absolute and final differences between Russian humanity and, let us say, American humanity. "One can remember," he writes in one of his memorable perorations, "that *some degree of conflict* and antagonism is present in every international relationship; *some* measure of compromise is necessary everywhere, if political societies are to live together on the same planet. Those who bear this in mind will be inclined to doubt whether there is such a thing as total antagonism, any more than there is such a thing as total identity of interests. Whoever sees it this way will realize that the illusion of total antagonism can be created only by a complete absence of effective communication; and for this reason he will be inclined to doubt, as I myself must confess to doing, whether an enemy with whom one can communicate is really entirely an enemy, after all."

*September 11, 1961*

# LEARNED HAND

## by Francis Biddle

Learned Hand was endowed with so many talents of heart and mind that it is difficult to choose those which were most characteristically his. First of all, it must be said that he was thoroughly normal in his gusto for living, excellently balanced. As a skeptic he discarded the comforting magic of absolutes and stood alone facing the adventure of life, while he felt its mysticism and asserted its values. Like Justice Oliver Wendell Holmes, whom he greatly admired, he was never cynical, because life without values seemed to him intolerable. He did not believe that his values were eternal, but they were his—courage, a sense of humor that kept things relative, the spirit of liberty which "is not sure that it is right" and seeks to understand the lives of others. Above all he was tolerant. Yet his tolerance never touched indifference, and he was passionate in his beliefs as well as his feelings. I shall never forget what he said at a meeting of the Law Institute in Washington, in May 1941, putting aside his prepared address, trying to make us realize what the fall of France meant to civilization, with an eloquence that made us ashamed that we had not felt as deeply about it as he felt.

To Learned Hand his friends were dear, and they felt his love. He was gay, and could be very funny. He was more companionable, more sharing than anyone I knew.

That Hand was imbued with a European culture made him no less of an American, even if it left him with a relish for irony. He was democratic to the core, yet was not betrayed into the clichés and moralistic preaching which to Europeans so often speak of the American mind. He hated cant. He spent his long and outstanding career as a judge trying to find where truth lay, not in any field of the abstract, but in dealing with the concrete issues of American life. If the virtues which he held worthy were those of his own generation, his conviction that life was change and growth enabled him to meet the problems of law—which are but reflections of life—with an open mind and consistent objectiveness. That under the Constitution federal courts were given the undemocratic power to overrule acts of the legislature made him cautious to exercise it. He insisted, as did Justice Holmes, whose philosophy of law he accepted, that personal convictions of judges should not be permitted to intrude into the decision of conflicting public policies. That his own were not eternal—however valiantly he fought to sustain them—made such a tolerant approach inevitable. He felt, as a consequence, that it was as improper for "liberal" judges to impose their views in reaching decisions as it had been for their conservative predecessors. A judge, he insisted, should act like a judge, not like a reformer.

*November 27, 1961*

# BEN SHAHN ON FALLOUT
by Frank Getlein

Of all the ingenious verbalizings put out to explain *Schmeerkunst*, the one I like best is the one that links it to the world situation from about 1945 to the present, as if it were compounded of the remembrance of Hiroshima, the anticipation of Armageddon, and the resulting intuition that life is not worth living. While you and I, slaves of a pettifogging logic, might follow such an intuition with a leap from the Top of the Sixes to the doorstep of the Museum of Modern Art, the *Schmeerkunstler*, unburdened by logic, takes a more pedestrian path to the same destination, sets up as an official Young American, and does a brisk business in Despair and in Paintings Proving that Painting is Past.

Well, it's a living and who are we to cavil at the way any man elects to earn his bread?

The only problem with the ploy is that sooner or later some real painter was bound to come along and demonstrate that those aspects of the recent past and threatened future which allegedly impose a kind of gibbering can also be the material for intelligible passion. Really, this should surprise no one. For centuries, after all, painters regarded the inevitability of the end of the world and the last judgment in somewhat the same horror-stricken way many now regard the possibility of the nuclear Big Casino. Yet hundreds of them managed to paint that nightmare, not at all as a bogey to frighten children, but as a dread certainty toward which mankind moved as steadily as the shadow of night moving across the earth. The artistic act of the human spirit in steadfastly contemplating that ultimate disaster and making the contemplation visible for others was in a sense the human mastery of the disaster. This is one of the functions of all the arts. There is no theoretical reason why the process shouldn't be applied to our present situation, and now it has been.

There is an added irony to the triumph of artistic intelligence over the fell clutch of nuclear circumstance, because the artist is Ben Shahn, an American painter who, in the view of the *Schmeerkunstlers*, was supposed to have dropped dead years ago, condemned as being interested in social justice, something no true artist should be allowed to bother his Young American head about.

Shahn's achievement is a series of ten paintings and fifteen drawings exhibited this fall at the Downtown Gallery under the title of "The

Saga of the Lucky Dragon." Far from shunning the "literary," Shahn employs actual letters to spell out his theme. The first, and the largest, of the paintings, a full seven feet high, is a stark portrait of a Japanese man sitting on a hospital bed with a placard: "I am a fisherman, Aikichi Kuboyana by name. On the first of March, 1954, our fishing boat, the Lucky Dragon, wandered under an atomic cloud 80 miles from Bikini. I and my friends were burned. We did not know what happened to us. On September 23rd of that year I died of atomic burn."

Thus the theme is bluntly stated. It is developed through the series in terms of pure paint and pure image, but in that first painting, the letters themselves are far from being an extraneous "literary" element. Although in English, they are based on earlier uses by Shahn of letters from the Hebrew alphabet. Taken together here, they are black tongues of fire, a leaping, living illumination of the passive fisherman awaiting his death.

The same qualities appear in the chief visual symbol devised by the artist, a figure, strongly linear, of a firedragon, combining the name of the unhappy ship, the spread of fear and fallout, and a beast of Shahn's dating back at least thirteen years and referred to throughout his brilliant Harvard lectures, "The Shape of Content."

The firedragon appears and reappears, changing his size and shape like a malignant amoeba. Japanese parents and children are somberly posed with the firedragon hovering on the horizon. "The Physicist" appears against a vividly colored checkerboard background suggesting a table of the elements. Masked, he holds up an X-ray plate and on it is the image of the firedragon. In one great drawing, the beast squirms inside a man's head. Elsewhere it contrasts with the similar movement of a flight of white birds gazed at by children. Finally, in a spreading horizontal painting, "We Did Not Know What Happened to Us," the firedragon is everywhere. The large painting is black, and in the blackness are seen the faces and clutching hands of men sinking beneath the waves. The waves themselves are delineated by the lines of the dragon, drawn in many colors against the black, spreading out to fill the world. It is as if the lights of the stars, reflected in the waters, have become the firedragon of our dreams.

Done mostly in tempera or gouache, the painting itself has a dry, scraped quality, familiar in much of Shahn's past work, but now ominously recalling a future memory of our own skin and the skin of the world at some possible point in our universal voyage of the Lucky Dragon.

*April 9, 1962*

# ROBERT FROST AT EIGHTY-EIGHT
by Adlai E. Stevenson

The alliance of poetry and politics is very old. Poets from Vergil and Dante to Frost himself have paid tributes to statesmen in their own stock and trade: verse. But what is to be done when the roles are reversed? What can I, a dealer in international politics, do for our renowned poet? What is *my* stock in trade? Perhaps I can make him a present of a problem—such as the cold war; or disarmament; or the rule of law. And I have many more. . . .

But I can tell you, in part at least, what the public servant has to give to the poet—it is the defense of the society in which the man like Robert Frost will still have, in his own words, "the freedom of my material, the condition of body and mind now and then to summon aptly from the vast chaos of all I have lived through." That is all a poet needs from society; the rest, the power to reveal truth and clarify paradox, he has inside himself.

In Robert Frost, the American people have found their poet, their singer, their seer—in short, their bard. Fortunately, Mr. Frost concurs with at least part of our judgment. In a quatrain, clearly aimed at lawyers and politics [sic] such as I have been, he says:

> So if you find you must repent
> From side to side in argument,
> At least don't use your mind too hard,
> But trust my instinct—I'm a bard.

He once defined a poem as he would define love. "It begins," he says, "in delight and ends in wisdom." I am grateful to him for describing with such precision the reason why, for me, his poetry lives and speaks. You hardly need to read two pages before you encounter the first of these delights—the sudden brilliant image of mankind's "outer weather"—that natural environment of tree and bird and stone which his words make more vivid than even our senses can—"the whirr of sober birds," the "whelming east wind . . . like the sea's return"— we smell, we taste, our eyes are freshened and renewed, we see better because the poet has seen for us.

And he is the poet of our "inner weather" too. No living poet describes more dispassionately and compassionately the sea changes of the human heart—or has more sly humor to debunk the pretensions and pomposities we mistake for living. Sometimes it is a casual aside:

A small bird flew before me . . .
He thought I was after him for a feather—
The white one in his tail; like one who takes
Everything said as personal to himself.

Sometimes the light tone and the punch line cover a sad and serious thought:

I turned to speak to God
About the world's despair.
But to make matters worse,
I found God wasn't there.

God turned to speak to me
(Don't anybody laugh)
God found I wasn't there—
At least not over half.

But humor—and beauty—do not alone make a bard. He begins in delight. He ends in wisdom. A lot of things, it seems, pass for wisdom these days—flagwaving, superpatriotism, frenetic business confidence of the don't-sell-the-country-short variety, conformity, anticonformity, the power of positive thinking. We'll find nothing like that in Robert Frost. His wisdom does not shirk the risk of suffering and injustice and disaster. It measures it. Indeed, not many poets have expressed anguish more directly:

A voice said, Look me in the stars
And tell me truly, men of earth,
If all the soul-and-body scars
Were not too much to pay for birth.

It is just because there is no naïve optimism, and the abyss is recognized for what it is—the possibility of ultimate despair—that Robert Frost's constant extolling of a quiet, unsensational, dogging courage is more than a conventional theme. It is an inspiration and a force.

I, for one, do not believe that these are days of halcyon weather for America or for the world. We need poets who help us to gird ourselves for endurance, and who walk with us on dark roads where the end is not in sight. And if you asked me to name one poem which enshrines for me the spirit in which as a nation we should confront our troubled future, I would quote you the last of these familiar lines:

The woods are lovely, dark and deep,
But I have promises to keep
And miles to go before I sleep,
And miles to go before I sleep.

*August 13, 1962 [James Agee]*

# NO USE TALKING
by John Updike

"Of my own writing have been as usual trying this and that and the other thing, finishing little or nothing. Most of it has hung somewhere between satire and what I suppose would be called 'moralistic' writing: I wish I could get both washed out of my system and get anywhere near what the real job of art is: attempt to state things as they seem to be, minus personal opinion of any sort. No use talking: for various reasons of weakness & lack of time I continually fall far short of, i.e. betray, things I know better than to betray."

Had James Agee been more productive of the poetic fiction he seemed destined to write, this book of letters—written over a period of thirty years to his boyhood teacher and lifelong friend the Episcopalian priest James Harold Flye—presumably would not have been published. Both the flap copy and Robert Phelps's introduction invite us to lament over Agee's aborted and tormented career. Phelps quotes an especially precocious early letter, written from Harvard, and asks, "How then did Agee do with his gifts what he did do? Why did he not write a dozen Chekhov-Shakespeare novels [the letter describes such an ambition] instead of a quarter of a million unsigned words for *Time* and *Fortune*?"

Why indeed? It is a good question; yet to ask it, in the form of a five-dollar book, is to reduce Agee to a question mark. A subtle insult hides in this homage. Phelps explains, "In Europe, works are all that are required of [authors], and they are honored accordingly. Here they must also use their bodies and personal histories and failures (above all, their failures) to make us *emblems*," and goes on to install Agee in the American pantheon "with these letters as his testament, and the image of his scattered vocation as his didactic emblem."

Rather unwittingly, these sentences take the pulse of a very sick literary situation. A fever of self-importance is upon American writing. Popular expectations of what literature should provide have risen so high that failure is the only possible success, and pained incapacity the only acceptable proof of sincerity. When ever in prose has slovenliness been so esteemed, ineptitude so cherished? In the present apocalyptic atmosphere, the loudest sinner is most likely to be saved; Fitzgerald's crack-up is his ticket to Heaven, Salinger's silence his claim on our devotion. The study of literature threatens to become a kind of paleontology of failure, and criticism a supercilious psychoanalysis of authors. I resist Agee's canonization by these unearthly standards. Authors *should* be honored only for their works. If Agee is to be remembered, it should be for his few, uneven, hard-won successes. The author of the best pages of *Let Us Now Praise Famous Men* and *A Death in the Family* owes no apology to posterity. As to "the quarter of a million unsigned words," surely a culture is enhanced, rather than disgraced, when men of talent and passion undertake anonymous and secondary tasks. Excellence in the great things is built upon excellence in the small; Agee's undoing was not his professionalism but his blind, despairing belief in an ideal amateurism.

The truth is that we would not think of Agee as a failure if he did not insist on it himself. "Meanwhile I am thirty and have missed irretrievably all the trains I should have caught." "Or briefly, though the impulse is OK,/I haven't, really, a damned thing to say." "I am depressed because whether I am to live a very short time or relatively longer time depends . . . on whether or not I can learn to be the kind of person I am not and have always detested; and because, knowing my own character pretty well, I know pretty well what my chances are, even though I will try." These letters brim with self-accusations. "I have a fuzzy, very middle-class, and in a bad sense of the word, Christian mind, and a very clouded sensibility." "I knew I had some self-pity; I even defend it, in moderation. But I didn't realize how much I have, and still don't sufficiently." "Another [fault] is the whole habit of physical self-indulgence; the only degree of asceticism or even moderation I've ever given a hoot for, let alone tried briefly to practice, has been whatever might sharpen enjoyment. . . . Another is in some way caring much too little whether I live or die." ". . . I have nothing good to say about myself. . . ."

Of course, in writing to Father Flye, Agee is addressing not only a priest but the embodiment of his boyhood aspirations. Agee was religious in preferring self-disgust and even self-destruction to any downward adjustment of these aspirations. "I would certainly prefer death to reconciling myself." Among the things he refused to be reconciled to was his own nature as a writer.

Alcohol—which appears in the first Harvard letters ("On the whole, an occasional alcoholic bender satisfies me fairly well") and figures in almost every letter thereafter—was Agee's faithful ally in his "enormously strong drive, on a universally broad front, toward self-destruction." But I think his real vice, as a writer, was talk. "I seem, and regret it and hate myself for it, to be able to say many more things I want to in talking than in writing." He describes his life at Harvard as "an average of 3½ hours sleep per night; 2 or 3 meals per day. Rest of the time: work, or time spent with friends. About 3 nights a week I've talked all night. . . ." And near the end of his life, in

Hollywood: "I've spent probably 30 or 50 evenings talking alone most of the night with Chaplin, and he has talked very openly and intimately." And what are these letters but a flow of talk that nothing but total fatigue could stanch? "The trouble is, of course, that I'd like to write you a pretty indefinitely long letter, and talk about everything under the sun we *would* talk about, if we could see each other. And we'd probably talk five or six hundred pages. . . ."

He simply preferred conversation to composition. The private game of translating life into language, or fitting words to things, did not sufficiently fascinate him. His eloquence naturally dispersed itself in spurts of interest and jets of opinion. In these letters, the extended, "serious" projects he wishes he could get to—narrative poems in an "amphibious style," "impressionistic" histories of the United States, an intricately parodic life of Jesus, a symphony of interchangeable slang, a novel on the atom bomb—have about them the grandiose, gassy quality of talk. They are the kind of books, rife with Great Ideas, that a *Time* reviewer would judge "important." The poignant fact about Agee is that he was not badly suited to working for Henry Luce.

He half knew it. "The only writing I do which approaches decency is on this job [for *Fortune*]—and on other stuff I seem to be pretty well congealed." Twelve years later, Agee *wants* "to write a weekly column for some newspaper or magazine—very miscellaneous but in general, detailed topical analysis of the very swift and sinister decline and perversion of all that might be meant by individualism . . . etc., etc." In praising Kafka, he observes curiously that Kafka appears "in a way totally uninterested in 'literature' or 'art' except in so far as they are his particular instrument for studying, questioning and suggesting more sharply than he otherwise could." Whereas Agee was far too "much moved and excited by Ideas—related with general existence and with art. . . ." Ideas—particularly the American idea of the Great Novel, literature as a Puritan Absolute—obsessed Agee, and hounded him out of contentment with his genius, which was for spontaneous, gregarious commentary rather than patient, eremitical invention.

In the last of these letters, mostly written from the hospital bed where his overstrained heart had taken him, there are hints of reconciliation. His work with the movies—the cooperative art par excellence—affects him rather cheerfully. His prose takes on crispness. The tortuous, grinding note of self-reproach diminishes. Looking back on his career, he is pleasantly "surprised I have gotten done even the little that I have." He coherently and masterfully sketches several script ideas—a scene from *Candide*, a moral (*and* satiric) film fantasy about elephants. His versatility, his ardent interest in "this and that and the other thing," were beginning to find channels; perhaps there *was* some use in talking. But his body was ruined, and abruptly his magnanimous spirit and eager intelligence vanished from the world of American letters, to whose Manichaean stresses he had been so sensitive, and whose opportunities he had been so ingeniously reluctant to seize.

*July 6, 1963 [A. Philip Randolph]*

## "THE CHOICE, MR. PRESIDENT..."

by Murray Kempton

It is not Asa Philip Randolph's style to embarrass Presidents of the United States in large assemblies; and so, when he came as a vice-president of the AFL-CIO to the White House along with three hundred other labor leaders, Mr. Randolph's brief comment on President Kennedy's televised speech on civil rights two nights before was at once a stately compliment and a measured reminder: "It was a magnificent speech, but it was, *unfortunately*, made rather late."

When the President had left the room and his audience was moving toward the outer air, a Southern "brother" approached Philip Randolph and asked where he could find someone from the Labor Department. "I got a problem to tell him about," he said. "The colored people are doing all right in my state. It's the white people I'm worried about. They're being discriminated against."

Randolph gravely escorted this stray over to the nearest Labor Department official and went away. He returned to Harlem amused but unsurprised; he is the only figure in the American labor movement who has, for twenty years, been able continually to surprise his country, but nothing surprises him.

His Brotherhood of Sleeping Car Porters is aged and fading; it never had more than 15,000 members and no more than 5,000 of these are working now. Porters with thirty years of service endlessly deal the brittle old playing cards in their recreation room on 125th Street in New York, awaiting their chance for an odd, infrequent extra run. The porters may strike any day for the forty-hour work week, which they alone among the operating railroad crafts have not achieved. They can expect the other unions to support their picket lines; this little group of old men could produce a national railroad strike. Nothing is new about their headquarters except the fresh picket signs.

The porter has always been poor and a menial; segregation created his job; the Pullman Company hired Negroes as porters because Negroes were inexpensive. And for most of the thirty-seven years of their union's history, the porters have taxed themselves for campaigns to destroy segregation on the railroads, but they seem to have been defeated by economic history. Their union has raised their pay scale to a basic $436 a month, which has made a porter's job one fit for white men—so fit, in fact, that occasionally a white youth comes to the Brotherhood in search of a union card; it cannot be given him, because there are not enough jobs for the old members, let alone new ones. There will be no white porters, and there will be no Negro engineers; the rule for employment on the railroads is not opportunity but seniority.

World War II was the best time they have known as workers. They used its rewards to finance Randolph's March-on-Washington movement, whose threat in 1943 won from Franklin D. Roosevelt the executive order which set up the wartime Fair Employment Practices Committee.

The first Freedom Rides into North and South Carolina and Tennessee were planned in Randolph's office in 1946. Bayard Rustin, a veteran of that first adventure into jail, remembers that everyone else had discouraged him until he came to Randolph. "It doesn't matter if you only get eighteen people," Randolph said then. "If you go down there, other people will rise and follow." He was looking seventeen years ahead as though they were the next day.

Ralph Bunche remembers traveling to Atlanta on the Seaboard line in 1947. South of Washington he went to the diner and was shown a table behind a partition. He looked at it, announced that he had not lived quite long enough yet to accept segregation and went back to his room.

"About half an hour later, my door buzzer buzzed. I opened it and there were two sleeping-car porters and a waiter from the dining car with trays neatly covered and they told me that they had decided to bring me this food, because no Negro, in their view, who refused to eat at that Jim Crow table would ever go hungry on a train where they served. They didn't mention it, but I took it that the food was with the compliments of the company."

The Brotherhood Building on 125th Street was the headquarters of Thomas Patterson, Eastern Supervisor of the Sleeping Car Porters Union, who once traveled to Wilmington, North Carolina, to negotiate with the Atlantic Coast Line. He was ejected from its dining car for refusing to sit at the segregated table. The next morning, Patterson completed his union business with a Coast Line lawyer; that afternoon, he sued the line for his humiliation on the diner. The railroad settled out of court and removed for all time its Jim Crow partition; Patterson gave his profits to the Brotherhood.

In 1955, Edward D. Nixon, a Pullman porter, summoned the Negro community of Montgomery, Alabama, to boycott its buses. Nixon knew that it would be politic to choose one of the Negro ministers as leader of the boycott. The youngest, and a stranger among them, was Martin Luther King of the Dexter Street Baptist Church.

"He didn't say much, and I didn't know whether to trust him. But he had the richest church and he could hurt us," Nixon remembered. "So then and there, I nominated him to head our committee. I figured on pushing him out so far that he couldn't run away. And, with that bad guess, we got Moses."

Such is the history which enfolds this old command post set away in a Harlem that has changed hardly at all. Three floors down are the displays of studios that offer tap, ballet and other lessons in how to escape to the great world, and the advertisements of employment offices that offer jobs for maids in New Jersey.

"What was your class at Harvard, Phil?" Franklin D. Roosevelt asked once, bemused by the massively cultivated tone of a man whose only degree was from Cookman College, a Negro high school in Florida. "Who is Randolph?" a World War II government lawyer asked as he brought in draft after draft of an F.E.P.C. order in 1943 only to be told that "Randolph" was not yet satisfied that any of them went far enough.

"I wish you hadn't said that, Mr. Randolph," Harry Truman answered when Randolph told him in 1948 that he would advise every young Negro to refuse to serve in the Army so long as it was segregated. Randolph answered that he was sorry to have to say it; and, when President Truman was restored to calm, he signed the order which integrated the armed forces.

In 1951, William Mills, a Pullman porter, escorted a detachment of American soldiers into his car at Spartansburg, South Carolina. The sergeant was a Negro; most of the men in his command were white. One of the white boys put his head out of the window and asked in the accent of the South, "Sergeant, what time we supposed to get off?" The sergeant answered and turned to see William Mills looking at him. "Yes," the sergeant said. "It's true. It's true."

Randolph is seventy-four, thinner than he used to be. Men who have worked with him for thirty years call him "Chief" and treat him like a piece of old china; he tires more than he used to and lies down for a nap in the afternoon, like any country lawyer.

His only vanity is his manners. He has lived all his life in Harlem; he travels to the outside world as the ambassador of a Negro union. He carries a courtesy so old-fashioned that the white men with whom he negotiates are sometimes driven to outsized rages by the shock that anyone so polite could cling so stubbornly to what he believes; it was from such a shock presumably that George Meany breached the customary decorum of an AFL-CIO convention in 1959 by rasping, "Just who elected you, Phil, to represent all the American Negroes?" Randolph, almost alone on the convention floor, had been persisting in his insistence that the AFL-CIO had been derelict in its promises about civil rights.

"Every now and then," says Bayard Rustin, "I think he permits good manners to get in the way and that he even prefers them to sound tactics. Once I complained about that and he answered, 'Bayard, we must with good manners accept everyone. Now is the time for us to learn good manners. We will need them when this is over, because we must show good manners after we have won.'"

Yet the Black Muslims trust Randolph more than they do any other Negro leader. When he organized a neighborhood committee on Harlem's economic problems, he invited Malcolm X, the local Muslim prophet, to join. There were objections from the respectable. Randolph replied that when any group of citizens offered a representative, it "would be most improper not to recognize him, even though it will, of course, be most unfortunate if some of the ministers decide they can't go along."

Malcolm X came to his office. Randolph patiently explained how the Negro and the white will have to live together and how wrong he thought the Muslims were not to think so. Then he congratulated the Muslims on their campaign against whisky and narcotics. "That," he said gravely, "may be the greatest contribution any of us have ever made," and arose to help Malcolm X on with his coat and see him to the door. Malcolm X has said since that all Negro leaders are confused, but that Randolph is less confused than any of them. Last spring the Muslims put a picture of this pacifist on the cover of their weekly journal.

"When Randolph began," says Bayard Rustin, "the Negro leader had the terrible problem of living by his wits. It was very important that there be one man who could not be corrupted. That man was Randolph. Even now, any time you have a plan and don't quite trust yourself, you go to Randolph and, if you are fooling yourself morally, you can trust him to point it out."

Randolph suddenly appears as the only figure who can reconcile the painful personal differences that have fallen upon the Negro protest movement at the height of its sweep and its fashion. We confront one of those occasions familiar in all revolutionary movements when doctrinal differences pass over into personal quarrels. Its moment of revelation came just after the murder of Medgar Evers, Mississippi secretary of the NAACP. Martin Luther King called an NAACP official to suggest that together they proclaim a day of national mourning and self-examination and was told that he was always rushing into cases where he had no place or business.

The alliance between King and the NAACP has always been uneasy. They have moved by different roads in the same direction, King mainly in the streets, the NAACP in the courts. King's young can seem irresponsible to the NAACP's middle-aged; and the NAACP's middle-aged can seem stodgy to King's young.

Randolph is alone among these leaders, because he neither feels hostility for, nor excites it in, any other of them. He is a pacifist in a native American tradition; before most members of King's nonviolent army were born, he was reminding the Negro of Thoreau's prescription to cast the total vote with feet and voice along with the ballot. He has a natural sympathy for King. Still, there are ways in which he is more moderate than the NAACP. While the association has been in open war with the AFL-CIO, Randolph has kept his friends there, offending them only on matters of principle. The porters remain as they have always been, moderate in the particular which involves manners, and radical in the general which involves principle.

Not even a malignant imagination could assign Randolph one side or another in the quarrel between King and the NAACP. King he judges to be not just a modest man but a humble one, which, for him, disposes of the NAACP's complaint. On the other side, he reminds the radical young how important it is to respect the association and Roy Wilkins, its executive secretary. "We must cultivate Roy," he tells them. "The association is the most important of all our organizations." He respects King because he has roused the poor Negro with results more consequential than any leader before him; and he respects the NAACP because it reaches the Negro middle class and can call upon its local chapters for hundreds of thousands of dollars in a real crisis; there is no other resource like this one.

Two months ago, Randolph had announced that he would call 100,000 Negroes to Washington to demonstrate against unemployment in October; it had seemed then just an echo of his 1943 march on Washington and scarcely relevant. Wilkins and King had different concerns and higher priorities, and without them, Randolph seemed reduced to the depleted resources of the porters. But then President Kennedy introduced his civil-rights bill; Washington had again become the center and Randolph's march the only certain item on the movement's agenda this summer. Randolph moved his march to August; he and King agreed to widen its scope to cover the civil-rights bill. There was suddenly the surprising prospect that Congress would debate these bills with thousands of Negroes standing outside.

Randolph and others were called again to the White House on June 22, just before the President was to leave for Europe. Mr. Kennedy said that he hoped that it wouldn't be necessary for Negroes to come to Washington in great groups while the debate was going on. Philip Randolph answered that he was afraid the choice was no longer whether Negroes came to Washington or not. "The choice, Mr. President, is between a controlled and nonviolent demonstration and an uncontrolled and violent one."

Mr. Kennedy answered that a President had many responsibilities and he wanted it made clear that he was not inviting them. Randolph's manners instructed him that Mr. Kennedy was talking for the record.

He returned to plan a march that would be unlimited in aim, and that would remember above all the needs of all the poor and displaced, whatever their color.

"The Negro people are just one other depressed area," he said the other day. "As long as there is unemployment, it's going to hit us. The Negro is in the position of the white hod carrier and the white longshoreman. I should like all the unemployed to come with us. We complain because the building trades have no room for Negroes, but the real trouble now is that these unions are designed for profit through scarcity. If the crafts were open to us, that could not, in the present economy, create more than 40,000 jobs.

"When we have won, there will remain the Negro sharecropper. We shall end, great as this is, with a very sharp disillusionment when the great rallies are over. We had this experience with sitdowns in the Thirties. We are basically a working-class group; we will not move unless we move with the rest of the working class."

More than anything else, Philip Randolph said. he would like to bring the displaced miners of Hazard, Kentucky, to Washington with him. He was silent just a moment, contemplating what all this sudden energy could mean, not just to the Negro, but to the whole United States. His secretary came in and reminded him that it was time for his afternoon nap. The Pullman porter, weary and depleted, has raised himself for just this one last effort to redeem his country.

*December 7, 1963 [The Assassination of John F. Kennedy]*

# ROMANS

by Murray Kempton and James Ridgeway

> Robert Frost wrote fifty years ago, "nothing is true except as a man or men adhere to it—to live for it, to spend themselves on it, to die for it." We need this spirit even more than money or institutions or agreements.
> —JOHN F. KENNEDY, November 18, 1963

By Saturday night, even the television seemed worn out by attempt and failure and ceased to comment and gave over to a succession of photographs of the columns and the windows and the corners of the White House and of the shadows of the great Lincoln head in Springfield and to a voice reciting, "Oh, Captain, My Captain." It is to be, then, the grand style. But the ship has not weathered every storm; Mr. Kennedy is not Abraham Lincoln; not because he is more or less, but because he is a remembered physical presence, and Mr. Lincoln an image of the plastic arts. One's own time is personal, not historical. Just how long will it be before many of us will want to read a book about the day Mr. Kennedy was shot?

The news of the President's assassination was given by a taxi driver to three gentlemen as they left a hotel on Arlington Street in Boston. They turned right around and hurried back inside to attend to their investments. Packed with students and businessmen, a shuttle plane from Boston to Washington waited for permission to take off, when the captain came on the intercom: "Folks, up here on the flight deck we've been listening to the news and the President is dead." There was only time to hear one woman say, "How dreadful" before three men went back to discussing plan specifications. A college student reading *Agamemnon* paid no visible attention. One of his notes read, "love-in-hate." The plane took off, the stewardess collected the money and started to serve drinks. Then the captain was back again. They had been listening to more news, that is, trying to listen to news, because their real job was to hear flight control. There had been a gun battle in Dallas; a patrolman was killed; the police had taken a man in a movie theater. Vice-President Johnson was now the President. The talk of business went on through this, and stopped only when the captain again interrupted to say that the new President had been sworn in aboard an aircraft. A few laughed.

They ask too much of us when they ask us to act up to the grand style. We are not an emotionally affluent people. And yet some of us always complained that Mr. Kennedy did not seem quite emotionally committed enough. But now someone remembered with special affection a moment late in the 1960 campaign. Mr. Kennedy was in a motorcade and the Democratic governor who was with him said how wonderful it was to feel the love with which these crowds pressed forward to feel the touch of their candidate. "Oh, dry up," Mr. Kennedy said. It seemed now somehow a special grace in him that he used only the real in emotion and abstained from fabricating the expected. He had too much respect for the grand style to counterfeit it; how much truer to him might we have been if we had come down in scale and if the many of us who must have remembered the lines from *Cymbeline* had thought them proper to speak:

> Fear no more the heat o' the sun
> > Nor the furious winter's rages.
> Thou thy worldly task hast done
> > Home art gone and ta'en thy wages.
> Golden lads and girls all must
> > As chimney sweepers come to dust.

*Cymbeline* is a Roman play. The Kennedys are a Roman family; America seems only a Roman crowd. For us alone in it, there is only a terrible irritation with God and with self and with every other face that is left.

Friday night caught most of the President's Cabinet away from the city. All that could be collected from his official establishment came to Andrews Air Force Base to meet the dead man come back from Dallas.

Everything mechanical intruded as it would intrude all weekend. The lights were vagrant, savage and aimless; the planes came and went on distracting, irrelevant missions. The face of Undersecretary of Commerce Roosevelt seemed the ruin of his father's. Every uncared-for lank of Senator Dirksen's hair, every fold under every chin seemed for the moment our own fault.

For we had lost in the instant the hope of beginning again. Reason might argue that the sense of a new start was already gone. The main story in the morning's *Washington Post* had detailed the exculpations of a Congressman who had made a 1,000 per cent profit from the stock of a company which had enjoyed his good offices with the Internal Revenue Service. The very Senate which dissipated in shock at the news from Texas had just before been waspishly disputing the privileges and emoluments of elective office. For weeks it had been hard to remember anyone in Washington talking about anything except who was getting what from whom. Mr. Kennedy seemed to be wasting in his city and to be nourished only by the great crowds in the countryside. The films from Dallas, painful as they were, reinforced the feeling that he was his old self only away from Washington. It could be argued then that we would see a time when we recognized that all that promise had been an illusion; but you need only look at hope lain dead to know how easy it is to look forward to regret. It had been less than three years since Mr. Kennedy had announced that a new generation was taking up the torch; now old General de Gaulle and old Mr. Mikoyan were coming to see the young man buried.

The great red-and-white plane of the President of the United States came to Andrews at last bearing all the transition in one horrid large economy-size package. There was a portable yellow elevator to bring Mrs. Kennedy and Attorney General Kennedy down with a casket that looked like a ship's chest. Half of Lyndon Johnson could be seen waiting in the open door behind them. Mrs. Kennedy's weeds as a widow had to be what some said was a strawberry- and some said was a raspberry-colored campaign suit.

Everything mechanical that did not intrude functioned badly; the elevator seemed to stall; Mrs. Kennedy tried a door of the ambulance, which did not work, and the Attorney General, with a deliberation unbroken as hers was, found one which did, and she was gone at last, the high Roman figure that she would be all weekend.

So Mr. Johnson came on, tall as ever but wearing the glasses which his image of himself has always thought unsuitable to state occasions, emptied by his misfortune of all his vanity, small and large, and of almost everything else. His lips seemed wet, his chin uncertain; there was a fear that he might be a man who would cry in public and who was there enough his better to blame him? He said something into the microphones that was identifiable only as being hoarse, broken and undeservedly apologetic, and then his new household gathered around him. And the eye as cruel to everyone else as the heart was cruel to self focused and saw only the hearing aid of an Undersecretary. The next morning, Mr. Johnson had repaired his interior and left off resenting himself, as all of us had better do if we are to get about our business.

As the people waited the passing of the cortege on Sunday some of them squabbled over who was to stand on the stepladder and shoot the first pictures and at what speed and lens opening. A mother trying to tune up a transistor radio said to a pouting child, "I want you to understand one thing. This is very important to me." Amidst the people came a teen-ager with a portable tape recorder. He stuck out a microphone and said, "Sir, on this day of national mourning how do you feel?" Coming away from the Capitol after viewing the bier, a man with a camera slung over his head said to another man with a camera, "Did you get any good pictures?"

One sat in the Senate press room away from the rotunda on Sunday night and read a wire service report on the tributes paid to the patriotism of Jack Ruby by the master of ceremonies of Mr. Ruby's strip parlor. There was a story about the good fortune of the Dallas citizen who had been in at the death with his movie camera and had sold the films to *Life* for $40,000. The National Football League had played its full Sunday schedule; every seat in Yankee Stadium was filled with mourners. One thought with respect—it was not possible to be grateful to anyone—of Randall Jarrell for having known enough soon enough to have written a book and called it *A Sad Heart at the Supermarket.*

Then a man spoke up and said:

"She came in with the children this afternoon when the rotunda was first opened and she was standing and waiting and the kid looked up at the dome and began to walk around, and she bent over and touched him and he looked up and she straightened her shoulders to show him how to stand at attention, and he did it for about ten seconds. You know, I wish it was a dynasty and the kid was taking over and she was the regent."

Monday was sunny and for those to whom life is a picture, the Capitol was the best and largest color television screen anyone could hope for. A boy sat on his father's shoulders, and his father told him to use the Number One setting. The band began "Hail to the Chief," the boy raised his camera and instructed his father not to move. Behind them a woman put a child on her shoulders; the child must have tickled her, because she kept laughing, comfortably, and this pleasant distraction continued until the coffin could be detected from its flag to be coming out and she left off and pointed her finger and said with undiminished gaiety, "See, there he is." One left and walked past a girl clutching a paperback. Then suddenly there was one man kneeling on the sidewalk, and it was impossible to stop and put a hand upon his shoulder and not to begin to hope that a chain might be put together again.

In front of St. Matthew's the crowd was quieter. The bands and the soldiers went by, the pipers last; and then, like thunder, there was Mrs. Kennedy with the Senator on one side and the Attorney General on the other and ramrods up their spines. And behind them, the powers and potentates of the earth; the Kennedys were marching with all of Madame Tussaud's in their train, as though Charles de Gaulle had been created a Marshal of France and Haile Selassie I the Lion of Judah only for this last concentrated moment. The powers and potentates waited; Mrs. Kennedy, for the moment made flesh again, gathered her children. Cardinal Cushing came down, under his miter, looking, to his credit, a trifle irritated with God; we could be grateful for the Catholics and grateful to them for providing one Cardinal who looked like a Prince of the Church.

And the children in their sunny pale-blue coats began walking with their mother up the stairs, the little boy stumbling only at the vestibule, and then they were gone. We had lived awhile with old Romans; now the doors were closing and we must make do with ourselves.

*January 11, 1964 [E. M. Forster]*

# THE MODERN MR. FORSTER
by Gilbert A. Harrison

Before calling on E. M. Forster at Kings College, Cambridge, I had gone with a friend to sit in the superb Henry VI Chapel. A service was on. Not a knee creaked, no voice broke, no word grated. The light, the windows, the stalls, stone and banners—all were perfection. I drifted from the chapel across the court and up the stone staircase to Mr. Forster's rooms, part of me left behind, another part beginning to anticipate the meeting.

He was all twinkle and solicitude, busying himself with seating us and with the sherry. I told him that I had just come from chapel service and was bothered. Why, since it was perfect, was I not moved? "Why," he burst out, "you weren't *meant* to!" He was delighted. That was what he thought of high-churchmanship. And what else could I tell him? "He enjoys hearing about escapades of any kind," Mollie Panter-Downes said of him in *The New Yorker*, on his eightieth birthday. "Then his glasses glint, his mustache twitches, his face creases into puckers of amusement, little gasps of gathering delight escape him, and out of this steady fortissimo bursts the helpless shriek of laughter . . ."

I recall little of the conversation we had that afternoon. The talk, like his room, was pleasant, almost intimate. . . . He was about to visit Italy and asked if I could recommend an inexpensive *pension* in Assisi. I could, but would it be right for him? "No, no," he said, "do *you* like it?" So I gave him the name, and he later wrote of the pleasure staying there had given him. He had liked the white pigeons and the grape arbor on the breakfast porch overlooking the valley. He had been trying, he said, to read what the scientists were writing, even some science fiction; but he found it hard; it was of another age. What age was he? I knew, but not from seeing him. He is eighty-five.

He long ago wrote five novels, part of a sixth, and a seventh (unpublished). But there are a great many fine short stories too, and the numerous essays, radio talks, tributes to writers, a history and guidebook of Alexandria, a biography of his great-aunt Marianne Thornton, a critique of the novel, the biography of his Cambridge friend, Goldworthy Lowes Dickinson, a report on the government of Egypt done for the Labour Party's research department, even a pageant play about England. It is remarkable he is thought of as "not having produced much." Every line speaks for the individual, for the possibilities of the spirit against brutality or indifference or coercive pride. In his 1931 report on Egypt, he says apropos of "the Egyptian character": "Up to 1919 the Egyptians were allowed such plebeian virtues as industry and good temper, but they were regarded as an inferior race, incapable of taking the initiative or of suffering for an ideal. This low estimate of them was not confined to Europeans; it was shared by the coreligionists in Turkey and in India. But hatred of the British has hardened the national character. The official view of this change is that it is due to propaganda. But propaganda is not a magic drug; it must appeal to something that already exists in men's minds, or its power evaporates. . . . Whether [Egyptian] patriotism has a constructive side we cannot tell until we give it a chance; at present it necessarily takes the form of rioting."

We cannot tell . . . but we must act as if we could. He ends a pamphlet on the Nazis, which he describes as "propaganda," this way: "Whatever the outcome of the war, we are in for bad times. But there are moments when each of us, however feeble, can feel within himself the strong hopes of the human race, and see beyond his personal death its renaissance, and the restoration of delight."

We live, he says, a stone's throw from the caves of Marabar ("a Marabar cave can hear no sound but its own"). Below, in the dark, all sound is echo—a dread and impersonal "Boum." But how are we to save ourselves from this horror, from fear, panic, withdrawal, even despair? "Love is a great force in private life," but in public affairs, "it does not work. . . . The fact is we can only love what we know personally. And we cannot know much." And so Mr. Forster settles for something less for the community—tolerance, which is "boring" and a "very dull virtue. Unlike love, it has always had a bad press. It is negative. It merely means putting up with people, being able to stand things. . . . [Yet] this is the only force which will enable different races and classes and interests to settle down together to the work of reconstruction."

Tolerance at least, affection at best, is the message of all the books. And a repugnance for fanaticism: "I have lost all faith in positive militant ideals; they can so seldom be carried out without thousands of human beings getting maimed or imprisoned." . . .

He wonders how "can we put any trust in personal relationships or cling to them in the gathering political storm?" Then he transforms the "we" to "I": "One must be fond of people and trust them if one is not to make a mess of life, and it is therefore essential that they should not let one down. They often do. The moral of which is that I must, myself, be as reliable as possible, and this I try to be. But reliability is not a matter of contract—that is the main difference between the world of personal relationships and the world of business relationships. It is a matter for the heart, which signs no documents." Against suspicion and indifference he asserts trust and concern.

In this age, personal relations may be despised ("I will not turn my back on Alger Hiss" was a remark for which Dean Acheson paid heavily); we are asked to put in their place some cause. Mr. Forster hates the idea of causes; if he "had to choose between betraying my country or betraying my friend, I hope I should have the guts to betray my country." His ultimate confidence (let it be betrayed) is in the private vision shared.

Hope without hallucinations. . . . "What is good in people—and consequently in the world—is their insistence on creation, their belief in friendship and loyalty for their own sakes; and though violence remains and is, indeed, the major partner in this muddled establishment, I believe that creativeness remains too, and will always assume direction when violence sleeps. So, though I am not an optimist, I cannot agree with Sophocles that it were better never to have been born. And although, like Horace, I see no evidence that each batch of births is superior to the last, I leave the field open for the more complacent view."

Civility is the cement of society, but it does not bind us to one another. In writing of India and of his sad conviction that good will is inadequate (for "the reactions to it are instantly cynical"), he says that "the only thing that cuts a little ice is affection or the possibility of affection . . . but it must be genuine affection and liking. It must not be exercised with any ulterior motive."

Here is the moralist without Belief; the reformer without program, the prophet of personal relations who knows how often they fail. Mrs. Moore in *A Passage to India* disappoints Dr. Aziz; friendship is not possible—"no, not yet." Mrs. Wilcox drifts in and out of Margaret Schlegel's life in *Howard's End*; there were hints of understandings, a trace of intimacy, then death and mystery. But not before Mrs. Wilcox had said: "We are all in the same boat, old and young. I never forget that."

Can the hero in wartime escape "the insolence of victory, the venom of defeat" Foster asks in a short essay, "Hymn Before Action." He cannot; "he drives into the battle rejoicing, and wins a great victory. But it is necessarily and rightly followed by disillusionment and remorse. The fall of his enemies leads to his own, for the fortunes of men are all bound up together, and it is impossible to inflict damage without receiving it." This was written in 1912.

In Belfast, Mr. Forster said a few words some years ago, in memory of an author he knew, Forrest Reid, whom he described as "elusive and sensitive, yet at the same time he was tough and knew his own mind. He preached no dogma, and yet all his work is characterized by what he himself has beautifully called a sort of moral fragrance. Its final impact is ethical. Behind nature and the indwelling power in her, behind Lagan and the Ulster countryside, behind Celtic or Hellenic fancies, behind his sympathy for youth and young people, for animals, for birds, there lurks that moral fragrance. Not moral precepts, but moral fragrance. There is a profound difference." The words will do for Mr. Forster himself.

He has never been pretentious about his work. He told an interviewer in 1952 that he had not "got down more than the people I like, the person I think I am, and the people who irritate me. This puts me among the large body of authors who are not really novelists, and have to get on as best they can with these three categories. We have not the power of observing the variety of life and describing it dispassionately."

He has dreaded war and mechanization and the spoiled landscapes and resisted them all. He has not been sure his kind of humanism would last very long. In 1935, he wondered whether writers like himself would not soon "be swept away." And "this being so, my job, and the job of those who feel with me, is an interim job. We have just to go on tinkering as well as we can with our old tools until the crash comes. When the crash comes, nothing is any good. After it— if there is an after—the task of civilization will be carried on by people whose training has been different from my own." Meanwhile, each may be redeemed by imagination, and partially redeemed by great literature, for great literature "transforms the man who reads it toward the condition of the man who wrote, and brings to birth in us also the creative impulse. Lost in the beauty where he was lost, we find more than we ever threw away, we reach what seems to be our spiritual home, and remember that it was not the speaker who was in the beginning, but the Word."

*February 8, 1964 [Norman Mailer]*

# WHY MAILER WANTS TO BE PRESIDENT
by Richard Gilman

It is possible to regard Norman Mailer as one of the prices we pay for widespread literacy. By the same token, it is possible to escape his presence by shrinking the area of your own literacy, by never looking at *Esquire*, being highly selective about *Commentary, Dissent, The Village Voice* and *The New York Review of Books*, giving a wide berth to Carnegie Hall and the Y.M.H.A. on certain evenings when you are in New York, not reading a newspaper for fear of coming upon another chapter of the life story, and in general making your way back to a simpler world in which the extreme limits of the ego were defined by field marshals and dictators, not writers.

Yet the world is rampant with Communication and the publishing of the Self, and Mailer may be suppressed but not the phenomenon which he represents and incarnates most aggressively, but to which we all contribute. Beyond that, there is a suspicion that it is worth staying open to Mailer, allowing ourselves, for the sake of what is harshly exemplary or paradoxically instructive in him, to remain exposed to his messianism, autocanonizations, tantrums, headstands, strip teases and deteriorating prose. . . .

In *The Deer Park*, Mailer wrote that "part of a man's style is what he thinks of other people and whether he wants them to be in awe of him or to think of him as an equal." There has never been any doubt that Mailer wishes us to be in awe of him, just as there should not have been any doubt that for all his rage against America he is held more tightly than any of his contemporaries in the grip of one of her chief horrors and blasphemies: the cult of success. It is not simply that he manages and promotes his career as though it were a movie star's; in his work, in the center of his journalism and even of his imaginative vision, success is the touchstone. . . .

To win absolutely or lose everything, such are the stakes Mailer has always played for. If it has therefore become impossible for us to respond to him freely as an artist or a thinker among others, reserving our notions of victory or defeat for wars, business enterprises and seductions, it is clearly because he will not let us. Out of his invincible and programmatic confusion of art and life, he has changed the game, compelling us, through intimidation, a finger on our guilt, a bait to our secret envy and frustration, to swallow him whole or risk

starvation. . . . He has made first literature and now politics a choice
between himself and everything else. . . .

"I hate everything that is not in myself," says Croft, the steely,
mystically brutal sergeant in *The Naked and the Dead*, who Mailer
has declared was the character he felt most closely identified with and
whom, in one guise or another, he has continued to emulate in his
frenetic assault on what exists.

Great prophets, true visionaries live apart and assail what is outside
themselves if it is a betrayal, and they are ultimately blessed for it—
it is what makes for revolutions in consciousness, the way intellectual
community makes for consolidation and continuity—but Mailer has
never been able to convince more than a coterie that he is one of them.
That this is true, that he has publicly existed as an *enfant terrible,* a
gang leader, a big-game hunter or the man who turns the party dangerous, but never as a hero or a seer, is one source of his misery and of
his compulsive return to the attack, and it is a central way to understand him in his present incarnation as pundit and would-be President. . . .

It has become a commonplace to say that Mailer is more interesting
for what he is than for what he says, but the two are mutually illuminating and, more stringently, leave no room for choice. . . . Toward
the end of his remarkably sentient but wild account of the first Liston-
Patterson fight, after describing how he had thrust himself absurdly
into the scene with a cakewalk up to the new heavyweight champion,
an imaginary left hook to his jaw and a claim to be the only man who
could make the return bout a financial success by handling its publicity,
he writes: "Once more I had tried to become a hero and had ended as
an eccentric."

Now it is crucial to Mailer's mystique of preternatural self-sufficiency
and his platform of ruthless candor that he always appears to be his
own speediest and most unappeasable critic; there is no beating him
to the draw whenever he knows—and knows that we know—that he
has made himself an especially attractive target. Yet the self-criticism
in the Liston piece, like all that which he continually issues as part of
the diary he keeps in public, is surely a great deal less candid and
thoroughgoing than he would have us think or than he himself
knows. . . .

Traditional self-criticism on the part of a writer, the kind that leads
to spiritual crises, flights into the desert, or painful revaluations of
style or attitude, is precisely what Mailer never undertakes, certainly
not in front of us, because it is of the essence of his willed thrust
against the consciousness of the age that he remain implacable, intransigent, and subject to no serious revisions from within. This is
indeed one source of his apparitional power, a center of his appeal; in
an era of bending spirits, provisional morals and accommodating tal-

ents, Mailer holds out the possibility of the self's eventual triumph through stamina, absolutism, Faustian hunger and autonomous light.

Pursuing this, he has become his own tiger whom he holds by the tail. He cannot let go of himself, yet he lives in the middle of the enemy camp. And this is why his self-disparagement must always be read as tactical, a sortie against our credulity, a bit of judo. . . .

The death of the man he had been measuring himself against once more brought Mailer to a partial, a tactical humility, while revealing how far along he is in his inability to see his ludicrous side. In his statement, Mailer confessed that "what one had written about Kennedy was not reverent" (his increasing use of the impersonal pronoun is no sign of a gaining humility but rather of a swelling sense of institutional grandeur, the writer as Sun King). But what it turned out he was mourning was the loss of the target, the fact that Kennedy would no longer be around for him to take shots at and thereby improve the atmosphere of political discourse.

It was, of course, the response we had expected. Mailer had been making it alarmingly clear that he was engaged in defining the President's existence by his own, as in some sense, it is necessary to say, we all were. But we were at a much lower and more innocent level of the game, we had not institutionalized ourselves into an alternative to the President or into his counterpart. . . .

Mailer, on the other hand, had incorporated Kennedy into his own mystique at the beginning, having claimed a crucial role in his election, by virtue of the *Esquire* report on the Convention. . . . Since then he had been making a new career of addressing the man in office in the manner of a temporarily exiled Nestor, with a lofty condescension to his utterances, which spoke of his conviction that the real center of political wisdom, if not of immediate power, lay in Brooklyn Heights and not in Washington.

This is what is so characteristic of Mailer, that he feels himself to be not simply *at* the center of whatever he is undertaking, the way other mortals feel whose talents make them aware that they have the power to affect the conduct and quality of existence, but the center itself, hotter than the sun. Out of this blaze of centrality issues unexampled political truth, keenest literature and social comment, the only quest for authenticity, the only life of heroic violence, the single siege being laid to a new morality and the unparalleled hunting down of the devil as a preliminary to trapping God.

Having arrogated the center to himself, Mailer has succeeded in obscuring the very notion of periphery, of marginal discovery and fragmentary truth. Even more, by declaring himself to be in possession of the answers, with a stranglehold upon them, he has made it almost impossible for us to see that his true significance lies in the questions, unanswered and perhaps unanswerable, that he has raised. . . .

One is either a mover and shaker or one is not. To insist on being one imposes a fearful strain, which inevitably withers and scatters the powers one does have. "I am imprisoned with a perception," Mailer told us in *Advertisements for Myself*, "which will settle for nothing less than making a revolution in the consciousness of our time." Yet rather than devoting all his energy to doing it, to producing solid and irresistible works that will do it, he continually claims it, with a growing desperation that can only have the result of making us think that somewhere he knows that he has failed.

And, of course, he has failed, he has not made anything like a revolution in our consciousness, but rather has produced a splash upon its surface. If he would be content with knowing it we would tell him that it has been a splash whose effect has been to have made us more aware of the depths. But he cannot be content with that, any more than a child can be content with knowing that he has had an effect on us but that we retain our independent and pre-existing being. What the child has then to do is grow and set among us a being of its own, equal to ours, perhaps superior; and what an ambition for revolution has to do is *create* the revolution, through works and acts that embody it. And Mailer, for all the rebelliousness he has set going and the air he has enlivened, has given us works and deeds that are too few, too limited, too erratic, problematic, fallacious, derivative or self-serving for any true revolution to have sprung from them.

"It is my present and future work which will have the deepest influence of any work being done by an American novelist in these years." Mailer wrote this about himself five years ago; it was not true then, it is not true now. . . .

At a turning point in his career, as he wrote in *Advertisements for Myself*, he came to feel that "it was more important to be a man than a very good writer." But as the same book demonstrates, what he set out to do was to try to become a bigger man, through an extension of experience, in order to then become an even better writer, though one of a different kind. He had behind him the early and enormous but misleading success of *The Naked and the Dead*, the debacle of *Barbary Shore* and the equivocal and debilitating triumph—minor successes both of esteem and scandal—of *The Deer Park*. Such effect as he had had was imponderable, a seepage into the public consciousness and no stick to its recalcitrance. . . .

From then on, with only the most sporadic and abortive returns to imaginative writing, but covering himself with the announcement that he had an immense new novel in gestation, he began to evolve into an artist-actor, into a quotidian prophet, a commentator as close to his audience as a scoutmaster plunging up the trail with his pack at his heels. He would attempt that "entrance into the mysteries of murder, suicide, incest, orgy, orgasm and Time," through a supremely ambitious yet hot-handed kind of journalism which could proceed without the screens and obliquities of art. . . .

In the columns he wrote for *The Village Voice* and the pieces for *Dissent*, both of which journals he had a hand in founding, he took up directly all those themes which had occupied him implicitly in his fiction or, more often, for which he had not been able to shape an imaginative mode: the deadness of American life, the imprisonment and suffocation of the ego, the radical need for a new basis of morality which would incorporate extremity, danger and perversion, the quest for heroism and apocalypse through sex and violent epiphanies, and finally the liberating role of the Negro, the Hipster and what he chose to call "existentialism."

It is this later triad of motifs—the Negro as postmoral man, the Hipster as contemporary hero, and existentialism as weapon and deliverance—that has come to subsume all of Mailer's concerns and that stands forth as the triple ground where his followers find him most energizing but where, from a vantage point outside the mystique, his capacity for evocation and for the destruction of stereotypes is seen to clash most angrily with his limited powers of analysis and his solipsistic thinking about the world.

It is an opaque region, filled with fragmentary knowledge, acute insights in isolation, brilliant descriptions and courageous confrontations, but also with misconceptions, romantic fallacies, grotesque theories and an unwearying ascription of universal meaning to what are clearly idiosyncratic notions. . . . It mistakes its dream for reality and its malady for salvation. . . .

Mailer's Hipster and Negro (who are, of course, frequently the same) are not to be found where he says they are, among us, and this is because they are his own creations. They are his space-men out beyond known society in the region he craves to occupy but from which he is barred by his self-consciousness, his whiteness, and his burden of culture. They are the selves he would be if he were not his own, singular autonomous egos sprung from mass life and psychic undifferentiation by ennui and oppression, the one coolly seeking "a sexual life which will suit his orgiastic needs," the other moving light-footed and exemplary in that area "where all situations are equally valid." . . .

At the heart of Mailer's vision of him the Negro dances on the end of a string whose other end was once attached to notions of "gaiety, rhythm and capacity for spiritual richness." That in Mailer the terms are now extremity, purifying violence and transmoral, Promethean re-creation leaves the Negro as unseen as before. . . . It is our exclusion of him from our simplest condition that destroys the Negro, but for Mailer he must function as the agent of a complex superlife.

So, too, the Hipster, the self-excluded. For Mailer, Hip "is an exploration into the nature of man, and its emphasis is on the Self rather than society." Go past the foolish, crippling dichotomy (everywhere in Mailer the romantic opposition of self and society functions as an intellectually reductive force while at the same time providing him with his momentum) and the point to be made is that such exploration is precisely what the Hipster is incapable of. With his very existence dependent on remaining isolate, uncommitted and closed to complexity, with his fingertips filed and his antennae raised in order just to survive—the Hipster is the outlaw, the victim and the secessionist, not the adventurer. . . .

In the same way that he mistakes the Hipster's victimized and jungle-trained consciousness for a liberation, Mailer inverts the Hipster's psychopathetic element and offers it as the sign of a new movement toward authentic being.

But the psychopath, far from being the intrepid Viking of the psychic seas, heroically "trying to create a new nervous system" for himself, is the arrested and agonized victim of precisely that attempt. He is pinioned and spread-eagled on the field of his own chaos by his refusal to accept his own nervous system and to allow it to link up with others so that, through the discovery of limitation and debt, he can come to the discovery of equipoise and possibility. . . .

"At the bottom the drama of the psychopath," Mailer writes, "is that he seeks love. Not love as the search for a mate, but love as the search for an orgasm more apocalyptic than the one which preceded it. Orgasm is his therapy."

Perhaps nowhere in Mailer's entire work is his fundamental confusion, . . . love as an orgasm, orgasm as therapy, been so starkly exhibited. . . . In his dream of an ever-intensifying personal and hermetic apocalypse and an ego wresting its health from the world through rape, Mailer comes eventually to place on the stage a figure who wrestles with impossibility, so that there is no drama but only an anguished sterile dance. . . .

What he is asking from politics in these essays, diatribes and calls to order is what it cannot give; we may speak of the art of politics but political procedures and truth are not the procedures and truth of art. A President is not "supposed to enrich the real life of his people," he is supposed to protect and preserve it, enrichment being precisely the function of the artist. There is a perennial and necessary tension between the protective and material function of politics and the transcendent and liberating function of art; and it is a tension that Mailer, like all romantics, cannot bear, so that he seeks to dissolve it. And doing this leads him to his most dangerous formulations, including the notion that "existential politics is rooted in the concept of the hero."

No, it could not be more wrong: totalitarian politics, mystical politics, the politics of immolation and disastrous ambition are rooted in that concept.

Something else remains true: . . . the fact that he is a guru to certain disciples has not been due at bottom to the soundness of his thought but to its irreverence, its rebelliousness and its plunges, blind and abortive as they may be, into regions that have not previously been invaded or that have been patrolled by "experts" whose professionalism insures that colonization will never take place.

Beyond that there is an emanation from Mailer, a cloud of discontent which bumps the stagnant heavens into motion. . . .

The poet C. Day Lewis once wrote that "it is sometimes more valuable to be proved wrong than to be right." Norman Mailer may not take comfort from it, just as he may not find it a relief to discover that he is part of the culture and not an alternative to it, but he stands among us as an exemplary instance of what Lewis meant. For by his ludicrous and self-misconstrued colloquies with devils and incubi, and his challenge to a wrestling match issued to the wrong angels but to angels nevertheless, he has kept the life lines open. He has not been right, but he has been present; and he has given us, by the ironic action of his voracious ego, a new sense of where our own selves are and what we might do to resurrect them.

*March 28, 1964 [Lyndon B. Johnson]*

## LBJ ISN'T JFK

by T.R.B.

Lovely spring is turning Washington yellow with forsythia, and the time has come at last to quit disparaging Lyndon Johnson because he isn't John F. Kennedy. He isn't, and that's that. He is a powerful figure in his own right who has already got Congress to pass the biggest tax cut in history; he is giving all-out support to the most far-reaching civil-rights bill in a hundred years; he has proposed a "war on poverty" which—even with superlatives drained off—remains a splendid bundle of beginnings; he will try to enact Medicare, and he will do his best with foreign aid in the face of a broadly hostile Congress and a generally indifferent public.

Mr. Johnson is operating in a world where the Opposition almost seems not to want to win. We have always suspected that of Goldwater: he told the Press Club here not long ago that he had thought seriously of withdrawing after JFK's death and continued only from loyalty to his friends; something of a defeatist admission, we thought. . . .

President Johnson is popular, but not too popular. His position is illustrated by the story of the thank-you note written by the little girl to her grandmother for the gift of a thimble. "Thank you, Granny," she wrote, "I like your present, but not very much." The approval of Mr. Johnson is widespread, but nobody can say how deep it is; it seems to lack both the passionate support and dislike that most leaders create in time.

As a matter of fact, this mood of muted approval may express something important within the country. Mr. Johnson elicited it in his hour-long TV interview, in which he did not make any slips, but evoked instead a feeling that was cozy, relaxed, comfortable and bored. Maybe the country wants to be bored a bit. Mr. Johnson implied that he loves everybody; that he wants to be a "prudent progressive," favors a "better deal," and just adores free enterprise. The viewer could snap off the set and turn to more interesting things, satisfied that Mr. Johnson was probably safe and sound, precisely the feeling the President probably sought to elicit.

Is Mr. Johnson, then, nothing more than an intelligent Eisenhower? He is a lot more, we think. He said about the civil-rights bill, for example, "I believe they [the Senate] can pass it and I believe they will pass it and I believe it is their duty to pass it, and I am going to do everything I can to get it passed."

Ike never made an affirmation like that in eight years, save perhaps about the dangers of galloping inflation.

Take twenty historians and ask them to write down adjectives that describe the typical American; then let half a dozen Johnson friends write down his predominant characteristics as they see it. There will be a close resemblance, we guess, between the lists. He is proud, sensitive, impulsive, flamboyant, sentimental, compassionate; he is a doer, not a thinker, and he won't alarm people (as JFK did) with startling new notions. He is optimistic, a worrier, quick-tempered, impatient, tough, hard-driving and boastful; he is earthy as Truman and tends to leave culture and art to his wife (who is a great asset, by the way). He is an exponent of moderation, compromise and manipulation, and on big issues he is careful and cautious. He works eighteen hours a day.

All the time he does corny things that embarrass ivory-tower intellectuals, like going around and turning the White House lights off;

but how many votes do intellectuals have? The man in the street understands the symbolism, and the businessman thinks that LBJ is somehow safer than JFK because "he isn't a spender." Well, we'll see.

*May 16, 1964 [James Baldwin]*

# EVERYBODY'S PROTEST PLAY

by Robert Brustein

> "Let us say, then, that truth, as used here, is meant to imply a devotion to the human being, his freedom and fulfillment; freedom which cannot be legislated, fulfillment which cannot be charted. This is the prime concern, the frame of reference; it is not to be confused with a devotion to Humanity which is too easily equated with a devotion to a Cause; and Causes, as we know, are notoriously bloodthirsty."
>
> *—Everybody's Protest Novel*

James Baldwin wrote these words fifteen years ago in an essay which still stands as the *locus classicus* on the subject of protest fiction; I imagine they sometimes return to haunt him in his dreams. *Blues for Mr. Charlie*, certainly, is the embodiment of everything he once professed to deplore, being "notoriously bloodthirsty" propaganda of the crudest sort, with little existence either as truth, literature, or life. Uncontrolled, hysterical, self-indulgent, employing a clumsy flashback technique and proceeding by means of a surprisingly flabby rhetoric, it is a play of thumbs—fashioned, I would guess, to gouge the eyes of the audience.

It is well known that Baldwin has radically changed his conception of himself over the past few years, suppressing the private side of his character to become an Official Spokesman for a Cause. I have not been among those who admired him in this new role, but I never assumed the decision was easy—or even wholly avoidable, for it may be, as Irving Howe suggests, that the Negro writer cannot find "freedom and fulfillment" until he achieves his Cause. On the other hand, Baldwin's rage, formerly authentic and precise, has begun to seem increasingly mechanical, trumped-up, and free-floating, while his self-righteousness has been expressed at the cost of complexity and scruples. In this play, for example, he is—despite a usually delicate awareness of the deadening effect of racial abstractions—dedicated to perpetuating stereotypes and doing so in a manner which can only create confusion or dissension. The characters have no life apart from narrow racial categories and the categories themselves are based on prejudice and prejudgment.

No doubt, Baldwin's material is partly to blame. Any work inspired by the Emmett Till case is almost automatically destined to be a melodrama. *Blues for Mr. Charlie,* however, simplifies the historical events even further—the stage is given over literally to a conflict between black and white, or Blacktown versus Whitetown. It is the author's apparent conviction now that all white men are Mr. Charlie, the oppressor, for they are characterized either as sadists and supremacists, burning with hatred for Negro men and lust for Negro women, or as vacillating liberals who befriend the Negroes only to betray them when the chips are down. As for the Negro characters, they enjoy more noble racial stereotypes: the Uncle Tom who redeems himself by fingering the murderer after a lifetime of subservience to him; the integrationist minister who finally determines to keep a gun under his Bible, and fight the white man with his own weapons; the strong-minded, white-haired grandmammy of the past generation who believes in pious passiveness; the angry hero who has returned from the North, furious at all the white women who have seduced him, to goad a Southern peckerwood into shooting him; the childhood sweetheart who is rather quixotically persuaded of the necessity for love ("I'm going to learn from Richard how to love! I won't let him die for nothing!") by the hero's angry life and violent death. Since many of these characters are also fixtures of the Broadway stage (Baldwin already manipulates theatrical clichés with the weariness of an experienced commercial dramatist), few of the actors are able to transcend the oppressive conventionality of their roles—though Al Freeman, Jr., is a handsome, vigorous actor, and Diana Sands has an affecting moment of grief—while Burgess Meredith, who directed the Actors Studio production, has been forced to give it the form of a mass meeting in a Union Hall, especially in the courtroom scene, where Black confronts White in angry turmoil, and witnesses detach themselves to deliver impassioned soliloquies downstage.

The most disappointing thing about the play, however, is not its aesthetic flatness, but rather its moral and intellectual deficiency. Particularly depressing is Baldwin's curious insistence on the superiority of Negro sexuality, especially since this is a myth which the author himself once took pains to explode. You would never learn from *Blues for Mr. Charlie* that segregation has social, political, or economic roots; like Tennessee Williams, whose *Sweet Bird of Youth* his play occasionally resembles, Baldwin has determined that the major cause of anti-Negro feeling is sexual envy. This suggests something of the incredible chauvinism which permeates the work—a strain as virulent here as anything to be found in White Citizens' Councils, and even less honest, since Baldwin attempts to vindicate his own feelings by victimizing his characters. (One finds the same desire to make hatred look virtuous in Leroi Jones's *Dutchman,* where the chauvinism and violence of the Negro protagonist are forced from him by a white woman who needles, provokes, and finally kills him—but the rage belongs to the author.) Here, for example, is Baldwin ventriloquizing through his hero, when he is crawling on the ground with three bullets in his belly: "White man! I don't want nothing from you. You ain't got nothing to give me! You can't eat, because none of your sad-assed chicks can cook. You can't talk, because won't nobody talk to you. You can't dance, because you've got nobody to dance with. . . . Okay. Okay. Okay. Keep your old lady home, you hear? Don't let her near no nigger. She might get to like it. You might get to like it, too." In contrast with the "dried-up white women" and the "faggoty white boys," however, Baldwin's Negroes are all extraordinarily virile, courageous, passionate, and alive, even to the point of displaying, during a dance hall sequence, a natural sense of rhythm.

At this point, the healthiest thing for spectators of both races would be to rise up and repudiate these romantic fabrications, and loudly too; but since the theater audience is far from healthy, the play merely sinks the white spectator deeper into an impotent, self-defeating guilt. (An index of this is the cowardly way in which the play was received by the daily reviewers—to praise inferior art, simply because it is produced by a Negro, is to let guilt turn into an inverted form of prejudice.) Worse than this, the play attempts to lacerate an ugly rage in the heart of the colored spectator; *Blues for Mr. Charlie,* for all its conventional gestures toward love, emerges finally as an inflammatory broadside of race hatred which will profit nobody but the author. If we are locked in the stereotypes that Baldwin conceives, and Negro and White can confront each other only in mutual distrust and anger, then we will have to assume that the Negro "problem" is still too crude for the stage; but such a work as Atholl Fugard's *Blood Knot,* with its more controlled form and deeper understanding, proves there is nothing inevitable about these oppositions at all.

The fault, I am afraid, lies not in the "problem" but in the author. The very terms we use to criticize Baldwin were learned in his school, since it is he, along with Ralph Ellison, who did most to make the Negro visible as a complicated human being. But considering all that Baldwin once knew and wrote, it is difficult not to conclude that *Blues for Mr. Charlie* is more a work of provocation than conviction—the author has tasted power and is rolling that taste around on his tongue. The ultimate difficulty, then, is not a racial difficulty at all; it is the difficulty of the modern intellectual, torn between the way of influence and the way of truth. This conflict has driven more than one gifted individual of our time to a sorry abuse of his talents, as well as to that almost pathological frustration that often accompanies it; and I suspect that much of the exasperation in this play stems from Baldwin's inability to reconcile the private and public aspects of his character. Until he does, however, he has ceased to illuminate our consciousness. Early in his career, James Baldwin declared it his ambition to be "an honest man and a good writer." In *Blues for Mr. Charlie* he is neither. There, the complex man of sensibility has been totally absorbed by the simplistic man of power—and that constitutes what Baldwin himself once called "his corruption and our loss."

# INDEX OF AUTHORS

# INDEX OF SUBJECTS

# New Republic

MAY 9, 1949

## PENTAGON CENSORS

By MARTIN AGRONSKY

## THE COMMUNIST TRIAL

By BRUCE BLIVEN

## MAX LERNER ON T. S. ELIOT

## HAROLD L. ICKES: ON
### FRISKING THE ALASKA INDIANS

15¢

The New Republic *as it appeared after World War II*
*(Redesigned by Lester Beall)*